mental ray® for Maya®, 3ds Max® and XSI®

mental ray® for Maya®, 3ds Max® and XSI®

A 3D ARTIST'S GUIDE TO RENDERING

BOAZ LIVNY

BICENTENNIAL

1807

WILEY

2007

BICENTENNIAL

WILEY PUBLISHING, INC.

Acquisitions Editor: Mariann Barsolo
Development Editor: Jim Compton
Technical Editor: Keith Reicher and Geordie Martinez
Production Editor: Christine O'Connor
Copy Editors: Judy Flynn & Kim Wimpsett
Production Manager: Tim Tate
Vice President and Executive Group Publisher: Richard Swadley
Vice President and Executive Publisher: Joseph B. Wikert
Vice President and Publisher: Neil Edde
Media Associate Project Manager: Laura Atkinson
Media Assistant Producer: Kate Jenkins
Media Quality Assurance: Kit Malone
Compositor: Happenstance Type-O-Rama
Proofreader: Candace English
Indexer: Ted Laux
Anniversary Logo Design: Richard Pacifico
Cover Designer: Ryan Sneed
Cover Image: Boaz Livny

Dear Reader

Thank you for choosing *mental Ray for Maya, 3ds Max and XSI: A 3D Artist's Guide to Rendering*. This book is part of a family of premium-quality Sybex books, all written by outstanding authors who combine practical experience with a gift for teaching.

Sybex was founded in 1976. More than 30 years later, we're still committed to producing consistently exceptional books. With each of our titles we're working hard to set a new standard for the industry. From the paper we print on, to the authors we work with, our goal is to bring you the best books available.

I hope you see all that reflected in these pages. I'd be very interested to hear your comments and get your feedback on how we're doing. Feel free to let me know what you think about this or any other Sybex book by sending me an email at nedde@wiley.com, or if you think you've found a technical error in this book, please visit http://sybex.custhelp.com. Customer feedback is critical to our efforts at Sybex.

Best regards,

Neil Edde
Vice President and Publisher
Sybex, an Imprint of Wiley

Dedication

To Jolie, Bill, Mom, Dad, Abigail, my family, friends, and students.

Acknowledgements

My thanks to the outstanding editorial, production, and compositing staff at Sybex and John Wiley & Sons, including acquisitions editor Mariann Barsolo and development editor Jim Compton, whose patience and support have been key to the production of this book. I would also like to thank production editors Christine O'Connor and Martine Dardignac, technical editors Keith Reicher and Geordie Martinez, copy editors Judy Flynn and Kim Wimpsett, and proofreader Candace English. ■ Special thanks to Sameer Shah, Yorie Kumalasari, and Santosh Sailesh Gunaseelan, who first unknowingly provided me with support and motivation for writing this book, then helped me prepare the educational support materials, and finally provided critique for chapters as well as images for the color gallery. I would also like to thank Patrick Walsh from Walsh Family Media and Dale Carman from Reel FX for their contributions to the color gallery. ■ Special thanks to www.RenderRocket.com, an online render farm that made their fantastic render services available for rendering the high-resolution cover image and some of the color gallery's images. They customized their services for my purposes so I can easily manage my projects and use custom plug-in shaders, and they provided constant technical support. ■ A very special thanks to my dearest Jolie, who encouraged and supported this ambitious project, and to Bill and my mom, who both motivated and pushed me to write this book. Without your support and encouragement, I would have never done it. To Gordon Skadberg, thank you for your support and constant interest in this book, providing me with help in explaining some of the more complex mathematical concepts presented in this book, and proofing them for accuracy.

About the Author

Boaz Livny is a lighting and shading artist, consultant, writer, and educator in New York, New York. Passionate about photography, a field that he explored for years before entering the digital world of 3D, he currently specializes in lighting and rendering, focusing on the photography aspect of 3D imaging, but is experienced in working the entire pipeline. He began his experience with 3D working for TV stations using 3ds Max and After Effects. During that time he also worked as a 3ds Max demonstrator for a Kinetix (the company that created 3ds Max) representative abroad. Eventually he made the transition to Softimage and then Maya, providing services for the film, TV, and architecture industries, giving him experience with all the host applications covered in this book.

From his New York studio, Vision Animations, Inc., he provides regular services, consultancy, and freelance support to clients and studios. Currently he is a primary consultant for the animated feature film *The Cool Beans: Humbucket Caper* from Walsh Family Media. He is a professor of master's-level courses at NYU's Center for Advanced Digital Applications (CADA) and bachelor's-level courses at the NYU Digital Communications and Media, McGhee division. Boaz regularly writes articles demonstrating advanced mental ray and Nuke techniques for *HDRI 3D* magazine, from DMG publishing. He also contributed chapters to *Mastering Maya 7* and *Mastering Maya 8.5*, both from Wiley.

CONTENTS AT A GLANCE

Contents

Introduction

Welcome to mental ray for Maya, 3ds Max, and XSI: A 3D Artist's Guide to Rendering, which provides an in-depth look at lighting and rendering techniques with mental ray. The book focuses on rendering technologies with mental ray, and how mental ray is implemented in each host application: Maya, XSI, and 3ds Max.

However, this is much more than a book about mental ray. It's a book on rendering technologies and techniques that just happen to be demonstrated with mental ray. The topics covered in this book provide essential background on light and camera fundamentals, as well as rendering technologies and techniques used with any advanced rendering software, be it V-Ray, Brazil, Final Render, RenderMan, or, of course, mental ray.

This definitive artist's guide provides several in-depth explanations about mental ray technologies and how they function, as well as camera, lighting, and shading principles. It shows you how these technologies can be used in each host application, along with advanced techniques. For example, you'll learn how to create complex shader trees in each host application with mental ray shaders. Because rendering is the final stage of 3D production—taking several 3D assets and converting them into an image—you will learn a great deal about 3D in general in addition to rendering.

The two primary motivations for the content and structure of this book are based on my personal experiences studying rendering technologies (PRMan and mental ray) and my perspective on how rendering and real-world photography intertwine. The latter refers to the fact that the sole purpose of rendering and 3D is to capture still images or animation in a synthetic environment as if they were actually photographed. For that purpose, the book explores my definition of *photorealism*—the process of taking images so that the environment appears natural and consistent with the content, including the lighting, shading, and photographic characteristics (depth of field, field of view, lens distortion, and so on). That environment, however, needn't be confined to the realism of a car commercial; it can be crazy characters in imaginary worlds.

Over the years I have found the search for valuable in-depth explanations of rendering with mental ray and the technology to be frustrating. In particular, I wanted to know more about how things really function behind the scenes so that I can use that knowledge to improve my workflow in 3D. CG may be a creative field, but unlike drawing, it requires a lot of technical know-how to accomplish coherent and well-prepared 3D scenes for rendering. Thus, fundamental to the book's structure is that each chapter takes a topic and reviews it in great detail with mental ray from the technical to the creative, constantly providing insight on a per-host basis for Maya, XSI, and 3ds Max.

The book is aimed at helping you become more confident in creating your art within a complex and technical environment. It encourages you to further research the advanced topics, be more observant of your surroundings, and become more knowledgeable about how to use mental ray or any other renderer to implement phenomena you observe.

What You Will Learn from This Book

Several tutorials on lighting and shading are available in books and on the Web. There are also several technical tutorials and books on rendering for shader writers and programmers. These are both attempts to deal with the same topic from different perspectives. This book is intended to bridge that gap, providing you with detailed explanations of how rendering algorithms function—whether for raytracing, shader construction, light simulations, or camera work—by providing technical insight into how they function, as well as how to use them creatively to improve your rendering practices. In today's CG marketplace, you need to both have creative skills and understand your tools in depth.

You will learn all about rendering technologies, including the underlying fundamentals of scanline and raytrace rendering. An introduction to optical physics and the nature of light will help you better understand shading and lighting in 3D, and you'll learn about cameras and photography, high dynamic range (HDR) imaging, advanced lighting and indirect lighting technologies and techniques, and shading tools and techniques. With respect to shading practices, these are some of the topics included:

- Basic and advanced shading models
- Custom shaders from online resources
- Environment, volume, and lens shaders
- Complex shader trees
- Texture mapping and texture coordinates
- Advanced raytrace shaders and physical shaders
- Subsurface-scattering shaders
- Natural material creation

Most important, many of us take for granted the simple process of using cameras, assuming we already know how to use them and understand their nature. That assumes we can start taking our own photographs in 3D and they will look professional. However, you must master the art of photography so you can bridge the gap between real-world photography and 3D. There is much to be said about light and cameras, their fundamental character, and how to use them in 3D. The goal is, then, to take that knowledge and apply it in 3D so that the images we capture look more aesthetic and real. This book will help you bridge that gap, constantly referring to real-world observations and how you can mimic them in 3D using mental ray or any other renderer.

Who Should Read This Book

This book is for anyone who is interested in learning about 3D software and wants to better understand the fundamental and advanced concepts behind generating images in 3D, including learning more about common terms. The focus is on mental ray lighting, shading, and rendering using Maya, XSI, or 3ds Max. This book is an essential tool for any 3D artist who is studying these topics for the first time or just wants to learn more about them. If you are already familiar with mental ray rendering, the book will help you have a more complete understanding of the tools and techniques used.

Every chapter demonstrates how a feature is implemented in mental ray and then shows how the mental ray functions are accessible in each host application. The demonstrations provide detailed explanations on a per-host basis so that intermediate to advanced users can learn about mental ray's technologies and apply that knowledge using their preferred host application. Thus, it's also a great book for users who are familiar with mental ray and are migrating from one 3D application to another; for example, if you're a Maya user who wants to learn more about XSI, the book's coverage of the same topics in both host applications lets you easily compare the differences while learning the nuances of mental ray with XSI and its interface. In all cases, the book can help you in filling gaps with respect to mental ray practices and how well they are implemented in each host application.

For beginners, the book covers all the host application paths for settings in the tutorials so that you can easily follow along. Furthermore, the first few chapters will give any beginner or advanced user a thorough review of 3D rendering programs and how they operate. However, many of the tutorials, although easy to follow, require that you are comfortable with your software of choice. You need to already know how to use cameras, lights, and shaders and execute renders in your host—for example applying shaders or projecting textures. This book then gets into those topics in more detail so you can use them more effectively and knowledgeably.

How to Use This Book

mental ray for Maya, 3ds Max and XSI: A 3D Artist's Guide to Rendering begins with an overview of the technology and ends with advanced shading and lighting techniques, exposing you to fundamental and advanced rendering, cameras, lighting, shading, indirect lighting, and subsurface scattering with mental ray, in that order. Ample cross-references allow you to approach any chapter that strikes your fancy and find relevant references for terms that are discussed in other chapters.

The book is intended to be used in two ways:

- I recommend you read through it at least once. It has been written in a way that you can read it on the road, on a couch, in bed, or at any place where you don't have a computer. Each chapter describes mental ray concepts in detail, as well as the mental ray options. Then at the computer, you can review the designated areas that deal with per-host settings and tutorials for Maya, XSI, and 3ds Max. In this way, you understand a topic in detail before approaching it on the computer. After reading it once, you will become familiar with mental ray as well as all the secrets, tips, and notes provided in various places throughout the book. You can then use the book as a reference when you need a recap of all the intricacies of a given topic.

- For your continuing work, the book will also serve as a must-have reference so that while working with, for example, Final Gather, you can open Chapter 14 and find explanations for all the Final Gather options and techniques. You can easily jump to any chapter and learn a great deal about a topic without reading previous chapters.

I recommend you definitely read Chapters 1 through 3, 5, 10, and 12 if you don't want to read the book from start to end.

Each host application has its own terminology for referencing the different settings. In Maya we use attributes, with XSI properties, and in 3ds Max parameters. Also with mental ray, these are referred to as options. Whenever you see any of these words, they are used interchangeably based on the application being referenced, or the mental ray option.

Finally, with respect to color, most of the figures in the book don't require color. Those that do are provided on the companion CD for each chapter. Figures that require seeing color are also placed in the book's color gallery so that you don't need to use the CD on a regular basis.

Reading the Book

The book focuses on mental ray the mental ray options for scene settings, special effects, and shaders. The integration of mental ray with Maya is applied in a way that most options (attributers) are labeled using mental ray conventional names. Thus, I use Maya's UI more often to display the mental ray options and discuss them in detail, for consistency with mental ray naming conventions. The same options are always further discussed in each host application, identifying their unique names, as well as the differences in how they are implemented, when applicable. Because the Maya UI appears a lot throughout the book, it is important to note that this is not a Maya book, but a mental ray book that tries to stick with mental ray naming conventions and then identify them in hosts within the discussion or in specific host-application sections.

Furthermore, the integration of mental ray differs in each host, providing different options and features that may not be available in each host. Thus, occasionally the book focuses on any of the hosts, showing their compatibility with a specific feature that may not be integrated in other hosts. On that topic there are two points worth noting:

1. You don't have to read those host-specific sections; however they will further your understanding as to mental ray capabilities.

2. Learning what you don't have makes it possible for you to seek alternative means for implementing those options, either by installing custom shaders, by using stand-alone mental ray where you can specify any feature, or by implementing custom output code or plug-ins in your preferred application, opening the door to additional features that you may not have known about without looking at the "bigger picture" that is mental ray.

If you don't fully comprehend a tutorial or topic discussed on a per-host basis, read the other host tutorials that may help you better understand that feature in your host.

How This Book Is Organized

The book is organized as follows:

Chapter 1, "Introduction to mental ray," introduces all things mental ray. It presents the mental images (.mi) file format and the mental ray stand-alone renderer, as well as how mental ray integrates with each host application. It covers the different fields that mental ray caters to and the advantages it provides. Throughout the chapter you will become familiar with important terminology, technologies, and the structure of mental ray as well as per-host command-line rendering and batch rendering.

Chapter 2, "Rendering Algorithms," introduces the fundamentals of scanline, ray-trace, and hardware rendering using mental ray. These fundamentals apply to all rendering software. You will learn how each render algorithm functions and become familiar with their relevant mental ray options, as well as how they are implemented in each host application. The explanations on the render algorithms and how they function are true to any advanced render software.

Chapter 3, "mental ray Output," teaches you all you need to know about mental ray frame buffers, their bit depth, and output formats. It covers important topics related to output settings, such as gamma correction and premultiplication. The topics are aimed at preparing images as final renders or for compositing passes in applications such as Nuke, Fusion, or Shake. The chapter begins to look at mental ray camera lens, volume, environment, and output shaders, as well as how you can implement them in host applications, including rendering passes and mental ray's multipass options.

Chapter 4, "Camera Fundamentals," continues the technical introduction to mental ray cameras. It looks at real-world cameras, how they function, and their photographic characteristics. You will learn how real cameras can be simulated in 3D with camera lens shaders and the mental ray camera options. The chapter is an extensive overview of the fundamentals of cameras regardless of mental ray.

Chapter 5, "Quality Control," explores several quality control algorithms and their options in depth. You will learn how to remove flickering, moiré patterns, and banding artifacts, as well as how to optimize the render for better performance. The chapter covers in detail sampling and anti-aliasing using mental ray's scanline, ray-trace, and rasterizer render algorithms. Topics covered include sampling, filtering, render diagnostics, and raytrace acceleration (BSP, Large BSP, and Grid). Each topic is explained in detail with mental ray options that are then further examined on a per-host basis.

Chapter 6, "Lights and Soft Shadows," looks at using light shaders, photometric lights, area lights, and raytrace shadows with mental ray. The chapter covers topics such as soft lighting and distance-based shadows. It looks in depth at the different light shader options, as well as using photometric light profile files and external tools to view light profiles. You will see how mental ray shaders can be used in each host application, as well as how they are implemented with host-specific lights.

Chapter 7, "Shadow Algorithms," builds on the light shaders presented in Chapter 6, looking in detail at shadow map shadows, detail shadows, and raytrace shadow algorithms. The chapter covers the technical aspects of controlling shadows in CG, presenting all the mental ray options, and how they are implemented with each host application.

Chapter 8, "Motion Blur," continues the discussion of cameras, covering fundamental concepts related to real cameras and motion blur. You will learn how motion blur is simulated with mental ray cameras and the different effects camera components have on motion blur, such as the shutter. The chapter examines motion blur with scanline, raytrace, and the rasterizer render algorithms, examining how you may accelerate motion-blur rendering. At the end of the chapter a sidebar introduces you to using mental ray motion vectors with compositing.

Chapter 9, "The Fundamentals of Light and Shading Models," is probably the most important chapter of this book. It is an essential introduction to all the following chapters, so it can be considered as the first chapter on indirect lighting and advanced shading techniques. In it you will learn about the characteristics of light in detail. The chapter introduces you to geometric optics, radiometry, photometry, high dynamic range imaging, and tone-mapping, including how all those topics are used in 3D. Then you will move on to CG shading models and how they are implemented in 3D and with mental ray base shaders. You will learn how lights and shaders define a surface's material character in depth and how mental ray materials are constructed, including their implementation in host applications. The purpose of the chapter is to provide a bridge between real-world surface and light characteristics and how to simulate those characteristics with shaders.

Chapter 10, "mental ray Shaders and Shader Trees," builds on the in-depth introduction to shaders and further examines how advanced shaders and shader trees are constructed with mental ray shaders. The chapter presents online sources for custom shaders along with installation guidance for these shaders in each host application. The chapter then proceeds to review mental ray physics shaders, glossy shaders, and the architectural material. In each host you will look at a complex shader tree for brushed metal using several component and complex shaders to generate the effect of brushed metal with anisotropic highlights and reflections. Through this tutorial you will learn a great deal about several mental ray and host-specific shaders.

Chapter 11, "mental ray Textures and Projections," is an important chapter for all 3D users. It reviews texture space and projections, looking at how UV coordinates are defined on surfaces. The same concepts apply to various principles in 3D, such as surface or texture rotation and translation. In this chapter you will learn how coordinates are extracted from surfaces as well as how they are controlled with a transform matrix. You will learn about the math behind the scenes enough to understand how texture placement and vector shaders function, followed by examples using mental ray shaders and host-specific shaders in host applications. The chapter also covers bump mapping, normal maps, texture memory–mapped images, image filtering, and pyramid images.

Chapter 12, "Indirect illumination," is an in-depth look at mental ray indirect illumination algorithms. Building on the fundamentals discussed in Chapter 10, this chapter looks at the tools and techniques for using global illumination and caustics. The chapter also covers participating media (PM) effects, which render atmospheric particles that interact with light, and how PM effects are used with global illumination and caustics.

Chapter 13, "Final Gather and Ambient Occlusion," covers an additional set of tools for indirect illumination. Final Gather is a hybrid of indirect illumination that deals with improving indirect light simulations with more detail and better environment sampling; the effect of the environment on the scene, particularly when using high dynamic range images or lighting. The chapter covers the mental ray physical sun, sky, and tone-mapping shaders, and how they are used with Final Gather. You will also learn about panoramic HDR images, their types, and how they are created with host applications and edited with external tools, such as HDR Shop. The chapter presents additional software for generating HDR environments. Finally, the chapter reviews the mental ray ambient occlusion shaders and how they are used with Final Gather, as well as how they can be used for rendering diffuse, reflective, and environment sampling passes for compositing.

Chapter 14, "Subsurface Scattering," shows how this effect can be implemented with mental ray using a combination of component shaders that fake the internal scattering of light or can be realistically simulated with an advanced physical shader. Both topics are examined in detail with examples using mental ray shaders in each host application. The chapter presents several external resources for learning more about subsurface scattering and acquiring the scatter properties of real-world surfaces. This chapter also presents the *bidirectional surface scattering distribution function* (BSSRDF) shading models with information on how they compare with the mental ray subsurface shaders. As a side topic, this chapter presents normal bump maps using one of the subsurface component shaders.

Hardware and Software Considerations

The book is about mental ray, which is the same regardless of the platform you choose to use, whether that's Windows, Linux, or OS X. In Chapter 1 of this book, you'll find instructions for executing batch renders from a command line or a shell, depending on the platform. Each chapter presents mental ray command-line commands or mental image file options for the option block. These are the same regardless of the platform.

With respect to the type of computer you need, most of this book was written on a laptop that has Maya, XSI, and 3ds Max installed. Even most of the figures for print (high resolution) were rendered on the laptop. Each option was thoroughly compared in each host to identify their nuances while rendering on the laptop so that I can safely say you don't need a supercomputer to get through the study phase. For generating complex scenes and rendering indirect lighting, you will want to use a computer with a relatively updated processor, preferably a dual processor or dual-core processor, and at least 2GB of RAM with a good graphics/video card from NVIDIA, ATI, 3D Labs, and so on, that has at least 128MB of memory. All these manufacturers produce low- to high-end products for computer-aided design (CAD). With respect to workstations, if you are unfamiliar with selecting a system that is right for you, Boxx computers provide well-prepared workstations customized for any host application and purpose (rendering, animation, and so on). I also recommend HP, which has a solid line of affordable to expensive workstations.

RENDER FARMS VERSUS YOUR MACHINES

An additional hardware consideration relates to the approach you take for managing high-end renders. If you work from a production studio, or have your own studio, generating production-quality images at HD resolutions using, for example, Final Gather and motion blur requires more than a workstation to complete rendering within a reasonable time. For that purpose you should consider using the mental ray stand-alone renderer, or use mental ray satellite (distributed rendering) across several computers (see Chapter 1). If you don't have the computer resources, or don't want to tie up your system with renders, you can outsource renders to render farms. For example, the cover image was rendered at HD 1080 (1920×1080 resolution), 300 DPI and with Final Gather and motion blur—too much for my workstation to handle.

Within the time span of one day, the online service www.RenderRocket.com provided me with FTP access and support so that I could set up my project and render it on their farm. The following day the image was complete, as opposed to a four-to-five-day render time on my 64-bit dual dual-core system with 8GB of RAM. Point is, my system is powerful, but sometimes you will need the extra help to get productions complete in a timely fashion, which plays an important role in building up your own service as well as keeping your machines productive. You should invest money in machines that allow creating art, which is different from machines designated for rendering. For example, for production you need good graphic cards with average dual-core machines and about 2 to 4GB or RAM, but not the several processors that are required for rendering. Those processors on an artist machine are wasted, as they are not used during creation, only rendering.

MAYA AND 3DS MAX USERS

Both these applications offer their own renderer and shaders. The book focuses on using the mental ray components and shaders in each host, but occasionally reviews host-specific techniques and shaders, as required. In both cases most of the host-specific shaders and functionalities are supported with mental ray. With 3ds max a lot of the advanced lighting (for radiosity) parameters are not supported by mental ray, such as some of the exposure control parameters. You will see in Chapter 1 how to read mental ray output, which typically identifies (with errors) the functions that are not supported. Also the help files will tell you which items are supported.

XSI USERS

XSI has duplicate settings in three instances. You have the render region and render settings, which utilize the same settings for different purposes (viewport preview vs.

final output). In this book I never refer to render regions, since they are the same as the global render properties. Just note that if you use a rendered region to fine-tune properties, be sure those properties are copied or manually implemented in the Render Options window. In addition, you have the Render Manager properties window and Render Options and Passes property windows, which offer a different approach to managing the same settings for rendering. In Chapter 1 a sidebar discusses the differences between these windows. Throughout the book, it is irrelevant which of the windows (Render Manager or Render Options) you use when specifying properties. The paths are the same in both windows.

TRIAL SOFTWARE

A great way to learn 3D is to experiment with trial versions. For each host application, you can obtain a free learning edition for noncommercial use or a trial version as follows:

- Maya has a Personal Learning Edition (Maya PLE) software that you can download from the Autodesk website (www.autodesk.com). Maya PLE is a special version of Maya that gives you free access to Maya Complete for noncommercial use.

- 3ds Max has a 30-day trial version that you can download from the Autodesk website (www.autodesk.com).

- With XSI you can get the Academic Edition of Softimage XSI 6 Advanced. It provides you with an academic license for XSI Advanced, including all the features of the professional version, with no limitations. However, you can not use it for paid work. You can download it at http://softimage.com/education/educationalpricing.aspx.

The Book's CD

The companion CD of this book is organized into folders by chapter, and each chapter has a folder for each host application (when relevant). In the host application folders you can find scene files. You'll find source images (textures) that apply to all host applications and figures in the chapter's root directory. You can copy them to your hard drive into a project directory for each host.

The CD provides the following:

- Images of figures that you need to view in color or in fine detail.

- Relevant movie clips mentioned in some of the chapters.

- Host-specific scene files, mostly for complex shading networks, including examples of some networks that are not covered in the book.

- Articles on relevant topics I've written for the *HDRI 3D* magazine, from DMG Publishing. For example, there's an article on texture-baking, a topic I could not cover in the book. Although it's a Maya article, the same principles apply in each host application. Another article covers compositing passes using Nuke, a compositing software developed at D2 software (Digital Domain) and now owned by The Foundry.

- Free high-dynamic-range panoramic images for environmental lighting with Final Gather or as a source for environment reflections. These are in the HDR Images folder.

- A collection of light profile files for photometric lighting, covered in Chapter 6.

A bonus chapter on surface approximation methods with mental ray; "SurfaceApproximationMethods" PDF file in the Chapters folder. This additional chapter introduces you to the tessellation process that converts 3D surfaces into polygons during rendering.

Contact the Author

You can contact the author at www.3darts.org. You can also email him at Boaz@3darts.org.

## CHAPTER 1

Introduction to mental ray

mental ray, a robust and independent rendering package, is well integrated within several 3D applications—Autodesk Maya, Autodesk 3ds Max, and Softimage|XSI, for example—as plug-in software. As a plug-in application for these host programs, mental ray specializes in generating photorealistic images, with an unsurpassed ability to re-create natural phenomena. As you'll see, it can also be used for creating nonphotorealistic contour renderings (NPRs). mental ray's photorealistic capabilities derive from an extensive set of tools that perform advanced camera, light, surface, and volume shading simulations. These simulations and the realistic renderings they allow lend themselves to various applications: architectural design, motion picture animation and visual effects, high-end television commercials, automotive and industrial design, and games. In a nutshell, mental ray provides outstanding render quality and an unsurpassed set of tools that cope with complex rendering challenges such as indirect illumination, volumetric lighting, memory handling and optimization, cross-platform network rendering, flicker reduction, and much more.

This chapter is an overview of mental ray, introducing the key terms and concepts that you'll examine in detail throughout this book. It provides a detailed introduction to what goes on in a mental images (.mi) file, not because I expect you to create such files by hand-coding but because understanding mental ray's functionality and settings lends to a better understanding of its features from within each host application. The chapter covers the following topics:

- **What Is mental ray?**
- **Why Use mental ray?**
- **The Structure of mental ray**
- **mental ray Integration**
- **Command-Line Rendering and the Stand-Alone Renderer**
- **mental ray Shaders and Shader Libraries**
- **Indirect Illumination**

What Is mental ray?

The main focus of the mental ray product technologies is the generation of photorealistic images, a process that requires complex computations using physics to simulate the way light behaves and interacts with surfaces. Light physicists have long been in pursuit of the definition of light, particularly for demystifying the *photoelectric effect*, which describes the reflection of light from surfaces and its physical characteristics and nature. Computer graphics (CG) software developers are particularly interested in applying the knowledge of lighting and its interaction within an environment, as well as its perception by the human eye, into shading and lighting models within their applications. This might explain why shading models developed by different scientists have inherited their names within our 3D applications. The Lambert shading model, for example, is the same in every application and provides the base model for all diffuse shading models; it is then extended to provide enhanced shading characteristics such as with a Blinn, Phong, Oren-Nayar, or any other shader. You will learn more about light and CG shading models in Chapter 10, "CG Shading Models and Light Primer."

mental ray is a product from a rich line of specialized tools developed by mental images GmbH, a company based in Germany. Most users, however, access mental ray primarily through OEM partners such as AutoDesk, Avid, and others. These partners offer mental ray both as an integrated render plug-in within their software with support for *satellite* rendering (also known as distributed rendering), and as a stand-alone renderer (sold separately).

mental ray Scene Description Language

At its core, mental ray is a fully functional 3D package that enables you to describe a scene consisting of geometric forms, surface materials, lights, environment shaders, and a camera using the mental images scene description language. For describing such scenes, mental ray does not provide its own user interface. Thus, you can simply describe a scene using plain text and a text editor, resulting in a rendered image upon execution. This sort of text file, known as a mental images file, is then executed from the command line simply by entering the default mental ray render command ray followed by a filename:

```
ray myfile.mi
```

Because of the efficiency and control it provides, this approach has many useful benefits for production houses that have the development resources, but not as many for the independent artist or smaller CG or CAD shop. Without a UI, mental ray is not very intuitive to use. These users normally would not consider purchasing a stand-alone render program; they are more likely to consider a package such as XSI, Maya, or 3ds Max, which provide a full set of tools and a user-friendly graphical interface. Artists with strong programming skills (and sometimes a computer science degree) can use the mental ray stand-alone package to further customize rendering as well as design several additional features; for example, using the C or C++ programming language, they can design custom shaders that can then be added to the mental ray shader libraries. This obviously requires familiarity with the scene description language, C or C++, and mental ray shader libraries and their implementation.

Most of this book assumes you are using mental ray from within a host, but it also refers to using stand-alone mental ray where appropriate. mental ray options are labeled differently within each package. I will always refer to mental ray options as they are implemented (labeled) in mental ray and then demonstrate how to access those same options from within the different packages. With mental ray, render options are defined within a mental ray .mi file's *options block*. The options block options can then further be overridden on the command line with stand-alone rendering using similar syntax for options found in the options block. In most cases, syntax presented in this book refers to command-line commands that may be used to override option block options. When an option is unavailable as a command-line command, the options block syntax is presented. Non–options block options, such as internal options for lights and shadows, are presented in their relevant context. These options and their syntax and execution become clearer as you read through this chapter.

Host Translators

When using mental ray through a host application, it is not necessary to be familiar with the mental images scene description language. In fact, no knowledge of any mental ray programmable features is required in order to take full advantage of mental ray. During the render, the host application will automatically translate the scene into a mental images format that is then rendered with mental ray. (For example, when a render is executed in Maya, we can see the command line progress feedback, shown in Figure 1.1, indicate that the current frame is first being translated prior to indicating any render progress.) Hence, mental ray can render an image directly from within these host applications without any need for you to manually provide any programmable settings or help with the translation process.

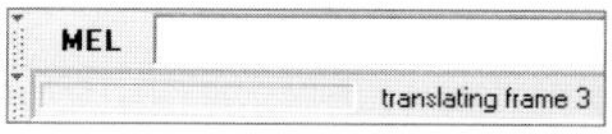

This sort of mental ray integration from within host packages provides access to most mental ray features. It is what makes mental ray a practical tool for the CG artist, eliminating the need for advanced technical skills and allowing you to focus on your art. The integration of mental ray within OEM partner packages that will be discussed throughout this chapter is achieved through a structural component known as the host translator program deals with translation, supporting mental ray features within host applications. Thus, the translator program interfaces between the host application and mental ray while executing renders, exporting .mi files, or calculating mental ray specific maps such as photon maps, final gather maps, and light maps. For now, let's discuss some of the requirements and

Figure 1.1

This feedback on the Maya command line indicates that the Maya scene is being translated for rendering with mental ray.

goals of industry professionals from a wide variety of professions, as well as how mental ray caters to their needs.

Why Use mental ray?

Professionals in the various fields that use mental ray have different purposes in generating images, and those differences are reflected in the ways they work with the software and how they customize their production pipeline. The different approaches may range from a simple out-of-the-box rendering to advanced customized tools developed in-house, such as with Sony Image Works, Industrial Light & Magic, and other large-scale production houses.

Architectural and Industrial CAD

With architectural or industrial CAD rendering, usually a focus on establishing realism based on physically correct calculations is imperative. Architecture professionals are particularly interested in drawing a realistic image that represents an environment's appearance at a particular time of day or with a specific type of artificial lighting. This may require using *light profiles* (provided by light manufacturers) that specify the exact light intensity and falloff characteristics of a particular light source. mental ray then adds to these light models additional abilities to simulate light bounce within that environment; this is known as the *indirect illumination* of surfaces by reflected light. (You can learn more about indirect illumination later in this chapter and in Chapter 12.)

Industrial designers usually aren't concerned with simulating specific lighting conditions, so they have the creative freedom to seek a more aesthetic lighting scenario over a physically correct one. Their rendering focuses on generating realistic characteristics for surfaces and their interaction with light. They need to simulate realistically how surfaces reflect and transmit light. For example, chrome surfaces, aluminum, "heavy" metal, plastic, brushed metals, translucent surfaces, and glass of varying thickness and type all interact differently with light.

Chapters 10 tand 11 will guide you through several approaches for creating complex surface shaders and custom effects. In both architectural and industrial design, render times can be quite long, but this is not normally a serious obstacle. These fields in many cases may require rendering only a relatively small sequence of frames for print, a high-end commercial, or a video presentation.

Entertainment

mental ray's photorealistic capabilities are equally important in the entertainment industry, but the sheer number of frames to be generated means that another component needs to be considered: time. While beautifully rendered CG images may greatly increase a film's appeal, they must also be generated in a timely manner. For this reason, film productions usually prefer to avoid using mental ray's powerful *raytracing* abilities whenever possible (see Chapters 2 and 5, "Rendering Algorithms and Quality Control,"), and they expect a fast turnaround in the production pipeline. In the entertainment industry, mental ray plays two different roles: one as a primary renderer for entire productions and the other as an additional renderer providing high-end realistic visual effects shots that emphasize realism.

For feature animated films, currently the norm is to use a RenderMan-compliant renderer, typically Pixar's PRMan, which provides a scalable and fast *scanline* renderer as well as a powerful raytracer when needed. However, some projects use more than one renderer in a production pipeline and divide the work among different studios that each assemble specific shots using their tools of choice. Typically, films that combine live action with 3D use mental ray more often than feature animations do. Some familiar feature films that have used mental ray in part or in full are *The Wild*, *The Matrix Revolutions*, *The Matrix Reloaded*, *Star Wars: Episode II*, *The Hulk*, *Terminator 3*, *Fight Club*, *Panic Room*, *Blade Trinity*, *The Cell*, *The Day After Tomorrow*, and *Walking with Dinosaurs*.

When simulated photorealism is used in films, it's is usually to create props or scenes that it would be too costly to build, such as spacecraft. But it also allows shots that otherwise would be impossible or too expensive to shoot. In some cases, mental ray is used to clone an environment or character into CG, enabling the director to obtain nonstandard camera shots. For example, in the Motion Pictures gallery on www.mentalimages.com, you'll find some images from *Panic Room*, a nonfuturistic film that at first glance does not appear to be loaded with special effects or 3D. It takes place in a New York City townhouse where everything appears to be real. However, it uses several shots that probably would have been impossible or at least very difficult to manually construct within a set. mental ray was used to render a replicate environment of the townhouse so that the nonstandard camera motions through the house could be shot. This sort of integration between real life and 3D requires a great deal of realism. Its goal is to prevent the viewer from distinguishing between real shots and CG-enhanced shots.

Games

In computer games, which are constantly evolving and offering more "realistic" experiences, the emphasis on complex, instantaneous interaction has always put high-end rendering out of reach. Enhanced CG requires complex shading models and lighting such as simulating indirect lighting. Games do not consist of images prerendered using mental ray or any other renderer; they run on a game engine that renders in real time. This real-time display is enabled using technologies that access and control hardware, through OpenGL or DirectX, and based on the hardware abilities such as with NVIDIA, 3DLabs, ATI, and other manufacturers' boards. The games industry bridges the technical gap by using mental ray's *light baking* options. Light baking is the process of converting surface shading and lighting from mental ray into texture maps that can then be applied to models. Thus, baked texture-map files may include surface-shading properties and their influence from direct and indirect lighting. In essence, textures can represent a *global illumination* (see the section "Indirect Illumination" later in this chapter) render that provides the indirect diffused light bounce within an environment, providing for more appealing texture maps for game environments and characters. You will learn techniques and considerations for light baking in Chapter 14, "Light Maps (Baking) and Complex Shaders."

The Structure of mental ray

In the following sections, you will learn more about mental ray rendering procedures, as well as its integration with other applications. The goal is to provide a solid understanding of mental ray technologies and abilities so that when you're evaluating rendering technologies, you will be able to weigh one advantage against another. Being more familiar with the core technology and its algorithms will enable you to make a better decision for your rendering approach.

A mental ray file, regardless of whether it was generated within a host application or was custom-made, typically includes information on the spatial arrangement of objects, their physical characteristics within a given coordinate space (*object space*, *camera space*, *world space*), and their influences from a variety of shaders. When rendering, mental ray transfers data by sampling shader color values, typically from surface points within the file (the 3D scene). These color values are then passed into a 2D *frame buffer*, which acts as a storage container for the different rendered data. Frame buffers typically store the four standard color channels that represent an image, *RGBA*. The R, G, and B channels each represent a different additive primary color (red, green, and blue) and A represents the alpha masking channel. Image data is always stored within frame buffers until the render process has completed and the frame buffer is ready to be written to a file on disk.

> mental ray also supports several other custom channels that will be discussed within the book (in Chapter 3, "mental ray Output"), such as the Z-depth channel and motion vectors.

Photorealistic rendering requires a lot of processing, so mental ray is structured in a form that maximizes performance during rendering. In Chapter 2, you will learn more about the different rendering algorithms mental ray uses, which include different algorithms for scanline rendering, raytrace rendering, and hardware rendering.

Modularity

An important aspect of mental ray's structure is modularity. That is, mental ray is divided into several separate modules that act as software components. Each module is essentially plugged in to mental ray and is responsible for providing very specific tasks. For example, the image (IMG) module will load, write, or convert images to *memory mapped images* (see Chapter 11, "mental ray Shaders and Shader Trees") during the render or when prompted to do so with the mental ray *imf_copy* utility (described in the section "mental ray Components and Application Files" later in this chapter). For example, you may use the imf_copy utility to convert image types, creating memory-mapped images by utilizing functions from the IMG module. Hence these modules, which are at the core structure of mental ray, are in fact "plug-in units," which, when combined, form a larger, more-flexible system with improved capabilities.

Another aspect of modularization is that all mental ray shaders are provided as external plug-in programs designed for very specific tasks. These external shader libraries provide a great deal of flexibility in developing custom tools and shaders, not just for programmers, but for artists as well. For example, it is fairly simple and straightforward for artists to append new shaders or shader libraries to mental ray, just as you can download and import shaders into XSI, Maya, or 3ds Max. With mental ray, a new shader can be implemented so that it is always available simply by adding its declaration file into the shader libraries and linking it to mental ray. Shader libraries can be found in mental ray's root directory for each package, as discussed in the section "mental ray Shaders and Shader Libraries" later in the chapter. With respect to modularity, shaders open the door to an ongoing development process, which not only adds new shaders through a shader library, but primarily leads to finding new and creative ways for blending several shaders into one complex shader tree, forming a more robust material shader for surfaces or any other special effects.

On-Demand Execution and the Geometry Cache

When a render is executed, mental ray constructs a *scene database,* which is stored within the *geometry cache* and contains all the relevant information mental ray currently requires for executing the render. In essence, mental ray manages the cache in a way that allows for information to be loaded and unloaded into the database while maintaining efficient memory handling. Beginning with mental ray 3.*x*, the scene information is loaded into the database on demand. Briefly, here's how mental ray's render management process works.

mental ray 3.*x* divides a render task into different *render jobs,* which are structured based on some form of dependency so that they may be executed in the most efficient way. In previous versions (2.*x*), mental ray would execute the render in consecutive phases. For example, all the geometry would first be loaded into the cache and then tessellated before a following phase could commence.

> *Tessellation* refers to all geometry—be it NURBS, polygons, or subdivision surfaces—in the scene that must be converted (tessellated) into polygonal triangles before rendering the geometry. This task has two primary phases: first loading the geometry into memory so the renderer is aware of its existence, and then tessellating it into triangles.

mental ray 3.*x* and later seek to optimize data flow with on-demand execution of jobs. Thus, jobs are executed when needed rather than in a predetermined order. A job can execute any type of task, such as tessellation, raytracing, calculating light maps, managing texture data, rendering portions of the frame, and so forth, all based on the job status and data flow. This means that memory can be handled more effectively. Essentially, during rendering, most of the data that is being provided by the geometry cache to ongoing jobs is stored in memory and within the machine limits. Note that the cache can store all types of information, which may include spatial positioning, geometric tessellation data, texture maps, photon maps, Final Gather points, and any other data it may require for rendering. As the cache grows, the memory usage increases gradually until the machine limit or a specified limit is reached. If the limit is reached, mental ray will dump certain information from the cache to enable an ongoing render. This job-based model helps mental ray 3.*x* improve memory handling and optimization.

Enabling Message Logging and Verbosity Levels

mental ray provides message logs that are output into the console window when rendering so that you can track the rendering progress as well as retreive render statistics on the "quality" of the render, which helps troubleshoot or further optimize a render. You can control what information is displayed by enabling different levels of verbosity by using the mental ray verbose command either from within a host application or on the command line. When using a command-line renderer, you enable verbosity by specifying the -v (flag) and a verbosity level, as seen here for mental ray stand-alone rendering, Maya, XSI (-verbose), and 3ds Max command-line rendering. The topic of command-line rendering is discussed further in the section "Using the Host Application's Command Line" later in this chapter.

COMMAND-LINE CODE	SOURCE APPLICATION
`ray -v 5 myfile.mi`	mental ray stand-alone
`render -r mr -v 5 myfile.mb`	Maya command line
`xsi -r -verbose "prog" -scene fileName.scn`	XSI command line
`3dsmaxcmd -v:5 "scenes\anim.max"`	3ds Max command line

The message log can be viewed in different places depending on the host application that is executing the render. When using the mental ray stand-alone renderer or command-line rendering, the message log appears in the console window, which you'll see in Figure 1.5 in the next section. There are seven levels of verbosity; each level builds on the previous level, introducing more information into the output console. In general, default verbosity is set to level 2, and when enabled (verbosity specified without including a specific level) it defaults at level 5. For most troubleshooting, and as a general method to keep track of render progress, verbose levels 4 and 5 are useful. The following table describes the different levels of verbosity:

VERBOSITY LEVEL	MESSAGES LOGGED
0	No messages
1	Fatal errors
2	Non-fatal errors

VERBOSITY LEVEL	MESSAGES LOGGED
3	Warning messages
4	Informational messages
5	Progress messages
6	Debugging messages
7	Verbose debugging messages

Follow the steps presented for each host application to enable verbosity:

Maya

1. From the top menu bar navigate from Render → Batch Render or Render Current Frame and select the options box to reveal their attribute windows, as seen in Figure 1.2 for batch rendering. Both have similar settings with a difference in purpose. The Render Current Frame executes a render in the Render View, and the Batch Render is used for executing animation sequences.

2. From under Verbosity Level dropdown list you can specify the message level as seen in Figure 1.2, where Progress Messages are highlighted. Maya offers verbose levels 0 through 6.

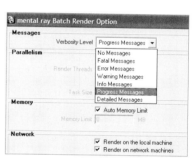

3. When rendering using the Render Current Frame attribute (or icon shortcut), Windows users will see the output displayed in the Maya Output Window; OS X users will see it within a console window. (OS X users, note that you need to run Maya from the Maya console for this to function correctly.)

4. When rendering using the Batch Render attribute the verbosity output is saved in the Maya Render Log text file. The file is located under the user\My Documents\maya directory. Note that in this mode the verbosity is not visible during the render in the Maya Output window.

Figure 1.2

Enabling verbose message output from Maya. You'll see the resulting messages in the Maya Output window, the Maya console (OS X), or in the Script Editor.

In previous versions of Maya (8.0 and lower), verbosity options are located under the Render Settings window → mental ray tab → Translation rollout.

XSI

1. Navigate from the top main menu or the Render toolbar (on the left side) to Render → Render Manager → mental ray tab (from the left column) → mental ray Render Options rollout → Diagnostics tab as seen in Figure 1.3. When per pass mental ray options are in effect use the Current Pass → mental ray Render Options, as further discussed in the sidebar "The Render manager in XSI 6.0".

2. You will see a list of verbosity levels under Logged Messages.

3. Enabling Progress messages as shown in Figure 1.3 will enable level 5 verbosity. XSI verbose messages offer levels 2 through 7.

4. When rendering within XSI, you can see the verbosity output within the Script Editor window.

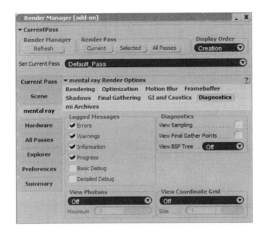

Figure 1.3

Enabling verbose message output from XSI. You'll see the resulting messages in the Script Editor.

3ds Max

1. From the Main Menu bar, navigate to Rendering → mental ray Message Window.

2. This window, as shown in Figure 1.4, enables both specifying verbosity levels and viewing the output results (mental ray progress) while rendering.

3. By specifying Information, you enable verbosity level 4. 3ds Max offers levels 2 (Open on Error), 6 (Debug), 5 (Progress), and 4 (Information) at the bottom portion of the mental ray Messages window. The top portion of the window also specifies information regarding the number of CPUs and threads that are being used during the render.

4. From under the Main menu bar Customize, select Preferences… to reveal the Preference Settings window. Under the mental ray tab → Write Message to File parameter enables specifying an output log file that stores the verbosity messages as plain text, based on the parameters defined under the mental ray Messages window. The Append to File will enable adding these messages into an existing log, rather then overwriting the file.

With all these host applications, using the command-line renderer allows you to specify any verbosity level, even if it does not appear within the host UI.

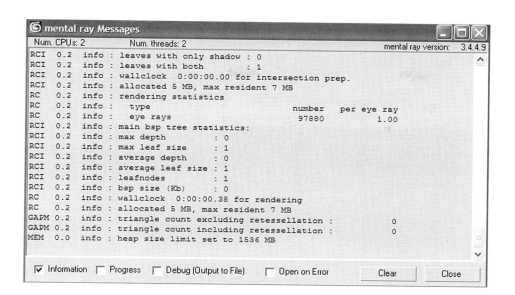

Figure 1.4

Enabling verbose message output from 3ds Max. The mental ray Messages window allows you to both set the verbosity level and see the output during rendering.

THE RENDER MANAGER IN XSI 6.0

The Render Manager window provides a more effective way to organize XSI passes and scene options. Essentially, the underlying concept is that settings are generally specified globally affecting all scene passes, however, you can then further apply independent per pass settings (overrides) when required. I will usually avoid any reference to scene (global) or per pass (local) options unless specifically required, as in both cases the mental ray options have the same relevance, just the context of pass or scene may differ. The concepts of passes and output are discussed in more detail in Chapter 3.

Consider that if you navigate in the Render Manger window to the Current Pass (in the left column) → Pass mental ray → mental ray Render Options rollout, the same mental ray options appear, which are tied with the global mental ray render options found under the mental ray tab (from the left column). Detaching this dependency is applied by pressing the Make Local to Current Pass option under Current Pass → mental ray Render Options → Rendering tab, which breaks the automatic linkage between global mental ray options (in the left column) and the current pass mental ray options. In both cases all the options are equivalent only with a difference in purpose, which is per pass, or globally for the scene. Once detached clearly the per pass options take effect.

In addition, the Current Pass → Pass Output tab also has a global dependency driven by the Scene tab (on the left column). It too can be disconnected by specifying different options under the Current Pass → Pass Output → Output tab. For example, if you look under the Scene tab, notice that the Scene Globals→ Scene Renderer dropdown list is set to mental ray, defining mental ray as the current scene renderer. If you look under Current Pass → Output → Pass Renderer dropdown list, notice that Use Scene Render Options is specified as a default, deriving the scene renderer from the previous (global) scene parameter. Thus you can always override this local option specifying the hardware renderer, or specifically specifying mental ray (if it differs from the scene global option). The same is true for the remaining options found under the Pass Output tab. Notice that when you begin to enable per pass options their relevant properties appear, enabling you to specify per pass overrides.

An Example of On-Demand Execution

Now that you understand how to output messages during rendering, let's look at what they tell you about on-demand job execution. Figure 1.5 illustrates part of the message log for a render using verbosity level 5. I've added labels and highlighting so that you can follow the discussion.

Figure 1.5

mental ray's message log in the console window. Here you can identify the render progress as well as troubleshoot problematic renders.

The first highlighted line reads as follows:

```
JOB 0.15 progr: 44.5%      rendered on Wiley.15
```

All lines are formatted in a similar way, providing information from various mental ray modules and jobs. From left to right, the line tells us that the module JOB (a general indication of the render progress of a specific job, or render task, unique to mental ray 3.*x* and up) is currently operating on the following machines and threads. The machine reference is the first number (0) followed by a decimal point and the thread number (15). Machine 0 indicates the client machine that initiated the render, the machine that is currently being used to submit the render. The following message deals with the type of message this line is providing and its verbosity level, hence a progress (level 5) message, which is then followed by a plain-English description for the current information. The description confirms that mental ray has completed 44.5 percent of the rendering on this machine (0 - Wiley) using thread number 15, which is clearly a progress message on the status of a particular job, hence a level-5 verbosity message.

In section A of Figure 1.5, the highlighted text reads as follows:

```
IMG 0.7 progr: opening texture F:path…, for reading
```

This line tells us that the IMG module is providing the progress message and that this module is currently loading a texture file into memory. The messages in section B begin as follows:

```
GAPM 0.5 info: created 16 tesselation jobs from object...
```

This line indicates that the GAPM module, which deals with geometry approximation, is creating new tessellation jobs. Note that 50.0 percent of the render has already completed and mental ray is still initializing new tessellation jobs during the render. This should provide some insight into how mental ray actually utilizes the on-demand rendering process in practice. That is, geometry will be calculated only when needed rather than as prerequisite for rendering.

Because mental ray (3.x and up) executes only on-demand jobs, it does not need to tessellate an entire scene, only the elements that are required by the jobs. This essentially enables mental ray to ignore geometry that is not needed for a particular frame, even if it exists within the scene. Only geometry that is needed for a given frame will be tessellated. Further, if geometry is no longer needed, mental ray can clear it from cache, freeing up space for new geometry based on demand. Of course, this approach also has disadvantages: If the memory limit is exceeded, mental ray may dump the cache of geometry that will be needed in a subsequent frame, or even within that same frame (the later is unlikely). If geometry is removed from the cache, then that geometry will need to be recalculated the next time it needs to be used, such as in a subsequent frame. This sort of memory-dump behavior may be required for extremely "heavy" scenes or machines with a low memory capacity. On the other hand, if mental ray recognizes that the geometry will be needed in subsequent frames or by other jobs, it will try to keep it in the cache as long as there is sufficient memory to support completing other ongoing jobs. Essentially, any type of data may be loaded or removed from the geometry cache, based on mental ray's ability to determine the best workflow for rendering. Thus, mental ray efficiently divides the scene into small jobs that optimize render times and improve memory handling, trying to follow the most efficient path while increasing memory gradually in a stable manner.

Images loaded into memory, whether texture files, light maps, or any other image file data, have a significant impact on memory usage. Notice that Figure 1.5 displays two RAM PF Usage indicators showing how the memory usage increased after loading in additional images between 40 percent and 50 percent of the render completion. mental ray tries to improve image handling in different ways. For example, additional boosts in performance are provided by mental ray's ability to consider partial *Shadow maps* that can be quite large in file size. (You'll learn more about shadow maps in Chapter 7, "Shadow Algorithms.")

Dividing a rendering task into jobs also helps mental ray maximize performance by taking advantage of multiple processors on a single machine (*thread parallelism*). With multiple machines, *network parallelism* enables mental ray to use all the available processors over a network of multiprocessor machines to execute jobs. This significantly increases the ability to process large frames and data. For example, a traditional nonparallel render would render a frame on each processor, separate from the other frames. With parallelism, one frame can be computed over several processors and networked machines. Hence, network rendering can take advantage of mental ray's abilities to divide a render into jobs and effectively distribute them over the network, efficiently handling the flow of data. mental ray 3.2 and above also supports Intel's *Hyper-Threading*, when it's available.

mental ray Integration

This book focuses on using mental ray as it's integrated with three of the most widely used packages: Autodesk (Maya and 3ds Max) and Avid (XSI).

XSI has always incorporated mental ray, which is its default software renderer and currently the only software renderer that ships with it. Maya and 3ds Max both added integration with mental ray as their users came to need an alternative rendering solution. For users, this seamless integration appears simple and straightforward; behind the scenes, however, is a complex integration based on ongoing technical development. The functionality that bridges between packages is quite complex, and the integration methods may differ between packages.

Currently, the best integration is within XSI, which is designed to render solely with mental ray. One of my favorite features about XSI, which is absolutely invaluable, is its ability to continuously update a rendered region regardless of the components that are being changed. Thus, XSI allows every change within the rendered region—including raytracing, global render settings such as sampling or diagnostics, and even indirect illumination features—to be updated, all interactively and while you view the rendered result. On the other hand, Maya's Interactive Photorealistic Rendering (IPR) view and 3ds Max Active Shade view both have limited abilities to display updates while you tweak mental ray–specific features; for example, neither software package supports displaying render settings or raytracing features, such as reflections, refractions, ambient occlusion, and indirect illumination simulations, among other mental ray–specific features.

Some mental ray functionalities and shaders exist only in one package or are better implemented in one package than in another. Examples include Maya's unique phenomenon shaders and comprehensive export settings (for .mi files), XSI's shader wizard that supports implementing new mental ray shaders, and 3ds Max's great implementation for mental ray's *multipass* rendering feature, which deals with saving separate mental ray sampling files and then merging them together (see Chapter 3).

The complex integration between host applications and mental ray is accessed through the mental ray application programming interface (API). This not only enables software developers to access all of mental ray's features; it also enhances their ability to further customize tools that integrate mental ray with their own application. This way, they provide a graphical user interface based on the different mental ray functions (modules) with support for controlling mental ray settings from within their host application (XSI, Maya, 3ds Max). Maya and XSI also provide their own mental ray stand-alone versions with their packages. Each package provides extended access to the host's customized integration and any plug-in tools they may have customized, such as shader libraries.

Typically, when you render a scene using mental ray, a translator program (discussed earlier under "Host Translators"), is used to translate the host application's scene description into the mental images scene description for rendering. Each package has its own scene description language as its backbone, which means that scene files from Maya, XSI, and 3ds Max are all translated into equivalent mental images (ASCII or binary) files, which can then be saved as an .mi file (mental images file) and rendered with the stand-alone mental ray renderer. Alternatively, host applications can execute renders directly from within their applications through the use of the mental ray API and the translator application.

Exporting an .mi File

The following steps can be taken to export an .mi file from host applications; note that they all offer similar settings, with Maya offering the most-robust settings for customizing the translator export. Figures 1.6, 1.7, and 1.8 show the different export settings from within each application.

MAYA

1. Navigate from the top main menu to File → Export All (or Export Selection if you just want to export a specific element).

2. From within the Export All Options window, select mentalRay from the File Type drop-down menu, as shown in Figure 1.6.

3. Notice that when the Export Selected Items Only check box (not seen in the figure) is checked, several additional settings appear, which enable controlling and customizing the translation process from Maya to an .mi file. Maya offers options to export specific features such as geometry that can then be externally linked into an .mi file (on-demand geometry) during rendering, or exporting mental ray shading networks as *Phenomenon* shaders (see the section "mental ray Shaders and Shader Libraries" later in this chapter).

4. After selecting the features you would like to export, you simply execute the command by clicking the Apply button from the lower portion of the window.

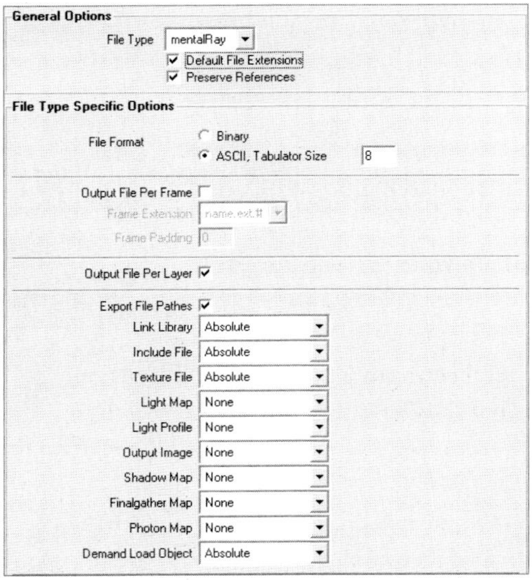

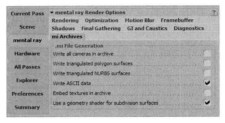

Figure 1.6

The Maya-to-mental-ray export dialog window (partial display). Here you control how Maya converts to mental ray .mi file formats.

Figure 1.7

The XSI-to-mental-ray export options found under the mental ray Render Options → mi Archives for a given pass, or globally for a scene.

XSI

1. Navigate from the top main menu or under the Render toolbar (on the left side) to Render → Render Manager.

2. From the mental ray tab (or the Current Pass tab) reveal the mental ray Render Options → mi Archives tab. As with all host applications, a number of features appear for controlling how these settings are exported, as seen in Figure 1.7. Notice that with XSI, you have an option to override the scene globals using the equivalent Current Pass options, as discussed under "The Render Manger in XSI 6.0" sidebar.

3. In the Render Manager window under Current Pass → Pass Output tab → Archive, the Scene Archiving property (when enabled) exports frames incrementally within an .mi file, a topic further discussed in the following "Incremental Frames" section.

4. After specifying the required settings, navigate from the main menu bar or the Render toolbar to Export → Current Pass (or any of the other options) to initiate the export. The files will be saved into the current projects "Render_Pictures" directory.

3DS MAX

1. From the main toolbar, select the Rendering → Render… (F8) window, which opens the Render Scene: mental ray Renderer window.

2. In the Render Scene: mental ray Renderer window, reveal the Processing tab → Translator Options rollout options. Within the Translator Options is an Export to .mi File section with some relevant settings, as seen in Figure 1.8.

3. When the Export on Render check box is enabled, an .mi file rather than an image is created when you render. After, after enabling this check box, click Render (as you would for initiating any render) to export the .mi file. The file will appear in the Render Output folder in your 3ds Max directory.

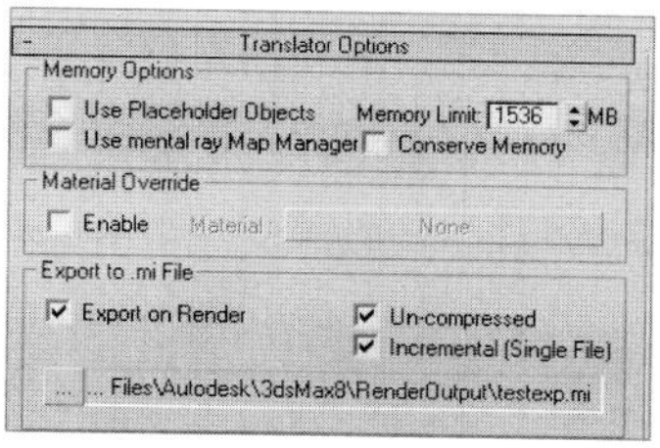

Figure 1.8

The 3ds Max Translator Options rollout for exporting .mi files from within 3ds Max

Commonalties between All Hosts

As with most mental ray features, there are several commonalities between these applications, and in this case they specify formatting options for exporting .mi files. All three applications derive most render options from their render settings as defined by the user. With Maya and 3ds Max, these would be the render settings you specify within the mental ray–specific render settings in each application and the Common render settings tab.

Some typical settings that are derived from the render settings into the exported .mi files relate to sequence frame length for animations as well as quality control settings. With Maya and XSI, these settings are also based on the current render pass (XSI) or the current render layer (Maya).

INCREMENTAL FRAMES

mental ray 3.*x* and up integrated a new approach with respect to describing animation within .mi files. This new approach refers to defining only changes that occur from one frame to the next, hence describing an *incremental* change. With this approach, rather than geometry or any other feature being described on a per-frame basis, only changes from the preceding frame need to be provided. Note that each package provides an option to export mental ray both on per-file basis (a file per frame) and as a single file that incorporates this new incremental approach. In 3ds Max, there is an Incremental (Single File) attribute, within XSI there is the same Scene Archiving property, and Maya outputs incrementally by excluding the Output File Per Frame option. Hence all three packages provide the same function in similar ways, and all describe incremental frames using the same mental images scene description structure.

> To see an example of this, export a sequence of about 10 frames from your application of choice and then examine the .mi file within a text editor. Try different settings from the export options and note how they influence the export.

The benefit of using incremental frames lends to optimizing rendering performance, as well as making .mi files more readable, by reducing the amount of clutter found within repeatedly redefined frames. For example, consider a camera traveling through an environment that requires only the camera's spatial position for each frame to change, in which case only the camera would appear in the incremental statements within the .mi file.

ASCII VS. BINARY EXPORT

Each host application also offers ASCII or binary export options for .mi files. Thus mental ray files can either be ASCII (*plain text* files) or binary files. ASCII-encoded files are human-readable text files, and each character (of any type) is represented by 1 byte. Thus, with ASCII-encoded files, there is a one-to-one mapping between characters and bytes. Binary files support compression, particularly of vector data, in a form that provides more characters to be represented by fewer bytes; hence the file can be smaller and not as user-friendly. Typically for editing .mi files, you would take advantage of the ASCII export features. Additional export features from these host applications relate to geometry tessellation, file linking, and declarations, among other features, which change how the host applications export .mi files.

mental ray Components and Application Files

As integrated into host software, mental ray consists of three main components: application files, *shader libraries,* and *shader declaration* files. These files are always stored within the root directory of each application. They include most of the base files that ship with mental ray, as well as additional files provided by the different OEM partners.

The additional files that each application provides are primarily the host's custom shader libraries, which describe host specific shaders found within that application. With XSI, as it is solely based on mental ray, these are actually custom shaders developed specifically for rendering with mental ray. In general, shader libraries provide for three main functions: converting application-based shaders to mental ray, integrating new custom shaders within the application, and loading the mental ray base shader libraries into the application. (You'll learn more about shaders in mental ray later in this chapter and in Chapters 10 and 11.) In Maya or 3ds Max, for example, their software native (not mental ray–specific) shaders can be found within the extended mental ray shader libraries (`mayabase.mi` and `3dsmax8.mi`, respectively) and are used to translate already existing "native" shading models into models that mental ray can support and render, hence integrating these shaders with mental ray rendering. The Paint phenomenon shader library, however, is a collection of mental ray–specific custom shaders that deal specifically with vehicle shading and have been integrated into Maya, providing new mental ray custom shaders that are not part of the mental ray base shader libraries or XSI, and 3ds Max, native (host specific) shaders.

Tables 1.1–1.5 summarize the different types of files typically included with host applications, and Table 1.6 shows their directory locations for mental ray source files.

APPLICATIONS	DEFINITION
ray	mental ray renderer (the mental ray executable file is labeled differently in host specific stand-alone versions.)
imf_disp	Image display utility. Type **imf_disp** into a command line console window to open this utility. Note that you may need to specify the utility's directory location; you can then use it to view mental ray–supported image formats.
imf_copy	Image copying and conversion utility. Used to convert to different image formats and to mental ray memory-mapped images (.map). Type **imf_copy** into the command line and then execute to see a list of supported flags and help.
imf_info	Provides image-related info.
imf_diff	A comparison utility for comparing images.
mkmishader	Used for writing shaders; creates C-based shader skeletons.
fg_copy	A utility that handles merging several Final Gather maps and is extremely useful at reducing Final Gather flickering. More on this in Chapter 13, "Final Gathering and Ambient Occlusion."

Table 1.1

Base Application Files Typically Included with Maya and XSI

Note that XSI and Maya use different versions of the ray *render command with their respective stand-alone versions. XSI uses the* ray3 *command and Maya uses the* mental ray render *command.*

DECLARATION FILE	SHADER LIBRARY
base.mi	base.dll or base.so
physics.mi	physics.dll or physics.so
contour.mi	contour.dll or contour.so
subsurface.mi	Subsurface.dll or subsurface.so
architectural.mi	architectural.dll or architectural.so
paint.mi	paint.dll or paint.so

Table 1.2

Shader Declaration and Shader Library Files Typically Included with Host Applications

With respect to the OS platform, shaders are Dynamic Shared Object (DSO) files on Unix-based systems and Dynamic Link Libraries (DLLs) on Windows-based systems.

DECLARATION FILE	SHADER LIBRARY
mayabase.mi	mayabase.dll
mayahair.mi	mayahair.dll
surfaceSampler.mi	surfaceSampler.dll

Table 1.3

Custom Shader Declaration and Library Files Included with Maya

DECLARATION FILE	SHADER LIBRARY
sibase.mi	Sibase.dll
motionblur.mi	motionblur.dll
softimage.mi	Softimage.dll
softimage.mi2	Softimage.dll
legacy.mi	Legacy.dll

Table 1.4

Custom Shader Declaration and Library Files Included with XSI

In XSI an some base and custom shaders exist, which are not ecessarily exposed in the UI. You can find the SPDL files used to declare these (unexposed) shaders within the different directories found in the installation path under; Softimage\XSI_6.0\Application\phenolib\spdl, for example, the mibase folder. The SPDL files can then be used to install unexposed shaders using the Plug-in Manager window, a topic further discussed in Chapter 10.

Table 1.5	DECLARATION FILE	SHADER LIBRARY
Custom Shader Declaration and Library Files Included with 3ds Max	3dsmax8.mi	3dsmax8.dll
	3dsmaxhair.mi	3dsmaxhair.dll
	physics_phen.mi	Physics_phen.dll
	lume.mi2	lume.dll

Table 1.6	APPLICATION	WINDOWS DIRECTORY
Directory Locations for mental ray Source Files	Maya	C:\Program Files\Alias\Maya7.0\mentalray
	XSI	C:\Softimage\XSI_5.0\Application\rsrc
	3ds Max	C:\Program Files\Autodesk\3ds Max 9\mentalray\ shaders_standard

Typically, an include folder contains all the shader declaration files and an additional lib folder includes the .dll *or* .so *shader libraries. Also note that C:\ simply represents the root drive; your actual drive may be different.*

The mental ray Initialization File (.rayrc)

Each application uses an additional file, named rayrc (or some variant), that defines and links mental ray shader libraries and also sets mental ray environment variables. The rayrc file is essential for mental ray's integration with these applications. It can be found within the same mental ray directories that include shader declaration files and libraries:

APPLICATION	RAYRC DIRECTORY	RAYRC FILE
Maya	Alias\Maya7.0\mentalray\	maya.rayrc
XSI	Softimage\XSI_5.0\Application\rsrc\	ray3rc
3ds Max	Autodesk\3ds Max 9\mentalray\	rayrc

The rayrc file is loaded when your application loads. It provides your application and mental ray with shader declarations and links to shader libraries so that you may render mental ray shaders from within these applications. Any additional shader or shader library that you would like to add to your application must first be declared and linked through this rayrc file. The following is a portion of the maya.rayrc file that deals with linking shader libraries and shader declaration files when Maya is started:

```
# Copyright 1986-2003 by mental images GmbH & Co.KG, Fasanenstr. 81,
D-10623
# Berlin, Germany. All rights reserved.

registry "{MRMAYA_START}"
        link    "{MAYABASE}/lib/base.{DSO}"
        link    "{MAYABASE}/lib/physics.{DSO}"
        link    "{MAYABASE}/lib/mayabase.{DSO}"
        link    "{MAYABASE}/lib/contour.{DSO}"
        link    "{MAYABASE}/lib/subsurface.{DSO}"
        link    "{MAYABASE}/lib/paint.{DSO}"
```

```
            link        "{MAYABASE}/lib/mi_openexr.{DSO}"
            link        "{MAYABASE}/lib/mayahair.{DSO}"
            mi        "{MAYABASE}/include/mayabase.mi"
            mi         "{MAYABASE}/include/base.mi"
            mi         "{MAYABASE}/include/physics.mi"
            mi         "{MAYABASE}/include/contour.mi"
            mi         "{MAYABASE}/include/subsurface.mi"
            mi         "{MAYABASE}/include/paint.mi"
            mi         "{MAYABASE}/include/mayahair.mi"
            echo        "mental ray for Maya - startup done"
      end registry

            $lookup      "{MRMAYA_START}"
```

Each .mi file listed within the rayrc file consists of shader declarations in plain text, using the mental images scene description language. The link statements are used to connect these declarations with the compiled shaders from their respective shader libraries. You can learn more about this integration in the section "mental ray Shaders and Shader Libraries" later in this chapter.

> With Maya 8, Maya 8 and 3ds Max 9 it will suffice to place new shader DLLs and .mi declaration files within the correct directories. There is no longer a need to add them to the rayrc file because those directoriesare searched for any available shader libraries and appended automatically. In Maya use the mentalray\include and lib folders, and with 3ds Max use the shaders_autoload\include and shaders folders. With XSI shaders are typically installed using .xsiaddon files that are unpacked into the user add-on paths. The topic of custom shaders and installation is discussed in detail in Chapter 11.

Command-Line Rendering and the Stand-Alone Renderer

Another powerful feature mental ray offers is a stand-alone renderer. In general, large productions or smaller high-end specialist production houses can get more from mental ray by using the stand-alone renderer for troubleshooting. They use it primarily for taking advantage of additional mental ray features that are not fully incorporated in host software packages and instead of, or as a means to develop render farms without a need to install host applications on render nodes (making it more cost-effective). mental ray has several features for fine-tuning renders and dealing with problems such as memory or flickering that can be improved while using the full power of mental ray, the stand-alone version. With the stand-alone renderer, most mental ray rendering options can be enabled, changed, or disabled directly by using override command-line commands while executing renders. For example, suppose you are rendering a Maya scene with the mental ray stand-alone renderer. After the host scene has been converted to an .mi file, you recognize that you need higher sampling values or more raytracing rays. You can just type in the appropriate flags and resend the render; you won't have to load the Maya UI, apply the changes, then resave and render the scene. In general for shader writers and technical directors, it is easier to write custom code that controls mental ray than to develop a plug-in for a host. For some, creating custom tools for rendering specific tasks may be easier with the stand-alone version rather than a host application.

> Currently, customized stand-alone packages are provided for Maya and XSI. 3ds Max requires you use the mental images stand-alone package.

Using the Host Application's Command Line

We have already covered the two main options for rendering with mental ray, one from within the host application and the other externally with the stand-alone renderer, in previous sections in this chapter. The stand-alone renderer obviously requires an .mi file and cannot render the host's native file format without translation. Another option for rendering is using the host application's command-line utilities. This means you can still use command-line rendering, but through the host's application and not with the mental ray stand-alone renderer. This sort of command-line rendering does not support using an .mi file, since it works exactly the same as within the host application. Thus, a Maya, XSI, or 3ds Max command-line render will use either an .mb or .ma (Maya), .scn (XSI), or .max (3ds Max) binary or ASCII file as a source file. Thus, rendering through these host command-line utilities, still requires that the host application utilize its translator to provide a mental images renderable file.

Some advantages of using command-line rendering are reducing memory the full host application normally requires when the UI is enabled, specifying batch render scripts that perform several render operations consecutively, and quickly specifying different render setting overrides. With respect to command-line overrides, you can use these overrides (*flags*) only within the limits of the host's supported flags. With Maya and 3ds Max, the available mental ray flags are very limited; hence their command-line utilities don't support the entire range of flags that exist with the stand-alone renderer. Each application provides an extensive set of flags for its native renderer, including common settings such as frame range, resolution, aspect ratios, and so forth, as well as some extended flags specifically for mental ray. XSI, as mental ray is its native renderer, supports the widest range of mental ray–specific command-line flags. Another point for consideration is that some shops develop in-house tools for their pipeline using Java, Perl, Python, or another programming language; these tools can then automatically construct and execute command-line (or shell) renders on a network by piping code for execution, provided the command-line utility they access supports the settings they wish to override.

In general, it is always better to render from a command-line utility rather than from within a package. Aside from reducing the amount of memory used on your machine, you gain the ability to list several renders within a command-line render script file known as a *batch render script*, discussed in the section "Batch Rendering." Command-line rendering can be executed directly in a command prompt window in Windows (or a shell in Unix-based systems) by typing the commands discussed in the next sections for each host application. Note that the path to the render utility with XSI and 3ds Max must be specified as part of the syntax; alternatively, if you navigate to that directory in advance, you can then execute the render without specifying the path. Let's look at an example of a command-line render using each host.

Command-Line Render Execution

On Windows systems, to open the command prompt, simply choose Run from the Start menu. You are then prompted for a program to execute. Type **cmd** into the text line and click OK to execute. The command-prompt window will open, typically in your default directory. With XSI and 3ds Max, you then need to either navigate to the directory where the render utility is located or specify that directory with the `render` command (see examples later). In addition, with all hosts you must specify the directory for the scene file that you wish to render or navigate to that directory and execute the command there, which then does not require you to specify a full path.

Note that you can change a directory in the command prompt by copying and pasting the directory using the `chdir` command-prompt command. For example, for the 3ds Max directory, enter the following:

```
chdir "C:\Program Files\Autodesk\3ds Max 9\"
```

Once the directory is set, in most cases you can then specify relative paths for the scene and image files from the current location. You will see the `render` command in the XSI and 3ds Max batch render script examples on the book CD; the following sections show how to use it with each host.

MAYA

With Maya, the command can be entered in any command prompt directory without specifying a path for the Maya render utility; however, you must specify a path for the scene file or navigate to that directory in advance. The following line can then be used to execute a render:

```
render -r mr -v 5 -s 1 -e 10 -b 1 "…path\fileName.mb"
```

This line, read from left to right, has the following meaning: `render` starts a Maya render, and the `-r mr` flag specifies that mental ray should be used (`mr` for mental ray, `sw` for software, etc.). Verbosity is specified with the `-v 5` flag, equivalent to level-5 progress messages. `-s 1`, `-e 10`, and `-b 1` specify start frame, end frame, and step increment frame, respectively. The path and filename are indicated at the end. If you type `render -r mr`

-help the -help flag provides a list of mental ray command line options you can review. Later, we'll look at using this command within a batch script.

XSI

With XSI, the command can be entered in any command prompt directory as long as you specify the full path, as in this example:

```
C:\Softimage\XSI_6.0\Application\bin\xsi -r
```

You can also use just the xsi command if you navigate to that directory before executing the command, or alternatively you can use the XSI-specific command prompt. You can find the XSI command-prompt under the Softimage program folder through your Start menu. In any case, you must specify a path for the scene file or navigate to that directory in advance. The following line can then be used to execute a render:

```
xsi -r -s 1,5,1 -verbose "prog" -scene "…path\fileName.scn"
```

This line reads from left to right as follows: xsi means start an XSI render, and the -r flag specifies rendering. Note that if you just type xsi and execute, the XSI application will launch. The -s flag is an abbreviated flag specifying the start, end, and step frames with comma-separated values. Verbosity -verbose "prog" specifies an output of level-5 progress messages, and the filename is indicated at the end. In general, the filename should be specified with a full or relative path, especially when using a script. If you type xsi -r -h the -h (help) flag provides a list of command line options you can review.

3DS MAX

With 3ds Max, the command entered in the command prompt must specify the full path to the render command; for example, on most Windows machines the path would be as follows:

```
C:\Program Files\Autodesk\3ds Max 9\3dsmaxcmd -?
```

The -? flag is a help flag that will list all the options for command line rendering. You can also use just the 3dsmaxcmd command if you navigate to that directory before executing the command. You can find that command in the the root 3dsMax directory. The following line is then used to execute a render from the 3ds Max 9 directory:

```
3dsmaxcmd -frames:0-10 -v:5 "scenes\filename.max"
```

This line reads from left to right as follows: 3dsmaxcmd means start a 3ds Max render. The -sframes:0-10 flag specifies the render frame range. Verbosity -v:5 specifies an output of level-5 progress messages, and the filename is indicated at the end. In general, the filename should be specified with a full or relative path, especially when using a script.

Batch Rendering

You can open a simple text file and list several lines (as seen in the following code), which will then enable batch rendering. As one render job completes, the next one can be executed. This sort of render list can be saved as an executable file. Within such a render script file, you may specify mental ray stand-alone renders or host command-line utility rendering. The following examples demonstrate an XSI command-line render script that renders separate files with different frames for each file.

Note that with XSI, you can only batch render continuously when using the XSI Batch render utility. I omitted the full paths, hence the three dots in the path directory. Note that with XSI (and 3ds Max), I first indicate a change directory (chdir) command so that the command prompt initiates from the correct directory, where the xsibatch.exe utility exists; without that, it will not find the utility:

```
chdir "C:\Softimage\XSI_6.0\Application\bin\"
xsibatch -r -s 1,10,1 -scene C:\...\fileName1.scn
xsibatch -r -s 10,20,1 -scene C:\...\fileName2.scn
xsibatch -r -s 20,30,1 -scene C:\...\fileName3.scn
pause
```

The pause command is another command-prompt command that keeps the command prompt open after rendering has completed so you may review render statistics; otherwise, once the render completes, the command prompt closes automatically. If you specify within the host to save verbosity output to a file, as demonstrated earlier under "Enabling Message Logging and Verbosity Levels", then you don't really need to use the pause command

If you type such a script into a simple text document, such as a Notepad document in Windows, you can save the script as a BAT (.bat) executable file simply by typing the name in quotes when prompted to save, as seen in Figure 1.9. For now, whether you are using Maya, XSI, or 3ds Max, I have provided batch-render scripts (for Windows systems) for each application in the Chapter 1 directory on the companion CD. Open these files and examine them; they should help you quickly and easily set up your own batch-render scripts. Note that you must adjust directories and filenames to match your system and files.

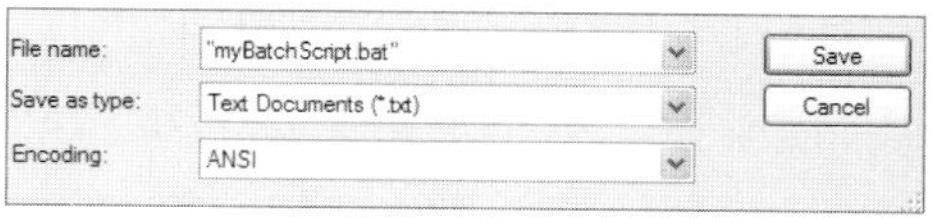

If you're using a Unix-based system (OSX or Linux), you can use the same syntax in a standard text file, but you must convert the file into an executable file through the terminal by executing the chmod a+x command.

Figure 1.9

Saving this plain text file as a BAT file creates an executable file that can be used to submit a render list to either a host command-line render utility or the stand-alone renderer.

mental ray Shaders and Shader Libraries

Shaders are the fundamental building blocks of rendering software. As you probably know from other applications, a shader is a program that determines the surface characteristics of an object in a 3D drawing. But mental ray shaders are far more than the typical surface shaders we commonly think of. There are material shaders, light shaders, geometric shaders, texture shaders, camera lenses, and more. You will learn a great deal about mental ray and its shader capabilities throughout this book. The mental ray shader libraries include an extensive collection of base and custom shaders. They include common shaders, like the familiar Blinn, Phong, Lambertian, and Anisotropic shaders, as well as the typical texture-placement shaders and light shaders that are commonly found within 3D packages.

Keeping these functions in external libraries enables software developers and mental ray users to easily integrate new custom shaders and shader libraries.

Shader libraries are collections of C- or C++-based shaders that have been compiled for mental ray and can be described as plug-in programs for mental ray. These libraries may include a cluster of shaders that handle numerous specific tasks. The declaration files describe these shaders and their options using the mental images scene description language. In essence, to use a shader you must effectively declare it within the mental ray .mi file. The mental images declaration files (.mi) essentially transfer shader information from these declaration files into the mental ray file. Once declared, they know how to interact with their counterparts from within the shader libraries. So you may think of these declaration files as your interface into the shader libraries.

Most mental ray shaders perform very specific functions. This approach lends itself to modularization and custom shader development. Because each shader is designed to handle a very particular task, shaders are not interdependent and can be used in various ways. For example, if you use a base *illumination* shader such as a Blinn, you can then connect it to a *sample compositing* reflection shader that provides reflections. Because the mental ray Blinn shader does not include a reflection shader, it can take advantage of a new and improved reflection, as you will see in Chapter 11. In contrast, if you used a host's Blinn shader, a reflection shader would already be part of its functionality and you could use only that built-in feature. Stripping down shaders to their base functionalities gives the developer more control in creating complex custom effects and reduces unnecessary duplication. In our example, the developer would need to write only the new reflection shader rather than a whole new Blinn shader, which obviously requires more work and provides less flexibility. The key concept behind this modular approach is to enable a flexible procedural approach for designing custom effects, combining multiple shaders in a way that provides for more-complex effects and more flexibility as well as a speedier development process.

Shaders provided by the 3D host applications are usually far more robust than a simple shader. Hence, some of these applications have already provided some sort of procedural shader tree based on several "simple" mental ray shaders. These shader trees are hidden from the user and typically combined by using mental ray's Phenomenon technology.

Phenomena

Shaders can be combined and interact with any other type of shader. For example, you may use a geometric shader to define a volume in the scene and then, using a variety of other shaders, apply a complex volumetric effect, or you could use several shaders to create a complex surface-shading effect such as subsurface scattering for skin. These shader graphs may be combined using several base mental ray shaders from the mental ray libraries (`base.mi`, `physics.mi`, `subsurface.mi`) that may include illumination shaders, light maps, sample compositing shaders, photonic shaders, environmental shaders, and essentially any type of shader. The process of compiling individual shaders into one of these compounds may be tedious and redundant. To spare you this effort, mental ray allows you to create a Phenomenon shader.

Phenomena are shader trees compiled from several other shaders, forming a complex effect. Once you have named and exported the Phenomenon, this new shader can be linked through the rayrc file (see " The mental ray Initialization File (.rayrc)" earlier in this chapter). The shader will then become available as a single node within each application. The entire shader tree remains hidden from the user so that the user has access to a single shader interface that essentially controls several embedded shaders from within the Phenomenon shader tree. The developer can create an interface for the new Phenomenon shader either within these applications or by editing the .mi file. Essentially, the creator decides what settings should become available from within the tree and manually links them to the shader interface.

Note that a phenomenon shader does not require a compiled shader library, as it is based on existing shaders. Thus only a declaration file is required that provides access to the shaders settings as well as the shader libraries that were used to derive this new shader. In production this tool can become very useful to streamline redundant shader trees and simplify the general process.

Indirect Illumination

mental ray is packed with tools to simulate the realistic interaction of indirect light with surfaces. As light reflects, it hits and "bounces" from one surface to the next. This explains why, although you most likely wouldn't have a light fixture under your desk, light that hits the floor would bounce and illuminat the entire region beneath the desk. This light interaction carries light energy and color from one surface to the next—a phenomenon known as *color bleeding*. To generate indirect illumination, mental ray uses a *Photon Map* that describes the contribution of indirect light on surfaces. Raytracing, in this case, is the process of emitting light photons from a light source and tracking its behavior throughout the scene. This sort of indirect illumination is used with the following mental ray features:

Global illumination is mental ray's primary indirect lighting feature; it calculates the indirect light bounce of diffused light. Diffused light in CG refers to the diffused color contribution from material shaders.

Caustic light, a subset of global illumination, represents the light behavior for surface reflections and refractions. As light reflects or refracts through surfaces, it typically magnifies in intensity and appears to focus or spread out based on surface characteristics. By using global illumination and caustics, you can simulate a wide range of light characteristics, which include diffuse, glossy, and specular light reflections. These light characteristics are discussed in detail in Chapter 10 "The Fundamentals of Light and Shading Models."

Participating Media refers to light scattering from particles suspended in air. This term is used to describe particles that participate in the illumination within a defined region. This is yet another powerful feature mental ray offers to simulate non-geometric effects that influence lighting. Typically, suspended particles of dust or smoke contribute by reflecting and absorbing light within a scene. This also has an effect on shadowing and direct lighting in the scene, as would any geometry that blocks or reflects light. You'll learn about participating media in Chapter 12, "Indirect Illumination."

Sub-surface scattering refers to the transmission of photons through translucent surfaces. Typically, this refers to skin, jade, wax, plastic, and several other types of surface where scattered light within the surface may become visible. mental ray enables calculating this sort of effect with a physical shader from the `subsurface.mi` shader library, which scatters photons within a surface. A second approach to simulating sub-surface scattering does not use photons to calculate sub-surface scattering but instead utilizes a complex shader that simulates the light influence across a surface based on *lightmaps* as well as certain parameters defined within the shader.

Final Gather is an additional feature that calculates indirect illumination, but unlike those just listed, it does not use photons to calculate its effect. The name refers to the "final gathering" of light influence in a scene. Final Gather is evaluated after global illumination (if enabled) has been calculated and before the render commences. This feature is based on casting rays into the scene from a hemispherical point on a surface and evaluating the total influence of light on that point, from the surrounding objects. This enables you to simulate the effect of light being occluded between surfaces in close proximity as well as simulate the influence from different light intensities derived from a high dynamic range (HDR) image.

Chapters 10 through 15 demonstrate and explain all of these features in great detail. You will first learn how light interacts in real life and then how that is translated and re-created using these indirect lighting algorithms. A solid understanding of light and surface behaviors will enhance your ability to control and predict the results of such simulations.

## CHAPTER 2

Rendering Algorithms

This chapter presents a detailed overview of the three rendering algorithms available with mental ray—the default scanline rendering, raytracing, and hardware rendering—and how they are used together and separately. The goal of this chapter is to help you better understand the fundamental rendering processes and the various considerations that will influence the decisions you make in preparing to render.

You'll learn about the differences between scanline, raytrace, and hardware rendering and their implementation and options in mental ray's host applications. Mastering this material is essential in order to optimize rendering, for the sake of both time and quality. The decisions behind an optimized render combine the "right" render settings for fast renders with the right approach for the development and execution of an entire shot sequence. Considerations such as geometric model resolution (triangle counts), texture formats and resolutions (image file size), special effects, and render passes all contribute to a successful project that leverages good scene construction to achieve render coherency. The chapter covers the following:

- ▪ **Introduction to Synthetic Lighting**
- ▪ **Rendering under the Hood**
- ▪ **mental ray Render Algorithms**
- ▪ **Scanline Rendering in Depth**
- ▪ **Raytrace Rendering in Depth**
- ▪ **Hardware Rendering**

Introduction to Synthetic Lighting

As we begin exploring rendering algorithms, it's important to remember that the ultimate goal of rendering a computer-generated image is to create realistic, finished surfaces by simulating the behavior of light in the real world. In CG, the process of surface shading is based on two main components: light shaders (lights) and their interaction with the surfaces' material shaders. However, as real light is far more complex than CG light, even the most basic light phenomena can become rather complex to re-create, such as *high dynamic range (HDR)* lighting, a topic covered in detail throughout this book. In CG, different rendering algorithms and complex shading models are used in an attempt to resolve these real-world complex shading challenges, providing more realism in 3D renders. Complex behavior can be partially accounted for by using techniques that rely on advanced raytracing algorithms such as indirect illumination rendering using HDR images, a topic covered in Chapters 12 and 13.

The main difference between synthetic 3D image generation and real-world observation is that in real life, light travels outward from a light source into the environment, interacting with surfaces both in its direct light path and in indirect light paths to define form, regardless of the viewer or recording device. Thus, in real-world conditions we instinctively think of light paths as initiating from a light source and traveling throughout the environment, reflecting light from different objects, and eventually reaching the eye, a camera's digital sensor, or film. In the realm of 3D rendering, we can perceive the environment as being defined by following eye paths from the camera's perspective into the scene, regardless of the algorithm. Each observation begins by theoretically following an eye's observation path from the camera position into the scene and examining the different color attributes for surfaces that collide within that path, such as texture, color, light, fog, and shadow influences. Thus, in the artificial world of 3D synthetic imagery, the relationship between the light source and the viewer is reversed. The procedures used to evaluate these "eye rays" differ between the render algorithms; scanline and hardware rendering don't actually follow any real "eye rays," (rather, they use other methods for evaluating the eye path), whereas raytracing simulates eye paths by evaluating triangle intersection along a given path through the scene, which is a more expensive form of rendering. These algorithms are all discussed in detail in the following sections and in Chapter 5, "Quality Control."

Our understanding of real-world lighting and photography significantly influences our approach to rendering practices, image formats, and output displays. Throughout this book we'll explore the topic of synthetic imaging and simulating real-world conditions using CG shading and lighting techniques. In Chapter 4, "Camera Fundamentals" and Chapter 9, "The Fundamentals of Light and Shading Models" you will learn more about the physics of light and cameras and their relevance to CG shading, photography, output formats, and even HDR images. The more you know about cameras and light, the more inspiration for your art you will find in even the simplest natural phenomena.

Rendering under the Hood

Rendering is the process of rasterizing 3D vector graphic information into 2D pixel graphics to create a raster image. To generate a raster image from 3D, the software must sample color values in 3D, optionally apply additional color processing, and then determine a final color value for each pixel. Basically, a *raster image* data type contains grayscale values for each pixel that are then interpreted as color channels within image viewers, such as the typical RGB channels. Rasterizing is typically referred to as the process of converting vector data into 2D non-vector data, just as vector-based applications you may be familiar with such as Adobe Illustrator or Macromedia Freehand do when you export vector data to a raster format, such as a TIF image.

In 3D rendering, there are two very different approaches: one is *software*-based rendering (both scanline and raytrace algorithms), and the other is hardware-based rendering using one of the two common 3D APIs—OpenGL and Direct3D—to utilize the computer's graphic processing unit (GPU) while rendering. Software rendering evaluates the scene pixel values sample by sample (even on sub-pixel levels) by utilizing scanline rendering and raytracing based on the scene's sampling levels and other related settings, further discussed in Chapter 5.

The other approach, which also uses scanlines (see the section "Scanline Rendering in Depth" later in this chapter), renders based on the hardware abilities, sending visible vertices to the GPU for geometry assembly and shading. Hardware rendering doesn't use the mental ray scene database (as discussed in Chapter 1); instead, it works with one triangle at a time, interpreting its related settings in "real time" but (unlike software rendering) not reading any information from scene database entries. Thus hardware rendering doesn't need to know about the entire scene and its settings; instead, the GPU works triangle by triangle to process and fill up all the resolution-dependent pixels. Although mental ray supports passing triangles for hardware rendering to the GPU, it is mostly a software-renderer independent of the GPU hardware. This chapter focuses on mental ray's software rendering methods and briefly introduces hardware rendering concepts and mental ray's integration with hardware. Software-based scanline rendering is the most commonly used algorithm with most rendering applications, and references here to "rendering" are to that method except where noted otherwise. All three methods are discussed in the following sections.

Sampling and Filtering

mental ray uses several approaches to measure a pixel's color value. These measurements are important because, as you'll see, different surface color properties are engaged by different color values and intensities. The methods of measuring the color values differ between the different render algorithms, but they all share one common denominator: *sampling*. Figure 2.1 demonstrates the typical software-rendering sampling process. Typically, evaluating a surface point consists of sampling color measurements from within the

3D scene (label E) based on the camera's *field of view* (label A) that correspond to the frame buffers (label B) pixel in question (label C). The same pixel can then be sampled more than once (sub-pixel sampling), as demonstrated with the arrows (label D) that are sampling the scene entities (label E) for the given pixel (label C).

Sampling is not necessarily restricted to the target pixel size with software rendering, and sampling values don't necessarily represent a final pixel value, on a per sample basis, but rather a step toward finding that final pixel value by *interpolating* (blending color values) a series of samples. Hence, sampling can occur on a sub-pixel level (*super sampling*), and vice versa, several pixels can be contained within one sample (*infra sampling*). In the case of several pixels within one sample, essentially only one sample is taken; this provides a color value for *n×n* pixels, resulting in obviously lower quality and faster render times. This method is a means for quick preview rendering.

It's imperative to understand that one pixel uses a single color value to represent several elements from within the scene (all contained within that pixel). Knowing how that value is calculated can help you control render quality, reduce flickering, and control render efficiency. The ability to sample pixels on a sub-pixel level greatly improves the interpolation of the final color result for each pixel and is a way of working outside the pixel's limitations.

Figure 2.1

The relationship between the camera, frame buffer, sub-pixel sampling, and 3D scene

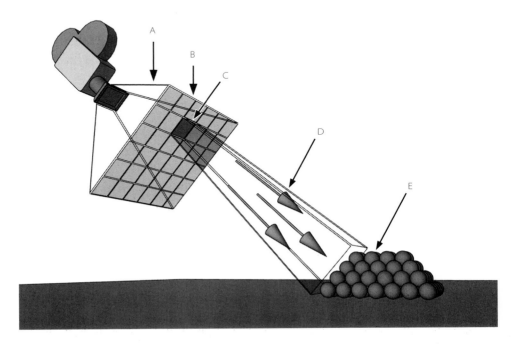

Aside from sampling, additional sample interpolation and sample *filtering* can be applied to provide the best possible color value for each pixel. Filtering methods are aimed at filtering samples into pixel colors in the frame buffer, improving how samples integrate with their neighboring samples before they reach the frame buffer.

Frame Buffers and Output

After sampling and filtering have completed, these values are stored as raster data within a frame buffer, which holds that information until it has completed rendering and is ready to be saved into an image file on disk. Before the image is written to disk, the frame buffer may also transfer that data to additional per-pixel postprocessing effects such as glows or blurring effects, to mention but a few.

Figure 2.1 illustrates the relationship between the camera, frame buffer, sampling, and 3D scene. In this case, as discussed earlier, the figure illustrates more samples taken than pixels. The Figure also illustrates the concept that one pixel within the frame buffer may represent several polygons within the scene.

> You'll learn more about frame buffers and their output options in Chapter 3, "mental ray Output."
> In Chapter 5, you will learn how to control sampling, filtering, and other quality-related settings.

mental ray Rendering Algorithms

There are three primary rendering algorithms that may be used with mental ray, along with different options within each primary algorithm. As mentioned, these algorithms are mostly software-based solutions because we are dealing with software-based rendering software:

- Scanline rendering, which encompasses three different scanline algorithms
  - The default scanline render algorithm, which is software-based
  - The *rasterizer*, previously known as *Rapid Motion*, which is also software-based
  - OpenGL accelerated rendering, which is software-based with hardware assistance
- Raytrace rendering, which is software-based
- Hardware rendering, which is hardware-based with software assistance

The following sections focus on the software-based solutions and their differences, then hardware rendering is revisited at the end of the chapter.

Although the product name implies that mental ray specializes in raytracing, scanline rendering algorithms are equally important and equally widely used. In fact, the software itself, as it evaluates a scene for rendering, determines which algorithm to use based on your input. The renderer is responsible for evaluating surface shader color values, atmospherics, and much more, and with each task mental ray will decide how to best interpret the surface based on the specified render settings provided by the user and placed within the mental images scene *options block* within an .mi file. The renderer can then decide whether to use raytracing or scanline rendering and in which form, as well as several other options that correlate directly to mental ray's render abilities, some of which can be seen here in a small excerpt from the options block of an XSI-to-mental-image file conversion:

```
options "Render Options"
   …
      shadow on
      trace on      >  enable raytracing rendering
      scanline on   >  enable scanline rendering
      hardware off >  disable hardware rendering (default)
      filter box 1.000000 1.000000
      face both
      trace depth 2 2 4
      samples -1 2
      samples collect 4
      contrast 0.2 0.2 0.2 0.2
      motion off
      task size 0
      caustic off       > Advanced ray trace features…
      globillum off     > Advanced ray trace features…
      finalgather off   > Advanced ray trace features…
      output on

   …
   end options
```

mental ray settings are defined within the *options block* inside .mi files. These options typically control the different render settings, which also can be overridden on the command line before rendering. When the command line is used, these options are referred to as commands and use a prefix flag (-). Also, when commands that contain more than one word, such as trace depth (seen in the preceding excerpt), are entered on the command line, an underscore rather then a space is used, as with the options block syntax. Within this book, the command-line syntax is used, and thus in the same commands under the option block, the prefix flag is omitted and the underscore is swapped for a space.

The different mental ray render algorithms may collaborate and render together, or they may be used as sole render algorithms. That is, mental ray may use only raytracing or only scanline rendering, or it may use both scanline and raytracing together. It may or may not use hardware rendering to boost software performance. Alternately, you may specify a render that is hardware-based, and thus mental ray will insist on using the GPU for hardware-supported features, such as basic shading and rendering, falling back on software for the more advanced features such as indirect illumination (a feature not supported by hardware). It's more common to combine the different software-based algorithms than to use either raytracing or scanline rendering alongside hardware rendering. Essentially, mental ray offers an approach that allows you to specify and tweak render algorithms for more-efficient rendering control. It is then up to you to find the best approach for each project or scene. By specifying an algorithm as well as its settings, you are actually defining the approach to several scene entities, such as reflections, refraction, motion blur, camera lens effects, indirect illumination, and much more, which are all enabled under the options block, provided their supporting algorithm (mostly raytracing) is also enabled.

Choosing a Method: Scanline or Raytrace?

When mental ray initiates a render, it will always begin by using the scanline render algorithm (unless that algorithm has specifically been disabled). If mental ray determines during the render that raytracing is required, for example to resolve a reflection, it will automatically switch to raytrace rendering. Scanline rendering evaluates the first *primary rays* cast from the camera's perspective into the scene; however, these primary rays are not raytraced. Instead, their path is inferred from information gathered in the scanline preprocessing phase (see "Scanline Rendering in Depth" later in this chapter). Typically, raytracing is initiated only when a *secondary* ray needs to be traced. Then, when the raytrace ray completes its evaluation, mental ray will resume scanline rendering until the next raytrace ray is required. In some renders, with scanline enabled, scanline rendering may never be used. For example, a depth-of-field lens effect requires each primary ray to be raytraced, so when it's enabled, the render will never initiate scanline rendering, utilizing raytracing for all primary rays. Thus mental ray will decide for itself when to trace a ray and when to only use scanline rendering, provided you've enabled those capabilities under the render settings.

If hardware rendering is enabled, the scanline process would utilize hardware methods to best evaluate all hardware-supported features, loading color values into the frame buffer. If raytracing is required, it may sample those raytrace features using software raytrace rendering, passing those values to the GPU, where they are then passed to the frame buffer and mathematically added to existing values, For example, color values calculated for reflections are added onto the non-reflective color values determined solely by hardware. This process is referred to as *layering* software and hardware rendering and is further discussed in the section "Hardware Rendering" later in this chapter.

Advantages and Disadvantages

Raytracing and scanline rendering differ primarily in the quality of sample precision and thus the method for evaluating a sample's color. Scanline rendering only needs to identify polygons directly in front of the camera and within a direct line of sight, while raytracing can examine surfaces by redirecting the line of sight, as with reflections and refractions. Thus, with scanline rendering, mental ray does not need to know where additional surfaces are located or even if they exist. For example, surfaces behind the camera have no influence on sampled points when raytracing is disabled, but when raytracing is enabled, they provide reflection color contributions. Therefore, if a surface point requires additional color evaluations, such as a reflected color from a nearby surface, raytracing at that point casts a secondary ray that looks for reflections or refractions based on the material shader requirements and thus provides a more accurate means in measuring color.

Because raytracing requires more information about these additional surfaces not in camera view, the time required for rendering is significantly increased. Thus, scanline rendering is an efficient and affordable means for rendering when you need only to evaluate a scene point by point without "seeing" the entire (reflected) environment. There are workarounds such as environmental mapping that provide "fake" reflections using texture projection (projecting color values from a bounding spherical or cubical environmental image) and are a means for simulating reflections using scanline rendering, omitting any raytrace rendering.

The comparison between hardware rendering and either of the software algorithms is essentially between software CPU processing and hardware GPU processing, and the advantages and disadvantages are based on hardware abilities, as well as on hardware rendering implementation in general. Hardware rendering is resolution-dependent and does not support sub-pixel sampling or high-resolution rendering, and it has little support for complex shading. In short, it is not really a competitive algorithm compared with software abilities. Hardware rendering is used when speed is an essential factor or when the development process is aimed at transferring mental ray shaders to a hardware-based platform, as with games.

Scanline Rendering in Depth

With scanline rendering, mental ray first preprocess the scene by sorting the scene triangles (polygons) into a 2D pixel array of Y and X coordinates, determining where each polygon should be placed. This array is essentially a projection of the scene using a direct line of sight from the camera's perspective, providing information on intersecting polygons. Within this array 3D values are represented by 2D pixel raster values, and not in 3D space coordinates. Even though depth (the Z axis) isn't represented directly, mental ray is still able to determine which object appears closer or farther from the camera based on the camera's depth range. Rendering is then simply the process of sorting the frontmost geometry within this pixel array based on the surfaces' spatial arrangement within the scene. This means that several triangles may line up at the same coordinates within the array so that polygons are overlapping. To sort depth, mental ray needs to resolve the triangle's location based on some scene depth measurement from the camera's perspective, which indicates where each polygon is located within the scene depth relative to other polygons at the same X, Y pixel coordinate.

Rendering can then be set to sample at a sub-pixel level based on the information gathered during the scanline preprocessing phase. With scanline rendering, once the frontmost object is identified, the object behind that surface may be ignored, and even removed from the cache memory. With hardware rendering, the preprocessing phase of determining polygon intersections and depth sorting can be extremely fast but not as accurate as its equivalent software-based preprocessing phase.

> With scanline rendering, mental ray's ability to sort depth properly depends closely on a proper setting of the camera's near and far viewing ranges because they define the accuracy of values used to define depth throughout the scene. In Chapter 3 you'll learn how to properly define the viewing ranges for scanline renders.

After preprocessing has completed (per render job), mental ray's scanline renderer can begin sampling points on the visible surfaces in the scene, ultimately resulting in a rastered image. One of the advantages of rendering on a per-pixel basis with scanline rendering is memory conservation. Only portions of geometry directly in front of the camera need to be in memory, so as the render progresses, different geometry segments can be loaded or unloaded based on demand and the polygon's spatial positioning. Hence surfaces that are behind the frontmost object or no longer needed may be removed from memory. This technique lends itself to mental ray's on-demand execution architecture, as discussed in Chapter 1, "Introduction to mental ray."

Scanline Render Algorithms

mental ray offers three different scanline algorithms—the default scanline renderer, the rasterizer, and OpenGL—plus a fourth option, turning off scanline rendering altogether.

The default renderer This option is the default software scanline rendering algorithm just described. This method also uses mental ray's primary sampling algorithm, further discussed in Chapter 5.

The rasterizer The rasterizer scanline algorithm provides two significant render improvements that primarily benefit film productions but are also useful for smaller productions. First, this algorithm sorts the scene depth much faster than with regular scanline rendering, which means mental ray can find the frontmost triangle faster and without considering all other triangles that line up directly behind it at the same pixel-coordinate position. Once it recognizes the first triangle based on a "first hit" from the camera's perspective, it can then ignore all the remaining triangles that are behind it. Essentially, the rasterizer does not bother to sort each triangle's distance from the camera in order to determine which one is in front; omitting this step improves the scanline render speed. Dealing effectively with dense geometry makes the rasterizer an attractive solution for rendering hair- or fur-intensive scenes.

The rasterizer can also accelerate motion-blur rendering. mental ray's motion-blur rendering can utilize either scanline or raytrace rendering without any significant difference in the result. When the rasterizer is enabled, only scanline motion-blur rendering is supported and raytracing motion-blur effects are disabled. This significantly improves render times, but the trade-off is that it doesn't support any raytrace motion-blurring features such as reflecting, refracting, or shadowing motion-blurred surfaces. However, the boost in performance the rasterizer approach provides is very significant and should always be considered when applicable. (You will learn more about motion blur with the rasterizer in Chapter 8: "Motion Blur.")

Is the rasterizer's sampling algorithm "better than" mental ray's default sampling algorithm? It does not provide the same amount of flexibility and does not support the same approach for sub-pixel sampling, although it can evaluate color on a sub-pixel level. However, it is particularly powerful when used to accelerate motion blur or troubleshoot large scenes that may have become difficult to render because of their geometric complexity. Some large scenes may have complex depth sorting for millions of triangles. Chapter 5 includes in-depth discussion on rasterizer sampling and characteristics.

OpenGL rendering   OpenGL rendering improves performance by using a computer's graphics card while determining the spatial arrangement of the scene before proceeding to render with a software render algorithm. The preprocessing scanline phases of intersecting surfaces and depth sorting can be quickly generated using hardware, which is faster than the equivalent calculations using software (but not as accurate). This process does not reduce the rendering quality because all the subsequent color-sampling evaluations are executed using software. OpenGL is used only to enhance the preprocessing phases; it is a supplement to software-based rendering and not an alternative method (as hardware-based rendering is).

One significant difference between OpenGL acceleration and hardware rendering is that with the former, mental ray will not allow hardware to do any shader evaluations. With hardware rendering, by contrast, mental ray does use hardware for shading. You'll learn more about that in the section "Hardware Rendering" later in this chapter.

The following excerpt of the render progress output for an OpenGL accelerated render (using Maya) shows that preprocessing is used for intersections and "primary rays," determining the visible triangles from the camera's view:

```
RC    0.2  progr: rendering
RCI   0.2  progr: opengl intersection rendering begin
PHEN  0.2  info : -------------------------------------------
PHEN  0.2  info : mayabase, compiled on Jul 19 2005.
```

```
PHEN 0.2  info : ------------------------------------------
RCI  0.2  info : opengl rendering time: 0.0 seconds
RCI  0.2  progr: opengl intersection rendering end
RCI  0.2  progr: begin intersection preprocessing
RCI  0.2  info : using OpenGL for eye rays
RCI  0.2  info : not tracing secondary rays
RCI  0.2  progr: end intersection preprocessing
```

Enabling scanline accelerated OpenGL rendering is fairly straightforward. On the command line you can use the -scanline opengl command, or you can use the same command within the options block of an .mi file. Within host applications OpenGL acceleration is available with Maya and XSI 5.1 and lower. XSI 6 and 3ds Max do not offer OpenGL acceleration. The topic of OpenGL acceleration may be fading out as CPU processor power increases and significantly reduces the requirement for GPU assistance, opposed to previous less capable CPU's.

Disabling scanline rendering You may wonder why it would make sense to disable scanline rendering explicitly when you already know that mental ray will select raytracing automatically if it needs to. The answer is simply to save the computer some work. Why bother calculating and sorting the scene for scanline rendering if you know that the entire scene requires raytracing? In these cases, disabling it will eliminate the scanline scene preprocessing phase. Also, if certain artifacts appear, or you are experiencing render problems (particularly due to depth precision), you may try disabling scanline rendering because raytracing generally provides more-accurate results without the typical scanline depth sorting process.

For example, it would make sense to disable scanline rendering within your host application if you're using mental ray's depth-of-field effect, which requires raytracing for every primary "eye ray" exiting the camera's lens. Likewise, poor scene depth may result when objects within near proximity appear simultaneously. They may appear to intersect each other when in fact one should be the frontmost surface. This may happen either because the camera's depth viewing range is exaggerated or because the objects are just too close for scanline depth sorting to properly determine which surface should appear first. Ray-tracing may resolve this sort of problem using its more accurate methods for evaluating the spatial arrangement of geometry within the scene.

Enabling the Scanline Render Algorithms

The scanline rendering options can be specified on the command line when using the stand-alone renderer, with the following flags:

```
-scanline [off | on | rasterizer | opengl]
```

With respect to scanline rendering, it only applies to primary rays, so in host applications you can specify whether or not to use scanline for primary ray color samples. To select them from one of the host applications, follow the procedures shown here.

MAYA

1. To open the Maya Render Settings window, start by pressing the shortcut icon or choose from the top menu Window → Rendering Editors → Render Settings. In the Render Settings window, under the Render Using drop-down menu, choose mental ray, and locate the Rendering Features rollout, seen in Figure 2.2, under the mental ray tab.

Figure 2.2

Maya's scanline algorithm settings can be found under the Rendering Features rollout in the Render Settings window.

2. The Primary Renderer radio buttons allow you to specify which algorithm is used for primary rays, which include the scanline, rasterizer, and raytracing algorithms. Note that when scanline or the rasterizer are enabled, they only determine the preferred algorithm and do not disable raytracing. Notice that raytracing is also seen enabled for secondary rays in Figure 2.2 under the Secondary Effects checkboxes.

XSI

1. Open the XSI Render Manager window from the top main menu, or under the Render toolbar (on the left side), Select mental ray → mental ray Render Options → Rendering tab. The render algorithms can be found under the Primary Rays → Type dropdown list, seen in Figure 2.3.

Regarding using the Render Manager, see the Chapter 1 "Render Manger in XSI 6.0" sidebar.

2. If you look in the mental ray Render Options → Optimization tab you can see the Primary Rays dropdown list again. Essentially the Rendering tab collects some of the basic properties found in other tabs, but not only. Essentially these two are then linked, change one and the other updates.

Figure 2.3

XSI's render algorithms can be found in the Rendering and Optimization tabs under the mental ray Rendering Options rollout.

3. Notice in the Optimization tab the Tile Size and Order properties (seen in figure 2.8). These options relate to the order and size of render tiles, a topic further explained in the sidebar "Tiling Order and Task Size" later in this chapter.

3DS MAX

1. For using mental ray with 3ds Max, you must first enable it as the Production renderer in the Render Scene window. From the Main Menu bar, navigate to Rendering → Render… (or press the F10 shortcut). Within the Render Scene window, you will find the Assign Renderer rollout under the Common tab, enabling you to specify mental ray as the renderer for the Production option.

2. In the Render Scene: mental ray Renderer window you will find the Rendering Algorithms rollout options under the Renderer tab, seen in Figure 2.4.

3. Under the Scanline title, the Enable check box correlates to the On/Off scanline options as cited earlier under "Enabling the Scanline Render Algorithms." Enabling this utilizes the default scanline algorithm.

Figure 2.4

3ds Max's scanline render algorithms can be found on the Renderer tab.

4. When scanline rendering is enabled, you can further select whether to utilize the rasterizer algorithm by selecting the Use Fast Rasterizer (Rapid Motion Blur) check box.

Raytrace Rendering in Depth

Raytracing introduces several advanced features and algorithms into the render process. At the most basic level, *raytracing* is really only another means of providing a more accurate color measurement for a sampled point on a surface. Raytrace measurements are more accurate because they sample points by "shooting" rays into the scene and then comparing each ray with the triangles in the scene to determine if they intersect. To clarify, raytracing does not really use rays, however it does evaluate triangle intersections along a given path in the scene, hence the term rays. mental ray offers three different algorithms that deal with dividing the scene into smaller segments, reducing the amounts of ray-triangle comparisons and accelerating the render time. These methods are described and discussed in detail in Chapter 5. Thus, raytracing refers to the process of casting rays into the scene from the camera's point of view; the rays then travel inward in direct paths until they intersect a surface. This initial phase of shooting rays into the scene for color measurements is referred to as *ray casting*. The ray casting algorithm was first presented by Arthur Appel in 1968.

TILING ORDER AND TASK SIZE

With mental ray's software rendering methods, the rendering process occurs tile by tile rather than line by line. From the host applications, you can control two tiling parameters that may affect overall performance: tiling order and the task (render tile) pixel size.

Tiling Order

For all three host applications, the default *Hilbert* tiling order optimizes the render in the most efficient way for job execution and render performance. It forces mental ray to use the scene database in the most logical order, which also optimizes memory handling when intensive geometric scenes are rendered. For efficiency, you should always accept this default. The other available tiling orders, which you might use diagnostically for viewing the render "pattern" in a different sequence on the screen, are Spiral with XSI; with 3ds Max they are Spiral, Left to Right, Right to Left, Top-Down, and Bottom-Up.

Task Size

The number of pixels contained within each tile is referred to as the *task size*. Task size can be set in the options block (as seen earlier in the excerpt in the "mental ray Render Algorithms" section) as well as on the command line. For the command line, the command is as follows:

```
-task_size [whole number - integer]
```

Task size is specified in square pixel regions and typically is automatically evaluated by mental ray within the host applications. When Task Size is set to zero, mental ray automatically resolves the task size based on internal computation and the target render resolution. Task size has some significant influence on sampling and filtering, which is described in detail in Chapter 5.

The task size can influence rendering speed in a couple of ways. Lower values generally take longer to render because fewer pixels are considered for each tile so there are ultimately more tiles to evaluate. With large scenes, however, setting lower values may help you troubleshoot a difficult render. In setting a tiling size for rendering across a network, you need to consider the other machines on the network. In general, a lower value will prevent slow machines from delaying the render, but too low a value will slow down the entire network.

As a general rule of thumb, the Task Size automatic setting is fine on single machines; however, when used with a network of machines, it doesn't evaluate their abilities. Thus when networking it is more feasible to examine different task sizes, and only if the render has become problematic.

SETTING TASK SIZE IN MAYA

1. From the Render menu set, Render menu, select the Batch Render (or Render Current Frame) option boxes to reveal their attributes.

TILING ORDER AND TASK SIZE *(continued)*

2. When the Auto Tiling attribute is enabled (default), the task size is automatically computed. If you disable the Auto Tiling attribute, then you can manually specify a value (pixel size) for the Task Size Attribute.

SETTING TASK SIZE IN XSI

1. With XSI, open the Render Manager and navigate to the mental ray Render Options → Optimization tab.

2. The Tile Size and Tile Order properties are used to control the size of each tile and the order in which it appears on the screen, respectively. (These options are shown in Figure 2.8, later in this chapter.)

3. As you can see, XSI then offers two tiling orders, Hilbert and Spiral, as well as an automatic task size, based on XSI's "best guess" for the scene, which usually should suffice. (But note the exception regarding network renders cited earlier.)

SETTING TASK SIZE IN 3DS MAX

1. In the Render Scene: mental ray Renderer window look under the Renderer tab. The Options section found under the Sampling Quality rollout provides control over these settings.

2. The Bucket Width setting correlates to the Task Size settings, as discussed earlier, and defaults to a 48x48 tile.

3. The Bucket Order option controls the tiling order and in this case offers several different orders to choose from, including the Hilbert, Spiral, Left to Right, Right to Left, Top-Down, and Bottom-Up.

Ray Casting

Ray casting provided a more accurate means for measuring color within the scene than the older and less-precise scanline rendering algorithm. The first feature film to make full use of ray casting, combining live action with 3D while relying solely on ray casting, was *Tron* in 1982, produced by the MAGI animation studio in New York. (Interestingly, it wasn't until more than 10 years later, in 1995, that the first fully animated scanline feature film was released: Pixar's *Toy Story*.)

Tron was a major event, if not the cornerstone of 3D feature-film production, using advanced ray casting algorithms to superimpose CG with real actors, making history. Remarkably, in the same year and using the same conceptual artist, Syd Mead, the unforgettable *Blade Runner* was released. *Blade Runner* remains one of the biggest influences on CG futuristic films, having opened the door to concepts such as genetic engineering, cloning, and futuristic environments. Where the creation of these environments such as with Blade Runner, relied on photographic effects and miniature sets, it now relies on advanced rendering algorithms along with the miniatures. Integrating all these elements with actors, backgrounds, and natural phenomena at times relies on some form of ray-tracing techniques, bringing realism into films such as *Terminator 3: Rise of the Machines*, a Warner Bros. film loaded with complex renders of reflective surfaces.

Raytracing

Raytracing, first presented by Turner Whitted in 1979, expanded on the ray casting abilities by including the additional reflection, refraction, and shadow ray algorithms. This means that as eye rays are cast into the scene, they can further trace these additional paths. As you've seen, the eye rays are typically referred to as *primary rays*, and the additional reflection and refraction rays are referred to as *secondary rays*. (Shadow rays are also a form of a secondary ray.) All these additional rays can be cast after primary rays intersect with a surface, if needed, based on the render options you specify for a scene, and of course the surface shader. For example, if you've enabled raytrace shadows, reflections, or refractions, then additional rays trace the path from the intersecting point to the next intersecting point, returning information about the color that should be visible on the first point of intersection. The traced path also can provide a means for measuring the distance between two traced points, which opens the door to advanced reflection, refraction, and shadow techniques and is discussed shortly, as well as demonstrated in detail within this book.

Raytracing always implies a change in direction for a given ray. Direct paths such as with plain transparency (index of refraction of 1) don't need to be raytraced; thus with nonrefractive transparent objects, scanline rendering (when enabled) will suffice. Raytracing is then enabled every time a specific shader requires the primary ray to change its direction, thus tracing direct segments in any direction. Furthermore, enhanced raytrace features also support more-accurate blurring of reflections (a more distant reflection should be more blurred) and more-accurate distant shadows (as a shadow falls farther away from the object, it both expands and blurs). You'll learn more about these topics in Chapters 6, 7, and 10.

In a nutshell, raytracing has evolved to provide more advanced features that have the ability to consider indirect, reflected, and refracted light contribution from the surrounding environment, as well as the total incoming *irradiance*, which enables utilizing HDR images for simulating real-world light intensities. Thus raytracing has expanded to consider the light energy reflected onto a point by other objects in the scene for indirect light contribution. In comparison to scanline software and hardware rendering, raytracing has access to the entire 3D environment, not just points directly in front of the camera, and provides increased accuracy in all aspects of image generation.

In Chapter 9, you will review in detail the different types of light-reflection characteristics, as well as how they relate to 3D shading models.

Also, with respect to cameras, the ability of raytracing to perturb the direction of a ray opens the door for implementing camera lens effects. Thus mental ray can faithfully reproduce several realistic lens characteristics (known as lens shaders) by bending the direction of the primary rays as they travel outward from the camera into the scene, a topic discussed in detail in Chapters 3 and 4. Another raytracing feature, known as *ray marching*, is the ability to evaluate ray measurements along a light path, determining the visibility of light; thus the raytracer may consider volumetric effects within the light's path that affect shadowing and lighting. If air or dust participates in the lighting of a scene, raytracing can then be used to evaluate the relationship between suspended particles in air by measuring the distance between each particle, a topic you will learn about in more detail in Chapter 12, "Indirect Illumination."

Combine these raytracing abilities and you are provided with a powerful approach for simulating realism. (Of course, this comes at the price of increased render times.) Almost all of mental ray's advanced tools rely on some form of raytracing effect. Raytrace features that incorporate advanced render algorithms, such as those used with indirect illumination, advanced shaders, and volumetric effects, are all covered in detail throughout the book, particularly in Chapters 10 through 14.

The Raytracing Process

As discussed earlier, raytracing is the process of tracing paths from a given point into the scene, investigating the influences cast upon that point from other surrounding points from within the 3D environment, and returning a color. Let's examine raytrace characteristics with Figure 2.5

Reflection and Refractions

In Figure 2.5, as a ray exits the camera, it is first evaluated at point A, the sampled point. Thus, at point A the surface shader is called and begins evaluating surface properties for that point based on its shader settings. If the surface is reflective, refractive, or both, the shader evaluation will determine whether a ray needs to bounce and thus cast a secondary ray into the scene to look for additional influence objects.

Assuming point A is reflective, a secondary ray is cast to point B. When the ray hits point B, the same process of evaluating the surface shader is repeated, this time for point B. If point B is nonreflective, a simple shader evaluation will return a reflective color value for point A's shader evaluation. However, if point B is reflective, an additional ray will travel, for example, to point C and begin yet another shader evaluation at point C. Thus,

Figure 2.5

The process of calcu-
lating reflection
bounces

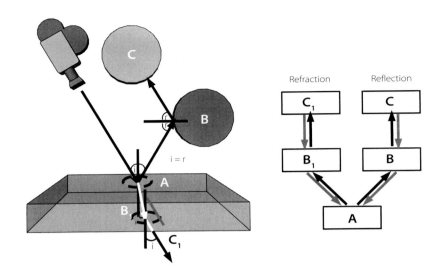

Figure 2.5

The process of calcu-
lating reflection
bounces

point C would return a reflective color to point B, which would then complete the surface shader evaluation for point B and return a reflective value for point A, as illustrated by the diagram within the figure. Black arrows represent the rays cast into the scene, and the gray arrows represent the returned values.

> The reflection angle of incidence is equal to the angle of reflection, as seen in Figure 2.5; hence reflections require mental ray to perturb a ray's path so that it can follow a physically accurate path into the scene, as with specular reflections (see Chapter 9), and then return accurate reflective values.

If point A is a refractive surface (index of refraction other than 1.0), then a refraction ray path is cast to point B_1, which is the bottom portion of the refractive container. At point B_1, another shader evaluation is executed to determine the color that should be returned to point A's surface evaluation, just as with point B (reflection example). If there are further refractions, then an additional ray would exit the container and travel to a theoretical point C_1. As with reflection rays, refractions follow realistic ray paths while evaluating so that rays perturb their direction based on real-world physics, in this case following *Snell's Law* of refraction. You can learn more about the physics of light in Chapter 9.

Raytrace Limits

With both reflections and refractions, the number of times a ray can bounce is based on the limits specified in the render settings (as described in the section "Enabling and Controlling Raytracing"). If reflections are set to a limit of 2 and refractions are set to a limit of 2, then you may expect up to a total of 4 raytrace rays to exist in the scene. Thus, each surface point may emit a secondary ray, reflection and refraction, which is permitted to "bounce" one more time within the scene before returning a color value because the reflection and refraction limit for each component has been set to 2, which includes the first secondary ray and one more additional ray.

Essentially, this means that in the case illustrated in Figure 2.5, as a secondary ray is cast from point A to B and then to C, if the reflection limit has been set to 2 the flowchart holds and the reflection values can be evaluated. Upon completion, the color values are transferred down the chain toward the first surface (point A), thus the initial surface that triggered the reflection request receives reflection colors influenced by both points B and C.

Max Trace Depth

A maximum raytrace limit can be set for the combined total of both reflection and refraction rays. In Figure 2.5 if the max trace value is set to less than 4 bounces and there is a requirement for evaluating 2 reflection and 2 refraction rays, then raytracing is forced to quit before completion. If the limit is set to 2, then mental ray can only evaluate 2 reflections or 2 refractions or one of each. This limit acts regardless of the reflection and refraction limits settings so that they can both be set to 10; however only a maximum of n max trace reflections may be evaluated. The fact that limits can be set independently allows you to tentatively set the reflections to a high value and refractions to a lower value and then limit the total of the two in a way that allows the renderer to make the best use of these settings, but within a reasonable range. Alternately, this also provides you with a fast option to troubleshoot or preview-render the scene with very low settings by changing only one attribute. As a rule of thumb, with raytracing, usually two raytrace evaluations will provide you with sufficient color evaluations; however, with refractions, if you do not provide enough refractions as required by the surface and the surface requires penetrating four times to evaluate the color, an unwanted value is usually returned, resulting in empty (black) spots within the image's RGB and alpha channels. We will examine these settings further in relvant sections throughout the book.

> Aside from setting these global settings, within each application, shaders and surface properties further allow you to specify raytrace limits, thus disabling or enabling raytracing for a particular shader or object. This extends these settings to a per-object or -shader basis and provides a means to further optimize raytrace renders.

Empty Space and Environment Reflections

If the ray limit is met or there are no other objects to reflect, the ray will terminate and return a color. If an environment shader exists, either globally in the scene or as part of a specific shading network, that shader will be used to calculate the reflection value. Note that this sort of reflection value, defined by an environment shader, does not utilize raytracing but is part of a projected shader, such as with a spherical environment shader.

In essence, several raytrace features can be easily reduced by using environmental projections to provide reflected color. We will look at creating these "fake" environment reflections in various contexts within the book. Note that the mental ray base reflection shader (a sample compositing shader) has a No-Trace (with similar labels in Maya, XSI, and 3ds Max) option that disables raytrace reflections altogether, regardless of the global settings. The underlying concept is that of using an environment shader to produce reflections for a particular surface. Sometimes, these environment shaders may be *panoramic images* of the scene itself, generated to reproduce reflections over several frames of objects that remain still. We will examine these concepts to some extent in shader-related chapters.

Enabling and Controlling Raytracing

The steps for enabling raytracing and controlling the different settings are almost identical for the three host applications. We will look at the raytracing stand-alone flags, and then locate them within the applications. Essentially, they have all been defined earlier in the section "The Raytracing Process." The following sections will focus on reflection and refraction, and you will further investigate raytrace acceleration methods in Chapter 5 and shadows in Chapters 6 and 7.

On the command line, with the stand-alone renderer, the following options are supported with respect to enabling raytracing, reflections and refractions, and max trace depth:

```
-trace [on | off]
-trace_depth [reflect] [refract] [max trace]
```

The -trace option enables or disables raytracing from participating in the render. -trace_depth, as discussed earlier, is used to limit the total number of times a secondary ray can bounce within a scene. This limit applies not only to the number of reflections or refractions, but also the total of both combined.

Maya

1. Navigate to the Maya Render Settings window, and under the mental ray tab, locate the Ray-tracing rollout, shown in Figure 2.6

2. The Ray tracing check box is used to enable or disable raytracing altogether, corresponding to the command-line -trace option. Note that the Ray Tracing check box correlates to the Rendering Features rollout → Secondary Effects → Raytracing check box seen in Figure 2.2. Thus if you change either one, the other will update automatically.

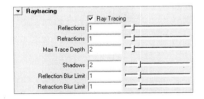

Figure 2.6

Maya's raytracing settings are found on the metal ray tab in the Render Settings window.

3. The Reflections, Refractions, and Max Trace Depth attributes are the same as the mental ray raytrace limiting options described earlier. These settings are the same with all applications.

4. The Shadows attribute limits the number of times a raytrace shadow can bounce and appear visible between one (reflective) surface and the next. Raytrace shadows are further discussed Chapters 6 and 7.

5. The Reflection Blur Limit and Refraction Blur Limit attributes supposedly control how many times blurred reflections may appear reflected or refracted. These attributes don't appear to function properly, the topic is examined in more detail in Chapter 10.

When you're using Maya shaders in a scene that will be raytraced, if you increase the raytracing limits under the Raytracing rollout, you must also specify correlating limits for the relevant shading networks, using the Refraction Limit and Reflection Limit attributes under the Raytracing Options rollout for reflective shading models, such as a Blinn or Phong shaders, as seen in Figure 2.7.

Maya raytracing shader overrides can collide with global settings if not planned carefully. Keep in mind the underlying concept of optimization—most surfaces don't require generating several bounced rays; however, when need be, you may increase the limit for that specific shader. Thus, with Maya you can set several limits on a per-shader level and then adjust those limits either globally or within the shader. One of the advantages with this approach is that it enables you to globally reduce the limits quickly while testing (without changing all your per-shader settings) and to prevent high global settings from affecting each shader. On the flip side, you need to remember to adjust these settings because they are always active when raytracing is enabled and they default to low values.

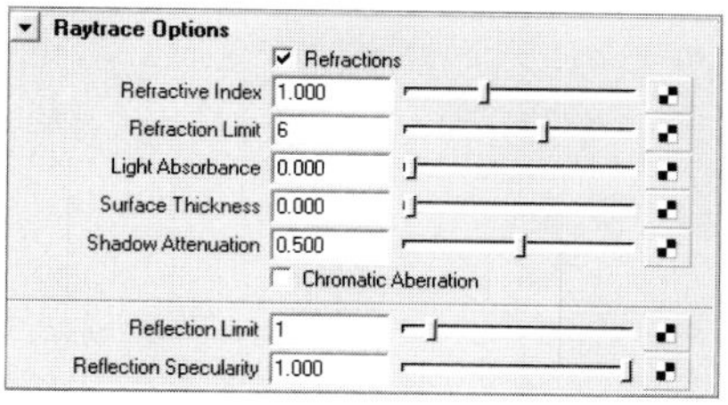

You can also specifically disable tracing reflections or refractions on a per-object level regardless of the shader or the global settings. This is achieved by navigating to the mental ray rollout in the Attribute Editor for the selected shape node (or from under the Flags rollout under a similar mental ray rollout on the transform node). On this rollout (under the shape node), you can disable both the Trace Reflections and Transmit Refractions attributes, which consequently will disable either of those raytrace features for that object.

Figure 2.7

Maya shader raytracing settings. These settings may unexpectedly confuse the user by limiting reflection or refraction rays.

Only native Maya shaders have raytracing limits; Maya mental ray shaders under the Create mental ray Nodes do not have these per-shader limiting attributes and are affected only by the global render settings.

XSI

1. Open the XSI current pass Renderer Options from the top main menu or under the Render toolbar (or in the Render Manager window). Select the Optimization tab, and locate the Secondary Rays - Depth section, shown in Figure 2.8.

2. Below the Secondary Rays - Depth title you can enable or disable raytracing rendering with the Enable check box, correlating to the command-line -trace option.

3. When Enable is checked, you can further specify the raytrace limits from under the Reflection, Refraction, and Combined properties, as seen in Figure 2.8. The Combined property correlates to the max trace depth option discussed earlier.

> Remember that XSI supports raytrace updates in its render region. If you want to see the effect "live," just drag the sliders up and down (under the Render Region Options) in a simple highly reflective scene.

> XSI shaders provide independent access to each type of ray; thus you may assign specific "rules" for the different raytrace rays, a topic discussed further in Chapter 12.

Within XSI you can further set raytrace overrides on a per-surface basis.

4. Open the Visibility tab for an object from the Explorer window (number-8 hotkey), and examine the Rendering tab, seen in Figure 2.9.

5. Under the Ray Visibility title, you can specify whether the surface is visible using the Primary check box. This option applies to primary rays, regardless of whether they are scanline or raytrace; thus, unchecking the Primary check box renders the surface invisible.

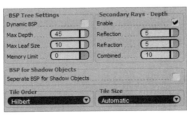

Figure 2.8

XSI's raytracing settings are found on the Optimization tab.

Figure 2.9

XSI per-object visibility settings enable specifying per-object surface-rendering properties.

6. The Secondary option enables casting secondary reflection or refraction rays for the object; thus when it's disabled, the surface will not render (will not "see") reflections or refractions, regardless of whether they are enabled as global settings.

7. Under the Reflection and Refraction titles, there are two options to further customize the secondary ray characteristics for both reflections and refractions:

    Caster disables the secondary ray for each raytrace feature. Thus when it's disabled, for example under Reflection, the surface doesn't ("see") render reflections of other objects in the scene.

    Visible enables viewing the surface in other reflected surfaces. Thus when it's disabled, the surface itself may render color, even reflection color (as when Caster is enabled), but the surface color will not appear in other surfaces that render reflections, essentially rendering it "invisible" to the other secondary rays.

Notice that several other raytrace overrides exist for other types of rays, such as with indirect illumination algorithms (not visible in the figure).

3ds Max

1. Navigate from the Main Menu bar Rendering → Render… to reveal the Render Scene: mental ray Renderer window. In the Render Scene window under the Renderer tab expand the Rendering Algorithms rollout (as in the previous 3ds Max scanline rendering tutorial), as seen in Figure 2.10.

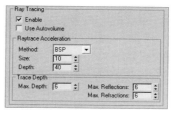

Figure 2.10

3ds Max's raytracing settings are found in the Rendering Algorithms rollout.

2. Below the Ray Tracing title, you can enable or disable raytracing rendering with the Enable check box, corresponding to the command-line -trace option.

3. When Enable is checked, you can further specify raytrace limits from under the Max Reflections, Max Refractions, and Max Depth attributes, as seen in Figure 2.10.

With native 3ds Max shaders, not mental ray–specific shaders, reflections and refractions also need to be enabled under the shader's Maps section, as seen in Figure 2.11. You can navigate to these settings for the selected shader in the Maps rollout in the Material Editor window.

Enabling the Reflection or Refraction attribute is not enough. You must also apply a reflection shader to the slot, such as the Reflect (Base) mental ray component shader or the 3ds Max Reflect/Refract shader, both seen in Figure 2.11 as Map #3 and Map #5, respectively. This process is identical to concepts presented in Chapter 1 for mental ray base shaders and component shaders.

Figure 2.11

3ds Max shader's Maps section, where you apply different shader types into the shader tree

Hardware Rendering

As graphics processing units (GPUs) improve over time, so does our ability to accelerate rendering using the GPU rather than the CPU. The most significant improvements in GPU technology directly relates to accelerating render performance at several different levels and can be seen within the increased hardware support throughout several renderers and host applications across the board. This integration more commonly relates to viewing and working with hardware shaders for hardware-based platforms such as games and not specifically for increasing software render speed. An example of this integration is seen with the extensive support for using and developing real-time shaders within all these host applications. For example, XSI enables viewing, editing, and troubleshooting Cg- (Cg stands for C-like programming language for graphics), OpenGL- and DirectX-supported shaders in real time, completely separate from any software renderer.

Terms such as *Cg*, *DirectX*, and *OpenGL* may be unfamiliar to CG artists working outside the "real-time arena," which tends to keep both worlds apart. The main gap between hardware and software rendering is in the approach to rendering. Hardware rendering deals with one triangle at a time, with no additional knowledge of the scene database. The GPU's sole purpose is to fill the frame buffer as fast as possible, providing real-time rendering. The objective of hardware rendering is to pass vertices through the GPU as fast as possible through the vertex and fragment processing stages (see "Programmable GPUs and Shader Trees" later in the chapter), filling up the frame buffer within the given resolution, as with, for example, real-time games. With software rendering, the resolution is not much of a factor, and theoretically, any resolution can be processed within a given time span and a properly set-up render, even if it requires rendering separate regions and then combining them within compositing. Another difference is that software can examine each pixel at the sub-pixel level, providing better aliasing and shading interpolation. The significant difference between both methods is then in the approach to rendering, where software can build a render more accurately, one sample at a time, regardless of resolution, whereas hardware initiates with the resolution knowing nothing about the scene and filling in pixels as fast as possible based on the resolution. One of hardware rendering's disadvantages for entertainment applications is its resolution dependence; you cannot render at a higher resolution than the system's graphics board supports.

Because (as you'll see) hardware rendering isn't a practical option for most users of mental ray's host applications, the following sections provide the book's only coverage of the topic, and we'll look at it in some depth.

GPU, Cg, OpenGL, and Direct3D

In the past, CPUs performed all the 3D calculations, transforming vertices to pixels and rasterizing 3D graphics within the CPU. The hardware only displayed the frame buffer after the per-pixel values had been fully calculated by the CPU. Today, software rendering still uses the CPU for rendering, but with much more powerful CPUs than in the past. One reason we still use CPUs is programmability. Although hardware has become extremely fast, it still doesn't support the same level of shader programmability and functionalities, such as raytracing or complex shading algorithms. Hence, the fact that hardware deals with one vertex at a time, filling up the frame buffer, obviously limits its ability to support advanced algorithms that require seeing other geometric objects in the scene, as with indirect illumination or other advanced raytrace features. Regardless of raytracing, most notable is the fact that hardware deals with a per-pixel value while software can perform several sub-pixel shader calculations and thus still is a preferred method for shading over hardware.

The GPU Advantage

GPUs have been developed to maximize speed and flexibility for hardware *vertex transformations* followed by *primitive assembly and rasterization*, creating vertices that have been lit, shaded, and placed within a specific pixel space as well as eliminating all unused vertices. The ability of a GPU to deal with such tasks in real time has some significant advantages over CPUs. In fact, GPU hardware can process hundreds of millions of triangles per second. As a result, your CPU can be relieved of these duties, which provides for a more efficient system pipeline by dividing render tasks between the GPU and CPU. Obviously, nowadays you may want to take advantage of the GPU while rendering without compromising quality, which is why OpenGL acceleration provides for a nice speed performance upgrade. Essentially it means that you allow the GPU to deal with vertex transformations, which in most cases will be much faster than the CPU, and then use the CPU for shading so that there is no hit to shading quality because of the GPU's limited shading abilities.

GPU Communication

To communicate with the GPU, we need to use one of two common APIs: OpenGL and Direct3D. OpenGL was developed on Unix-based systems by Silicon Graphics in the early 1990s as a means to provide a programming interface that is aimed at interfacing with the GPU. Direct3D, developed by Microsoft, is a component of the DirectX framework. Direct3D is also an interface for communicating 3D through the GPU. Currently OpenGL is the cross-platform standard, supported on Windows, Mac OS, Unix, and Linux, and thus the most accessible system. Direct3D is available only for Windows systems and most likely will stay that way as part of the Microsoft DirectX multimedia framework.

These APIs expect to receive compiled shader programs that are then passed as instructions into the GPU for processing. Using these sort of compiled shaders is referred to as *static compilation*. The shaders are written for DirectX or OpenGL, compiled by the programmer, and then passed to the API using one of these two interfaces. Thus, when you use these interfaces for hardware rendering with mental ray, you also need to provide, based on your system, a set of precompiled shaders that support either Direct3D or OpenGL, such as the mental ray `migl_base.dll` shader library, which provides OpenGL base shaders.

mental ray Hardware Shaders

When hardware rendering is enabled, mental ray automatically looks for hardware shaders that are named exactly the same as the software shaders used within the scene. The difference is that hardware shaders have a unique prefix or postfix to help identify them as hardware shaders. Cg shaders can be provided as source code without precompilation (see the following section), and mental ray searches for these .cg shader files within a specified path. These shaders would have the software shader name in addition to a postfix, such as with `mib_illum_phong_v.cg` or `mib_illum_phong_f.cg`, which stand for the two different hardware shader types vertex (_v.cg) of fragment (_f.cg) shaders, and in this example cor-relating to the `mib_illum_phong` base shader. When searching for a compiled OpenGL or Direct3D shader (or a shader library), mental ray expects a prefix such as `migl_base.dll`, which would provide a hardware shader library equivalent to the base.dll shader library. These prefixes for shader libraries are as follows:

PREFIX	TYPE
`micg_`	Cg shaders
`migl_`	OpenGL shaders
`misl_`	Direct 3D shaders

Cg, OpenGL 2.0, and HLSL

The high-level Cg shading language provides a solution for *dynamic compilation* of shaders while executing a render. Cg shaders can be used with any platform API and regardless of the hardware as long as the system supports the Cg compiler, or the Cg shader has already been compiled. Thus, Cg shaders are not NVIDIA-specific and can work on, for example, ATI hardware systems. With Cg, you can simply specify the shader code using the C-like programming language, which is then compiled at runtime when the render is executed and passed to the GPU through the platform's API. Thus, Cg comes as a solution to the lower-level static shading interfaces used with OpenGL and Direct3D.

Cg has been developed by NVIDIA in close collaboration with Microsoft, offering a more flexible programming language to interface with the GPU through Direct3D or OpenGL. The collaboration between NVIDIA and Microsoft has resulted in the high-level shading language (HLSL) for DirectX 9.0, which is equivalent to Cg, and Cg and HLSL can be used interchangeably with Direct3D on Windows systems. Similarly, OpenGL 2.0 also has extended the basic OpenGL support for a more robust shading language that extends the vanilla base-shader abilities of hardwired (nonprogrammable) hardware rendering to a more flexible programmable shader approach.

The importance for mental ray users is that when using Cg-specific shaders, you can describe (Phenomenon shader-equivalent) *shader trees* that are compiled upon render execution, assuming your system can link with the Cg runtime routine supporting dynamic Cg compilation. Essentially, whenever you render, the Cg code is first compiled by the Cg compiler for the specific graphics system's platform (DirectX or OpenGL) and in accordance with the GPU's supported abilities. Thus, Cg provides a common ground and flexibility to access any environment as well as avoid a tedious development cycle.

The Cg Advantage

The connection between all these technologies and the GPU is that shaders that process the appearance of 3D renders are all processed within the GPU. Thus the Cg program, which interfaces with the GPU through either OpenGL or Direct3D, executes within the GPU every vertex and fragment shader (see "Programmable GPUs and Shader Trees" below), repeatedly if necessary, until the shader process has finished evaluating. Essentially, with mental ray, when using Cg you can simply provide the source code for several base component shaders, which when combined form a complex shader tree, and then compile upon render execution. These component shaders rely on a programmable GPU to then execute several shader mathematical operations repeatedly, in many "passes," evaluating a Cg-equivalent Phenomenon shader. Figure 2.12 shows the approach to rendering with Cg shaders as apposed to equivalent OpenGL or Direct3D shaders.

Programmable GPUs and Shader Trees

Hardware shading abilities have come a long way, from supporting vanilla base shaders to being able to support shading trees. Shading trees are the backbone of any good 3D application; you develop a shader graph by connecting several different elements in a certain "tree" form, creating a complex effect. Supporting shader trees requires programmable third-generation or later GPUs. That is, for a shader to provide mathematical color-evaluation instructions, the GPU must be capable of interpreting and executing those instructions. A programmable GPU supports receiving such instructions through the OpenGL and Direct3D 3D APIs using Cg, GLSL, or HLSL precompiled shaders. Note that although you may pass Cg (only) shaders uncompiled, by the time they reach the GPU they have been compiled using the Cg runtime compiler.

In the past, the vertex and fragment operations were not programmable. They were hardwired hardware operations; thus, once in the GPU, they could only perform specific tasks that represent vanilla base shaders and not shader trees or programmable user-defined procedures, a topic further described in the next section.

Figure 2.12

**The hardware flow
using Cg, OpenGL,
or Direct3D shaders**

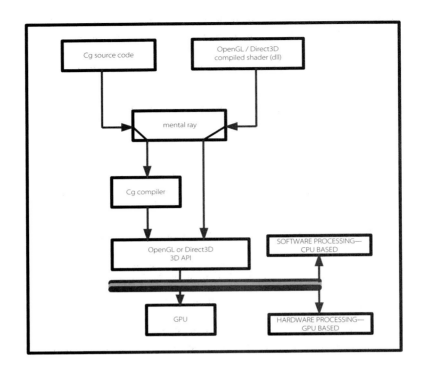

These advances in technology that have opened the door for programmable vertex and
fragment processing enable us to specify specific mathematical operations for execution
within the GPU. This essentially opened the door for programmable shader trees, which
can be very quickly processed by the GPU and match low-level Phenomenon shaders (see
Chapter 1, "Introduction to mental ray").

Using such shader trees through compiled fragment shader instructions utilizes the
increasing abilities of advanced graphics boards to perform (basic) decent shading calculations. So in addition to accelerating 3D, hardware rendering now allows us to render an
entire image based on the hardware's GPU abilities.

Vertex and Fragment Stages

The hardware pipeline first deals with tasks such as vertex transformations, screen positioning, and vertex prelighting. These are followed by the primitive assembly stage, which
creates the geometric form using the vertices, and finally fragments are configured for
execution. Vertex transformations are responsible for defining the visibility of objects and
their placement within the frame buffer. Fragments are essentially per-pixel shading operations that process color, textures, and the final output of each pixel. In essence, a single
triangle may have several fragments associated with it, and as GPUs have expanded to
support programmable shader instructions, mental ray commonly passes Cg fragment
shaders that specify a set of mathematical color operations to be executed within the GPU.

Thus, both vertex and fragment shaders can be passed at render time from mental ray to the GPU through one of the APIs discussed earlier, and as a result, the GPU may process several consecutive tasks until it has finalized the color for a pixel. This process is similar to compositing, as several passes are layered together to resolve a per-pixel color; fragment shaders may initiate a set of instructions that layer together several different color processes for each pixel, and at lightning speed. Figure 2.13 illustrates the processes that are carried out during hardware rendering.

mental ray Hardware Rendering

Currently, hardware rendering is a practical option only for stand-alone mental ray users. (Although Maya allows you to specify hardware rendering, you still need to provide supporting shaders as well as customize the render for hardware support.) Thus, hardware rendering currently is not an "out-of-the-box" solution. You may, however, find that it can greatly accelerate render times, and so you can research it further with your application and the onboard hardware through the mental ray help files. This section outlines some of the concepts behind mental ray hardware-based rendering.

Figure 2.13

mental ray and GPU flowchart

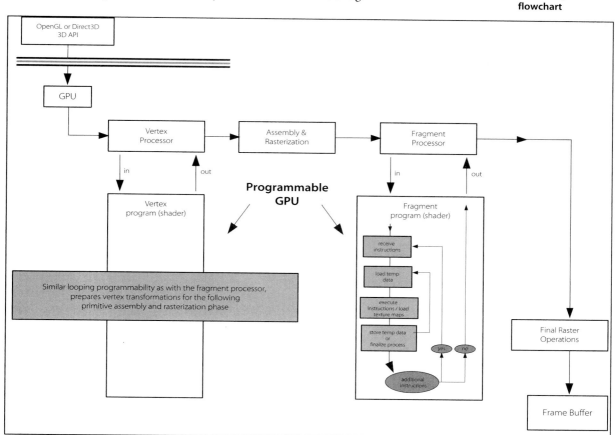

The fundamental concept is *layering*. This process refers to repeatedly rendering elements one at a time, based on the current shading task. This method forms an optimized render flow based on executing tasks in the "best" order. Essentially, hardware layering uses many data sources to evaluate each task that may originate from a hardware shading calculation, from a prerendered map such as a shadow map, or from a software rendering task. The execution would first initiate with the software-based tasks that may require the generation of a photon map, or shadow map, and then follow through to the hardware-based stages. Texture maps or light maps are typically passed into the GPU when called for by a fragment shader.

Hardware can deal exceptionally well with image files (within the onboard memory limits), but it can't deal with advanced algorithms such as raytrace abilities, so such data must be compiled into texture maps so that hardware rendering can leverage those advanced render features. Thus, as texture maps may represent a multitude of different effects that include indirect illumination light maps, shadow maps, environment shaders for non-raytrace reflections, and any other color contributing maps, hardware rendering may use them to add their colors into the color evaluation of a particular fragment shader. In essence, this process can be broken into two basic forms: mental ray hardware rendering can either read in precomputed image map files that the user has supplied on disk or precompute them during the render stage, on the fly, thus layering software rendering (scanline or raytrace) on top of hardware rendering, eventually passing the software computations to hardware rendering. One of the advantages of doing a poor job in preparation is that hardware rendering may fall back on software rendering when need be, so you are "covered" for all render tasks. However, this may impact the usefulness of the hardware render approach. It is important to note that mental ray is then responsible for layering and executing these tasks through the GPU based on providing the resources, regardless of their origin.

Hence, hardware rendering will use all available resources, initiating with any required software tasks followed by the hardware tasks (any number of times), passing color values to the frame buffer. This process can be extremely fast and have a significant impact on render times. Although reducing render times is an attractive notion, you also must consider hardware rendering's limitations, both in general and those specific to your hardware.

Hardware Rendering Capability Parameters

The following sections list some hardware rendering architectural implementation issues, capabilities, and limitations.

IMPLEMENTATION

Hardware rendering imposes on mental ray some implementation characteristics of its own:

- Hardware rendering has no knowledge of the scene and thus copes only with one triangle at a time, adding its color values within the frame buffer. This approach is significantly different than software rendering, which sorts the scene with a scene database, evaluating and distributing jobs based on the entire scene, as discussed in Chapter 1.

- With hardware rendering and OpenGL acceleration, the preprocessing phase is done on the client machine, and then the render is distributed between the different servers.

CAPABILITIES

As a result of hardware limitations, mental ray tries to increase capabilities using some workarounds, improving render quality.

- mental ray provides two approaches for increasing hardware render quality:
  - *Supersampling* enables increasing the frame buffer size so that, theoretically, pixels are sampled on a sub-pixel level, as the frame buffer is then scaled down to the original size.
  - *Multisampling* enables hardware to sample each triangle several times, each time passing the color to the frame buffer and eventually resolving a better color solution.
- Hardware rendering copes efficiently with texture maps, as cited earlier, and can sort depth complexity and determine triangle visibilities at a faster rate than software. Providing premade texture maps enables layering software solutions for complex shading algorithms during rendering using hardware shading.

LIMITATIONS

There are several limitations with respect to hardware, especially when compared with a top-level renderer such as mental ray.

- Only supports the RGBA (red, green, blue, and alpha channels) and Z depth frame buffers at a limited bit depth.
- Low-quality preview motion-blur abilities.
- Per-pixel sampling, which does not support sub-pixel sampling, so there is less accuracy when resolving shader colors.
- Limited memory for storing texture maps. Although processing images with hardware is efficient, this is true only for images within the hardware's memory abilities (to load).
- mental ray supports rendering partial shadow maps, requiring shadow information only for visible shadows. With hardware-based shadows, by contrast, the entire shadow is calculated; so with hardware rendering you cannot leverage mental ray's (fairly new) ability to consider partial shadow data.

Hardware Rendering Setup

As the setup process for hardware rendering with mental ray can become inconvenient for most users who are not familiar with hardware shaders and technologies, this section is aimed at pointing out the mental ray–related options and their usage. To enable hardware rendering, use the following commands and options, either in the options block of an .mi file or on the command line:

```
-hardware [off|on|all] [cg|native|fast] [force]
```

These options specify a specific order for hardware render execution, as well as define whether or not hardware rendering can fall back on software rendering. You may specify a command as follows:

```
-hardware all cg native fast force
```

Hardware command-line commands instruct mental ray to do the following:

on specifies that any objects with specific instructions to render in hardware (meaning if the object has a specific hardware-on option within its declaration inside the .mi file) will first try rendering hardware before falling back on software.

all means that mental ray will attempt to first render all objects using hardware rendering before falling back on software.

off obviously disables hardware rendering altogether and is the default. You can see the hardware options block option set to off in the options block excerpt as mentioned in the section "mental ray Render Algorithms" earlier in this chapter.

cg specifies that mental ray should first attempt to use Cg shaders, which are the only shaders mental ray can use for compiling basic shader trees, as discussed earlier.

If Cg shaders are unavailable, native instructs mental ray to then look for programmable precompiled OpenGL 2.0 or HLSL shaders.

If native fails, it will fall back on fast, which uses only hardwired nonprogrammable OpenGL shaders, provided they exist.

If force is specified, mental ray forces all the geometry to render using hardware, disabling software rendering. If Force is disabled, mental ray would first try resolving hardware shading in the specified order (cg native fast), and if all those fail, it would use software rendering as a fall-back option. This option forces objects to render based only on the on, all, and off specifications.

Enabling Hardware Rendering in Maya

In Maya, when exporting .mi files, you can enable these features from under the .mi default options. These options should be accessed preferably when mental ray is selected as the current render type. Once mental ray rendering is enabled, you can access the hardware render settings by entering the following line into the script editor:

```
select -r miDefaultOptions;
```

Figure 2.14

mental ray hardware render settings within Maya

Once you've opened the Attribute Editor, locate the bottom Extra Attributes tab, where you will see the hardware rendering settings, equivalent to the command-line options discussed earlier, seen in Figure 2.14. You can also select the miDefaultOptions node in the Outliner window when the Display menu → DAG Objects Only attribute is disabled.

mental ray Output

This chapter tackles mental ray's output features, including camera shaders and custom passes. We begin with the relationships between mental ray's data types and bit depth as a foundation for understanding image formats. Frame buffers control render output and so you'll learn about the different mental ray frame buffer types and their bit depths and purposes throughout this chapter. In the section "mental ray Cameras," you'll begin outputting custom frame buffers and specifying global shader effects. You'll achieve this through camera output statements and shaders. Camera shaders are used to add background environments, volume effects (such as fog or mist), 2D postprocess effects (such as glow effects), and lens effects that influence the cameras' photographic characteristics. In addition the chapter begins to look at external resources for custom shaders that can be used for customizing your host application's abilities.

This chapter covers various topics that influence all the other topics discussed throughout the book. It can be considered as a book within a book on advanced render techniques and as a preparation for compositing 3D. You may want to return to this chapter after you finish the book to recap all the topics discussed here, The chapter covers the following topics:

- **mental ray Data Types**
- **The Frame Buffer**
- **Frame Buffer Options**
- **mental ray Cameras**
- **Output Statements**

mental ray Data Types

Before we dive into the topic of mental ray output, image formats, and frame buffers, you need to know some basic terminology as well as how images are stored. The following sections will gradually build these concepts so that you feel more confident with all the different frame buffer and image output options available with mental ray.

Image bit depths are specified as either *n* bits per channel or *n* bits per pixel. Per channel bit depth refers to the bit depth of each channel independent of the total of all three (RGB) or four (RGB+A) channels. When you combine all these RGB color channels, the result is referred to as a *per-pixel bit depth* (per image). Thus, a single channel may contain 8-, 16-, or 32-bit depth values, and a three-channel image (excluding the alpha channel) may contain 24, 48, and 96 bits per pixel, respectively.

A three-channel (RGB) 24-bit per-pixel image provides more color combinations than the human eye can see, so any bit depth greater than 8 bits per-channel leads to unnecessary file sizes and color ranges. If you're rendering a 16-bit or 32-bit per channel image (64–128 bits per-pixel image), you most likely intend to further postprocess the image with Photoshop or compositing packages, in which case you require a higher bit depth to avoid color artifacts such as banding as well as have more control over the render exposure.

> When using a compositing software, higher bit depth images help maintain the image's integrity after being exposed to several filters or color corrections. It also opens the door for applying custom tone-mapping corrections to correct for over exposure.

Image Channels and Color Values

By default, all color image formats typically use three channels to store the RGB color values as grayscale shades in each channel. It is the image viewer software that interprets the first channel within an image as a scale of red values, the second as a scale of green values, and the third as blue values, providing, in the case of an 8-bit per-channel image, 24-bit color, also commonly referred to as True Color within monitor display settings. The per-channel grayscale values that interpret as shades of color represent the luminance values (brightness) for each color channel independent of the other color channels.

Primary and Secondary Color Values

RGB primary colors, when combined, provide any shade of color from the visible spectrum. The RGB color model is described as additive because colors are formed by adding light—generated by phosphors in the monitor—in the three primary colors. Essentially, a render view (background) can be thought of as a black "blank canvas," corresponding to a value of zero. As values are rendered, their values are added together, increasing in value and relative brightness. When all three colors are combined at their highest possible value

(255 on a 0–255 scale), the color appears as white, which can be thought of as the exposure limit; any value greater than 255 will appear as white.

With print, CMYK colors are used to process color values. CMYK color is described as subtractive because the colors we see are the colors reflected back to us after other colors are absorbed by the inks or pigments. This can be thought of as a process of removing color values from white, revealing darker shades of color. With 3D rendering, we primarily use RGB color; any conversion to CMYK color is applied later in a graphic imaging application such as Adobe Photoshop. See the side bar "Calibration in a Nutshell".

The Alpha Channel

The fourth channel is typically used for storing a masking channel, such as the alpha channel but not only. This channel should be considered as an additional grayscale channel not encoded to any specific color because it is not automatically (by the image viewer) encoded with any of the primary RGB colors; it is simply a black-to-white grayscale channel that is used to store any form of data as grayscale values. For example, high dynamic range (HDR) images store the three standard RGB channels and use the fourth (alpha) channel to store an additional exponent value, as further explained later in this chapter in the section "Intro to HDR Images," and in Chapter 9, "The Fundamentals of Light and Shading Models."

Intro to Multichannel Images

Beyond these standard four channels, additional channels may also be stored, providing a multichannel image. For example, an image may store the RGBA channels and an additional fifth Z-depth channel, supporting five channels within a single image file. Today, one of the most significant formats is OpenEXR, an HDR format that supports storing any number of additional channels. It can store different grayscale channels that can then be interpreted as color channels within supporting compositing packages such as Nuke, Shake, and Digital Fusion. For example, an OpenEXR image can have the following 10 channels, representing the RGB color pass and alpha channel, RGB specular pass, and an RGB environment pass: RGBA+RGB+RGB. Each RGB combination represents an "independent" image that is stored within the OpenEXR image and can be accessed easily in compositing, mostly with Nuke that has superior abilities for compositing with multi-channel OpenEXR images.

OpenEXR images (the multi-channel approach) provide for easier handling of data within compositing applications and conserve disk space. Encoding any of the additional channels (beyond the first 4 RGBA channels) as R, G, and B channels is applied within the compositing software. The section "Output Statements" later in this chapter discusses multichannel rendering for compositing purposes.

You can find an article I wrote on compositing multichannel images on the companion CD in the PDF file labeled "Nuke Compositing", offering a detailed look at using such images with Nuke. Nuke is a compositing application owned by The Foundry (UK) that was developed in-house at Digital Domain.

Bit Depth and Data Types

Bit depth and data types determine the range of values and the precision used to represent data (color value) in an image file. Numeric data types are distinguished by the range of values they can represent, and whether they are natural or rational numbers. A single bit, of course, provides two options, 0 or 1 (off or on), offering either black or white, and is thus the smallest unit of data on computers. As we increase the bit depth, we get a larger range of options and thus an ability to define grayscale shades between white and black. With 8 bits per channel we have 2^8 grayscale values per channel, providing 256 (natural numbers on a number line scale) color options per channel, which is commonly referred to as the byte data type. A byte is used to represent clumps of 8-bit data. So you may refer to a 3-channel (RGB) 8-bit per-channel image as an image with 3 bytes per pixel. A 16-bit image (2^{16}) provides 65,536 color values per channel, utilizing with mental ray the integer data type.

The byte and integer data types offer different ranges of whole number values (natural numbers) that are used with 8 to 16 bit frame buffers. Thus bytes and integer data types are nondecimal point numbers, such as 1, 2, 3…256. Floating-point data types are used with 32-bit images, which support a wider range of values, as well as rational (decimal point) numbers. With 32-bit images, the increase in bit depth enables floating-point images to store a larger range of values (2^{32} per channel) and also supports using several decimal points that represent a fractional value such as 1÷10000, using 0.0001, providing more accurate precision while describing a gradation between two values, such as between 0.0 and 1.0. To avoid confusion, note that in mathematics, the term rational numbers is used to describe a fractional number. The main comparison between 8- to 16-bit images and 32-bit images is in the available range of values they use to represent a gradation from black to white and not as much how they choose to represent those values (integer vs. floating-point values). Most important is the fact that floating point images can store values that exceed the 0 to 1 range, a topic further discussed throughout this and other chapters. Table 3.1 illustrates the relationship between bit depth values and their data types that are used with mental ray (discussed further shortly).

Table 3.1

Bit Depth and mental ray Data Types

DATA TYPE	BIT PER CHANNEL	COLOR RANGE PER CHANNEL	BITS PER PIXEL	COLOR RANGE
Byte	8	0–255	24 ($2^{8 \times 3}$) (three channels)	16,777,216
Byte	8	0–255	32 ($2^{8 \times 4}$) (four channels)	16,777,216 + transparency
Int_16 (short) unsigned	16	0–65535	48 ($2^{16 \times 3}$) (three channels)	281 trillion
Int_16 (half) unsigned	16	-32,768–32,768	48 ($2^{16 \times 3}$) (three channels)	281 trillion
Int_32 unsigned	32	4,294,967,295	32 ($2^{32 \times 1}$) one channel - used only with the mental ray tag frame buffer)	4,294,967,295 Natural numbers
Float	32	-3.4×10^{38} – 3.4×10^{38}	96 ($2^{32 \times 3}$) three channels)	4,294,967,295 A rational number range (decimal point)

Bit Depth and File Size

High-resolution images are among the largest computer files, making storage space a valid issue for anyone working with them. When we store an image (or any file type), we measure its size in multiples of bytes: kilobytes (1,024 bytes), megabytes (1,048,576 bytes), and so forth. We can estimate the disk space required by a particular image (ignoring any compression or additional encoded data) by looking at its bit depth, and its pixel resolution. For example, a 1024 ×1024-pixel image (sometimes described as a 1k image) stored as a single 8-bit grayscale channel would require 1,024 kilobytes (1 megabyte) per channel; when using three 8-bit channels, it requires 3 megabytes on disk:

```
(X × Y resolution) × channels × bytes per channel = file size (in bytes)
```

$$1024^2 \times 3 \times 1 = 3{,}145{,}728 \text{ bytes}$$

When represented as MB the result is divided by 1k as follows:

$$3{,}145{,}728 \div 1{,}024^2 (X \times Y\, resolution) = 3 \text{ MB}$$

As you can see, a 1k image using three 8-bit channels requires only 3MB of disk space; however, when you increase the bit depth per channel, the file size significantly increases. The same image with an additional alpha channel (RGBA) and at 16-bit (2 bytes per channel) requires 8MB, and at 32-bit, (4 bytes per channel) requires 16MB per image. Most file formats, however, provide some form of compression to reduce the file size.

The Frame Buffer

A *frame buffer* is a resolution-dependent temporary image with a given number of channels and bit depth. Frame buffers are generated when you render and are used to store color values in memory until the rendering phase has completed (frame buffers can also be temporarily written to disk) and the output image can be written to disk using a specified file format and data type. Because frame buffers are required to maintain these per-pixel values during rendering, they may represent any supported data type (listed in Table 3.1) that is required for the rendering. These data types are associated, as cited earlier, with channels and a bit depth defining their purpose their purpose, for example, the typical 8-bit RGB and alpha channels, or a 32-bit Z-depth channel, among others.

By default, mental ray will render an image using an 8-bit per-channel frame buffer, representing the output image format's supported bit depth (for example, 8-bit TIF), unless you specify a greater output bit depth. Thus, the default frame buffer channels and bit depth correspond to the four 8-bit RGBA color channels in a 32-bit per pixel image. This provides three color channels as well as an alpha channel, all at a bit depth adequate for most viewing purposes.

Thus, mental ray data types represent the number of channels and bit depth used for a given output image within each channel. In the same context, data types also define the numerical precision in which data is stored (float versus integer). Typically the mental ray frame buffers are referred to by their data type (as seen in Table 3.1), for example byte, integer, or floating-point data type frame buffers. Thus the default frame buffer is referred to as a byte data type because each channel's color value is represented with a single byte, offering the commonly used 8-bit four-channel (RGBA) image format, providing 256 shades of gray per channel and 16,777,216 color variations.

Normalized Values

In most image applications—digital cameras, rendering formats, and scanners, for example—the bit depth usually ranges from 8 to 16 bits per channel. As you can see, the range of colors between 8- and 16-bit images can be expressed using different numerical values, but the value always represents a range from black to white. To address the difference in value range, mental ray always uses *normalized* ranges so that the range from black to white is described as fractional values from 0 to 1 instead of 0 to 255 or 0 to 65535.

When mental ray outputs an image to the chosen image format and bit depth, mental ray converts these normalized values to match the target bit depth format by multiplying its range by the current normalized value. For example, a 50% gray RGB color, a normalized value of 0.5 per channel, is multiplied by 256 when saving to an 8-bit image, adapting to the 0 to 255 nondecimal range; a color value of 128 is used for each of the RGB color channels.

> In most contexts, *normalizing values* refers to remapping any range of values so that it fits into a 0 to 1 range. In this case, normalized values are remapped to the output range.

32-Bit Depth and Super-Whites

Hardware devices such as monitor displays, scanners, cameras, and printers are limited to displaying only colors within the range of black to white, and more accurately, within a range of a given *contrast ratio*. Contrast ratios describe the gradation in value from the darkest to the brightest values in an image, which is not limited to a given range in real life lighting conditions; however, with display devices the contrast ratio range is limited by the device's display abilities. For now we are only concerned with a range from black to white.

As color is represented by numerical values, hardware devices such as those cited above have no use for colors beyond the numerical range of their supported colors. Values in excess of white are referred to as *super-brights* or *super-whites*; these values always appear as white in an image viewer or on paper (print); for example, a value of 1.2 on a scale of 0 to 1 (black to white) will appear as white within an image viewer. To clarify, these output devices do not visually differentiate between colors beyond the scale of white even if they exist within the image. As you'll see, however, mental ray can make use of these super-bright values.

With 8-bit and 16-bit data types, values greater than the permitted range are either scaled down within the 0 to 1 range or clipped to that range so that values do not exceed the 0 to 1 range. For example, an 8-bit image utilizes a 0–255 range describing black to white, and if a value of 300 were received, that value would be either clipped or scaled down to the valid range, a value not greater than 255. Clipping values results in the removal of any super-bright data from an image, and scaling refers to the remapping of color values so they "fit" into the given range, such as with *tone-mapping* operations.

Super-whites can be stored only in limited image formats that typically support at least 32-bit per-channel color, or HDR images that can use 8-bit images to represent a virtually limitless range; more on that later. Thus mental ray can store values in excess of the 0 to 1 range (black to white) using 32-bit floating-point data types or HDR images. Values that are not clipped to the typical 0 to 1 range maintain their numerical integrity and thus maintain the relationship between values (the contrast ratio) even if they exceeded the 0 to 1 range. Although we can store such super-bright values, they can not be visually perceived in image viewers. In practice, storing such super-bright values allows us to control light intensities, remove overexposure, and more, all topics that will be discussed over the course of this book, beginning with the discussion of overexposure in the section "Frame Buffer Options" later in this chapter.

Intro to HDR Images

With HDR images (RGBE), the alpha channel is used as an exponent (E) channel, known as an *exponential notation* (see Chapter 9), that is used to represent each channel's "real" value outside the 0 to 1 range and in fact practically within any range. This sort of image format supports value ranges that can better represent real-world ranges of light intensity. The problem HDR imaging addresses is that the dynamic range of light humans can perceive (expressed as a contrast ratio) is much greater than most of today's output devices' display abilities. (Tomorrow's devices, however…) For example, monitors have specific contrast ratio ranges that describe their display qualities, but this range is far smaller than the visible range perceived by the human eye.

Thus HDR images can use 8-, 16-, or 32-bit depth where the fourth channel is used as an exponent value so that the range evaluated mathematically is far greater than the typical 8-bit range. With HDR images, the difference of using 8 to 32 bits per channel really only addresses the mathematical precision of the values (gradation) and the file size and not so much the range, because again, the expression can evaluate to represent any range regardless of the bit depth.

In most cases 8-bit HDR images are more then adequate for reproducing images with a high dynamic range.

Not every image format supports HDR data. Typical formats are the radiance HDR format, ILM's OpenEXR format, or the floating-point TIF formats, as well as mental ray's CTH format. HDR images and their significance on photography and 3D imaging and their characteristics are discussed in detail in Chapter 9 as well as used with advanced lighting examples in Chapter 13.

Color Values and Sampling

When mental ray renders, regardless of the output format, it samples each color channel value as a 32-bit floating-point value, and only then converts these values to the specified output format (8, 16 or 32-bit) before storing them in the frame buffer. This means that within the 3D domain, color values can represent contrast ratios within a high dynamic range, similar to HDR images. This characteristic has significant impact on rendering. For example, consider that during rendering, shaders add values from material shaders, light shaders, indirect illumination, and so on, the color values for a given shaded point often exceed the standard 0 to 1 range of an image, giving us super-white colors. The fact that mental ray renders using a high dynamic range can affect how you select an output format and describe values (lights and shaders) in the 3D scene.

First consider that 32-bit buffers store the values in a linear fashion, a one to one mapping with the color acquired during the rendering stage. Thus the colors are not further modified as they are stored within the buffer, maintaining their integrity, be it a value of 0.05 or 500. Clearly this process also requires an image format that supports 32-bit data while storing these values on disk.

Then consider that when using lower bit depth buffers (8- and 16-bit), mental ray still utilizes a 32-bit process that represents a contrast ratio between the darkest and brightest colors acquired from sampling. And so, if the contrast described within the scene exceeds a range of 256 values, only a given portion of those values can be effectively represented using an 8- or 16-bit buffer. The result is two fold.

1. Artifacts such as banding may appear due to a lack of accuracy in representing gradations using lower bit depth buffers. The precision of fractional numbers acquired while sampling with a 32-bit process is greater than the precision of lower bit-depth buffers.

2. Lower bit depth buffers only consider values within that 0 to 1 range clipping values in excess of 1, hence values are easily omitted from being properly stored or represented within a 16-bit and lower image format.

Thus, while defining lights and shaders, to some extent you also need to consider how colors are evaluated for the frame buffer, providing colors that are adequate for the range of its selected data type (8 bit, 16 bit, etc.). mental ray provides some options for controlling how colors are scaled or clipped to match the range with 16-bit and lower frame buffers. The topic of balancing light and shader values is further discussed in Chapter 9.

Primary and User Frame Buffers

Before rendering begins, mental ray can create and maintain up to six standard "built-in" frame buffer types as well as additional user-defined frame buffers. The standard frame buffer types include RGBA, Z-depth, motion vectors, normal vectors, coverage, and tag labels. The primary frame buffer (RGBA), a four-channel data type frame buffer (at any bit depth), is responsible for storing per-pixel color and transparency values that correlate directly to the output image RGB and alpha (transparency) channels.

> Throughout the chapter, the term *primary frame buffer* refers only to the RGBA (main) frame buffer and when referred to as plural, as with *primary frame buffers*, it refers to the six built-in frame buffers listed above. The term *standard frame buffers* is also commonly used to describe the primary frame buffers.

The primary frame buffer is the minimum requirement for rendering images. The remaining five buffer types act as assisting frame buffers. They are created on demand to support specific shader calls, typically for postprocess effects that require a specific type of information. Examples include 2D postprocess depth of field or motion blur effects. Post-process shaders with mental ray are referred to as *output shaders* and are further discussed in "mental ray Cameras" later in this chapter. As frame buffers are used to represent per-pixel values, they can only be used with per-pixel operations. They are used to output custom channels for compositing (essentially a form of postprocess effects) or with output shaders that apply postprocess effects during rendering.

mental ray frame buffers can be output to disk in specific image formats. These formats may be either host specific, to support a target data type and precision, or one of mental ray's image formats. mental ray's formats, as a matter of convenience, directly correlate to the different frame buffer types, discussed next. Each frame buffer can then be stored either using one of the mental ray formats or using a host-specific format correlating to that format's data type. For example, if three 32-bit channels are required, either use the mental ray format or an equivalent 32-bit TIF image. The following sections describe the frame buffer types and recommended bit depth to help correlate them with supported output formats. Further, in each case the mental ray format is specified. It should be clear that the concepts of saving frame buffers as images is nothing more than the process of storing data (value) in image files that have a given number of channels and are at a given bit depth. In most cases, host applications may force you to accept a host-specific format which is fine, as long as it has adequate bit depth and supports the channels you require.

> Most custom buffers use 32-bit output to guarantee a high degree of precision while processing postprocess effects or for compositing purposes, where a high precision is required in order to avoid any resulting artifacts after the effects have processed.

The Z-Depth Frame Buffer

The Z-depth frame buffer, a 32-bit single *floating-point* channel frame buffer shown in Figure 3.1, represents the scene depth based on the camera's viewing plane. mental ray provides the ZT image format for exporting Z-depth images, or you most likely will use your host-specific Z-depth format.

Z-depth is used for depth sorting with per-pixel effects, such as depth fading, 2D fog, or fast depth-of-field post-process effects. For example, a 2D depth fade would require the use of both the RGBA primary frame buffer and the Z-depth frame buffer to calculate the relationship between the RGBA colors and the scene depth. It can fade an image over distance by inverting the Z-depth values and multiplying by a fade value, so that if the farthest point from the camera is assigned a value of 0 and the closest point a value of 1, as surfaces get farther from the camera they fade to black.

Figure 3.1

The Z-depth frame buffer can be used for compositing 2D postprocess effects with mental ray or a compositing application such as Nuke, Shake, and Digital Fusion.

You can see in the figure that in mental ray's Z-depth output, white represents the farthest point from the camera, and black is the closest point to the camera. This color interpretation for depth is the opposite of that used by other rendering applications. Typically these values would be inverted for image processing.

Z-depth postprocess effects, whether with an output shader or in a compositing application, a high level of accuracy is required for representing a transition over distance as means for avoiding unwanted artifacts, and thus you should always use (and export) 32-bit floating-point Z-depth passes.

The Motion Vectors Frame Buffer

The motion vectors frame buffer, a three-channel 32-bit-per-channel floating-point data type frame buffer, stores motion vectors typically for 2D (postprocess) motion blur effects. Motion vectors are exported using the MT mental ray format and represent the vertex motion and velocity in a color-coded form so that it can then be used by output shaders or with vector motion blur effects within compositing applications. When rendering motion blur 2D postprocess effects, mental ray creates the primary RGBA frame buffer and a motion vectors frame buffer and maintains them until the 2D motion blur effect has been processed. With respect to outputting the motion vectors frame buffer as a pass, mental ray motion vectors are not easily used with compositing applications, however, there are other custom shaders and plug-ins that you can use more effectively. You can see an example for a motion vectors pass with the image labeled "LMV Motion Vectors" on the companion CD, under the Chapter 3 directory. The topic of using motion vectors for 2D motion blur is further discussed in Chapter 8, "Motion Blur."

> With depth of field and motion blur effects, updating a render sequence can take several hours. This wait time is the Achilles heel of 3D rendering. Too often, even though the 3D counterpart is much more realistic and physically accurate, it is also significantly slower, so a quick 2D solution becomes much more attractive in most production-driven cases, as demonstrated with motion blur in Chapter 8.

The Normal Vectors Frame Buffer

The normal vectors buffer uses three 32-bit floating-point channels to store the surface normal directions in a color-coded form using mental ray's NT image format. Normal vectors are used to describe the surface normal aim direction at a given point, typically in world space coordinates. Green is used for the up Y vector, red for positive X vector, and blue for positive Z vector, as seen in Figure 3.2 (on the CD, you'll find a color version named "Normal Vectors").

X = Red   Y = Green   Z = Blue

Figure 3.2

The normal vectors frame buffer produces a color-coded image representing the surface's orientation within the scene's coordinate space.

To fully explain normal vectors, it's actually useful to see them in grayscale. Figure 3.2 shows the primary color channels separated so you can distinguish between the different color values. (You can see this separation for any image simply by viewing channels individually in the host application's "flip book" utility, in a compositing package, or in Photoshop.) In the grayscale image, white represents on a scale from 0 to 1 a value of 1, which in the case of the red channel is 100 percent red, whereas a 0.5 value provides 50 percent red, as a gray value. Remember that the channels are grayscale gradations from 0 to 1, encoded with color by the viewer. Thus, a value of 1 in any of the three RGB channels corresponds directly to the positive direction for that X, Y, or Z axis, corresponding to the R, G, and B channels respectively. Thus 100% red refers to the positive X axis. As you can see in the figure, each channel indicates the direction of its correlating positive X, Y, and Z axis with white. You can tell by looking at the figure that the camera is looking directly at the sphere where the world's Y axis points up, as indicated with the white color under the Y-Green label. Black colors in the figure represent the opposite (negative) side for that axis (normal direction), which in color is drawn using secondary colors (the result of mixing the primary colors). To fully understand the color interpretation take a look at the color image noted above.

By now it should be clear that color in CG is a very significant source of information for processing postprocess effects either with shaders or in compositing, and thus not just a visually pleasing aspect of an image.

Normal vector values may be required by some output shaders for applying effects that require information about a surface's normal aim direction. It is more common to use normal vectors as texture maps for bump mapping rather than output frame buffers. The topic of normal maps for shading is further discussed in Chapters 11 and 14. In a nutshell, the process of color coding images based on the normals directionality allows you to take a high resolution model, and *bake* a normal map. Baking refers to exporting an image that contains the normal vector output as color, just as with the normals frame buffer, but only as a texture map. The map contains within it the directional information of the high-resolution surface's geometry in a color-coded format. You can then apply that normal map as a *normals bump map* texture to a lower resolution model. Bump mapping shaders use normals to perturb (bend) the direction of the geometries normals based on image files, in this case it will use the normal data to control the lighting across the surface, based on the data extracted from the higher resolution model. Thus it provides a means for transferring surface properties from a high-resolution model to a low-resolution model so that you can mimic the same interaction of light on the lower-resolution model; its shading.

Most significantly, the game industry uses normal texture maps to define how a flat plane with a simple texture can perturb light so it appears to have a 3D form, such as a wall that appears to have pipes stretching across the surface or bricks bulging out.

The Object Labels Frame Buffer

The tag frame buffer creates a 32-bit single integer channel frame buffer that stores tags (also called labels) that list objects within the scene. Essentially this is the only buffer that uses 32-bit depth with integer precision instead of floating-point precision. Integer precision is used so that each label may have a unique number, thus the objective is to provide a clear color separation between separate labels and not a smooth gradation, as with Z-depth or motion vectors. This buffer uses the mental ray TT image format.

An output shader uses the information it contains to identify objects or groups of objects; for example, a tire may comprise several independent surfaces grouped as "one" tire. The object labels then act as ID tags, helping output shaders determine how to process effects on the pixels associated with those object IDs. Thus a label may or may not be unique to a single object; it can also be shared by several objects that require similar processing, and are defined by the user. After rendering a scene, you can view this frame buffer in the image viewer and see the different objects identified by label color, as shown in "Object Labels" in the Chapter 3 folder on the CD. This frame buffer may appear to provide a sort of masking ability, based on the object's label. However, it does not provide sufficient precision to be applicable as a compositing pass. In the section "Output Order and Output Shaders" later in this chapter you will see an example of using this object labels frame buffer with a 2D postprocess fur shader.

The Coverage Frame Buffer

The coverage frame buffer can use a single channel 32-bit floating-point frame buffer or any other precision to represent pixel *coverage*. This buffer can then use a grayscale range of values to represent objects that have more pixel coverage within a pixel so that the dominant object's coverage is represented. This frame buffer with mental ray is stored using the ST format. Coverage can be used with other frame buffers to help prioritize objects that are dominant within a pixel, so in a way it can help the accuracy of other frame buffers by determining the most influential surface per pixel. This sort of specialized buffer is more useful in the hands of a shader developer, who creates custom programs that process various effects that may require this sort of specialized information.

All these frame buffers are specifically used with shaders, and in most cases, if you have no use for them in compositing, you would not bother to output them. Shader writers, however, can choose which frame buffers they require for processing an effect and thus have more use for specifying them. Finally, as cited earlier, for compositing, the Z-depth and motion vector frame buffers have the most usage and are more commonly exported as separate image passes.

User Frame Buffers

Aside from the six "built-in" frame buffers, which are created on demand, mental ray 3.4 and later also supports any number of additional user-defined frame buffers. Typically these buffers are meant to assist some sort of 2D output shader postprocess effect or to output specific color information, such as separate color passes for diffuse and specular color components. Users define the user frame buffer data type so that it supports their specific

objectives, so mental ray allows user-defined frame buffers to be of any data type. In Figure 3.3 you can see the XSI properties for a new user frame buffer. As you can see, the Type property allows you to select any of the frame buffer data types discussed above so that the new user frame buffer labeled My_User_Buffer_01 may be any of the following types: Color (RGBA), Grayscale (single channel), Depth, Normal Vector, Vectors / Motion Vectors, and Object Label.

Consider that when all the color information is stored within the same RGBA primary frame buffer, there is no color separation; you can't store just a specific color component (ex. the reflection, specular, shadow, or other color). Thus user frame buffers are used to provide separation, where you can store specific color passes, such as the reflection, specular, shadow, or indirect light colors, to mention a few, in separate frame buffers that are then saved as separate image files on disk, used as passes for compositing. We return to user frame buffers and passes shortly, in the section "mental ray Cameras," and see an example of their implementation within XSI. You can also see the Nuke Compositing article noted earlier on the CD.

Frame Buffer Options

Frame buffer options enable us to deal with different types of color ranges and how they are stored on disk. These options enable us to control how floating-point color evaluations are converted to a specific frame buffer data type and output format. They are used to define whether an image is 32 bit or 8 bit, *premultiplied*, *interpolated*, *dithered*, and so forth as well as whether its *gamma corrected*. All frame buffer options must be entered within a mental image file's options block.

One advantage of frame buffer options in mental ray 3.4 (and up) is that frame buffers can be saved on disk during the render, in a temporary file until the render has completed. This enables mental ray to better handle memory when several buffers are required, such as with multiple user frame buffers, effectively enabling mental ray to use the memory for more pertinent information. Also, during sampling, mental ray can examine each buffer for contrast thresholds, so that a change in contrast from any one buffer may result in additional samples. The topics of sampling and contrast thresholds are described in detail in Chapter 5, "Quality Control."

mental ray frame buffer settings are offered at different levels and different integrations within each package. We'll look at the mental ray options first and then identify them within host applications.

mental ray Frame Buffer Options

The following options control how colors are combined into pixels and how color and transparency are handled with respect to the image's bit-depth format:

- Interpolation vs. padding
- Premultiply
- Colorclip
- Desaturate
- Gamma
- Dither

The *Colorclip*, *Gamma*, and *Desaturate* options deal with controlling color with frame buffers that maintain a (16-bit or lower) 0 to 1 color range. These options are not relevant with 32-bit data types; however, they must be set accordingly, as discussed in following sections, so they don't "damage" the desired results. Premultiply in most cases should be enabled, unless you intend on compositing different elements (ex. a character, room, phone, and chair) and color correcting them, hence an option that is intended for compositing purposes. Let's look in detail at all of these options with the following sections.

Interpolation vs. Padding

This option defines whether sample values are blended together. When a frame buffer is *interpolated*, it will blend the samples for a given pixel, producing an "averaged" result. A *padded* frame buffer, by contrast, simply stores the first or last received value (depending on the buffer's data type); samples are not blended together. Padded frame buffers would not suffice for evaluating good "beauty" pass color renders. We specify frame buffers in the mental ray options block, prefixed with an interpolation option, either a plus (interpolated) or a minus sign (padded). The primary frame buffer (RGBA) is interpolated and thus referred to as +RGBA frame buffer. Thus custom user buffers that deal with extracting color passes should also be specified as interpolated frame buffers.

Premultiplication

The Premultiply option is specified on the command line as

```
-premultiply on | off
```

This option, referred to as *premultiplication* in compositing, controls how transparency values are stored within the RGB and alpha channels. Unless you specifically know that you need an *un-premultiplied* image, which is an image that has not been premultiplied (as described in this section), you should always leave this option enabled. Premultiply mathematically multiplies each RGB color channel by the alpha channel value. By doing so, this option preserves the correct transparency values for each of the RGB color channels. For example, an RGB value of 0.9 multiplied by an alpha value of 0.2 (R*A, G*A, B*A), will result in a 0.18 value for each color channel. Essentially premultiply is a per-pixel operation that matches the RGB intensity for a given pixel with the corresponding alpha channel transparency.

The premultiply option is intended for 16-bit and lower image formats, since those images utilize a 0 to 1 value range. However, with 32-bit buffers (and output) the color values are greater than 1, so if premultiplication is applied on 32-bit buffers, color values that are multiplied by an alpha value of 0.5 (50 percent transparency) may still provide RGB color values in excess of 1, and hence are not an accurate representative of transparency for compositing purposes. For example, consider a pure color of blue that is set with a value of 500 (R=0, G=0, and B = 500), when multiplied by 0.5 it equals 250 which still provides a full intensity blue color, without appearing any darker (transparent). However, in a 0 to 1 range a color value that can not exceed 1, when multiplied by an alpha below 1, will correctly represent a transparency within the RGB channels and of course correlating to that pixels alpha value.

Another form of transparency is applied along an object's edge as it recedes into the background. Anti-aliasing (Chapter 5) attempts to provide a smooth gradation for this transitional phase. If the background color is set to black (the default in host applications), the surface color will transition to black; that is, the surface itself changes color as it is composited over the black background by blending both (surface and background) colors together. If you have a composite of several passes and you intend to apply color or value corrections, you inevitably would adjust the transition color from the surface to the background while applying color corrections, rather than just adjust the surface color. Consider that the transition color represents the current surface's color after it has been premultiplied and thus corrected for transparency. If you change that value it no longer represents the correct transparency value. In the case of a transition to black, if you increase the brightness of an image in compositing, this would influence the "fade to black" transition, which should maintain the same gradual "darkening" value throughout the transition. However, adjusting brightness will in fact also brighten the transition, creating visible artifacts along the transition.

Figure 3.41 later in this chapter shows artifacts from applying incompatible postprocess shaders to premultiplied images with 3ds Max effect shaders, which apply a blur color effect that creates a clear black outline around spheres that are rendered over a white background.

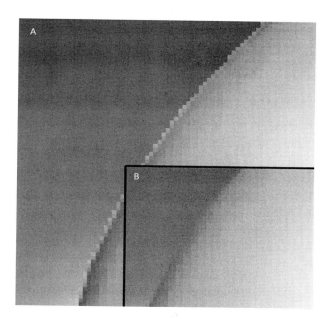

Figure 3.4

Premultiplied and un-premultiplied compositing. Notice the artifacts along the premultiplied color-corrected image (A) compared with the unpremultiplied image with the same correction (B).

COMPOSITING PRACTICES AND PREMULTIPLICATION

Based on the discussions above, when compositing different elements together you want to apply all the color corrections to the un-premultiplied image; an image that has not been multiplied by its alpha channel. Then, when you are satisfied and ready to composite it over a background image, use a premultiply operator in your compositing application to premultiply the foreground by its alpha. You can then composite it using an *over* operation. An over operation is a standard compositing term (math operation) that refers to layering two images (a premultiplied foreground image and a background image) together based on the alpha channel of the foreground (top) image like this:

$A + (B \times (1-a))$

This means that the foreground A (premultiplied) is added with the background B. The background is first multiplied by 1 minus the foreground's alpha value. This means that where the foreground alpha is equal to 1 (white / opaque) it will result with 1 - 1 which is equal to zero, and vice versa for values of 0 which will equal 1. This has the effect of inverting the foreground alpha and multiplying it by the background, effectively cutting out a hole in the background image so that the foreground colors can fit into that hole without increasing in intensity; remember they are mathematically added together so that if you don't cut a hole with the foreground's alpha, the values of both layers add up together.

Since the image has been premultiplied in compositing after color corrections and before the composite (over) operation, it assures that the correct color values between the background and foreground will blend together along the edges, where a transition is defined using values from 0 to 1. Thus, by correcting an un-premultiplied image, you can adjust the color without concerning yourself with such artifacts. Figure 3.4, image B shows how the transition is maintained using the same composite *flowchart* (composite tree) used for image A; however, an un-premultiplied image was used rather than the premultiplied image. After a color correction has been applied, the image was premultiplied by its alpha and composite over the background using an over operation.

UNPREMULTIPLIED RENDER CHARACTERISTICS

When premultiplication is disabled, especially with transparent surfaces, we typically see two noticeable characteristics. The first is that the transparent areas are filled with the surface's color. For example, suppose a transparent solid blue glass is placed over an empty background. With premultiplication disabled, instead of appearing darker from the influence of the black background "visible" through the glass, that transparent area is filled with a solid blue color, showing no transparency in the RGB channels and a gray transparent level in the alpha channel.

The other noticeable characteristic is that in the surface color's transition area (edge anti-aliasing) over the background's empty space, the surface edge color is exaggerated outward from the object. For example, if the surface were green, a green color as well as the specular color would extend outward from the surface to compensate for the area of transition (as shown in Figure 3.5 D, Premultiply off). In the color version on the CD (named "Color Clipping"), notice how for labels C and D (where Premultiply is off), you can see how the green color covers the entire surface (seen as brighter values in print) and gets brighter thanks to the specular component instead of fading to black, as with the section labeled B (premultiplied) that preserves the transparency.

This should all make sense now that you examined the compositing process. If the image is not multiplied by the alpha (unpremultiplied), it will not show any transparency and thus maintain its correct surface color throughout its surface area and over the edges' aliasing areas. You can then change blue to red, premultiply it, and arrive at a correct premultiplied image that is ready to be superimposed over a background image.

Color Clipping

The colorclip option is specified on the command line as follows:

```
-colorclip [raw | rgb | alpha]
```

It controls how mental ray treats sample color values that exceed the 0 to 1 range, providing values suitable for the selected frame buffer's data type bit depth. With 16-bit and lower frame buffers, the RGB and alpha clipping options enable you to prioritize a color clipping method; how values are clipped to the 0 to 1 range. These options scale the range of one value (ex. RGB values) to the other (ex. the alpha value), thus maintaining either color or alpha intensity and always clipped at a maximum value of 1. The raw mode, discussed shortly, is the only mode that permits values outside the 0 to 1 range and is used by default with 32-bit images.

RGB AND ALPHA MODES (16-BIT BUFFERS AND LOWER)

Figure 3.5 illustrates the relationship between RGB and alpha color clipping. It shows both RGB color and alpha channel renders with various settings. In all cases, the surface shader used a horizontal gradient texture to define transparency and a solid green color is used for color as well as an overexposed white specular color to pronounce the effect color clipping has on specular highlights.

The alpha gradient seen under label D represents the "real" shader's alpha gradient, which was used in all cases. The only changes applied to all these images are color clipping modes and premultiplication. The figure is hard to interpret in black and white, thus I recommend you locate the color plate on the companion CD. In black and white, brighter color indicates a higher value of green, where the brightest colors indicate specularity, and as color value transitions to black, the transparency influence is taking effect.

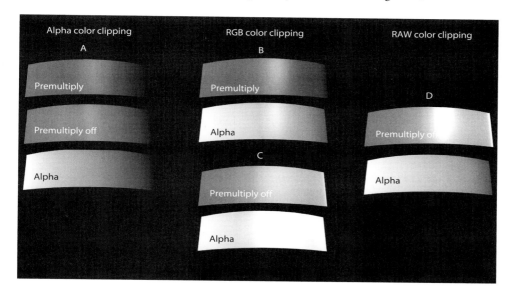

Figure 3.5

Color clip comparisons. These images show RGB, alpha, and raw color and alpha channels, respectively.

In these discussions consider that with an HSV color scale the V parameter defines the color intensity (brightness). In the same context, on an RGB color scale each channel has its own intensity defined with its numerical value, where higher values for the R, G, and B color channels are also considered brighter colors. The following discussions refer to value often and thus can be interpreted either as the per-channel value or the HSV V value. Also remember that the alpha channel only has one channel that defines its intensity.

The RGB Mode

RGB color clipping will prioritize color over alpha by first conforming the alpha values to the RGB values' intensity so that the alpha intensity, if need be, is raised to conform to the surface's intensity. In the figure under RGB color clipping (B), you can see how the alpha channel has adjusted to match the surface's value, specifically noticeable with the specular highlight in the center of the surface. Notice how that highlight carries through from the RGB channels to the alpha channel, which makes the alpha channel look like a glossy surface. With alpha color clipping (A), the alpha channel (third one down labeled Alpha) shows no such highlight. Clearly you can see how RGB color clipping affects the alpha channel.

The Alpha Mode

With alpha color clipping, transparency is preserved and RGB values are clipped to preserve the alpha intensity. Look at alpha color clipping in Figure 3.4A. The first premultiplied version shows how the green surface is multiplied by the alpha, preserving the transparency. Most noticeable is that the specular component has been scaled down by the alpha, as its part of the RGB color values. The alpha gradually loses intensity along the surface, so at the mid point it has already scaled down by some percentage, and at that point we have a specular highlight that should be much brighter (even overexposed), When the RGB values are multiplied by the alpha, however, the intensity is lost. Thus alpha color clipping may lead to unwanted results, so it should only be used if you are sure that you need to prioritize transparency over color.

Factoring Premultiplication

If premultiplication is enabled, as in Figure 3.4A and B, the RGB color values are premultiplied by the alpha channel after color clipping has been evaluated, based on the selected color clipping mode. Thus the color clipping mode is first used to clip colors based on the mode, and then premultiplication takes effect. When premultiplication is disabled, as in C (under RGB color clipping), notice how the surface color is much brighter and, as cited earlier, the color and specular components are carried through the surface's transparent areas and over the surface edges. This is exactly the type of unpremultiplied image you want to use for compositing color corrections, as discussed earlier under "Compositing Practices and Premultiplication".

Also notice, under C, how the alpha has also been affected by RGB intensities, raised in this case to the unpremultiplied RGB intensity. Because mental ray tries to match intensity of either RGB or alpha channels when rendering 16-bit and lower images based on the specified color clipping mode. Thus, when premultiply is disabled the RGB color clipping mode provides an alpha channel that preserves the unpremultiplied RGB colors values and eliminates any real representation of the surface's transparency within the alpha channel. In such a case, you may want to render a separated alpha pass and then during compositing after applying any color corrections, premultiply the RGB image by the separate alpha pass to determine its effect on the transparency. With respect to compositing, if you premultiply the alpha pass by the color pass in the compositing application you will still lose the RGB intensity. As a workaround consider that if you render specular color as a separate pass you can still composite surface transparency while maintaining highlights, as each is handled (composited) as a separate component.

After Effects users, notice that when you import images into After Effects you are immediately prompted to indicate if the images are premultiplied or not. The topic of premultiplication is at the backbone of every composite tree that deals with superimposing CG over other images.

With alpha color clipping, when premultiplication is off, you can see how the RGB colors scale to a lower grayer color (A), because the RGB colors are still scaled down by the alpha channel. These modes and premultiplication provide for different variations in how you use the options. When alpha color clipping is selected and premultiplication is disabled, the results are similar since both methods conform the RGB color channels to the alpha intensity. Typically you should prefer RGB color clipping because you don't want to lose highlight color values.

Remember, all these discussions only apply to 16-bit and lower images.

RAW MODE AND 32-BIT COMPOSITING

The raw color clip mode allows colors outside the normal 0 to 1 range and thus enables RGB colors that contradict the alpha value, as seen in Figure 3.5 D where the raw mode is selected, premultiply is disabled, and a 32-bit image data type is selected. As you can see, the alpha value is maintained, as with alpha color clipping, and the RGB color is maintained as with RGB (unpremultiplied) color clipping, both values contradicting each other. If premultiplication is enabled, the RGB colors will look like the premultiply image seen under label B, however, the alpha channel will not conform to the RGB values and maintain its integrity, as seen under image D. Thus the RGB and alpha channels will still contradict in value, however, the appearance of a premultiplied image is present. Note that the RGB values will support super-bright values, for example, the brightest areas seen in the highlight under B (when rendered as 32-bit raw) may carry values such as 2 or 20, both significantly higher than the 0 to 1 range.

mental ray will only store erroneous values when using 32-bit frame buffers with the raw mode (32-bit buffers default to the raw mode).

Desaturation, RGB and alpha color clipping, and gamma correction are all disabled with 32-bit frame buffers. They all represent methods for adjusting "real" values to values that are in the 0 to 1 range as well as values that don't contradict in value (RGB and alpha), opposed to 32-bit images that offer values outside the 0 to 1 range using raw values that may contradict in value, for example an image that has a fully transparent alpha with bright RGB colors.

Compositing 32-bit Images

Let's look at the significant differences between using 32-bit images and 8-bit images in compositing. Figure 3.6 shows side by side two columns of rendered images, one at 32 bit and the other at 8 bit, and in both cases using the RGB channels with no alpha channel. (The 32-bit image is not an HDR image.) The images were generated using an infinite point light emitting a strong bright light that forms a large overexposed circular region over a checkerboard surface. Notice that after the brightness for the 8-bit image is scaled down, a smudge of gray color remains. The pattern there is lost because those values no longer exist; the colors have been clipped to within the 0 to 1 range. The 32-bit image maintains the relationship of values over the 0 to 1 range, and so when the exposure is scaled down, the pattern reveals itself. This permits powerful compositing editing without loss of data and avoids the need for re-rendering to recover lost data.

Figure 3.6

An infinite point light reveals the pattern behind the overexposed areas with 32-bit images. Contrast this with the 8-bit image, which has lost any relational data for those values.

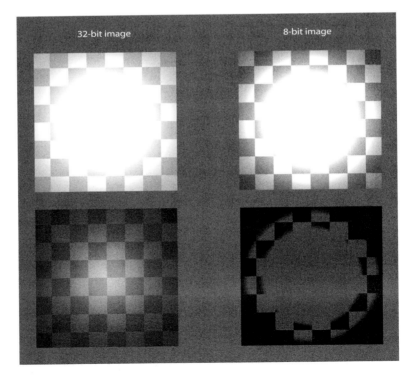

In compositing, it is always better to use 32-bit images that enable you to preserve the relationship between color values and thus correct overexposure on-the-fly rather than by re-
rendering. It also provides for better color correction and effect abilities without introducing
artifacts into the image due to the increase in precision, as discussed earlier.

Desaturation

The Desaturate option is specified on the command line as follows:

```
-desaturate on | off
```

Desaturation is an option that should be used with the 16-bit and lower images. It provides a means for maintaining the ratio between color values that exceed the 0 to 1 range,
relatively scaling down values into the 0 to 1 range so that their relative brightness (contrast) is maintained. Figure 3.7 shows two images side by side, both clipped using RGB
color clipping. Notice how the specular highlight appears flat in the nondesaturated image
(left), and how it appears to maintain some level of gradation in the desaturated image
(right) as mental ray reduced some of the color values in excess of 1 into the 0 to 1 range,
rather than just clip them at 1. This method is not a tone mapping operation that effectively handles a non-linear remapping of image values, as discussed in Chapters 9 and 13,
rather a loose hack that reduces the intensity locally, which may or may not suffice. As
cited above, overexposure is best handled in compositing when using 32-bit images, or by
carefully specifying shading and lighting values in the scene so that they do not easily
exceed a 0 to 1 range.

When values exceed the 0 to 1 range, but not significantly (ex. 1.2, 1.5), the desaturate option
will usually provide adequate results.

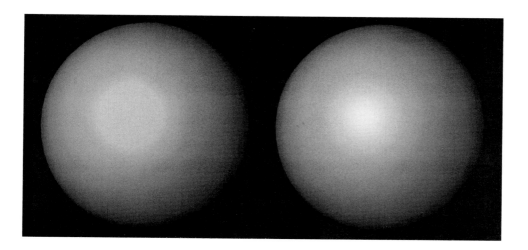

Figure 3.7

**Desaturation
enables us to scale
down super-bright
colors so that they
maintain a visible
intensity gradation
within images at
16 bits and lower
bit depths.**

Dithering

The Dither option is specified on the command line as follows:

```
-dither [on | off]
```

Dithering is a method that introduces noise into the image to minimize artifacts caused by linear gradations. Typically, *dithering* is a term that is used in reference to print; when pixels don't correspond directly to dots per inch with the printer, dithering is used to introduce more dots (noise) for representing equivalent pixels. In 3D, dithering is used in part for film production when the render will be printed to film. mental ray dithering is not really distinguishable and is primarily aimed at removing the chances of artifacts, such as banding.

Gamma Correction

The Gamma option is specified on the command line as follows:

```
-gamma [value]
```

Gamma is a term used to describe the display characteristic of monitors with a mathematical equation that represents how values from black to white are displayed. Monitors display light values in a nonlinear fashion, thus color values between 0 and 1 will not reproduce at the same intensity (grayscale shade) on a monitor, typically appearing darker than they are. The voltage sent to the monitor defines the monitor's response curve to light, which describes a nonlinear transition of voltages for a given light intensity (grayscale value), and as the intensity increases, more voltage is required for reproducing the correct brightness.

The equation used to derive the display intensity at a given gamma (a monitor-specific gamma) is then the color (pixel) value raised to the power of the gamma, and so the display brightness equals x^{gamma}. Most monitors today use a gamma of 2.2 to 2.5 (for PC monitors), so ball-parking this value may be sufficient. This equation then represents the display characteristics for the monitor, and so a pixel value of $0.5^{2.2}$ is roughly 0.22. Clearly a 50 percent gray displayed as a 78 percent gray appears darker, which then requires a gamma correction to adapt to the given monitor's response curve.

Images captured or created using a linear curve to represent value distribution between 0 and 1 would obviously appear too dark on monitors, and so we apply a gamma correction to boost their intensity. This way, if we need to display a 50 percent gray, we need to correct the image's gamma so that 50 percent gray equals a 75 percent gray (closer to white). Thus, when sent to the monitor it appears as 50 percent gray. The equation used to derive a corrective gamma curve is applied in the same way as when extracting gamma, thus $x^{inverse\ gamma}$; the inverse of the gamma. To determine the inverse gamma value that we should use, we divide a value of 1 by the monitor's gamma(1÷gamma), providing us with a gamma-corrected value that we can use for rendering. In the case of a 2.2 gamma that value is 0.454 (1÷2.2). Thus when you want to correct a 2.2 gamma you should apply the gamma option with a value of 0.454.

To help clarify these equations and how they affect gamma, let's look at Table 3.2. Using the equations cited above, Table 3.2 shows a few different linear intensity values and their equivalent value (intensity) based on a 2.2 gamma display monitor, referred to as monitor gamma Y in the table; it shows you how a gray value will appear on a typical PC monitor without applying any gamma correction. The last column utilizes a gamma correction value of 0.454, as cited above, displaying the result of raising each gamma value Y to the power of 0.454. You can see how the last column almost (because I only used three digits precision past the decimal point) reproduces the exact initial intensity values listed under the first column (the source intensity). Thus it corrects the Y gamma values so that they will appear on a 2.2 monitor correctly, using the same intensity values seen in the first column; the source image.

LINEAR VALUE X	$X^{2.2}$ (MONITOR GAMMA Y)	CORRECTED GAMMA ($Y^{0.454}$)
0	0	0
0.25	0.047	0.249
0.5	0.217	0.499
0.75	0.531	0.749
0.85	0.699	0.849
0.95	0.893	0.949
1	1	1

Table 3.2

Intensity values based on a 2.2 gamma.

It's important to emphasize that gamma only affects values between 0 and 1 not inclusive of 0 and 1. Thus it generates a non-linear curve that starts at 0 and slowly increases in value as illustrated in Figure 3.8 above gamma 2.2. Figure 3.8 illustrates the relationship between a linear curve, gamma curve, and a gamma-corrected curve, correlating to the table above where the first column is the linear curve, the second column is the gamma curve, and the third column is the gamma-corrected curve. The gradient renders under each of the illustrated curves show you the following:

Gamma 1 shows a gradient that represents the target image; it shows what a linear black to white gradation should look like when it appears correctly.

Gamma 2.2 shows how such an image (gamma 1) will look on a monitor without gamma correction; the image appears darker throughout the gradation until it eventually turns white.

Gamma 0.45 shows the result of applying a gamma correction; the image appears correctly on screen and looks identical to the source (target) image seen under gamma 1.

Notice how 0 and 1 define the bounds of the gamma curve, where in-between values are affected by the monitor's gamma. For this reason, gamma correction is only applied to images that are in the 0 to 1 range, hence images that are 16-bit and lower, as discussed above. With 32-bit images you can't apply any gamma correction; more on that later.

With mental ray's gamma correction option, use the inverse value to select the gamma correction you desire, as discussed in this section. Thus for a 2.2 monitor gamma use a value of 0.454, not 2.2. Some applications expect you to enter the monitor's gamma value (2.2) and they do the math behind the scenes, which is not how mental ray handles gamma correction values.

Figure 3.8

Gamma curves and correction

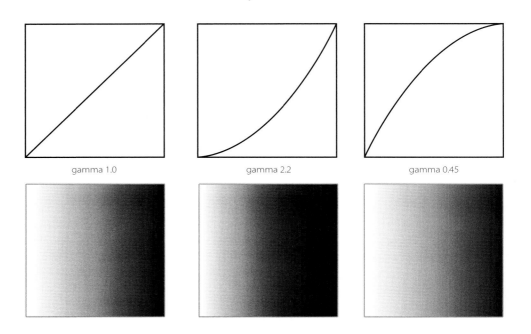

The rendered grayscale values may appear incorrect in print, see the "Gamma Curves" image provided in the Chapter 3 folder on the CD.

Gamma can be corrected by hardware or software—usually by software on Windows computers. Software gamma correction can be done either automatically, as with Photoshop, or manually as with the mental ray gamma option. With Macs, typically there is a built-in gamma correction of 1.4, which is slightly lower than the actual gamma correction of 1.8 that is required, and thus Macs use some hardware gamma correction (which does not mean that you can't also use software gamma correction of course). Note that if you render on Macs with the intention of displaying the image elsewhere (TV, PC monitors, etc.) you need to apply software gamma correction to the image, since the Mac's hardware gamma correction is not imprinted in the image; it will appear darker on other screens.

GAMMA CORRECTION IN 3D

With respect to rendering, when viewing your images on a monitor, a gamma correction has already been applied to textures from digital images, so you would not need to do so yourself. The only reason for you to apply gamma correction is if you are using source material that is still represented as a linear transition from black to white and thus would require a gamma correction to appear correctly on the monitor. mental ray by default renders images with a gamma of 1, which means it doesn't change the gamma of the source material, and so unless you need to change this value, it should stay at 1. If, for example, you wanted to apply a gamma correction of 2.2, you would use a value of 0.45 for the gamma correction, entering the inverse of the monitor's gamma. However, for the purpose of lighting you do need to apply gamma correction. That is, 3D lighting is applied linearly, thus the spread of light always appears to dark. As a result, you may try adding more lights into the scene, or using stronger source lights, which has the effect of creating various overexposed areas without a natural transition of light. The topic of gamma correction and it's implications on lighting is discussed and demonstrated in more detail in Chapters 9 and 12 with indirect lighting.

Gamma Correction and Texture Files

If you want to work in linear space, you should remove the gamma correction before importing texture image files into 3D or within the package, such as with XSI's gamma property for shaders, with Maya's gamma shader, and with 3ds Max's LUT and gamma correction window (see host tutorials below for details on their gamma options). The reason is, image values in gamma-corrected images are represented in a non-linear fashion (as seen in Figure 3.8 above), whereas color values in 3D are added mathematically in a linear fashion; a linear space. Thus, all the color values used with shader math should be represented using their correct linear value and not the gamma corrected value. Then, during rendering the gamma correction is applied (or re-applied) while color values are passed to the frame buffer with a lens shader, as a postprocess, or in compositing.

> Remember, the gamma correction is only relevant to 16-bit and lower images, unlike 32-bit images that are always linear (see the discussion on 32-bit images above). Also, images that are used for shader functions, such as bump mapping, displacement mapping, or masking are not used in the same context as other image files, meaning they are not used to provide color output for visual purposes, rather values for some internal effect. These images don't need to be gamma corrected; they should be linear before using them within the application since their values are used to create an effect where, for example, a 50 percent bump is applied using a 0.5 gray, not the equivalent gamma corrected value of 0.729, a much higher value.

The only problem with applying gamma correction relates to the bit depth of the image. Since gamma correction shifts the distribution of values, it can also reduce the quality of an image with low-bit-depth images, which is why it is better to use 16-bit buffers when gamma correction is applied; it reduces the likelihood of banding artifacts.

Workflow Considerations

I always render an image using a 0.454 (2.2) gamma correction value applied. In this way I can see how the light should spread in the scene while I specify light and shading values. It gives me a correct indication for how the render should look like once finalized. Then, before I execute a final render, I set the gamma value back to 1; a linear gamma without any gamma correction. I then select a 32-bit output format and render.

In compositing (or Photoshop) I set the image viewer to display the sRGB color space (discussed in Chapter 9), which is similar to a gamma correction of 2.2. In some applications I would just set the application viewer's display gamma to 2.2. It allows me to apply all the compositing effects and color corrections to an image while viewing it with gamma correction, as well as using a high bit depth so that artifacts don't appear as a result of compositing effects when using lower bit depths. When the composite tree is finalized, as a last composite operation, I set the gamma correction value to 2.2 and render. Alternatively, in Nuke, I select to output the image to the sRGB color space which has a similar effect.

> If you render 32-bit images without gamma correction (a gamma value of 1), when you open the image in Photoshop it will appear with a gamma correction of 2.2 automatically. The topic is further discussed in Chapters 12 and 13.

Note that I don't usually use a full 2.2 gamma correction since it has the tendency of reducing the contrast, thus I use lower gamma correction values, such as 1.8 which produces a more cinematic gamma appearance.

> It is better to render at a high bit depth, process the image, and then apply gamma correction as a final stage.

Finally, here are a few points of consideration from a practical user perspective:

1. Do you need to remove gamma from all the images before rendering with gamma correction? No. It's not the most practical (or easy) approach to remove gamma from all your source material. If one or two textures in the render appear to become too bright due to gamma correction, you may want to remove gamma just for those images.

2. Should you attempt to remove gamma from procedural shaders? No, they are usually fine as is, if they appear to bright adjust their color properties as you do for normal shader properties.

3. Do you need to use gamma correction to fix light distribution so that it appears more natural? Absolutely yes!

4. Is it better to apply gamma correction in compositing? Depends; when you use lens shaders for gamma correction, the correction is applied on a per sample basis and may provide better quality images without artifacts. For postprocess gamma correction, a pixel based operation, you should probably leave the gamma correction for the compositing stage.

5. Is it a confusing topic? It is indeed, and still needs a lot of work in host applications to become more user friendly. In fact, XSI has completely removed the gamma option from its render settings.

If the light distribution is corrected for gamma, the lighting will appear more natural; your primary concern. All the other considerations should be handled visually, modifying texture values without necessarily dealing with gamma correction or removal. It will allow you to keep a safe distance from getting too technical while focusing on your art rather than on whether the texture or image files have been properly treated for gamma correction.

Frame Buffer Options in Host Applications

The topic of user frame buffers is further discussed throughout the chapter with mental ray cameras, as frame buffers and their output format are dependent on camera statements, options block options, and custom shaders.

The topic of frame buffer options in host applications is divided into two parts that are the frame buffer options discussed above (mental ray Colorclip, Premult, Desaturate, and Dither options) and how frame buffers are exported, including the primary frame buffer, additional primary frame buffers (Z-depth, motion vectors, etc.), and user frame buffers. Let's examine how the host applications handle mental ray frame buffer options and types as well as introduce the frame buffer and user frame buffer export options. After we review each host application's options, we then take a look at managing user frame buffer output using a set of powerful tools available from online resources.

With user frame buffers, the primary RGBA frame buffer will render a full image using the different color components, whereas user frame buffers extract those components and store them in individual image files. Thus the compositing process is based on using the user frame buffer's color passes, not the primary frame buffer pass, which represents the complete image where all the different color contributions are combined.

Maya

Maya offers two separate levels of interaction with mental ray output options. First, you'll find a variety of render output attributes in the Render Settings window → Common tab. In this tab, you can easily specify image formats and output channels without customizing the mental ray frame buffer. In the Render Settings → mental ray tab → Framebuffer rollout, there are several additional attributes for customizing specific mental ray frame buffer options, thus further customizing the output format, its bit depth, and data type.

In the Common tab, the Image File Output section offers the basic RGB, Alpha, and Depth (Z-depth) channel export attributes, as well as commonly used image formats, such as TIF, JPG, IFF, TGA, and more. When mental ray is selected as the current renderer, the same Image Format drop-down provides a similar list of image formats and mental ray–specific formats, including CT, TT, MT, NT, CTH, ST, and others. The mental ray–specific image formats correspond to mental ray frame buffer data types, such as motion vectors (MT), Z-depth (ZT), normal vectors (NT), and so forth, as discussed earlier. In addition, when mental ray is enabled, you also see the OpenEXR, HDR, and TIFF uncompressed (tif) formats. The OpenEXR, HDR, and TIFF uncompressed (tif) formats support HDR images and 32-bit images; all these formats support raw data. The TIFF uncompressed (tif) format also supports storing higher DPI values.

> With the TIFF uncompressed format you can render a 32-bit image at 300 DPI and then modify it in Photoshop, as required for most print related tasks.

Our focus in this section is on the mental ray Render Settings → mental ray tab → Framebuffer → Primary Framebuffer rollout shown in Figure 3.9, which controls mental ray–specific frame buffer settings: image channels, bit depth, data types and render options. By

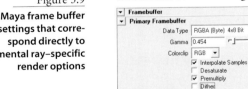

Figure 3.9
Maya frame buffer settings that correspond directly to mental ray–specific render options

default, the frame buffer is set to RGBA (Byte) 4×8 Bit, which is the default 8-bit frame buffer, so when Maya renders, this would be the frame buffer used for storing output color values before writing that data to the selected image file and format (selected from the Common tab → Image format list).

The frame buffer Data Type drop-down list is used to select the bit depth, channels, and data type for the frame buffer.

For example, selecting RGBA (Byte) 4×8 Bit will render four channels (RGBA), each using a byte size data type, the default buffer. Alternatively, the Depth (Float) 1x32 Bit option renders a single-channel 32-bit floating-point depth buffer into a 32-bit supporting image format. There is also an RGBE 4x8 Bit HDR image format, so you can render HDR images with mental ray; this option also requires that you select an appropriate HDR image format such as the mental ray .cth format, the radiance HDR format, or ILM's OpenEXR format, which all support the (E) exponent channel.

Below the Data Type drop-down list, there are additional attributes including Gamma, Colorclip (drop-down list), Desaturate, Premultiply, and Dither, all of which behave as described earlier. In Figure 3.9 you can see a common setup for rendering, correlating to our discussions on frame buffer options where the Colorclip attribute is set to RGB color clipping and the Gamma attribute is set with a value of 0.454; a gamma correction for a common PC display based on a 2.2 gamma curve. Also, you can see that frame buffer is set to Interpolate Samples (interpolated versus padded), as it should be so that samples are averaged for "beauty" color output.

OUTPUTTING SEVERAL PRIMARY FRAME BUFFERS

The problem with selecting a data type under the Primary Framebuffer rollout is that it only supports one data type export. To clarify, it will only render the selected data type as output. However, as discussed earlier, one of the advantages of frame buffers is that several frame buffers can be exported during the execution of a single render. For example, you may select the RGBA (Byte) 4×8 Bit data type for color but then also add a Z-depth channel. To do so, you can enable the Depth channel (Z-depth) attribute under the Common tab → Renderable Cameras rollout. When enabled, the Z-depth will render its value into the output image file as a fifth channel in addition to the RGBA channels (with IFF file formats), or as a separate IFF file placed in the same render directory (when the primary output format doesn't support adding a Z-depth channel, for example with TIF images).

In addition to this common practice with Maya you may want to export motion vectors, or any other primary frame buffer during the render, in which case the Primary Framebuffer rollout doesn't provide you with additional export options as noted above; you can only select one data type and enable the Z-depth under the Common tab. To output additional buffers during the execution of a single render, select the render camera and reveal its attributes in the Attribute Editor window. Under the mental ray rollout → Output Passes rollout, shown in Figure 3.10, you can enable additional primary frame buffers for output by listing both output statements and shaders (shaders are discussed later) after clicking the Create button.

Figure 3.10 shows a list where three different output passes for Z-depth, coverage, and normals are listed and rendered in addition to the primary buffer that is selected under the Render Settings window (typically the RGBA color buffer). Thus, in the case shown in Figure 3.10, each rendered frame will produce four image files on disk including the primary and the three additional frame buffers shown in Figure 3.10.

Figure 3.11 shows the window that appears after clicking on the Create button. Under Frame Buffer Type, you can select the type of frame buffer that you want write to disk, identical to the Render Setting's Framebuffer → Primary Framebuffer rollout → Data type attribute discussed above. In the same context, the Interpolate Samples attribute will specify whether the buffer is interpolated or padded.

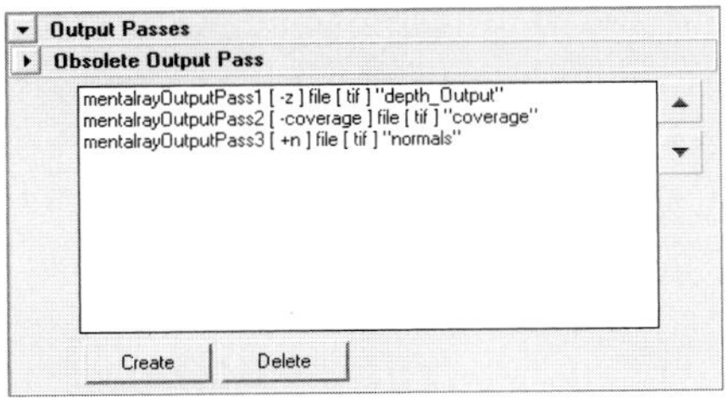

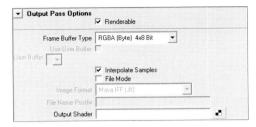

Figure 3.10

Maya enables you to list several output frame buffers under the camera's Output Passes rollout.

Figure 3.11

The Output Passes list enables you to specify whether you want to output custom frame buffers or apply output shaders during the render.

The File Mode attribute specifies whether this listing acts as an output statement or output shader (output shaders are discussed under "mental ray Cameras" later in this chapter). When it's enabled, the File Name Postfix and Image Format attributes are also enabled so that you can specify the output image format and file name. Note that the name you specify will be appended to the file name indicated in the Render Settings → Common tab. Also note that for sequence numbering (animation) in the Common tab you should set the Frame/Animation ext: attribute to name.ext.# so that the custom buffer labels are appended before the numbered sequence.

I highly recommend that you experiment with a simple scene while outputting common buffers, such as depth and normal buffers that are easy to view in image viewers. Once you manage the first step try exporting a small animation sequence of 5 frames and importing it into a compositing application. You should first see that you fully understand the process of exporting custom buffers as well as making use of them in compositing before using it for production purposes.

> Listing output frame buffers in the Output Passes list allows you to write several images to disk during a single render rather than one at a time.

MAYA USER FRAME BUFFERS

User frame buffers, although they can be created within Maya, currently have little or no application for the standard user. They are only partially integrated into Maya; mostly part of a development cycle and an option for advanced users. Basically, they are not useful unless you plan on adding custom mental ray text to the scene, editing the scene within an .mi file, or have a custom output shader that requires using additional frame buffers, which would then be specified by the shader (most likely). Essentially, mental ray user frame buffers are only created when needed, so if they are not specified within a specific output statement, or shader, there is no reason to create them.

The User Framebuffer rollout in the mental ray Render Settings window offers a shortcut for enabling or disabling custom frame buffers by clicking the Open Editor attribute button. This button opens the miDefaultOptions node attributes in the Attribute Editor window. We discuss this window on several occasions throughout the book; essentially it offers a more complete listing of mental ray options, some of which are not available in the Render Settings window. In this case, under the Frame Buffers rollout you click the Create button to create new user frame buffers, similar to the process described above with the Output Passes list on the render camera. The list discussed above deals with outputting images using any of the built-in primary frame buffers, whereas this list offers you the ability to create new user frame buffers. When you click Create you can then select any output format for the user frame buffer. User frame buffers are specified with index numbers, a topic discussed in detail under "Output Statements" later in this chapter. As cited above, this process is still a work in progress development and is not functional unless you plan on writing custom shaders that can write color data to specific frame buffers.

> The section "Online Resources for Exporting Custom Passes" introduces a powerful set of tools for efficiently managing user frame buffer export options with Maya and mental ray.

XSI

XSI is geared solely for rendering with mental ray, which means there is no separation between the mental ray frame buffer output settings and the host application (XSI) settings; they go hand in hand. The Render Options properties in XSI that control frame buffer output options are found under various tabs in the Render Manager window. Let's begin by reviewing the frame buffer options discussed earlier, found under the mental ray → Framebuffer tab.

THE FRAMEBUFFER TAB

The Framebuffer tab, shown in Figure 3.12, provides the frame buffer options discussed earlier, under the Color Control and Advanced Settings sections shown in the figure. Let's briefly review these options:

1. The Dither 8-bit Framebuffers and Desaturate colors when clipping properties correspond to the mental ray dither and desaturate options.

2. The Premultiply with Alpha property corresponds to the premultiply option, when enabled images are premultiplied by the alpha.

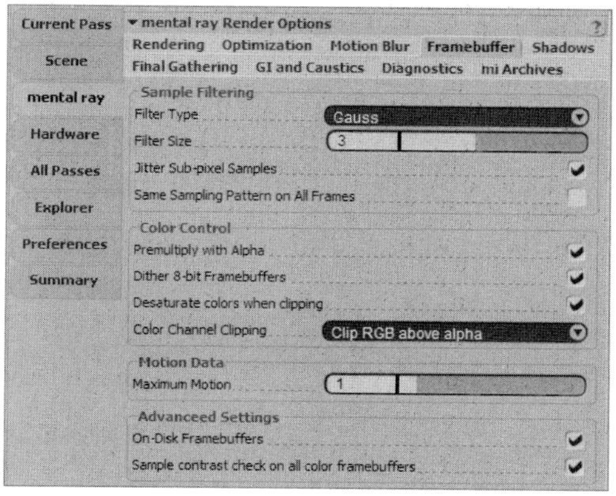

Figure 3.12

The Framebuffer tab enables specifying the mental ray frame buffer options.

3. The On-disk Framebuffers property enables temporarily storing frame buffers on disk and thus improves memory handling when several frame buffers need to be written to file. This is typically useful for when you use several user frame buffers or render very high resolutions.

4. The Sample contrast check on all framebuffers property, as mentioned earlier, enables mental ray sampling to compare contrast values in all the frame buffers when determining the adaptive sampling level. See Chapter 5 for sampling and contrast checks.

5. The Color Channel Clipping property drop-down list has labels that may appear somewhat confusing in comparison to the mental ray color clip options discussed earlier. These labels act as follows:

    1. The Clip alpha below RGB option corresponds to RGB color clipping.

    2. The Clip RGB above alpha option corresponds to alpha color clipping.

    3. The No Clip option corresponds to raw color clipping.

THE OUTPUT TAB

In the Render Manager window → Current Pass → Output tab , you can control the per pass (for the current pass) RGBA primary frame buffer's output options as well as list additional primary and user frame buffers for output using the Render Channels Output list shown in Figure 3.13.

GAMMA IN XSI

XSI 6 and higher removed the mental ray gamma option from the render properties. To apply gamma correction you can use a custom lens shader such as the tone-mapping shader discussed in Chapter 13, "Final Gather and Ambient Occlusion." Alternatively there are online shaders that you can install and use to apply gamma correction as well as remove gamma correction from textures, on a per image basis; recall that in a linear workspace you may want to remove gamma from image files that are already gamma corrected if those images will be exposed to a gamma correction during the render. The sRGB color space, discussed in Chapter 9, is similar to a standard gamma correction for a 2.2 display; images in sRGB appear similar to gamma corrected images. The purpose of the sRGB color space is to set a standard correction for web display. You can find two custom shaders as well a discussion on the topic of gamma and the sRGB color space online at:

    http://www.xsi-blog.com/archives/133

From there you can also download two shaders (sRGB_utils); a lens shader for gamma correction and a texture shader used to remove gamma from image files. Currently the link that provides these shaders as a downloadable Zip file resides at: http://perso.orange.fr/harry.bardak/data/sRGB_Utils.zip

Figure 3.13

The primary frame buffer, its name, image format, and channels are seen listed under the Render Channels Output property.

Figure 3.14

The frame buffer properties can be edited in a properties window by selecting the frame buffer listing and pressing Edit… under the Render Channels Output list shown in Figure 3.13.

The default listing shown in the figure refers to the primary RGBA frame buffer outputted with each render. When you select it (click anywhere within the listing) and click on Edit… you can modify its properties in the pop up window shown in Figure 3.14. As you can see in the figure, under Output you specify the file name seen as [Pass]_[Framebuffer] by default, which defaults to the name of the current pass and the frame buffer name. The frame buffer name is seen under the Render Channel property in Figure 3.14 as well as under the Channel column in Figure 3.13.

Under the Output Format section three drop-down lists offer the properties that control the current frame buffer settings; the frame buffer listed under Render Channel seen as Main in the figure. The Main frame buffer correlates to the primary RGBA frame buffer. The first drop-down list selects an image format, the second drop-down list selects the rendered channels (ex. RGBA, RGBE, RGB, etc.) and the third drop-down list selects the per-channel bit depth. When you select an image format the other two drop-down lists automatically update to include within them relevant (supported) settings for that image format. For example, when TIFF is selected, as shown in the figure, you can then select either RGB or RGBA for the render channels and set the bit depth to 8 bits, 16 bits, or Float (from the third drop-down list). Thus these three drop-down lists specify an image format, its channels, and bit depth.

As another example, if you render HDR output using the Radiance HDR (.hdr) image format, then you will see that the RGBE channels (the E exponent channel is required for HDR formats) are enabled at 8 bits without any options for changing the channels or bit depth properties (see Chapter 9 for more on HDR image formats), demonstrating how these options only offer relevant settings for a given image format.

OUTPUTTING PRIMARY AND USER FRAME BUFFERS

To output additional primary frame buffers (Z-depth, motion vectors, normals, tags, and coverage), you can append them to the list seen in Figure 3.13 by clicking on the Add... property. When you click on Add you are prompted in the Create Framebuffer From

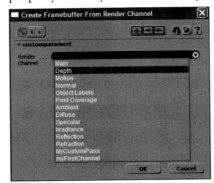

Render Channel window, shown in Figure 3.15, to select which frame buffers you want to append to the list. As you can see in the figure, the Render Channel property drop-down list enables selecting any of the standard built-in frame buffers as well as any user frame buffers that are currently defined for the scene (user frame buffers are clarified shortly). Once you select a frame buffer and click on OK a new entry is added to the Render Channels Output list, as shown in Figure 3.16.

In Figure 3.16 you can see various standard and user defined frame buffers have been added to the list. The checkmark on the left of each listing specifies whether that listing will be used to output an image during the render. The checkmark correlates to the Enabled property checkbox seen in Figure 3.14; both disable or enable the selected frame buffer. As you can see in Figure 3.16, the Depth channel, referring to the standard Z-depth frame buffer, is disabled (no checkmark) so that it will not output a Z-depth pass when a render is executed. You can modify the properties for any of the listed channels by selecting the listing and pressing Edit... as seen earlier with the primary frame buffer and Figure 3.14. As you can see, for the Depth channel the mental ray ZT image format is used. You could

Figure 3.16

The Render Channels Output lists several primary and user defined frame buffers to be rendered when a render is executed.

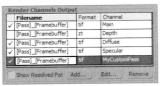

then edit that listing and change the image format used to store the Z-depth to a more compatible format; a format that is supported by your compositing application which may be ZPIC (Softimage Z-depth), RLA, OpenEXR, or any other format.

Trial and error experimentation will help you identify the formats that are best suited for your work environment.

XSI User Frame Buffers

In Figure 3.16 you can also see that additional user frame buffers have been added to the list, including Diffuse, Specular, and MyCustomPass. User frame buffers in XSI are offered as additional predefined user frame buffers or user frame buffers that you manually construct. In the Render Manager window under Scene → Scene Render Options → Available

Channels tab, shown in Figure 3.17, you can see a list of all the available frame buffers for your scene, globally. All the frame buffers highlighted in gray (brighter in the figure) refer to the six built-in primary frame buffers, and those highlighted in green (darker in the figure) refer to custom user frame buffers. The first six listed user frame buffers are provided by XSI for you, allowing you to separate any XSI render pass into several sub-pass components that output specific color information to image files during the execution of a single render (for each rendered frame), including the Ambient, Diffuse, Specular, Irradiance, Reflection, and Refraction frame buffers listed in Figure 3.17. These buffers can be added to the current pass (or any other pass) by pressing the Add... property under the Render Channels Output list and selecting the frame buffer form the list shown earlier in Figure 3.15.

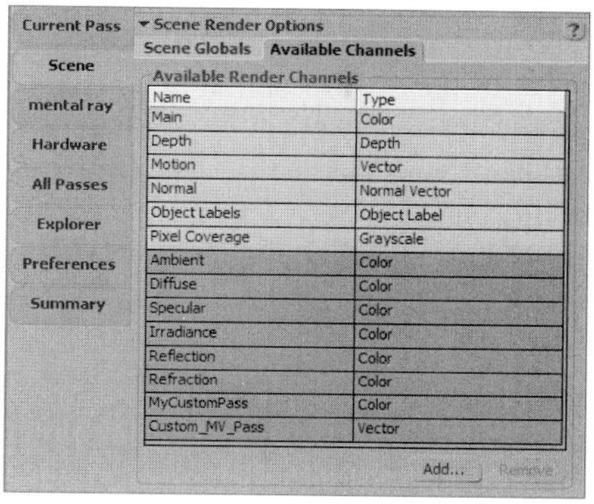

Figure 3.17

The available frame buffers for a scene, which can be used with any XSI pass, are seen under the Available Channels list in the Render Manager window

By listing several of these predefined user framer buffers, during the render of a single frame, several additional customized frame buffers are output with specific color information, as instructed by their relevant user frame buffer.

Creating User Frame Buffers

As you can see in Figure 3.17, two additional user frame buffers that I manually created are present in the list. They are MyCustomPass (RGBA color buffer) and Custom_MV_Pass (a motion vectors frame buffer). To create these buffers press the Add... property shown in Figure 3.17 under the list. You are then prompted with the Create Render Channel window shown earlier in Figure 3.3. In that window you label the frame buffer with the Name property and set its data type with the Type property. As discussed earlier, any user frame buffer can be set to one of the six default data types (seen listed in Figure 3.3) that are Color (RGBA), Grayscale (single channel output), Depth, Normal Vector, Vectors / Motion Vectors, and Object Label. In the case of figure 3.17, MyCustomPass is set as an RGBA color pass and Custom_MV_Pass is set to render motion vectors.

To actually make use of these buffers, they must receive some color information from shaders in the scene; they don't automatically know from what surfaces they should extract color values. Thus you need to further customize the scene so that they are connected to certain shaders. This process is only true for user frame buffers that you manually define. The other six XSI user frame buffers (diffuse, specular, etc.) already know how to extract those colors form shaders, thus they don't require additional customization.

Let's look at some practical examples for using user frame buffers, such as those that I added to the list in Figure 3.17.

1. The custom color user frame buffer (myCustomPass) can be used to extract color from a collection of surfaces in the scene that you want to further tweak during compositing. For example, the scene is very slow to render and you are not completely satisfied with their exposure or color values. Exporting them as separate buffers (passes) allows you to further modify those surface colors during compositing.

2. With respect to the motion vectors pass, you may want to output the motion vectors for specific surfaces (that are in motion) so that you can modify their motion blur effect independently of other surfaces in compositing. A more advanced approach for motion vectors, based on the discussion on custom motion vectors in a sidebar at the end of Chapter 8, is to use custom shaders (LMV shader) to create color (RGB) motion vector passes. In Chapter 8 you will see how you may want separate motion vector passes for different components in the scene. Using such custom passes, in this case a color pass from a custom shader, would allow you to specifically output motion vectors for individual surfaces using a user defined frame buffer.

3. You may want to render the output from volume light effects into a separate frame buffer so that it becomes easier to fine-tune its effect during compositing.

To apply the connection between user frame buffers and shaders, shown in Figure 3.18, follow these steps:

1. In the Render Tree window, graph a shader tree for a given surface.

2. From under Nodes → Render Channels you can select to create a shader that corresponds to the type of output you need. For example, in Figure 3.18 I want to output the color from the Cook-Torrance shader labeled A into an RGBA color user frame buffer (myCustomPass in Figure 3.17). Thus, I created a Store Color In Channel shader seen labeled B. You can see the other channel types in the figure labeled D, corresponding to vector, scalar, Boolean, and integer output data types.

3. I connect the output from the Cook-Torrance shader labeled A to the Color_StoreInChannel shader labeled B. I then connect that shader to the Material Surface property input labeled C.

4. To select a user frame buffer, under the Color_StoreInChannel shader properties, the Render Channel property drop-down list is used to select any of the predefined user frame buffers available from the list shown in Figure 3.17. Only relevant user frame buffers will appear; frame buffers that have the same data type (color, vector, etc.).

In this way, you create an in-between shader that resides between the surface material and the illumination shader (or any other shader) which is used to pass the color (or other) data from the source shader (labeled A) to a user frame buffer (labeled B).

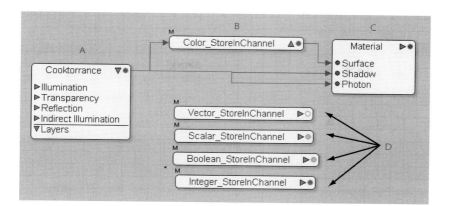

Figure 3.18

A shader tree in XSI used to output color values from the illumination shader (A) to a custom user frame buffer with the shader labeled B

We will look at the implementation of these output stalemates later in the chapter in the section "mental ray Cameras."

3ds Max

3ds Max tries to collapse all the global settings for export into common tabs for all renderers (mental ray, 3ds Max, V-Ray, etc.). In doing so, in my opinion, it has both neglected to provide several important settings and included some nice additional settings not commonly found in other host applications.

> 3ds Max image formats and channels, with respect to mental ray, are integrated in a completely different way than with Maya or XSI. This is not necessarily a disadvantage. 3ds Max does offer users a lot of flexibility, especially with channels using the OpenEXR, RPF, and RLA formats. However, the frame buffer options discussed throughout this chapter are not derived from mental ray–specific parameters and thus can be accomplished in various different ways. We will look at some of these options in this section.

3ds Max has not included the premultiply, desaturate, dither, and colorclip options as mental ray render parameters. On the other hand, 3ds Max's extended support for output image formats such as OpenEXR provides for some nice options not found in Maya or XSI. Further, 3ds Max is currently the only host application to support *multipass rendering*, a topic further discussed at the end of this chapter.

For gamma correction, you need to navigate through the Customize → Preferences… → Gamma and LUT tab. In this window you can specify 3ds Max postprocess gamma correction. To enable gamma correction, enable the Enable Gamma/LUT Correction parameter checkbox and then specify a gamma correction value with the Gamma parameter. The values you specify here are opposite to those discussed earlier in the chapter, meaning for a 2.2 gamma correction use the value of 2.2 not 0.454.

With respect to the primary frame buffer settings, you will find the following under the Render Scene: mental ray Renderer window → Renderer tab → Sampling Quality rollout → Options section a Frame Buffer Type setting offering you a selection between 16- or 32-bit frame buffers.

Under the Common tab → Render Output → Files, if you select an OpenEXR image file format and go into the setup (or click Save), an additional window, shown in Figure 3.19, appears, providing some advanced features for multichannel images, a hot topic these days. Under the Extra Channels to Save section you can add additional images for output based on the primary frame buffers discussed above as well as some 3ds max–specific custom frame buffers. Notice the Pre-Multiply Alpha setting in this window; it enables or disables premultiplication. You can also find similar settings for other image formats such as the RPF image format. If you select a TIF image format then a Gamma Correction parameter is provided. You can select to use the system defaults which derives the gamma correction value from the gamma parameter discussed earlier (in the Gamma and LUT preferences tab), or use the Override parameter to manually specify a gamma correction override value.

3ds Max applies its gamma correction as a post process so that it is best to apply it in compositing. For testing, set the gamma correction you require, such as 2.2, under the Gamma and LUT preferences tab so that while you render you see a gamma corrected render in the viewport render window, and then remove that gamma correction before executing a final render, as discussed under the Gamma Correction section earlier in this chapter.

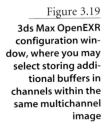

Figure 3.19

3ds Max OpenEXR configuration window, where you may select storing additional buffers in channels within the same multichannel image

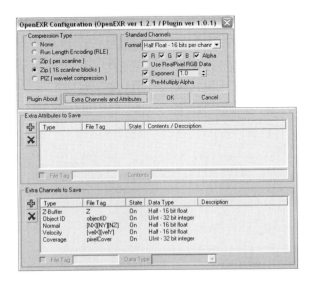

Essentially, with 3ds Max it appears that regardless of the render settings, the alpha always corresponds to the mental ray Colorclip option RGB setting. Thus the alpha intensity is raised to match the RGB values so that specular highlight intensities are maintained, as discussed earlier.

EXPORTING ADDITIONAL FRAME BUFFERS

To export additional frame buffers, as discussed earlier, either use the Extra Channels and Attributes button seen in Figure 3.19 to add additional channels into an OpenEXR image (similarly within the RPF format options) or set each channel to render into separate image files. In Figure 3.20, you can see the Render Scene: mental ray Renderer window → Render Elements tab and rollout.

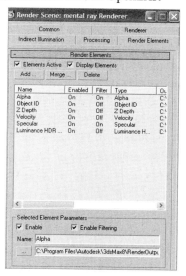

Figure 3.20

The 3ds Max Render Elements options enable you to output several different color properties and frame buffers into separated image files.

Here you can select Add to enable outputting other user frame buffers or primary frame buffers during the render. This window is one of the nicest features within 3ds Max with respect to mental ray output. It enables selecting several custom passes as well as the primary frame buffers and appears to function well. For each element added, you will find options for specifying the output file format and location, along with occasional other options. With these settings you can then easily export all the primary frame buffers, including the motion vectors, normal vectors, object ID, and so forth, each into a separate file.

The Render Elements passes (listed in the window) execute each render as a separate render rendered consecutively. However, when you choose to specify additional output channels for the EXR format, as cited earlier, the current render will include those output channels without executing additional consecutive renders. If you choose to export a mental images file for stand-alone rendering, when several render elements are specified, each will be exported into a separate .mi file for rendering.

In Chapter 8 we look at rendering motion vectors for compositing motion blur in a sidebar at the end of the chapter. That sidebar is based on using the Render Elements window to render motion vectors output for compositing. With respect to mental ray user frame buffers, there are external shaders for 3ds Max that can be used to better implement user frame buffer output with mental ray, as discussed in the following topic.

Online Resources for Exporting Custom Passes

With all host applications, there are various shaders online that can help you better develop your scenes for custom output, such as rendering separate passes into individual image files or into a single OpenEXR multichannel image (discussed later in this chapter) during the execution of a single render. Pavel Ledin, aka Puppet, is the author of a collection of powerful shaders for managing custom output for mental ray standalone rendering as well as through Maya, XSI, and 3ds Max. These shaders offer several advanced shading and lighting options aside from their user frame buffer context discussed here. His p_MegaTK shader tools enable you to specify various user frame buffers for export into OpenEXR or other image formats, as shown in Figure 3.21, a Maya screen grab. You can find the most current collection of shaders at: http://www.puppet.cgtalk.ru under Download → Shaders_p (current version) → p_MegaTK. You can also use the puppet shaders for each host application provided on the companion CD under the Custom Shaders folder → Puppet Shaders folder (not guaranteed to be the most current collection). In the folder under the Doc folder (as well as on his site), you will find tutorials and detailed explanations on how to use these shaders in practice. Please see the Licensing page in the documents for more information on using these shaders or their source code (provided in the Zip files). Basically he provides a BSD license.

In Figure 3.21 you can see that the Mega TK passes Out Format is set to Single OpenEXR which, will render all the buffers specified under the Output passes rollout as additional channels within a single OpenEXR image file. Also, note that all the primary built-in buffers discussed earlier can be enabled under the Mental Ray Standard Channels rollout seen contracted in the figure. Using the shader requires using custom illumination and light shaders that are provided with the MegaTK shaders that write their output color values to the user frame buffers seen under the Output Passes list in Figure 3.21; you must specify shaders to output color to specific user frame buffers.

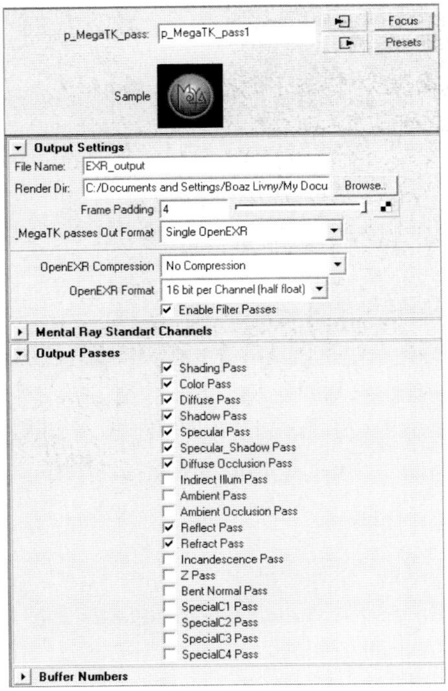

Figure 3.21

Puppet's p_MegaTK shader collection enables you to output several different color components (user frame buffers) during the execution of a single render.

To clarify, when a shader outputs its color values, it sends that output to the primary frame buffer, for example, if you want the reflection color values to output to the user frame buffer for outputting a reflection pass, the shader would need information on that user frame buffer so that it knows to send the reflection colors into that specific frame buffer. Thus you can see how the user frame buffers are tightly integrated with shaders while determining the distribution of color (or other) values across several user frame buffers.

Resources such as these custom shaders significantly improve your abilities to create more efficient renders, where several user frame buffers are extracted and written to image files during the time frame of a single render rather

cutive renders. After all, the various color values such as specular and
e present as independent components during the render; mental ray
shader contribution values during the render as discussed in Chapter 9,
me buffers merely allow you to record those values before they are
r, outputting each as an independent image file for compositing pur-
s discussed above, you can construct your own user frame buffers to
he channel output shaders, which reduces the requirement of using
rs.

using such custom shaders in host applications, in Chapter 10 you will
nstalling such shaders. With respect to the puppet shaders, their help
CD will walk you through the installation process in each host applica-
l that you experiment with these custom shaders after you are very comfortable with using mental ray and compositing passes. Also, as cited above, these shaders
offer far more than just output passes. Their advantages will become clearer as you learn
more about mental ray shaders in Chapters 9 to 11.

INDEPENDENT RENDER JOBS

There are actually two approaches to rendering passes, only one of which is discussed in this
chapter. The first consists of outputting passes during the execution of one render, meaning
that the frame is rendered once and during that time it outputs several image files based on
your requirements, as discussed per host in the sections above as well as with the puppet
shaders. This is the approach of using user frame buffers to define custom passes.

However (using a different method with each application), you can also render passes
consecutively. For example, first you might execute the diffuse pass, then a specular pass,
and so on, and each pass is then a separate render job, executing independently. Thus, in this
case a separate pass might as well be considered a separate render scene altogether and has
nothing to do with how you specify mental ray output options. To do this, Maya offers *render
layers*, XSI has *passes*, and 3ds Max has *render elements*. Each of these lets you define particular
settings that can then be executed. For example, you might first render the foreground and
then the background and define different shading options with each render, such as reflection
or diffuse colors. Maya and XSI have similar abilities for specifying object and shader overrides
per render layer or pass (respectively), and so you can prepare a scene for compositing and
then execute several consecutive renders that result with all the color passes you require.
You can learn more about compositing passes in the article on "Nuke Compositing" available
in the companion CD.

The topic of each hosts' methods for defining these separate render passes is beyond the
scope of this book. It's a host-specific approach (not mental ray–specific) for organizing your
scene into several separated render passes, which is not as render time efficient as when
using custom user frame buffers that handle this process during a single render.

mental ray Cameras

mental ray cameras have three primary objectives: to simulate the photographic characteristics of a real camera, to specify environmental and postprocess effects, and to specify output files and formats. With respect to host applications, mental ray cameras to a certain extent act as both the render settings and camera settings. In the following sections, you will see how all of these settings come together within mental images files.

Virtual Cameras with mental ray

3D virtual cameras are typically characterized as pinhole cameras, which are the simplest form of imaginary camera. Pinhole cameras don't use lenses to perturb light as it enters the camera; they simply provide an opening (the hole) that exposes film to light. Thus pinhole cameras don't focus light onto the film as does a lens. Instead, they record the scene simply perceived through the camera's *field of view*. Essentially, this means that 3D cameras don't account for lens distortion and accurate perspectives. The cameras we use in 3D can simulate a wide range of camera characteristics, such as capturing a wide field of view only possible with wide angle lenses, however, as with a pinhole camera, a wide-angle focal length would not yield the same result as when using a wide-angle lens (at the same focal length), which distorts the path of light, focusing more light from various angles onto film.

> In Chapter 4, "Camera Fundamentals," you will learn more about how real-life camera characteristics are translated into CG cameras and about the relationship between real cameras and virtual cameras.

For a virtual camera to simulate a real lens, paths of light must be raytraced as they focus through the lens. This can be achieved through the use of a *lens shader* that describes the lens's physical characteristics. Once a lens shader is applied to a mental ray camera, mental ray can realistically reproduce not only perspective, but also the focal depth (depth of field), lens distortion, or any other lens effect (such as *chromatic aberrations*) provided you have an appropriate lens shader that defines these effects mathematically. Chapter 4 discusses lens shaders extensively.

If you look at Figure 3.22, you can see the same image rendered with a wide-angle lens effect (A) and without a lens shader (B). The image labeled A uses a *barrel* distortion lens effect to simulate how a wide-angle lens would affect the projected image, by increasingly distorting light paths closer to the lens rim as well as capturing a wider field of view. Thus both images A and B are rendered using the same camera settings (placement and focal depth), however image A shows more of the room than image B. Barrel distortion effects are common to wide-angle (converging) lenses. As the lens focal length gets shorter, a wider angle can be recorded, eventually resulting in a near-180° image, which at that point is referred to as a fish-eye lens that commonly posses a high-level of lens distortion.

The virtual camera can simulate wide fields of views and their effect on perspective without a lens shader, the equivalent of an "advanced" theoretical pinhole camera. However, the addition of lens shaders then adds that extra realism, allowing for the kinds of lens distortion seen with real-world cameras as well as a more accurate perspective.

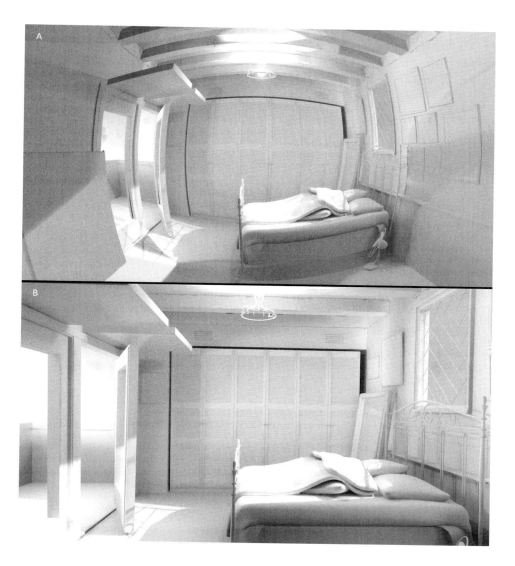

Figure 3.22

Rendering with lens effects to simulate the barrel distortion effect found with wide-angle lenses

mental ray Camera Declaration Block

Let's look at a mental images file (.mi) camera declaration block. I have numbered comments for each section so you can easily refer to them in following discussions:

```
camera "perspShape"

resolution 640 480
    aspect 1.33333
    aperture 1.41732
    frame 3 3.
    clip 0.1 1000.
    focal 1.37795

    # 1. mentalray Output Pass
    output "+rgba" "iff" "firstRender"

    # 2. mentalray postprocess 2D shader
    output "+rgb_fp,+z" = "depth_fade" (
                "near_depth" 1,
                "far_depth" 15
                 )

    # 3. mentalray final Output Pass
    output "+rgba" "tif" "test_cam.tif"

    # 4. mentalray lens shader

lens "maya_dof" (
        "focusDistance" 5.,
        "fStop" 5.6,
        "focusRegionScale" 1.,
        "lensSamples" 4
                )
    # 5. mentalray volume shader
    volume = "mib_volume2"

    # 6. mentalray environment  shader
    environment = "mib_lookup_spherical2"
end camera
```

You can see that the declaration block is broken into two segments. The first section under the camera statements (before comment 1) includes settings for render resolution, the camera's aperture, the lens's focal length, and the image aspect ratio. Chapter 4 discusses all of these settings, which directly relate to camera and lens characteristics. These characteristics add realism when used with a lens shader during the render as shown in

Figure 3.22 image A. Without a lens shader, they merely determine perspective and field of view. The `frame` option simply notes the frame sequence that should be rendered, and `clip` defines the clipping planes (discussed in the section "Depth Sorting" later in the chapter).

Followed by the camera settings, you find in the following order mental ray's output statement (1), output shader (2), an additional output statement (3), lens shader (4), volume shader (5), and environment shader (6). All these show how mental ray cameras use a variety of different shaders and options to process environmental effects, camera effects, and render output. Let's take a closer look at all these shaders.

Output, Volume, Environment, and Lens Shaders

All these shaders can be assigned internally from within your application, or added into an exported .mi file when rendering with the standalone renderer. These shaders either ship with mental ray or can be implemented into your application through the mental ray .rayrc file, as discussed in the section "mental ray Shaders and Shader Libraries" in Chapter 1.

Output Shaders

An *output shader* affects frame buffer pixel values to produce its visual effect; it's a 2D postprocess effect that operates on per-pixel color values. For example, the shader in this statement requires the primary frame buffer as a floating-point frame buffer and the Z-depth buffer for producing a depth fading effect:

```
output "+rgb_fp,+z" = "bfade1"
```

Output shaders then apply their effect on a per-pixel basis and have no effect on sampling. The significance of output shaders is that they are faster to render and are executed in order, so several shaders can be "stacked" to execute in a specific order. We look closer at the significance of output order later in this chapter under "Output Order and Output Shaders".

Maya and 3ds Max currently have not yet implemented any postprocess output shaders, with the exception of contour shading and the architectural library exposure shader. The exposure shaders (architectural library's exposure simple and photographic shaders) can be used either as an output or lens shader. From the shader resources cited in this chapter and Chapter 10 you will find various output shaders that you can use. XSI does provide some useful 2D postprocess shaders such as 2D fur, glows, and depth of field, among others.

For Maya and 3ds Max you can experiment with some of the output shaders kindly provided by Jan Sandstrom (www.pixero.com) on the companion CD in ChapterFiles/CustomShaders/Pixero in the Maya and 3ds Max folder. Try using the JS_Glare output shader. Each shader has some relevant information within the Zip file.

One nice output shader is a glare shader from the Lume shader library (an additional collection of mental ray shaders). It creates a glare effect around the brightest areas of the scene. It also allows you to specify whether you want to render solely the glare effect (good for compositing), or the effect super imposed over the image. In Figure 3.23 you can see an example of the glare effect rendered in XSI in overlay mode (you only see the effect of the glare). In this case the glare Quality property is set high so that it appears to glare from everything in the scene (all the various intensities). With lower Quality property values the glare effect will focus only on the brightest areas of the scene as demonstrated in the Color Gallery image "Physical Lighting".

Figure 3.23

The Lume shader library glare output shader effect rendered in XSI

In Chapters 9 and 10 you will learn more about the custom shader resources presented throughout this chapter, as well as installation tutorials.

Lens, Volume, and Environment Shaders

The most significant difference between lens, volume, and environment shaders and output shaders is that they are applied at the scene level and influence sampling, and thus the order in which they are applied has no significance with respect to output statements. As seen in the camera declaration block above, they all appear after the output statements (4–6), unlike the output shader (2), which appears within the output statements (1 and 3).

LENS SHADERS

Lens shaders almost always apply a distortion effect to simulate realistic lens characteristics, as discussed earlier. Currently, each host application provides different lens shaders in addition to the depth of field lens shader. XSI and 3ds Max also provide the additional Lume shader library. Figure 3.22 image A was rendered using the Lume shader library distortion lens shader available in XSI and 3ds Max.

Another useful lens shader from the Lume collection is the wraparound shader. It allows you to render a 360° *spherical panoramic image* (for panoramic image types see Chapter 13), as shown in Figure 3.24, which can then be used for reflection maps to accelerate rendering. Reflection maps are discussed in more detail next. When you render panoramic spherical images, the resolution should be set at a ratio of 2:1 such as 1024 × 512. Note that there are other shaders and tools in host applications that can be used to produce panoramic images; the wraparound shader is just one of them. We return to lens shaders in detail in the following chapter, with respect to depth of field.

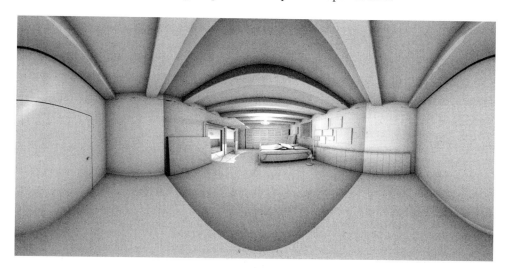

Figure 3.24

Rendering spherical panoramic images for reflection maps with the Lume wraparound shader

If you have the lume.dll shader library you can easily add it to Maya as explained in Chapter 1. The include (.mi shader declaration file) and AETemplate files are provided by Jan Sandstrom (http://www.pixero.com) on the companion CD in ChapterFiles/CustomShaders/Pixero in the Maya folder (LumeTools for Maya.zip).

ENVIRONMENT SHADERS

Camera environment shaders are used to bound the scene with a 2D environmental image, which can be used to provide a background color, reflection color (reflections of the environment), and a source of illumination for indirect illumination such as with final gather, all topics discussed throughout this book. One key advantage of environmental shaders is that they act as shader projections and do not require a geometric surface for visibility. Thus geometry is not tessellated during the render; colors are sampled from the environment projection. These images may be panoramic images, commonly provided as either *cubic* or *spherical* images as shown in Figure 3.24; a spherical panoramic image.

Each application offers different methods for applying (projection-mapping) these shaders into the scene (mental ray projection-mapping shaders are discussed in Chapter 11).

As noted above, environment shaders can be used to apply non-raytrace reflections by extracting the reflection color values for a surface from the environment projection. This means that the environment behaves like any other color texture mapped on a shader, where in this case, the reflection color is acquired by sampling values from a spherical texture projection rather than by raytracing the scene. Thus, a prerequisite to faking reflection is rendering the scene as a panoramic image, as shown in Figure 3.24, which can then be used to project reflection colors on surfaces placed within the scene, for example on a mirror or on the windows.

It is a common practice with advanced reflection shaders to raytrace reflections of geometry in the scene and then add the environment reflection using a simple color sampling process, without raytracing. Furthermore, various shaders allow you to limit the distance raytrace rays can travel into the scene before the environment color is sampled from an environment shader, a topic demonstrated in Chapter 10.

In the camera declaration block excerpt, you can see a mental ray spherical environment applied to the camera. When an environment shader is applied on the local level with a surface material's environment color, it provides reflection colors for that surface material only, opposed to when applied with the camera which provides environmental colors that are "seen" by all the shaders in the scene; of course only shaders that actually are specified to sample reflections. Thus camera shaders are used extensively in host applications to specify an environment.

Host applications offer common mental ray environment mapping techniques, such as with spherical, cylindrical, and cubical mapping, discussed on a per-host basis in the following tutorials.

VOLUME SHADERS

Volume shaders are used to define volumetric effects such as volume fog or mist. Volume shaders applied to cameras act as global volumetric effects that influence the entire scene. When volume shaders are applied on a per-object level, they apply a "foggy" effect within the surface's volume. Volume shaders can be used with transparent surfaces such as within "mystical" crystal balls, within a cone that represents car headlights, or within a room. The topic of mental ray materials and their shader inputs (volume, environment, illumination, etc.) are discussed in detail in Chapter 9.

The most basic volume effect can be applied with the mental ray mib_volume base shader, which has a Max option that defines how far you can see into the scene. When applied to a camera it defines a gradual fade from the camera's perspective into the scene;

it fades the scene over distance to the specified volume fog color as shown in Figure 3.25. The mental ray mib_volume shader (in XSI the Volume_fog is an improved version for the same shader) also has a Lightrays option that attenuates the light's influence in the scene based on the fog density. In other words, when disabled the light influence on surfaces is unaffected by the fog, and when enabled the light gradually decays as it passes through the dense medium, as it does in real life. Note this only affects the light's intensity on surfaces and does not create a volume light effect for the source lights, such as with a light beam. For the purpose of light beams, each host application offers host-centric shaders that are geared towards volume light effects, as well as the mental ray participating media shaders discussed in Chapter 12.

One nice feature about mental ray volume shaders is that their foggy influence can be seen in reflections and refractions, which is not always the case with volume shaders found in various applications.

Figure 3.25

Fading a scene over distance using the mental ray mib_volume volume shader

A better implementation for a volume fog effect is with the Lume shader library mist shader available in XSI and 3ds Max. It provides more control over fading the fog over distance using various options. It also has an ability to layer the fog (fade) from the ground up so that you can create a low layer of mist. The shader is applied to a camera's volume shader input just as with any other global volume effect shaders. The shader options are straightforward and easy to use.

Applying Camera Shaders

In the following chapters we'll use camera environment, lens, and volume shaders within host applications. Let's quickly identify them within each application and see how you may apply them as mental ray camera shaders.

Maya

In Maya, you can apply these camera shaders directly under a camera's mental ray tab in the Attribute Editor, as seen in Figure 3.26.

Figure 3.26

Maya mental ray camera settings for shaders and output statements

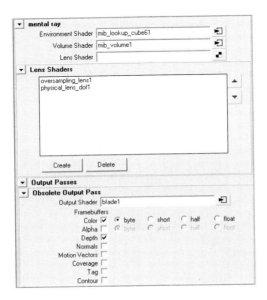

Notice that you can select to map environment, volume, and lens shaders, as shown in the figure. Under the Lens Shader tab you can further list several consecutive lens shaders if need be. The physical_lens_dof1 (depth of field) shader listed in the figure is further discussed in Chapter 4.

Under Output Passes (Primary Output Passes → Secondary Output Pass rollout in Maya 2008) the Output Shader attribute allows you to apply 2D postprocess shaders. Notice how both the Color and Depth attributes are selected under the Framebuffers section. These specify the type of frame buffers that should be maintained (used) with this shader, equivalent to the excerpt seen in the camera declaration block earlier:

```
output "+rgb_fp,+z" = "bfade1"
```

When you map any of these shaders, the mental ray Create Render Node window → mental ray tab pops up, allowing you to select a shader from the relevant tab. For example, for a depth fog, you may select the Mib_volume shader (discussed above under Volume Shaders) from the Volumetric Materials tab, which adds a simple distance-based fog effect to the scene. Figure 3.25 was rendered using this volume shader.

From the Environments tab in the Create Render Node, you can select to map the Environment Shader attribute on the camera with one of the various mental ray environment shaders, as seen mapped with a cubical environment in Figure 3.26. Note that these shaders can also be used to map surface shaders for local (per-shader) effects. You can also apply these environment shaders to Maya's "default" camera's Environment → Background Color attribute. We will look at using these shaders in other sections of the book as they become required. Figure 3.28 shows a Maya camera graphed in the Hypershade window, revealing how all these shaders are connected to the camera, including volume, output (bfade1), environment, and lens shaders, which were all connected by dragging and dropping these shaders over their relevant camera attributes shown in Figure 3.26.

Figure 3.27

A Maya camera shader graph in the Hypershade window, displaying environment, volume, output, and lens shader connections to the camera

THE IMAGE BASED LIGHTING ENVIRONMENTAL NODE

In the Render Settings window under the mental ray tab → Environment rollout, Maya provides the image based lighting attribute. If you click on Createan additional light node is created in the scene, which can be seen under the Lights tab in the Hypershade window (or in the Outliner window) labeled mentalrayIblShape1. This node physically appears as a bounding spherical wire frame geometry in the 3D views, however it is rendered as a non-geometric projection. Its appearance in the viewport makes it possible for you to easily view and align (rotate) the background image. This node is referred to as the *image based lighting* (IBL) node, providing various attributes for applying image based lighting techniques in Maya.

The IBL node offers a means for mapping the environment with a more robust set of tools, specifically tuned for indirect illumination effects. It is used to map an environment image as with a camera shader but also allows you to use that image for image based lighting; the process of emitting direct lighting from a dome of directional lights that surround a scene, where each light acquires its intensity and color from the mapped environment image. It also allows you to emit photons for indirect lighting in a similar fashion. The topic of IBL techniques is discussed in more detail in Chapter 13. In the context of this chapter, we are interested in using it simply to apply an environment image as a non-geometric projection.

In the Attribute Editor window, the IBL node's Image Based Lighting Attributes rollout offers the Mapping, Type, and Image Name attributes to load environmental images, as seen in Figure 3.28. Loading images is rather straightforward, as follows:

1. Set the Type attribute to Image File.

2. Specify (or browse to) a file path and name under the Image Name attribute.

3. If the image is a spherical image (may be spherical or angular, see Chapter 13), such as the one seen in Figure 3.24, set the Mapping attribute to Spherical,

Most environment images that you may have from texture libraries default to spherical mapping.

The Render Stats tab offers several visibility options for the environment; Figure 3.29 demonstrates their effect on rendering. Let's review them quickly.

Figure 3.28

The image based lighting (IBL) node attributes for loading and displaying environmental images in Maya

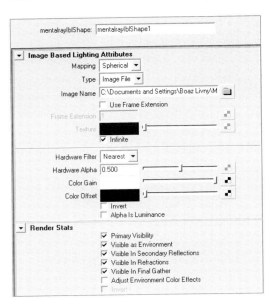

Figure 3.29

A comparison between the different Render Stats attributes with the IBL node

Primary Visibility enables rendering the environment into the background, as shown in image A. However, the appearance of the IBL node as a colorful background is depended on some other settings. With respect to our discussions on frame buffer options earlier in this chapter, when the Colorclip attribute (under the Render settings window → Framebuffer rollout) is set to Raw, the environment image will not affect the alpha (background) and appear to render in full color in the RGB channels; this is what you typically want from a background image. If the Colorclip attribute is set to RGB, the environment image's RGB values will be used as intensity values for the alpha channel, as shown in Figure 3.29 image B (image B displays the alpha channel). With RGB color clipping, the environment will render as a colorful background image in the RGB channels, however, for compositing purposes the alpha channel is not usable. When the Colorclip attribute is set to Alpha, the environment image will not appear to render at all, because it is set to match a zero alpha value, making it invisible in all the RBGA channels.

Visible in Secondary Reflections enables or disables any additional reflections after the first one has rendered, as seen in image C. Notice how you can see the first reflection level on the floor and sphere; however, the sphere's reflection on the floor doesn't show reflections from the environment, and thus the floor reflects a black "empty" sphere. The same is true for the floor reflected on the sphere, where you can't see the environment color reflect across the floor.

Visible as Environment enables or disables the first reflection bounce, meaning the first secondary ray. However, when it's disabled (and when Visible in Secondary Reflections is enabled), additional rays will still appear (second reflection bounce), as seen in image D. Clearly you can see that the environment is being reflected form the sphere onto the floor and vice versa, but the remaining areas of the floor and sphere, which represent the first reflection level, appear empty.

If you find it a bit confusing, I recommend you experiment while changing these attributes using a simple scene, such as the one shown in Figure 3.29. The rest of the settings relate to indirect illumination and image-based lighting and will be further examined when we discuss final gather in Chapter 13.

OUTPUTTING OUTPUT SHADERS AS PASSES

In the Output Passes tab (discussed earlier in the Maya frame buffer tutorials) under the camera's mental ray rollout → Output passes (Primary Output Passes in Maya 2008), shown in Figure 3.30, you can further list both output statements (demonstrated earlier) and output shaders by clicking Create. Figure 3.30 shows several different output passes and shaders that are applied in a given order; the order defines a sequence of execution for output shaders and statements (output files).

Figure 3.30

Maya enables you to list several output statements and shaders in this window.

Notice that first an output shader is applied, and then a Z-depth buffer and a motion vectors buffer are written to file, each as an independent pass. These passes are followed by another output shader and then another output file, this time as an HDR image. Listing these primary frame buffers within these lists enables you not only to execute postprocess effects in order, but to output several other primary frame buffers during the execution of a single render, as discussed in the previous Maya tutorials and in the section "Output Statements" later in this chapter. In this case, each frame will produce three image files on disk and process two output shaders. The last output shader will only affect the last output statement because they depend on the order in which they are listed.

Figure 3.11, displayed and discussed earlier, shows the window that pops up after you click Create. In the previous tutorials we looked at adding output statements (outputting frame buffers to file) to the Output Passes list. In this section we look at adding output shaders to this list. When File Mode is disabled, you can use the Output Shader attribute (grayed out in Figure 3.11) to map additional output shaders. Essentially, if you are using an output shader, for example the contour shader, by listing it here after an initial output statement you may select to first write the image to file without the effect, and then process the effect and write an additional image using a second output statement, which can then allow you to composite these layers in compositing software. Thus in such a case you would have three items listed: output statement, output shader, and output statement.

> If you want to list a sequence such as the one presented here, you don't need to apply an output shader under the Output Passes → Obsolete Output Pass rollout → Output Shader attribute shown in Figure 3.26; omit that entry and use only the Output Passes list shown in Figure 3.30.

XSI

With XSI, you apply camera lens shaders under the camera's properties and global output, volume, and environment shaders under the current pass options (or in the Render Manager window). We use lens, environment, and volume shaders in various chapters throughout the book, starting with Chapter 4.

Figure 3.31

The XSI camera lens shader list

From the Explorer window, select and display the camera (General) properties window for your camera. You will find the Lens Shaders tab, shown in Figure 3.31, under the Camera rollout. Using the Add and Inspect property buttons you can append new lens shaders to the shader stack and inspect their properties. As you can see in the figure, a depth of field lens shader has been added as well as a tone mapping shader, both shaders discussed in detail in Chapters 4 and 13. If you select Add and browse through the XSI lens shaders you will find a True_lens_emulator shader that can be used to simulate barrel distortion (and various other effects) as illustrated earlier in Figure 3.22 image A.

For environment, volume, and output shaders, open the current pass render options, shown in Figure 3.32, via Render → Edit → Edit Current Pass. Under the Default_Pass (or other pass name) rollout you can add global effect shaders in the Environment, Output, and Volume Shader stacks (lists) just as with the camera lens shaders. Notice how the output shader stack has three entries. These shaders are executed in the order of appearance as discussed under "Output Order and Output Shaders" later in this chapter.

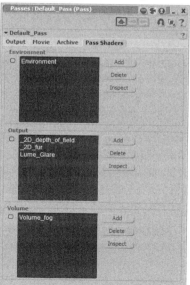

Figure 3.32

XSI's current pass options reveal both the global effect shaders and the cameras output shaders, which with mental ray are all applied at the camera level.

ENVIRONMENT SHADERS

The Environment shader seen in the Environment shader stack is an important shader that is used extensively throughout the book with indirect illumination and as a source for environment reflections. When you click on the Inspect property button for the environment shader, the Environment properties tab, shown in Figure 3.33, opens. In this window you can specify several options that define how the environment appears and is used during the render.

The New property button allows you to load a new environment image from disk, or select an existing one that is present in the scene. (You should already be familiar with the process of loading and using image files in XSI.) Once an image is loaded, the Environment Mode drop-down list is used to select a projection mapping method for the (ideally panoramic) image; typically you'll use Spherical mapping as discussed earlier and shown in Figure 3.24. We return to the topic of environment projection mapping in Chapters 10, 11, and 13, where Chapter 13 discusses panoramic image types in more detail.

Under the Intensity section, the Background, Reflections, and Image properties define the intensity of the image for that given purpose using values from 0 to 1. A value of 1 renders the image fully opaque (full color), and as the value decreases to 0 its intensity declines and becomes fully invisible at a value of 0. The Background property is used to specify the visibility of the environment image as background color. The Reflections property defines whether the background is visible in reflections, at a value of 1, or invisible to reflections as the value approaches 0. And the Image property is used to specify the influence the image has in final gathering, a topic discussed in Chapter 13.

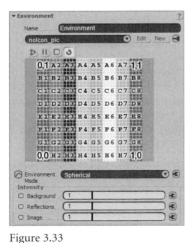

Figure 3.33

The XSI environment shader properties window

Figure 3.34

The image clip properties window allows you to apply color corrections and set the exposure for an environment image.

After you load an image, select the Edit property in the Environment properties window (Figure 3.33) to open the image (Clips) property window, shown in Figure 3.34. If you selected to load an HDR environment image, then under the HDR and OpenEXR properties you can define the exposure of the image during rendering using the Exposure (f-stop) property. It will define how bright (positive values) or dark (negative values) the image appears to the three properties in the Environment properties window; Background, Reflections, and Image. The most significant influence this property has on rendering is on how the image appears in the background when you include it as a visible background image (appears rendered) and with final gather. The topic of HDR images, exposure, and their usage in rendering is demonstrated throughout this book, particularly in Chapters 9 and 13.

If you click on the Enable Effects property, shown in Figure 3.34, you can further color correct the image using the Color Correction properties seen below (not included in the figure). You can also blur the image with the properties found under the Blur section. Blurring an image has several advantages in 3D, for example, it can help remove glossy reflection artifacts when the image is an HDR image, and it can help render environment sampling effects using the occlusion shader using a low sample value rather than a high sample value; if the image is already blurred fewer occlusion samples are required to produce the glossy effect (see Chapters 10 and 13).

If you select the Cubic_mapping_6 environment shader (in the Environment shader stack) and inspect its properties, you will see that each projection (front, right, left, back, top, and down) has its own tab where you can load an image. Since each axis receives an image, the projection method is cubical mapping and there is no need to further specify a mapping technique.

VIEWING THE CURRENT PASS NETWORK

From the Explorer window, under Passes you can select the default pass (or other pass) and graph its network in the Render Tree window, as shown in Figure 3.35. In this figure you can see how all the shaders discussed above are applied to their relevant inputs for the current pass. To see the lens shader inputs, you would graph the camera instead.

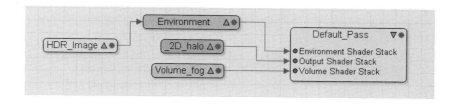

Figure 3.35

XSI's current pass graphed in the Render Tree window. You see all the global shader inputs applied at the pass level.

3ds Max

In 3ds Max, you apply camera shaders in the Render Scene: mental ray Renderer window → Renderer tab → Camera Effects rollout → Camera Shaders section, seen in Figure 3.36. In this window you can apply lens, output, or volume shaders using the three Lens, Output, and Volume parameters seen mapped in the figure. Each shader has been mapped with a relevant shader from the Material/Map Browser window.

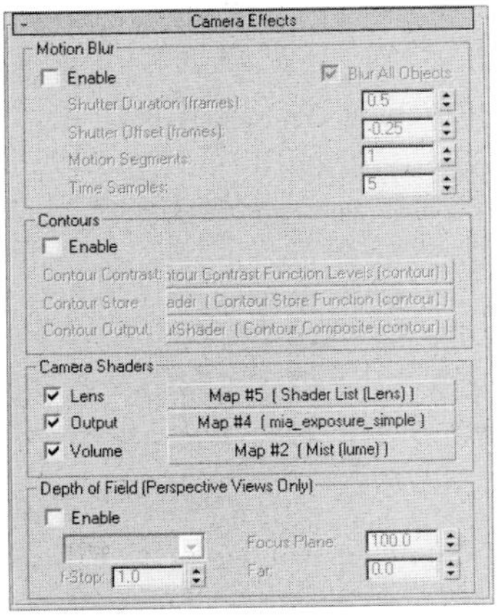

Figure 3.36

3ds Max Camera Effects settings rollout, where you apply lens, output, and volume shaders

When you choose one of these shader options, the Material/Map Browser window opens, enabling you to select from the available shaders for the shader type you selected. For lens shaders, the Distortion (lume) shader mimics the effect of wide-angle lenses, as seen in Figure 3.22. The WrapAround (lume) is another nice lens shader that allows you to export spherical panoramic images of the scene, rendering 360 degrees, as seen in Figure 3.24.

If you select one of these shaders, you can then display its settings in the Material Editor window by dragging from the Lens parameter to an empty slot in the Material Editor window. Alternatively you can click the Get Material icon (the first icon on the left under the material slots) to load the camera shader from under the Scene list in the Material/Map Browser window. Once the shader is loaded, you can tweak its settings, as shown in Figure 3.37 for the Lume Distortion shader. This shader's options allow you to specify the barrel effect's intensity by increasing the Amount factor, simulating lens distortion for a wide-angle lens.

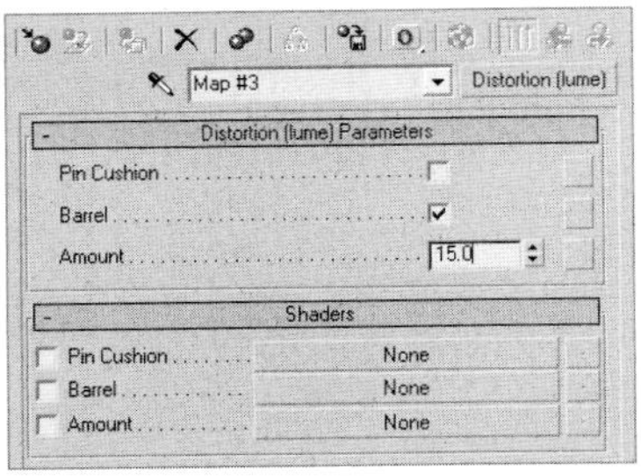

Figure 3.37

The Material Editor enables you to edit settings for the camera shader. In this case, the Lume Distortion shader is displayed.

If you want to list more than one shader for any of these three camera shaders, then your 3ds Max offers shader list shaders. Notice that in Figure 3.36 the Lens parameter is mapped with a Shader List (Lens) shader that I selected in the Material/Map Browser window. When you drag this shader into the Material Editor window and examine its parameters, you will see that you can list several shaders in what is known as a *shader stack*. Figure 3.38 shows the shader stack for the lens shader. As you can see in the figure, two lens shaders have been stacked in the list. You can add a shader using the Add Shader parameter and inspect its parameters by double-clicking over its name in the list.

Figure 3.38

Shader list shaders allow you stack several shaders for a given purpose; lens, environment, volume, and output effects.

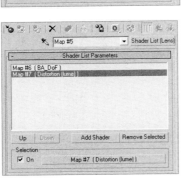

3ds Max has several shader list shaders that are designated for specific tasks. In the Material Editor window press the Get Material parameter to view all the available shaders in the Material/Map Browser window. Figure 3.39 shows a small segment of shaders that can be seen in the Material/Map Browser window that are used as shader lists. As you can see, each of the shaders under the Camera Shaders section has a correlating shader list shader that can be used for stacking several shaders for that specific purpose.

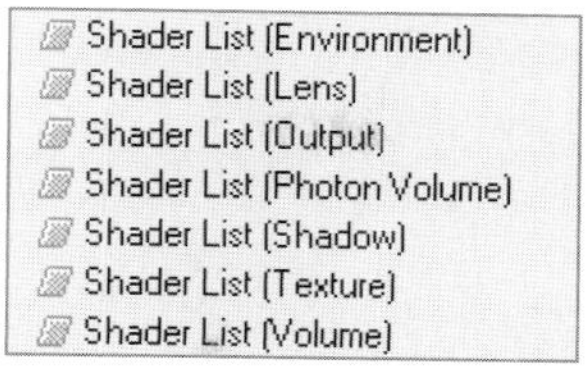

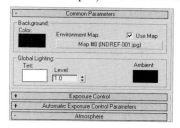

Figure 3.39

3ds Max has various shader list shaders that can be seen in the Material/Map Browser window

ENVIRONMENT SHADERS

To apply Environment shaders, navigate from the top menu Rendering → Environment to open the Environments and Effects window, shown in Figure 3.40. Under Environment Map you can simply add an image by selecting the mapping option, choosing Bitmap from the Material/Map Browser window, and then navigating to the image file on disk. You can then drag the bitmap shader to the Material Editor and edit its projection method.

When using spherical images, such as the one seen in Figure 3.24, under the bitmap shader Coordinates rollout in the Material Editor, select the Environ parameter radio button and select Spherical Environment from under the Mapping drop down parameter. The topic of 3ds Max projections is discussed in detail in Chapter 11 and the topic of loading HDR images is discussed in Chapter 13.

Figure 3.40

Applying Environmental shaders in 3ds Max through the Environment and Effects window

Note that you can also use the Atmosphere rollout in this window to apply 3ds Max-centric volume effects such as fog, but this may create color artifacts such as banding when rendering with mental ray. In the Effects tab, you can also select 3ds Max postprocess effects that currently don't appear to be fully compatible with mental ray. For example, these outputs shader effects are applied on premultiplied images, producing artifacts that relate to "outlining" surfaces when extending their edges, as seen in Figure 3.41 with the depth of field effect.

Figure 3.41

3ds Max centric effects are not completely compatible with mental ray and may cause artifacts, such as when applied to premultiplied images.

Depth Sorting

mental ray's ability to properly sort depth depends on the camera's near and far viewing range. Known as *hither* and *yon* planes with mental ray, they define the visible scene range from the render camera's perspective. The depth represented within this range has tremendous influence on the quality of scanline rendering, influencing scanline abilities to identify the distances between polygons that line up at the same pixel coordinates. With scanline rendering, the depth from the camera is represented by a grayscale scalar value. When clipping planes are set to an optimal distance, this guarantees that the best value distribution for the scene is being used without wasting values within empty space. In some cases, even optimal values do not provide for efficient depth sorting, and in those cases the render can be set to use only raytracing; alternately, the scene can be divided into foreground and background elements (passes) that can be rendered independently, thus more efficiently, and then composited.

For example, if you have a black to white 0 to 1 gradient range, consider the difference between using 0.1 percent or 0.01 percent of that range to represent your scene depth instead of 0.95 percent of the same range, as illustrated in Figure 3.42. This range is constantly being evaluated by the camera for each frame, and if ignored it can lead to unwanted flickering and polygon (partial or full) overlapping (intersecting) for close proximity polygons. This occurs only with scanline-based rendering because raytracing uses a different algorithm (not dependent on depth projections) for sorting distance and can resolve depth-related artifacts, but at the expense of longer render times.

Figure 3.42

Setting the near and far camera viewing range has tremendous influence on scanline rendering.

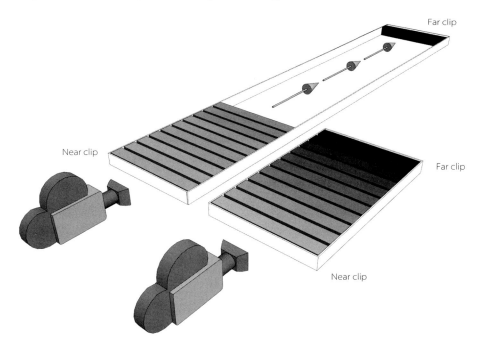

One problem arises with clipping with respect to animated scenes that "travel" over a large distance. As objects get farther away from each other, the range of the scene expands. In cases where clipping is automatically derived, artifacts may appear, and when it is manually specified, sections of the scene may be clipped. To prevent this, all you can do is be aware of these settings and make sure they are within a reasonable range.

For controlling the near and far clipping settings within host applications, use the following options for a selected camera:

HOST	CAMERA CLIPPING SETTINGS
Maya	Camera Attributes → Near (and Far) Clip Plane.
	Auto Render Clip Plane should be disabled, or it overrides the clipping values.
XSI	Camera → Primitive tab → Clipping Planes → Near (and Far) Plane. Notice you can use the buttons on the side to either clip to the selected object's bounding box or the entire scene's extent. The entire scene may be suitable in most cases.
3ds Max	In the Modify panel, under Parameters → Clip Manually → Near (and Far) Clip
	Clip Manually must be enabled for clipping control; you see the results within the viewport.

Output Statements

Throughout this chapter you have been introduced to the topics of frame buffers and output options, particularly the topic of rendering passes using primary and user frame buffers. These topics are advanced and should be used once you feel more confident with everything else mental ray. You may want to return to this chapter once you have completed the book as its content reflects on various aspects of using mental ray. The topics of frame buffers and output options are concentrated in this chapter to avoid spreading them across several chapters in the book; these topics cover beginner to advanced principles and techniques and thus you don't have to understand everything here at a first read.

The implementation of user frame buffers and passes is actually more complex within host applications than in mental image (.mi) files, where few statements are used to clearly represent the camera's output. This section presents all the topics discussed earlier as they are implemented in mental ray. It serves two purposes that are:

1. If you use the standalone mental ray renderer, you will be able to read the code and modify it beyond what your host application offers. In the same context, exporting .mi files from your host and examining the output statements can help you better understand, or verify, what your host application does when it renders with mental ray.

2. No single host application offers the entire range of mental ray's abilities in this area; looking at these options in mental image files provides more extensive coverage of these topics as well as a better understanding for them in your host application.

As discussed throughout the chapter, an advantageous approach to rendering with mental ray, especially when using the standalone renderer, is to create output statement passes, which enable you to output multiple passes at once during a single render execution. There are four aspects of this process:

(a.) You can output any of the six primary frame buffers into separate image files. You've already seen how to do this in the host applications.

(b.) Output order is also significant when output shaders are being used. Maya users have seen how they can list different output statements and output shaders in a given order under the Maya camera's Output Passes list earlier in this chapter.

(c.) You can also leverage user frame buffers to output different color passes through the execution of one render, as seen with XSI and with the p_MegaTK shaders provided by Puppet. We also briefly look at OpenEXR formats that can store unlimited channels (in "Outputting User Frame Buffers" later in this chapter). In the same context, you saw the OpenEXR multipass export options earlier in Figure 3.21 with the Puppet shader.

(d) Finally, among mental ray's output options there is *multipass* rendering, which enables you to save sampling frame buffers on disk to help deal with complex scenes. This option is demonstrated through 3ds Max, the only host application that offers it as a built-in feature.

Outputting Frame Buffers

One aspect of rendering passes with mental ray, explored within this chapter, is its ability to specifically set different channels (primary frame buffers) for output, such as RGBA, Z-depth, and motion vectors. Because each output is provided within a separate image file, they can use different bit depth settings at varying precisions (floating vs. integer) independent of the other outputs. Thus you can specify rendering color passes (RGBA) at 16 bit, providing for high-quality images, and rendering a Z-depth pass at 32 bit (floating point) for better quality Z-depth in compositing.

mental ray uses the following line for defining output, as seen in the camera declaration block earlier in this chapter:

```
output "+rgba" "iff" "firstRender.iff"
```

Left to right, this line says that the primary frame buffer, always referred to as +rgba (the data type), will save an IFF (Maya file format) image file to disk using an image labeled firstRender.iff. Using this syntax, you can list all the data types (passes) you wish to export. Let's see how this is achieved through XSI and the resulting output.

With XSI, as you saw in Figure 3.16, for each render pass you can enable all the primary frame buffers (and user frame buffers) to render during the execution of a single file. With Maya, you saw that you can load them under the camera's Output Passes list, and with 3ds Max, you saw that you can include them within image formats such as the OpenEXR format but not specify that they render into separate image files, as with Maya or XSI.

By enabling additional frame buffers for export, you actually specify additional output statements that are added into the .mi file upon execution. The result is shown in the following excerpt from an XSI-to-.mi-file conversion, showing how all these data types are listed:

```
camera "Camera_Root/Camera/Camera"

    output "-z" "Zpic"  "Render.1.zpic"  # Z Depth
    output "-m" "mt" "Render.1.mt"       # motion vectors
    output "-tag" "tt" "Render.1.tag"    # labels
    output "-n" "nt" "Render.1.norm"     # normals
    output "+rgba" "pic" "Render.1.pic"  # primary color
… (omitted irrelvant camera statements for this example)
end camera
```

In this case, there will be five resulting images for each rendered frame, which have all been declared under the camera's output declaration. Each of these, as you see, uses a different data type (-m, -z, etc.), corresponding to its relevant frame buffer that is then stored as an image on disk—for example, the line:

```
output "-m" "mt" "Render.1.mt"
```

uses the motion vectors frame buffer (-m) to store motion vectors in a mental ray MT (file format) on disk, labeled Render.1.mt. Each host application then offers methods for outputting these sorts of camera output statements using a different approach, as described in "Frame Buffer Options in Host Applications" earlier in this chapter.

> I recommend that you specify various primary frame buffers for output and export a .mi file, then look at the camera declaration statement in the .mi file to see how your host exports these statements in this way.

Output Order and Output Shaders

Using mental ray's output statements, you can also output your render in stages, outputting an image to file before processing a 2D postprocess effect, and then output another image after the effect has been processed, as seen in the full camera declaration block earlier in this chapter(a Maya-to-mental-images conversion). Output shaders and output statements both deal with the rendering at the frame buffer level, so specifying different output shaders or statements in a particular order will define an order-based set of frame buffer instructions and postprocesses. To recap on the mental ray Camera Declaration Block seen earlier in this chapter, consider these following lines:

```
output "+rgba" "iff" "firstRender"
output "+rgb_fp,+z" = "depth_fade" (
               "near_depth" 1,
               "far_depth" 15
               )
output "+rgba" "tif" "test_cam.tif"
```

The first statement will write a file to disk called firstRender.iff, and then the second statement will process a depth fade postprocess effect on the primary frame buffer. Notice that the second statement also includes the parameters for the depth fade effect. At that point, yet another output statement is required for writing the result from the postprocess depth fade effect to disk, seen with the third output statement. Thus the third statement outputs the primary frame buffer after the postprocess effect has been applied. If you do not explicitly set the order so that output shaders are executed before output statements, they typically appear first in the camera's declaration block output list so that they are processed before any image files are written to disk.

When output shaders are used, the frame buffers that the shader requires for processing are also included within the statement, as seen here from an XSI export using two output shaders (the first is the 2D_depth_cue shader, and the second is a 2D_fur shader):

```
output "+rgba,-z" = "Camera_Root/Camera/_2D_depth_cue"
output "+rgba,-z,-n,-tag" = "Camera_Root/Camera/_2D_fur"
```

As you can see, the depth cue output shader requires both the primary frame buffer and the Z-depth frame buffer, and the fur shader requires in addition the normals and object labels frame buffer. This should make sense because you can assume that for a fur postprocess effect, mental ray requires knowledge of scene depth and the surface normal direction for determining the fur's growth aim direction, and of course it also needs to identify the objects that grow fur within the frame buffer's pixel space, so object labels provide a unique ID to help identify these fur-growing objects within the scene. This example illustrates how the primary frame buffers are used specifically with output shaders, or as passes for compositing.

You don't see the output shader options in these two excerpts because they call on shaders that have already been specified (declared) elsewhere in the mental image file.

Outputting User Frame Buffers

For compositing, it is likely you will need images with varying bit depth and different channels. One in-production advantage relates to compositing passes so that light color and intensity (overexposure) can be adjusted without re-rendering and effects such as motion blur and depth of field can be added and tweaked interactively rather than with very long time-consuming renders. For effects such as motion blur and depth of field, you would need to output the Z-depth or motion vectors frame buffers as cited earlier.

Chapter 8 looks at a production proven technique for using motion vectors in compositing.

User frame buffers typically target rendering custom color channels that are not included with the primary frame buffers and may represent color passes such as diffuse, specular, and shadow. Again, each host provides an approach for creating custom passes —Maya's render layers, 3ds Max's render elements, and XSI's passes. However, these output options refer to separate render files and not user frame buffers that are output during the execution of a single render.

Such built-in user frame buffers are available with XSI, offering a set of custom color passes that execute during a single render, as discussed earlier.

These color passes use custom shaders that store specific color information within user frame buffers and then output them during the render. User frame buffers must be declared with a relevant data type (RGB, Z-depth, etc.) before being used, which is specified in the mental images options block as seen with the following excerpt from an XSI-to-mental-images export:

```
frame buffer 0 "+rgba"
frame buffer 1 "+rgba_fp"
frame buffer 2 "+rgba_16"
frame buffer 3 "+rgba_fp"
frame buffer 4 "+rgba"
frame buffer 5 "+rgba"
```

Notice how each of these frame buffers is applied with a data type and index number. You can see the same passes enabled within XSI in Figure 3.43. Each pass is provided with a target image file, channel data type, and bit depth precision. So it is clear that various color passes at various bit depths and formats may be outputted with user frame buffers. The diffuse and irradiance passes are set to use a 32-bit floating point buffer, and the specular pass uses a 16-bit buffer; all three have corresponding frame buffer data types seen in the preceding excerpt for frame buffers 1, 2, and 3. Notice that all these buffers are also specified as interpolated (plus sign) buffers that use averaged color values for the pixels, commonly so with most "beauty" color pass outputs.

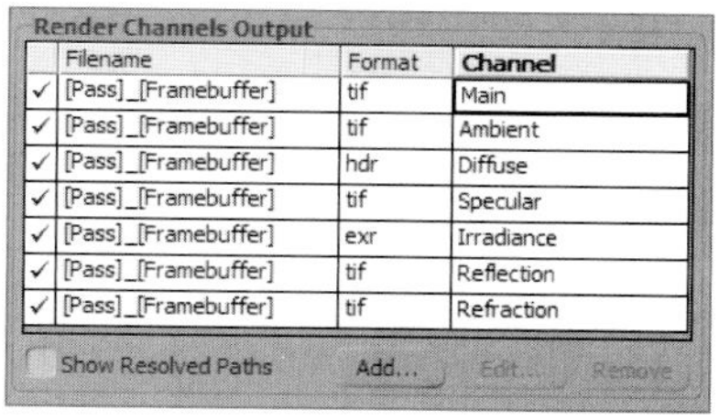

Render Channels Output			
Filename		Format	Channel
✓ [Pass]_[Framebuffer]		tif	Main
✓ [Pass]_[Framebuffer]		tif	Ambient
✓ [Pass]_[Framebuffer]		hdr	Diffuse
✓ [Pass]_[Framebuffer]		tif	Specular
✓ [Pass]_[Framebuffer]		exr	Irradiance
✓ [Pass]_[Framebuffer]		tif	Reflection
✓ [Pass]_[Framebuffer]		tif	Refraction

Show Resolved Paths   Add…   Edit…   Remove

Figure 3.43

XSI per pass user frame buffer output, which will then create several images on disk for each rendered frame containing the requested color information

These same user frame buffers are then used within the camera's declaration block to specify their image output format, as seen in the following camera declaration excerpt for the same XSI scene:

```
camera "Camera_Root/Camera/Camera"
      output "+rgba" "tif" "Main.tif" # primary buffer
      output "+fb0" "tif" "Ambient.tif"
      output "+fb1" "hdr" "Diffuse.hdr"
      output "+fb2" "tif" "Specular.tif"
      output "+fb3" "exr" "Irradiance.exr"
      output "+fb4" "tif" "Reflection.tif"
      output "+fb5" "tif" "Refraction.tif"
   … camera options omitted
   end camera
```

The ideal is that when you execute a render, during that render you can save several additional passes to disk representing these diffuse, ambient, reflection, shadow, and luminance passes, among others. The advantage is that rather than executing several consecutive renders, you execute one render that outputs all these passes during each frame's render, so the time in which a single frame is rendered provides several different passes on disk for the purpose of compositing. In this case the diffuse pass is rendered as an HDR image, the specular as a 16-bit image, the irradiance as a 32-bit image, and the remaining passes are rendered as 8-bit images.

Multi-Channel Output

Another significant advantage of user frame buffers is that rather than outputting separate image files for each pass, when using formats such as the OpenEXR format, all these passes can be added into an individual image. Hence the OpenEXR format enables you to specify one image file on disk that would contain four color passes within one image, representing, for example, 14 color channels in the following order:

- color pass -RGB channels,
- Alpha channel
- Z-depth channel
- Shadow - RGB channels
- light - RGB channels
- specular - RGB channels

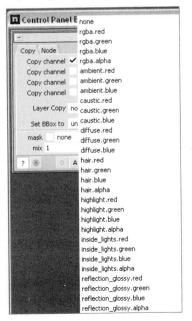

Figure 3.44

OpenEXR channels seen within Nuke for a multichannel OpenEXR image file

Figure 3.44 shows the drop-down list for an OpenEXR image in Nuke, displaying all the additional channels that are present within the file. The long list of channels shows all the color channels stored within this image. As you can see they are organized in a way that allows labeling sets of channels so that you can easily identify, for example, the caustic RGB channels while compositing. See the Nuke Compositing article on the companion CD for more information on compositing with OpenEXR images.

With 3ds Max, you can output primary frame buffers with some extra channels, as seen under "Host Application Frame Buffer Options" earlier in this chapter, into multichannel images. In addition, under the same section I briefly introduced the Puppet p_MegaTK shaders that allow you to export a single multichannel OpenEXR image from each host application. Currently, none of the host applications provides a built-in straightforward method for outputting such multichannel passes into a single EXR file, but I hope we will see more support for these features in the future. In production environments, these abilities are already being applied using custom plug-ins for mental ray and host applications.

Multipass Rendering

Multipass rendering is yet another camera-based output and shader option. With mental ray, multipass rendering refers to rendering separate elements (ex. surfaces) and then merging them together using sampling frame buffers. The strength behind multipass rendering is with respect to rendering complex "heavy" scenes with a lot of geometry, so you separate the scene into specific elements and then combine them later using a *merge* shader.

Most artists approach this sort of compositing, using a Z-depth pass and the color image files within a compositing application. Essentially, compositing surfaces in a 2D application is based on a per-pixel depth composite that is dependent on the precision and resolution of the Z-depth pass. Thus, while objects are being composited with a Z-depth pass, the quality of the composite is based on the available resolution of both the images and the Z-depth pass and not on several sub-pixel samples as with 3D rendering.

Multipass rendering resolves any pixel limitations by enabling you to combine elements (in depth) on a per-sample basis rather than a per-pixel basis, providing more accurate results. Remember that sampling may be achieved on a sub-pixel level, which means that elements are then merged at the sub-pixel level.

The process is based on storing *sampling frame buffers* on disk and then using them to merge samples rather than pixels with mental ray. Sample compositing can therefore be processed only through mental ray, not a compositing package. Also, it is very easy to apply it if you either have the standalone renderer or are using 3ds Max, which currently is the only software that provides built-in multipass rendering features. With Maya or XSI, you would simply add the `pass write` and `pass read` options into the camera's declaration block (as demonstrated later with standalone rendering).

One more important note: you can effectively combine sampling passes, but if the sample algorithm changes between passes (from default sampling to the rasterizer, for example), the samples will not align correctly.

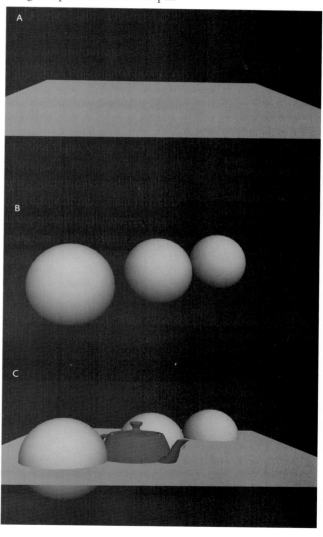

Figure 3.45

Images A and B represent the data that has been stored in sampling frame buffers on disk. Image C shows a multipass merging of these two passes as well as the scene (teapot).

Let's look at writing and merging sampling frame buffers using 3ds Max and the camera options for the .mi file. Figure 3.45 shows three stages of rendering, A, B, and C. A and B represent pass files that were written to disk, and C shows how both those pass files, including an additional element from the "live" scene (the teapot), are all merged.

To re-create this for yourself, create a scene with various intersecting elements and three layers (optional). Hide any objects that shouldn't get rendered into the first-pass "partition," seen as A in the figure. The first stage requires writing the pass files to disk using mental ray's `pass write` option. The option to write sampling frame buffers to disk is entered under the camera declaration block as follows:

```
pass write "file path and name"
```

In 3ds Max this process is applied as follows:

1. Under the Render Scene: mental ray Renderer → Processing tab → Render Passes section (seen in Figure 3.46), open the file browser (…) , specify a name and path, and enable the Save parameter. Render the scene.

2. In the specified directory, a new file has been created that contains the sampling information; it is not a viewable file.

Figure 3.46

3ds Max multipass rendering export and merging options, where we can effectively split up heavy scenes into separated sampling frame buffers

3. Toggle the visible objects in the scene with the hidden ones, rename the pass file from the Save option (so you won't overwrite the previous pass file), and render again. Leave at least one other object invisible for a third pass.

Currently these pass files represent the different objects in the scene, as seen in Figure 3.45 images A and B, each represented in a separate pass file.

Now let's merge them together, as well as with additional objects in the scene, meaning at three levels that include both pass files and any other objects in the scene. To read passes from disk as well as render in the current scene elements, the following pass statement is used:

```
pass merge
       read [   "", "pass file 1", "pass file 2" ]
```

The first set of double quotes refers to the current scene, meaning the visible objects, and in the case of Figure 3.45, it refers to the teapot (in image C), which was not available in both pass files.

To apply the new pass files, simply enable the Merge parameter and load them in using the Add button (they are seen loaded in Figure 3.46) and render. Once the render has completed, you should have successfully merged all the pass files with the scene elements, as seen in Figure 3.45 image C.

## CHAPTER 4

Camera Fundamentals

Our understanding of real-world lighting and photography significantly influences our approach to rendering practices, image formats, and output displays. Photography normally attempts to reproduce images that represent real-world conditions as seen by the human eye. Learning how images are reproduced with real-world photography leads us to a better understanding of the requirements for creating such images from scratch when using 3D software. The process of rendering plays two significant roles: it must re-create the environment (with advanced rendering algorithms) and re-create the effects of the camera. The amount of work you invest in an animated short or still image will take you only so far if you can't use the camera.

In this chapter, you will learn fundamentals of the camera and how to apply that knowledge in practice using the mental ray camera. This chapter includes the following topics:

- **Camera Basics and Aspect Ratios**
- **Camera Lenses**
- **Host Application Settings**

Camera Basics and Aspect Ratios

One of the most important aspects of film production—whether it's a short independent film or a high-tech feature film—is the camera. The better a virtual camera can simulate a realistic camera's photographic abilities, the more the viewer will be convinced that the shot is genuine. Virtual cameras used to superimpose computer-generated imagery on live-action shots need to match the same image aspect ratio, focal depth, perspective, and so forth as the live-action camera. But that's only part of the equation. You also need to make sure that render settings correlate to equivalent camera settings within the 3D host applications. That is, each application (Maya and XSI more than 3ds Max) provides separate controls over render settings and camera settings. The camera settings provide control over simulating real camera characteristics and render settings simulate display devices so that, ideally, the virtual camera and render settings are parallel to real-world cameras and monitors, where one deals with acquisition and the other with display.

Understanding real-world cameras will help you simulate photographic qualities. For example, good slow-motion photography is typically recorded at faster speeds, and thus there will be less motion blur as well as less focal depth, both topics further discussed in the following sections.

Before examining the internal settings within each host application, let's examine some camera fundamental mechanics and terms and then examine how those fundamentals are applied within host applications.

The Transport Mechanism

We use the term *camera transport mechanism* to describe the internal process within a camera. A basic camera model consists of a *film back, film gate, claw, shutter, lens*, and *film* or *digital sensor*. In Figure 4.1, you can see a basic illustration of the camera's transport mechanism. The claw (not illustrated because it has no equivalent in computer graphics) is used to pull down the film using the sprocket holes (along the film's sides) while the shutter is closed so that the next frame (film) gets placed between the film gate and the film back. The film back, which is the area directly behind the film, defines the size of the film or digital sensor—35mm, 16mm, and so forth. As you can see in the figure, the film gate acts as a window through which each frame is exposed to light that penetrates through the lens. Hence, the film gate defines the area on film that is exposed to light, and thus the frame's horizontal and vertical (X, Y) scale.

The Transport Speed

Transport speed is commonly measured as frames per second (fps). It defines the time interval in which the transport mechanism can perform a cycle of loading a frame, opening and closing the shutter, and then repeating the process. In essence, the transport speed makes the illusion of motion possible because the human brain retains images for a fraction of a second, allowing a new image to be "loaded" into memory between exposures. This is known as *persistence of vision*; it enables the illusion of motion that the mind perceives while watching alternating still images projected on a screen. This book's discussion of CG will deal with the time interval the shutter remains open, exposing the film to light, and, and capturing motion blur effects on film. Controlling that time interval enables you to control the amount of visible motion blur by means of customizing shutter time and shutter angle characteristics, all topics discussed in this chapter and in Chapter 8, "Motion Blur."

For *slow motion*, special cameras film at higher speeds, such as 48fps, and the film is then projected at the normal speed of 24fps. Essentially, this means that if you render an animated sequence at a higher frame rate, you can also reproduce quality slow motion by playing the sequence back at normal frame rates.

Shutter Speed, Shutter Angle, and Motion Blur

A shutter is a device that, based on a *shutter speed*, opens and closes in front of the film gate, exposing the film to light. With still cameras, the shutter typically operates like an opening door or a sliding curtain that can rapidly open and close. For simulating real motion cameras in CG, the shutter interests us to the extent that it influences some photographic phenomena, mostly motion blur and depth of field. Depth of field is not influenced by the shutter, rather by how the shutter and iris are balanced together to produce an exposure level. With cameras, motion blur is visible in images because, during the exposure time, the film captures moving objects at different stages of their motion and, as the exposure time increases, so does the amount of visible motion blur. Both depth of field and motion can be simulated in a very realistic manner with mental ray. In this chapter, you'll look at simulating depth of field, and in Chapter 8 you will learn more about motion blur.

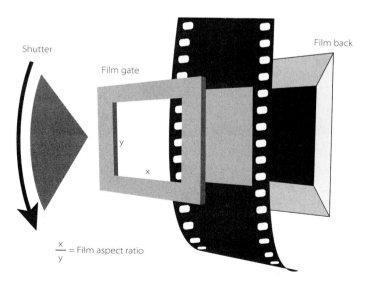

Figure 4.1

The transport mechanism

Typically, with motion cameras, the shutter is a circular disk mechanism, known as a *rotary disk shutter*, that constantly rotates in front of the film, as illustrated in Figure 4.2. The two images on the top illustrate the shutter at two different points during the exposure time. Further, the shutter's shape (seen as the gray triangle that is pivoted to rotate around the polygonal shape) may be open to a greater or lesser degree based on the *shutter angles* value, measured in degrees. Thus, the number of degrees the shutter is open, as with the different examples on the lower portion, regulates the amount of time film is exposed to light during the time a full 360° cycle is performed.

Obviously, larger shutter angles, as with the 180° compared to the 30° shutter angle, permit more light to enter the camera during the shutter cycle. For our purposes this cycle is referred to as the time interval, which determines the shutter speed, and will be examined in detail in Chapter 8.

In essence, the relationship between the shutter speed (cycle time) and shutter angle define the amount of light that penetrates during each cycle (the time interval). For example, a shutter angle of 180° will expose the film to light throughout half of the time interval (cycle), and a 90° shutter angle will expose the film to light for one quarter of the time interval, thus the relationship between shutter angle and shutter speed help regulate the amount of light that is exposed to film.

Further, the combination of the shutter speed, shutter angle, and the aperture f-stop defines the *exposure level*, a term used to describe the overall light exposure to film, based on all the influential mechanisms that take part in regulating light exposure. Let's look at the aperture settings next. In Chapter 8, you will learn how to simulate a virtual shutter angle with mental ray.

Figure 4.2
Shutter angle

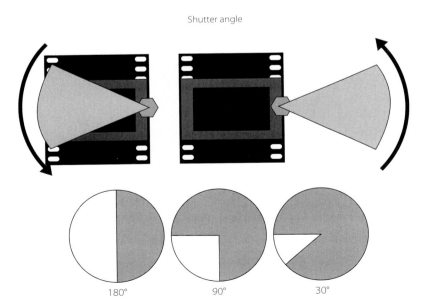

Shutter angle

180°   90°   30°

Apertures and Image Aspect Ratios

The aperture determines the amount of light that can pass thorough the lens. In essence, the lens uses an internal *iris diaphragm,* which is a thin metal plate that has a small opening in the center that regulates how much light can penetrate through the lens, measured in *f-stops* (f-stops are further discussed in the section "Camera Lenses" later in this chapter). The diameter of the opening is then the aperture size, measured in f-stop values. However, the term *aperture* can also be used in reference to the *film aspect ratio.* In 3D applications, this second meaning is confusingly distorted. With CG the "aperture" refers solely to the film gate's X and Y measurement scale, not the film aspect ratio or the aperture's f-stop value. With mental ray, as you will see later, the camera declaration aperture [n units] option is measured as the horizontal axis of the aperture (the film gate's horizontal axis) in camera space units.

> The iris is a lens-specific mechanism, whereas the shutter is a camera-body mechanism; both regulate light exposure, commonly referred to as the *exposure level.*

The film aspect ratio is acquired by dividing the film gate's horizontal scale by the vertical scale (X/Y), as seen in Figure 4.1. This aspect ratio is also commonly referred to as the *image aspect ratio* within host applications. The aspect ratio value describes the relationship between the horizontal and vertical axes of the film gate's opening, which is also referred to as the film aperture with film cameras. Thus, film aperture may represent an f-stop value or a film gate ratio. Typically, this ratio is either 4:3 (1.333 image aspect ratio), as with most video formats, or 16:9 (1.77 image aspect ratio), as with HD formats.

Changing either the film gate ratio or film back size will have several effects on camera characteristics, including image aspect ratio, field of view, focal depth, perspective, etc. A change to any of these settings will affect all of the other settings proportionally to accommodate the new settings. For example, if you change the X, Y scales for the film gate, then you will see the aspect ratio automatically correct itself for these new values. We further look at defining the aperture in CG in the tutorials later in this chapter, where you will see how your host application implements these terms for simulating film back, film gate, and the aperture (aspect ratio), and the relationship that exists between these settings.

> With respect to proportions, note that if you double the aperture scale (X and Y), you will still maintain the same aspect ratio; however, the film back scale has actually increased and will affect the field of view, as discussed in the "The Film Back" section later in this chapter.

Pixel Aspect Ratio

Typically, if you are using the same format to film as well as to project, you would want the render settings and the camera settings to match in size proportionally so that they both use the same image aspect ratio. When dealing with computer monitors, film formats, and even HD formats, pixels are said to have a 1:1 aspect ratio, and thus are known as square pixels.

Figure 4.3

Pixel aspect ratios

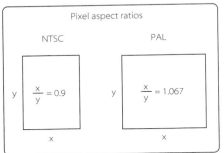

Other output media, however, don't use square pixels. With digital video recording (DV) devices and NTSC and PAL televisions (VHS), the pixels are compressed in a way that they are either taller than they are wide (NTSC) or wider than they are tall (PAL), as illustrated in Figure 4.3. Complications arise when we create graphics on computer displays using square pixels and then output to one of these devices that use non-square pixel ratios.

Notice that with square pixel ratios, the pixel aspect ratio, like the image aspect ratio, is derived by dividing the horizontal axis by the vertical axis:

$$X \div Y \text{ (horizontal/vertical)} = \text{pixel aspect ratio}$$

With NTSC and PAL displays, you must compensate for their non-square pixel aspect ratios. When outputting images, there can be only one image aspect ratio; you don't output two separate ratios. Thus, before rendering, you must specify an aspect ratio that accounts for the pixel aspect ratio's effect on the image aspect ratio. mental ray then will compare the aspect ratio derived from the render X and Y resolution settings (which is based on square pixel ratios) with the provided aspect ratio. When pixels are non-square, the provided aspect ratio is derived by multiplying the pixel aspect ratio by the image aspect ratio, a topic further explained later in this chapter. To clarify, if the render resolution aspect ratio (derived from the X and Y render settings) is different than the provided aspect ratio, it means that mental ray still needs to "stretch" the resolution pixel array so that it fits within the provided aspect ratio the same number of X and Y pixels, and by doing so mental ray outputs pixels that are non-square. Figure 4.4 shows a simple example of how this equation is used to derive the pixel aspect ratio for NTSC D1 video.

The line next to (a) refers to the standard used with NTSC video, which is the 4:3 ratio, equal to a 1.33 image aspect ratio (based on non-square pixels). Images rendered for NTSC video should have the same 1.33 image aspect ratio. Under (b), you see the standard NTSC D1 resolution of 720×486, which when divided provides for a 1.48 image aspect ratio, which is different than the 4:3 standard ratio. Thus, this aspect ratio obviously does not match the NTSC standard aspect ratio; so why is this resolution used as the standard for rendering NTSC D1 video? If you look at the figure, you can see that when (a) is aligned over (b), the NTSC standard (a) is taller than the render resolution (b) because NTSC pixels are taller than they are wide. Thus, you correct the NTSC render for the NTSC standard

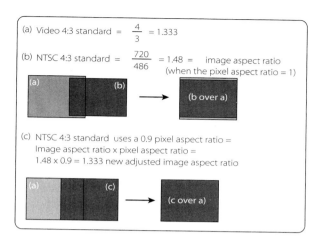

Figure 4.4

Derived pixel aspect ratio in NTSC

by multiplying the image aspect ratio by the pixel aspect ratio, arriving at the new corrected image aspect ratio, which essentially matches the NTSC standard 4:3 ratio (1.333), stretching the pixels to match that new aspect ratio.

When rendering, you can provide the image aspect ratio and the pixel aspect ratio separately. The host application translator does the math behind the scenes so that it provides mental ray with a correct aspect ratio value.

> If you forget to correct for video aspect ratios, the result will be that round objects will appear stretched along the Y axis with NTSC and squashed along the Y axis with PAL, even though on your monitor they appear correctly. Remember, your monitor uses square pixels, so essentially, if something appears incorrectly on your display, chances are it will appear correctly on the output monitor.

The Film Back

One of the main characteristics of photography that influence an image's appearance is the camera's *field of view (fov)*. The field of view describes the camera's visible viewing range, a value derived from the film back, the film gate aspect ratio, and the lens's *focal length*. Let's first examine the impact that film back size has on the field of view.

Figure 4.5 illustrates the relationship between the film back and the field of view. As the film back scales up, so does the field of view, because there is a larger region within the camera's body that can receive light penetrating through the film gate. Within each host application, you can specify either a larger film back or a larger film gate (seen in the tutorials later in this chapter) and have the same effect as increasing the field of view. For clarification, in 3D host applications the film gate's horizontal and vertical scale (typically in mm) and film back are tied together so that essentially an increase in size for either component results in an increase of the other component (film gate or film back), as well as an increased field of view. Thus, you can conclude that larger X, Y aperture settings provide for larger film backs and gates and thus a larger field of view.

Figure 4.5

The camera's film back size is one of the factors that determine the visible field of view.

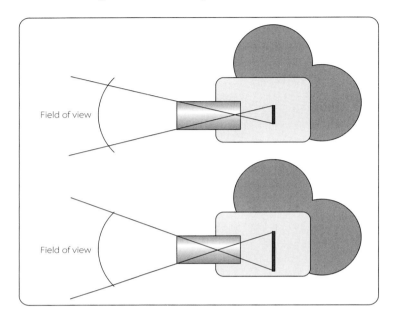

Camera Lenses

There are three commonly used types of lenses: normal, wide-angle, and telephoto. (Other lenses, such as fisheye, are not commonly used in 3D.) Lenses are classified based on their *focal length*, which is the distance from the lens to the film and defines the lenses' magnifying abilities as well as influences the field of view and *focal depth*. Focal depth simply refers to the region within perspective where focus is maintained, defined as the distance between the closest point to the camera that is in focus and the farthest point in focus. The following sections look at the topics of focal length and depth, field of view, and the role of f-stops before turning to the lens shader that mental ray provides for controlling depth of field.

Focal Depth and Perspective

As described earlier, a camera's focal length is the distance between the lens and the film, measured in millimeters. The focal length determines the perspective and focal depth of the shot. *Perspective* refers to the perceived distance between subjects in the shot. With a wide-angle lens, subjects appear unnaturally far from the camera, as well as farther from each other, and thus wide-angle lenses exaggerate perspective, distorting subjects. Telephoto lenses have the opposite effect, bringing subjects closer to the camera as well as to each other, and thus "flatten" perspective. Figure 4.6 demonstrates the influence focal length has on focal depth using different lenses.

Figure 4.6

The effect of a camera's focal length on focal depth and perspective

Telephoto lens

Normal lens

Wide-angle lens

As you can see, telephoto lenses (top image) are good at rendering with less distortion as well as less depth of field. Notice how the distance between objects, as well as the overall distance from the camera to the end of the scene, appears relatively smaller than with the wide-angle lens (shorter focal length), seen on the bottom. Again, focal depth, or depth of field, is largely based on the lens type, thus a telephoto lens produces a shallower focal depth, providing for a smaller region in focus. In contrast, a wide-angle lens has a greater focal depth, providing for more focus in the shot. Thus the shorter the focal length (wide-angle lens), the more exaggerated the distance will appear between subjects and the greater the focal depth, as opposed to telephoto lenses that contract distance and provide less focal depth. The next section looks at measurements that range from telephoto to wide-angle lenses as well as their effect on the field of view.

Field of View

Field of view is another component that is significantly influenced by both the film back size and the focal length. Earlier you learned about the influence of the film back dimensions, and now you can add the lens focal length into this equation. Normal lenses use an average horizontal width field of view of 20° to 25°. Because the film gate's horizontal and vertical scales differ, they dictate a different field of view value along either axis, unless of course you use a theoretical square film gate. Typically, in the host applications, the field of view is based on the horizontal axis.

Film back corresponds directly to different film stocks, and the focal length value correlates to lenses such as wide-angle or telephoto lenses, so you may conclude that smaller film stocks use shorter focal lengths to represent a normal lens; larger film stocks require longer focal lengths to reproduce the same perspective. For example, 35mm film using a 50mm focal length provides for a normal lens at about 23° of field of view; however, if you use a 16mm film with the same 50mm lens, then the field of view changes to about 12°, creating the effect of a telephoto lens. Figure 4.7 demonstrates the effect different focal lengths have on field of view (using the same film back), and as you can see, the shorter the lens, the wider the viewing angle.

ZOOMING AND DOLLYING

A zoom lens allows you to adjust the focal length by shifting the lens's distance from the film within a given range. Hence, when you perform a zoom as opposed to a dolly, you are changing the camera's focal length and thus changing several camera characteristics, such as the depth of field and perspective. So when you need to translate a camera's position in a CG scene, you should always dolly (physically move the camera) unless you specifically want to animate a change in perspective.

Common focal lengths for 35mm, 16mm, and 8mm cameras are listed in the following table:

LENS	35MM	16MM	8MM
Wide-angle	25mm	15mm	9mm
Normal	50mm	25mm	12mm
Telephoto	65mm	45mm	25mm

All three host applications provide means for simulating the relationship between the focal length and the field of view. As the camera's focal length changes, or the film type (film back or film gate) changes, the field of view (also referred to as *angle of view* in some applications) will automatically adjust to accommodate the changed setting. However, notice that if you increase the focal length, as with a telephoto lens, the field of view gets narrower but the film back will not change because the change in focal depth influences only field of view, the perception of perspective, and depth of field. Conversely, changing the field of view will force the application to adjust either the focal length or the film back to accommodate the new angle, and typically the change would influence the focal length but not the film back because the film back is a more static setting.

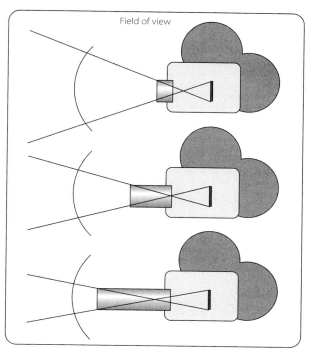

Figure 4.7

The effect of focal length on field of view when used with the same film back

Depth of Field and F-Stops

Within the camera lens, the *iris* simulates a pupil's iris expanding and contracting based on sensitivity to light. The iris then controls the aperture's diameter, controlling the "pupil's" size. What the term *f-stop* really describes is a relationship between the aperture diameter and the focal length of the lens.

A *stop* is said to halve the light intensity that can penetrate the lens, "stopping" a portion of light from reaching the film. Typically, f-stop values are provided in increments of one stop, so that each change doubles or halves the amount of light based on the power of 2. The aperture's diameter opening in millimeters can then be derived by dividing the camera's focal length by the f-stop value; thus as 50mm lens, using an f-stop value of 11 (*f/11*), provides for an aperture opening of 4.5mm. Essentially, higher f-stop values provide a smaller aperture opening. More-advanced cameras allow you to change the stop increment by a third, or half stop, rather then a full stop. In CG, because you can basically enter any value, you have the opportunity to choose any range for the f-stop value.

With respect to camera phenomena, the f-stop value defines to a great extent the focal depth of the image. Depth of field is then said to be broader with higher f-stop values and narrower with lower f-stop values; the higher the f-stop value, the smaller the aperture and the more in focus the image will appear. Common f-stop values start at 2.8 and range upward, generally between 5.6 and 12 with motion cameras. Figure 4.8 shows two renders of the same image using different f-stop values. An f-stop value of 2.8 was used for the image on the left, and more of its apparent depth is blurry; for the image on the right, an f-stop value of 11 was used, providing a smaller diameter and an image with more focal depth.

Exposure Levels

By now it is clear that real cameras enable us to use different methods to control light exposure, and the shutter speed and shutter angle (discussed earlier) and the aperture f-stop to regulate it. These settings provide unique methods for tweaking different photographic phenomena such as motion blur and depth of field. Ideally, you can reach the same specific exposure level balancing the shutter and f-stop values. With respect to exposure level, photographers will argue that there can be only one right exposure for each shot. If you consider that focal depth really refers to the range in focus within a shot (defined by the iris) and motion blur obviously refers to the amount of blurriness motion objects have (defined by the shutter), both shutter and aperture provide for controlling very different photographic phenomena. As each of these mechanisms regulates light, they can be balanced so that one phenomenon is more (or less) pronounced than the other. You can then conclude that while simulating a real camera, if there's fast motion (a horse running) and the shot has very little motion blur, you would also expect to see very short focal length because the iris would be larger to provide more light, compensating for the small shutter angle (or fast shutter speed).

The iris also defines the light contrast ratio that can be acquired during the exposure time, a topic discussed in more detail in Chapter 9, "The Fundamentals of Light and Shading Models" as it directly relates to HDR imaging and lighting characteristics. Ideally, you balance the shutter settings with the iris to reach the perfect exposure level for a shot.

Figure 4.8

The effect of changing the f-stop value on the focal depth in a frame: (left) f/2.8; (right) f/11

On cameras, if you increase the f-stop by one stop and decrease the shutter speed by one step, you are said to achieve the same exposure level. However, the difference will be in the photographic phenomena that are emphasized, and thus balancing these two can produce the same exposure level but provide different photographic characteristics. For fast motion, photographers prefer using faster shutter speeds and thus fast motion usually has less depth of field and less motion blur because a larger iris diameter compensates for the faster exposure time. Such characteristics should be considered when attempting realistic camera simulation with CG.

In the following sections, we will look at controlling these settings with mental ray and within host applications.

mental ray Depth of Field Lens Shader

mental ray ships with a physical lens shader that accurately mimics depth of field. The shader, seen as a lens shader (camera shaders are discussed in Chapter 3, "mental ray Output") under the camera's declaration block, is relatively simple:

```
camera "myCam"
    ...
    lens "physical_lens_dof" (
        "plane" -10.0,
        "radius" 0.1,
            )
end camera
```

The shader takes in two parameters, plane and radius. The plane option defines the distance from the camera in camera space. Cameras always look down their negative Z axis, so if an object appears 10 units away from the camera in a direct line of sight, you would enter -10 for the plane value. The radius value defines the amount of focal depth that will be visible. In essence, radius defines the diameter for the aperture's opening—the lower the value, the smaller the aperture—and thus we can say that lower values are equivalent to higher f-stops, both providing small apertures. Good values range from 0.1 to 1. All three host applications provide similar settings, as well as more custom-made settings that drive this shader in a logical manner. For example, within host applications, you can also define the aperture by specifying f-stop values rather than using a radius value.

When the physical lens shader is used with any host application, depth of field will always account for the relationship between focal length and the aperture f-stop, as discussed. So if you specify an f-stop and then change the focal length, this consequently will affect the visible focal depth during rendering; hence, lens shaders achieve realism. This holds true whether you are using the host's depth of field settings or mental ray's physical shader specifically (see the host-specific tutorial later in this chapter for examples on using depth of field).

Rendering Depth of Field

As discussed in Chapter 3, lens shaders (including mental ray's depth of field shader) require raytracing, so even if you disable raytracing when using (most) lens shaders, they will re-enable raytracing. For example, the following excerpt from a Maya render shows the mental ray output messages at render time.

```
SCEN 0.2  progr: begin scene preprocessing for frame 1
PHEN 0.2  info : shader "maya_dof" sets scanline off
PHEN 0.2  info : shader "maya_dof" sets trace on
```

Before this render was submitted, raytracing was disabled, and as you can see, mental ray automatically enabled raytracing and disabled scanline rendering because each primary ray is required to be a raytrace ray and so scanline rendering is insignificant, as discussed in Chapter 2. This behavior occurs with each host application because it is a mental ray characteristic and not host specific.

The Price of Power

Depth of field is a very powerful and very expensive raytrace shader that requires taking more samples for visually pleasing results (samples are discussed in Chapter 5, "Quality Control"), and thus you will find that you may use high-quality settings and experience very slow render times. The reason higher samples are required will become clearer as you examine light paths, particularly with glossy shaders and environment sampling. This hit in render performance is one of the reasons we may prefer using a 2D post-process depth of field shader. Alternatively, we can export the Z depth pass and use a depth of field (Z blur) effect within a compositing package; this provides a visually interactive method for tweaking depth of field, but with less accuracy. Don't forget that in most cases, you're looking for a visually pleasing, time-sensitive result, not exact optical simulation.

Host Application Settings

Now we are ready to look at the host applications' camera settings for aperture, film back, film gate, lenses, and depth of field.

As you saw in the previous chapter, mental ray uses a few simple lines to describe the camera's render options. Each host application provides several options for controlling camera settings based on its own approach to camera render options and then behind the scenes uses the translator to convert these settings to render settings. Regardless of the application, the result is the same because the renderer (not the host application) defines the render abilities. In the case of cameras and render settings, all three host applications offer a multitude of options for tweaking these related settings. Note that as mental ray simplifies these settings, the host applications have customized theirs to provide you with more-intuitive settings. Let's get started.

Film Aspect Ratios

When film aspect ratios are delivered on SD (4:3 TV, standard definition), the film is adjusted to fit the screen by matching either the horizontal or the vertical axis with the display's equivalent axis. Typically, film is shrunk into the screen by matching the horizontal axis. This approach, also known as *letterboxing*, results in black bars on the top and bottom of the TV screen, as illustrated in Figure 4.9. It's used because we do not want to distort the image by forcing the film to conform to video standards, so we normally prefer a smaller but undistorted image, as seen with common wide-screen DVDs when viewed on 4:3 standard TV sets. Figure 4.9 also shows the cropping used to maintain the vertical axis on a 4:3 TV screen and the *pillar boxing* used to display a 1.77:1 HD format on a 1.85:1 wide-screen film screen, theatrical display.

As seen in Figure 4.9, an alternative to letterboxing would be enlarging and cropping the image along the vertical lines. Obviously this is less attractive because portions of the film are cropped out of view. Typically this sort of alignment can be found with non-wide-screen DVDs that have been adjusted for TV display. Personally, it's the reason I prefer getting wide-screen DVDs; although the image is smaller, I get the entire picture rather then a cropped-down version. I'm surprised film producers haven't outlawed this sort of crime.

Letterboxing is getting more common as displays get bigger, but when viewing on a small screen, there's a big trade-off for maintaining the true aspect ratio with wide-screen films. Try watching *Lawrence of Arabia* on a 20-inch TV.

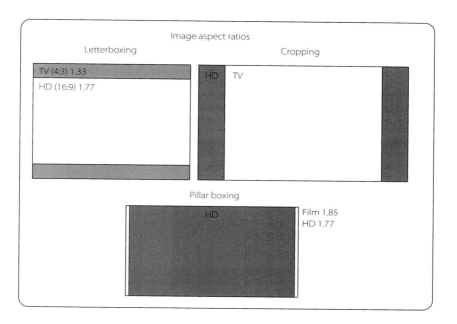

Figure 4.9

Image aspect ratios

When converting HD to 35mm 1.85 projection, a common practice nowadays, the HD's vertical axis is matched with the film's vertical axis, and the horizontal is then centered and slightly smaller than the film's scale. This makes HD a possible format for film because HD's and film's aspect ratios are relatively similar; HD uses a 1.77:1 aspect ratio compared to a 1.85:1 aspect ratio with film. Both formats also use 24fps, and HD supports *progressive* formats, which are non-interlaced images, so each frame is a high-resolution still image, as with film. Once HD has been matched along the vertical axis, there are black bars along the side of the image, making up for the smaller horizontal length. This format is known as *pillar boxed*, as seen in Figure 4.9.

Maya

With Maya, the camera settings provide several controls for fine-tuning the camera. Let's take a quick look at some of the relevant settings, shown in Figure 4.10. To access these settings, select the camera and look at its shape node in the Attribute Editor window.

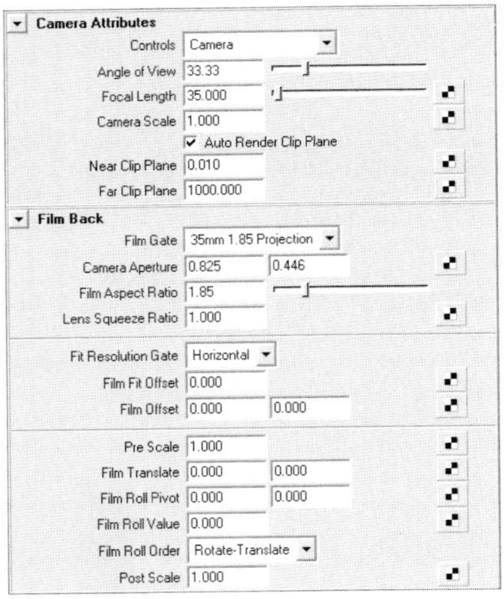

Figure 4.10

Maya's camera settings enable us to control the three primary camera characteristics: aperture, film aspect ratio, and film gate.

Camera Attributes

The Camera Attributes rollout provides general settings for the camera's field of view as well as the render clipping planes. The Angle of View attribute directly correlates to the camera's field of view. The Focal Length attribute dictates the size of the camera's lenses. Notice that when you change one of these settings, the other automatically conforms to the new setting, as discussed earlier in this chapter in the section "Camera Lenses." Because the field of view is based on the camera's focal length and the film back size (Maya's Camera Aperture attribute), if you change the Angle of View attribute, either the Focal Length or the Camera Aperture size will need to conform, and in this case Maya automatically adjusts the Focal Length attribute, maintaining the camera's aperture size.

The Auto Render Clip Plane option should in most cases be disabled; it is better to control the clipping planes yourself during scanline rendering than to allow Maya to automatically dictate a different range for each consecutive frame. When Auto Render Clip Plane is disabled, the Near and Far Clip Plane attributes below it define the camera's visible range, a topic further discussed in the section "mental ray Cameras, Depth Sorting" in Chapter 3.

The Maya Film Back

The Film Back rollout provides essential settings that dictate the camera's film characteristics. Notice that there is no specific film back setting; rather, the film back size is derived from the Film Gate attribute and the Camera Aperture attributes. If you look at the Film Gate drop-down menu, you can see that there are several presets for cameras. If you need HD, however, you would have to create custom settings because these presets cover a small range of cameras. If you select the 35mm 1.85 Projection preset, notice how Camera Aperture, Film Aspect Ratio, Angle of View, and Focal Length all update to represent that camera type and lens. Essentially, the Camera Aperture scale dictates the film size, so if you increase these values proportionally (X and Y axes seen with the two numerical inputs next to the Camera Aperture attribute), you will maintain the Film Aspect Ratio (also referred to as film aperture in the discussions earlier) and the same Focal Length value; however, the Angle of View value will change, as discussed earlier. Clearly the field of view is dependent on the camera lens focal length and the film back. To quickly examine the relationship between different camera components with Maya, you can try the following:

1. Set Camera Aperture to 0.5 and 0.4 and Focal Length to 50.

2. Note that as you defined the film gate's X, Y relationship using the Camera Aperture setting, the Film Aspect Ratio setting updates to represent that ratio automatically (1.25).

3. Note that the angle of view should now be equal to 14.48°.

4. Change Camera Aperture to 1 and 0.8.

5. Notice how the field of view in the camera view has changed. The new Angle of View value is set to 28.50°.

6. The change in Camera Aperture scale has changed the cameras lens type from a telephoto lens to a normal lens by scaling up the field of view. As the film back size grows, so will the field of view for a given lens (unchanged Focal Length). This topic is further discussed in the section "Camera Lenses" earlier in this chapter.

Try individually changing each of the camera attributes discussed in this section while examining their affect on other attributes.

The Lens Squeeze Ratio attribute is used to simulate anamorphic cameras by "squeezing" twice as much data within the film's horizontal axis, which is then "unsqueezed" during projection, providing an expanded wide-screen image. Notice that if you select the 35mm Anamorphic Film Gate preset, the Lens Squeeze Ratio value changes to 2. Also, you can see from under the Film Gate drop-down list that a 35mm film back can have different film gates and image aspect ratios, as discussed earlier in the chapter.

Display Options: Matching Resolutions

Maya provides a few ways of displaying the film and render resolutions in your view, as well as the relationship between them. Because the camera and render settings are in fact separate from each other, the ideal is to match them so that the render provides a correct

Figure 4.11

Maya's camera Display Options rollout provides options for comparing how the render and camera settings align.

image. You enable these displays via the view's drop-down list, as you probably already know. Figure 4.11 shows another method: the Display Options settings available in a camera's Attribute Editor window (scroll down to see them). Use these options to see if your render settings and camera settings align properly.

Let's use a small tutorial to learn more about film and render aspect ratios.

1. Select from the camera Film Gate drop-down list the 35mm 1.85 Projection setting, as shown in Figure 4.10. Also, create a plane and a couple of basic primitives for reference in the scene.

2. Set the preset render setting Image Size → CCIR 601/Quantel NTSC, which can be found in the Render Settings window under the Common tab.

3. In the camera's Display Options rollout, enable the Display Film Gate and Display Resolution attributes (seen enabled in Figure 4.11), and look in your view (you should maximize the camera view).

4. Change the Overscan attribute to 2.000, and notice how both film gates shrink in the view. The Overscan attribute does not affect any camera characteristics; it just enables you to view film gates that might be hard to see, essentially expanding the view but maintaining the camera's proportions to the scene. Notice how the film gate appears as a dotted white line, which, not surprisingly, does not match the resolution gate (solid white line) image aspect ratio.

5. Under the camera Film Back attributes, shown in Figure 4.10, you may use the Fit Resolution Gate drop-down list to control how the film gate is scaled (enlarged or shrunk) with respect to the resolution gate, as an attempt to match resolutions without distorting the film aspect ratio. Select the Horizontal option (which should be the default).

This produces letterboxing (discussed earlier) as the horizontal (X) axes of both the resolution gate and the film gate are matched. Thus, they have the same horizontal length and their aspect ratios are maintained, but their vertical axes differ.

6. Now try selecting Fit Resolution Gate → Vertical to match the vertical axis (Y) for the film and resolution gates. Notice how the film gate now extends outward, along the horizontal axis, passing the resolution gate's border lines (also discussed earlier), resulting in the film's sides being cropped to match the resolution gate.

Device and Pixel Aspect Ratios

As discussed earlier, digital video (D1) pixel aspect ratios are non-square. To derive a corrected aspect ratio for non-square pixels, the film aspect ratio is multiplied by the pixel aspect ratio.

With Maya, you can find the Film Aspect Ratio attribute under the camera Film Back attributes, as seen earlier in Figure 4.10, and the Pixel Aspect Ratio attribute under the Image Size rollout in the Render Settings window, shown in Figure 4.12.

The Device Aspect Ratio attribute is used to represent the corrected aspect ratio. Thus, mental ray is interested in this attribute only when rendering. The device aspect ratio is automatically calculated based on the pixel aspect ratio and the render resolution Width and Height values aspect ratio. To clarify, let's use a simple test:

1. Set the Presets attribute drop-down list to CCIR 601/Quantel NTSC.

2. Set Pixel Aspect Ratio to 1.

Notice how the Device Aspect Ratio value has change to 1.48, which is the correct ratio for 720/486, as discussed earlier in the section "Pixel Aspect Ratio."

Note that when you're using square pixels, the Device Aspect Ratio attribute should match the camera's Film Aspect Ratio attribute, in which case both render and camera aspect ratios will match. This is the ideal method for matching camera settings with render settings. For example, if you select the 35mm 1.85 Projection preset for the camera (as we did earlier) and for render settings select the HD 1080 preset, you will see that the gates almost match perfectly. To get a perfect match, under the camera settings change the Film Aspect Ratio attribute to match the HD Device Aspect Ratio that represents an HD image's aspect ratio of 1.777. The moment both aspect ratio attributes are matched, you see a perfect overlap in the view for the resolution and film gates (provided the Pixel Aspect Ratio attribute is set to 1.0). Thus, the only time you should not enter the same value for the Film Aspect Ratio as the Device Aspect Ratio attributes is when pixels are non-square. In that

Figure 4.12

Maya Render Settings window for specifying the image aspect ratio and resolution settings

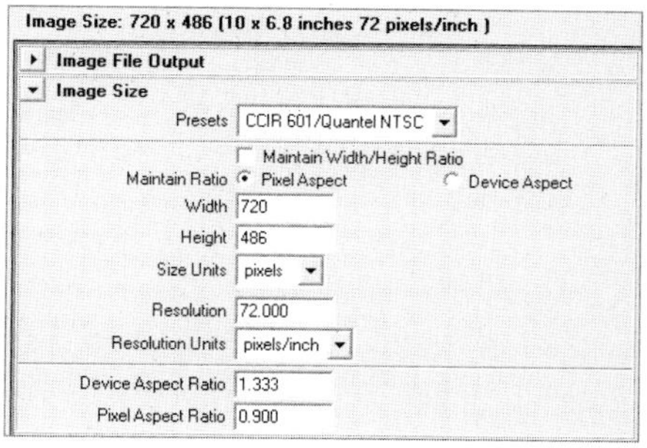

Image Size: 720 x 486 (10 x 6.8 inches 72 pixels/inch)

▸ **Image File Output**

▾ **Image Size**

Presets | CCIR 601/Quantel NTSC ▾

☐ Maintain Width/Height Ratio
Maintain Ratio ⦿ Pixel Aspect ◯ Device Aspect
Width | 720
Height | 486
Size Units | pixels ▾
Resolution | 72.000
Resolution Units | pixels/inch ▾

Device Aspect Ratio | 1.333
Pixel Aspect Ratio | 0.900

case, you need the Width and Height settings (as shown in Figure 4.12) to represent the same camera ratio, and then the Device Aspect Ratio value will be derived by multiplying this ratio by the Pixel Aspect Ratio value.

Because the camera will always use square pixels, you can't get a perfect overlap for the same aperture size (film gate) and render resolution settings, due to non-square pixels. Thus, with NTSC or PAL formats, the camera gate should be set to match as close as possible, for example a Film Aspect Ratio of 1.48, and then the resolution (1.33 with D1 video) gate should be used as a visual reference for the render region. Essentially, this allows you to mimic more accurately a DV camera with proper perspective, accounting for non-square pixels during the render.

Depth of Field

Maya, unlike XSI, doesn't have any postprocess 2D depth of field effects because it doesn't ship with any 2D output shaders, so you can only use the physically correct (but more time-consuming) raytrace lens shaders. In the Hypershade window under Create mental ray Nodes under the Lenses rollout, you will find the physical_lens_dof shader. This shader can be connected as a camera's lens shader in the camera's Attribute Editor under the mental ray rollout → Lens Shaders input attribute, as seen in Chapter 3 (in the section "Output, Volume, Environment, and Lens Shaders"). This is mental ray's depth of field shader, with the characteristics and settings discussed earlier.

Alternately, Maya's custom depth of field shader, which is based on the same lens shader, provides a nicer approach to controlling depth of field. Navigate through the camera's Attribute Editor to the Depth of Field rollout, shown in Figure 4.13. Maya's Depth of

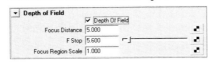

Figure 4.13
**Maya Depth of Field
camera settings**

Field attributes reflect real camera settings rather than the erroneous values used to define the aperture opening, as with mental ray's Radius option.

The Depth of Field check box enables a custom mental ray lens shader. When Maya renders, it attaches a Maya mental ray custom shader as a lens shader under the camera's statement block using the following declaration:

```
camera "perspShape"
    ...
        lens "maya_dof" (
            "focusDistance" 14.3246,
            "fStop" 5.6,
            "focusRegionScale" 1.,
            "lensSamples" 4
                )
end camera
```

Notice how Maya's depth of field attributes appear as options under this custom lens shader within the camera's declaration block. If you are using the stand-alone renderer, you could also try improving render quality by increasing the Lens Samples option value within the .mi file.

DEPTH OF FIELD SETTINGS

In the Attribute Editor, the Focus Distance attribute simply represents the focus point in the scene, and thus the point with the sharpest focus, known as the *focus plane*. The F Stop attribute relates to realistic f-stop values, so you typically would try using a range from 2.8 to 11 as discussed earlier in the section "Depth of Field and F-Stops." The Focus Region Scale attribute simply enables you to visually scale the "circle of confusion," increasing the area within focus by a more "creative" means.

To determine the focus distance, you should either select an object in the center of the desired focus region or place a locator at that position. With the object selected, enable the Heads Up Display → Object Details attribute from under the top menu bar Display menu item, which reveals a collection of settings info in the viewport window, including Distance from Camera.

The Distance from Camera value is the value you need, so by selecting the object at the focus point, you can easily retrieve the distance value from the viewport. Make a note of it and then enter it manually for the Focus Distance attribute under the camera's Depth of Field rollout.

CREATING A CONTROL FOR ANIMATING THE FOCUS DISTANCE

With animation, you may prefer to use a locator to determine the focus distance automatically instead of constantly copying values into the Focus Distance attribute. That is, it may make more sense to visually place a locator in the scene, or even animate it, and then have the Focus Distance value automatically update, opening the door to some nice "in and out" of focus animation.

Let's look at some simple steps to achieve this sort of control. You can refer to the scene Maya_Animated_DOF.mb in the Chapter 4 Maya folder on the CD as a reference.

1. Create a new scene and place some primitives and a floor plane within it.

2. Create a distance-measuring tool by choosing Create → Measure Tools → Distance Tool, and then click twice within the scene to place the two locators that are used as both ends of the measured distance. The two locators and a distanceDimensions node appear in the Outliner window.

3. Select locator1 and parent it under the camera; then zero out its Translate X, Y, and Z transforms in the channel box so that it is centered in the camera.

4. With the second locator (locator2) you have two options: parent it under an animated object so that it follows it during the animation, or manually place (or animate) it at the desired focus plane in the scene.

5. You now want to connect the Distance attribute from the distanceDimensions node to the camera's Focus Distance attribute. You can easily access the Distance attribute through the Connection Editor window, or use a bit of MEL (Maya Embedded Language) to drive these connections.

6. Enter the following code into the script editor all on one line, then highlight it and press Ctrl+Enter to execute the command. Before doing so, consider the following points:

   - This is the Connect Attribute command, equivalent to using the Connection Editor, and you can read about it under the Help → MEL Command Reference.

   - The attribute names need to match the names in your scene, so the distanceDimensionShape1 should match the name in the scene, as should the camera name match your camera. If you're using the perspective camera (not likely, and not recommended), then just make sure to reparent the locator under the camera when you reload the scene, as that hierarchy will typically disconnect.

   - When the attribute names are correct, you can execute the script (note a space is required between the locator and camera names in the script).

   ```
   connectAttr -f distanceDimensionShape1.distance
       cameraShape1.focusDistance;
   ```

At this point, you should be able to verify that as you move locator2 in the scene, you can see the Focus Distance under the cameras attributes update. Note that you can open the Attribute Editor and disable the option under List (Attribute Editor top menu) → Auto Load Selected Attributes so that the Attribute Editor remains focused on the camera attributes as you translate the locator in the scene without the Attribute Editor switching back to the locator attributes. Further, you can run some render tests to verify that as you move it around, different areas in the scene fall into focus, as with the provided scene file.

XSI

With XSI, camera settings provide several controls for fine-tuning the camera. Let's examine some settings relevant to our earlier discussions. You can navigate to these settings by selecting the camera in the Explorer window and pressing Enter on the keyboard. Alternatively, because with XSI each pass is associated with a camera, you can open the camera settings through the current pass by choosing Edit → Edit Current Pass from under the menu bar Render menu, and then press the Pass Camera → Inspect button, revealing the Camera property window. Look under the Camera rollout → Primitive tab, shown in Figure 4.14.

The Primitive Properties Tab

The Primitive tab provides general settings for the camera's field of view as well as the film format. The Field of View → Angle option directly correlates to the camera's field of view. The Horizontal option below it dictates whether the Angle value represents the vertical or horizontal field of view. Typically, *field of view* refers to the horizontal axis.

The Format → Standard option provides several presets for cameras. If you select the NTSC D1 4/3 720x486 preset, notice how the Pict. Ratio and the Pixel Ratio options automatically update to represent the correct settings for non-square pixels and image aspect ratios. With XSI, the Pict. Ratio option represents the corrected aspect ratio, correcting for non-square pixel aspect ratios when need be. The Pixel Ratio attribute below it has no significant effect on the renderer and is not used to derive pixel aspect ratio information for correcting the picture aspect ratio. Instead, it's used only for rotoscoping. Thus, if you had imported a rotoscope footage sequence that has non-square pixels, this Pixel Ratio option would need to be set to match the imported footage's pixel aspect ratio in order for you to match 3D with live action correctly.

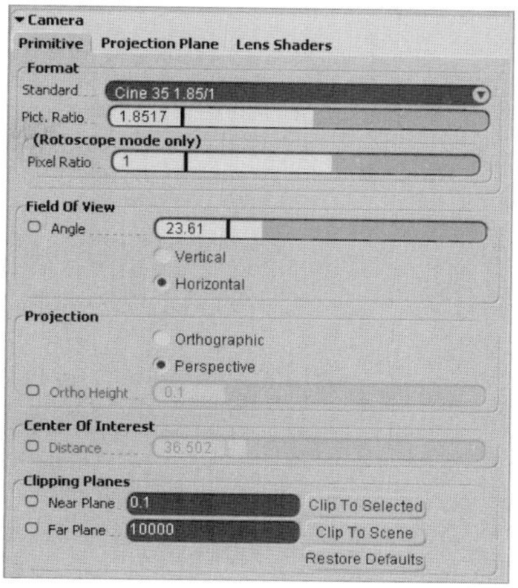

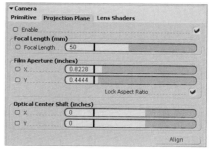

Figure 4.14

XSI camera settings enable you to control the three primary camera characteristics: aperture, image aspect ratio, and film gate.

Notice that the camera's clipping planes for both the near and far distances can be set at the lower portion of this tab, as seen in Figure 4.14. This correlates to the discussion on depth sorting in the section "mental ray Cameras" under "Depth Sorting" in Chapter 3. You can either set it manually or use one of the three auto-evaluation buttons on the right.

The Projection Plane Properties Tab

Before we can examine the influences of camera focal lengths and film backs with XSI, you need to become familiar with an additional window. Figure 4.15 shows the Projection Plane tab in the Camera properties window.

The Focal Length option dictates the camera's lens size. Notice that after enabling the Enable check box, you can manually adjust the aperture size from under the Film Aperture X and Y options. The Film Aperture options refer to the film gate's X, Y scales, and film back size, as discussed earlier in the chapter.

Because the field of view is based on the camera's focal length and the film back size, if you change either the Focal Length value or the Film Aperture X and Y options, the field of view will need to conform. When you change the Focal Length setting, the Field of View Angle option (on the Primitive tab) automatically updates, conforming to the lens's new focal length. Conversely, if you change the Angle option (Field

Figure 4.15

The XSI Camera settings Projection Plane tab, where you can further customize camera characteristics such as the aperture and focal length

of View), then only the Focal Length option conforms on the Projection Plane tab, maintaining the camera's aperture size, as specified with the Film Aperture X and Y values. Essentially, the Film Aperture X and Y options dictate the film size, so if you increase this value proportionally, you maintain the same Pict. Ratio and Focal Length values but the Angle value will change. To quickly examine these characteristic with XSI, try the following steps:

1. On the Primitive tab, set the Standard option to the Cine 35 1.85/1 preset, representing 35mm film, using a film aspect ratio of 1.85 (theatrical projection).

   Notice that the Pixel Ratio option is set to 1, which means that, if you use rotoscoping, the image's pixel aspect ratio should match square pixels, as with film formats.

2. On the Projection Plane tab, enable the Enable check box and set Focal Length to 50. Make sure Lock Aspect Ratio is enabled (by default it should be) so that if you change one of the Film Aperture axes, the other proportionally adjusts.

3. Open the Primitive tab. The Field of View Angle option should read 23.61. With a 35mm film back, this represents a normal lens focal length, as with a 50mm lens (for this example, any Angle value will suffice).

4. Change the angle to a more telephoto field of view, such as 11, and press Enter. Notice how the view immediately updates.

On the Projection Plane tab you will see that as you changed the field of view, the Focal Length option has updated to a value of 108, conforming to an appropriate focal length, matching that field of view, and the film back size. In this case the new settings represent a telephoto lens, where the field of view is narrow and the focal length is longer.

5. Change the Focal Length value back to 50, and confirm that the Angle value has returned to 23.61.

6. Double the Film Aperture X option from 0.8 to 1.6 and notice how the Y value also updates proportionally.

   Notice that the angle of view has now changed to 44.2, representing a wider-angle lens, which results from using a larger film back at that focal length.

The change in Camera Aperture scale has changed the relationship between the camera and the lens. Basically, we simulated converting 35mm film to 70mm film (a higher-quality expensive film stock). As discussed earlier, the film back size and focal length influence a lens's field of view from telephoto to wide-angle lenses. By scaling up the Film Aperture value while maintaining the same Focal Length value, we have changed a normal lens to a wide-angle lens, a topic explained earlier in the section "Camera Lenses."

If you disable the Lock Aspect Ratio option and change the Film Aperture X and Y values to 0.4 and 0.3, respectively, notice that on the Primitive tab, the Pict. Ratio option has adjusted to the 1.333 aspect ratio. If you change the Pict. Ratio value to 1.48, you will see that the Film Aperture X and Y will conform to this new ratio, using 0.4 and 0.27 for the X and Y values, respectively.

Render Settings and Pixel Aspect Ratios

How do you match the render settings with the camera settings? The answer is relatively easy. Navigate to the Render Manager window → Scene → Scene Globals tab and locate the Scene Output Resolution section, shown in Figure 4.16.

The render settings and the camera settings are similar; including image and pixel ratio properties. The Aspect Ratio property correlates to the camera's Picture Ratio property, and the Pixel Ratio

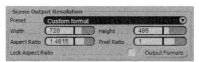

Figure 4.16

XSI's render output properties, where you can match camera and render settings to a specific film/video standard

property, found under the Scene Globals tab, defines the pixel ratio used with the render output, as discussed earlier under "Pixel Aspect Ratio." To customize these settings, you can select Custom format from the Preset property list, as I've done to set up the screen shot in Figure 4.16. Once Custom is set, the properties become editable. Furthermore, if you navigate to the Current Pass → Output tab → Pass Output Resolution properties, you can enable the Override Scene Render Options property checkbox and specify per pass output options. Let's examine some of the pixel aspect ratio theory discussed earlier in this chapter with a quick tutorial on render settings.

1. Select NTSC D1 4/3 720×486 from the Preset drop-down list (under Scene Output Resolution properties).

2. Now change the selection to Custom format so the NTSC settings remain in the area below and are now enabled. Make sure Lock Aspect Ratio is enabled.

3. Change Pixel Ratio to 1. Notice that Aspect Ratio has not changed but the image Width and Height properties have adjusted to represent the current picture ratio.

4. Disable the Lock Aspect Ratio check box and change Height back to 486. Notice how Aspect Ratio now conforms to 1.48, representing the NTSC resolution image aspect ratio for square pixels.

As discussed earlier, because NTSC uses square pixels, when you change the Pixel Ratio setting back to 0.9, you arrive at the standard picture ratio ratio for NTSC DV. mental ray uses the Aspect Ratio value for its aperture[n value] camera option value when rendering.

Matching the Camera and Render Settings

You've tried manually entering values into the render settings, but what if you want to specify a format and transfer it to both the render settings and to the camera? If you click Output Formats, a new window opens, Output Format.

The Output Formats window allows you to specify custom settings, just as within the Render Options window; however, when you click Apply Now, you can select whether or not to apply these new settings to both the camera and the render settings, as shown in Figure 4.17. Note that the properties don't always update correctly, so inspect the results.

Figure 4.17

XSI options for applying the Output Format settings for both render and camera settings. You can also apply timeline and default settings here if need be.

Depth of Field

XSI provides both a physically correct depth of field lens shader and a postprocess 2D depth of field effect output shader so that you don't need to raytrace depth of field.

DISTANCE TO CAMERA

To be able to use depth of field, you will need to input a value for the focus plane, which is the center point within the focal depth, the area that has the "most" focus. Deriving this value is simple. To view the distance from an object to the camera, select the camera view's eye icon, which opens the Camera View properties list, or reach the same list through the top menu by choosing Display → Attributes. Enable the bottom option, Distance to Output Camera. Now within the camera view, the distance to the camera from the selected object is displayed in front of the selected surface (Figure 4.18). That distance value should be used as the focus plane when adjusting the depth of field effect.

Figure 4.18

Distance to Output Camera display in XSI camera view.

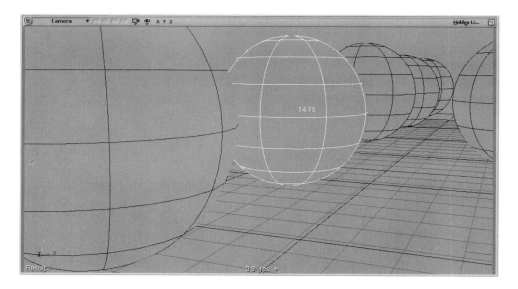

Switch to Bounding Box display to clearly see the distance value; it can become hard to see through surrounding geometry.

APPLYING THE OUTPUT SHADER

With XSI can you can choose to use the mental ray 2D output shader. To select the output shader, navigate through the Render menu, Edit → Edit Current Pass, and then select the Pass Shaders tab in the properties window. Under Output, select the Add property and load the 2D_depth_of_field shader. Once it's loaded, select the shader in the shader stack and click Inspect to load its properties, shown in Figure 4.19.

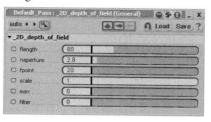

The 2D_depth_of_field will render the depth of field using the Z depth frame buffer to determine scene depth. As this is an output shader, the settings are all defined within this tab and not derived from the camera's aperture, focal length, and f-stop (as they are with the lens shader, discussed later). You can use the Flength attribute to define a focal length, Naperture to specify an f-stop aperture (as discussed earlier), and Fpoint to select the focus plane within the image. For the focus plane, you should use the value you derived for distance from camera, as described earlier. The rest of the settings are creative tools to fine-tune the effect. Both Scale and Max are used to exaggerate or tone down the effect by controlling the *circle of confusion*, which refers to the areas outside the focal depth region, meaning the areas that gradually go out of focus. As with f-stops, a higher value in this case will produce more blur, and lower values will maintain more focus.

Note that the first three settings are meant to specify the camera's characteristics, as we discussed in the sections earlier, so that the effect mimics a realistic camera. Even so, when you're rendering 2D depth of field, the result will not be as accurate as it would be if you used the lens shader, discussed later, but may prove to be a very fast compromise that looks just as good.

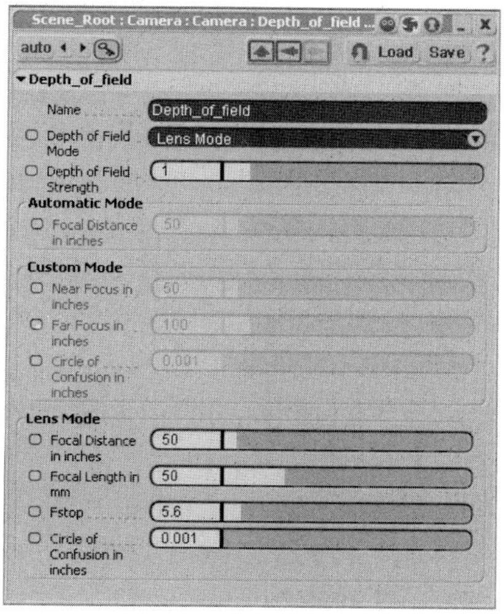

THE LENS SHADER

From the Explorer window, reveal the camera and navigate to the Lens Shader properties tab (discussed in Chapter 3). Select Add to reveal the available lens shaders, and add the Depth_of_field shader. Once it's loaded, select the Depth_of_field shader in the shader stack and click Inspect to reveal the properties seen in Figure 4.20.

Figure 4.19

XSI depth of field 2D output shader properties

Figure 4.20

XSI Depth_of_field lens shader settings provide various ways for controlling the depth of field.

XSI provides three approaches to specifying the depth of field for the physically accurate depth of field shader. Located in the Depth of Field Mode drop-down menu, they are the automatic, custom, and lens modes.

Automatic Mode This mode utilizes the same options as with mental ray's physical shader. The Depth of Field Strength option refers to the mental ray radius option; good values range from 0 to 1. The Focal Distance in Inches option refers to the plane option, determining the distance from the camera to the and the surface in most focus.

Custom Mode The custom mode is a more visual way to control depth of field. You specify the near and far ranges for the focal plane using the Near and Far Focus in Inches options. The Circle of Confusion in Inches setting defines the falloff region where objects fall out of focus; higher values will increase the region and produce more blur.

Lens Mode Lens mode is my preferred mode. In lens mode, you specify these attributes based on your understanding of camera characteristics. The Focal Distance is the distance to the focal plane. As with the other options, this value should be derived based on the distance from the surface to the camera. You can use the Focal Length value to override the focal length you specified for the camera. To avoid doing that, consider copying your camera's Focal Length value (under the Projection Plane tab) to this option. Circle of Confusion, as with the other settings, is used to specify the scale of the region in focus, so you can creatively scale the intensity of the effect. With XSI you can creatively scale the depth of field effect interactively while viewing the render region update—again, one of XSI's best features.

> If you load the lens shader's Property Editor window and lock the settings, you can then select the sphere in the scene to compare the distance value in the viewport with the one applied with the Focal Distance in Inches option. If you tumble the view, you will notice that the value doesn't automatically update in the Property Editor window. In order for this value to update, you must change the time (move the time slider to a different frame), which refreshes that distance value.

ANIMATING DEPTH OF FIELD

With XSI, you can attach the Focal Distance in Inches option to any object in the scene so that, as the object moves, the focal distance updates, enabling you to easily animate in and out of focus effects. Once you have the lens shader inspection window open and you can see the Focal Distance in Inches option, you can use the following steps to apply this connection. (you may examine the scene XSI_DOF from the Chapter 4 XSI folder in the companion CD).

1. Right-click over the animation icon to the left of the option, and select Set Expression.

2. In the Expression Editor, remove the value that appears in the editing pane (the bottom-half input area). Then from the command bar menu, select Function → Distance → To

Camera, which loads the following script into the editing pane (you can also type it in directly):

```
ctr_dist_cam( <elem1> )
```

Replace the `<elem1>` placeholder code with the name of the object you want to use as a target distance. In this case I used `sphere8`, as shown in Figure 4.21. (Note that you must either enter the name of the object postfixed with a period as in the figure, or select the object from the command bar Object menu button.)

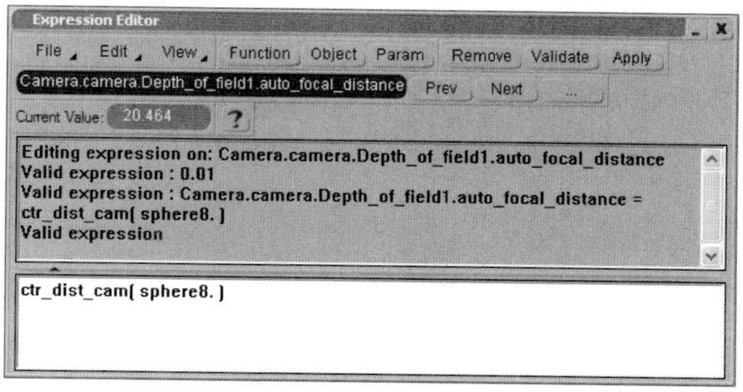

3ds Max

With 3ds Max, the camera settings provide little control over fine-tuning the camera separate from using the render settings, and in fact the camera doesn't have any explicit film gate or film back settings. Settings such as the film aperture are derived from the render settings, and thus render settings automatically "update" the camera. With 3ds Max, you still have all the abilities to specify particular cameras, but using a narrower approach than with Maya or XSI.

Let's take a quick look at the relationship between the render settings and the camera settings. Figure 4.22 shows the settings in the Modify tab for a selected camera (you must first create a camera).

Parameters

Let's look at the top section under Parameters, where you see the main camera lens settings. The camera's characteristics divide into two equally important factors: the film back and shutter (hence the camera body), and the lens and iris. With 3ds Max, these camera settings are then used to control the lens, providing general settings for specifying the camera's field of view and focal length as well as render clipping planes. The Stock Lenses options provide a few common lens focal lengths that you can choose from. When you select one, it updates the Lens field to display that lens's focal length and updates the FOV value to represent the new field of view.

With respect to the Clipping Planes options, you should always verify that these settings are optimized when using scanline rendering. Notice that by default Clip Manually is enabled. If you disable Clip Manually, you'll see in your scene the influence of Near and Far Clip, and you can adjust those settings visually until both settings are optimized, as discussed in Chapter 3 under "mental ray Cameras" in the "Depth Sorting" section. It is always better to manually set these ranges than to allow the host application to automate them.

The FOV option directly corresponds to the camera's field of view, and the Lens option dictates the camera's focal length. Notice that when you change one of these settings, the other automatically updates, conforming to the new setting. Because the field of view is based on the camera's focal length and the film back size, if you change the FOV option,

Figure 4.21

XSI's Expression Editor window allows you to apply custom connections; in this case, it is used for animating depth of field.

Figure 4.22

3ds Max camera settings enable you to control the camera lens focal length.

either the Lens setting or the camera's aperture size (within the render settings) will need to conform. In this case, 3ds Max automatically adjusts the Lens option, maintaining the camera's aperture size. Conversely, if you change the Lens setting, the FOV will also update, conforming to the new value. Thus with 3ds Max, you can see that the camera settings are really lens controls, and the relationship between these settings and the camera film type is then specified under the render settings, as shown in Figure 4.23.

Figure 4.23

3ds Max render settings control the camera's film aperture size.

Render Settings (Output Size)

In the render settings under the Common tab, you can find the Output Size options that specify the aperture. In Figure 4.23, I have selected Custom as an output option, which will be discussed shortly. You can select common presets such as the 35mm 1.85:1 (cine) preset camera from the Output Size drop-down list. Also notice that the Image Aspect ratio and Pixel Aspect ratio are provided. If you choose the NTSC D-1 (video) preset, you will see the Pixel Aspect ratio update to 0.9 and the Image Aspect ratio update to 1.333. The Width and Height settings then provide you with further control over the aspect ratio you want for rendering and thus can be used to specify the aperture size. The following steps show more about the powerful relationship between these render settings and your camera.

1. Create a new scene with a plane and some primitive geometry for reference, as well as a new camera. Set the viewport so the camera's view is visible, and keep the camera selected and its Parameter options visible in the Modify tab. Right click over the Camera name in the viewport and enable the Show Safe Frame parameter.

> You can enable the Lock Selection icon on the bottom of the max screen to keep the camera selected.

2. Open the render settings so you can adjust settings there, and view the influence on the camera.

3. Select the 35mm 1.85:1 (cine) preset camera. Notice that under the camera settings, only the Lens value updates. For example, change the camera preset to the NTSC format and you will see that the Lens value changes. Then, when you change it back, it will update again.

When you change the camera type through the render settings, the lens updates to maintain the same field of view. With 3ds Max the field of view is prioritized so that if you change render settings, you still maintain the same FOV value. However, the Lens value must change to provide the same FOV value when a different film back is used. Thus, as the Aperture Width value displayed in the render settings window changes, the lens also changes to accommodate that change. In this way, 3ds Max respects all the camera fundamentals we discussed earlier under "Field of View". And when using depth of field, or any other lens shader, these camera render characteristics affect the result.

4. Select the Custom preset as seen in Figure 4.23. Notice that with Custom selected, all the grayed-out options are now available. Essentially, enabling you to control the film back, focal length, and field of view for the rendered camera.

> Note that these render settings determine the aperture for all cameras in the scene, so you may think of render settings as the camera's body and any cameras within the scene as additional lenses.

5. Either set the Image Aspect ratio to 1.77 or change the Width to 1280 and Height to 720 to specify a common HD format. Notice how when you specify one of these settings, the other updates. Pixel Aspect should be set to 1.0.

6. Set Aperture Width to 25 and look at the camera settings. As you can see, the FOV is set to 50°, which provides for a wide-angle lens using a 26mm focal length.

7. Set Aperture Width to 35 (the FOV is maintained) and set Lens to 26mm, matching the previous lens. Notice how the FOV has now grown to 67°, confirming the relationship we discussed earlier between the film back size (Aperture Width), focal length, and field of view.

8. You can use the drop-down options to the right of FOV to select whether the FOV output value represents a horizontal, vertical, or diagonal field of view. This has no effect on the camera, just the value you wish to view, and as noted, usually these terms refer to horizontal fields of view.

Depth of Field

3ds Max has several options for depth of field, not all of them meant to be used with mental ray. There are only two relevant options that work well with mental ray. These options are lens shaders that render depth of field. Let's quickly take a look at their settings.

> There is an additional postprocess 2D depth of field that you can select from the Effects window, but I will not discuss it here because it applies its effect on a premultiplied image, resulting in black outlines, so it is not really useful to us.

CAMERA DEPTH OF FIELD

In Figure 4.22 (camera settings), notice the Multi-Pass Effect area. When Enable is checked, you can select the Depth of Field (mental ray) option from the drop-down list. Once this is selected, the Depth of Field Parameters area reveals the mental ray relevant settings, in this case only an F-Stop value for the camera. As you know, you must also set the camera focus so that it knows where the focus plane is. This is set with the Target

Distance option (below the Multi-Pass Effect drop-down list) and should be set as the distance from the camera to the center of the focal depth.

With 3ds Max, it is easy to control depth of field animation such as in-out focus effects by animating the camera target. The Target Distance value is then derived from the camera's target so that translating or animating it in the scene enables you to visually set the focus point in the scene. Note that you could also easily parent the camera target to another animated object so that the focus plane will always be determined by that parent surface.

> You can always convert a free camera into a target camera from under the camera's Type drop-down menu, then select the target and translate it.

PERSPECTIVE DEPTH OF FIELD

Figure 4.24 shows the render settings Depth of Field (Perspective Views Only) area, which can be found within the Renderer tab → Camera Effects rollout under the Render Scene window.

Figure 4.24

3ds Max Perspective Depth of Field display

These settings are used to control depth of field when the default perspective view is used for rendering, and thus have no effect on other cameras in the scene. Once Enable is checked, you can select two options for setting depth of field from within the drop-down menu. The F-Stop option then provides two settings, F-Stop and Focus Plane, which are exactly the same as the F-Stop and Target Distance settings for camera depth of field.

For the perspective camera, you can also select In Focus Limits, which provides an alternative option for specifying depth of field. This option simply enables you to manually set the focal depth circle of confusion, the area that falls out of focus, by specifying a Near and Far (gradually decreasing) range. The focus plane can be specified using the Focus Plane option, defining the center of focus.

As mentioned, 3ds Max provides several abilities for re-creating cameras and camera effects. All these settings are then rendered with mental ray, so it is irrelevant how an application determines the settings. Eventually they all go to the same renderer, which will then render physically correct camera characteristics.

Quality Control

When you are ready to start rendering final images, you will be challenged with optimizing settings that control various aspects of image quality in light of the time constraints you face. These settings include *anti-aliasing*, raytracing, geometry tessellation, and advanced features. You'll need to achieve acceptable render times while still properly handling raytrace acceleration, flicker reduction, and problems like *banding* and *moiré patterns*.

This chapter focuses on some of the more powerful render settings, which control how colors are evaluated and how raytracing is optimized. Later chapters cover settings that contribute to resolving other problems and in the context of specific topics. For example, Chapter 13, "Final Gather and Ambient Occlusion," shows how to resolve Final Gather flickering. (The most common render problem, flickering is usually caused by very thin objects, poor depth coherency, fine detailed texture maps or procedural textures, and advanced lighting techniques.) The first part of this chapter clarifies the intricacies of sampling and filtering and shows how to optimize these settings. The second part focuses on improving render times by tweaking raytrace acceleration, particularly the BSP tree for optimal rendering times. The chapter covers the following topics:

- **Sampling and Filtering in Host Applications**
- **Raytrace Acceleration**
- **Diagnostic and BSP Fine-Tuning**

Sampling and Filtering in Host Applications

Anti-aliasing is applied during rendering to resolve flickering and artifacts. To control the anti-aliasing quality, we apply sampling and filtering techniques that help blend colors together so they appear consistent over a series of frames. The key function is that of averaging colors so that several points from the scene are "consulted" when determining a per-pixel color, thus eliminating the possibility of getting different results every frame for the same surface area.

Sampling and Filtering Settings

Sampling and filtering instructions are set within the .mi file's options block or in the host application's render settings or overridden on the command line with mental ray stand-alone rendering.

Host applications mostly provide the same sampling and filtering options, located in similar tabs with similar labeling. The relevant settings are Samples Min and Max, Jitter, Sample Lock (in XSI called Same Sampling Pattern on All Frames), Contrast Threshold, and Filtering (type and size). Figures 5.1, 5.2, and 5.3 illustrate these settings within each host application. These settings can be found within each application under the following paths:

HOST	PATH
Maya	Render Settings → mental ray → Anti-aliasing Quality rollout
XSI	Render → Renderer Options → Rendering and Framebuffer tabs
3ds Max	mental ray Renderer → Renderer → Sampling Quality rollout

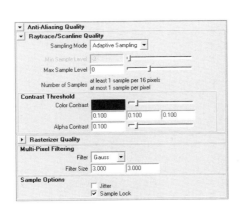

Figure 5.1

Maya sampling and filtering attributes

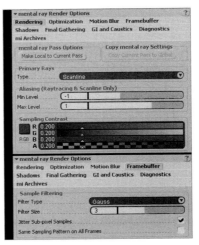

Figure 5.2

XSI sampling (A) and filtering (B) properties

Anti-Aliasing

The main purpose of sampling and filtering is to control the *anti-aliasing* quality of the rendered image to provide the best possible render quality for the 3D scene. Aliasing refers to two primary types of artifacts (and motion artifacts) that appear while rendering. The first is *object* aliasing, which is the stair-step jaggedness along a surface's edge against a background or another surface. Anti-aliasing is used to soften the edge and provide a better transition between edges. Figure 5.4 shows this artifact on the left and the result of applying corrective anti-aliasing on the right.

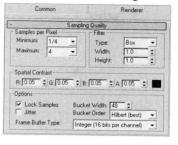

Figure 5.3

3ds Max sampling and filtering settings

The second type of aliasing artifact involves shading interpolation, where sharp changes in contrast, caused by a texture's characteristics, can appear jagged, meaning they may appear more pixelated, not reproducing fine detail visible in the texture. The left side of Figure 5.5 shows this effect, caused by using a noise procedural texture on a planar surface; on the right is the result of corrective anti-aliasing. Notice how the aliased version (on the right) appears as a low-quality image, and in the anti-aliased version the noise is clearer, particularly the fine-detail high-frequency (grainy) noise.

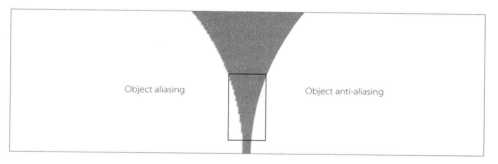

Figure 5.4

(left) Object aliasing artifacts along a surface edge; (right) the result after applying corrective anti-aliasing

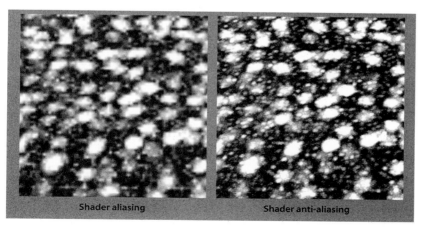

Figure 5.5

(left) Shading aliasing artifacts; (right) the result after applying corrective anti-aliasing

Shader artifacts, especially when there is motion in the scene, can cause flickering because each frame may reevaluate a different color for the same surface points. That is, with each frame a different color value may be sampled for the same surface area, resulting in shimmering or flickering as the sampled colors change. Even if you apply high-quality anti-aliasing settings, this sort of flickering may be hard to eliminate for very high-frequency noise textures or several thin objects, especially if they are placed in near proximity.

The left side of Figure 5.6 demonstrates several thin objects placed in near proximity, creating moiré patterns over most of the image. You can see how low sample qualities can misinterpret the scene, "skipping" the space between objects and applying one color over several pixels, another example of poor aliasing. The moiré pattern is caused because the surfaces don't always appear when they should; thus, they appear to come and go based on the samples that where taken, resulting in these pattern artifacts. The image on the right demonstrates the difference after applying high-quality anti-aliasing settings; the moiré patterns are gone, and each thin surface is distinguished from its neighboring surface.

> Note that a better example for this figure is on the companion CD, not limited by print constrains.

Anti-aliasing then is used to average neighboring sample colors for a given area, evaluating a better per-pixel color on a per-frame basis and reducing the chances of unwanted artifacts for both object and shading aliasing. As a user you have a lot of control over anti-aliasing. For example, you can produce a smoother, softer color solution or a sharper one (as with sharpening filters commonly found in image editors). The concepts for controlling anti-aliasing and relevant settings are the focus of the following sections.

Figure 5.6
(right) Moiré caused by the pattern of fine lines, and (left) the result after applying corrective anti-aliasing

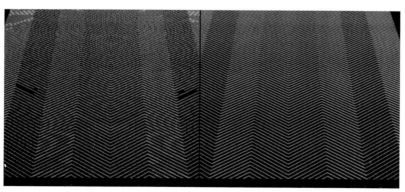

Moiré patterns　　　　　　　　High anti-aliasing settings

Sampling

Sampling is the primary step taken for determining the color value for a point within a scene. As discussed in previous chapters, mental ray samples color values within the scene using a set of primary eye rays that are either scanline or raytrace. *Primary eye rays* is a theoretical term used to describe an observation of the scene from the camera's perspective, which is achieved with scanline or raytracing algorithms, as discussed in Chapter 2, "Rendering Algorithms." These primary rays are the minimum requirement for rendering and are always "cast" into the scene. After sampling, filtering methods are used to average the sampled colors into per-pixel colors, determining the final per-pixel color value sent into the image frame buffer based on a collection of primary rays' sampled color values. The sampled color may or may not have used additional raytracing rays (secondary rays) for evaluating reflections, refractions, and shadows, among other raytracing abilities.

In Chapter 3, "mental ray Output," we showed how mental ray uses two frame buffers: one holds the final per-pixel values, and the other, an intermediate frame buffer, holds sample values. Essentially, the render flow process begins with samples, which are stored in the sampling frame buffer temporarily for each render tile (see the sidebar "Tiling Order and Task Size" in Chapter 2). When each render job has processed all its required samples, filtering commences. Thus samples for each render tile are filtered into per-pixel color values that are then sent into the image frame buffer. The fact that sampling and filtering are done per render job, and thus per tile, has important ramifications, further discussed in the following section. Also note that, as discussed in Chapter 3, additional color instructions such as color clipping, premultiplication, and desaturation are further used to set the final per-pixel color value for each pixel within the image before the value is stored in the image frame buffer.

Sample Blocks

Sample blocks determine the relationship between sampling and pixels. mental ray samples use square sample blocks. Each block represents one sample in the scene. These blocks may contain any number of pixels (an approach known as *infrasampling* or *undersampling*), or there may be several sample blocks within a pixel (an approach known as *supersampling* or *oversampling*). Figure 5.7 illustrates the difference, using × symbols to mark sample locations. The supersampling illustration demonstrates four samples within one pixel; the infrasampling illustration shows one sample for four pixels. It is clear, then, that the sampling setting determines the relationship between sample blocks and pixels. You can also see that with mental ray, each block is sampled at its corner rather than in the center as with other software's sampling algorithms and the rasterizer (discussed later under "The Rasterizer Alternative"). If the sampling setting is set to zero, which equals one sample per pixel, the sample block is the same size as a pixel; hence, in such a case, one corner sample is taken for each pixel. By sampling the corners, mental ray provides a more efficient approach to filtering and anti-aliasing.

Figure 5.7

mental ray infra- and supersampling

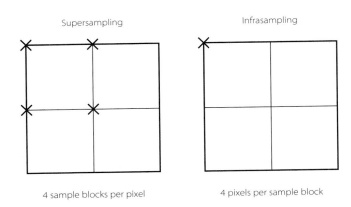

Because sampling occurs at block corners rather than in the center, the bordering edges between the render tiles will share sample locations. These border samples are not shared between the different render jobs, and thus sample information is not passed from one tile to the next, resulting in the resampling along border edges seen in Figure 5.8. Although this approach may seem time-consuming, it is not necessarily a disadvantage. With multiple processors or with network rendering, it is less efficient to share sample information because each tile is an independent process and it would defeat the purpose of having certain tiles "wait" for values from other tiles to either complete rendering or pass information over the network. This sort of sample overlapping is also influenced by filtering and is further discussed in the section "Filtering" later in this chapter.

Figure 5.8

Overlapping samples at border edges, between tiles

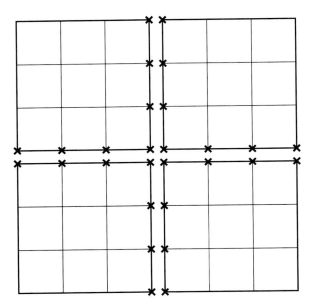

Sampling and Adaptive Sampling

Sampling is controlled with two primary settings, Min and Max sample values, as well as two additional optional settings, Default Min and Max sample values. Additional options that fine-tune sampling are Contrast Threshold, Jitter, and Sample Lock. With respect to their influence on sampling, Contrast Threshold is the most significant and influential option. In stand-alone mental ray, the sampling command is inserted in the .mi file's options block or can be overridden on the command line with the following syntax:

```
-samples [min][max][defmin][defmax]
```

The sampling settings within host applications, as seen earlier in Figures 5.1, 5.2, and 5.3, are set using the following options:

APPLICATION	LABEL
Maya	Number of Samples (Min, Max Sample Level)
XSI	Sampling (Min and Max Level)
3ds Max	Samples per Pixel (Minimum, Maximum)

With Maya, the Sampling Mode attribute dropdown list, seen in Figure 5.1, allows you to select a predetermined relationship between the Min and Max Sample Level attribute values. When set to Adaptive Sampling, the Max Sample Level is automatically set at two values greater then the Min Sample Level. At Fixed Sampling, their values are always equal (use for fast motion blur, see Chapter 8). The Custom Sampling option allows you to define both values independent of the each other.

The Min and Max values provide for an adaptive sampling range so that additional samples, up to the maximum value, may be taken if the minimum value is not sufficient. The decision whether sampling values are satisfactory or additional samples should be taken is based on comparing color contrast between samples using a *contrast threshold*. Thus, mental ray sampling is adaptive and can expand into finer sampled regions. Figure 5.9 illustrates the adaptive sampling process; let's follow the steps and, in the process, better define contrast threshold.

When sampling initiates, only as many samples as specified in the Min samples setting are taken. You can see this in section A, using the upper-left. The entire outer frame (A) represents one Min level sample block. The other corner samples in gray on the outer edges illustrate samples from the neighboring sample blocks (not illustrated). After each four neighboring samples are taken, they are compared and evaluated using the contrast threshold, which determines whether additional samples, up to the Max sample level, should be taken. Assuming you provided two sample levels, the first represents the first set of samples, seen as the outer edge samples for each sample block, and the second represents

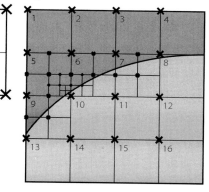

Figure 5.9

Adaptive sampling with mental ray

the additional samples that can be taken, adaptively if required. In this case, the contrast threshold required additional samples, and thus sample block A is divided into four more sample blocks. After this division, only three additional samples are taken; they are represented by the dark gray (smaller Xs) samples long the center lines. Notice that each of these additional samples represents the top corner sample of a sample block within the initial block.

Using the more detailed illustration seen in section B, we can further examine contrast threshold. We can assume that each numbered block represents a sample block equal to one pixel in size. Contrast threshold determines the adaptive nature of sampling by comparing contrast between samples for each color channel (RGB) and the alpha channel separately. Thus contrast threshold provides four option settings, one for each color channel. The lower the contrast threshold value (see the section "Setting Contrast Threshold"), the less contrast is allowed between samples, requiring additional samples to be taken for areas with greater contrast. Let's assume that blocks 7, 8, 11, and 12 are sampled and compared. mental ray identifies the difference in contrast between the gray areas within samples 11 and 12 in comparison to samples 7 and 8. The result is that sample block number 7 is then adaptively subdivided, and three new samples are taken. After the new samples are compared (within block number 7), mental ray recognizes that the difference in contrast is still higher than the allowable range.

For illustrative purposes, I left that area un-subdivided so you can see the adaptive process continue under block 6, where the additional third-level subdivision is being sampled. Similarly, the next block to the left (5) shows another level of subdivision. As long as you provide a max sample value that supports additional subdivisions, mental ray will continue to compare four samples and subdivide them, essentially forming a sub-pixel loop.

Every time mental ray recognizes that additional sampling is required, it will subdivide into four new blocks and then start sampling each of them and comparing contrast, starting with the first block. If the first block requires further subdivision, mental ray will subdivide it before moving on to the next block. Subdivision sampling proceeds recursively through each block until either the max sampling level has been reached or the contrast threshold falls within the allowable range.

SETTING CONTRAST THRESHOLD

In stand-alone mental ray, you can set the contrast threshold options on the command line or in the .mi file's options block using the following options:

```
-contrast [R][G][B][A]
```

From within the host applications, you can set a contrast threshold for each color channel and the alpha channel, as shown in Figures 5.1, 5.2, and 5.3, using the following options:

APPLICATION	LABEL
Maya	Color Contrast and Alpha Contrast
XSI	Sampling Contrast (RGBA)
3ds Max	Spatial Contrast (RGBA)

In each host application you can see four sliders (and a color picker) that are used to specify the contrast value. Essentially, if all four sliders are set to a value of 0.5, you may expect very few additional samples to take place, as a high range of contrast between samples is allowed. However, lower values greatly increase the chances of additional adaptive sampling taking in areas with changing contrast, and thus increasing the anti-aliasing quality by examining color shifts in finer detail. You will learn more about balancing sampling values with contrast threshold later in the chapter. For now, let's clarify the sampling arithmetic used to determine the number of samples equivalent to each sample level.

SAMPLING MATH

The x number of samples allowed for both Min and Max values is based on the values you specify for each option and the following equation, n being the value you provided:

$$2^{2 \times n}$$

Table 5.1 illustrates the number of samples allowed with different sampling values and their relationship to pixel resolutions.

SAMPLE SETTING (POSITIVE VALUES)	NUMBER OF SAMPLES PER PIXEL (SUPERSAMPLING)	SAMPLE SETTING (NEGATIVE VALUES)	NUMBER OF PIXELS PER SAMPLE (INFRASAMPLING)	
0	1			Table 5.1
1	4	-1	4	**Sample Settings and Pixel Resolutions**
2	16	-2	16	
3	64	-3	64	
4	256	-4	256	

Clearly, increasing the sample value greatly increases the number of samples taken within a single pixel. For example, with sample Min set to −1 and sample Max set to 2, mental ray will first sample using 1 sample for 4 pixels. Then, if the contrast threshold requires additional samples, mental ray can recursively subdivide three more levels, for 16 sample blocks within each pixel. Thus, if that area requires the maximum samples taken, sampling ranges would be from 1 sample per 4 pixels to 64 samples within the same 4-pixel block. Particularly with raytracing, there is a big difference in render time between 1 sample and 64 samples, which leads me to the next point: the ability to recursively subdivide areas with contrast change greatly improves render abilities. Suppose your image has one small region that has a change in color (maybe centered in the image), while the surroundings share the same color (for example, black). Why bother oversampling in those black areas when you can get away with even 16 pixels within 1 sample block until the contrast threshold recognizes that change in color near the center and transitions to 16 samples per pixel, saving you a lot of render time? You'll see this sampling process in action later in the chapter, in the section "Diagnostic Sampling," which takes another look at adaptive sampling using a diagnostic render that visualizes the samples taken.

High Max sample values greatly increase render times and should be used with care.

JITTER

Jitter is another method of dealing with flickering or unwanted artifacts caused by banding and moiré patterns. As shown in Figure 5.10, jitter offsets the sample location for a given sample block so that it is no longer placed at the corner. The sample is then placed somewhere within the sample block randomly, so that the sampling pattern has some variation in sample locations. This helps avoid banding, where changes in color may appear with visible gradual changes rather than a smooth transition. And to minimize moiré patterns, it helps offset the samples so that certain areas that may constantly be "missed" by the sample algorithm can be picked up.

Figure 5.10

The jitter technique offsets a sample block away from its corner to minimize banding or moiré artifacts.

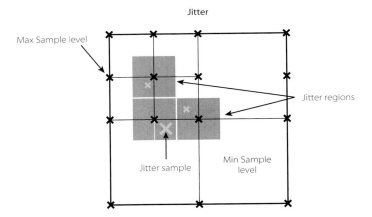

Jitter can be enabled in each host application using the Jitter setting, seen in Figures 5.1, 5.2, and 5.3. You can enable it in an .mi file's options block or specify it on the command line using the following command:

```
-jitter [1(on)|0(off)]
```

SAMPLE LOCK

Sample Lock forces mental ray to "lock" the sampling pattern used when rendering motion sequences. The same sampling pattern will be reused with consecutive frames, which can force mental ray to reproduce similar sampling results and reduce flickering. Alternatively, reusing the exact same sample pattern may reproduce moiré patterns or banding between consecutive frames, in which case it should be disabled and Jitter should be used.

Sample Lock can be enabled in each host application using the Sample Lock option (Lock Samples parameter in 3ds Max), seen in Figures 5.1, 5.2, and 5.3. With XSI, it's enabled with the Same Sample Pattern on All Frames property. Within .mi files, Sample Lock is enabled in the options block or overridden on the command line using the following command:

```
-samplelock [on|off]
```

Default and Per-Object Sampling

Sampling values can also be applied on a per-object basis, under an object's declaration within an .mi file. Thus, you may specify sampling at three different levels: the main (primary) global level, additional default values, and per object. This chapter mainly focuses on the primary sampling values, which constrain the two other settings to the primary sampling value range. Both default and per-object sampling may override each other based on which provides higher settings, but both are limited to the bounds set by the primary setting. Essentially, your primarily concern is with setting the Min and Max sampling values and not as much with the additional default or object sampling values. In fact, as this is being written, only Maya offers straightforward settings for both default and object sampling values without the need to add custom text or manually edit .mi files. Note that the per-object sampling values can be very beneficial for optimizing rendering, as seen in the example in the section "Diagnostic Sampling."

MAYA USERS

Maya users can enable the object overrides in a shape node's Attribute Editor window under mental ray → Min Max Object Sample Limits. Enabling this feature allows you to manually set the limits for both Min and Max sample levels. With Maya, you can also change the default sample values under the miDefaultOptions node attributes in the Attribute Editor window, under Sampling Quality → Sample Defaults → Object Samples → Min Object Samples and Max Object Samples attributes.

> The miDefaultOptions node can be selected in the Outliner window after mental ray is enabled as the current render type and you disable the Display → DAG Objects Only attribute in the Outliner window.

Diagnostic Sampling

Diagnostic sampling is a method of visualizing the sample pattern within a rendered image. It can help you verify that you are not "wasting" samples by oversampling in sparse areas and helps you see if enough samples are being generated in detailed areas. Visually seeing the sample distribution helps you learn a great deal about the adaptive nature of sampling.

Diagnostic sampling can be enabled on the command line, inside the .mi options block, or from within the host applications. The command-line syntax is as follows:

```
-diagnostic samples [on|off]
```

The paths to these settings are shown in the following list. Select the sample related option for enabling sample diagnostics in each host, as seen selected in Figures 5.11 to 13.

HOST	PATH
Maya	Render Settings → mental ray → Diagnostics rollout
XSI	Render → Renderer Options. → Diagnostic tab
3ds Max	mental ray Renderer → Processing → Diagnostics rollout

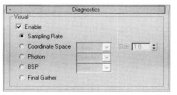

Figure 5.11

Maya Diagnostics tab, with Diagnose Samples enabled

Figure 5.12

XSI Diagnostic tab, with View Sampling enabled

Figure 5.13

3ds Max Diagnostics tab, with Sampling Rate enabled

XSI users can interactively tweak sampling values while viewing the diagnostic samples update in the render region, making it easier to set the sample values, a great sample values, a great benefit of XSI's interactive render region!

Figure 5.14 illustrates diagnostic sampling in action. This tool helps us visualize several sample-related components. The render tile size can be seen with a red line along the tile boundaries (seen as black grid pattern in print), subdividing the render image based on the tile render size. Visualizing the tile size can help you identify problematic areas where one edge doesn't follow through into the next tile, in which case you could change the tile size (see the sidebar "Tiling Order and Task Size" in Chapter 2).

Figure 5.14

Sample diagnostic render of two identical images with and without raytracing

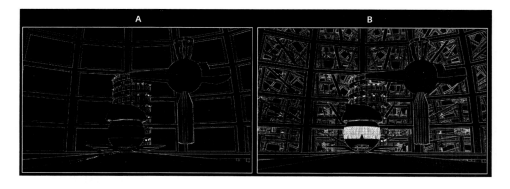

Samples are visualized using a grayscale value. Areas in black have not been sampled at all, and areas that appear grayscale have been sampled at some sample level; finally, areas in white are areas that have been sampled at the Max sample value. You can learn a lot by examining these images and testing different sample settings using simple primitives. Notice the difference between A and B in Figure 5.14. Raytracing is disabled in the image labeled A, and it's enabled in the image labeled B. As you can see, it is easy to identify the sample pattern in the mirror surfaces picking up the reflections and to clearly see how samples follow edges along the surfaces.

In Figure 5.15, you see the sample pattern output for different Min and Max sample levels for the same image. Image A was rendered with the same Min and Max level of -2. This level means that for every 16 pixels, there will be one sample, and as both levels are set to the same rate, there is no ability to further subdivide and thus no ability to sample adaptively. Hence, image A appears identical throughout the entire image and does not distinguish contrast changes. Similarly, image B is rendered with the same Min and Max sample levels, and hence also is nonadaptive. In image B, the sample levels are set to zero, thus generating one sample per pixel, and that is why the entire image appears white; each pixel receives one sample, which is its max sampling level.

Image C demonstrates adaptive sampling using a Min level of -1 and Max level set to 2. Clearly, in image C you can recognize the adaptive nature of sampling and distinguish the areas where max samples were used to render this noisy texture, which is applied to both the oval sphere and the plane surface. Thus, as the samples get brighter, more samples are used in those areas.

In Figure 5.16, you can see the same three images using the same Min and Max levels of 0 and 2. The differences in this figure are changes in contrast threshold. Notice that all areas in the image are at least at some gray level. Since the Min level is zero, each pixel is sampled at least once, and thus the entire image receives a gray coating. However, areas that have been sampled at the Max level are in white. A contrast threshold of 0.1 was used in image A, 0.06 was used in image B, and 0.03 was used in image C, for all color channels in each case. As you can see, the lower the contrast, the more samples used to recognize the changes in contrast in the noise texture. By now you should have a clear picture of the relationship between sampling, contrast threshold, and render tiles.

Figure 5.15

Adaptive and non-adaptive sampling

Figure 5.16

**How changing the
contrast threshold
value affects
sampling**

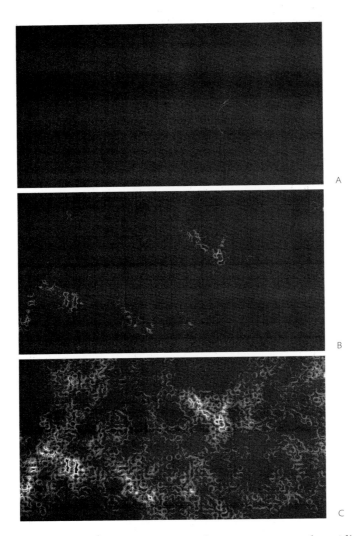

One last example demonstrates how you can control sampling at the per-object level, as discussed earlier in this chapter in the section "Default and Per-Object Sampling." Figure 5.17 demonstrates the difference in sampling after applying a lower per-object sampling rate to the plane in image B. Image A has no overrides and uses the same global settings as image B for Min and Max sampling. The image's Min and Max sample levels are set at 0 and 2, respectively. In image B, the floor's Min and Max sample levels are set to −1 and 1. Notice that although a −1 value was entered for the floor's Min level, you can recognize that all areas across the floor have received at least one sample, demonstrating how the scene's global settings define the range. Thus, setting the scene with a Min sample level of zero acts as an override for the object's ability to sample at less than zero, restricting it to the 0 to 2 range. Also, you can see that the floor's samples are not white at any point, showing that the Max level of 2 was never reached because the floor's Max level is set to 1. Also note that since the sphere is reflecting the floor, the samples on the sphere, which include reflections from the floor, are also bound by the floor's sample rate. Therefore, only areas outside of the floor's influence that are not limited by object sample overrides are able to reach the max sample level, in this case the top half of the sphere, outside the plane's reflective area.

Balancing Sampling Values and Contrast Threshold

A combination of high maximum sampling values and low contrast values provides for higher-quality rendering as well as longer render times. To find the optimum balance within your time constraints, you should always increase the contrast threshold sensitivity (by decreasing the contrast values) before increasing the sampling level. This way, you make sure that the current Max sample value is being properly used before increasing the number of samples. Use the diagnostic mode as shown earlier to verify whether max sampling is being used effectively. If a lower contrast threshold value does not provide the desired result, you can then increase the sample level by one. With the contrast threshold, you can make changes that vary by some decimal point, but with samples, you always want to increase one level at a time because there is a tremendous difference between, for example, 16 samples and 64 samples per pixel. Remember, each of these samples with raytracing may lead to several secondary rays, bringing the render to a crawl, a topic discussed in detail later in this chapter in the section "Raytrace Acceleration."

Normally, good sampling testing values range from -3 to 0 Min, Max respectively). For final render, typically 0 to 2 is sufficient and acceptable in terms of render time. Contrast test values can range from 0.1 to 0.2 for each color channel. For final render, you may use values below 0.1, in the range of 0.04 to 0.1. The alpha contrast value should be set to a low value only if you need to use the alpha channel for compositing. If you will not need an alpha channel, this value should ideally be set to 1 so that it doesn't have an impact on the render time by rendering a high-quality alpha channel. Preferably, you can disable the alpha channel altogether, which may be the best thing to do in such cases, depending on your compositing intentions.

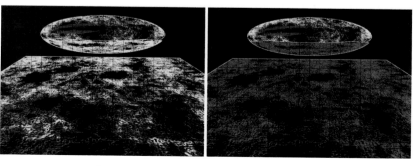

A   B

Figure 5.17

The effect of applying different per-object sample overrides

EDGE FOLLOWING

mental ray supports *edge following*, which is a method of following contrast along an edge until the end of the render tile. Thus, even if neighboring sample blocks have satisfied their contrast lookup and found nothing, if a the lookup within a different sample block finds an edge, it can follow that edge back into the previously sampled blocks, forcing them to further subdivide within a given render tile. This backtracking is a smart mechanism to ensure that thin objects, which can easily be missed, can be followed once they are identified in another block. The fact that it is restricted to a given render tile may cause a problem because the next tile may not pick up the object and then artifacts appear. In such a case, you may try increasing the tile size, thus providing a better chance for thin objects to be picked up as well as followed through a larger area. Aside for changing the tile size and setting the global sampling, you have no direct influence on how mental ray executes edge following.

Filtering

After the sampling phase has finished (for a given render tile), the samples are then filtered into pixels. The filtering process is based on filter width and height values that dictate the number of pixels contained within the filter, extending outward from the center of the filter. Essentially this means that a filter size of 1×1 pixels will contain one pixel and a filter size for 2×2 will contain four pixels, spanning one pixel outward from the center of the filter as shown in Figure 5.18. As you can see, the filter size is used to dictate how many samples are used for filtering from within a filter region.

Figure 5.18

Filtering samples into pixels and the relationship between filters and render tiles

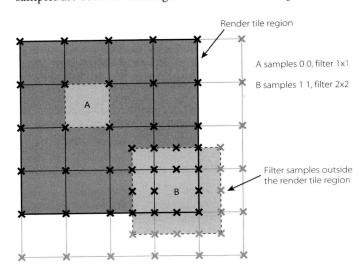

Render tile region

A samples 0 0, filter 1x1

B samples 1 1, filter 2x2

Filter samples outside the render tile region

Filtering uses a weight value that represents the amount of influence each sample has on the filtering process. The max weight is applied at the center of the filter region and then gradually changes toward the filter edges, representing the influence of samples along that path and, again, dictating their influence in the filtering process. Different filters have an effect of either blurring or sharpening an image, based on the filter size and type. The filter type dictates the relationship between the filter size and the sample weight (see the section "Filter Types" later in this chapter). Thus, filtering is an essential phase in averaging color samples into pixels based on the filter size and type.

Figure 5.18 demonstrates the filtering process and its relationship to render tiles and samples. Let's assume we are using a filter width and height of one pixel, as seen in section A, which is then equal to the size of one sample block, covering one pixel in size. As you can see, in this case, filter A will use four samples, one belonging to that pixel and an additional three samples from neighboring pixel corners, showing one of the advantages of using corner samples with mental ray, a topic further explained later within this section.

Consider that the render tile is defined with the heavy black border labeled "render tile region" and that samples from outside this region belong to neighboring render tiles. What happens if we try filtering the samples at the lower-right pixel labeled B? Assume that we increased the sample level to 1 using four samples per pixel and increased the filter size to 2×2. There are not enough samples within this render tile to use with a 2×2 filter size. In theory, mental ray needs to retrieve other samples from neighboring tiles to fill in the gap, as illustrated by the lighter-gray bounding box, which extends outward from the filter center, one pixel in each direction, thus extending outside the render tile region. But render tiles don't share sample information, so in cases like this where the filter size along render tile edges requires extending outward from the tile region, more samples are taken to fill in the gap. With heavy renders, this can have significant impact; for example, if you use a 10×10 filter region, it will resample several pixels that belong to other render tiles, using the sample settings levels to define the number of samples taken, which may require several sub-pixel samples. Also, keep in mind that if these additional samples require ray-tracing for evaluating color, this can lead to a significant hit in render performance. Thus, filtering forces mental ray to resample along tile borders, based on the filter size. With heavy rendering, it is recommended that you keep filter sizes at their minimum default rather than increasing them.

The fact that corners rather than centers (as with the rasterizer) are sampled for each sample block benefits filtering. With a sample block of one pixel size, there are four samples along a pixel's edge, one from its own sample and an additional three neighboring samples. The filtering process is based on a size in pixels, so if a filter size (such as the Box filter type) is equal in size to one pixel, it will use those four samples for filtering instead of just one. With the rasterizer, resolving this sort of problem requires increasing either the number of samples or the filter size, as the rasterizer samples in pixel centers, and thus a filter of one pixel in size would use only the available samples from within that pixel. With the default corner sampling, however, we get more information about each pixel without taking more (time-consuming) samples, using the neighboring sample blocks samples.

Filter Settings

Filter settings are entered in the .mi file's options block or overridden on the command line using the following settings:

```
-filter [clip][box|triangle|gauss|mitchell|lanczos] [width] [height]
```

This command selects one of five filter types—Box, Triangle, Gauss, Mitchell, and Lanczos—and defines their width and height in pixel sizes. The `clip` option clips negative filter values to zero, as with the Mitchell and Lanczos filter methods (see Figure 5.19 in the next section, "Filter Types").

Within host applications the filter settings can be found in the same locations shown earlier in Figures 5.1, 5.2 (label B), and 5.3. The relevant filter settings are filter type, where the filter type is selected from a drop-down box, and the X, Y width and height for the filter, in pixel units. These options are labeled as follows in the host applications, under their filtering sections:

APPLICATION	LABEL
Maya	Filter
	Filter Size
XSI	Type
	Filter Size
3ds Max	Type
	Width
	Height

Note that the filtering values have default, recommended filter sizes; however, you are not limited to these sizes and can change them. Settings above these recommended values may increase render times and make images blurry or oversharpened. Essentially, you should change the filter size only to correct artifacts or reduce blurriness. Note that the filter clip option is available only for stand-alone rendering and is not yet available within host applications.

You should try rendering some detailed texture using different filter types and sizes and then zooming in on the image and examining the different results.

Filter Types

Figure 5.19 illustrates the five different filter types you can use, and Table 5.2 summarizes their effects.

FILTER TYPE	DEFAULT SIZE	RESULT
Box	1×1	A square filter that evenly weights all samples during filtering.
Triangle	2×2	A gradual linear transition; decreases the weight from the center outward. Can result in a bit of blurring.
Gauss	3×3	Provides for a smooth falloff, resulting in a blurred result.
Mitchell	4×4	Higher-order filters that have the effect of sharpening because they fall below the zero weight while filtering.
Lanczos	5×5	Same as Mitchell, but provides more sharpening.

Table 5.2

Filter Types and Default Sizes

All the filters except Box create some form of gradual change in weight from the center, so they should be used with filter sizes greater than 1×1. Their influence decays outward (as seen in Figure 5.19), and thus they need more samples to transition over or their effect is minimal. Again, the default sizes are recommended starting points for each filter, and normally you would either leave them at that default value or increase them. For example, the Triangle filter, as it transitions over a 2×2 pixel area, will use the full weight of the original center pixel and half the weight over the neighboring pixels as it gradually decreases to zero weight. Thus, when filtering, it better blends the samples between the center of the filter and the neighboring samples within the filters pixel size, resulting in a bit of blurring.

The Rasterizer Alternative

The rasterizer uses a different non-adaptive sampling algorithm. This algorithm is particularly good at dealing with accelerating motion-blur rendering and rendering scenes with several polygons (such as hair or fur) that overlap in

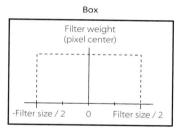

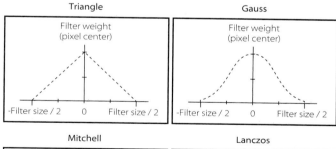

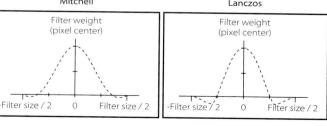

Figure 5.19

Filter types and their weight falloff influence from the filter center outward

the same pixel space, as discussed in Chapter 2 in the section "Scanline Rendering in Depth." The rasterizer sample settings can be set in the .mi options block, overridden on the command line, or set within host applications. Note that the rasterizer has changed between mental ray versions 3.3 and 3.4. In version 3.3 the rasterizer was known as Rapid Motion, and in version 3.4 it has been renamed the rasterizer and also changed. We will look at these settings based on version 3.4.

Rasterizer Options

When the rasterizer is enabled, the following commands are used to control it:

```
-scanline [rapid or rasterizer]
-samples_collect [value]
-shading_samples [value]
-samples_motion [value]
```

The first line is used to enable the rasterizer. (For information on enabling the rasterizer from each host application, see the section "Scanline Render Algorithms" in Chapter 2.) Some of the other three settings can be found from within host applications under the following paths, which display the windows shown in Figures 5.20, 21 and 22. The following table provides the paths to rasterizer settings within the host applications..

HOST	PATH
Maya	Render Settings → mental ray → Anti-Aliasing Quality → Rasterizer Quality rollout
XSI	Render → Renderer Options → Rendering tab
3ds Max	mental ray Renderer → Renderer → Rendering Algorithms rollout

The labels used for the rasterizer options with each application, which are further discussed later, are as follows:

APPLICATION	MENTAL RAY EQUIVALENT	LABEL
Maya	Samples Collect	Visibility Samples
	Shading Samples	Shading Quality
	Samples Motion	Motion Samples
XSI	Shading Samples	Shading Samples
	Samples Collect	Pixel Samples
	Samples Motion	Motion Samples
3ds Max	Samples Collect	Samples per Pixel
	Shading Samples	Shades per Pixel
	Samples Motion	Time Samples (Fast Rasterizer)

These settings are enabled in host applications only when the rasterizer (or Rapid) is selected as the scanline algorithm; see Chapter 2 for more details about the rasterizer.

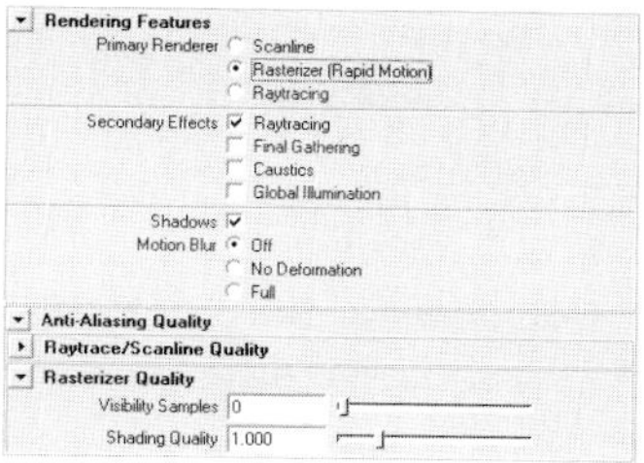

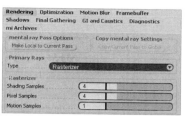

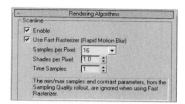

Figure 5.20

Maya rasterizer sample settings

Figure 5.21

XSI rasterizer sample properties seen after the rasterizer is enabled.

Figure 5.22

3ds Max rasterizer sample settings

MAYA

In Maya, the Motion Samples option is found under the mental ray default options (miDefaultOptions node discussed earlier under "Default and Per-Object Sampling") and is not available from the Render Settings window. To display these options, as an alternative to selecting the node in the Outliner window, make sure the Attribute Editor window is open and mental ray enabled; then type the following command into the command line or script editor and press Enter to execute:

```
select -r miDefaultOptions;
```

In the resulting Attribute Editor display, go to the Rendering tab, where you can now see all three rasterizer options, including Motion Samples.

Rasterizer Sampling

The rasterizer differs significantly from mental ray's default sampling algorithm. Sampling is not adaptive with the rasterizer, and samples are taken in pixel centers rather than corners. The rasterizer also differs in its approach to sample collection by separating shading samples from visibility samples. With the rasterizer, the Shading Samples option is tied to the geometry tessellation. Instead of the usual method of sampling the scene with primary rays, where at each point of intersection a shader is called to evaluate that point's color, with the rasterizer, mental ray first collects the shading information on a per-pixel basis, shading triangles within a pixel dimension as many times as required by the Shading Samples option. Once the shading has been distributed for all surfaces in the scene—that is, once the surface has been subdivided into per-pixel-shaded triangles—those values are cached with the geometry. This allows for a significant improvement in motion-blur rendering as the shading samples "travel" with the surface. As objects move over a given distance within the time interval of one frame, these shaded triangles "drag" their shading value with the surface and so the object does not have to be resampled several times within a frame's Shutter Open and Close time interval and along that motion path. You will learn more about the rasterizer and motion blur in Chapter 8, "Motion Blur."

After shading samples have been evaluated, the Samples Collect option is responsible for defining the density of visibility samples taken within each pixel, sampling the shading samples from the geometry, much like the Samples option with the other mental ray algorithms. The Samples Collect option is defined as the n number you provided multiplied by itself, thus producing $n \times n$ samples per pixel, as shown in Figure 5.23.

Figure 5.23

Samples Collect sample distribution for the rasterizer

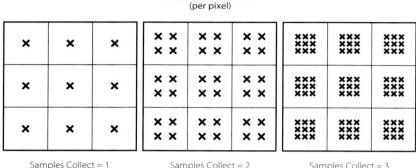

Samples Collect values
(per pixel)

Samples Collect = 1
1 sample per pixel

Samples Collect = 2
4 samples per pixel

Samples Collect = 3
9 samples per pixel

When you set the rasterizer options, the default value for the Samples Collect option is set to 4, generating 16 samples per pixel. The Shading Samples option is a linear (non-adaptive) value also representing a per-pixel value, so in mental ray 3.4, you cannot take fewer samples than pixels with the rasterizer (as you could in version 3.3).

The Samples Motion option dictates whether additional samples are taken with motion blur. This option is needed because caching the shading values with the rasterizer can lead to dragging of reflections across the scene. To reduce this problem, the Samples Motion option allows you to increase the number of shading samples taken within a given time interval. Thus, as the object moves within the shutter open and close time, additional shading samples may be taken, up to the number specified by this option. The rasterizer sampling characteristics with respect to motion blur are further discussed in Chapter 8.

To take advantage of multiple samples per pixel, you need to have multiple shading samples per pixel. Since the sample-collection phase gathers samples for the filtering process, if you specify a high Samples Collect value, then you should also increase the Shading Samples value so they support gathering a collection of color samples during the collection phase. Another point of consideration relates to filtering. As discussed earlier, filters are applied on a per-pixel resolution, and because the rasterizer samples are taken in pixel centers, a filter size of one pixel will have only one sample to filter. Thus, for filtering to have an effect, you would need more than one sample per pixel or a larger filter size.

As the rasterizer is primarily a motion-blur acceleration method (or an alternative algorithm for rendering dense geometry, such as hair), we will look at it in more detail in Chapter 8. Note that the rasterizer can also be very good at rendering complex scenes that have a lot of depth, as well as provide another way to offset the samples, if the default sampling method produces artifacts.

Raytrace Acceleration

Chapter 2 introduced scanline rendering and the basic concepts of raytracing. This section provides a closer look at raytracing and the three raytrace acceleration algorithms available for calculating raytracing. The different scanline rendering algorithms affect image quality as well as rendering time, but the raytracing algorithms are aimed only at improving render times and have no effect on image quality. This might be one reason users are not as familiar with these settings. After all, why bother learning about these algorithms if the image will look the same? The answer is simple: knowing how to set raytrace algorithms can reduce per-frame render times by a very significant factor.

Raytrace Algorithms

Raytracing requires the renderer to compare each ray with every triangle in the scene, determining whether that ray intersects with a surface. With ray casting (primary rays), the sampling number determines how many rays are cast into the scene, whether you're using infrasampling or supersampling. For example, if you set a sample level of 1, you will cast four rays into the scene for every pixel, and each of those rays needs to be compared with every triangle to find any intersections. You can see why raytracing requires so much computation. Each ray must be compared with all the triangles, and not just those directly in front of it because it has no knowledge of triangles in its path until it finishes the comparison process. So you may conclude that higher sampling forces more comparisons between rays and triangles to determine intersections, increasing the render time.

In order to focus exclusively on raytrace rendering, this discussion assumes that scanline rendering is disabled. As the process of raytracing is discussed, however, the advantages of using scanline rendering for primary rays should become clear.

BSP, Large BSP, and Hierarchical Grid

mental ray provide two algorithms for dealing with these ray-triangle comparisons in a logical method: the *Hierarchical Grid* and *Binary Space Partition (BSP)* algorithms. The BSP tree algorithm is mental ray's primary raytracing algorithm, used in most cases, and there is also a subset algorithm, known as *Large BSP*. These algorithms are responsible for dividing the scene into smaller segments, so that a ray can be compared with fewer triangles. The theory for good raytracing render times is to minimize the number of such comparisons. Thus the fewer ray-triangle comparisons, the faster the render.

These algorithms divide the scene into a collection of 3D "containers" that attempt to separate triangles evenly based on two main factors that you control: the number of containers permitted and the number of triangles within each container. Once the scene is subdivided into these containers, known as *voxels*, a ray can evaluate which voxels it passes through while traveling through the scene. The renderer can then compare it only with triangles found within those voxels, significantly reducing the number of comparisons required. I described this separation process as an "attempt" because mental ray is constrained to the number of voxels you provide. A voxel, then, can contain either additional voxels or triangles. Voxels that contain only triangles are referred to as *leaf nodes*.

The Grid and BSP algorithms differ in their approach to dividing the scene into voxel containers. Grid divides the scene into a grid of containers evenly, and each container can then be further subdivided into smaller containers within it. BSP is an adaptive method that has a treelike structure that subdivides the scene unevenly based on areas that require more voxels. The Large BSP variant enables mental ray to use disk swapping more effectively to balance the memory. Disk swapping basically enables mental ray to efficiently swap the portions of the BSP tree that are available in memory, pushing and pulling data in and out of memory as required. Large BSP utilizes the same BSP settings but with a more complex tree structure that is better at handling large scenes and is a bit slower than the BSP algorithm. The BSP method is the fastest rendering algorithm for single-processor machines, and if the scene runs into memory problems or has millions of triangles, the render may come to a crawl, in which case it would behoove you to try using the Large BSP algorithm as an alternative. The Grid algorithm is also fast, especially with multiprocessor machines, and is efficient at handling large scenes and conserving memory, which is typically useful for scenes that have a fairly even distribution of triangles. In most cases, certain aspects of raytracing benefit from using the BSP tree, which provides more control for minimizing the number of voxels and localizing them to solve complexity in random areas of the scene, where a lot of geometry actually exists. In all cases, the voxel subdivision process will terminate when all voxels have their leaf nodes, which contain the triangles, as seen in Figure 5.24.

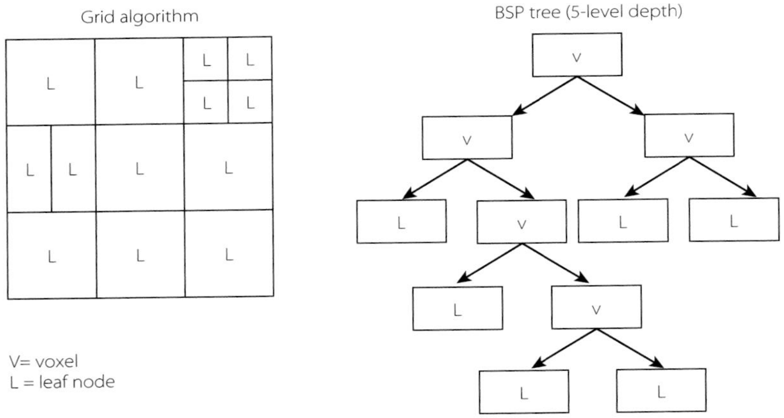

Figure 5.24

BSP tree and Grid algorithms illustrated in 2D, which poses three dimensions in reality

Voxel Depth and Size

With voxels you provide a depth (max subdivision) value, which represents a fixed limit that mental ray will not exceed; no additional voxel subdivisions will occur past this number. For example, if the depth is set at three, then each voxel (in addition to the first primary voxel) can split twice, and thus with BSP the first voxel is split into two, dividing the scene into two new voxels. Each of those voxels can also split into two, essentially creating three voxel layers and four leaf nodes for the entire scene, as seen in Figure 5.24, which shows five levels of depth. With the Grid algorithm, a limit of three means that each voxel in the grid can subdivide twice, forming smaller partitions. However, to evaluate how many leaf nodes exist, you would need to know the size of the grid in relation to the scene. A grid of four cubes may produce eight leaf nodes after one subdivision, provided all the voxels required subdivision.

Another component that you control is the max size of triangles within each voxel (*voxel size*). If there are not enough voxels (voxel depth) to evenly distribute triangles based on the triangle limit (the voxel size), mental ray will exceed the size limit, adding in more triangles, but it will not exceed the number of voxels. Hence, mental ray ranks voxel (depth) limits over triangle (size) limits. The result may be a voxel that has an excessively high number of triangles since it has reached the max depth subdivision level.

An excessive triangle count means that as a ray enters a leaf node, a very high number of triangles need to be evaluated. Balancing between the number of allowable voxels and the voxel size (max number of triangles) can become a tedious trial-and-error process. There are a few techniques and scripts you may use to make this process easier; they are covered in the following sections along with the settings for each algorithm.

Larger depth values for voxels require more memory for storing as well as a longer preprocessing stage. If memory use becomes excessive, mental ray is forced to unload data temporarily to disk (disk swapping) and then reload it when needed, which slows down operations. The Large BSP algorithm is better at handling such tasks. Also, as cited earlier, the more triangles that exist within a voxel, the longer it takes to evaluate raytrace intersections, which means that you need to find the right value for depth. In general, voxel depth has a more significant impact on render time than the voxel size. As these topics are discussed further, keep in mind that the values you use on one machine will not necessarily be right for another machine because memory has a significant influence on how many voxels can be created without disk swapping.

The remainder of this chapter focuses on mental ray's primary acceleration method, which is the BSP algorithm, and methods for fine-tuning BSP settings. The options and settings for Grid are presented and are similar to the BSP settings, so an understanding of BSP should suffice for understanding the Grid algorithm.

Raytrace Acceleration Settings

You can set raytrace acceleration within an .mi file's options block or on the command line:

```
-acceleration [bsp|largebsp|grid]
```

The BSP options are as follows:

```
-bsp_depth [max depth value]
-bsp_memory [max memory in mb]
-bsp_size [max triangle per voxel]
-bsp_shadow [on|off]
```

And the following lines show the Grid options:

```
-grid_depth [max subdivision level]
-grid_resolution [x_res][y_res][z_res]
-grid_size [max triangle per voxel]
```

In the host applications, you can access the options shown in Figures 5.25, 5.26, and 5.27 via the following paths:

HOST	PATH
Maya	Render Settings → mental ray → Raytracing → Acceleration rollout
XSI	Render → Renderer Options → Optimization tab
3ds Max	mental ray Renderer → Renderer → Rendering Algorithms rollout

Table 5.3 summarizes the equivalent settings within each host application:

Table 5.3	MENTAL RAY OPTIONS	MAYA	XSI	3DS MAX
Raytrace Acceleration Options in mental ray and Host Applications	Acceleration [BSP | Large BSP | Grid]	Acceleration Method drop-down menu	BSP Tree Settings → Dynamic BSP checkbox[1]	Raytrace Acceleration → Method drop-down menu
	BSP depth	Bsp Depth	BSP Tree Settings → Max Depth	Depth
	BSP size	Bsp Size	BSP Tree Settings → Max Leaf Size	Size
	BSP shadow	Separate Shadow Bsp	Separate BSP for Shadow Objects check box	Unavailable
	BSP memory	Unavailable	BSP Tree Settings → Memory Limit	Unavailable
	Grid depth	Max Depth	Unavailable	Depth
	Grid resolution	Resolution	Unavailable	Resolution
	Grid size	Max Size	Unavailable	Size

[1] *Acceleration method in XSI defaults to BSP, and no Grid option is available. When Dynamic BSP is enabled, the large BSP acceleration algorithm is used.*

Grid Resolution

This value determines the 3D dimensions for the grid. If only one value is entered, it is used for the X, Y, and Z size of each voxel in the initial grid. Essentially, here lays the big difference between Grid and BSP: where BSP initiates with one voxel, subdividing where needed, Grid initiates with a grid of voxels based on the scene size in these dimensions. Host applications offer only one value, so by default it is not possible to provide three separate values unless you use a stand-alone renderer. A value of zero allows mental ray to compute a recommended scale during rendering.

Figure 5.25

Maya raytrace acceleration algorithms

Size (BSP and Grid)

Both algorithms have a size factor that controls the number of triangles to be used per voxel. If the triangle count has exceeded this size limit within a voxel, two additional voxels are created, provided the max depth supports additional voxels.

Increasing this size value can have the following effects:

- It increases the render times, as more triangles exist within each voxel.

- As fewer voxels need to be generated, less memory is required. Essentially, this means that on occasion you may consider increasing the size to lower memory usage and thus improve performance.

- By increasing the size, you lower the max leaf size, which represents the voxel that contains the most triangles. As cited earlier, the depth has priority, so some voxels may greatly exceed the max size value. Increasing the size helps lower that max value, distributing more triangles into other voxels, as you will see in the section "Diagnostic and BSP Fine-Tuning" later in this chapter.

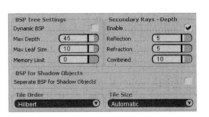

Figure 5.26

XSI raytrace acceleration found under the Optimization property tab

Decreasing this size value can have the following effects:

- The BSP tree grows in depth as it tries to accommodate the size factor, thus requiring more memory to store fewer triangles in more voxel leaf nodes.

- More voxels with fewer triangles also means fewer ray-triangle comparisons, which can boost render times and increase memory usage.

- The max leaf size can grow, so there may be a few voxels in dense areas of the scene that greatly exceed the max size value. This doesn't necessarily mean the render will slow down, since the value is low in most of the scene, but it is one of the values you will try to reduce, as demonstrated in the "Diagnostic and BSP Fine-Tuning" section.

Figure 5.27

3ds Max raytrace acceleration algorithms

Voxel Depth (BSP and Grid)

The depth represents the number of voxel subdivisions, for both BSP and Grid algorithms. As the depth factor scales up, more memory is required to hold these additional voxels. Each voxel needs to remember which triangle is placed within it, and with motion blur it also needs to remember which triangle is within it at a particular time interval through the motion-blur shutter open and close time. Thus in the case of motion blur, two or more voxels may be required to remember the same triangle that passes through it during the motion-blur time interval. The impact of motion blur on BSP statistics and tuning is further discussed in the "Diagnostic and BSP Fine-Tuning" section. Regardless of motion blur, higher values can accelerate render times provided the system has sufficient memory for the BSP tree. If the memory limit or the available memory on the system is exceeded, mental ray is forced to write data to disk, slowing down the render process. For resolving this problem, you can either decrease the depth factor or try using the Large BSP algorithm. Additional influences and considerations for setting the depth value are further discussed in the "Diagnostic and BSP Fine-Tuning" section.

Memory Limit (BSP)

The memory limit is used to prevent mental ray from exceeding a specific value in megabytes while recursively subdividing the scene. This essentially impacts the BSP depth as memory increases. The default value of zero results in no specific memory limits, which in most cases is fine. No memory limits also means that mental ray may use the max depth limit if applicable.

> The impact of too low a memory limit may unnecessarily force mental ray to start disk-swapping data, resulting in a very noticeable impact on render times.

Shadow BSP

As raytrace shadows also are evaluated using the BSP tree, a separate BSP tree can be evaluated for shadow rays. The shadow BSP enables mental ray to further optimize the render for evaluating shadow rays with fewer triangles because mental ray will create a BSP tree structure only for shadow-casting surfaces. This reduces significantly the number of triangles in each voxel and optimizes the number of triangles in the overall solution.

Diagnostic and BSP Fine-Tuning

When mental ray renders, if you set the translation output to info messages (verbose level 5; see Chapter 1, "Introduction to mental ray"), you will see useful fine-tuning information. Here is the output log for the BSP tree statistics:

```
RCI  0.3  info  :  main bsp tree statistics:
RCI  0.3  info  :  max depth         :  30
RCI  0.3  info  :  max leaf size     :  733
RCI  0.3  info  :  average depth     :  23
RCI  0.3  info  :  average leaf size :  22
RCI  0.3  info  :  leafnodes         :  14170
RCI  0.3  info  :  bsp size (Kb)     :  1192
```

Each of these outputs provides further insight into the current BSP optimization and its progress. Let's examine each of the messages, which are briefly described in Table 5.4.

LOGGED MESSAGE	DEFINITION
Max Depth	The maximum depth level that was reached during the render
Max Leaf Size	The maximum number of triangles contained within a voxel during the render
Average Depth	The average depth reach during the render
Average Leaf Size	The average number of triangles per leaf node
Leaf Nodes	The number of voxels used to store triangles; the higher the number, the more memory require
BSP Size (Kb)	The actual memory used for storing the BSP tree

Table 5.4

Raytrace Acceleration Output

The render was set with a BSP size of 25 and depth of 30, and as you see in the output log, Max Depth has reached the maximum allowable depth value. You can also see in Max Leaf Size that the densest leaf node contained 733 triangles, which is far greater than the limit specified with the BSP size setting. Average Depth (23) shows that in most cases, fewer voxels were created than the provided setting of 30. From Average Leaf Size (22), you can see that on average, fewer triangles where placed inside voxels. All together, 14,170 leaf nodes were created for this render.

Fine-Tuning BSP

Once you have retrieved the BSP message log, you can analyze the results and test some settings. There are many points to contemplate while choosing a good setting. In general, you don't want to have your leaf size set to a high value because it would defeat the purpose of optimizing raytracing. That is, if the leaf size is set to 100, it is likely that the max depth value you provided will never be reached. This means you're not taking advantage of that max value and you're forcing more ray-triangle comparisons within each leaf node. But suppose you set the leaf size to 1, provide a good depth value, and let mental ray do the rest. This too will be very inefficient because mental ray will put one triangle in each voxel until it reaches the max depth. Then, because they can not be further subdivided, the remaining triangles will be placed in those last leaf nodes, forming a dense collection of triangles in few voxels. This too would result in a very slow and inefficient rendering.

A good approach to optimizing BSP settings is usually to start with values from 10 to 20 for the leaf size and 30 to 40 for the depth size. Large scenes typically require more depth, so you may try 40 to 50 as a starting point in such cases. Tables 5.5 and 5.6 show the render values used for both BSP depth and size, the render time, and the resulting output statistics from mental ray. The numbers in the Settings Used column in Table 5.6 refer to the column headings (1, 2, 3, and so on) in Table 5.5.

Table 5.5

Render Statistics for The BSP Tree

OUTPUT STATISTICS	1	2	3	4	5	6
Max Depth	25	30	35	35	40	40
Max Leaf Size	4471	1873	961	961	531	531
Average Depth	21	26	31	31	34	32
Average Leaf size	35	16	9	12	8	13
Leaf Nodes	56,909	197,321	54,3578	375,138	860,342	330,054

Table 5.6

Render Settings Used and Render Times

SETTINGS USED	SIZE	DEPTH	RENDER TIME
1	15	25	1:23.09
2	10	30	33.14
3	10	35	29.66
4	15	35	30.59
5	10	40	30.36
6	20	40	31.69

For fine-tuning BSP, you will normally follow a trial-and-error process that requires applying specific settings, taking note of those settings, and re-rendering. After rendering has completed, take note of the info messages results (as seen earlier), including the render times. By comparing render times and the information from the info messages, you should be able to reach the optimal settings.

In Tables 5.5 and 5.6, you can see that depth has the most influence by comparing 1 and 2. Typically, low depth values have the greatest influence on render times. At some point, there will be a middle ground where render times will be relatively close, gradually increasing as seen with 2 through 6. You can learn more about BSP settings if you look at the first case (1). Notice that the average leaf size is greater than the size provided for the render. Clearly this means that mental ray was forced to, in most cases, exceed the size limit for the voxels. Normally, for the average leaf size you should aim for a value lower than the one you provided for size; thus, large average leaf sizes are some form of a warning sign. From the other tests, you can see that as the depth increases, fewer triangles exist in the max leaf size and more leaf-node voxels are created. In this case, the optimal setting would have been numbers 3 or 4.

> Note that resolution and anti-aliasing settings have no effect on BSP settings, so while testing, you should use lower settings to improve render times. You should also make sure scan-line rendering is disabled so you can get a worst-case scenario while fine-tuning the settings.

When you reach the point where an increase in depth results in slower render times, you may try either increasing the leaf size at a lower depth or reducing the depth size. The most important part for BSP fine-tuning is finding that point on both sides of the BSP render settings range where any change results in an increase in render time. Thus, there should always be some optimal setting that spans across a certain depth and leaf size that will provide for an optimal render time.

> Note that changing BSP settings have an impacts only render times and does not influence in any way the rendered image or its raytracing abilities.

Motion Blur BSP Settings

With motion blur, as cited earlier, a single triangle may pass through several voxels. This means that the scene, for the purpose of the BSP depth, actually has many more triangles. In this case, you may use different BSP settings to help deal with the increase in triangle count. Normally the approach is to reduce the depth, as increasing it will not help with the additional triangle count. Because the triangles may span several voxels in motion, it is inefficient to increase the voxel depth; it would never be able to resolve the triangle count, as voxels are not divided in time. In addition, the triangles exist only for a fraction of the time within each voxel, which makes it even harder to estimate the results. Thus, you should maintain a smaller voxel size, assuming the triangles are not always present in each voxel, for a given time within the motion-blur time interval.

XSI

For fine-tuning BSP with XSI, there is a fantastic script that allows you to select an increment for the depth setting, start frame, and number of frames to render. These settings are then used to run several consecutive renders. This script essentially allows you to specify the range you think may contain the best settings and then execute the script, maybe as an overnight render. The script executes these settings on top of your best-guess setting (the depth value you had initially set), recording the results so that when it has finished processing, it provides you with what it thinks will be the optimal settings. You can get the script from the following path: Net View → render → BSP tree Tuner v.(x). The script should open in your window as seen in Figure 5.28.

Because the BSP Tree tuner script is obtained online, its location or version may change, so it's best to let XSI find the URL.

Diagnostic BSP Rendering

In addition to running your own BSP test renders, there is a visual tool that can be used for diagnosing raytrace acceleration. the diagnostic options can be found in the same sections where the sample diagnostics examples discussed earlier are found (see Figures 5.11, 5.12, and 5.13). The following option can be used on the command line:

```
-diagnostic_bsp [depth|size]
```

And the options listed here can be used from within the host application:

APPLICATION	LABEL
Maya	Diagnostics → Diagnose Bsp → drop-down menu (Depth or Size)
XSI	Diagnostics → View BSP Tree drop-down menu (Depth or Size)
3ds Max	Diagnostics → Enable checkbox → BSP → drop-down menu (Depth or Size)

The diagnostic mode presents a color scheme that goes from blue (lowest depth) to green, yellow, orange, and red. The red sections represent the max depth level, meaning areas that reach the max level you provided. Typically you would like to see orange-red areas rather than a lot of red. Orange-red means those areas approach the max level, with some leaves at max. Solid red probably means you should either increase the size or provide a larger depth value. Both BSP Depth and Size indicate the scene status using the same color scheme; however, as depth also provides an indication for size, I find it the more useful diagnostic method.

Figure 5.28
XSI BSP Tree tuner script

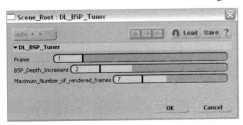

As you can see, these methods offer a means for visualizing the depth and leaf size within the scene using this color-coded system. In the Chapter 5 Color Images folder on the CD, the Diagnostic Color Coding image has BSP Depth selected as the diagnostic method. As you can see there, the scene is subdivided more in areas that have more triangles. This colorful diagnostic method can help you troubleshoot certain objects in the scene as well as find some good starting values for BSP testing. It is not an alternative to actually performing some test cases to make sure you are on the right track, as with the examples presented earlier in the section "Fine-Tuning BSP." If you are determined to avoid any raytrace BSP testing, you should at least run a few of these colorful diagnostic renders to help alert you to any really bad settings or a very problematic surface. Again, the impact of the right settings can become a matter of hours, not just seconds per frame!

In practice, you should rarely use high size values, and as cited earlier, good starting points range from 10 to 20. For depth, if the scene is very large you should try ranges from 30 to 50 as a starting point. For motion blur, reduce the depth size by 10 to 15 percent. While rendering, you can examine these settings in the diagnostic mode and then choose a few that you think will provide the best results and leave them as a batch render overnight for testing.

When you run BSP tests, to get a real indication for the render times you must disable the diagnostic modes. You cannot analyze the BSP statistics for render times while using this diagnostic method because the diagnostic render time is more representative of how long it took to preprocess the tree and provides output info on the render statistics. In such cases, the render times are not in any way a representative of real rendering times. For example, if you render two different depth values, such as 10 and 40, the preprocessing phase for the 40 may be a couple of seconds longer and result in a slower render. However, when you render in color you will find that the 40 may be 300 percent faster. Thus, the diagnostic modes are good for visual interpretation and reading the statistics for BSP settings.

## CHAPTER 6

Lights and Soft Shadows

This chapter introduces light shaders, area lights, and soft shadows. You will learn how the basic mental ray lighting models (infinite, point, and spot lights) are defined and how more-complex lighting models, including area lights, are enabled. Area lights allow for realistically simulating two significant light characteristics, *light wrapping* and *distance-based shadows*, to form realistic *soft shadows*. In this chapter you will learn how to control lights and raytrace shadows. In Chapter 7 you will learn more about raytrace shadow algorithms (optimization settings) and shadow mapping, and in Chapter 12, you will use area lights in practice, as well as other advanced indirect lighting techniques, to provide a more complete light solution.

In this book I assume you are familiar with basic direct lighting scenarios such as three-point lighting and the techniques for implementing lights within your host application. This chapter provides a solid understanding of mental ray light shaders and their implementation. It also looks at render considerations, especially with compute- and time-intensive features such as area lights to simulate realistic light characteristics. For an introduction to lighting techniques, I highly recommend *3D Lighting: History, Concepts, and Techniques* by Arnold Gallardo (Charles River Media, 2000).

The chapter covers the following topics:

■ **mental ray Lights**

■ **Area Lights**

■ **Host Application Settings**

■ **Light Profiles**

mental ray Lights

mental ray provides a basic light model through which you define various light types for direct illumination. There are four common light types: point, spot, infinite, and infinite-with-origin lights. If we look at a simple excerpt from an XSI light shader, you see the simplicity of this "initial" lighting model:

```
light "Light" = "soft_light" #applied light shader
        #base settings below
        origin 0 0 0
        direction 0 0 -1
        spread 0.866025
        #additonal (optional) settings for shadow maps and indirect
        #illumination below
        shadowmap on
        shadowmap resolution 512
        shadowmap softness 0.002
        shadowmap samples 20
        energy 7500 7500 7500
        exponent 2
        caustic photons 10000
        globillum photons 10000
    end light
```

Notice that we don't explicitly declare a light type. Instead, we define the type by declaring some combination of settings with the direction, origin, and spread options. For lights specified within your host application, some combination of these three options will be used to define a light model. In this example, because the host has declared all three options, mental ray knows the light is a spot light. For point lights, only origin is provided. If only direction is specified, it's an infinite light, and if both origin and direction are provided, then it's infinite with origin. The infinite light casts infinite parallel rays within a scene regardless of its placement, and infinite with origin is a directional light that has a "back" side relative to its origin, so light will not cast on objects that are positioned behind the light. (This type is not supported in all hosts.)

Light Shaders

The basic light model acts as a component shader so that complex lighting models can be achieved by combining different component shaders to add effects such as texture projection, light effects, and light profiles (used to simulate real-world light models). The common ground is that the base shading model selects one of four light types, and then additional options or light shaders are appended for specific light characteristics. For example, the excerpt in the preceding section created a spot light shader.

The basic light model handles five types of primary options:

- Basic light type options (defining the light type)
- Area light options
- Photon emission options
- Shadow maps
- An additional light shader through which other options are applied.

The base shading model excerpt in the preceding section used this statement: light "Light" = "soft light" to incorporate a spot light shader. Here is the definition of the soft light shader:

```
shader "soft_light" (
    "mode" 1,
    "color" 1 1 1 0,
    "intensity" 0.75,
    "shadow" on,
    "factor" 0.75,
    "atten" on,
    "start" 1,
    "stop" 100,
    "spread" 5,
    "use_color" off,
    "energy_factor" 0.75)
```

This is XSI's default light shader implementation, which is added with each light type (point, spot, and infinite), providing additional light options. You can see that this XSI shader provides more specific spot light settings, such as attenuation and cone radius, as well as a light color. Various different light shaders can be appended to the base light declaration through your host application, or by manually inserting them within .mi files.

As you can see, both the light's base declaration and the light shader (regardless of the host application) have settings for the light's falloff over distance, its spread, and its *penumbra* falloff. The spread option in the base shader excerpt is simply a definition of the light radius, providing the angle for projected light. Light shaders, in this case XSI, then add additional properties such as the cone property (found under the lights property editor in XSI) that defines the second inner radius (the light penumbra), providing a softer falloff along the outer cone radius. The factor option refers to shadow opacity, defining the shadow transparency while superimposing shadows (the umbra) over surface colors. All these and more are typical settings that can be achieved in any host application as seen under "Host Application Settings" later in this chapter).

When shadows are enabled through the light shaders, they default to raytrace shadows unless a shadow map is explicitly specified with the base model, as seen in the first excerpt. Specifying a shadow-map option tells mental ray not to use raytrace shadows. Thus, once shadows are turned "on" within the light shader, shadow-map options can then also be enabled.

Another important light characteristic is light decay over distance. Light in host applications may simulate no decay, linear, or inverse square falloff decay, typically applied using a light exponent falloff. With mental ray the exponent that describes a light's falloff is controlled in various ways by different light shaders, such as the mental ray spot, physical, photometric, and CIE D illuminant light shaders, to mention but a few. Typically, mental ray's basic light shaders use attenuation start and stop values to define the light's falloff range, and physically accurate light shaders, such as the physical light shader, use an inverse square falloff decay as with real light.

Most native Maya and 3ds max light types have corresponding mental ray shaders, so you can use them effectively; you can also connect alternative mental ray–specific light shaders, which are all declared through the host during the render translation.

All host applications provide controls for determining whether a light affects diffuse shading, specular shading, or both. This ability is especially important with lighting strategies and with indirect illumination, where you may want to affect only a single shading component, such as diffuse. One problem when using a complex lighting scenario involves multiple specular highlights on objects. By default, all these light types affect specularity, so when you add fill lights, you're adding additional highlights into the scene. This sort of "artifact" is one of the telltale signs of a poor lighting job because the objective of fill light is not to add highlights but to help define form. In any lighting scenario, consider which lights should affect both diffuse and specular and which should be diffuse only.

Umbra and Penumbra

The *penumbra* is the region where the *terminator line* divides light from shadow, as seen in image A in Figure 6.1. The light penumbra is the partially occluded light region, transitioning from fully occluded light (*umbra*) to un-occluded light. Penumbra transitions can be relatively smooth, both from the shadow's umbra to light and along the light's terminator line, as seen in image A in Figure 6.1.

With respect to shadows, area lights provide the benefit of simulating shadow falloff more realistically than shadow maps or plain-vanilla raytrace shadows, which create shadows that are either pixilated (a result of depth-map shadows), very sharp, or unrealistically blurred. In Figure 6.1 B, the shadow simulates some form of penumbra falloff using an area light's soft shadow.

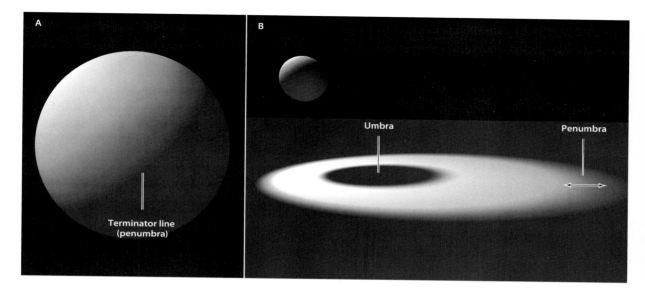

Figure 6.1

Defining umbra and penumbra regions

Area Lights

mental ray provides an additional set of options, which you can add to the base light shaders options to enable area lighting, discussed later in this chapter in the section "Area Light Settings." Area lights can be enabled regardless of the light type (which is also an "option"); however, the base light model should specify either a point or spot light type, and thus area lights should not be used with infinite light sources.

Let's first review some of the area light's illumination characteristics.

> Chapter 12, "Indirect Illumination," will discuss physically accurate lighting in detail and will look closely at using area lights for realistic light simulation.

Area Light Characteristics

Real-world light travels toward an illuminated point from various directions and of course from light sources of various sizes and shapes. The light source may be as large as an open window or as small as a lamp. When we apply lighting in CG, there is no real representation of the light's size or of light bounce (indirect illumination), which is why we need to apply several fill lights, compensating for the misrepresentation of a light's physical characteristics.

One of mental ray's advantages is its ability to apply area lighting instead of just light from infinitely small light sources. The concept behind area lights is to define a region that emits light from various points within it, similar to using an array of infinitely small lights.

With area lights, mental ray distributes several lights within the defined area light region, sampling their effect in the scene. We can control the number of lights that are randomly distributed along the width and height (U and V coordinates) of the area light region. The light region may take several forms, which may be either 3D (such as a sphere) or 2D (such as a flat rectangular shape). You will learn more about light-distribution options and shapes in the section "Area Light Settings" later in this chapter.

Figure 6.2 demonstrates the distribution of light from a light array (using infinitely small point lights) in comparison to an area light. For the area light (image B), an array of 3 × 3 (samples) lights has been provided, similar to the 3 × 3 light array over the same area shown in image A. Note that the white-bordered region and the circular shapes seen in image A only identify the point light locations and region using simple shapes with a constant shader. The standard point light array (A) doesn't provide any smooth interpolation between shadows, and shadows maintain focus through the chairs, forming sharp alternating stripes on the floor, a typical characteristic of plain-vanilla raytrace shadows, which don't diffuse over distance. Notice that in both cases, the coverage "shape" the shadows form is similar; it's similar because the light's spread behind the chairs is based on the effect of light emitted to that direction from a given angle and with a given size. So you can see that the point light array and the area light cover similar areas and cast similar shadow patterns. However, the area light (B) provides for two significant improvements: First, both the light and the shadows are softer because they are sampled in a much more effective way, providing a more aesthetic solution that re-creates natural light spread, unlike the sharp shadows seen in image A. Second, the diffused shadows also reduce the likelihood of flickering artifacts that might be caused by the shadows' sharp alternating lines, as seen in image A.

Figure 6.2

Area lights provide for simulating an array of lights from a given region to resemble a large light source. They utilize a more efficient sampling process than light arrays and provide more realistic results for both soft lighting and distance-based shadows.

The two primary advantageous of area lights are realistic light wrapping and distance-based shadows. Both of these advantages are made possible by the light's physical scale, unlike the standard infinitely small light models typically used with 3D CAD applications.

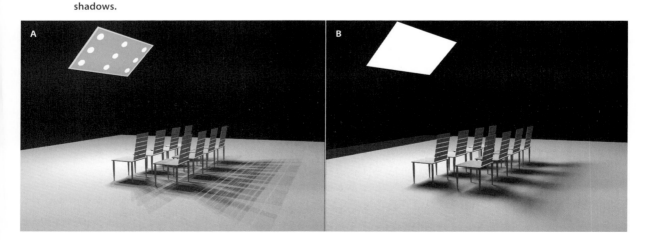

Light Wrapping

When light from a large area illuminates an object, it "wraps" around it, providing diffused soft lighting, which usually provides aesthetic high-quality lighting, far more realistic than the unsophisticated lighting of infinitely small source lights. Figure 6.3 shows why. With infinitely small source lights, the light "rays" travel from a given point only (A) rather than from a large region (as with B and C). Because we can define a region with area lights, we can then better simulate soft lighting that wraps around surfaces, illuminating what otherwise would fall into umbra regions and thus providing both softer lighting and shadows. As you can see, the rays from both corners of the area lights in B and C wrap around the cylinder based on the light's scale. You can conclude that a given point on a surface is influenced by several light rays cast from different emission points (from the area lights region), some of these rays may travel in an unhampered direct line, or alternatively pass occluding (shadow-casting) surfaces; others may even transmit through transparent (e.g. colorful glass) surfaces, and thus the total incoming light (*irradiance*) at a given point may be influenced by several different color-influencing factors, contributing to a more realistic rendering of light. We will refer to this figure in the following sections as we examine shadows.

Figure 6.4 illustrates the effect of a large area light when lighting a cylindrical shape. All the cylinder vertex normals are perpendicular to their faces, providing a faceted appearance so that you can easily recognize the gradation along the geometry surface. In image A, you can see the relationship between the area light's size (rectangular shape) and its effect on light wrapping. Notice how the area light illuminates the cylindrical shape past its midpoint (the terminator line), which with an infinite light would be the last point to receive light, as seen in image B1. Also notice in image A the shadows' diffused appearances,

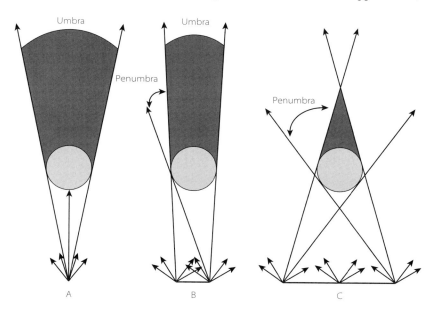

Figure 6.3

The effect of source light size. A is an infinitely small light source; B and C are two area light sources, which demonstrate light wrapping and distance-based shadows.

corresponding to Figure 6.3 C. Thus, as the area light scales up in size, more faces receive light, even those past the surface midpoint (aligned with the numbers), where the face normals are perpendicular to the light aim direction, as seen in the numbered examples in Figure 6.4 labeled B1 through 5, where each image is rendered with a larger area light source, making the cylinder more susceptible to light, wrapping illumination effects.

> In the image "indirect illumination effects" in the color section, you can see an example of soft light, demonstrating the advantages of area lights. As you can see there, the light has a nicer spread on the surface and feels more realistic than a more linear CG infinite light.

Figure 6.4

Area lights enable light to "wrap" around surfaces, even past their midpoint, which with standard lighting can be achieved only using fill lights.

Distance-Based Shadows

One of the more expensive tasks we face is softening a shadow's falloff, providing a more natural "soft shadow" look. Soft shadows can be accomplished in various ways, based on whether you choose shadow maps or raytrace shadows and whether you want to emphasize realism or just provide a "creative" shadow blur, such as with a Photoshop blur effect. The more you focus on realism, the more render-expensive the task becomes.

Figure 6.5 demonstrates render equivalents for Figure 6.3 A, B, and C. Image A demonstrates the typical plain-vanilla raytrace shadow, which solely provides a sharp shadow and lacks any penumbra definition, so only the umbra is present. If you increase the scale of the light, maintaining a relatively small source light compared to the illuminated object, the penumbra light falloff will begin to appear, and as the area light region scales up, the shadow umbra contracts, simulating distance-based shadow falloff. Thus the effect of *distance-based shadows* is the result of shadows that receive light rays from various directions, illuminating areas behind occluding objects (shadow areas) more accurately. Thus the effect is dependent on various directions of light, a direct result of the area lights scale.

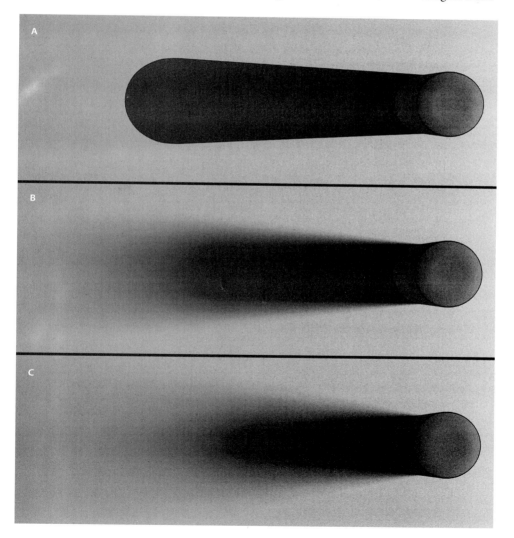

Figure 6.5

A comparison between different shadow methods for producing natural soft shadows: (A) basic raytrace shadow, (B) area light source smaller than the occluding object, (C) area light source larger than the occluding object

Notice that as a shadow falls farther away from the shadow-casting surface, the penumbra region (blur) increases, diffusing the shadow as light rays "reappear" behind the surface. However, when the light source size is infinitely small, as in A, the shadow falloff lacks the realism of light wrapping and soft shadows. Both B and C demonstrate distance-based falloff; in image C, an area light that is somewhat larger than the occluding surface is used, providing a different realistic appeal than with image B's smaller area light source. Similarly, you can see a completely diffused shadow, created by a very large area light source, in Figure 6.4 image A. The different area light sizes can then be used to apply more realistic lighting, as well as introduce different moods and hint at the scale of the light source, such as a flask light in comparison to a flood light.

As the source light is closer to the surface, the light's intensity is more powerful and the shadows are sharper. With lights farther from the surface, the lighting and shadows appears softer and more diffused, requiring more sampling to produce high-quality images.

Point and Spot Area Lights

As cited earlier, area lights are either spot or point light types. The result is very different with each light type. Point area lights typically are better for simulating long light sources (fluorescent lights), illuminating along a given distance, and spot area lights are better for simulating localized soft lights, such as halogen reflector lights, illuminating in a given direction. The term "long" refers solely to the area light shape scale, which can be scaled nonuniformly. With spot area lights, the light maintains the spot light's spread, appearing as a larger source light, such as a flood light, localized to a given area. Figure 6.6 demonstrates the differences between using long spot and point area lights (columns A and B, respectively). As you can see, the point area light (B) provides better lighting than the spot area light when a long light source is used. You can also see that the spot area light maintains the cone's angle, but "stretches" the light emission along the area light's shape (length), which is why it is better suited for uniformly scaled light sources than with a long stretched light. Notice how the shadows in the top figure of column B (point light) better resemble a fluorescent light's shadow characteristics, spreading light realistically behind the surfaces as expected from a fluorescent light. With the spot light, however, the shadow simply appears "enlarged," unnaturally stretched along the area light shape. Spot area lights project their shadows similar to the way light projectors do, mimicking a shadow from a large or distant uniform light source, as seen in column A. Clearly point lights are more efficient at simulating long area-light source shadows opposed to spot lights.

Figure 6.6

The effect of using a long area light with both spot and point light sources

Area Light Settings

Area lights are enabled by adding additional options within the light's declaration block in the .mi file. The following excerpt shows how a spot light is converted into an area light.

```
light "spotLightShape1"
    = "spotLightShape1:shader"
        origin 0. 0. 0.
        direction 0. 0. -1.
        spread 0.93

#the following 4 rows are the area light declarations
        rectangle 0 2 0    # shape type, U edge (coord)
                  2 0 0    # V edge (length xyz coordinate)
                  8 8 1 2 2 # sampling High, and Low
        Visible            # light visible in render
    end light
```

As you see, the area light options are added onto the main light shader, the base structure, and in this case, a spot light. The area light declaration specifies the three following options, as seen provided in the same order in the preceding lines of code:

```
[shape type] [shape dimensions] (*first two rows above)
[u, v sampling][use low level][u, v low sampling]
[visibility]
```

In the excerpt, the area light options use a rectangular area light shape (always centered on the light), with U and V lengths of 2 units determining the area light scale. Different area light shapes use different scale settings, as you'll see in the following section. In the excerpt, the five numbers that are identified as sampling settings (8 8 1 2 2) have a significant influence on both quality and render performance. In the following sections, you will learn how to use these settings, as well as examine their rendering characteristics.

> Note that in all these discussions on area light shadows, I refer solely to raytrace shadows. Shadow maps should not be used with area lights, even though you are "permitted" to enable them within host applications.

Area Light Shapes

There are six types of area light shapes, and as you'll see, not all of them are provided in each host application. They are listed in Table 6.1.

Area light shapes can simulate a multitude of light effects. Rectangular area lights can be used to fill in windows, simulating a large light spill into a room or long fluorescent lighting that casts light downward, such as in a store or parking lot. Disc-shaped lights can resemble large round projectors, or even strong flashlights that produce softer lighting. 2D shapes emit light 180° along the front side of the area light and can be seen with the sudden transitions from light to dark in the two top images in Figure 6.7.

Table 6.1
**Area Light Shape
Options**

SHAPE	SCALE	COMMENTS
Rectangle	U and V vectors	2D 180° light scatter
Disc	Aim vector, radius	2D 180° light scatter
Sphere	Radius	3D 360° light scatter
Cylinder	Axis vector, radius	3D 360° light scatter
Object	Derived from shape	Instanced shapes that may be used for light emission*
User	Derived from shader	Light shader that implement a geometric light shape for light emission*

Not implemented in any usable form within the host applications, and noted here only for completeness

Figure 6.7

Area light shapes influence light spread within the scene.

3D area light shapes provide for 360° of light emission, and so their entire surroundings will be illuminated. Typically, you would use the cylindrical shape to simulate neon lights, or other types of long light sources, and the sphere-shaped light to resemble omnidirectional lights. Both types are seen in the lower section of Figure 6.7 projecting light in all directions.

> Clearly the shape and scale of the area light (in 3D) has tremendous effect on both the visual results and the rendering performance.

Visibility

The Visible option enables the area light's shape to appear in the rendered image as a visible light source, as seen in the images in Figure 6.7. Regardless of whether the light source is visible to primary rays, it is seen in reflections, providing a nice "glowing" light effect based on the light's intensity. It can be seen reflected in various figures throughout this chapter.

Area Light Sampling

As you saw in the base light excerpt, five numerical values (8 8 1 2 2) are used for sampling, representing the following settings:

U, V sampling

Low level

U, V low sampling

U, V SAMPLING

Area lights use an internal mental ray algorithm to calculate the number of light sources randomly distributed within the area light region. The distribution density is based on the two first sampling values (8 8), which define a relationship between the light distribution within the area light's shape along the U and V coordinates—for example, the height and width for a rectangular area light shape. U, V sampling is then used to define the number of emission points mental ray calculates within the area light region, controlling the quality of the area lights' rendering, particularly with penumbra transitions. The lower the sampling value, the more artifacts tend to appear in the penumbra region for the light because fewer emission points are sampled. Figure 6.8 demonstrates the difference between high and low sample values. As you can see, the higher the values (image A), the more samples taken and the smoother the transition over the penumbra region, as opposed to low sampling used with image B.

> The area light shape has a significant effect on sampling values. When using 3D shapes, you should consider that the light distribution is 360° around the light shape and so requires sampling larger regions in the scene, producing much slower render times.

Figure 6.8

Light sampling enables you to improve the quality of the light along its penumbra transition and soft shadows. A shows higher sampling values, and B shows lower sampling values.

As you know, all types of shapes in 3D use 2D UV (texture space) coordinates for determining how a texture is mapped across their surface, as with NURBS surfaces. mental ray then defines the area light's emission distribution (density) by mapping the light distribution along the shapes' U and V coordinates. Area light shapes such as the rectangular or disk shapes are relatively uniform in scale, and so you may use uniform values for UV

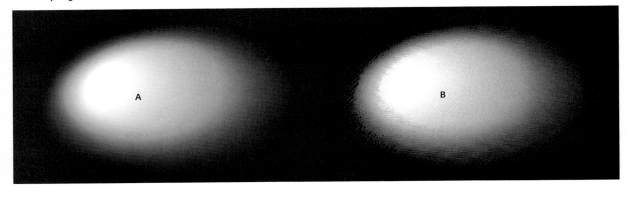

sampling values, distributing lights evenly along their uniform shapes. Spheres and cylinders, as you know, when unwrapped provide for a longer coordinate along the U axis, as seen in Figure 6.9. With mental ray area lights a sphere or cylinder shape U coordinate runs along the "equator," and when unwrapped into 2D texture space, it's significantly longer than the V coordinate, correlating to width versus height, respectively.

When dealing with non-uniform shapes, particularly after scaling (such as a rectangle or cylinder into a fluorescent light), you should consider using the same relative ratio for the area light sampling U and V values. For example, a rectangular area light that has been scaled to a width of 10 units and a height of 1 unit to provide a fluorescent light would use values such as 20 and 2 (U:V) or some compromise such as 15 and 4, which still provides more samples for the longer axis. In contrast, if a cylindrical shape is used for simulating long light sources, then the ratio might be more like 20 and 8, because the V coordinate wraps around 360°, requiring more rows of lights (8) to cover the entire U length. Note that as cited earlier, mental ray uses these numbers to derive a relationship and density; the actual number of light sources used is greater than the specified number.

Let's look at optimizing sampling when dealing with area lighting in either reflections or refractions.

LOW LEVEL AND LOW SAMPLING

Two additional sampling options, low level and low sampling, are enabled by adding their numerical representation into the sampling statement, as seen in the excerpt earlier with the three last numbers (1 2 2). These options are optional; if they are not specified, high sampling values (8 8 in the excerpt) are used for all area light sampling.

Low level is used only to enable low sampling, much like an on/off switch. When set to a nonzero value (1), low sampling is enabled. The low level value also selects the level of secondary rays that use low sampling values. For example, if set with a value of 3, then after 2 reflections or refractions, low sampling values will be used (instead of high sample values) from the third level of reflections (or refractions) and until that current ray stops bouncing (reflecting) in the scene. Low sampling is then used to define the area light sampling quality

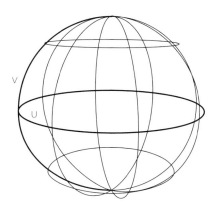
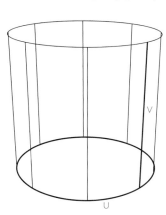

Figure 6.9

Sphere and cylindrical UV texture coordinates are non-uniform scales, requiring non-uniform light distribution relative to their scales.

as it appears in reflections or refractions. Providing lower sampling values can improve performance while rendering. Area lights, especially with very soft shadows, can be very time-consuming renders, but reflections or refractions do not need to maintain the same sampling integrity as direct lighting regions.

> Low sampling values should generally maintain a similar ratio as "high" sampling, using smaller values. However, nothing is set in stone; the final determination should be based on the visual results.

Figure 6.10 demonstrates the relationship between sampling and low-level sampling with reflections. Image A has low sampling disabled (low level is set to zero), and so the same sampling values were used for both the direct light and shadows and the reflected light and shadows. Images B and C have low sampling enabled (set to 1) and used a much lower low sampling value for optimizing the area light's appearance in reflections. As you can see, image B is a more direct 1:1 reflection, and so some artifacts (grainy shadows and light penumbra) appear in that image. However, in many cases the reflection is not applied in such a 1:1 relationship because the reflective surface may take any form. Image C shows a more practical case, where the 100 percent reflective sphere surface deforms the reflection and shrinks it into a smaller region. Note that the low sampling is sufficient for the sphere, effectively optimizing the render. More samples are used where needed (the direct light), and fewer are used for the reflected light.

Figure 6.10

The benefits of applying low sampling for rendering area lights in reflections or through refractions

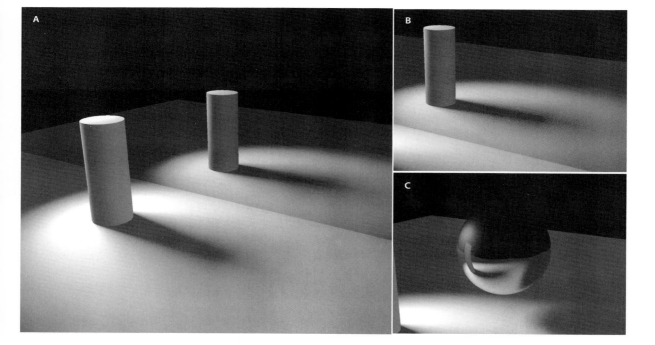

Remember that 3D doesn't really use mirror-like simulations to pick up reflections; rather, reflections are "additional images" generated by rendering ("looking") through the reflection's perspective, and thus lower sampling can significantly improve overall render times.

Host Application Settings

Now we can examine the host applications' general light settings for source lights, particularly area light settings. We'll use raytrace shadows because they are the only shadow type compatible with area lights. In Chapter 7, "Shadow Algorithms," you will learn about shadow maps. Of course, raytracing must be enabled in the global render settings, with appropriate reflection, refraction, and shadow limits for viewing raytrace characteristics.

The last section in this chapter provides insight into using light profiles with Maya and 3ds Max.

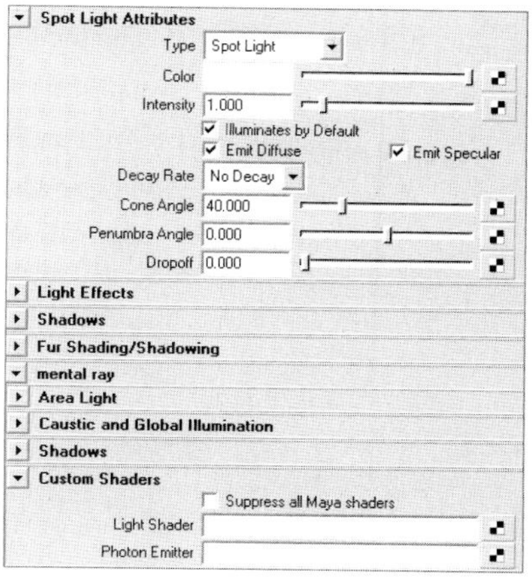

Maya

Maya provides a variety of light sources, all compatible with mental ray except for the volume light type. The point, spot, area, and directional light sources all have an additional mental ray rollout with mental ray–specific attributes, seen in the Attribute Editor in Figure 6.11. The "global" light settings are derived from the Spot Light Attributes rollout (similarly labeled with each light type), such as Color and Intensity, light falloff (Decay Rate), cone (Penumbra Angle), spread (Cone Angle), and so forth (based on the light type) also shown in Figure 6.11. Cone Angle and Penumbra Angle are only used with spot lights, and Decay Rate is not used with directional lights. In this chapter, we'll primarily focus on the mental ray Area Light, Custom Shaders, and Light Profile (available with point lights) rollout attributes and raytrace shadow casting.

Under the Custom Shaders rollout, the Light Shader attribute provides a means for mapping custom mental ray light shaders. You can map mental ray light shaders either by selecting the checkered box or by creating the shader in the Hypershade window and then dropping it over the empty mapping link. In the Hypershade window, under Create mental ray Nodes → MentalRay Lights, you can find several mental ray light shaders, listed in Figure 6.12.

Custom Light Shaders

Once you map the Light Shader attribute with a custom light shader, mental ray will determine which Maya light settings should be overridden by this shader during rendering. Some of these light shaders, such as mib_cie_d and mib_blackbody, provide the *Kelvin scale* for specifying *color temperature* and an additional scalar value to determine intensity (brightness). The mib_light_photometric shader allows you to specify light

Figure 6.11

Maya's spot light attributes, displaying the mental ray rollout for mental ray–specific light settings

Figure 6.12

In the Hypershade window, under the mental ray Nodes rollout, you can find various light shaders.

profiles; see the section, "Light Profiles," later in this chapter for more details on using light profiles with Maya. The mia_physicalsun shader is used for realistic light simulations with the mia_physicalsky lens shader and final gather, a topic further discussed in Chapter 13: "Final Gather and Ambient Occlusion".

The physical_light shader is used for simulating physically correct lighting models, and is primarily used with indirect illumination simulations that require accurate light evaluations. This shader imposes a realistic inverse square light falloff rate and raytrace shadows, without an option to change or disable these settings. Let's briefly review its attributes:

The Color attribute allows you to control light intensities using light energy specified as RGB color values. If you click on the Color attribute, the Color Chooser window opens and you can see that the RGB values are set by default to 1000. As with real-world *radiance*, light energy can be specified using values beyond the 0–1 range, providing a high dynamic range of light within the 3D environment.

The Cone attribute works only with mental ray spot and spot area lights, defining an additional inner cone angle. The result is similar to using the Cone Angle and Penumbra Angle (using a negative value) with Maya spot lights. A value of zero provides for a harsh penumbra, and a value of one provides for a smoother falloff.

Threshold defines a minimum illumination value, below this percentage light influence has no effect; it is not cast at all. You can use the Threshold attribute to control the light's influence region. By increasing its value you contract the light towards its brighter areas. Threshold is mostly intended for optimizing rendering; areas that receive very little light are cut out and will not be sampled..

The Cosine Exponent attribute is used only with mental ray area lights (rectangular or disc shapes) as a means for contracting the illumination area. For example, an area light aimed downwards in a room casts light on the walls from a given height, so that an increase in value will push the light influence downwards, providing for a narrower light region. In a way it's similar to Maya's Cone Angle attribute defining the general light region, but also changes the light ratio from bright to dark. In Figure 6.7, the two area lights (rectangular and disk) are attached to a physical light shader and the Cosine Exponent attribute was used to render a nicer falloff from the area light and outwards.

Most of these shaders' abilities can also be achieved through Maya's light shader, such as specifying an inverse square decay rate, as well as specifying high RGB color values for intensity, To better understand the character of light and the terms cited above, see Chapter 9: "The Fundamentals Of Light and Shading".

Shadows—General

Typically, with Maya you enable shadows under the light's Shadows → Depth Map Shadow Attributes or Raytrace Shadow Attributes. With raytrace shadows, the Shadows → Raytrace Shadow Attributes rollout, seen in Figure 6.13, enable both Maya and mental ray raytrace shadows regardless of the light type or whether its an area light or standard light. The Shadow Color attribute, as expected, enables you to apply a color value for the shadow. Shadow Color also sets the shadow umbra transparency value, and thus defines both transparency and color with shadows.

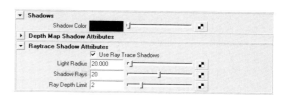

Figure 6.13

Maya's Shadows rollout enables mental ray raytrace shadows and shadow color control with all light types.

Raytrace Soft Shadows

Using the Raytrace Shadow Attributes rollout, you can simulate distance-based shadows. Increasing the Light Radius attribute provides a penumbra falloff for the shadows region, as seen in images B and C in Figure 6.5. This provides for a semirealistic shadow that simulates a real size light source for shadow casting only. Note that although the shadows appear to wrap around the object, the light itself will not exhibit any light wrapping effects, as discussed earlier under "Light Wrapping". As the Light Radius attribute increases, the penumbra's "blur" increases, requiring more samples to reduce visible grain, providing a higher-quality render. Additional samples are introduced through the Shadow Rays attribute; a value of 20 is usually a good sampling starting point.

Maya—Raytrace Shadow Limits

Ray Depth Limit is an extremely important attribute; it defines how many times a raytrace shadow may be seen in the scene. This value needs to be increased along with the Render Settings → mental ray → Raytracing → Shadow Trace Depth attribute, which is the same setting on a global level. It will not suffice to increase just one of these setting if the other remains low. Both settings deal solely with the visibility of raytrace shadows, defining the number of levels shadows appear on, penetrate through, or reflect on other surfaces.

Figure 6.14 illustrates Ray Depth Limit values. The two upper images (A and B) are of a transparent plane on top of an opaque plane, showing the effect on refractions, and the lower two (C and D) show reflections. For both images on the left side (A and C), the value of 1 was used, so only direct shadow light effects are visible. In the two images on the right (B and D), the value is increased to 2 for both Ray Depth Limit and Shadow Trace Depth (locally and globally), and we see the effect on both reflections and refractions. The increased value enables us to see the shadow through the refractive surface (B) and in the reflective surface (D).

Maya mental ray Area Light attributes

For area, point, or spot lights, the light's Attributes → mental ray → Area Light options offer mental ray–specific attributes for enabling area lighting, as seen in Figure 6.15 for a spot light.

Once the Area Light attribute check box is enabled, the current light functions as an area light. The Type attribute specifies the area light's geometric shape, which is immediately made visible in the viewport (centered on the light). Specifying the size for the light is then simply a matter of scaling the light in the viewport as you would with any other object, or you can enter numeric values into the Channel Box X , Y, and Z scale transform options (Z scale is applicable with 3D area light shapes only).

Figure 6.14

Maya shadows can be limited to penetrate or reflect *n* number of times based on the Shadow Trace Depth attribute: (A) refraction with Shadow Trace Depth = 1; (B) reflection with Shadow Trace Depth = 2. (C) reflection with Shadow Trace Depth = 1; (D) Refraction with Shadow Trace Depth = 2.

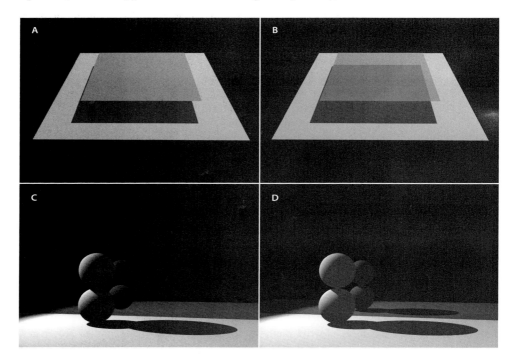

Although you may scale lights into any nonuniform shape, such as a flat sphere, mental ray will render using only the Light Shape types it supports. For example, the mental ray sphere shape uses a radius, thus the scale will export a radius value, rendering a uniform sphere, regardless of any nonuniform shape you may have defined. The same is true with a cylinder that takes a length and radius, so that nonuniform length is supported with a given radius.

Use the Visible check box to render the area light as a visible light source. High Sample Limit with a value of 1 (or greater) enables the Low Samples attribute. Both High Samples and Low Samples work as described in the section "Area Light Sampling" earlier in this chapter, where the first value represents the U sampling (length) and the second value represents the V sampling (height).

Figure 6.15

Maya mental ray area light attributes under the mental ray rollout → Area Light

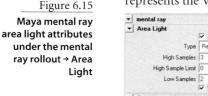

As of Maya 8, the Area Light rollout has been removed from point lights (unfortunately); instead, the Maya area light should be used. If you create a spot light and enable the mental ray area light attribute, you can then convert the light type to point light, maintaining the area light settings even though they are not visible. This workaround is primarily for "older" scenes that have been constructed with point area lights.

The Maya Area Light source light is not a real mental ray area light. Thus to avoid confusion, note that Maya's area light type (shape) is irrelevant (as an area light); however, when Area Light → Use Light Shape is enabled, the mental ray area light shape appears on top of Maya's area light shape (mental ray's shape always prevails). The settings are also a bit different, where for both High Samples and Low Samples only one numerical input is provided correlating to the U samples, as discussed earlier. Currently (Maya 8) the area light is exported using that value as n samples on U (only), and a default value of one for V samples regardless of your intentions. With Maya 8 and 8.5 (currently), when you save a scene and reload it the area light settings are reset (you loose your settings). You can download a corrective script from www.Highend3D.com; search for "area light" under Maya downloads.

XSI

All of XSI's light types are supported by mental ray. Their tight integration means that XSI provides many component base shaders, integrated into the light options and not as separate mental ray light shaders. XSI provides the three base light types: infinite, point, and spot. It also provides an additional two area lights, neon and light box, XSI also provides an additional option for creating a light rig, comprising several infinite lights that base their color intensities on image color values (HDR images are especially useful with this technique), also known as *image-based lighting* techniques.

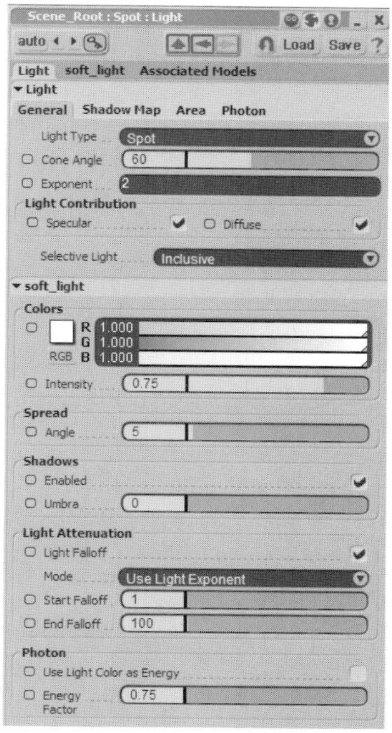

If you look at the light settings for any of these lights, such as the spot light in Figure 6.16, you see how XSI implements its default light shader. Under the Light rollout, four property tabs appear: General, Shadow Map, Area, and Photon. The common ground for all these tabs is that they are part of the base mental ray shader structure and not part of the light shader. Thus, all these top-level tabs are equivalent to the light shader settings seen in the base light excerpt earlier in this chapter under the "mental ray Lights" section. The soft_light properties rollout seen in Figure 6.16 is in fact the same light shader appended to the base light shader model, seen in the excerpt examples earlier—the default XSI light shader.

This chapter examines both the General and Area property tabs. The General tab provides the mental ray base shader settings for options such as origin, direction, and spread, which are defined by setting the Light Type option and selecting a Cone Angle value.

The Exponent option provides a "null" value that may be used by some mental ray shaders to determine light decay and, in this case, used by the standard soft light shader that is automatically created with each primitive light.

Figure 6.16

XSI base light settings and the soft light shader

Under the soft_light → Light Attenuation, the Light Falloff option enables you to control light decay either by using a linear or nonlinear decay rate. When Light Falloff is enabled the Mode → Use Light Exponent utilizes the Exponent option (under the General tab) to control light decay, a value of 2 represents inverse square falloff (recommended with physical simulation of light). If you set Mode → Linear then you can use the Start and End Falloff option values to set a specific linear falloff range.

The Soft Light Shader

The XSI soft light that appears within each light's hierarchy provides a combination of different light-specific settings, similar to mental ray component light shaders and shadow shaders (discussed in the next chapter). Under the soft_light → Shadows section, once Enabled is set, XSI will render shadows. By default shadows are raytraced unless shadow maps are explicitly specified; thus the Enabled option acts as a global on/off switch for shadows. Umbra allows you to specify a color value and transparency level for shadows. In addition to the default light shader, XSI also includes the physical sun and sky shaders (architectural library), which are further discussed in Chapter 13.

XSI Area Lights

XSI provides two "ready-made" area lights. The light box creates a rectangular area light, using a spot source light and a uniform height and length for the area light's (square) region. The neon light is an area light that also uses a rectangular shape, but scaled along the X (U) axis to mimic a "longer" source light. In other words, these two light types are point and spot lights with area lighting enabled.

For all lights, area lights are enabled under the Light → Area property tab, shown in Figure 6.17. Note that with infinite lights, this option doesn't actually function because mental ray doesn't support infinite area lights. As you can see, most of mental ray's area light options are available.

The Visible in Render option enables area light visibility, and the Geometry drop-down list provides the four standard shapes (not including user and object).

The Samples fields provides the U and V general sampling values (length and height respectively), as discussed earlier. Unfortunately, as this book is being written, low sampling has not been implemented. However, you can insert low sampling into an .mi file with stand-alone rendering. Low sampling is expected to become available in future releases.

The Scaling and Rotation X, Y, Z fields enable control over the shape. mental ray takes different settings for the different shapes. Sphere and Disc Geometry types use only the Scaling X to define radius. Cylinder uses both Scaling X and Y to define the scale along the axis and the radius. Rectangle uses Scaling X and Y to determine the rectangular shape. All four are visible in the viewport. Also, all four use all the rotation values to orient the area

Figure 6.17

XSI Area tab for enabling area lights

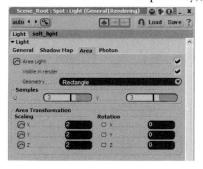

light shape; however, I recommend that you orient the "entire" light physically in the scene rather than through the rotation settings as they can provide unpredictable results.

> With XSI, when a light is selected, you can use the B hot key to enable modifying its properties visually within the scene, including properties such as the lights inner and outer cone spread (penumbra), as well as the area light size. The Tab key is used to toggle between the "live" settings that are modifiable. After creating a point or spot light primitive (with enabled area lighting), press the B key to enable this mode, and then press the Tab key to toggle to the area light modification mode. When the area light shape outline appears brighter (a bit thicker too), then by placing the cursor over the outline and pressing the left mouse button, you can visually adjust the area light scale in the viewport interactively.

3ds Max

3ds Max lights, both standard and photometric, are supported with mental ray, including daylight system lighting. However, not all their settings are used with mental ray. If you create any spot, point, or directional light and look at its settings in the Modify panel, you will see some mental ray rollouts alongside the 3ds Max rollouts, as in Figure 6.18 (bottom two rollouts).

Under the Spotlight Parameters (similarly labeled with omni and directional lights), the Hotspot/Beam and Falloff/Field options act as equivalents to mental ray's spread and cone options, respectively. Additional nice features are the cone types, Circle and Rectangular, which are supported. Overshoot is not supported. Directional lights act as "infinite lights with an origin," meaning that if a directional light is placed between two objects, only the lower surface will be lit.

Photometric Lights

It's a great advantage that mental ray supports all the photometric lights, including an implementation of mr sky and mr sun shaders (equivalent to the IES sun and sky shaders), which can be used with the daylight system and Final Gather to produce realistic lighting. The daylight system improves the approach to simulating particular lighting, and a particular time of day and location, as well as enables a high dynamic range of light (brightness). The daylight system utilizes the mr sun to mimic a strong key light (sun light) and the mr sky to mimic the environment that is typically used with image-based lighting techniques, a topic covered later in this book under Chapter 13, "Final Gather and Ambient Occlusion."

Essentially, photometric lights (regardless of the daylight system) provide extended settings for simulating natural and artificial direct lighting. All photometric lights obey the laws of physics, applying inverse square falloff, as well as dynamic range of light. Some of these photometric lights are very similar to custom mental ray light shaders, such as the CIE D illuminant light shader, enabling you to specify light color using *color temperature*

Figure 6.18

3ds Max lights have various settings, not all supported by mental ray.

Figure 6.19

3ds Max has a variety of photometric lights aimed at providing more real-world settings for defining light colors and intensity, all supported with mental ray.

based on the standardized *Kelvin scale* plus an intensity value for specifying brightness. The light energy (brightness) can even be specified using candelas units (*photometric luminance* units), as seen in Figure 6.19. From the Color drop-down list, you can choose from various standardized light models often used in the architectural market. Notice that D65White is selected in the figure, referring to a light color temperature of 6500 Kelvins, correlating to standardized white light. We will discuss lighting topics, including Kelvins, color temperature, and more in Chapter 9, "The Fundamentals of Light and Shading Models" 3ds Max's photometric lights also support light profiles, as with mental ray's photometric shader, a topic discussed at the end of this chapter.

mental ray Rollouts

3ds Max has four mental ray rollouts, two of which are seen in Figure 6.18. The mental ray Indirect Illumination rollout is discussed in Chapter 12: "Indirect Illumination." The mental ray Light Shader rollout (seen expanded in the bottom of the figure) enables you to map mental ray–specific light shaders. If you select Light Shader, the Material/Map Browser window will open, offering the standard mental ray spot, point, and infinite light shaders. You'll also find an ambient occlusion shader that provides a global (rather than per-object) occlusion effect for the entire scene. Occlusion techniques are covered in Chapter 13. If you map the Light Shader option with the occlusion shader (or any other shader), you can then view its settings in the Material Editor by selecting Get Material → Scene list and then selecting the light shader from the existing shader list.

Settings for the mental ray spot light shader (mapped to the Light Shader setting) can be seen in Figure 6.20, where you can easily identify all the settings we discussed earlier for light color, shadow, and shadow transparency, attenuation start and end, and an attenuation falloff multiplier. It's impractical to use these shaders rather than the 3ds Max lights unless you are using a custom shader that extends abilities already provided with 3ds Max lights. However, if you want to know more about mental ray shaders, this is one good way to become familiar with them.

> In the mental ray Light Shader rollout seen in Figure 6.18, the Enable check box must be enabled for the light shader to operate, an easy setting to miss.

mental ray Shadows

In the General Parameters → Shadows drop-down list you will find an additional mental ray tab, mental ray Shadow Maps, which is the only tab for controlling shadow maps with mental ray. Shadow maps are discussed in detail in Chapter 7, "Shadow Algorithms." For raytrace shadows, you select the Ray Traced Shadows option, which enables mental ray raytrace shadows and provides the additional Ray Traced Shadow Params rollout (seen in Figure 6.18) for controlling the shadow settings. The Color setting controls shadow color and transparency. A black color produces a fully opaque shadow, and white produces fully transparent. These raytrace shadows are used to enable both standard raytrace shadows (for non-area lights) and area lights alike.

mental ray Area Lights

3ds Max provides mental ray area lights as two additional standard light types: mr area spot and mr area omni found in the Modify panel → Create tab → Lights. The mr area spot provides only 2D flat area light shapes (disc and rectangle), and the mr area omni, provides 3D area light shapes (sphere and cylinder). Area lights are in fact only an additional light option, as discussed earlier, and so these 3ds Max area lights are exactly the same as the spot and omni standard lights, but with the added mental ray area light functionality. When other renderers are used, these lights still function as spot and omni lights, but without the (mental ray) area light functionality.

When you create one of the mental ray area lights (mr Area Omni or Spot), an additional rollout, Area Light Parameters, appears with mental ray's area light settings, as shown in Figure 6.21. When you press on either the Height or Width setting temporarily (holding down the left mouse button), an iconic display for the area light region appears around the light in the viewport, enabling you to visually tweak its size.

The On setting enables the area light, and Show Icon in Renderer enables the area light visibility, making the light source visible in the render. You select the area light shape from the Type drop-down list. The Radius setting or the Height and Width settings define the area light's size in the scene, depending on the shape. Samples provide the U (height) and V (length) sample settings, as discussed earlier in the section "Area Light Settings." The low sampling option is not currently available with 3ds Max.

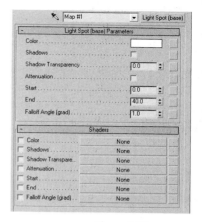

Figure 6.20

mental ray's spot light shader settings in the Material Editor window

Figure 6.21

3ds Max mental ray area light settings rollout for the mr spot light

Light Profiles

The mental ray photometric custom light shader supports adding realistic light models by means of light profiles known as Illuminating Engineering Society (IES) photometric files or Eulumdat profiles. Both are plain-text descriptions of light intensity and falloff, corresponding to various light types and light fixtures provided by light manufacturers. They are used to realistically simulate physically accurate lighting for architectural renderings or light simulations. Light fixture descriptions can mimic both direct and indirect light. *Indirect* in this context refers to light that is not aimed directly at the environment, meaning light fixtures that spread light, for example, upward onto a wall; the light then bounces around, providing the environment with softer lighting. Essentially these light profiles can then describe light models that in real-world terms are used as both direct and indirect light sources, some a combination of both, providing direct lighting as well as additional indirect lighting.

Thus, light profiles can represent the physical shape of complex lighting fixtures, not just a "lightbulb." They are in-fact another type of area light with an embedded light shape that defines direct or indirect lighting. The disadvantage is that the shadows are not affected by the light's shape, as they are with mental ray area lights, so shadows don't spread correctly and distance-based soft shadows aren't supported. You should not use area lights with light profiles; as both are area light sources and the two don't work well together.

Light profiles can only added to mental ray point lights and will only emit light in the angles and directions as defined by the light profile's description (emission and form). These profiles can then represent lights such as fluorescent, halogen and A-lights (incandescent lamp), to mention a few, as well as more complex light fixtures, light reflectors (reflectors focus light, as with spot lights), and flood lights, spreading light in specific directions and intensities, as seen in Figure 6.22 under label A (the Render window).

Light profile preview renders and plotted diagrams can be viewed in an IES Viewer. You can find one on the web if you search for IES viewers. Andrey Legotin has generously provided his viewer for free (seen in Figure 6.22), it may still be available under the following link (you need the installer to see rendered previews):

http://www.cgarena.com/freestuff/tutorials/max/ieslights/

You can see the viewer interface in Figure 6.22. When a profile is selected in the browser window, that profile is then plotted in the orthogonal diagram seen in Figure 6.22 under label B. Once it is selected, you can then click the render icon labeled C to view a render preview of the light scatter. In this case, you can see that the selected light scatters both direct and indirect light. Thus, these plotted lines illustrate the light scattering directions and decay. The inner dark line (red in the viewer) can be thought of as the attenuation start point, and the brighter outer line represents the falloff directionality and intensity, towards the attenuation end point. When rendering these lights with mental ray participating media effects, or just volume light effects (in 3ds Max) you will see a render that appears similar to the viewer's preview for a given profile.

Both figures 6.23- and 24 show the same image rendered using different light profiles, demonstrating both direct and indirect lighting. In Figure 6.22 the top row demonstrates an incandescent light, on the left you can see the plotted diagram and the rendered preview, then on the right you can see the result of rendering the profile with volume light in 3ds Max. The same has been done with a strong HD outdoor light that scatters in more directions, as seen in the lower row with the plot, preview render, and 3ds Max render. In Figure 6.23, on the right you can see light reflectors were used as well as indirect lights along the wall sides, and as you can see, light spreads upward from the point lights. On the left side of Figure 6.23, fluorescent direct lighting was used, and as you can see, the quality of light distribution differs between both images.

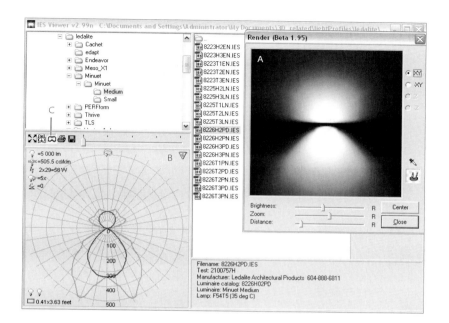

Figure 6.22

Andrey Legotin's IES viewer displaying the plotted orthogonal view and a rendered preview for a selected light profile IES file.

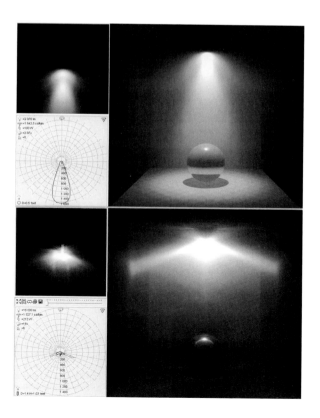

Figure 6.23

Two examples for light profiles, where each row uses a different light profile and shows the plotted diagram, the render preview and a 3ds Max render using volume light.

In figure 6.24 the room is still dark; thus for a full solution you would need to use either additional fill lights or indirect illumination, mimicking the light distribution more realistically. Also, when using light profiles, consider that they define light decay in real-world units, so the scene may need to be built in real size, matching the correct light distribution. When used for creative purposes only, it may not be necessary to match in scale because you can further tweak their intensity and falloff using the light shader settings.

You can download light profile files from light vendors over the Web, from these sites, for example:

```
www.lsi-industries.com/products.asp
www.lightolier.com/
www.lithonia.com/
```

I have provided a collection of light profiles for experimentation in a light profiles folder in the book's CD under a LightProfiles folder.

Light Profiles with Maya

With Maya, you can use the mental ray photometric shader as a light shader with a point light and then through that shader attach a light profile. Better yet, you can attach IES light profiles directly to the point light (only point lights) using the Light Profile attributes under the Light Profile rollout in the mental ray section of the light's Attribute Editor, as shown mapped in Figure 6.24.

Once the Light Profile attribute is mapped, a mental ray light profile node is created, as seen in Figure 6.25. This node enables you to load either IES or Eulumdat files, both representatives of light characteristics, as discussed earlier. More commonly you will obtain IES files over the Web.

Note that the point light's orientation becomes significant with light profiles because they represent the light's directionality. Once the light profile is attached, you can then enable raytrace shadows and use other common light settings to control the light's color and intensity. With light profiles, Maya's ability to create fake soft shadows using the shadows Radius attribute (discussed earlier), is extremely beneficial, as light profiles by default cast unrealistic sharp shadows.

Light Profiles with 3ds Max

With 3ds Max, you can use the photometric lights to attach light profiles. As cited earlier, you should not use photometric area lights (the free or target area lights) with a light profile, even though you can technically do so. Note that photometric area lights export as point lights, with the area light option enabled, as with the mental ray area light examples in this chapter. Thus you can use these area lights with mental ray, but without light profiles. You can control sampling from the Area Light Sampling rollout → Num. Samples, however this only provides U samples, and not V samples, as with the mental ray area lights.

To attach a light profile to a photometric light, after you create a photometric light (linear or point), in the Modify tab under the Intensity/Color/Distribution rollout → Distribution dropdown list, select the Web parameter as seen in Figure 6.27. When Web is enabled you can then load a profile from the Web Parameters rollout → Web File parameter button, seen mapped with a profile (95111702) in the figure.

In 3ds max, once a profile is attached to a photometric light, the lights physical geometric shape in the viewport changes shape to represent the scatter characteristics. This shape is derived from the outer line of the profile plot, as seen in the diagrams in figures 6.22 and 6.23. The shape helps estimate the light scatter direction and characteristics so that you can easily orient and aim the light in the scene.

Notice that the plotted lines seen in the orthogonal view in the IES viewer also provide information on the light intensity in photometric and radiometric terms. These units, for example luminous power (lumen), expressed as lm in the viewer (top entry depicted

Figure 6.25

Maya's point light provides this additional Light Profile mental ray rollout for mapping IES photometric files.

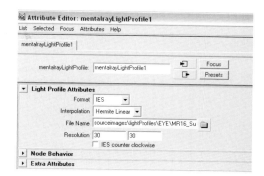

Figure 6.26

Maya's light profile node enables loading IES or Eulumdat files into either the mental ray photometric shader or the Maya's Light Profile attribute on point lights.

Figure 6.27

3ds Max photometric light parameters used to load light profiles.

with a light bulb icon), correlates to the same values seen in 3ds Max under the Intensity/ Color/Distribution rollout. Make sure to select the appropriate measuring technique as the lm radio button to compare with the luminous power, you should see the same value. Furthermore, you can use the Multiplier parameter to scale the light proportionally for the scene.

Under Atmospheres & Effects rollout you can enable the volume light effects. Doing so will help you visually see the scatter characteristics of the light, as well as, provides for much nicer renderings when using light profiles.

## CHAPTER 7

Shadow Algorithms

With 3D applications there are essentially two types of shadows: depth-based shadow map shadows and raytrace shadows. The focus of this chapter is on shadow maps and the algorithms that mental ray uses to calculate raytrace and shadow map shadows. In Chapter 6, "Lights and Soft Shadows," we looked at raytrace shadows with area lights, and in this chapter we'll focus primarily on shadow map techniques and algorithms. The host settings for both shadows and lights are very similar. As usual, we'll first review the underlying algorithms and then show how to implement them with mental ray command-line rendering and in the host applications. This chapter covers the following topics:

- Shadow Algorithms

- Raytrace Shadows

- Depth-Based Shadows

- Stand-Alone and Host Settings

Shadow Algorithms

mental ray provides both raytrace and depth-based methods for rendering shadows. The raytrace methods are offered at various levels of complexity, allowing us to realistically mimic distance-based shadow falloff and decay, as discussed in Chapter 6. For example, raytrace algorithms (*ray marching*) also allow for measuring the light influence on suspended particles in air (known as participating media), and raytrace shadows enable you to examine the effect of such participating media effects on shadowing, producing what are commonly referred to as *volumic shadows*. As always, raytrace algorithms can be more "render expensive" than depth-based algorithms, but they are more accurate, providing a great deal of realism while respecting the physical and atmospheric (participating media) effects on light and shadow.

Shadow maps, as the name suggests, provide a method for storing shadows within image files, known as a *shadow map files*, for the purpose of reusability. This technique is widely used in animated feature films. mental ray provides three shadow map algorithms: OpenGL shadow maps (which this chapter discusses only briefly), the shadow map (also known as fast shadows) algorithm, and a more advanced algorithm known as detail shadow maps (similar to deep shadows in Pixar's RenderMan). All shadow map algorithms offer optimization, although with some compromise in quality. For example, shadows are limited by the shadow map file's resolution. By contrast, raytrace shadows have no such dependencies.

Shadow Shaders

Several shaders influence a surface's color appearance, primarily the surface's illumination shading model (Phong, Blinn, etc.). Most mental ray illumination shading models provide a limited set of options that deal with ambient, diffuse, and specular shading components. Essentially, the surface's material shader calculates color properties for a given point in space (the sample location). This color evaluation is dependent on all of the connected component shaders that manifest that surface material (shading model). For example, aside from the illumination component shader, additional transparency, reflection, refraction, and shadow component shaders can be used to manipulate or contribute to the final color for each sampled point. While evaluating light influence on a surface, mental ray light shaders use the material's shadow shader to determine the shadow color and intensity. Thus the shadow value is not automatically derived from the illumination shading model (Phong, Blinn, etc.) or a transparency component shader as you might expect. Essentially, shadows other than default plain-vanilla (opaque) shadows are applied through component shadow shaders, providing very specific functionality. We discuss component shaders and color evaluations in more detail in Chapter 9, "The Fundamentals of Light and Shading Models."

Shadow shaders are not supported with shadow map shadows; however, they are supported with detail shadow maps and raytrace shadows, providing control over shadow color and intensity.

Fortunately, with host-specific shaders, host applications automate the shadow shader for you. Typically the shadow color and intensity is derived from the surface's shader transparency settings. Thus with a transparent surface the shadow intensity is derived from the host shader's transparency value. Furthermore, if you want specific shadow colors to appear (not just a gray shadow) you must also include color as part of the transparency value (or mapped texture). For example, while setting the transparency value within a color chooser window using HSV, if you set the hue to green (H), saturation (S) to 1 (100%), and value (V) to 0.5 (50% gray), you will render a semitransparent green shadow. Figures 7.1 and 7.2 demonstrate connections between component shaders and the material shader for a surface model in Maya and XSI, respectively. In both host applications, the same mental ray component shaders have been used. You can see that the shader trees are in fact identical in both cases. In both, a Phong component illumination shader is driven through the transparency component shader to enable transparency. The transparency shader is then connected to the material. An additional shadow shader can be seen connected to the shadow input, applying shadow transparency and color as shown in Figure 7.3.

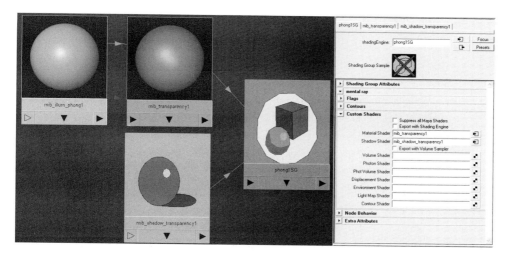

Figure 7.1

mental ray material and shadow shaders applied to a surface's shading group in Maya

Figure 7.3 illustrates a semitransparent green surface over a floor plane with a shadow-casting light from above. In image A there is no shadow shader, and the surface will render completely opaque regardless of its color and transparency values. Image B utilizes a shadow shader for specifying transparent intensity as a grayscale value; thus the shadow appears gray (transparent). The shadow shader used for image C applies both intensity and color, which means that the shadow has a green tint providing both color and transparency. The image is black-and-white here, but you can see the color version, "Shadow Shader Transparency and Color," in the Chapter 7 folder of the companion CD.

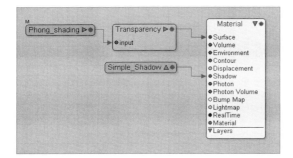

Figure 7.2

mental ray material and shadow shaders applied to a surface's material in XSI

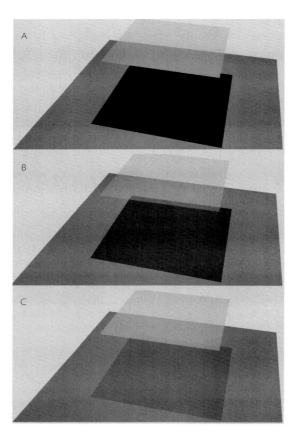

Figure 7.3

The effect of shadow shaders on shadow transparency and color value

mental ray Color Gallery

On the following pages, you will find images from film and commercial mental ray applications, along with examples of techniques described in this book. Some of these are more complete images created using certain techniques, such as indirect illumination and physical shaders, while others are purely color references for topics discussed in the chapters. These images are referenced and, in most cases, discussed further in the chapters. Each image also has a brief description of the techniques or effects demonstrated. In most cases, images that are references have more elaborate descriptions in their relevant chapter.

ABOVE: An example of mental ray motion blur. Here you can see how texture color and reflections are motion-blurred based on the rotational direction of the surface. **BELOW:** The water bottle was rendered with direct light, caustics, and Final Gather. You can see the HDR environment image reflected in the chrome sphere. Notice the caustic patterns that form on the wall.

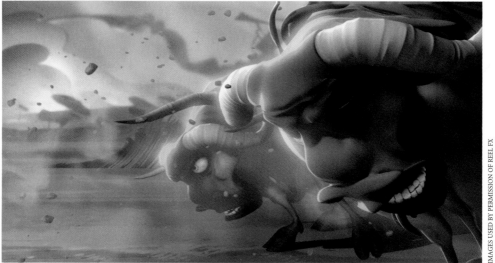

These are images from the Disney Pictures feature animated film *The Wild*; they were created at Reel FX using mental ray for rendering and Nuke for compositing. Reel FX created a theatrical dream sequence that is implemented in the film as a self-contained, highly creative piece.

These images were created and produced by Walsh Family Media LLC (WFM). WFM is dedicated to providing inspiring, fun-filled, and cutting-edge content through their characters, called the Cool Beans. If you are interested in the Cool Beans project, you can find information at www.thecoolbeansmovie.com and www.walshfamilymedia.com. The images shown on this page and on the opposite page above are concept renders from WFM's first feature film, entitled *The Cool Beans: Humbucket Caper*. The film is about two Cool Bean brothers finding the soul in music and life.

LEFT: Daddy Bean takes some time out to collect his thoughts and ride the tack. **RIGHT:** These two cute girls are called Kiss-Ups; they are a type of flower born to help people. Kiss-Up 1 and Kiss-Up 2 work for the Kernel, the biggest man in show business.

ABOVE: The Kernel takes a hot butter bath in his studio, Marigold Records, while the Kiss-Ups attend to his needs. This image was produced by Walsh Family Media LLC (WFM). **BELOW:** This is an image from Yorie Kumalasari's thesis animation short, *Grounded*, completed at CADA, NYU. It is truly a fantastic short about a bird who really wants to fly.

ABOVE: This is an image from Sameer Shah's thesis animation short, *Voyager*, presented at CADA, NYU. The project was rendered with mental ray as individual passes and composited with Shake. Some of the passes included participating media passes for atmospheric effects. **BELOW:** This is an image from Santosh Sailesh Gunaseelan's thesis animation short, *Metamorphosis*, which was completed at CADA, NYU. The project was rendered with mental ray as individual passes and composited with Shake.

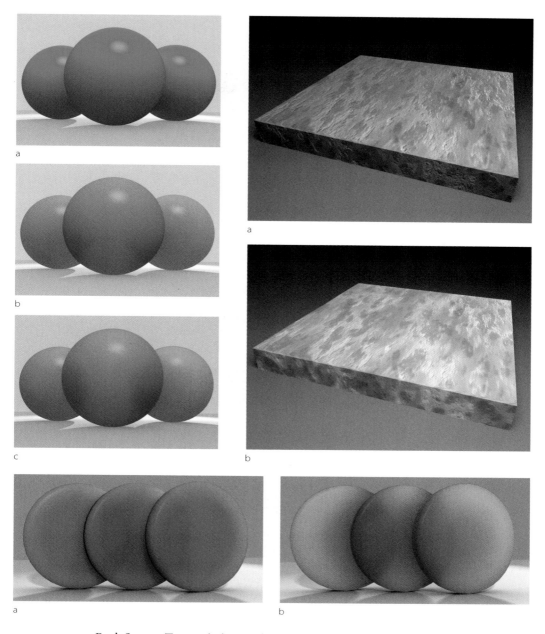

ABOVE LEFT: Back Scatter Transmission. In image a, the subsurface scatter depth is set to 10, in b to 50, and in c to 150. **ABOVE RIGHT:** Marble Subsurface Scattering (SSS) Plate. This is an example of subsurface scattering using the nonphysical shaders. Image a displays only external surface scattering, and image b shows the subsurface effect, providing a more natural appearance. **BELOW:** Subsurface Scale and Falloff. This is an example of scale conversion using the nonphysical subsurface shaders. The front scatter color is set to green, and the back scatter is set to red. The scale conversion factor changes from a value of 1 (a) to a value of 10 (b). As you can see, image b is brighter and more translucent.

a

b

Photon Counts: These images illustrate global illumination and participating media (PM). **IMAGE A**: A low photon count and a large radius (to remove artifacts). The result is flat lighting, and the color bleeding from the red wall appears to stretch further out, which is a result of using a large radius. You can also see some radius artifacts that appear as big spots on the wall behind the kitchen. In this image, only the lights in the living room cast photons. **IMAGE B**: Here the photon count and accuracy were significantly increased, and the radius was decreased. Also, the two stove lights have been set to cast photons. The detail has improved particularly near corners, and the color bleeding doesn't appear to stretch. In both images you can see PM effects near the window and over the stove, the room is defined as a transmat volume, and only the external light and stove lights are connected to the PM shader.

a

b

ABOVE: Photon Trace Limits. This color image supplements the discussion of photon trace limits. Increasing the global illumination trace limits from those used in image a to those in image b makes the photons bounce around (reflect) more and provide additional illumination and color bleeding. You can achieve a similar effect by using Final Gather rather than increasing the trace depth, which will also remove global illumination splotchy artifacts. **BELOW:** SSS Displacement Mapping. This is a reference for the discussion of displacement mapping with subsurface scattering. In the image, you can see displaced cylinder primitive shapes rendered with the nonphysical subsurface shader.

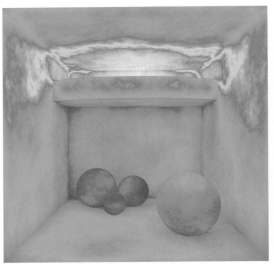

a   b

TOP LEFT: Stained Glass. This image illustrates the effects of caustics on shadows and color transmission. The transparent glass transmits its color onto the floor with caustics, the shadow is opaque, and the caustics contribute the irradiance and color effect on the floor. **TOP RIGHT**: Brushed Metal Plate. This is the rendered color plate for the brushed metal tutorial in Chapter 10. It shows anisotropic highlights and reflections that follow the metal's brushing direction. **BELOW**: Photon Density. Diagnosing photon renders using a color-coded image that represents the density of photons. You can see the denser areas in image a appear in red. In image b, you can see the effect of photon merging to reduce the density of close-proximity photons in the photon map.

a

b

ABOVE: Photon Shaders and Color Bleeding. The red wall and sphere are assigned the same photon shader as the green sphere, which is a green photon shader. Thus, they reflect green photons into the scene, which is not inline with their direct lighting illumination shader that renders them as red surfaces. See Chapter 12. **BELOW:** LDR versus HDR. This is a color reference for the Chapter 13 discussion of dynamic range. Image a shows the influence of Final Gather using a low dynamic range image; image b shows the effect using the high dynamic range version of the same background image. The lighting has more contrast and color influence in image b thanks to the high dynamic range.

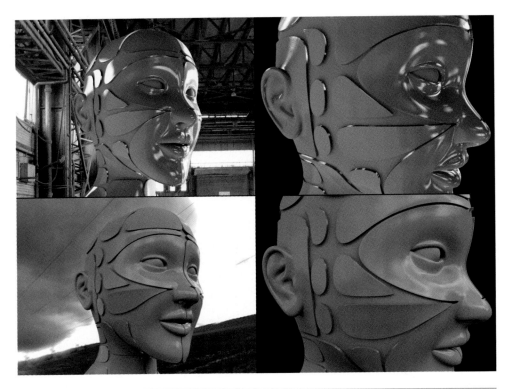

ABOVE: 2D HDR Color. These images show the differences provided by using environmental HDR images. Each row shows two perspectives using the same HDR image. The HDR images on this page are from real environments (photographed), whereas the plate above on the opposite page shows similar results using 3D generated HDR images. See Chapter 13.

BELOW: Sun and Sky Lighting. This is an example of a spherical HDR panoramic image generated using the mental ray architectural sun and sky shaders, discussed in Chapter 13. For clouds I used Maya fluids. The ground is cropped to save print space.

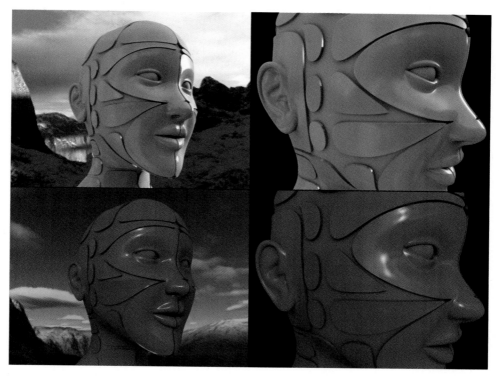

a

b

c

ABOVE: 3D HDR Color. Compare this with the 2D HDR Color image on the facing page. For these images I used environmental HDR images generated using the Terragen software from Planetside software. **BELOW**: Ambient Occlusion Environmental Sampling. The image demonstrates the effects of using the mental ray occlusion shader for environment sampling discussed in Chapter 13. The apples on the left and center use different HDR images where you see the different color influences from sampling an HDR environment. The apple on the right has a much lower spread value that provides a more specular (not as glossy) reflection appearance. The black is from the occlusion effect.

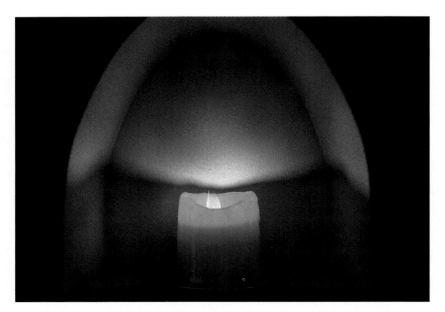

ABOVE: Candle Physical Subsurface Shader (SSS). An example of a physical subsurface shader, as discussed in Chapter 15. This image demonstrates the transmission of light through a candle. Notice that caustics transmit through the candle, inherit its color, and apply it to the walls below the candle top (indirect lighting). **BELOW:** Physical Lighting. This was rendered with global illumination, and Final Gather. In this image, photons are emitted from the light source in the room and from an area light outside the window. Final Gather is used to remove GI artifacts, improve the diffuse illumination, and capture luminance values from an external HDR environment image. I used physical shaders in all cases for consistency, as discussed in Chapter 12.

Glass Shark Comparisons: Above you can see the shark rendered with the dielectric shader, and below with the architectural material. In both cases caustics and participating media effects are enabled. The architectural material provides more control over glossy transmission such as with frosted glass. These comparisons are references for the discussions in Chapters 10 and 12.

ABOVE: Jade Physical (SSS). This is another example of a physical subsurface shader from Chapter 15. This one simulates the transmission of light through jade using caustics. For the counter I also used a physical shader, which is the architectural material. **BELOW:** Participating Media Effects. This image shows different source lights participating in illuminating the atmosphere. The entire scene is encompassed within a volume container applied with a participating media shader. The Maya ocean shader was used for the ocean. I rendered the components as independent passes and composited them in Nuke.

You've seen that for surfaces to render transparent color shadows, a shadow shader needs to be defined with its own color settings, and within host applications many materials automatically (behind the scenes) transfer material properties to shadow shaders. Again, the key point is that although a light casts the shadow and a surface material defines surface properties, the shadow information is provided through a separate shadow shader. The importance of shadow shaders will become more apparent as we examine different shadow methods and their ability to cope with color and transparency.

Raytrace Shadows

Raytrace shadows utilize different shadow algorithms (applied globally) that specify how shadows are evaluated behind the scenes. The three algorithms are Regular, Sort, and Segment. Raytrace shadows allow us to simulate a wide range of realistic shadow effects, and they support shadow shaders' transparency and color values, unlike shadow map shadows, which render only opaque shadows.

In the Chapter 6 procedures for area lights, you saw how to simulate realistic raytrace distance-based soft shadows. This section focuses on more technical differences between the three raytrace shadow algorithms, and how you choose an appropriate algorithm.

The Regular and Sort Shadow Algorithms

Both the Regular and Sort algorithms provide for basic raytrace shadowing needs and are sufficient for most cases. When a material requires a light shader to evaluate a shadow for a given point (using the shadow shader if present), rays are cast from the light shader to any intersecting polygons between the light and the shaded point, within that "light path." Thus, any existing polygons within that path are treated as occluding objects that may cast transparent or fully opaque shadows.

Figure 7.4 illustrates the similarities and differences between the Regular and Sort shadow ray algorithms. One ray points to surface A, a fully opaque surface, and the other to surface B, which is a semitransparent surface. The transparency can be seen in the resulting shadows on the floor and on surface C. With both the Regular and Sort algorithms, the rays are evaluated from the source light to the surface in question, as implied by the arrows' directionality. Also, in both cases, once a fully opaque shadow has been evaluated, the shadow evaluation process terminates. Thus, if 10 objects line up between the light and a surface, the moment one of those surfaces returns a fully opaque shadow value, the remaining surfaces are ignored and rendering may continue. If all the surfaces are transparent, then all the surfaces would contribute to the shadow, at least until those shadows cumulatively produce an opaque shadow, at which point the shadow evaluation terminates.

Figure 7.4

Regular and Sort shadow raytracing

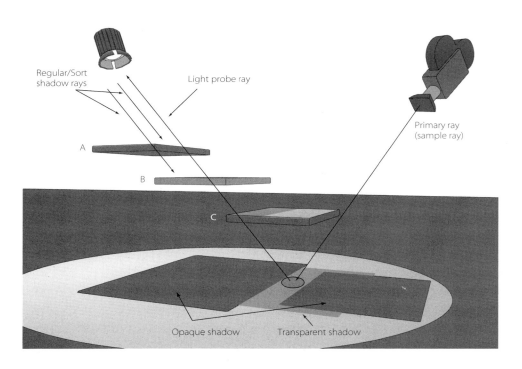

When a surfaces shadow evaluation commences, a *light probe ray* (seen in the figure) determines which lights in the scene may affect that point. Essentially, these probe rays ignore any occluding surfaces and are only a means for determining which lights are in a direct line of sight with the point in question. Once the Regular or Sort algorithm initiates for a given light, the light examines the polygons within its line of sight, one at a time. With repect to the Regular shadow algorithm and the rays seen cast to points A and B in the figure, any of these rays may be evaluated first regardless of the order in which the surfaces appear from the light. Thus, the ray that leads to surface B may evaluate first, resulting in a transparent shadow, which would lead to another shadow evaluation that may hit either one of the two remaining occluding surfaces (A or C). Obviously, as both are fully opaque, the next shadow ray would terminate the shadowing process, so in this case only one additional surface would be taken into account. Hence the Regular mode does not sort occluding polygons in any given order; it evaluates shadow values randomly until there are no more occluding polygons or the shadow is fully opaque, in both cases terminating the shadowing process.

The Sort shadow algorithm sorts all objects in order of appearance from the source light before initiating any shadow ray evaluations. Hence it will examine the surfaces in the correct order, which means that in the scenario in Figure 7.4, surface A is evaluated first. This surface is fully opaque, so the shadow ray terminates there without considering surfaces B or C. Sort is not commonly used within these host applications, because the sorted list it produces is required by very particular shaders that are not really part of any host application. Most shaders that require the Sort algorithm automatically override the global settings, enabling the Sort option.

> The Regular algorithm is the fastest for evaluating raytrace shadows because it does not require sorting all the surfaces into a particular order before evaluating the shadow rays, and thus should be used in most cases.

Because both methods provide information on the distance between a source light and a shadow-casting (occluding) surface, depth-fading volume effects are supported with raytrace shadows, accounting for the light decay over distance. This, however, does not account for the distances between occluding surfaces themselves (for example the distance between A and B in the figure). It accounts only for the distance from each surface (A, B, or C) to the source light. The Segment shadow algorithm provides that additional and valuable information, as discussed next.

The Segment Shadow Algorithm

The Segment shadow algorithm builds on the abilities of the previously discussed algorithms (Regular and Sort) by evaluating the distances between each occluding surface (polygon) within the light's path. This more complex shadow algorithm supports volumetric effects shadows such as through dust or smoke clouds. Figure 7.5 illustrates the segmented shadow process from a point on a surface to the light source, emitting a new ray at each intersection (occluding) point. The segmented shadow method provides that valuable information on the distance relationship between occluding points within the ray's path and how they will affect shadow values. Most importantly, these distance values can also be calculated for nonexistent (theoretical) points within volumetric containers, such as volume fur, light, or smoke effects. Essentially, the Segment shadow algorithm provides an ability to calculate the influence of suspended particles in air (dust or smoke) on shadows (from volumetric effects), an expensive but well-appreciated render ability.

Figure 7.6 demonstrates the differences when using Regular or Sort (A) and Segment (B) with a particle cloud. As you can see, only the Segment shadow method produces shadows on the surface and self-shadowing within the cloud. If there are no volumetric effects (i.e., volume fur, participating media, and particle effects) present in the scene, there is no need for this level of sophistication in evaluating shadows and it's better to use the Regular shadow algorithm.

> Physical shaders, such as the architectural material, deal with complex light transmission and absorption effects that benefit from the segmented mode; it supports simulating the influence of light absorption on shadows through a volume (surface).

Figure 7.5

**Segment shadow
raytracing**

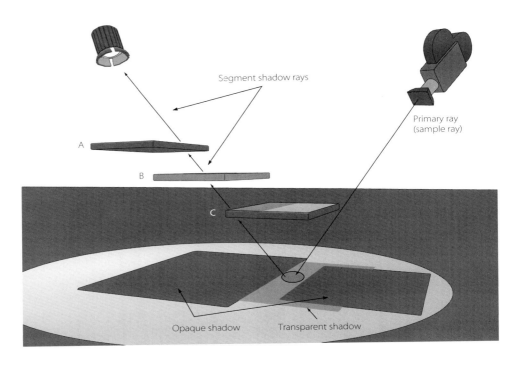

Segment shadow rays

Primary ray
(sample ray)

A

B

C

Opaque shadow   Transparent shadow

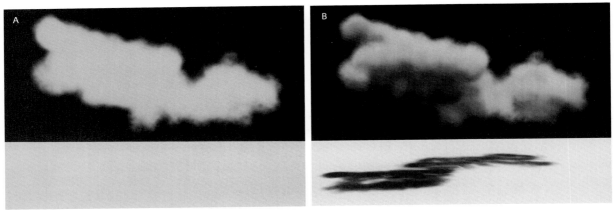

Figure 7.6

**(A) Regular (or Sort)
shadowing; (B) Seg-
ment shadowing.
Notice the self-shad-
owing in the particle
cloud as well as on
the surface.**

XSI

In XSI, particle effects have a Self-Shadowing property that is used for specifying volume shadowing, as illustrated in the lower portion of Figure 7.7. You can navigate to this property through the Explorer window for a given particle system by choosing ParticleOP → PType → Particle_Billboard. This option requires only that shadows are enabled; it does not depend on the shadow method used. XSI seems to use an internal mechanism to overwrite the shadow algorithm used whenever needed, so it is not essential to specify Segment or Regular. Essentially, this means that you can always use Regular and rely on XSI to switch to Segment when self-shadowing is enabled.

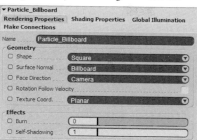

Figure 7.7

XSI has a Self-Shadowing property that enables inner volumetric shadowing between particles and with volumetric effects.

Depth-Based Shadows

As mentioned earlier, shadow map files can be saved on disk for reusability with static (nonchanging) shadows, such as with interior spaces. Reusing shadow maps requires mental ray only to load the shadow map files into memory, and if several maps exist, loading them can have a significant impact on memory and render performance. The larger the map files (image resolution) the slower the preprocessing phase and the more memory-intensive they become, as with high-resolution textures.

> The advantage of shadow map reusability can quickly become a disadvantage if there are several high-resolution shadow map files.

To optimize shadow map rendering, mental ray 3.4 and up supports rendering partial shadow maps, which is more efficient than loading shadow maps from disk because only the required segment is calculated rather than the entire shadow. Thus, when rendering without reusing shadow map files, mental ray will consider only the relevant shadowed areas and not evaluate an entire map. This eliminates the overhead of loading several maps of high resolutions or calculating shadows for the entire scene. Essentially, when a shadow map is stored on disk, the entire shadow will be evaluated before rendering can commence. For example, if there is a very large region in shadow, such as a coliseum with thousands of shadow-casting elements, and only two percent of that region is required for a given frame; calculating the shadowing effects for only two percent is more efficient than precalculating an enormous shadow map file or several files of very high resolution.

The following section first reviews the Shadow Map shadow algorithm, which is used by default when shadow maps are enabled. After reviewing shadow map concepts with the default algorithm, we will further explore the differences between this default algorithm and the more advanced Detail shadow maps algorithm, with a brief look at OpenGL shadows.

Shadow Map Shadows

Unlike raytraced shadows, *depth-based* shadows are based on a visual projection of the scene as seen from the light's perspective, as in Figure 7.8, similar to a Z-depth pass from a camera's perspective. Here, a grid of X×Y pixels (B) is used to record the scene from the light's perspective (A). Each pixel in the shadow map is responsible for recording several elements from within the scene, as seen through each pixel's line of sight. Thus the ability of a shadow map to properly define shadow boundaries in the scene is based on the amount of detail it can record within the shadow map file, and limited by the overall shadow map pixel resolution. Figure 7.9 shows a shadow map file; you see how grayscale color values depict the distance between the occluding surface and the light, where darker colors are closer to the light and brighter colors are farther away. Obviously, the more pixels that are present, the finer the detail is in the shadow map. Figure 7.9 is a high-resolution shadow map file, hence the smooth outline of the sphere's outer boundary.

Note that mental ray stores depth-based colors in the opposite order compared to other packages, where brighter colors are usually closer to the camera.

Figure 7.8

Resolution-dependent shadows are based on the resolution of the grid that is used to store the scene projection seen from the light's perspective.

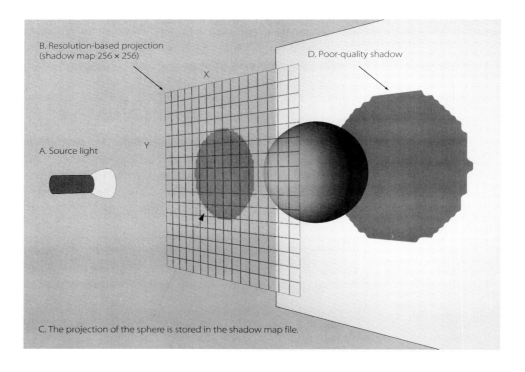

B. Resolution-based projection (shadow map 256 × 256)

X

D. Poor-quality shadow

A. Source light

Y

C. The projection of the sphere is stored in the shadow map file.

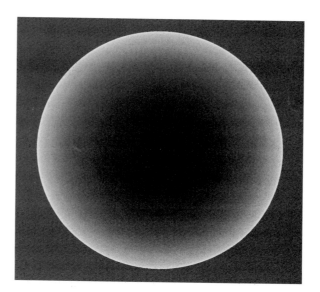

Figure 7.9

A high-resolution shadow map file demonstrates how distance from the light is stored as grayscale values seen from the light's perspective.

The shadow map file, also known as a *depth map*, is thus a prerender depth pass that is used to sample object distances from the light. Thus, for each shadow map pixel, the distance to the shadow-casting polygon closest to the light is recorded using a grayscale value as a measurement of distance.

Rendering Shadow Map Shadows

During rendering, when mental ray needs to decide if a point is in shadow, it compares the distance from that point to the shadow-casting light with the stored depth map distance for that point. Figure 7.10 shows both the distance to the light from the point in question (on the wall), referred to as distance B, and the distance from the closest light-occluding point (the sphere), referred to as distance A. Distance B is compared with distance A, the stored shadow map distance. Because the shadow map file never "saw" the wall, the stored value is representative of distance A, not distance B. When the renderer recognizes a difference in distance between the depth map value and its current evaluation, it knows whether that surface should receive a shadow or not. Clearly in this case, as distance A in the depth map is shorter then distance B, mental ray can conclude that a light-occluding (shadow-casting) polygon exists between the light and the point used to reference distance B, and thus that point is in shadow.

When comparisons produce the same distance values, a point can then be interpreted as either in shadow or not, typically causing self-shadowing artifacts.

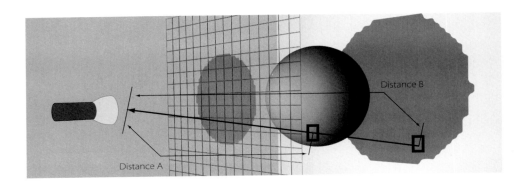

Because depth maps provide information only about distance between objects and shadow-casting lights, the camera has no way of identifying transparency or shadow color. Essentially, shadow map shadows always render as opaque shadows regardless of actual surface properties, merely validating the presence of occluding objects.

For fine-tuning depth-based shadows, increasing the resolution will usually not resolve poor shadow quality, flickering, self-shadowing, or other unwanted artifacts unless other optimization measurements are taken, such as blurring the shadow penumbra (see "Soft Shadow Maps" later in this chapter) or properly framing the shadow map projection, as discussed next. Optimizing shadow maps is not a step-by-step process you must follow because several factors influence shadow quality. Understanding the following topics will help you better approach and troubleshoot shadows in your scene.

Using Shadow Map Real Estate Effectively

You always need to have as much shadow map resolution "real estate" as possible. If you have one sphere covering a 32×32 pixel region in a 1024×1024 shadow map file, most of that map is wasted. In Figure 7.11, the sphere labeled A makes good use of the available pixel resolution in a high-resolution shadow map file, so the recorded pixel values provide reasonable detail along the sphere outline. If the same sphere were poorly framed, using only a smaller potion of that resolution (B), the high resolution would be essentially wasted. The sphere labeled C illustrates "zooming" in on sphere B, demonstrating the resulting shadow map with poor shadow map framing, where there is no way for properly reproducing the sphere's outline in shadows due to a lack in pixel coverage.

Clearly, proper coverage of surfaces in a resolution-based depth shadow is essential for productive results. Hence, increasing shadow map resolution may not always improve shadow quality if the current resolution is not properly utilized.

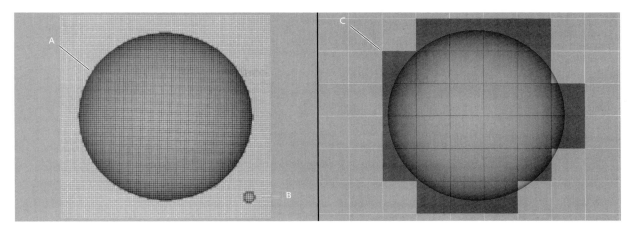

Figure 7.11

Shadow map framing is key to quality shadow maps, where "wasted" pixels (B and C) produce pixelated shadow maps.

Here are some considerations you should be aware of, as well as some recommendations you can use to optimize shadow map real estate:

First and foremost, spot lights by nature limit the visible angle of light and by doing so limit the angle used to capture the shadow projection. By contrast, point lights and infinite lights will consider a larger region. Point lights project shadow maps for each axis, and infinite lights see the entire scene from a given direction; thus they are forced to "condense" a large area into the given resolution.

Point lights require evaluating all six directions (positive and negative XYZ directions), while spot and infinite lights "look" only in one direction. This means that point lights are more expensive because six projections and shadow map files need to be calculated and written to disk. With respect to resolution, all six projections are "squeezed" into the provided resolution, so with point lights you may need higher resolutions. To clarify, if the resolution is set to 512×512 pixels, then that resolution is used collectively for all six projections, and not independently for each projection.

mental ray calculates shadow maps only for objects that have a shadow flag enabled, meaning only shadow-casting surfaces are framed within the shadow map file. In your host application, any object that is not meant to cast shadows should have its shadow flag disabled so that the shadow maps can focus only on shadow-casting objects. This is significant with point and infinite lights that "see" the entire environment within the shadow map file. Unless you reduce the number of objects that appear as shadow-casting surfaces, these lights are likely to produce poor-quality shadows regardless of the resolution specified. Limiting the shadow-casting surfaces to a specific region allows mental ray to do a better job at framing the shadow map around the shadow-casting objects only. Disabling shadows in host applications is achieved for a selected object as follows:

HOST	SHADOW-CASTING FLAGS
Maya	Shape attributes → Render Stats → Casts Shadows
XSI	[None] Under the object Visibility properties window, the Rendering tab → Shadow → Caster property
3ds Max	Right-click over geometry → Object Properties → Rendering Control → Cast Shadows

As an animated object moves from point A to point B, the distance between objects in the scene can gradually increase. For example, consider two objects that begin to move in opposite directions; as they get further away the distance between them grows. Also consider that during the time each frame is rendered, the same shadow map resolution is used, and as the objects get further away, they each have less resolution real estate within the shadow map file. The result is an animated shadow that gradually decreases in quality (with an increase in pixelated artifacts) until the shadow is completely useless. Possible solutions might be to enable raytrace shadows or to parent inverse shadow-casting light pairs to each object (discussed next). The latter means that a specific spot light field of view will be used regardless of the object's position, thus maintaining the same resolution real estate and quality over several frames.

Inverse shadow casting light pairs assure that a specific spot light field of view will be used regardless of the object's position, thus maintaining the same resolution real estate and quality over several frames.

With large scenes, it can become cumbersome to cover the entire scene range with one shadow map. Increasing the shadow resolution to a very high value is inefficient because the distribution of objects within that shadow file still remains inefficient. One workaround is to use several shadow-casting spot lights to localize the shadow maps, dividing the region into n shadow map files.

INVERSE LIGHTS

You probably don't want to cast light from all these additional points, but it is easy to use an inverse light to negate the contribution of direct illumination and maintain only shadow. That is, you create a shadow-casting spot light (at any intensity), and then duplicate that light in place and invert its intensity to a negative value. For example, the first spot light has an intensity of 0.8 with shadow casting enabled; the duplicated light will then have a −0.8 intensity and shadow casting disabled. Each pair of such lights will contribute only shadow to the scene because their illumination contributions cancel out. Note that their placement as well as their spread must be identical. When using this technique, you typically add the scene illumination from a "master" key light (or lights) that doesn't cast shadows and then use additional inverse light pairs to spread better-quality localized shadow map shadows around the scene.

Soft Shadow Maps

Figure 7.12 demonstrates the result of rendering with a low-resolution shadow map (A) vs. a high-resolution shadow map (B). In A, pixel artifacts appear along the sphere's edge, but in B we have a more finely detailed outline; however, you still see the pixel patterns.

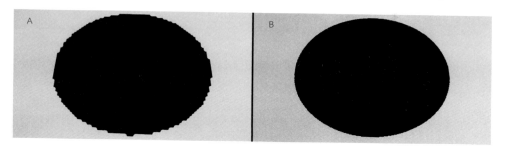

Figure 7.12

Low-resolution shadow maps vs. high-resolution shadow maps, where fewer pixel artifacts can be seen

Shadows appear more natural when they have a bit of softness. A softer shadow penumbra can help "blur" the pixelated artifacts caused particularly by low-resolution shadow maps. Ideally, if you apply some penumbra blur, you can get away with lower-resolution shadow maps, optimizing the use of memory by avoiding higher-resolution maps.

mental ray provides two options for fine-tuning the quality and amount of softness along the shadow map penumbra. These options are entered under the light declaration block in an .mi file and are as follows:

```
shadow map softness n
shadow map samples n
```

The softness option is used to set the size of the blur (in actuality, it's a filtering process) along a shadow's outline, forming a soft penumbra region. The samples option is then used to determine the quality of the blur. The higher the Samples value, the more time required for rendering the shadow. Figure 7.13 shows soft shadows that have been applied to the same shadow maps shown in Figure 7.12. Both shadows now appear acceptable. Note that Figure 7.13 Image A uses only a quarter of the shadow map resolution (256×256) that was used in image B (1024×1024). Notice that A appears far more blurred than B, because the artifacts along the low-resolution shadow map required more blurring (a higher softness value) to achieve an acceptable result. The impact of a higher softness value also requires that more samples be taken. Image A used over 40 samples and B used only 20; thus fewer samples were required to smooth out the smaller penumbra region seen in B. How do all these settings (including resolution) intertwine in optimizing shadow maps using soft shadows?

- With lower-resolution maps, a larger soft region is required to eliminate pixel artifacts, and thus more samples are also required.

Figure 7.13

**Low-resolution
shadow map soft
shadows vs. high-
resolution shadow
maps. Fewer arti-
facts are visible
when the shadow
penumbra region
appears blurred,
making the
low-resolution
version acceptable.**

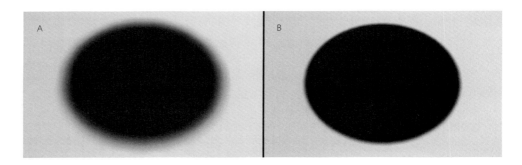

- Low-resolution maps can significantly improve memory handling (loading images into memory), especially when several shadow maps are used. However, they are more processor-intensive while calculating the softness (filtering). Thus the number of samples and the size of the penumbra blur can reduce render times when high values are used.

- Higher-resolution maps are more memory-intensive. However, they produce finer (thinner) soft shadow penumbras, using lower values with both softness and samples.

The decision should be based on balancing acceptable penumbra regions (without pixelation) as well as avoiding high sampling values when possible. Sampling values that are too high can slow down render performance. However, if several maps are used, then you should try keeping resolution as low as possible, especially when you consider that there are several other textures in the scene.

Even with very high-resolution shadow maps, pixel artifacts can still appear, and so a slight application of softness is always beneficial for achieving good results.

Woo and Bias Shadow Maps and Self-Shadowing

Our discussion of shadow maps so far has omitted the issue of how depth values are stored and of *self-shadowing* artifacts. mental ray provides two internal algorithms for storing depth values. They are referred to as the *Woo* and *Bias* algorithms, and they are available regardless of whether you use shadow map shadows, detail shadow maps, or OpenGL shadow maps (except that OpenGL doesn't support the Woo algorithm). The Woo algorithm is also commonly known as *mid-distance* shadow mapping, and is the default algorithm used unless the Bias algorithm is specifically specified.

Consider that mental ray as a renderer doesn't distinguish between surfaces, so in essence the shadow map provides information on shadowed polygons based on their distance from the light. Thus, a single flat surface that spans a large distance may store different depth values for points across its surface, based on the surface angle and distance with respect to the light, as seen in Figure 7.14.

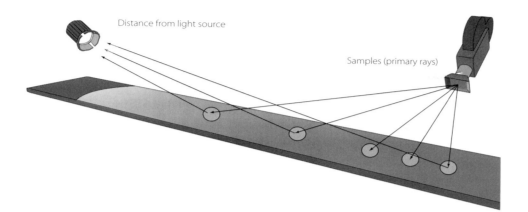

Figure 7.14

Depth values, distance from light, and surface angle

Notice that the camera is looking relatively directly at the surface. However, the shadow map will contain shifting depth values as the surface within the depth map gets farther away from the light. Figure 7.15 shows the same render with shadow maps enabled (using the Bias algorithm). Notice the faint banding along the surface. These are *self-shadowing* artifacts, caused by the comparison between several points that appear to have a gradual increase in distance from the light's perspective To clarify, since the shadow map is resolution dependent, a single pixel may contain depth values for several sampled points along the surface. Now consider that the closest point to the light is stored as the depth value. During the render, sampled points that are also represented by that same pixel (in the shadow map) will appear farther away from the light then the stored depth value. In such a case the renderer assumes that they fall in shadow, as a result of poor depth representation when using resolution dependent shadows. Increasing resolution may provide for a better result but is no means to resolving such artifacts.

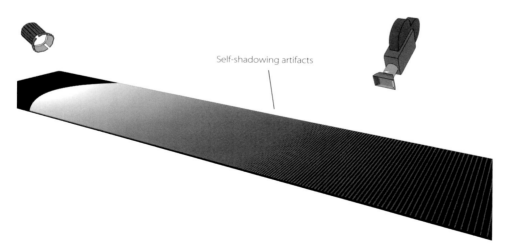

THE WOO ALGORITHM (DEFAULT ALGORITHM)

To avoid self-shadowing artifacts, the Woo algorithm simply stores the middle distance between two shadow-casting points that line up behind each other in the same line of sight for a given shadow map pixel. Figure 7.16 illustrates the middle distances on a sphere using three x, y, and z labels. Further, surfaces that have no other shadow-casting points behind them are stored as null values, meaning they won't have any representation in the depth map, such as the floor (even if its shadow-casting flag is enabled).

Figure 7.16

The Woo algorithm, also known as mid-distance shadow mapping, stores the middle distance between two shadow-casting points, preventing most self-shadowing artifacts.

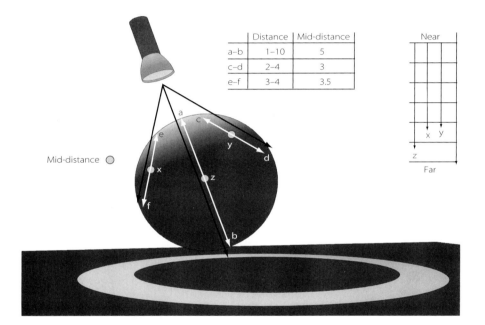

	Distance	Mid-distance
a–b	1–10	5
c–d	2–4	3
e–f	3–4	3.5

In Figure 7.16, points c and e are prone to self-shadowing as discussed earlier. However, if the stored depth value represents the mid-distance between a–b, c–d, and e–f, then those depth values essentially represent distances that are farther away from the light than the actual points a, c and e. To clarify, when the renderer samples points around the vicinity of c and e on the surface, those points that are represented by the same pixel in the depth map will be compared with the mid-distance depth values, and they will appear closer to the light then the stored depth values (x, y, and z). Thus, using mid-distance depth values prevents self shadowing artifacts because their depth representation will not place them farther away from the stored depth value. You can see that point a is closest to the light, but once its middle distance (z) is evaluated with the point that appears directly behind it (between a–b), its depth value changes from 1 to 5, as seen in the chart in the figure. Thus any sampled points in the vicinity of a will compare with a depth value of 5 instead of 1.

While comparing the distance between sampled points and the light, with the distance stored in the depth map, points that appear farther away from the light than the depth value fall into shadow.

In Figure 7.17 A, a Woo-based depth map image, you can see how the sphere gradually shifts from white to black. Remember, mental ray uses white for storing values farthest from the light, and black for points closest to the light. Essentially, this depth map is reversed from our expectations because of the Woo algorithm's mid-distance values. Thus, there is no chance that any of these points leading to the sphere's outer edge would self-shadow because these depth values place them farther from the light than their actual positions. In Figure 7.17 B, you can see the result of storing several objects as well as a floor (which is not present in the depth map because it is the last shadow-casting surface). Notice how each sphere appears uniform in color, all sharing similar mid-distance values that are aligned with respect to distance from the camera. You can conclude, then, that when surfaces occupy smaller portions in the depth map (meaning that a smaller angle of view from the light's perspective is required for framing those objects), it is more likely they will share similar mid-distance values and appear as uniform colors, unlike the gradation that is apparent in image A. Fortunately, none of these surfaces would self-shadow, also they are properly distinguished from each other so that one surface may cast a shadow on the following surface.

As the mid-distance values between two polygons in the same line of sight are stored, each sphere stores the mid-distance between its front side polygons and back side polygons. Thus, each sphere appears independent of the other spheres and the correct color scheme is visible where dark colors place the front-most sphere closer to the light. The advantage of the Woo method, then, is that distances are exaggerated so that two points on the same surface will not self-shadow, but they will shadow on a surface that appears farther away from their mid-distance point.

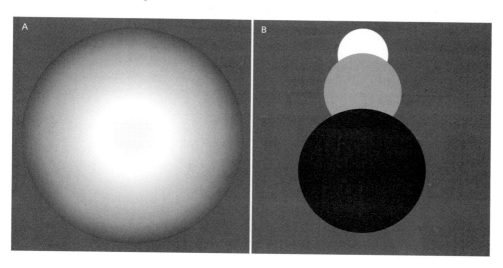

Figure 7.17

Two depth maps using the Woo algorithm

Problems arise, however, when the mid-distance between two surfaces that line up under the same pixel space appears as a shorter distance than that of neighboring points along the top surface. For example, in Figure 7.15, the long floor surface can easily become a problem if two such surfaces exist in very close proximity and both are shadow-casting surfaces. Figure 7.18 illustrates the problem where the distance a represents the middle distance between the top and bottom surfaces, which is stored in the shadow map when the point numbered 1 is sampled from the lights perspective. The depth map pixel indicates that the three sample points (1–3) use the same depth value (same pixel) for evaluating their distance from the light. Notice that the distance between the sampled points is greater than the distance a, which a appears to repeat several times. In this case points 2 and 3 will fall into shadow. The result will be that after a given point, self-shadowing artifacts appear because the mid-distance between both surfaces is shorter then the distances between points on the surface that gradually get farther away from the light. Clearly a lot of long flat surfaces in close proximity to each other, with varying distances from the light are prone to self-shadowing artifacts. In such cases, the Woo algorithm "breaks" and you can try using the Bias algorithm as an alternative.

Figure 7.18

The middle distance between two surfaces, when too low, can cause self-shadowing artifacts.

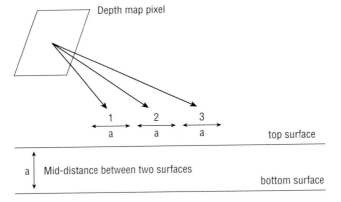

THE BIAS ALGORITHM

The Bias algorithm provides you with a means of defining the depth offset rather than automating it based on the mid-distance value. mental ray's Bias option takes numerical values that are added to the current depth value, so if a depth of n is evaluated for given point, the new depth will be $n + bias$. For example, if the depth is 1.3 for a given point and the bias is set to 0.1, then the new depth will be 1.4. Adding these values eliminates the chances of self-shadowing because the point in question will appear closer to the light than its stored depth value and thus provides for an adequate solution. On the flip side, wrong bias values can lead to either banding or moiré patterns caused by self-shadowing. Figure 7.19 shows an image packed with artifacts caused by Bias values that are too low. Notice that although the light is from above, the entire sphere appears in shadow because each point falls into shadow.

Figure 7.19

Bias values are harder to fine-tune, and poor value selections can lead to a multitude of shadow artifacts.

Figure 7.20 shows the same depth maps seen earlier for the Woo algorithm (Figure 7.17), but in this case the Bias algorithm is used. In A you can see depth values that more accurately mimic what you might expect to see in depth maps, representing the real distances from the light as points on the sphere gradually recede from dark to brighter values. This is a more predictable result than with the Woo algorithm. In B you can see that the floor is in fact included, unlike with the Woo algorithm that stores it as a null value (because it's the last shadow-casting surface). On the other hand, you can tell that there is fine gradation in the depth values across all the surfaces, which can lead to self-shadowing artifacts because these depth values don't clearly place those points farther from the light (as the Woo algorithm does). The Bias value is then added to each of these depth values during rendering to place them at a safe distance from the light without compromising shadowing.

Assume that the distance between shadow-casting point A and shadow-receiving point B is n units. When specifying Bias values, you want to select a value that is smaller than that n distance, the distance between two objects in the scene. Thus the bias value should remain lower than the shortest shadow-casting distance between a shadow-casting and -receiving point in the scene. If the bias is larger than that distance, the shadow-receiving point will not receive shadow, and if the bias is too short a distance, self-shadowing artifacts will appear.

Figure 7.20

Bias depth maps are more predictable in their visual appearance; they place objects at their "real" distances more accurately and by doing so are more prone to artifacts.

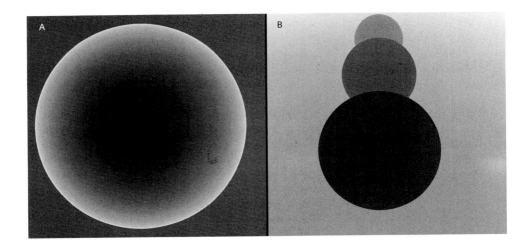

Detail Shadow Maps

Detail shadow maps use a more advanced algorithm, which supports some nice improvements over regular shadow maps. Detail shadows accept shadow shaders and thus can determine color and transparency by recording additional data, such as the alpha and color values along a specific "light-ray," with the depth map. As noted earlier, the default shadow map algorithm provides only for plain-vanilla opaque shadows, as shown in Figure 7.21, image A. In Figure 7.21, image B, you can see that detail shadow maps respect both color and transparency (you'll need to look on the CD to see the color version, "Detail Shadow Map Color").

With motion-blurred shadows, shadow maps outline only the blurred region, producing a "smudged" shadow effect. Figure 7.22 shows the differences between regular shadow maps and Detail shadows, where the shadow map (A) appears opaque, stretching along the motion blur distance and the Detail shadow map (B) appears to respect both color and motion blur transparency (you can see the color version, "Detail Shadow Map Motion Blur," on the CD). The ability to respect shadow shaders is a typical raytrace feature, available with this more robust depth-based shadow algorithm. When combined with the rasterizer, you can save a lot of render time while optimizing motion-blur rendering, as discussed in Chapter 8 "Motion Blur."

Figure 7.21

Characteristics of shadow maps and Detail shadow maps compared for transparency and color

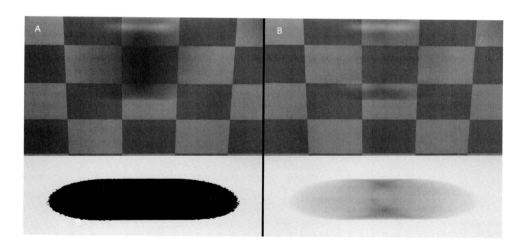

Figure 7.22

Shadow maps and Detail shadow maps compared for motion blur shadows

Detail Shadow Sampling

The Detail shadow map algorithm also allows supersampling on a per-pixel level (for depth map pixels), providing a good alternative to raytracing shadows. When enabled, two additional mental ray options are available (under the light block in the .mi file):

```
shadowmap detail samples n
Shadowmap accuracy n
```

The samples option enables you to increase the per-pixel sampling for each pixel in the depth projection, which provides for much better results because samples are averaged to produce more precise color values per pixel. The accuracy option controls a depth offset value by determining when additional depth values should be taken into account. After a sample has been taken for a given depth, the accuracy value is used to determine the minimum difference between this depth value and the next depth value that can be taken into account.

Figure 7.23 shows two rendered samples where the accuracy value increases and so does the base distance between the surface and the shadow. Accuracy is meant to help optimize render performance where samples are taken in an efficient manner, not offsetting the shadow from its position. Too low a value will cause mental ray to spend more time evaluating evaluating per-pixel samples, and too high a value will end up pushing the shadow away, as seen in Figure 7.23. If an accuracy value is set to zero, mental ray will evaluate a "best guess" value, which should suffice until you feel more comfortable with these settings .

Figure 7.23

With detail shadow maps, the accuracy value is used to limit the number of points sampled for the shadow by a set depth factor. Too high a value will cause artifacts such as shadows to move out of place.

The Detail algorithm does not produce reusable shadow map files. Detail shadows calculate only the required region on a per-tile basis, storing those values in the shadow map file on the fly. As rendering progresses, more tiles fill in the shadow map file, even through consecutive frames, so essentially this method should not be used with a stored shadow map file. Remember that with stored shadow maps, the entire shadow is first evaluated, which defeats the purpose of using this algorithm. Further, you cannot view these maps as with regular shadow maps in an image viewer, and detail shadow maps are not compatible with regular shadow maps and vice versa.

OpenGL Accelerated Shadows

OpenGL shadow maps allow hardware to calculate the shadow maps extremely fast, limited only by the hardware's abilities. There is not much to say about OpenGL shadows except that the technique is very similar to scanline OpenGL acceleration; it rapidly compiles the depth projection. See Chapter 2, "Rendering Algorithms," for more information on hardware implementations.

Because mental ray supports rendering partial shadow maps, it may require fewer shadow map calculations. With OpenGL shadow maps, partial shadow maps are not supported. This means that rendering OpenGL shadow maps is less desirable because they would consider an entire depth shadow rather than a partial shadow. A further limitation is that OpenGL shadow maps have no notion of objects in the scene; as discussed in Chapter 2, hardware deals with one triangle at a time, filling in the frame buffer. The result is that only Bias shadow maps are supported, which, as cited earlier, require careful fine-tuning.

Stand-Alone and Host Settings

For each host application, there are both global and local options for setting shadow methods. Typically, at the global level you may set whether raytrace or shadow maps are enabled, and on the local level you can specify which (per light) method is used. Both shadow maps and raytrace shadows can be applied using different light sources. As cited in Chapter 6, mental ray defaults to raytrace shadows with a shadow on statement under the light shader unless a shadow map statement is provided for that light shader. In any case, with raytrace shadows, you must choose one of three algorithms—Regular, Sort, or Segment—as a global setting, not local, just as a BSP tree is a global raytrace acceleration algorithm for the entire scene.

Let's identify both raytrace and depth-based shadow options within host applications, on both global and local levels.

Global Settings

In host applications, the global render settings, seen in Figures 7.24, 7.25, and 7.26, can be found in the following paths:

HOST	GLOBAL SETTINGS PATH
Maya	Render Settings window → mental ray tab → Shadows
XSI	Render Options window → Shadows tab
3ds Max	Render Scene window → Renderer tab → Shadows & Displacement rollout

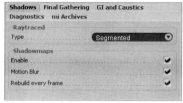

Figure 7.24

Maya global settings for shadows

Figure 7.25

XSI global settings for shadows

Figure 7.26

3ds Max global settings for shadows

Specifying Shadow Algorithms

The following options can be entered in the .mi file's option block or as a command-line command using the -shadow option:

```
-shadow [off, on, sort, segment]
```

These settings are equivalent to the three raytrace algorithms previously discussed—Regular (on), Sort, and Segment—and can be found within the host applications under the following drop-down lists, as seen in Figures 7.24, 7.25, and 7.26:

HOST	SETTINGS
Maya	Shadows → Shadow Method (Simple is Regular.)
XSI	dropdown list
3ds Max	Shadows → Mode (Simple is Regular, and the Enable check box turns shadows on.)

In each of the host applications you enable shadows with the On option (Simple or Regular), and you can specify more advanced raytrace algorithms (Sort or Segments) or disable shadowing altogether (choose Off in Maya, choose Disabled in XSI, or clear the Enable check box in 3ds Max). Disabling shadows disables both raytrace and shadow map shadows; shadows will not be generated at all. When On is selected (Simple or Regular in host applications), shadows are enabled, be it raytrace shadows or shadow map shadows. The only condition for shadow maps is then explicitly specifying additional shadow map options on a per-light basis, regardless of whether the shadow algorithm is set to Regular, Sort, or Segment.

Shadow Map Algorithms

The following options can be entered in the .mi file's option block or as a command-line command using the -shadowmap option:

```
-shadowmap [off, on, opengl, detail]
-shadowmap [motion, nomotion]
-shadowmap rebuild [on, off, merge]
```

This shadowmap command is also applied on a per-light basis with additional settings (such as specifying the shadow map file). For now we are interested in selecting shadow map algorithms, enabling motion-blurred shadow maps, and rebuilding shadow map files. These options are labeled as follows within the host applications, as seen in Figures 7.24, 7.25, and 7.26.

HOST	OPTION	HOST SETTINGS
Maya	Shadow algorithm	Shadow Maps → Shadow Maps check box and the Format drop-down list
	Motion Blur	Shadow Maps → Motion Blur Shadow Maps check box
	Rebuild/Reuse	Shadow Maps → Rebuild Mode radio buttons
XSI	Shadow algorithm	Shadowmaps → Enable check box
	Motion Blur	Shadowmaps → Motion Blur Shadow Maps check box
	Rebuild/Reuse	Shadowmaps → Rebuild Every Frame check box
3ds Max	Shadow algorithm	Shadow Maps → Enable check box
	Motion Blur	Shadow Maps → Motion Blur check box
	Rebuild/Reuse	Shadow Maps → Rebuild check box

XSI and 3ds Max Detail shadow maps are specified at the light level, and they both don't support OpenGL shadow maps.

THE DEFAULT SHADOW MAP ALGORITHM

With Maya, 3ds Max and XSI, the on and off mental ray options are provided by checking and clearing the Enable (Shadow Maps in Maya) check box, as seen in Figures 7.24, 7.25 and 7.26. With all hosts, when shadow maps are enabled, mental ray uses the standard Shadow Map Shadows algorithm.

DETAIL SHADOW MAP SHADOWS

Detail shadow maps with Maya, XSI, and 3ds Max are specified on the local level on a per-light basis. This means that if you select Detail shadow maps for a specific light, it will override the global setting for that light and render Detail shadows. Detail shadow maps are further examined on the local level later in this chapter. With Maya, you can specify Detail shadow maps using the Detail option from the Shadows → Shadow Maps → Format drop-down list, applying it as a global override to all the lights that cast shadow maps in the scene.

REBUILDING SHADOW MAPS

As discussed earlier in this chapter, one of the advantages of shadow maps is reusability. With host applications, the settings described in the following paragraphs apply.

When the rebuild shadow option is set to off, shadows are read from a file, so mental ray looks for the shadow map file on disk. With Maya, you can specify shadow map files under the light's attributes (see "Local Host Settings" later in this chapter). 3ds Max enables you to specify the shadow map file in the Shadows & Displacement rollout, with the Use File check box and path. With XSI, this process is hidden from the user, and although you may choose to disable the Rebuild every frame check box, you have little control over specifying the shadow map file.

When `rebuild` is set to on (Rebuild All and Overwrite radio button in Maya), mental ray constantly rebuilds shadow maps; the file is re-created for each frame. It's important to realize that unless shadow maps are rebuilt while you're creating the scene, you may have unexpected results such as missing shadows or shadows misplaced because the placement of objects in the scene may have changed. Figure 7.27 illustrates the effect of turning off the `rebuild` option and then rendering a frame after the sphere has been moved (image B). As you can see, the shadow map renders the same as with image A regardless of the new position. A new shadow should have been generated, but instead the old one remains.

Figure 7.27

Disabling the `rebuild` shadow option forces mental ray to read the shadow map file on disk (provided such a file exists) and may cause unexpected results with objects that have moved.

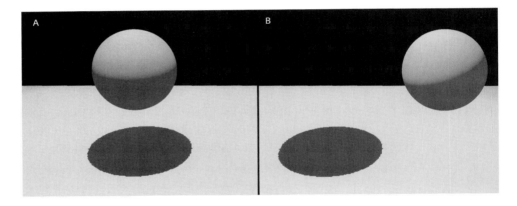

Keep in mind that mental ray's abilities to calculate only partial shadow maps may override the benefits of reusability.

MERGING SHADOW MAPS

The `merge` option is currently available only within Maya (Rebuild All and Merge radio button). Merge allows you to combine different shadow map files into one shadow map file so that data from a previous shadow map evaluation can be appended with new data from the current render. mental ray will only calculate changes to the shadow map that include depth values for surfaces that appear closer to the light than the depth values stored. Thus, it reuses existing data, and corrects for scene changes when necessary. Merge is not supported with Detail shadows.

Local Host Settings

The following sections identify shadow map settings on source lights for the mental ray features discussed in previous sections (locally). You have already reviewed the raytrace local settings in Chapter 6.

Enabling mental ray Shadow Maps

Figures 7.28, 7.29, and 7.30 show local shadow map settings for source lights, which may either be point, spot, or directional lights. These settings can be found in the following paths for a selected source light (note that directional lights may not support all these settings). These paths can be navigated only when a source light is selected:

HOST	GLOBAL SETTINGS PATH
Maya	Attribute Editor window → mental ray tab → Shadows rollout
XSI	Scene_Root: Light property editor → Shadow Map tab
3ds Max	Modify panel → mental ray Shadow Map rollout

MAYA

With Maya, you simply disable the Derive from Maya attribute check box seen in Figure 7.28. You can then further select Detail Shadow Map check box, also seen in the figure from the Shadow Map Format drop-down list. All the shadow map settings are further discussed in the section "Controlling Shadow Map Properties."

> Maya's Depth Map Shadow attributes (Dmaps) should not be used with mental ray. Thus, you should always disable the Derive from Maya check box that uses Maya specific shadow map settings to control mental ray shadow map settings.

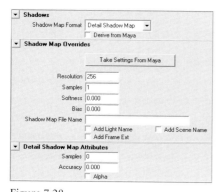

Figure 7.28

mental ray shadow map settings for Maya source lights

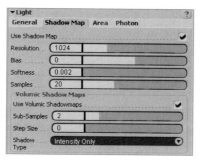

Figure 7.29

mental ray shadow map settings for XSI source lights

Figure 7.30

mental ray shadow map settings for 3ds Max source lights

With Maya, within the Render Settings window under the mental ray tab, if you have Shadows → Shadow Maps → Format drop-down list set to Detail (on the global level), all shadow maps, whether or not specified as Detail on the local level, will render as detail shadow maps provided the Shadow Map check box is enabled for the light (locally). Derive from Maya check box is disabled

On the local level, the Shadow Map File Name attribute (text input) enables you to specify a shadow map filename. You can postfix it with the light name, scene name, and frame extension, decreasing the chances of accidentally overriding the same filename. Once you enter a name into this field and render, if the Reuse Existing Maps radio button is selected (Render Settings window → mental ray → Shadows → Shadow Maps), mental ray will reuse that saved file rather than calculating a new shadow map file.

XSI

With XSI, under the Shadow Map property tab (shown in Figure 7.29), the Use Shadow Map check box enables shadow maps, and the Use Volumic Shadowmaps check box enables Detail shadow maps. All the shadow map settings are further discussed in the section "Controlling Shadow Map Properties."

3DS MAX

With 3ds Max, to enable mental ray shadow maps you must first enable shadows under the light's General Parameters rollout; choose Shadows → On and then select mental ray Shadow Map from the drop-down list, as seen in Figure 7.30. When both these conditions are met, mental ray shadow maps are enabled, assuming they are also enabled on the global level, as cited earlier. In the following sections, we look at enabling Detail shadow maps and relevant settings.

Controlling Shadow Map Properties

Table 7.1 maps the mental ray features discussed earlier in the chapter to host-specific option names for the corresponding settings. The following sections show how to apply those settings.

Table 7.1
mental ray Features and Host-Specific Options

MENTAL RAY SHADOW MAP OPTIONS	MAYA	XSI	3DS MAX
Resolution [n(xn)]	Resolution	Resolution	Map Size
Softness	Softness	Softness	Sample Range
Samples	Samples	Samples	Samples
Bias	Bias	Bias	Use Bias

continued

continues

MENTAL RAY SHADOW MAP OPTIONS	MAYA	XSI	3DS MAX
Detail	Shadow Map Format drop-down list → Detail Shadow Map	Use Volumic Shadowmaps check box	Transparent Shadows → Enable (intensity only)
Enabling color transmission	Not applicable. Both intensity and color are enabled by default.	Shadow Type drop-down list → Intensity Only or Full Color	Transparent Shadows → Color
Detail samples	Detail Shadow Map Attributes → Samples	Sub-Samples	Samp./Pixel
Accuracy	Detail Shadow Map Attributes → Accuracy	Step Size	Merge Dist.

INTENSITY AND COLOR TRANSMISSION

With XSI and 3ds Max, you can specify whether detail shadows will consider just intensity values (grayscale transparency) or both intensity and color. With XSI, set the Shadow Type drop-down list to either Intensity Only or Full Color. With 3ds Max, under Transparent Shadows check both the Enable and Color check boxes. Maya simply uses color if it is present.

As discussed under "Shadow Shaders" earlier in this chapter, with all host applications the shadow color and transparency are derived automatically from the surface shader's transparency settings. You can also use a texture file to map color with an image such as stained glass, as seen in color in "Detail Shadows" on the Chapter 7 folder on the CD.

Maya and XSI

Maya uses the shader Transparency attribute, and XSI uses the shader's Transparency → Mix Color → Color property, and in both cases an image may be mapped for color and intensity.

3ds Max

3ds Max uses a shader's Opacity setting to derive transparency (intensity) as grayscale values. For color, you can use Extended Parameters → Advanced Transparency → Type → Filter to specify a transparency color (seen in Figure 7.31). Note that while mapping an image or using color shadows, you should use the same color/image for both the Filter color and the Opacity color, maybe even the Diffuse color, as seen mapped with a bitmap on all three settings in Figure 7.30 and used for the render "Detail Shadows" seen in the Chapter 7 folder on the CD.

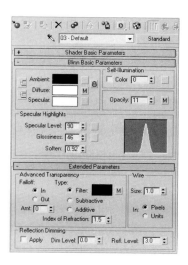

Figure 7.31

3ds Max shader settings for enabling color transmission in Detail shadow maps

SOFTNESS AND SAMPLES

The Softness setting (see table 7.1) for specifying the penumbra blur depends closely on the resolution and is very sensitive to values. Typically, lower-resolution maps will need higher values and more samples to provide a nice soft shadow. Start testing with very low values such as 0.001 to 0.01. If you don't see a shadow but do see artifacts, it could be that the Softness value is too high and the shadow is too blurred to be recognizable. If you do see the shadow and it appears grainy, the Samples value is too low.

With respect to the Samples option, it is relevant only when Softness has been applied. You can use a low value such as 4 while defining the Softness (penumbra radius), rendering with lots of shadow artifacts as seen in Figure 7.32, image A, and then once you're satisfied with the radius, increase the samples until the gradation appears smooth, as seen in Figure 7.32, image B.

Figure 7.32

Specifying low samples produces artifacts (A) but helps quickly define the shadow map penumbra blur radius; then higher samples can be used to smooth out the result (B).

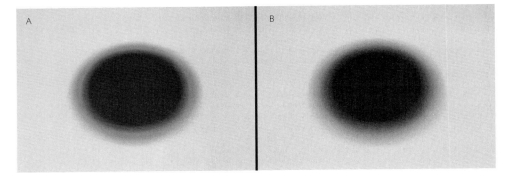

OTHER SETTINGS

To choose between the Woo and Bias depth-value algorithms discussed earlier in the chapter, you simply enable or disable the Bias algorithm. You do this by specifying a Bias value (see Table 7.1). Thus, when Bias has a nonzero value, the Woo algorithm is disabled.

The section "Detail Shadow Maps" discussed how to balance the Detail Samples and Accuracy settings (see Table 7.1). Note that the higher the Samples value, the more processing is required for each shadow map file. Each pixel is sampled based on the n value you enter, $n{\times}n$ samples. When Accuracy is set to zero, mental ray will evaluate a value for you. Remember that the accuracy value should never be too large because the shadow will shift away from the surface, as discussed earlier. Accuracy is meant to reduce the number of depth samples considered while rendering, improving render performance.

## CHAPTER 8

Motion Blur

Motion blur can be used to add a great deal of realism to mental ray renders. Adding motion blur not only provides an extra touch of photographic realism, it also provides for smoother animation. Objects that move fast with no blur simply appear "wrong" and "rigid," and so motion blur helps smooth the visual appearance of object translation over several frames. Be sure to complete both Chapters 4 and 5 before beginning this chapter. In Chapter 4, "Camera Fundamentals," you learned about camera characteristics such as shutter angle and speed; this chapter focuses on using mental ray to simulate the effect those elements have on motion blur. Chapter 5, "Quality Control," discussed sampling on a per-frame basis as well as the different render algorithms mental ray provides, which have a significant effect on motion-blur rendering. The chapter covers the following topics:

- **mental ray Motion Blur**
- **Motion Blur Options**
- **Motion Blur Render Algorithms**
- **Host Settings**

mental ray Motion Blur

Motion blur in mental ray realistically simulates camera motion blur, handling both standard features, such as correctly blurring surface texture colors, and advanced features, such as indirect illumination effects (i.e., global illumination, caustic light, and final gather). In film, there are two primary causes for motion blur, both illustrated in Figure 8.1: the motion of objects in front of the camera during the shutter interval (A) and movement of the camera so that anything within the camera's view appears blurred (B). Also, as seen in B, if both the camera and an object are in motion, then as with real cameras, the environment would blur but not the object, because its visual cues remain static in the "eyes" of the camera. Accommodating all these features provides yet another powerful tool for simulating realism.

Figure 8.1

mental ray simulates realistic camera motion blur for both moving objects and cameras.

The following sections look at the motion-blur options you can control in mental ray on the global and per-object levels, and the concepts underlying those options. As usual, the last section of this chapter will show how to implement those options in the host applications.

Motion-Blur Options

The mental ray options used to control motion blur are specified on the global level in the .mi options block (or on the command line). The following command-line options (or options block options) are used:

```
-motion [on | off]
-shutter [delay time (optional)] [open time]
-motion_steps [number of steps]
-time_contrast [r,g,b,a]
```

The motion on or off option enables or disables motion blur on the global level. It's not necessary to specify this option because specifying the shutter option will enable motion blur. However, the motion option must be included if you plan to export render passes for compositing, as explained in the sidebar ""Using 2D Motion Vectors in Practice" at the end of this chapter.

Shutter Time

mental ray simulates motion blur by realistically mimicking a camera's shutter time interval. In the following sections the term *time interval* may take on two meanings; one being the time between two consecutive frames referred to as the *frame time*, and it may also be used as reference to the time a shutter remains open during each captured frame, referred to as the *shutter time*. A combination of both shutter speed and shutter angle is used to define the shutter time in real cameras, as discussed in Chapter 4. The option for controlling motion-blur shutter time is as follows:

```
-shutter [delay (optional)] [time]
```

The mental ray `shutter` option can be used either with a single numerical value or with two values for both `shutter delay` and `shutter time`. `shutter time` defines a time interval for the shutter, from the beginning of the frame until the shutter closes. If the `delay` option is also present (optional), it defines a delay time at the beginning of the frame, defining a shutter start time. Thus `shutter time` and `delay` define the shutter open and close times respectively. Figure 8.2 illustrates the shutter time characteristics and their effect on motion-blur rendering.

In Figure 8.2 (A), you can see the horizontal scale representing the frame time interval during one frame. The `shutter` option specifies the period of time the camera can "see" the surface during the frame time interval. A shutter time of 1 (the default setting) means that the surface is visible throughout the entire frame time. The shutter time stated as 0.2–0.7 means that the shutter will open only after a delay of 0.2 of the time interval and will close at 0.7 of the frame time, effectively remaining open for only 50 percent of the frame time.

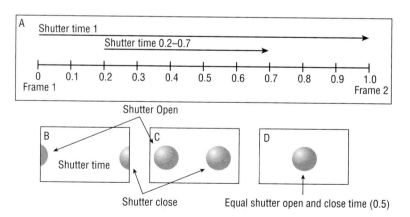

Figure 8.2

The `shutter` **option's effect on shutter time characteristics with mental ray**

A shutter open for only 50 percent of the frame time essentially simulates a camera shutter angle of 180°, as discussed in Chapter 4.

How does a 50 percent shutter time affect a 3D camera with mental ray?

First and foremost, the object will be less motion-blurred, as with a real camera, where faster shutter times produce less motion blur.

A set number of samples are taken during the shutter time, so a faster shutter time will take the same number of samples, for example over 50 percent of the time period (and distance), improving render quality. Motion-blur sampling is further discussed in the section "Motion Blur Sampling."

Also, the object's position is examined (at minimum) at both ends of the shutter time. Basically, an offset in shutter time or delay will offset the visible position of an object.

Let's examine the effect different shutter times have on a spherical object, illustrated in the three screens in the lower half of Figure 8.2 (labeled B, C, and D). Screen B corresponds to the first timeline in A and represents a shutter time of 1. Because mental ray visualizes the surface at both ends of the frame time, in this case the shutter time represents the entire distance over which the camera can see the object moving during that frame time interval.

Screen C corresponds to the second timeline in the section labeled A, where the shutter time has been reduced by 50 percent by specifying a shutter delay of 0.2 and a time of 0.7. In this case, the surface is seen by the camera only during the middle segment of that frame time, so the motion blur will only appear to span across that range of time, a shorter distance than with screen B.

Finally, screen D demonstrates the effect of using the same value for both shutter delay and time (open and close times). Essentially, the surface will render in the middle of the frame (if both are set to 0.5), because at 50 percent of the frame time the object is placed exactly between the frame start and end time. Thus if you specify the same value for both shutter delay and time, the surface is only rendered at that time, appearing, in this case, in the center frame. Further, because the shutter theoretically never opened, motion-blur effects are not rendered. To clarify, the lack of motion blur is because the shutter opened and closed instantaneously, so the object never appeared to move, and thus no visible change in position can be perceived by the camera.

Figure 8.3 demonstrates different shutter times for a rotating surface. For the first image (the least blurred), an almost identical shutter delay and time was utilized, and so the surface is placed in the middle distance between its position at that frame and the following frame. For the following images, increasing values in shutter time were used: 0.4 and 0.6, 0.3 and 0.7, 0.2 and 0.8, and 1.0. As you can see, the longer the shutter remains open, the more motion blur is captured in the image.

As you can see, mental ray utilizes a camera shutter to control motion blur; however the shutter does not realistically simulate different light intensities captured throughout different shutter times as with real cameras. With a real camera, longer shutter times provide more light exposure. With 3D, however, you define light properties with a lighting model and then mental ray uses the shutter settings to simulate only the effects of motion blur; thus all these shutter settings only causes mimicking motion-blur effects.

Figure 8.3

Increasing shutter time has the effect of increasing the motion blur visible in the shot.

Motion Steps

As noted earlier, our discussion of shutter time considered only the position of a surface at both ends of the shutter time interval. When mental ray calculates motion blur, it samples the position of the object along a path. By default, this path is derived by "drawing" a direct line from the surface or vertex position at the shutter open time to its position at the shutter close time. The option for controlling the number of motion steps is as follows:

```
-motion_steps [number of steps]
```

Figure 8.4 illustrates this concept, where a sphere has a nonlinear trajectory as it travels from point A to B. If the motion_steps number of steps is set to 1, mental ray simply blurs the line from point A to B using a linear path, assuming that's the correct motion trajectory, regardless of points 1, 2, and 3.

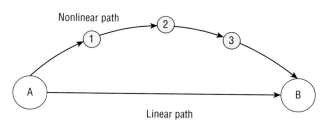

Figure 8.4

A surface may travel in a nonlinear path from point A to B. However, unless a motion_steps **value is specified, mental ray will fail to recognize the in-between positions.**

For mental ray to recognize the correct path, both transformation matrices and vertex motion vectors (both discussed shortly) can be declared several times within the shutter time. When you do so, mental ray receives additional information about the different positions of objects or vertices during that shutter time, effectively identifying points 1, 2, and 3 in Figure 8.4. Thus, more "steps" evaluated during the shutter time requires more transformation or vertex declarations for placing those surfaces correctly during the time interval period, consequently increasing the render time, particularly with vertex motion vectors.

Figure 8.5 illustrates motion steps with three horizontal lines that represent the shutter time using different "step" values. The line labeled A ("motion steps 1") represents the default, where a linear line is used to draw the path from point A to B. For the lines labeled B and C, as the Motion Steps value increases, so does the number of transform matrices or motion vectors used to define the surface position during that time. In the two images seen below, the differences are clear. Notice how the image under motion steps 1 appears to have a direct line of motion blur between the start and end positions of the blur. The second image, using 8 steps, provides for a rounder and more accurate motion trajectory.

Figure 8.5

Motion steps can be used to add transform matrices or motion vector data to surfaces and vertices respectively, improving the motion trajectory sampled during motion blur.

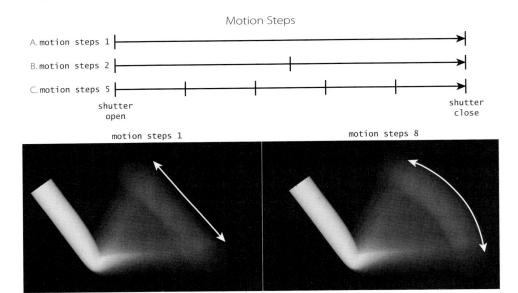

To clarify, the Motion Steps option has nothing to do with sampling quality; it deals with only where the surface is placed at particular points during the time interval. When using rotational motion such as with a tire, as seen in Figure 8.6, it is important to provide additional motion steps, but you should use as few as possible. With transform motion blur, you can specify up to 15 steps; however, you should really use under 6 steps with vector motion blur because it has a significant influence on render times.

Motion Blur Sampling

Motion blur sampling requires adding a third dimension to sampling: time. A technique known as *temporal sampling* factors in additional time samples that are taken during (along) the shutter time, based on spatial (XY pixel dimensions) samples. There are two approaches to temporal sampling: One approach is more render-intensive and precise; it is the default mental ray algorithm, which we'll refer to as *time contrast*. The other is typically (but not exclusively), used with the rasterizer; it is known as *fast motion blur*. The following sections examine and compare both approaches.

Figure 8.6

Rotational motion requires motion steps to maintain the integrity of the surface's motion during the shutter time.

Temporal Sampling (Time Contrast)

The option for controlling the number of temporal samples is as follows:

```
-time_contrast [r,g,b,a]
```

This sampling process is used to collect color information on the surface's appearance at equally spaced time periods. Unlike Contrast Threshold (discussed in Chapter 5), which controls spatial sampling quality for non-motion-blurred surfaces, the Time Contrast option determines the number of temporal samples that are taken during the shutter time.

Figure 8.7 illustrates temporal sampling in the section labeled A. Two horizontal lines represent the shutter time. As you can see, with a time contrast of 0.5, two separate time periods are sampled during the shutter time. Below that you can see that a contrast of 0.1 yields 10 samples during the shutter time, providing for higher quality because the surface is sampled more closely during the shutter time. The sample density is then approximately $1 \div n$ number of samples (the inverse value), n being the time contrast values you specify.

In the section labeled B in Figure 8.7, the shutter is open only for part of the frame time, and so contrast values depict only samples taken within the shutter time, not the frame time. Thus, n number of samples will be taken within the shutter time based on the equation cited earlier.

In host applications and with stand-alone mental ray, the Time Contrast option is specified per color channel, including the alpha channel. Since these "color" values depict sample intervals, not color comparisons, they should remain identical in all cases except with the alpha channel. If there is no need for an alpha channel, you might as well leave it at a value of 1, removing its sample density. In theory, applying separate RGB values can produce more accurate sampling for a given color channel, so if the entire scene is blue, you might want to take more blue samples and not bother examining the red and green channels. This, of course, is not really practical for most applications.

Figure 8.7

Time contrast samples are taken at equally spaced time intervals during the shutter time (which may or may not be the entire frame interval) and in a density that is approximately inverse to the specified contrast values.

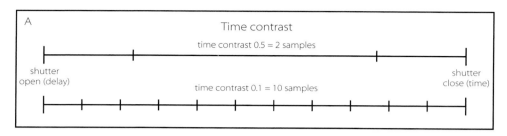

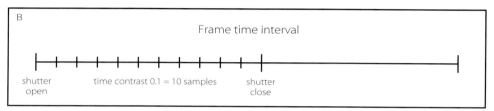

Figure 8.7

Time contrast samples are taken at equally spaced time intervals during the shutter time (which may or may not be the entire frame interval) and in a density that is approximately inverse to the specified contrast values.

With motion blur, time contrast greatly affects quality. You can reduce graininess and artifacts by increasing the sample density (decreasing the time contrast values). Essentially, adaptive spatial sampling is handled by the contrast threshold values, whereas temporal samples define the number of temporal samples taken for each spatial sample. The min and max sample levels, as with non-motion-blur rendering, define to a great extent the render quality and render time by specifying the number of samples, and thus the number of temporal samples that are taken per pixel. With still images for print or display (i.e., a photograph), higher time-contrast quality is required for a smooth motion-blurred result; however, with fast-motion pictures, grainy artifacts are not as noticeable to viewers, allowing you to compromise on quality and benefit the render time without a noticeable difference.

> When setting the Time Contrast option in host applications you should use higher values such as 0.2 for testing, maybe even for production. Typically a value of 0.1 provides very high quality.

Fast Motion Blur Sampling

The rasterizer uses a different sampling algorithm, which also influences motion-blur sampling. Recall that the rasterizer utilizes a nonadaptive sample algorithm, sampling in pixel centers (sample arrays per pixel), as discussed in Chapter 5. It doesn't use time contrast settings or the min and max sample settings to define quality. Instead, it uses a fast motion blur sampling algorithm. Fast motion blur will sample every spatial sample (regular sample) at a unique (different) time period, as seen in Figure 8.8 under label A. ("Rasterizer/fast motion blur"). Thus each rasterizer sample is placed at a different time period, providing random temporal color samples throughout the shutter time interval.

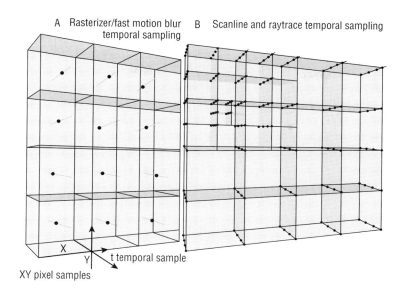

A   Rasterizer/fast motion blur
    temporal sampling

B   Scanline and raytrace temporal sampling

X

Y   t temporal sample

XY pixel samples

Figure 8.8

**Temporal sampling
with standard time
sampling and fast
motion-blur
sampling**

Fast motion blur can also be used with the default scanline or raytrace algorithms independently, whether or not the rasterizer is enabled. mental ray enables fast motion blur when you set all the Time Contrast RGBA values to 0 and set an equal min and max value for the Samples option. The sample values will still reflect the overall nonadaptive density of samples taken on a per-pixel level; however, in this case each spatial sample is placed at a different time period as illustrated (for the rasterizer) in Figure 8.8 A. Notice when the default render algorithms are used the samples are positioned according to the block (corner) sampling method discussed in Chapter 5. Time contrast sampling (not fast motion blur) may become quite dense when most of the frame is in motion because each spatial sample (for moving elements) will also take several additional temporal samples, as cited above and illustrated in Figure 8.8 B. Clearly fast motion blur decreases render times by taking only one temporal (spatial) sample per sample point, rather then several temporal samples based on a spatial sample point and the time contrast density (value).

> Fast motion blur should be used to optimize motion-blur render times when most of the frame is in motion.

Transformation vs. Deformation Motion

mental ray uses two methods to calculate surface motion: one is based on transformation matrices and the other on motion vectors, the latter referring to surface deformation. Transformation relates to blurring surfaces in translation (translation, rotation, and scaling) without considering any surface deformations. Deformation applies to vertex-level transformation, typically in dynamic simulations such as cloth or water simulations or character deformation such as with a character rig (bone systems) or facial expressions driven by morphing targets.

mental ray stand-alone enables you to specify transformation or motion vector motion blur on a per-object level. With transform motion blur, additional transform matrices are appended under the surface's `transform` matrix, as you can see in the following excerpt using the `motion transform` matrix:

```
instance "polymsh1"
    "polymsh1/Polygon Mesh"
    visible on
    shadow on
    trace on
    transform
        0.73 0 0.67 0
        -2.43 0.99 -1.17 0
        -0.67 0 0.73 0
        -0.10 3.22 -0.096 1
    motion transform
        -0.64 0 0.76 0
        1.0 0.99 -1.59 0
        -0.76 0 -0.64 0
        0.09 3.22 -0.10 1
    material ["polymsh1/DefaultLib/Material2"]
    ()
end instance
```

The first `transform` matrix is present regardless of motion blur and provides information on the object's position and orientation at each frame. The `motion transform` matrix provides additional information about the surface's position at the end of the shutter time.

For deformational motion blur, this `motion transform` matrix is not used because it does not depict the rearrangement of vertices at the object level. Instead, motion vectors are provided for each vertex. Thus, if a surface definition typically includes the placement of each vertex in object space, then additional similar statements are added to include the position of each vertex within the shutter time. The difference, then, is that motion transforms provide information about surface transformations (translation, orientation, and scale), and with deformation, per-vertex placement coordinates are provided. Clearly the per-vertex processing and rendering is more processor-intensive, so per-vertex motion vectors should be used only when deformations are required.

Figure 8.9 demonstrates the differences between the two methods. The figure utilizes a cylinder that has been "skinned" (enveloped) to a rig and animated. In addition a sphere has been parented to the bottom joint (as the hand). The cylinder is deformed by the rig, but the sphere is only translated, inheriting motion from its parent. Essentially, transformation motion blur will suffice for the sphere as seen in the section labeled A. For motion-blurring, the cylinder motion vectors are required, as seen in the section labeled B, in which motion vectors were utilized.

You should always prefer the transform motion blur algorithm because it is a faster algorithm that does not account for each vertex on motion-blurred surfaces.

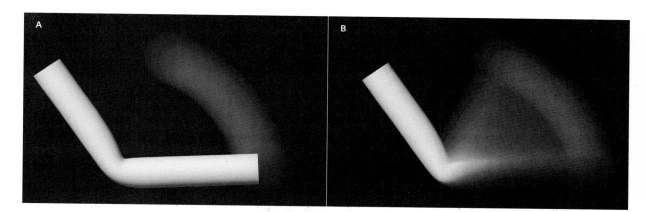

Motion-Blur Render Algorithms

Figure 8.9

Simulating an arm motion with a skinned cylinder and a parented sphere, where the cylinder requires motion vectors but the sphere requires only transformation matrices.

mental ray can use the default scanline renderer, the rasterizer, or raytrace rendering for motion blur. Essentially, the differences between these algorithms are in their support for raytracing features and sampling algorithms.

mental ray doesn't require you to explicitly set which algorithm is used for simulating motion blur aside from selecting the rasterizer over the default scanline algorithm. With the default scanline and raytrace algorithms, disabling one or the other is irrelevant as the sampling algorithm is the same and the rendered result will appear very similar, aside from the fact that raytracing is more precise. Obviously, if you disable raytracing, raytrace features will not be visible, and when both scanline and raytracing are enabled, mental ray decides for itself which algorithm to use. To clarify, if the scene has no raytrace features such as shadows, reflection, or refractions, the result of motion blur will appear almost identical in both cases. Further, if detail shadows are used for shadow maps, as discussed in Chapter 7, "Shadow Algorithms," the resulting shadow will appear similar to a raytrace shadow. Thus, raytracing really only adds reflection or refraction abilities as well as advanced raytrace features such as the global illumination, Final Gather, and similar concepts that can all be motion-blurred.

When both scanline and raytracing are enabled (scanline set to On, which is the default), raytracing features such as reflections (or any other raytrace feature) appear on motion-blurred surfaces, and the motion-blurred surfaces appear motion-blurred in reflections and refractions. In contrast, when both the rasterizer (scanline set to Rapid) and raytracing are enabled, one of the primary differences relates to how motion-blurred surfaces appear "seen" in reflections or refractions on other surfaces, as well as how they acquire reflection or refraction color (referring to the motion-blurred surfaces themselves). Essentially, the rasterizer's motion-blur effects are not visible to secondary rays; however, surface raytrace color values (reflection and refraction) are collected during the rasterizer's sample collection phase for a surface, before motion blur is evaluated. Thus, the rasterizer may examine a surface that has reflection colors and then motion-blur it using those colors. Also, the motion blurred surfaces themselves will not appear motion blurred to other reflection or refraction rays (on other surfaces). Let's examine these characteristics with the three samples, A, B, and C in Figure 8.10, as well as in the following section:

> For image A, default scanline and raytracing were utilized, and thus you see the motion-blurred surface appear in the mirror reflection and the raytrace shadows appear motion-blurred. Note that the surface and shadow closer to the camera are seen reflected on the mirror behind them.

> For image B, the rasterizer was utilized with raytracing enabled. You can see that the raytrace reflections and shadows appear visible; however, they don't account for motion blur. Thus rasterizer motion blur is not "seen" (....secondary raytrace rays):, or calculated with raytrace shadows.

> For image C, the same setting as image B (rasterizer and raytracing enabled) were utilized; however, detail shadow maps have been used rather than raytrace shadows, and as you can see, the shadows appear blurred both to primary rays and secondary rays but the sphere's motion blur is not reflected. Only detail shadow maps will properly render motion blur and are even seen in reflections. Detail shadow maps are discussed in Chapter 7.

For motion-blurred shadows, you should only use either detail shadow maps or raytrace shadows. Further, raytrace shadows should be enabled only if you are not using the rasterizer, unless the motion-blurred object is not casting a shadow.

Rasterizer Motion Blur

By now it's clear that the rasterizer scanline algorithm has significant impact on motion blur on many different levels, including sampling, temporal sampling, raytracing, and render speed. Faster motion blur is the key advantage of the rasterizer, making it a very attractive alternative to the more time-consuming default scanline or raytrace motion-blur rendering, especially when raytracing is not required. Let's look at some rasterizer characteristics that affect reflection or refractions on motion-blurred surfaces.

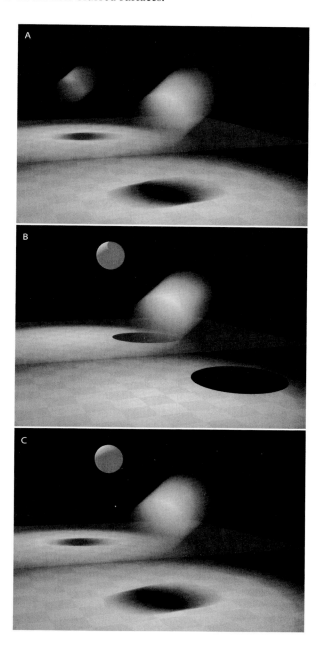

Figure 8.10

Motion blur with (A) the default scanline algorithm and raytracing, (B) the rasterizer with raytracing, and (C) the rasterizer with raytracing and detail shadow maps

Rasterizer Motion Samples and Raytracing

In Chapter 5 you learned about the rasterizer, and that it caches surface shading results. These cached surface colors are also used with motion blur. To clarify, after the shading values have been collected, fast motion blur samples are taken at different stages during the shutter time interval, discussed earlier under "Fast Motion Blur Sampling." Thus the Sample Collect option (phase) "draws" the surface in its temporal position, whereas the Shading Samples option provides surface colors that are not acquired over time, even though the position of the surface may have changed. The result of using these cached color values with temporal sampling primarily influences the color of reflections and refractions, where sampled colors appear dragged over time. Fortunately, the Samples Motion option provides a workaround for improving reflection or refraction quality during the shutter time. Motion samples can be entered into the .mi options block or the command line as follows:

```
-samples_motion [int value]
```

Motion samples are used to better simulate sampling at different segments of the time interval. Essentially, additional shading samples are collected within the time interval, providing for "corrected" reflection colors. Using motion samples enables mental ray to retrieve additional reflection or refraction samples, reducing the dragged appearance of reflections or refractions on motion-blurred surfaces. Figure 8.11 illustrates these concepts by comparing raytrace motion blur and rasterizer motion blur.

Image A simply shows the scene without motion blur. The middle cube is fully reflective and a texture gradient is used on the two additional cubes.

Image B shows standard raytrace motion blur. The surfaces and their textures are properly blurred, as are reflections. Notice the reflection appears "in-focus" and the surface appears blurred "under" the reflection, so the reflection samples don't translate with the surface, as expected. Also, notice that you can see more of the environment reflect along the "longer" surface; the surface appears longer because of motion blur.

Figure 8.11

A comparison of raytrace motion blur with the default algorithms and with the rasterizer as seen on motion-blurred surfaces.

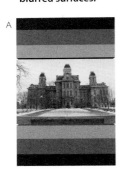

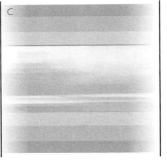
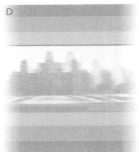

Image C shows the rasterizer using a Samples Motion option value of 1, the default setting. The reflections, as well as all other colors, translate with the surface. This demonstrates the dragging effect of reflections with the rasterizer.

Image D shows a Samples Motion setting of 6. As you can see, the reflection quality improves, but it is still not nearly as clear as with the raytracing render. For many purposes, this sort of reflection will suffice because motion-blurred surfaces typically move too fast for a viewer to accurately distinguish these differences. Thus, using high motion sample values helps improve motion-blur quality for reflective or refractive surfaces.

Tiling Artifacts

One problem with motion samples is that tiling artifacts can appear. As you know, each tile is a separate render job and different sample values may be generated per tile. With the rasterizer, the tile size affects the visible artifacts, as seen in Figure 8.12. Notice that a smaller tile size is used in the image on the left with the smaller artifacts, and as the tile size increases, the artifacts appear larger (right image). This is common to rasterizer motion blur and is more pronounced with high Samples Motion values that capture reflections. Basically you need to decide when it's too noticeable, and when it "passes" without the viewer noticing artifacts.

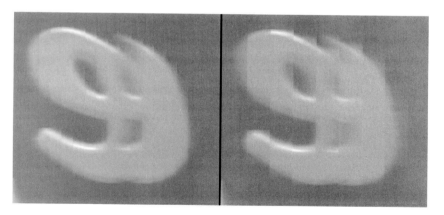

Figure 8.12

Different tile sizes affect the visible artifacts with the rasterizer, especially with higher Motion Samples values.

Host Settings

All three host applications offer similar settings for controlling motion blur, and they also offer their own additional settings. Host-specific settings act as queries, asking you what you would like to achieve and then translating as well as possible to mental ray those settings, using all the options discussed earlier in the chapter. For BSP settings, it's recommended that you reduce the BSP depth size about 10 percent when using motion blur, a topic discussed in detail in Chapter 5 in the section "Raytrace Acceleration." Also, with host applications, unfortunately the choice between transformation and motion-vector motion blur is applied only at the global level and not on a per-object level. Thus, when you specify either method, every scene element will receive either motion vectors or motion transformations. Fortunately, you can specify which objects are considered for motion blur by disabling their motion-blur flag under their surface properties in Maya and 3ds Max. Let's look at each host briefly to identify its settings as well as note some of it unique host-specific settings.

Maya

With Maya, as discussed in Chapter 2, mental ray attributes are found in the Render Settings window as well as under the mental ray default options (miDefaultOptions node). Figure 8.13 shows the mental ray motion blur attributes, seen in the Render Settings window under the Motion Blur rollout. You can also display the mental ray options in the Attribute Editor by typing the following into the script editor and executing:

```
select -r miDefaultOptions;
```

In Maya 8.5 instead of typing the script you can press the Primary Framebuffer→ Open Editor button from the mental ray Render Settings window.

When you execute this command, you can find the additional Motion Samples option (for the rasterizer) under the Rendering rollout, which is currently not available in the Render Settings window.

Figure 8.13

Maya's render settings for mental ray motion blur

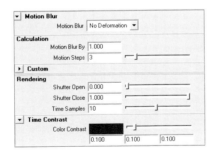

From the Motion Blur drop-down, you can enable motion blur by selecting one of the motion blur methods: No Deformation (Transformation) or Full (Deformation). Both options correlate to the previous Linear or Exact options (Maya 8.0 and lower). No Deformation and Full correlate to mental ray transform or motion vectors, respectively, as discussed earlier under "Transformation vs. Deformation Motion".

All the attribute naming conventions in Maya 8.0 (and lower) are still present (for the same attributes) under the miDefaultOptions node.

Shutter Close (overall shutter time), Shutter Open (previously Shutter Delay), Time Samples, and Motion Steps work as described earlier in the chapter and utilize almost identical mental ray naming conventions for their attributes. Note that the Time Samples option is identical to the Time Contrast→ Color Contrast options seen in the figure, however utilizes integer values instead of fractional values. (These options correlate to the previous Time Contrast RGBA options in Maya 8.0 and lower, where the Color Contrast attribute accepts the same value range as the previous Time Contrast RGBA attributes.) Thus Time Samples enables you to enter an integer amount of temporal samples per spatial samples without considering the inverse interpretation as discussed earlier. Notice that as you increase the value for Time Samples, the Color Contrast value automatically adjusts to read a correlating value, for example, a value of 10 Time Samples is equivalent to a Color Contrast value of 0.1, providing 10 temporal samples per spatial sample.

Under the Rendering Features rollout in the Render Settings window, you can enable the Rasterizer through its radio button. When it's enabled, the Anti-Aliasing Quality→ Rasterizer Quality→ Visibility Samples and Shading Quality attributes become available, as discussed in Chapter 5, as well as Motion Samples (only visible in the miDefaultOptions node) attribute, discussed earlier under "Rasterizer Motion Blur".

Do not confuse Motion Steps and Motion Samples, where one deals with transformation matrices and the other with rasterizer time sampling respectively.

When you want to exaggerate the motion blur effect, you can use the Motion Blur By attribute, prolonging the shutter time interval. Note that you can also specify exaggerated motion blur times by increasing the Shutter Open values (times) to exceed a value of 1. However, if the surface is rotating as with a propeller, a shutter time up to a value of 1 will effectively utilize Motion Steps, reproducing nonlinear motion blur, along the propellers rotational path. When a value greater than 1 is used, additional points past that shutter time (of 1) are not evaluated with Motion Steps and appear linear.

Clearly, if you want to exaggerate the motion, it is better to use the Motion Blur By value because it will spread the shutter time (and Motion Steps) equally within that increased time factor. You can disable motion blur on a per-object level by using the surface's Render Stats rollout attributes in the Attribute Editor. When using Deform motion blur doing so will significantly reduce the translation process for objects that don't require per vertex motion vector data.

Fast Motion Blur

For fast motion blur (not in the rasterizer mode) you simply need to set the Time Samples value to zero. Unfortunately in Maya 8.5 you can't set the Time Samples (or Color Contrast) in the Render Settings window to a value lower then 0.1. Thus to set Time Samples to zero, you need to open the miDefaultOptions in the Attribute Editor (as cited above) and there you can se the Time Contrast (for RGBA) to zero, which will update the Time Samples option in the Render Settings window.

Back in the Render Settings window you also need to set the Sampling Mode to Fixed Sampling (equal Min and Max Sample Level values). Remember that the value used for sampling defines the overall density of motion samples when using fast motion blur.

XSI

To enable motion blur with XSI, enable the Enable Motion Blur checkbox in the Render Manager window under Current Pass→ Pass Output→ Default_Pass (or other pass name)→ Output→ Pass Motion Blur as seen in Figure 8.14 A. This switch obviously corresponds to the mental ray Motion (On / Off) options.

You can find the same option under the Render menu→ Render→ Pass Options property editor.

The additional XSI motion blur settings used to fine tune motion blur are found under the Scene Render Options (seen in Figure 8.14 B), and the mental ray Render Options (seen in Figure 8.14 C) property editors (or in their equivalent Render Manager tabs).

Scene Options

The scene options in the Render Manager window under Scene (tab)→ Scene Globals→ Scene Motion Blur Settings (Figure 8.14 B) allow you to define the motion blur time interval.

The Speed option defines an overall time interval for the motion blur. The Offset option defines an offset time for starting the time interval count. These options, although similar, do not correlate to the shutter delay and shutter time options discussed earlier under "Shutter Time". To clarify them, Speed defines the relationship between the overall time interval and the frame time. A Speed value of 1 spans across one frame, values greater then one will extend the time interval beyond an interval of one frame, and lower then one values contract the motion blur, as with faster shutter times. The Offset doesn't change the time interval length, only its initial time, so that if you increase the Offset value the motion blur will appear to shift forward in time.

The dropdown menu seen in Figure 8.14 B, (across Speed) defines when the motion blur is evaluated with respect to the frame time. Simply put it dictates where the first motion blur transform (or motion vector) is a considered, acting as an additional offset option. Start on Frame begins with the current frame, End on Frame begins in the previous frame thus appears farther back in time, and Center on Frame is clearly the in between of both the start and end frame options. Thus these three options (in the dropdown menu) specify the general time interval placement, and the Offset option further offsets the interval starting time (from that starting point), and Speed defines the range of the interval for which motion vectors or transform matrices are generated (as required).

The Deformation Blur checkbox (also seen in figure 8.14 B) enables motion vectors, correlating to the mental ray motion vectors discussed earlier under "Transformation vs. Deformation Motion". When Deformation Blur is disabled, only transformational motion blur is calculated.

mental ray Options

The scene options define a custom time interval for the mental ray Shutter (shutter time) and Delay (shutter delay) options that are found in the mental ray Render Options (for a given pass) property editor. You can navigate to these options in the Render Manager window under Current Pass→ Pass mental ray→ Motion Blur tab, as seen in Figure 8.14 C. Delay controls the shutter delay or start time within the time interval, as defined by the Speed option.. Shutter is then the shutter time, which, when Delay is set to 0, specifies the overall shutter open time within the Speed interval.

Shutter times greater than 1 will exaggerate motion blur, however, motion steps (transformation matrices or motion vectors) are only evaluated for the shutter times that range from 0 to 1. That is, you can exaggerate motion blur appearance by increasing the Shutter option to exceed a value of 1, but with nonlinear motion (such as a propeller), the motion path will change and appear linear from a shutter time of 1 and higher. The Shutter and Delay options correspond to Shutter Close and Shutter Delay options in XSI 5.11 and earlier.

> To effectively exaggerate shutter times that span past a time interval of one frame, use the Speed option which evenly distributes the motion steps along the overall (Speed) time interval, and within the range of time specified with the Shutter and Delay options (assuming Shutter does not exceed a value of 1).

The Sampling Contrast (Sampling Threshold in XSI 5.11) options correlates to mental ray's Time Contrast option, as discussed earlier under "Temporal Sampling (time contrast)". The Motion Steps→ Transform option correlates to the mental ray Motion Steps option, and Deformation correlates to motion vectors. Thus both these settings (respectively) specify how many transformation matrices or motion vectors are generated for use during the time interval. Clearly for motion vectors the Deformation Blur option seen in Figure 8.14 B needs to be enabled.

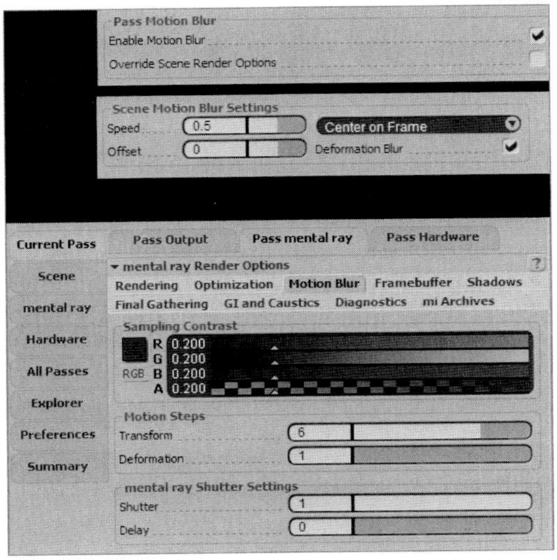

Figure 8.14

**XSI render settings
for mental ray
motion blur**

Rasterizer and Fast Motion Blur

Under the Render Options → Rendering property tab, you can enable the Rasterizer under Primary Rays→ Type dropdown menu. After you enable the rasterizer the Rasterizer options appear (below the Type dropdown menu), and you can further set the rasterizer Motion Samples property that corresponds to mental ray's Samples Motion option discussed earlier under "Rasterizer Motion Blur", as well as other rasterizer settings discussed in Chapters 2 and 5.

For fast motion blur (not in the rasterizer mode) simply set the RGBA Sampling Contrast values to zero, as well as set the Min and Max Level options to the same value (non adaptive). Remember that the value used for Min and Max Level defines the density of motion samples with fast motion blur.

3ds Max

In 3ds Max, mental ray motion blur is controlled and enabled from the Renderer → Camera Effects → Motion Blur section under the Render Scene: mental ray Renderer window, shown in Figure 8.15. The Enable option obviously corresponds to the mental ray motion (on or off) option. Shutter Duration refers to the mental ray Shutter (time) option, defining the motion-blur shutter time interval. Shutter Offset is the shutter delay time. Both Shutter Duration and Shutter Offset can be specified to exceed the time frame of a single frame. If you specify a Shutter Duration value that exceeds 1, the motion blur will appear exaggerated, spanning across the time frame of more than one frame. This provides you with an added ability for exaggerating motion blur. Motion Segments correlates to the mental ray motion steps option, as discussed earlier.

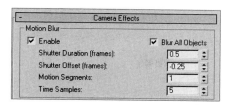

Figure 8.15

3ds Max render settings for mental ray motion blur

The mental ray Time Contrast option is specified with the Time Samples setting in 3ds Max 9 and up. As you see, the time contrast RGBA dependency has been removed; instead, a single value is used to depict the amount of temporal samples taken throughout the shutter time. In previous versions the Renderer → Sampling Quality rollout → Contrast → Temporal RGBA values were used as discussed earlier under "Motion Blur Sampling."

Also, under the Renderer tab → Rendering Algorithms, you can enable the rasterizer with the Use Fast Rasterizer check box. When the rasterizer is enabled under the Camera Effects rollout (Figure 8.15) the Time Samples option changes to read "Time Samples (Fast Rasterizer)," depicting that this setting now controls rasterizer motion samples, corresponding to mental ray's `samples motion` option, as discussed earlier under "Motion Blur Sampling." Essentially when you enable or disable the rasterizer the Time sample option toggles between mental ray's `time contrast` and `samples motion` options.

The Blur All Objects check box enables motion blur for everything in the scene; when it's disabled, motion blur can be specified per object by selecting the object and right-clicking to display its Object Properties window, shown in Figure 8.16. The Enabled check box enables motion blur for that object. None or Object specifies whether the object appears motion-blurred, and the Image radio button has no relevance with mental ray.

Note that per-camera Multi-Pass Effect → Motion Blur (seen in the Modify tab for a selected camera), doesn't affect mental ray; thus the settings discussed in this section are the only settings that mental ray recognizes.

Notice that with 3ds Max you cannot explicitly specify which method is used with respect to transform or motion vectors; these decisions are made automatically by 3ds Max. Essentially, both methods are supported. Note that if raytracing is disabled, motion blur is still rendered with the scanline or rasterizer methods. I only point this out as it contradicts information in the 3ds Max help files, which (at the time of writing) claim that raytracing must be enabled.

Figure 8.16

3ds Max per-object motion-blur settings

USING 2D MOTION VECTORS IN PRACTICE

Mental ray's motion vectors are not compatible with compositing applications, and as discussed in Chapter 3 under "The Motion Vectors Frame Buffer," they are mostly used with mental ray's own output shaders, which know how to interpret the per-channel values correctly. To use 2D motion vectors with compositing software, you must install both a custom mental ray shader to extract motion vectors, and plug-in software for the compositing application that can use those motion vectors.

XSI's built-in compositing software, along with Digital Fusion, Shake, Combustion, After Effects, and others support using a vector motion blur plug-in from RE:Vision Effects, Inc., called ReelSmart Motion Blur. You can get a fully functional demo version for your compositing software at `www.revisionfx .com`, under the Products menu. Once installed, the RSMB vector blur plug-in will be available in your compositing software. An FAQ (under Support on the plug-in's product page) describes in detail how to use the shader with Maya and XSI, and the Render Elements with 3ds Max 8 and up.

The mental ray shader can be found at

`http://www.alamaison.fr/3d/lm_2DMV/lm_2DMV_ref.htm`

Here you will find information about using the shader, as well as downloads for each host application. Note the following comments for each host:

- XSI users can download and install the XSI add-on from the XSI Plug-in Manager window. For more information on installing add-ons see Chapter 10, "mental ray Shaders and Shader Trees," or refer to the help files.

- Maya users can download the zip file (`lm_2DMV.v2.0p.zip`) that contains the shader DLL and mental images (.mi) declaration file, which need to be placed in the mental ray include and lib directories (see Chapter 1, "Introduction to mental ray"). You will also find a link to another site where you can get the Maya AETemplate file; this goes in your installation directory under \Maya8.5\scripts\AETemplates, as well as an XPM file that goes in your icons directory. The template file defines the UI seen in the Attribute Editor window.

- 3ds Max users cannot use the LMV shader; as an alternative you need to use the Velocity pass in the Render Elements window. You can find the specifics under the FAQ section of the RealSmart Motion Blur support page.

Motion Blur Options

For using the LMV shader, the only real requirements are that motion blur is enabled as deformation blur, not transformations, and that the shutter delay and open time are set equally, for example to 0.5. By doing so you ensure that mental ray exports motion vector color values, which the RealSmart Motion Blur plug-in requires. Essentially, the custom mental ray shader outputs a color pass that stores motion vector data using RGB values. Thus if the those values are affected by motion blur (that is, if they appear motion-blurred), the motion vectors color pass values are then useless. Thus by setting equal shutter open and delay times, as described earlier in this chapter, you guarantee that the motion vectors pass will render without unwanted blur.

Using the LMV Shader in Maya and XSI

The LMV shader needs to be applied to all the surfaces that require rendering motion blur; other surfaces ideally should be hidden or also have the shader applied. Like any other shader, it doesn't require a custom output pass, just a normal RGBA frame buffer at preferably a higher bit depth, such as 16-bit. You would also render a beauty pass for all the elements without motion blur, which are then motion-blurred in compositing using this shader's motion vectors color pass. First you need to enable verbosity for info messages and execute a test render for a selected frame that exhibits the most intensive motion blur during the animation. The verbosity output will indicate the motion vectors displacement factor (in the last output row) with the following message:

```
PHEN 0.4  info : [lm2DMV_v2] >> Max Displace -> 143 pixels
```

You will need to note the Max Displace factor for the compositing stage, as well as enter it into the LMV shader's Normalize option before rendering the animation sequence. Because different surfaces may have different displace factors, such as a rotating blade of a plane in comparison with the motion of the plane, you may want to render different elements individually (in separate passes), as I have done with the following example. At each stage I note the displace factor, apply it to the shader, and then render the sequence.

Using RealSmart Motion Blur

When all the passes are ready you can load them into your compositing package; I'm using XSI for this example. As you can see in the flow chart, I used three RSMB vector nodes, each applied to a different element: the clouds (Maya fluids; I attached the LMV shader to their color and removed incandescence), the propeller, and the plane. The RSMB vector node takes two inputs: the color pass and the motion vectors pass generated with the LMV shader (or in 3ds Max with Velocity Render Element). I then composite them together using simple Over nodes.

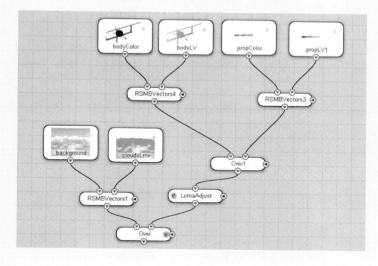

If I had not separated the different elements, I would get artifacts from the propeller, which moves much faster than the plane. Also, the plane is moving with the camera, so motion blur is much less significant than with the propeller. You can see in a rendered version labeled A how all these elements appear motion-blurred. Note that motion vectors don't include information about the placement of the object within the time interval of one frame, only a suggested direction, so I cannot simulate a full 180° rotational motion although there is a limit to how far you can go; for most purposes you can get really decent results that appear almost identical to the mental ray motion-blurred results. The image labeled B was rendered with mental ray, and as you can see the results are similar to the composited version labeled A.

## CHAPTER 9

The Fundamentals of Light and Shading Models

This chapter introduces the fundamental light and imaging concepts that are the backbone of shader construction and advanced direct and indirect illumination. The purpose is for you to understand absorption, reflection, and transmittance characteristics of direct and indirect light in the scene, and how those characteristics are implemented with shading models. Real-world light and photography concepts are the foundation of 3D rendering, particularly when you're attempting to re-create natural phenomena, so I'll cover them in some depth. Nonetheless, understanding light, and particularly its dual nature as both wave and particles, is a complex and fully loaded topic that cannot be adequately covered in just one chapter, so I'll point you to further resources. Like other rendering software, mental ray develops camera, shading, and lighting models based on the science of optics, and although some of the information presented in this chapter is advanced for most beginner to intermediate users, advanced users might argue that the coverage is too brief. These concepts are essential knowledge for professionals working as technical directors and lighting/shading artists.

This chapter begins with a brief history of the science of light, including its basic characteristics, followed by more-advanced concepts that build on image synthetics. The chapter then covers how you can sample real light through photography to help reproduce a realistic range of light in 3D using high dynamic range (HDR) photography and concepts. Finally, along with the following chapters, this chapter examines mental ray shaders and shader networks; Chapter 10, "mental ray Shaders and Shader Trees," and Chapter 11, "mental ray Textures and Projections," focus on demonstrating how to create and use these shaders and shader trees in host applications. The main purpose of this chapter is to explain necessary concepts and terms that are the foundation for using shading models (illumination shaders), advanced light simulations, and compositing color, topics that are all covered in the following chapters. This chapter covers the following topics:

- **The Fundamentals of Light**
- **Light Transport and Shading Models**
- **mental ray Shaders**

The Fundamentals of Light

The perception and interpretation of light is greatly influenced by the different viewing devices, whether a human eye or a camera's film or digital sensor. Light perception and behavior considerations are at the forefront of photorealistic imaging. To render a realistic image, you must mimic the natural behavior of light and its interaction with surfaces, as well as understand how it's perceived by recording devices, be they digital media or film stock.

A History of Light Theory

Scientists and philosophers since Pythagoras and Aristotle in ancient Greece (about 500–300 BCE) have experimented with light and hypothesized about it. Newton, Huygens, Maxwell, Hertz, Plank, Einstein, Bohr, and others have all contributed to the evolving field of optics. The focus of their efforts has been twofold. On the practical side, they developed the science of optics, creating modern optical lenses for telescopes and cameras that magnify and transmit light. Their efforts also led to experiments with propagating *electromagnetic radiation* such as radio waves and electric current. On the theoretical side, as their experiments with light led to discoveries of optical phenomena such as *interference, diffraction, chromatic aberrations,* and the *photoelectric effect,* they also hypothesized about the fundamental character of light.

The modern science of optics really began during the 17th century with Willebrord Snell's (1591–1626) discovery of the law of refraction, which mathematically explained how light redirects through matter. During that time, scientists struggled with the question of whether light manifests as a wave or a stream of particles. Robert Hooke (1635–1703) had set forth the wave theory by conducting experiments with *diffraction*—the propagation characteristics of a wave as it passes an obstruction, bending and changing directionality, as shown in Figure 9.1, which illustrates the *double slit* experiment of Thomas Young (1773–1829).

Dielectric substances are concentrations of matter that transmit light through their different layers, redirecting light several times. The term *interface* is commonly used to refer to the substance's internal compound (layer matter) such as with thin film coatings, liquids, oily substances, metals, and so on. Typically several different substances can be layered to create a specific coating, utilizing different interfaces, for the purpose of controlling light, such as reflecting specific wavelengths, absorbing others, and redirecting them through the coating. The path light takes through a dielectric is then subject to constant change based on the interface, specifically the substance's index of refraction, a topic further discussed in "Geometric Optics and 3D" later in this chapter. In 3D we deal with the transmission between interfaces, for example, air to glass, glass to liquid, and so forth, such as when using the mental ray dielectric shader, demonstrated in Chapter 10.

Diffraction

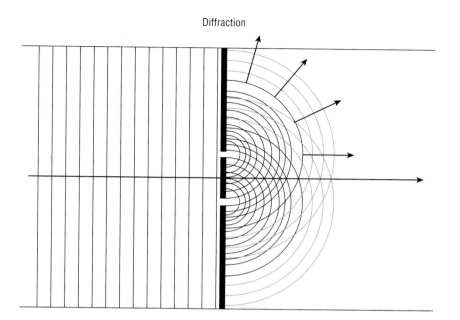

Figure 9.1

Diffraction describes the propagation of light as it interacts with obstacles, as shown with Thomas Young's double slit experiment.

Hooke also studied *interference patterns (color fringes)* that appear in thin *dielectric* films, similar to the colorful display seen in oil spills or substances with an "oily" nature. The effect of interference (further described shortly) is yet another phenomenon that supports the wave theory.

Throughout the 18th and 19th centuries, the concept of light developed as a medium that vibrates through the *aether*, which was thought to be "atmospheric matter" that enabled light to propagate through its substance. However, it was unclear whether light propagated as a wave through the aether or was a stream of particles. Sir Isaac Newton's (1642–1727) *light emission theory* leaned more toward the corpuscular (light as a particle) assertion based on his experiments, even though his work supported both wave and corpuscular theories. Newton objected to the wave theory primarily because he could not validate it enough to support it and valued empirical fact over hypothesis. His important observation of the prism effect, in which *white light* disperses into different colors, led him to conclude that white light in fact comprised several colors that have their independent corpuscular characteristics.

Around the same time, Christiaan Huygens (1629–1695) embraced the wave assertion, correctly observing the laws of reflection and refraction and discovering *polarization* (see the sidebar "Polarization in 3D" later in this chapter). He also established that light changes speed as it traverses through matter of varying densities. In the 18th and early 19th centuries,

Newton's theories received greater regard, almost automatically rejecting theories of light as a wave from Huygens, Euler, Young, and others.

Early in the 19th century, Thomas Young and Augustin Jean Fresnel (1788–1827) independently furthered Huygens' wave theory by asserting the *principal of interference*. Interference, a wave characteristic, explains how two undulations with similar frequencies traveling in the same direction in space and in close proximity join. The effect of super-imposing waves either can be can be either constructive or destructive, amplifying or can-celing each other out, which results in a new wave amplitude, as shown in Figure 9.2.

Interference

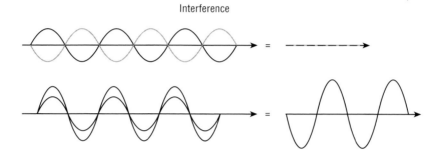

Figure 9.2

Interference describes the effects of two waves, at different amplitudes, traveling along similar paths.

By observing the effects of interference and diffraction through the double slit experi-ment (see the earlier Figure 9.1), Young was able to further the wave theory accretion. Using the double slit experiment, he projected a coherent light source through two narrow openings and accounted for the interference patterns of light that appeared on the screen, as shown in Figure 9.3. The patterns are caused because of diffraction and interference, where diffraction changes the direction of light (through the two slits) in a way that causes the light to ripple (as shown in the earlier Figure 9.1). Then the effect of interference results with those waves superimposing on each other and forming patterns of light on the screen, as shown in Figure 9.3. You can theoretically compare the effect of interference with a ripple effect in a pond, where some waves cancel out (no light) and others magnify (brighter light).

As a result of his experiments with light, Young concluded that the color of light is based on different wavelengths. He also explained that color fringing appears because of interference. You can think of this as the effect of separating wavelengths into groups with different frequencies and color, where interference magnifies some and cancels others, forming color-fringing effects based on the wavelength's associated color. There are other fringing effects (birefringence) that are due to polarization, as discussed in the sidebar "Polarization in 3D." The topic of color fringing as a result of waves dispersing into their components is a topic further discussed throughout the chapter.

Figure 9.3

Interference patterns appear to form a pattern of visible light streaks on a screen.

Even though these discoveries by Young and Fresnel contradicted Newton's corpuscular theory, the wave theory still met rejection. Fresnel further built on the law of refraction, defining the *Fresnel equations*, which describe the amplitude of light as it refracts and reflects. With transparent surfaces, these equations account for the balance between reflected and refracted light, which is an important surface shading characteristic. Balancing the total reflection from a surface based on the viewing angle is commonly referred to as *Fresnel reflections*. Because a surface cannot be fully refractive and reflective at the same time, the incident light needs to be weighed correctly to determine the proper balance between the reflection and refraction intensities, based on the incoming light intensity, the surface normal, and the angle of view. This chapter further discusses all of these topics.

By 1825, the efforts of Young, Fresnel, and others led to the widespread acceptance of the theory of light as different undulations through the aether, rather than a stream of particles; however, that was not the end of the debate.

Even nowadays, the understanding of light and its fundamental character is still considered debatable, reflecting the complexity of this topic.

Light as Electromagnetic Radiation

While these experiments and hypotheses were being debated in the field of optics, Michael Faraday (1791–1867), who was studying electric and magnetic forces, found an interdependent relationship between light and electromagnetism. Brilliantly, James Clerk Maxwell (1831–1879) merged the theories of optics and electromagnetism, describing light as *electromagnetic radiation*. He concluded that electromagnetic (EM) radiation propagates itself in the form of a wave through the aether and at the speed of light.

While experimenting with EM radiation, Heinrich Rudolf Hertz (1857–1894) discovered the *photoelectric effect*, the emission of electrons (energy) from matter. The emission from matter refers to discrete bursts of energy that are dependent on the incoming light energy.

Hertz was puzzled by the fact that projecting more light on a surface increased only the number of emitting electrons and not their energy. Essentially, the energy is dependent on the light frequency and not the "amount" of light, as will become clearer throughout the following sections. Hertz embraced the assertion of light as a stream of particles, because at that time the phenomenon of liberating electrons from matter could not be rationalized with the wave model.

The Birth of Quantum Mechanics

Essentially, EM radiation can be described as particles possessing ballistic behaviors or as waves demonstrating interference and diffraction. In the 20th century, Max Plank (1858–1947) came up with a constant that quantified independent light packets with a given energy value. His experiments led him to believe a relationship exists between the absorption and emission of energy that is dependent on an oscillator's frequency (the photoelectric effect). The oscillator refers to the atomic particles that excite electrons into emitting from matter. Plank was more lenient toward the wave accretion than the corpuscular theory, which is somewhat contradicted by his own experiment. Regardless, he found ways of rationalizing the wave accretion, particularly as his immense breakthrough was mostly hypothetical at the time, based on certain predetermined assumptions and lacking the means to provide a more concrete rationalization for the character of light.

Albert Einstein (1879–1955) furthered rationalized the treatment of the photoelectric effect with his corpuscular theory that quantized light with *photons*, using Plank's constant. Einstein also determined that the aether is nonexistent, that light travels through empty space, and thus that light does not require a substance to support undulations (its motion).

The new corpuscular theory evolved into describing photons as massless elementary light particles that manifest as part wave and part particle, a dual nature. Essentially the two very different physical attributes of light (particle and wave) are reconciled thorough the field of *quantum mechanics* using a wave/particle duality assertion. Based on Max Plank's experiments, Einstein further validated the direct connection between a photon's energy, which is dependent on a wave *frequency,* as described with the following equation, where h is Plank's constant and v is the frequency:

$$E = h \times v$$

Thus, photons, the most elementary form of light, are massless particles that osculate through a vacuum at a constant speed (the speed of light) carrying energy and momentum. They are timeless particles that propagate through space and time, and their energy is never lost; it's only absorbed by matter. When photons interact with matter, energy that is not absorbed is either reflected or transmitted. Essentially, at a given *threshold frequency* photons are said to either emit electrons or get absorbed. The threshold refers to the minimum energy required to liberate electrons from matter; thus, photons below the threshold are absorbed, and photons above the threshold are cause for discrete energy bursts, which liberate electrons from the surface. For physicists, these individual packets of energy are the foundation for quantifying light flux (power), as discussed in the section "Radiometry Measurements" later in this chapter. The particle nature of light is applied in math and 3D applications based on the field of *geometric optics*, a topic further discussed in the section "Geometric Optics and 3D" later in this chapter.

> *Geometric optics* describes light behavior, its propagation, and its interaction with matter while making several assumptions about light. By doing so, it makes it possible to describe light characteristics using mathematical equations that we use in 3D to create shaders and simulate light.

The Physical Nature of Light

So far we have already referred to EM radiation, photons, and waves repeatedly, so let's examine their characteristics and influence on color and brightness to better understand the perception of light.

Wavelength

The *wavelength* (λ) is the distance between the peaks and troughs of a wave, as illustrated in Figure 9.4 (between points A and B). The *amplitude* is the magnitude of the wave, and with respect to light, it defines brightness (as relative intensity). *Frequency* is defined as the number of cycles per second, referring to the number of waves that pass a given point per second. Frequency is measured in hertz, where a single cycle per second is equivalent to one hertz (Hz), and millions of cycles per second are referred to as megahertz (MHz).

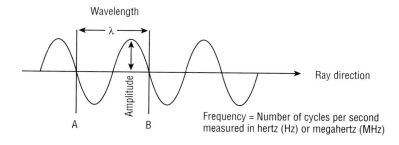

Wavelength

Ray direction

Amplitude

A   B

Frequency = Number of cycles per second
measured in hertz (Hz) or megahertz (MHz)

Figure 9.4

The wavelength, amplitude, and frequency all influence the characteristics of light.

EM Radiation

EM radiation refers to a pair of oscillating waves (at right angles) that are part magnetic and part electric, propagating in various directions over time and space. EM radiation, its energy, and its visual appearance can be charted as shown in Figure 9.5. The EM spectrum wavelengths span from one extreme to the other without a specific end point on either side. The range typically depicted in charts spans from radio waves (very long wavelengths) to gamma rays (extremely short wavelengths). Longer wavelengths possess a more wave-like nature (that is, radio waves); with shorter wavelengths, the wavelength becomes more negligible, and the radiation takes a more particle-like nature, referred to as *rays* (that is, X rays, gamma rays, and so on).

Figure 9.5

Electromagnetic radiation and the visible spectrum

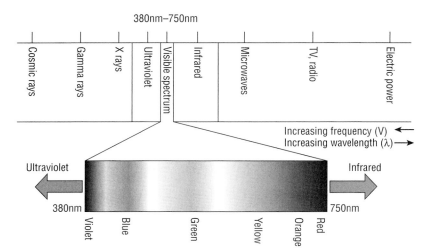

Based on the equation cited earlier ($E = h \times v$) that reconciles light's dual nature, you can conclude that as the frequency increases (shorter wavelengths), the energy increases. Energy also takes the form of heat, where an increase in energy results with a proportional increase in temperature. Thus, there is an interdependent relationship between the frequency, the energy, and the temperature. As discussed earlier, hertz cannot increase the energy of liberated electrons merely by adding more light, because only a change in frequency can cause a change in energy.

The Visible Spectrum

The term *light* refers to the *visible spectrum*, a small range of wavelengths that are perceived as color by the human eye, also shown in Figure 9.5. The visible spectrum spans from red (longer wavelengths) to violet (shorter wavelengths). You can see the color version in the EM Radiation image in the Chapter 9 folder on the companion CD.

The visible spectrum wavelengths are typically measured in nanometers (nm, where one nm is equal to one billionth of a meter) and range from 380–750nm. As you can see, different wavelengths are associated with different colors, known as the *color temperature*. The association of a wavelength with a given color is based on experiments that examine the observation of color (visible radiation) on a surface that is gradually increasing in temperature, shifting in hue. Thus, as the interaction of light with matter results in the heating of matter, absorbing and emitting energy of different wavelengths, the color of a surface is related to its current color temperature, as well as its light scattering (and absorbing) characteristics. Color temperature is measured using *kelvins* (see the section "The Kelvin Temperature Scale").

With respect to light scattering, different surfaces scatter light by reflecting certain wavelengths while absorbing (or transmitting) others based on the surface's "natural" color. The diffuse color of a surface is then a balance between the incoming radiant energy at a given frequency (color temperature) and the surface's scattering characteristics.

THERMAL VS. REFLECTED RADIATION

Light radiates from matter as either *reflected* or *thermal radiation*, providing the sensation of color. Thermal radiation relates to matter that is going through a chemical process, such as a burning filament. Reflected radiation relates to wavelengths that are reflected or transmitted through matter.

Essentially, as a surface is showered in light, the surface gives off heat based on its *current energy*, a threshold at which specific wavelengths are reflected rather than absorbed. As the surface temperature increases, longer wavelengths are absorbed and shorter wavelengths are reflected. This explains why surfaces that are gradually heating, such as over a fire, shift in hue from red to blue.

THE HUMAN EYE

In the human retina, *cones* and *rods* are the receptors for color and brightness, respectively. Cone receptors deal with the perception of color (chromaticity) and use three receptors that are sensitive to different wavelength ranges, which are long, medium, and short. These wavelengths ranges correlate to red, green, and blue temperatures respectively. Rods allow you to determine relative brightness, correlating to the light's amplitude (brightness), which is a measurement of *luminance power* that describes monochromatic values.

THE KELVIN TEMPERATURE SCALE

The Kelvin (K) scale measures color temperature based on degrees Celsius, offset by 273°. The scale assumes zero as an absolute zero temperature (to avoid negative Celsius degrees). Thus, at zero (-273° Celsius), the Kelvin scale depicts a hypothetical state where no heat (energy) is present. Visible light ranges approximately from 1700K to 16,000K.

The process of referring color measurements to temperature is based on *blackbody radiation*. This term refers to an experiment of observing the reflected color from a black surface that theoretically absorbs all incoming energy. The sensation of color is then solely derived by the energy the surface emits rather than a surface color. Thus, blackbody radiation allows us to observe the emitted radiant energy as color temperature while the surface temperature increases. The perceivable colors are then referred to by a temperature on the Kelvin scale that corresponds to a specific wavelength color.

It is common for light vendors to refer to a given light type by its Kelvin scale. It is also common for digital cameras to provide the Kelvin scale as a means for determining white balance, as discussed next. With kelvins, we can easily relate to a specific light intensity, such as D65, which is a daylight standard of 6500K.

> By convention, we refer to units of the Kelvin scale as *kelvins*, not degrees or Kelvin degrees.

Color Temperature and Photography

In photography, *white balance* relates to selecting a suitable color temperature (kelvin) for an image. Film and digital sensors don't have the same ability of the human eye to observe light as "white" under varying (or changing) light conditions. In essence, each image will have a white balance corresponding to a certain color temperature that appears as "white light."

Wavelengths that are greater or smaller than that balanced point will appear as colors, based on their relative color temperature. To clarify, the human eye has an "automatic" white-balance control (*chromatic adaptation*) that adjusts to lighting conditions. Wavelengths that are above or below that "white balance" appear to inherit their relative color temperature. Typically you see this sort of effect in a room that is illuminated from both indoor and outdoor lighting. Most of the light appears white, but the light entering from outside will usually have a bluer tint, whereas the light from a lamp will have a warmer tint. With cameras, it's important to set the white balance for the given light conditions. For example, if the white balance is set to dim light conditions and you then use that same white-balance in brighter conditions, all the colors will appear to have a bluer tint. These simulations of light are another important factor when designing the lighting scheme with direct and indirect illumination.

Wavelength Dependencies

All the previous sections are aimed at clarifying the different wavelength characteristics and their influence on perceivable light and color. The significance of wavelength dependency refers to the fact that every wavelength has its unique scattering characteristics and color temperature. Thus, the reflection and refraction of light are wavelength-dependent effects, where different wavelengths scatter in different directions. In 3D, shaders such as the Cook-Torrance shader or a custom lens shader enable per-wavelength effects, considering short, medium, and long wavelengths. The topic of mental ray shaders and their relevance to wavelength characteristics is discussed in detail throughout this chapter. Note that mental ray (3.4) enables specifying color profiles. One such profile even supports rendering spectral (wavelength) color effects using custom shaders; however, currently you cannot easily select color profiles without editing an .mi file manually and rendering it with a stand-alone renderer.

Light Perception and Synthetic Imaging

The human eye can perceive a much greater range (contrast ratio of light intensity) than artificial capture and display devices—typically varying by several orders of magnitude—but even that range is limited compared to the range of light intensities that physically exist. The methods and units of measurement with respect to *light energy* are based on *radiometric* or *photometric* terms and their relative measurement units.

So far this chapter has referred to light color as wavelengths of varying size and has neglected that real-world light consists of an infinite number of different wavelengths, not a single wavelength. Thus, light manifests itself as a collection of varying wavelengths (color) and amplitudes (brightness/intensity) that also vary in direction and time. Therefore, the perceived light color is based on multiple wavelengths and their relative intensities (amplitude). For example, if longer wavelengths predominate, the perceived color will show a red tint. The measurement of light intensity using precise radiometric (*radiance*) measurements, or equivalent photometric measurements (*luminance*), is significant to 3D rendering, particularly with indirect illumination.

With physically accurate simulations of light (indirect illumination), radiometric measurements are used to measure the influence of light in the scene, simulating light interaction with surfaces. Radiometry is part of the geometric optics tool set for mathematically describing light. Rendering is then based on radiometric measurements of light taken within the scene, where light is modeled in accordance to the geometric optics light model. You can see how 3D image generation heavily relies on the physics of light, as well as its measurements.

> Radiometric measurements are the backbone of shader design, where mathematical expressions are used to describe the interaction of light with matter. (See the section "The BSDF Functions" later in this chapter.)

Photometric measurements are equivalent to radiometric measurements, but they're adjusted for human (or photographic) perception, as discussed shortly in the section "Photometry Measurements." Thus, both sciences deal with light measurement; radiometry deals with a linear representation of light intensity, and in photometry the relationship is nonlinear, based on human perception. With synthetic imaging and 3D, tone-mapping techniques are applied to adjust linear measurement of light to a nonlinear (photometric) representation that better resembles how the scene (real-world environment) is perceived by a human eye. The following topics provide a clearer introduction to light-measurement fundamentals. Then, after briefly exploring these fields, we can further examine their relationships to visual perception, digital imaging, and shader illumination models.

Radiometry Measurements

Radiometry is the science of precise measurements of *radiant energy*, measured in joules; it measures the amount of photons at a given point. *Radiant flux* (Φ) is a measurement of radiant energy per unit of time (average flux over time) in watts (joules per second), as it is incident on, transmits through, or emits from matter. *Matter* refers to a radiation source that produces reflected or thermal radiation, regardless of whether the energy is perceptible to the human eye (within the visible spectrum range). In other words, radiometric measurements deal with radiant energy as an absolute value of *radiant power* (a term that's interchangeable with radiant flux), such as when we say that a light source emits 60 watts.

FLUX DENSITY

In addition to radiant flux per unit of time, we also consider radiant *flux density* projected onto, or emitted from, a given surface area over time, referred to as *irradiance* and *radiant exitance*. Both are measured in watts per square meter (watts ÷ m²), factoring in the surface area of a radiant source (or target). Thus, these measurements provide insight into the influence of light over a given surface area, as illustrated in Figure 9.6.

Irradiance

Irradiance can be found in host applications as a shader property typically used with indirect illumination, providing a means to fine-tune the total incoming radiant power from the surroundings, cast upon a given surface area. In other words, this measurement is used while rendering to evaluate the total light influences from several radiant sources (based on radiance measurements), across a surface area. For example, a radiant source casting 100 watts on a surface area of 2 square meters (the area in question), is equal to an irradiance of 100 ÷ 2 watts per square meter, as shown in Figure 9.6 under "Irradiance." Thus, in this case, every point on the surface, receives 50 watts/m².

Radiant Exitance and Radiosity

Radiant exitance, also known as *radiosity*, expresses the exitance (emission/reflection) of radiant flux from a given surface area. Thus, radiant exitance can express radiant flux emitted from a light source, such as an area light that has an emission area (not infinitely small) or radiation cast from (or through) a surface as reflected radiation, typically referred to as *radiosity*. As you can see in Figure 9.6, it is the opposite of irradiance, and thus, if we say that the area light is casting 100 watts from a 2-square-meter surface area, then the radiance exitance from the area light's surface (from each surface point) is equal to 50 watts per square meter (assuming it's uniformly distributed).

While converting a point light to an area light you will notice that the area light casts more light into the scene, as both use the same light intensity value (defined by the user) with the difference in flux density; the area light actually has a means for representing area flux (radiant exitance). Thus, a point light emitting 50 watts provides less light opposed to a rectangular area light of 2 units in size that casts 50 watts/m^2.

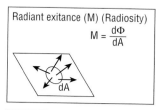

Flux (Φ) per unit of area

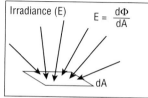

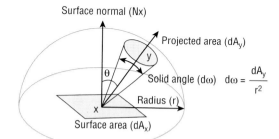

Radiance (L)
(flux per unit, projected area per unit, solid angle)

$$L = \frac{d^2\Phi}{d\omega dA \cos\theta}$$

Hemispheric coordinates over a sampled point X

Figure 9.6

Radiant exitance, irradiance, and radiance measurements.

Radiant exitance is used with radiosity, a subdivision mesh technique that divides a scene into patches for calculating the radiant exitance in the scene, which is a diffuse global illumination algorithm. Thus, radiosity is a radiometric-dependent algorithm for measuring radiant exitance from every subdivided patch, conducting a global illumination simulation. In a similar way to radiosity, mental ray uses a technique known as *photon mapping* to calculate global illumination without a mesh subdivision dependency; therefore, it does not require tessellating the scene into patches. You'll learn more about that in Chapter 12, "Indirect Illumination."

RADIANT INTENSITY AND RADIANCE

The distribution of flux in a given direction is referred to as *radiant intensity*. This measurement accounts for infinitely small light sources that cast light in a given direction over a certain area that is subtended with a solid angle on a hemisphere around the emitting source (point). A solid angle is a means for extending a 2D circle into 3D for various mathematical calculations. To clarify, look at Figure 9.6 under the "Radiance" area. The solid angle $d\omega$ defines an area (dA_y) on the hemisphere around point X. This area, dA_y, represents a projected region from point X on a hemisphere around that point (X) that is measured as radiant intensity projected over a solid angle.

A solid angle is calculated by dividing the projection area by the square radius of a hemisphere, as shown in Figure 9.6. Theoretically, when the hemisphere radius is at a value of 1, the solid angle is equal to the projected area value. The solid angle is measured with steradians (sr), and radiant intensity is measured in watts per steradian.

RADIANCE

Radiance is the complex measurement of radiant density (area flux) flux projected in a given direction within a solid angle. As illustrated in Figure 9.6, it's a measurement of watts per square meter per steradian [W ÷ (steradian × m^2)]. Radiance can be used to describe both emitted radiation (radiant exitance) and received radiation (irradiance), over a surface area, and within a specific direction and solid angle. In other words, it can calculate the different radiant contributions that comprise the overall radiant exitance or irradiance related to a surface based on the incoming or outgoing direction of flux.

With indirect illumination simulations, this is the most influential measurement because it determines the visual appearance of the surface based on the direction and solid angle of a radiating source. It enables the renderer to evaluate influences from several light-emitting or -reflecting elements in the scene, based on their directionalities and sizes. A common reference to indirect illumination is that of solving the *radiance equation*, which is an equation that describes the complex distribution of radiance in the scene. The techniques discussed in Chapters 12 and 13 deal with solving radiance in the scene for indirect light; the radiance reflected, transmitted, or absorbed by surfaces in the scene, and the particles in the air such as dust.

You will soon see how shading models depend on radiance while defining illumination models, basing the results on the angle between the surface normal and the direction of the light source. In Figure 9.6, the angle θ between the direction to the light source and the surface normal determines the influence of light on a shading point from a given direction and intensity (flux). With indirect illumination, the renderer is required to calculate the radiance incident on, transmitted through, or reflected from surface areas in the scene, such as the area labeled dA$_x$ in the figure.

Radiance is subject to the inverse square law, which describes the falloff rate of radiant flux over distance, and its intensity is inversely proportional to the square of the distance from the source; this results from the increasing spread (angle) of light as it travels away from a point over time. Thus, with respect to radiance, light flux is measured as projected energy in a given direction within a solid angle, as shown in Figure 9.6, which forms a "radius" of decreasing (spreading) radiant power at increasing distances. Note that the radiant energy itself does not attenuate over distance without interacting with matter; it only spreads over a larger area while maintaining its energy.

Photometry Measurements

Photometry is the science of measuring luminance power as perceived by the human eye. Thus, photometric measurements deal with the visible spectrum and its relationship to visual perception. These measurements divide into *scotopic* and *photopic* vision measurements. Scotopic vision relates to dim light conditions, such as night lighting, where the human eye's perception is more monochromatic because it depends on rods more than cones, opposed to photopic vision that distinguishes color more accurately using cones in our retina.

The human eye's ability to perceive light color (*chromaticity*) and brightness (*luminance*) is described by the *luminosity curve*, as shown in Figure 9.7, which has been standardized by the Commission Internationale d'Eclairage (CIE), known as the CIE 1924 photopic luminosity function and also as the V(λ) curve (V-lambda). The luminosity function provides a standard curve that describes the human observer's sensitivity to light using photopic vision, as well as a different sensitivity curve for scotopic vision. The luminosity curve is used to correlate between radiometric and photometric energy. In other words, it provides the photometric equivalent of a radiometric measurement adjusted for human perception. As you can see in the figure, human photopic perception is most sensitive at (around) 550nm, a yellow-green color.

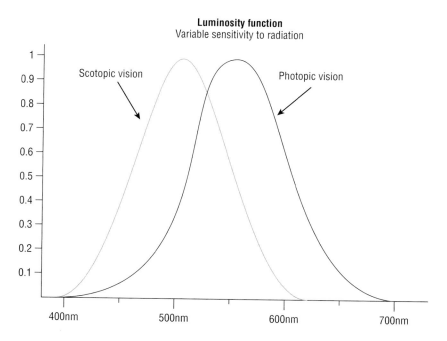

Figure 9.7

The luminosity function charts the human sensitivity to light and color with photopic and scotopic vision.

THE IMPORTANCE OF PHOTOMETRIC MEASUREMENTS

Photometric measurements are significant in 3D image generation with respect to the light brightness as perceived by the human eye (or film). Primarily, the luminance values define the contrast range visible on film (or to our eyes), as influenced by radiance from an environment.

Luminance is then a photometric term used to describe the *luminous power* (flux) perceived by an observer, over time and per unit projected area and solid angle based on the luminosity function. Photometric measurements are equivalents to radiometric measurements, as they have been described earlier in the chapter, with the difference that they are adjusted for human perception and use the term *luminance* rather than *radiance*. Conceptually, it's similar to gamma correction that describes the nonlinear representation of brightness with a monitor (see Chapter 3), just not within a range such as 0 to 1 (as with gamma) but instead as relative brightness of the scene. In contrast to luminance, radiance deals with absolute energy, as with indirect illumination that is not bound to human perception.

Typically, photometric luminance measurements are provided in orders of magnitude (powers of 10) and measured in candelas per square meter (cd/m^2). For example, star light measurement is 10^{-3}, whereas direct light is 10^5, describing a perceivable brightness range. These ranges become significant with respect to the differences between the human eye, acquisition, and display device abilities to capture and display luminance values of much smaller ranges.

COLOR SPACES AND PERCEPTION

In 1931, based on the $V(\lambda)$ luminosity function, the CIE standard observer XYZ color space was defined. It mathematically describes color dependent on human perception using three functions: $\bar{r}(\lambda)$, $\bar{g}(\lambda)$, and $\bar{b}(\lambda)$.

These color components are graphed in a similar way to the luminosity function, describing a *color-matching* function. The term *color-matching* means the standard observer XYZ color space mathematically plots these three functions in a way that enables re-creating (matching) any color combination based on human perception. To clarify, by using three RGB primary colors as independent monochromatic light projectors, participants are asked to control the intensity of each light so that they re-create a target color. This is accomplished by projecting colors on a screen and visually comparing the result with the target color. The measurement of the intensity of each projected light color is used to define the $\bar{r}(\lambda)$, $\bar{g}(\lambda)$, and $\bar{b}(\lambda)$ color-matching functions that are then used to define color spaces. Thus, color spaces standardize the results of such experiments into a diagram that can be used for color lookups, plotting three functions based on human perception.

Color spaces are used to describe a relative gamut of color for a given device, in comparison to a human observer's gamut. Today, different color space models exist, each specifying a range of colors that can be reproduced with that model (color space) relative to human perception. The CIE *xy* chromaticity diagram is commonly used to represent the human visual gamut of color, where the wavelength is specified around the outer border of the shape, as shown in the image here, starting at 380nm and going around to 700nm. As you can see, each wavelength also has a corresponding xy location on the diagram. Color profiles are charted relative to that diagram and define a gamut for artificial devices, such as the ones shown for Adobe RGB (1998) and the sRGB color spaces here; these are two common spaces. You can look at the CIExy1931 image in the Chapter 9 folder on the companion CD.

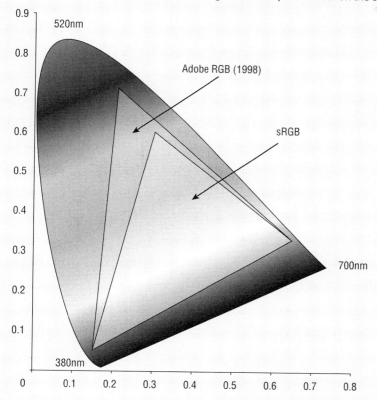

Color spaces and profiles have several purposes. With respect to our field of imaging, they are used to match the color of a shot to a specific gamut of a target media, be it film, broadcast TV, or print. They are also used for adjusting the monitor display and correcting the gamma using a color profile that matches the monitor's ability to reproduce color using three RGB channels. The sRGB color space is theoretically similar to applying a gamma correction of 2.2 that has been standardized with graphics and image display on a screen intended for web delivery. Digital cameras usually use sRGB or Adobe RGB (1998) color spaces so that when the image is brought into the computer, it appears with the correct luminance, as discussed in Chapter 3 with respect to gamma correction. The sRGB color space provides for more vivid colors and contrast because it has a smaller gamut of color that is more inline with the range of colors that can be vividly reproduced on a screen.

Geometric Optics and 3D

Geometric optics is a simplified subset of quantum mechanics that we use with CG to simulate light. In CG we make several assumptions to simplify the simulation of light while weighting-in important light phenomena using a *render equation*. The render equation is a mathematical process of weighting the total distribution of light based on all the scene properties, including direct light, indirect light, surface materials, participating media, and more. All these equations are evaluated using the laws of physics to mathematically describe light propagation.

With the wave theory, light propagation is explained based on common wave characteristics such as interference, diffraction, and polarization. Interference and diffraction have already been discussed earlier. The importance of the wave model is its relationship to perceived color, which is a wavelength-dependent phenomenon. In computer graphics, the wave model is not simulated as a wave of different lengths but as direct rays, similar to the particle assertion. Hence, CG simulations of light are limited to reflectance and transmittance, neglecting any diffraction or interference wave phenomena. Also, the geometric model assumes that light travels instantaneously, ignoring that light transmits through different media at different speeds. In a nutshell, this simplified method allows us to simulate the general behavior of light as it interacts with surfaces; however, phenomena such as the *dispersion* of different wavelengths through matter are not typically supported.

LIGHT DISPERSION

The dispersion of light means that light changes its speed as it travels through matter. The change of speed is referred to as a ratio (Snell's law of refraction) known as the *index of refraction* (IOR). This ratio represents the difference between the speed of light in a vacuum and the speed of light in matter. With respect to the refraction of light, matter is described as either dispersive or nondispersive media. Dispersive media refract different wavelengths using a different IOR so that the light fans out into its component wavelengths, as in Newton's prism experiment. Note that "white light" may be comprised of any collection of wavelengths as cited earlier; thus, when light fans out into its separate wavelength components, you observe the spectrum of colors (wavelengths) that manifested the incident light. So, the IOR through dielectric dispersive mediums is a per-wavelength phenomenon based on a relative change in speed as light propagates through matter. These types of effects are rather complex to simulate; in most cases, they are achieved by creative means rather than a realistic shader effect.

A typical phenomenon seen in photography and real life is *mirage effects*. When we discuss the path and speed of light in vacuum, we neglect atmospheric effects such as air density. Mirage effects are caused by a change in temperature (and thus densities) in the atmosphere. As light travels through the atmosphere, it changes speed through different densities and thus appears to refract (bend) the image that is perceived by the observer.

POLARIZATION IN 3D

Polarization describes the oscillation directionality of the electric and magnetic components of the electromagnetic spectrum relative to the light's travel direction. To clarify, consider a ray of light traveling along the Z axis; polarization describes the oscillatory directionality and phase (waves that are in or out of sync) of the electromagnetic wave components perpendicular to the travel (Z axis) direction along the X and Y planes.

We will not return to the topic of simulating polarization effects in 3D, so this sidebar provides a quick example of doing so, based on shaders discussed in detail throughout Chapter 10. Polarization typically attributes to birefringence effects of light, which is the effect of a ray of light that splits into two rays as it refracts through a thick anisotropic surface such as a calcite, creating the complex visual effect of seeing doubles as both rays actually refract at an offset index of refraction, as shown in here.

Birefringence effects are not simple to simulate in 3D and can be achieved by layering two refractive shaders where each has a different index of refraction. However, doing so will refract only one and then the other without layering them together in a way that they appear to split into two components. To remedy this, I use a complex shader tree that layers two mib_glossy_refraction shaders together to create the effect of anisotropic double refractions, as shown in the shader tree here. I also use the mib_texture_rotate shader to rotate one of the refractions so they appear at an angle to each other by relying on the theories discussed in detail in Chapter 10. You can find the Polar.mb shader tree for Maya in the Chapter 9 folder on the companion CD.

continued

continues

Consider that as an alternative you could render two refraction passes with different indices of refraction for the same surface. You could then mix these passes inside a compositing program, providing an easier alternative for constructing birefringence effects.

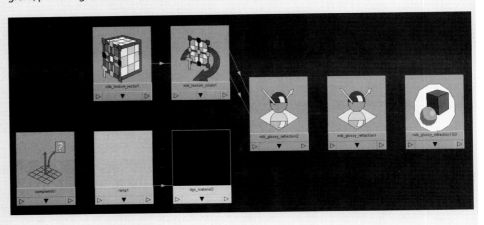

You could simulate such effects using a transparent surface with a noisy texture applied as the index of refraction so that the image randomly bends, mimicking a mirage effect. Further, you could fine-tune the effect using a gradient mask so that the effect is more pronounced in a certain area, such as closer to the ground.

CHROMATIC ABERRATIONS

Chromatic aberration refers to the dispersion of light as it refracts through a lens and onto a film or digital sensor. As the angle of incidence between the light rays and the lens increases, as with a wide-angle lens, the different wavelength of light may take on different paths. Essentially, by separating wavelengths, you see noticeable color fringes in photographs where the light dispersed unevenly through the lens. Light dispersing into its component wavelengths is even more noticeable with lens flares. Therefore, chromatic aberrations are another (wavelength-based) photographic characteristic that in most cases is not properly simulated in 3D. Some shaders offer chromatic aberration or dispersion as shader options, but they are merely hacks and not actual simulations of light dispersion through the lens.

Light behaviors based on the laws of geometric optics are discussed with their relevance to mental ray shaders in the following sections, which define the characteristics of absorption, reflectance, and transmittance with matter.

High Dynamic Range (HDR) Concepts

Our eyes constantly adapt to changing light conditions, "balancing" their sensitivity for optimal visibility, a phenomenon referred to as *chromatic adaptation*. The eye's ability to adjust for different light intensities enables us to see relatively clearly under different conditions and through a high dynamic range of light—particularly when the shift in dynamic range occurs over a large distance, as when observing a sunrise.

With 3D light simulations, when re-creating the natural lighting of an environment, HDR images allow us to use light luminance values captured on set, in a real environment, as a "source" for light within 3D. The use of a high dynamic range of light is significant on two occasions, both typically used with indirect light simulations:

- When we use real-world lighting acquired with HDR images to light our scenes, as cited earlier. This technique is dependent on HDR images and is the focus of this section.

- While physically modeling light transport in the scene with physically based light shaders. This technique is solely constructed in 3D and simulates the transport of a high dynamic range of light. Chapter 13, "Final Gather and Ambient Occlusion," discusses this topic and the architectural Sun and Sky shaders.

The topics of HDR images, capturing techniques, and HDR editing software are becoming essential tools for the 3D artist. In the following sections, you will become more familiar with the importance of terms for HDR imaging.

Human vs. Digital Perception

The photometric measurement of light in real-world conditions is not a black-to-white range but a measurement of contrast between the darkest and brightest intensities perceived by the human eye. That range is commonly referred to as a *high dynamic range*, where it effectively has limitless luminance ranges. To clarify, the range does not start at black (or zero) but instead at the darkest visible light, and it ranges to the brightest light. The range is a contrast ratio that effectively represents the real-world luminance. The difference between humans and artificial devices (film or digital sensors) is in the extent of light seen vs. captured.

With digital cameras, f-stops represent the range of light that is captured so that you may consider six f-stops to capture a contrast ratio of 2^6, which is equivalent to a ratio of 64:1, a very low dynamic range. The human eye, theoretically at a fixed pupil size (fixed f-stop), is estimated to perceive around 14 stops (more than 16,000:1), whereas cameras can theoretically capture at perfect exposure settings up to nine f-stops. The pupil is not fixed and does adapt to light conditions especially over distance, as noted earlier, and can theoretically perceive around 24 f-stops of light intensity, a ratio of more than 16,000,000:1. Thus, a camera's digital sensors (or film) typically remains within a low dynamic range (LDR) that can reproduce a limited contrast ratio between the brightest and darkest recorded values. Color values that exceed the sensors' ranges are overexposed. The purpose of HDR digital imaging is to capture the same light range as perceivable by the human eye (and to take advantage of even greater luminance ranges).

The purpose of HDR imaging is then to reproduce what the human eye can see, not what artificial devices can capture and display. Because of this difference, HDR images are referred to as *scene-referred* images, and LDR images are *device-referred* images, based on the device's capabilities rather than the actual scene luminance. (Note that *scene* refers to the environment in question, not a 3D scene.)

HDR Imaging and Display

HDR display and capture devices are beginning to emerge, but they are expensive and still far from being commonly used. Instead, with most display devices, you need to use a two-stage process to present an HDR range of luminance in an LDR environment using an LDR image file such as a JPEG or TIF. The process of reproducing such an image has two parts: compiling an HDR image using all the LDR images and *tone mapping* the HDR image to an LDR image.

COMPILING HDR IMAGES

HDR photography consists of acquiring several versions of an image at different exposure levels. The use of several exposures enables us to capture a higher dynamic range than possible with one single exposure. Each exposure displays a different range of light from the scene, as shown in Figure 9.8. The figure presents a collection of six images captured in a warehouse at different exposures. Image 1 appears underexposed, capturing the details outside the warehouse (the sky and other building details). Image 6 is overexposed, capturing the details in the darkest shadows within the warehouse. The gradual difference shown from 1 to 6 demonstrates the different luminance ranges captured at different exposures.

Figure 9.8

Several images taken at different exposures that capture a higher dynamic range, which enables us to reproduce a more accurate image representing a higher dynamic range

As an observer, I could clearly see the blue sky and details outside the warehouse as well as inside; however, the camera captures only a limited portion of details with each exposure. If you combine all these images into one, you can reproduce an image that more accurately represents the scene, representing a human-perceivable range of light with a tone-mapped LDR image.

Using a program such as HDR Shop or Adobe Photoshop, you can compile a sequence of different exposures, as shown in Figure 9.8, into an individual HDR image. This file will then internally hold all the information from the different exposures; however, you can display only one exposure at a time on the screen. That is, HDR images possess a wider dynamic range than most output devices (monitors) can display. You can use HDR Shop to view the information stored at each exposure one at a time by setting the current exposure with the plus and minus keys. (HDR Shop is covered in Chapter 13.)

In Figure 9.9, you see a waveform in Fusion (compositing software from eyeon Software, `www.eyeonline.com`) that describes the range of luminance in an image. I marked the 0 to 1 range along the bars under each label. The waveform allows you to inspect the luminance for broadcast purposes so that you can assure an image is within a broadcast-safe displayable range, which is an even smaller range shown with dashed lines along the bars in the figure. In image A, you see an HDR image graphed where the range by far exceeds the 0 to 1 range and in fact spans far outside the figure's border. All the values outside the 0 and 1 range are then not displayable on any device and appear as black or white.

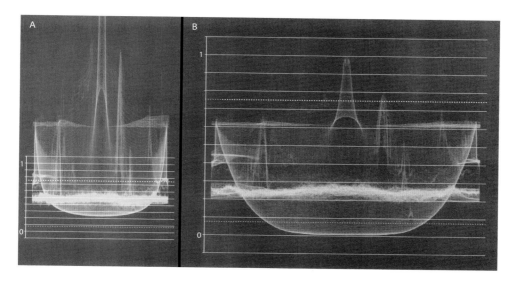

Figure 9.9

A waveform displays the luminance range of an HDR image (A) and an LDR image (B).

Tone mapping

Tone mapping refers to balancing the different exposures into an LDR image that realistically reproduces what a human eye may have perceived under those viewing conditions. It is the process of transforming HDR data from several images into an LDR image that can be displayed on most output devices. In Figure 9.10, which is a tone-mapped version of the warehouse HDR image, the details from outside and inside the warehouses are visible. Thus, tone mapping enables us to remap the distribution of values in a nonlinear fashion, from several exposures into one perceivable image that does not appear overexposed or underexposed. This process effectively takes values that are far greater than a 0 to 1 range and maps them to a 0 to 1 range so they don't appear overexposed, as shown with the waveform example in Figure 9.9 image B; the tone-mapped LDR image of the HDR image seen under image A.

Figure 9.10

Tone mapping enables us to remap the values stored within an HDR image into a lower dynamic range that more accurately represents the visual perception of the scene.

Normal images cannot reproduce data from overexposure, but with HDR images we can reproduce an image using data captured throughout the different exposures, as shown with the waveform in Figure 9.9 image A. The same image as an LDR image would have a flat line across the 0 and 1 boundaries, clamping any value outside that range. In contrast, HDR images maintain that data, allowing us to correct overexposure and tone-map the images so they appear closer to that of human perception.

HDR IMAGES AND 3D

For 3D rendering, tone mapping is less important, because we are primarily interested in the HDR data present in the image for illumination purposes. Thus, our purpose is not image display (as with showing a friend a photo) but luminance light measurements recorded within the HDR image as a source for illumination in the 3D scene. Although we cannot display HDR images without tone mapping, the 3D software does identify HDR per-pixel values regardless of the current exposure. While extracting values for indirect illumination simulations, the per-pixel value corresponds to the overall luminance, as shown with the waveform in Figure 9.9 image A.

Thus, in 3D we simply provide an HDR image that contains a dynamic range representative of a real scene, which is used to render richer lighting and reflection effects. If you downloaded HDR Shop, notice that as you move the cursor over the image, the RGB per-pixel values are displayed on the lower bar of the UI. Those values represent the per-pixel luminance in the image regardless of the exposure. Thus, if you leave the cursor at a given point and increase or decrease the exposure (with the plus and minus keys), the value will remain the same, because it's not dependent on exposure but represents the overall scene luminance.

> Using HDR images and LDR images with indirect lighting is not comparable. HDR images provide much richer colors and value, as shown in the color insert "HDR vs. LDR Rendering."

Thus, when you change the intensity of an HDR image in 3D, you are not changing exposure but actually changing the image range, as with Photoshop or compositing. To clarify, if you use a simple color gain operation (multiply) and set it to 0.5, you are scaling the high dynamic range to half, not actually selecting a different exposure. Creatively speaking, it is similar to adjusting exposure because as a result the lighting gets darker or brighter, but with a lower dynamic range of detail. It is better to leave the HDR image untouched so that the high dynamic range is not tampered and set the exposure in HDR Shop; setting the exposure defines the default exposure used for viewing as well as influences the intensity (brightness) of the rendered scene without reducing the dynamic range. Also, consider that you can render HDR images as output so that the exposure of the render can be manually adjusted in compositing. That ability is also available when you render 32-bit (non-HDR) images, as discussed in Chapter 3; but with HDR images, the available range is even greater than with 32-bit images, as discussed next.

> Maya, XSI, and 3ds Max all have at least one tone-mapping shader from the mental image architectural library that you can use to tone map renders when using physical simulations of light and physical shaders. The tone-mapping shader from this library is primarily intended to balance the render when using the physical Sun and Sky shaders, which use realistic illumination values. We will examine these shaders in Chapter 13.

LDR vs. HDR Image Formats

We must differentiate between image bit depth and brightness. When we render at a given bit-depth, as discussed in Chapter 3, the range of values that can be used to express the color shift from black to white is based on the image's bit depth and its precision. Higher bit depths provide for more accurate gradation from black to white. However, the increased precision does not provide a means to represent luminance correctly, only an increased precision within a given low dynamic range.

HDR images are typically stored in 8-bit files, where the alpha channel is used as an exponent value for each pixel, referred to as an *exponential notation*. The notation, especially with 32-bit HDR images, allows representing values by raising the RGB channel values to the power of 10 multiplied by the exponent in the alpha channel, such as $5.632^{10 \times n}$, where n is the exponent. In this case, the value is already larger than that capable of being stored in a 32-bit image (see Chapter 3 for 32-bit images). The resulting range of values is virtually limitless, representing the varying luminance intensities, not limited to a black-to-white linear range. If you use 32-bit images, the improved precision of the HDR image's color values reduces the chances of visible artifacts in gradation between the values, such as banding; however, it has no significance on the exposure range. When used with 3D, you really need a reference only for luminance, not a nice-looking image. If you intend on using the HDR image as a background, you should tone-map the HDR image and apply it as a background in compositing.

> When rendering, you can output either HDR or OpenEXR image formats, which are both HDR image formats.

As discussed in Chapter 3, gamma encoding is used to remap the intensity of color values in LDR images, by manipulating the gamma curve within the 0 to 1 range, remapping the luminance for low-dynamic-range display devices. In contrast, HDR images use a gamma curve of 1 (linear) because it represents the full dynamic range of the scene. Both gamma correction and tone mapping deal with remapping the luminance values of each color channel using a customized nonlinear curve to maximize color reproduction. The significant difference between the two is that gamma is used to remap the distribution of values that are already within a 0 to 1 range, whereas tone mapping is used to remap values from a high dynamic range into a lower dynamic range between 0 and 1.

Light Transport and Shading Models

mental ray attempts to reproduce the interaction between surfaces and light, mimicking several natural phenomena as a means to reproduce realism. Shading models are the basis for reproducing surface response to light, typically manifested as complex shader trees within host applications that are piped through a surface material.

FURTHER RESOURCES

Because this book is primarily focused on mental ray rendering, the topic of light is to some extent beyond the scope of this book. What I've provided here is simply an introduction to optics and the physics of light. I highly recommend that you pursue these topics further. Some valuable resources include 3D lighting and synthetic imaging books as well as some online resources such as Wikipedia (http://wikipedia.org). For photographic and HDR imaging, refer to www.cambridgeincolour.com and www.debevec.org.

Our primary concern with respect to rendering concepts deals with the light absorption and scattering characteristics of the surface material, be it metal, stone, glass, plastic, ceramic, and so on. Advanced shading algorithms attempt to consider the absorption and internal scattering (translucency) of materials such as those just cited. In real-world conditions, most surfaces exhibit some degree of subsurface scattering that may appear as a shallow layer of internal scattering or as deep scattering, such as with wax, minerals, liquids, and so on.

The Bidirectional Scattering Distribution Function (BSDF)

Most surfaces are not easily re-created with 3D because of their internal light-scattering characteristics. The primary focus of most shading models (that is, Lambert, Blinn, Phong, Cook-Torrance, and Ward) is on external light scattering, neglecting the effect of subsurface scattering on a surface's appearance. These shading models use various illumination models to resolve light transport in the scene. The illumination model is a function known as the *bidirectional scattering distribution function* (BSDF), a model for light transport. The shading models are the various shaders that examine the light at a shading point during rendering. They may be simplistic (Lambert, Phong, Blinn), physically correct (Cook-Torrance, DGS), and empirical (Ward, Strauss, Lafortune) shading models (discussed in the sidebar "Shading Model Types").

Internal light scattering that influences a surface's materialistic visual characteristics can be simulated with advanced shaders, be it "fake" workarounds or actual (physically correct) subsurface scattering calculations. We further discuss these more complex approaches to surface rendering in Chapter 14, "Subsurface Scattering."

SHADING MODEL TYPES

The Lambert and Phong shading models provide visual feedback that is detached from physical accuracy. They utilize the most elementary BRDF (BRDFs are a subset of BSDFs discussed in the following section) functions and provide an ad hoc solution, which is a basic means for shading in CG. The Lambert shader deals with diffuse light only, and the Phong shader adds specular highlights. In contrast, physical models such as the Cook-Torrance shader utilize complex illumination models (BRDF) that consider natural surface and light characteristics that are substructure microfaceted (Lambertian) reflectors, Fresnel reflections, wavelength dependency, and energy conservation

continued

continues

(discussed in more detail later in this chapter). The visual result of using more physically accurate shading models opposed to simplistic models becomes apparent when rendering complex surface types.

In the image shown here, you see two rows labeled A–F that compare the qualities of light using the Cook-Torrance and Phong shaders. The geometry on the top row (A–C) uses a Cook-Torrance shader, and the bottom row (D–F) uses a Phong shader. A large area light casts light into the scene, and you can see how each shader's BRDF simulates the reflected light at three different angles. You can see that the qualities of the reflected light with the Cook-Torrance shader are visually more pleasing and accurate than with the Phong shader. Notice how the reflected intensity in A–C shifts with the perspective (viewing angle), as opposed to the Phong shader (D–F) that maintains the same intensity. Also, the visual appearance of the area light is better simulated in the top row. The Blinn shader would provide similar results to the Cook-Torrance shader because they are similar aside from minor differences in their BRDFs (particularly wavelength dependency and energy conservation) that make the Cook-Torrance a more physically accurate shader.

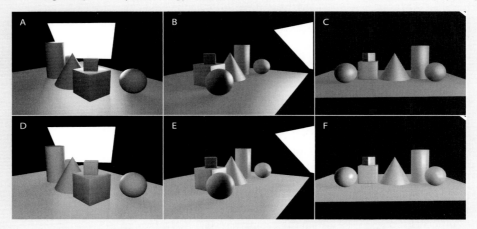

Also, for the purpose of realism, some shaders known as *empirical shaders* use scientific values to describe reflectance, such as the Ward and LaFortune shading models. Empirical shaders provide "fast" realism based on scientific accuracy, rather than applying complex shading mathematics to simulate the interaction of light with a surface. In other words, they use BRDFs that don't mimic realism based on accurate math but try to get as close as possible based on observation, mimicking what we would expect to see. One form of empirical shader, such as the Lafortune shader, allows us to use measurements of light reflectance gathered with scientific experiments. The results are then applied to the shader in a form of a database of reflectance data. Thus, the shader doesn't have to calculate physically accurate simulations; the shader has to only fit the data to a given condition, which is a much faster approach to rendering shading models. Visually, empirical models provide for very realistic results that are in line with the physical shaders, but they require fewer calculations.

You have already seen an empirical light shader in Chapter 6, "Lights and Soft Shadows," when we used light profiles with a photometric shader and provided the shader with scientific data describing the light intensity, spread, and decay. The shader model types are discussed in more detail throughout the chapter.

The BSDF Functions

BSDF consists of two component models: the bidirectional reflectance distribution function (BRDF) and the bidirectional transmittance distribution function (BTDF), as shown in Figure 9.11. For the most part, we'll focus on BRDF as a function that describes surface reflectance; however, the same concepts are true with BTDFs.

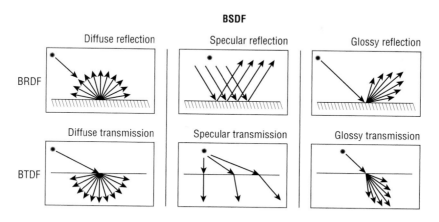

BSDF

Diffuse reflection   Specular reflection   Glossy reflection

BRDF

Diffuse transmission   Specular transmission   Glossy transmission

BTDF

Figure 9.11

BSDF light models utilize DGS reflectance and transmittance characteristics to describe a shading model.

THE FUNCTION

The BRDF function is a four-dimensional mathematical function that considers two incoming dimensions and two outgoing dimensions and can be written like this, where Φ is the radiant flux and θ is the angle relative to the surface normal (the subscripts i and r refer to incident and reflected):

$$f_r = (\Phi_i, \theta_i, \Phi_r, \theta_r)$$

The function maps the relationship between the radiance (radiant flux) cast from a source light and in a given direction (relative to the surface normal), as well as the radiance from the surface in a given direction relative to the surface normal. Thus, the BSDF calculates the surface reflectance considering the radiance (a term described earlier) cast on a given shading point from a given direction and solid angle.

BSDF equations make several assumptions about the behavior of light, neglecting subsurface scattering and assuming that light reflectance and transmittance occurs from the same point on a surface. Essentially these models dictate that incident light is reflected from the same point of incidence, as shown in Figure 9.11. They ignore the possibility that incident light may penetrate and bounce around internally before exiting at an offset position, as with translucent materials. Making such an assumption neglects the absorption of light caused by internal scattering, and therefore the reflected light may appear amplified in comparison to the same surface in real life. BSDF models also assume that light is cast from an infinitely small light source, ignoring the random spread of light from a given direction as a function of radiant exitance over a source light's emission area.

The mathematical complexity of the illumination model can be written to represent either a more empirical or a more physically correct shading model (see the earlier sidebar "Shading Model Types"). For example, in a shader that observes the conservation of energy, BSDF functions would need to consider that the reflected radiance is smaller or equal to the incident radiance ($L_r \leq L_i$), as with the Cook-Torrance shader. This means that on such a shader, the reflected light can never exceed the incident energy. (For more on energy conservation, see the section "Balancing Light Transport" later in this chapter.)

Heuristic and empirical BSDF models consider only the reflected light, ignoring energy conservation as well as wavelength dependencies. Thus, incident (and reflected) light is always considered as white light, without considering the wavelength dependencies, as discussed earlier in "The Physical Nature of Light." Some shaders, such as Cook-Torrance or other advanced spectral shaders, employ wavelength dependency into the BSDF. By doing so, the BSDF can consider the degree of light scattering based on its spectral wavelength characteristics and can be written like this, adding a wavelength dependency to the function (the λ character):

$$f_r = (\Phi_i, \theta_i, \Phi_r, \theta_r, \lambda)$$

BIDIRECTIONALITY

Another reflectance characteristic is reciprocity, which explains why BSDF is described as "bidirectional." This means that for a given point on the surface (v), if you swap between the locations of the viewer (Θ) with the light (L), the BRDF (f_r) function will still provide the same result so that the following relationship applies:

$$f_r = (v, \text{L} \rightarrow \Theta) \text{ or } f_r = (v, \Theta \rightarrow \text{L})$$

Both statements are correct; hence, reciprocity can be written as follows:

$$f_r = (v, \text{L} \leftrightarrow \Theta)$$

This presents a BRDF that states that for a given point v, you can measure the reflectance regardless of whether the light and viewer swap locations. Not all shaders provide reciprocity; for example, the Phong shader does not respect this rule, which is one of the reasons it's considered a simplistic shading model.

DISTRIBUTION

Each surface may exhibit *diffuse*, *glossy*, and *specular* (also referred to as *spread* or *mixed*) light scattering, as well as some combination of all three types. Diffuse, glossy, and specular (DGS) reflections deal with the reflection of light as defined by the laws of physics and as shown in Figure 9.11. Essentially, highly polished or mirror surfaces (shiny surfaces) reflect light rays in a mirror (specular) direction. Diffuse and glossy surfaces simulate light that scatters in more than one direction, providing a more diffused appearance. You can also see in Figure 9.11 that with respect to these characteristics, DGS light reflection acts the same for reflection or transmission but in opposite directions. The difference between DGS reflection or transmission is then in how focused the scattered light appears and whether the light scattering is *isotropic* or *anisotropic,* a topic discussed in the section "Anisotropic vs. Isotropic Reflections" later in this chapter.

Both reflectance and transmittance light distribution can be drawn using different *lobes* that describe the light-scattering characteristics (directionality and intensity) relative to the surface normal. Figure 9.12 shows three lobes on polar coordinate systems. In image A, you can see the fundamental concept behind drawing lobes based on a standard BRDF such as a Phong shader. The light source hits the origin, a shading point in question, and then the arrows determine the reflection intensity and distribution in 180° around that point (similar to the images in Figure 9.11), which is a 3D hemisphere above the shading point. If you consider that the inner circles in the chart represent intensity, then the length of the arrows defines the light intensity in a given direction.

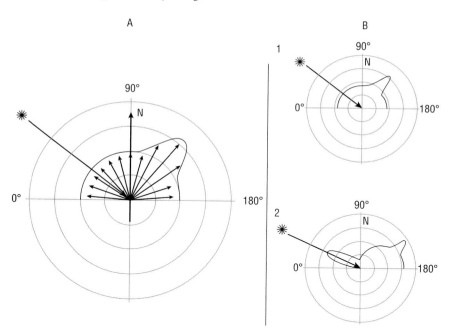

Figure 9.12

Drawing lobes on polar coordinates simplifies the process of visualizing the light reflectance model (its BRDF).

To simplify illustrating reflectance around a shading point, we can draw a line around the arrow's outer borders. We then easily visualize what the reflective lobe looks like, as shown in image B. The top illustration (1) is representative of a standard shading model such as a plastic ball that reflects more in a mirror specular direction, and the lower illustration (2) represents a surface that exhibits retro-reflections, which are reflections that reflect specular light back toward the light source as well as in mirror directions.

Diffuse, Glossy, and Specular Reflection

Let's examine each of the light reflection and transmittance characteristics illustrated in Figure 9.11. We can then further examine how these characteristics are implemented with shaders in the following sections. Note that, at minimum, most illumination shading models have diffuse and specular components, and some, such as the DGS physical shader, also have a glossy component. If the glossy component is not present, the specular component determines the glossy nature of the reflected source light (highlights), a topic discussed in detail throughout the reminder of this chapter.

SPECULAR REFLECTION

Figure 9.13 illustrates the law of reflection. As you can see, the angle between the incident light and the surface normal (perpendicular to the surface face) is equal to the angle between the reflected light and the surface normal ($\theta_i = \theta_r$). Thus, with specular reflections, an observer will see the same form (the reflecting source) reproduced on the receiving surface.

Figure 9.13

The law of reflection is used for rendering specular reflections in CG.

Specular reflection

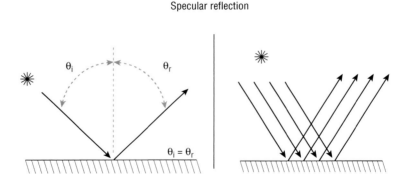

Typical reflective surfaces are mirrors, polished metals or woods, marble, surfaces with additional clear coatings such as vehicles (clear-coat shaders), and translucent or fully transparent surfaces such as water, glass, and oil, to mention a few. Basically these highly reflective surfaces don't possess harsh surface grooves such as with diffuse surfaces, which enables them to reflect more mirror images.

DIFFUSE REFLECTION

Diffused light reflects uniformly in a hemisphere over a given shaded point on a surface, as with powders, cloth, and paper, where the surface appears the same regardless of its orientation, as shown in Figure 9.14 image A. Diffused light reflection is more pronounced with rough surfaces, where the interaction with light across the surface causes multiple interreflections for a given ray, as illustrated in Figure 9.14 image B. In such cases, a measurement of surface luminance would provide the same result regardless of the viewing (measuring) angle. Thus, for a given angle on incidence, the light intensity is uniformly reflected in all directions, as shown in Figure 9.14 image A.

Diffuse reflection

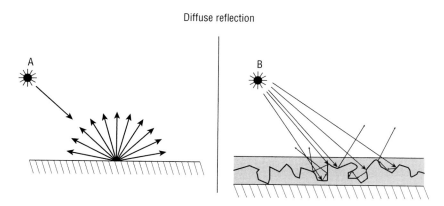

Figure 9.14

Diffuse light reflects uniformly from each surface point, based on the light ray's angle on incidence.

Real-world diffuse light reflection is the foundation for mental ray's global illumination feature set, in which a surface's diffuse color is a result of incident light from light sources, as well as reflected (indirect) light from surrounding surfaces (the environment). When using only direct illumination, the surface doesn't receive indirect diffused radiation; it receives only direct thermal radiation from a light source, as well as glossy or specular reflections. Thus, the diffuse color component in shading models is used to portray the effect of both incident light and environmental (bounced) light influences. With direct illumination, the diffuse component portrays only diffused direct light influences; in many cases, the diffuse color is either influenced with additional fill lights or the shader's ambient color is mapped with a texture as a means for mimicking bounced light influences.

Lambert's Cosine Law

Almost all shading models provide a diffuse component based on Lambert's cosine law. This law describes the intensity of diffused light as dependent on the angle of incident light, as shown in the following equation and in Figure 9.15:

$$E_r = E_i \times \cos(\theta)$$

The energy of the incident light (E_i) is multiplied by the cosine of the angle between the incident light vector (direction to the source light) and the surface normal vector, which is a dot product equation. As the angle between the surface normal and the directional vector to the light increases (up to a perpendicular angle of 90°), the intensity of the light decreases. This happens because the cosine of 90 equals 0, and the cosine of 0 equals 1; therefore, at perpendicular angles (90°) the diffuse light will terminate, and as the angle declines to zero, the reflected light will increase in intensity. In Chapter 12 you can see a complete example for a dot product equation to better understand its importance in lighting and shading.

Figure 9.15

Lambert's cosine law

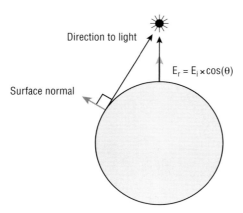

Lambert's cosine law

This leads us to another understanding of light interaction in CG models. Because light is cast from an infinitely small source, the diffuse component always terminates as the angle between the light and the surface normal reaches 90°. In real-world conditions, however, light wraps around surfaces because light sources are typically not infinitely small and because additional light is reflected from nearby surfaces (diffused indirect light bounce). Hence, area lights, which have a larger light-emission region, provide softer light and a more aesthetic appearance. They do this by extending the terminator point along a surface, as discussed in Chapter 6.

GLOSSY REFLECTION

Glossy reflections are present with surfaces that are not perfectly polished mirror surfaces—in those that possess some degree of surface grooves. These surfaces are less rough than diffused surfaces, representing a middle ground between diffuse and specular reflections. Figure 9.11 shows the characteristics of glossy reflection. Glossy reflection spreads light in a given direction, not uniformly across the surface, where the predominant angle represents the specular reflection.

Figure 9.16 illustrates the differences between specular and glossy reflections, as well as between isotropic and anisotropic reflections (discussed next). Image A demonstrates specular reflection, where incident light on the floor reflects a mirror image of the environment. Image B demonstrates glossy reflection, where the reflection is clearly present; however, it appears blurred because the incident light is reflected in more than just one direction. Essentially, surfaces of such nature (glossy) possess a sharper, more specular reflection for objects that are closer to their surface than those placed farther away. You can see that as the chair appears farther away from the floor, its reflection tends to appear glossier than specular. Thus, one of the advantages of glossy reflections is that they provide for distance-based reflections. Image C demonstrates a complex mental ray shader that provides for real anisotropic reflections that are dependent on the orientation of the surface, as discussed next. We will look at simulating all these types of reflection with mental ray shaders in Chapter 10, particularly the DGS shader, mib_glossy_reflection shader, and the architectural material in host applications.

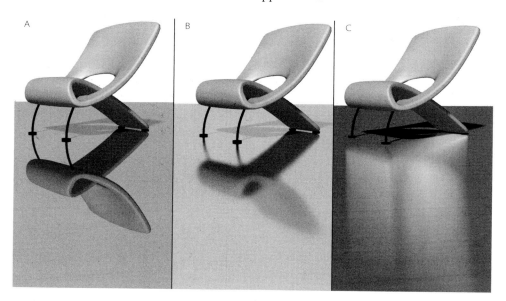

Figure 9.16

A comparison between (A) specular, (B) glossy, and (C) anisotropic glossy reflections

Anisotropic vs. Isotropic Reflections

You've seen that when light interacts with a surface, the reflected light characteristics depend on the surface's smoothness or roughness. With most surfaces in CG, the light reflection is always isotropic. With isotropic surfaces, the roughness of the surface is not spread out to follow a particular direction; there are no streaks or grooves across the surface as with aluminum or brushed metals. Instead, the roughness is scattered uniformly across the surface. Because the grooves don't possess a particular pattern, isotropic light reflection is not dependent on the angle of the surface relative to the viewer. In contrast, anisotropic surfaces have grooves or microgrooves predominantly in a given direction. The result is that the reflected light that interacts with the grooves reflects in a predominate direction, perpendicular to the grooves. With anisotropic surfaces, one of the more significant effects is that the surface reflection appears to change based on the surface orientation and the viewing angle. If you rotate an anisotropic surface, the glossy reflection will appear to change. Also, surfaces with long microgrooves such as brushed metals appear to stretch reflections across the entire surface, perpendicular to the grooves, as shown in the Figure 9.16 image C and diagrammed in Figure 9.17.

Figure 9.17

Anisotropic reflec-
tions occur when
surface grooves flow
in a particular direc-
tion, capturing and
stretching glossy
reflections perpen-
dicular to their
direction.

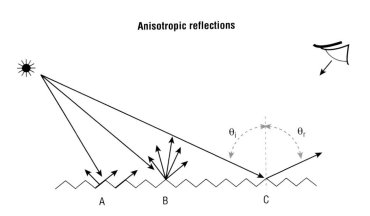

Anisotropic reflections

To better understand anisotropic reflections, let's consider the highlights that appear along surface edges such as with beveled edges that capture highlights. In Figure 9.17 the anisotropic microgrooves that emerge from the surface create a pattern of ridges and troughs. Labels A–C each demonstrate a different characteristic of anisotropic reflections.

In Figure 9.17 label A we can see that the reflected light is primarily captured along the ridges. Also, notice that light that falls into the troughs on the side facing the light is reflected back in that direction, toward the light. Thus, only light that hits directly, or reflects internally, on the side facing the viewer becomes visible. In any case, the intensity of that reflected light will be less than that of the reflected light along the ridge tops (label B). There we see that light that hits the ridge tops scatters in various directions, providing for the appearance of anisotropic glossy reflections. Thus, along the ridge top (a beveled edge), the surface perturbs (bends) and provides various directions for specular reflections. As the (vector-to-light) angle between the incident light and the surface normal increases (along the ridge top), the light intensity will decrease, forming a directional-dependent glossy reflection.

In Figure 9.17 label C we can see that as long as there is an angle below 180° between the incident light and the ridge, the anisotropic reflection will continue to capture and reflect glossy highlights, showing how these ridges act as microscopic reflectors that stretch the highlights. Essentially, these explanations provide insight into why anisotropic surface reflections appear perpendicular to the surface grooves, as well as why the reflections stretch across the surface as shown in Figure 9.16 label C.

Considering all these characteristics, it's clear that anisotropic reflections are mostly glossy reflections in which several microgrooves provide a glossy directional-dependent reflection.

The mental ray Ward shader provides a means for simulating an anisotropic shader's specular highlight only, which can be mapped with a texture to simulate light dispersion, as discussed next. In addition to the Ward shader, the mental ray glossy shaders and the architectural material found within host applications provide for simulating real glossy anisotropic reflections that stretch the reflection across the surface. We will review all these characteristics in host applications in Chapter 10.

ISOTROPIC AND ANISOTROPIC DISPERSION

Another component of isotropic and anisotropic reflections deals with light diffraction. In the earlier section "Light Dispersion," we focused on that light disperses into its different components as it travels through dispersive materials. With respect to anisotropic or isotropic light reflections, dispersive surfaces will cause the different wavelengths of light to fan out, causing white light to reveal its spectrum of color, as seen in oil stains, soap bubbles, and on CD Rom's to mention a few.

With isotropic dispersive surfaces, the light reflection (wavelength dependent) is typically shown as color fringes in highlight rims (see the Cook-Torrance shader later in this chapter). With anisotropic surfaces, as the reflection is stretched along the surface perpendicular to the grooves, the light diffraction causes the reflection to reveal longer streaks of color as the reflection fans out across the surface, of course revealing the spectrum of colors that manifested that light. This effect is typically noticeable with CDs, where as you rotate the CD, you can observe the different colors of light, and you can see that the reflection is direction-dependent based on the grooves and the viewing angle, as with all anisotropic surfaces. You can simulate iridescence effects (light dispersion) using the TEK2SHOOT shader presented in Chapter 10 Table 10.1 (Maya and XSI) as well as by mapping the specular color of an anisotropic shader using a gradient ramp (more on that later).

Diffuse, Glossy, and Specular Transmittance

The transmittance of light through matter provides for several effects based on how light reflects, refracts, absorbs, and disperses in a dielectric medium. The most significant components that affect transmittance are whether the medium is dispersive, its absorption level, and its IOR. Dielectric media are resistant to radiation, absorbing and slowing down the transport of light through the medium. The absorption level can be calculated using the *Beer-Lambert law*. The topic of dispersive matter was introduced earlier in this chapter in the "Light Dispersion" section.

SNELL'S LAW OF REFRACTION

With respect to light transmittance, rays that transport between two different media with different IORs follow Snell's law of refraction, as shown in Figure 9.18. The law of refraction defines the relationship between the angle of incidence and angle of refraction, as shown in the illustration. When the angle of incidence is parallel to the normal ($\theta=0$), then the light transmits in a straight path, without bending (refracting). In contrast, for a given ray (labeled b) at a given angle of incidence, referred to as the *critical angle* (θ_c), the light reflects rather than refracts, as noted with the condition for θ_c (shown in the figure).

Figure 9.18

Snell's law of
refraction

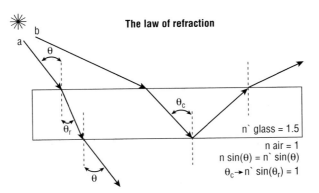

Figure 9.18
Snell's law of
refraction

In the case illustrated in Figure 9.18, the leftmost ray (a) travels from air into glass at a 30° angle of incident. The air has an IOR of 1, and the glass has an IOR of 1.5. As the ray penetrates the glass, it perturbs (bends) and continues to travel into the dielectric at an angle of 10.5°. When the ray exits the material, it re-enters air and resumes its initial direction, which has a 30° angle. In all cases, the transport of light through different dielectrics, be it air, water, glass, or any other transmitting medium, will follow Snell's law of refraction. Clearly, for simulating such surfaces, you should use the correct IOR for realistic simulation of transmission. Here are some common IOR values for reference:

SURFACE TYPE	IOR
Vacuum	1.0
Air	1.0003
Ice	1.31
Water	1.333
Ethyl alcohol	1.361
Turpentine	1.472
Benzene	1.501
Plexiglas	1.51
Crown glass	1.52
Flint glasses (light)	1.58
Dense glass	1.66
Fused quartz	1. 46
Diamond	2.419
Amber	1.55

In 3D it is common to overlook that a refracted ray bends twice—once as it enters the medium and once as it exits, as shown in the figure. The second refraction is overlooked, so the ray actually continues to travel at a wrong angle, resulting in inaccurate results by not correcting for the angle when exiting the medium and moving back into air, as in the example illustrated with the (a) ray. In Chapter 10 we will discuss these considerations with the mental ray shaders in more detail.

THE BEER-LAMBERT LAW

Another significant effect of dielectric media on light transport is light absorption. The absorption depends on two primary factors: the distance light travels through the medium and the density of its substance. Clearly, shorter distances within the surface will absorb less light than larger distances, and as such, they will refract more light through the medium. For example, green glass will show less coloration in thinner areas than in thicker areas that absorb more light, possessing more of a green hue, as shown in the image "Glass Shark Comparisons" in the Color Gallery. Notice how the glass is more absorbent along the shark's body than through the shark's fins. Both examples also demonstrate Fresnel reflections (discussed next) along the surface rims, a common effect with glass surfaces.

In addition to calculating the absorption through solid surfaces, the Beer-Lambert law can also be used for participating media effects (covered in Chapter 12), measuring light absorption between water droplets or particles present in the atmosphere.

> The mental ray architectural material and dielectric physical shader support simulating light absorption.

SPECULAR AND GLOSSY REFRACTION

The manner in which light spreads internally can be diffuse, glossy, or specular refraction. In most cases, we deal with specular refraction, which is typically seen when we place a pencil in water, where the refraction offsets the surface but maintains its focus. You can see this with the submarine example shown next. Diffuse refraction deals with the light that spreads uniformly inside a translucent surface, which is a subsurface scattering effect, which is not simulated with most refractive shaders (more about that later). Glossy refractions are then a blurred refraction as shown with frosted glass, crushed ice, or objects that submerge into deep sea.

The Fresnel Equations

Discovered by Jean Augustine Fresnel in 1834, the Fresnel effect states that the perceived light reflection and refraction change based on the viewing angle. It basically states that incident light both reflects and refracts and that the amount of reflection or refraction is based on a set of rules. Thus, the Fresnel equations determine the relationship between reflected and transmitted light intensities across a surface, balancing the incident radiant energy. When you observe water or glass over a long distance, as the glancing angle increases, the surface becomes more reflective than refractive, making it impossible to see through the surface. The most common example would be standing in a pool or the ocean so that as an observer you can see through the water in your vicinity, and as you look farther away the water becomes more reflective.

Figure 9.19 demonstrates specular refractions and Fresnel reflection with a refractive water surface. At facing angles, you see clearly into the water; however, as the angle between the viewer and water increases (along the edges), the water becomes more reflective, showing the outer area of the tub.

Figure 9.19

Fresnel reflections are balanced based on the viewing angle.

Fresnel reflections are not limited to transparent surfaces and are common with highly reflective surfaces. For example, metals or clear-coat covers (on vehicles) appear to reflect more specular reflections at glancing angles; thus, as the angle between the surface and observer increases, the surface possesses more specular reflections. In Chapter 10 you'll look at balancing reflections and refractions using physically correct light-transport simulations with mental ray shaders.

You can see examples for glossy and clear glass, absorption and Fresnel effects in the color inserts called "Glass Shark Comparisons." The images also show how caustics and participating media effects are affected by the absorption of a surface, all topics demonstrated in detail in the following chapters.

mental ray Shaders

mental ray ships with a collection of shader libraries that provide both standard and physically correct shading models. Table 9.1 lists the mental ray shader libraries that are typically included with host applications. mental ray shaders either are simplistic or empirical shading models that are not physically correct but render fast, or are more advanced physically correct shaders that provide realism. Realism is achieved by using shaders that employ more accurate BRDFs (simulated based on physical optics) that account for energy conservation, Fresnel reflections, absorption, and wavelength effects, as discussed throughout this chapter and in the sidebar "Shading Model Types."

SHADER LIBRARIES	PURPOSE
Base	This provides a collection of common and special-purpose component shaders (discussed in the next section).
Physics	The architectural and physics shader libraries offer physically correct (energy-conserving) shading models that are typically used with indirect light simulations. Both libraries are discussed in "Physical Shading Models" later in this chapter and demonstrated in Chapter 10.
Architectural	In addition to the previous description, this library offers light, sky, and tone-mapping shaders for rendering high dynamic range lighting scenes typically with Final Gather.
Subsurface	This offers a variety of complex shaders for translucent and "deep" subsurface light scattering. This library is examined in detail in Chapter 14, "Subsurface Scattering."
Contour	This is used for nonphotorealistic rendering (NPR), offering a wide range of 2D post-process effects using output shaders that can draw surface contours.
Paint	This provides additional shaders that extend the base library's abilities, specifically for designing vehicle shaders, typically used for car commercials. These shaders offer robust control over surface specularity and reflectivity using the mental images car paint phenomenon shader.
Lume	This offers an additional collection of custom shaders, typically as a plug-in library, available with XSI and 3ds Max some of which have been discussed in Chapter 3.

Table 9.1

mental ray Shader Libraries

The Base Shader Library

The mental ray base shader library provides the majority of the common isotropic and anisotropic illumination shading models that you are already accustomed to (Lambert, Phong, and so on). In addition to these shading models, the base library provides a collection of component shaders that act as texture, environment, sample compositing, data conversion, and light, as well as other shaders, as discussed in Chapter 1, "Introduction to mental ray." Table 9.2 lists the base shaders, most of which you can find in each host application (hosts may omit certain shaders).

Table 9.2	CATEGORY	SHADERS
Base Shader Library Component Shaders	Illumination	Lambert
		Phong
		Blinn
		Cook-Torrance
		Ward
		Ward derivatives
		Hair
	Volume	Volume
		Fur
	Photon	Photon basic
	Shadow	Shadow transparency
	Sample compositing	Reflect
		Refract
		Transparency
		Opacity
		Continue
		Dielectric
		Two sided
		Refraction index
		Ray marcher
	Raytracing	Glossy reflection
		Glossy refraction
	Occlusion elated	Ambient occlusion
		Fg occlusion
		Bent normal env
	Texture space mapping	Texture vector
		Texture remap
		Texture rotate
		Bump basis
		Bump map
		Bump map2
		Passthrough bump map
	Textures	Lookup
		Lookup2
		Filter lookup
		Checkerboard
		Polka-dot
		Polka-sphere
		Turbulence
		Wave

continues

CATEGORY	SHADERS
Environments	Lookup spherical
	Lookup cube1
	Lookup cube6
	Lookup background
	Lookup cylindrical
	Lookup spherical
Data Conversion	Color alpha
	Color average
	Color intensity
	Color interpolate
	Color mix
	Color spread
Light	Point
	Spot
	Infinite
	Photometric
Light utility	Blackbody
	cie_d
Lightmap	Lightmap write
	Lightmap sample
Lens	Lens clamp
	Lens stencil

The shader names omit irrelevant prefix labels such as mib_ (mental images base library), illum, and texture, and they are not necessarily organized in the same order as shown in host applications (mainly for clarity). Also, the table doesn't list geometry shaders.

So far we have used shadow, displacement, and light shaders, as well as camera lens, output, environment, and volume shaders, and most of these appear in Table 9.2 as part of the base shader library. As you can see, this library provides a wide range of shaders. Not all of these are meant to be used solely with surfaces, but also can be used as source lights and camera (lens and environmental) effects. In the following sections and in Chapters 10 and 11, we will utilize several of these shaders in host applications, showing how they can be used to form complex shaders (shader trees). You also further examine examples with the physics and architectural shader libraries, correlating them to the previous discussion of light transport models.

mental ray Materials

The sole purpose of a material is to apply the connection between different shader types and surfaces. A material acts as an overall shader program that "collects" within it different shader functionalities for a given surface, comprised of nine possible categories (types) that are shown in Table 9.3. We have already used some of these connections, as with the shadow shaders in Chapter 7, "Shadow Algortihms."

Table 9.3

Material Connections for Different Shader Types

SHADER TYPE	PURPOSE
Illumination	Provides the primary connection used to apply a shading model to a surface, with the purpose of defining the light transport character of a surface with respect to the direct lighting in the scene. The illumination connection is also referred to as *surface* or *material* in hosts, as shown in Figures 9.20, 9.21 and 9.22.
Photon	Provides an illumination model for use with indirect illumination only (photons). The shader evaluates the transport of energy and color between different surfaces in the scene (color bleeding). Thus, indirect illumination simulations don't utilize the illumination shader, only the photon shader, as you will see in Chapter 12.
Shadow	Provides a connection for shadow shaders, as discussed in Chapter 7.
Volume	Enables volumic effects within containers (surfaces) such as smoke, mist, haze and fire to mention a few. See "Participating Media (PM) Effects" in Chapter 12.
Photon volume	Is equivalent to the photon and illumination shader relationship described earlier. This shader is then used to apply volumic effects with indirect illumination photons, making them visible as smoke, or mist (and more) in the air, within the surface boundaries.
Environment	Applies environmental reflections by projecting texture colors onto a surface. We have already referred to environment shaders with cameras; in a similar way, they can be connected to a surface to avoid raytracing environment reflections.
Displacement	Used for displacement mapping, as discussed in the CD excerpt called "Surface Approximation Methods."
Light maps	Used for writing color data to image files on disk, such as surface luminance or texture colors. This light-baking process is also commonly referred to as *texture baking* or *render maps*. We will use light maps in Chapter 14.
Contour	Used with contour shaders from the contour shader library for NPR rendering (see Table 1 in the CD excerpt called "Surface Approximation Methods"). This book does not cover these shaders, other than using them in the CD excerpt as a means to see geometric tessellation during rendering, drawn as contours along the surface edges.

Aside from the illumination shader, each additional category may (optionally) be piped with a shader (or shader tree) that provides relevant information. Figure 9.20, Figure 9.21, and Figure 9.22 show the mental ray material connections in each host application, where you apply the different shader connections. The illumination category is the only required category that defines a surface's primary shader characteristics (BSDF), which is its light transport model. If that material is used with indirect illumination simulations, then a photon shader is also required (see Chapter 12 for more details on indirect illumination). Thus, the material pipes several component shaders, each providing some specific functionality. Further, for each category, a complex shader can be used, utilizing several component shaders (forming a shader tree) before the top node of the tree connects to the material's illumination input. Note that the top node isn't necessarily an illumination shader; it may be a sample compositing or data conversion shader such as the opacity opacity, reflection, or color mix shaders, as shown in Figure 9.20 and Figure 9.21. Thus, component shaders take the illumination model, such as a Blinn or Phong shader, and then process the output color before passing it into the material's illumination input, as with the common practice of mixing color from various shaders.

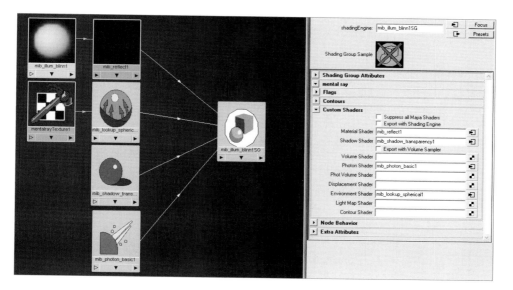

Figure 9.20

Maya Material connections for the Maya Shading Engine and the layout shown in the Hypershade window

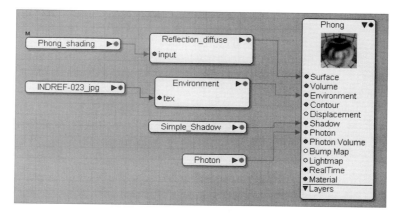

Figure 9.21

XSI simple shaders connected to a material that reveals all the possible shader connections in the Render Tree window

Figure 9.22

3ds Max mental ray material shown in the Material Editor window and the lay-out shown in the Schematic view

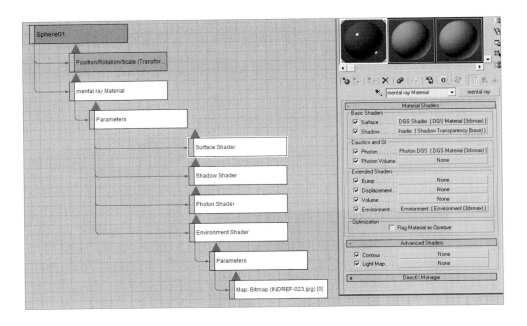

Figure 9.22

3ds Max mental ray material shown in the Material Editor window and the lay-out shown in the Schematic view

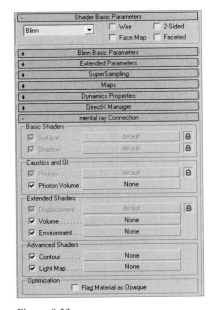

Figure 9.23

3ds Max mental ray Connection menu for a Blinn material reveals the mono-lithic nature of standard shaders

Monolithic Materials

Monolithic materials are shaders, like the architectural (mia) material, that provide all the internal material connections and functionalities built into a single shader interface. Typically these are host-specific shaders that utilize several component shaders and provide illumination (diffuse, transparency, refraction, reflection, and so on), shadow, and photon shader support.

Figure 9.23 shows a 3ds Max Blinn shader's mental ray Connections; you can see that the Surface (illumination), Shadow, Photon, and Displacement mapping links all appear locked, because they are all driven internally through the main shader settings. Similarly, you can see in Figure 9.24 that XSI's monolithic (host-specific) Phong shader drives three connections to the material: Surface, Shadow, and Photon. You are not required to apply additional photon or shadow shaders to retrieve transparent shadows or to use indirect illumination support when using host-specific shaders in Maya, XSI, and 3ds Max, because all of them provide monolithic "all-in-one" shader solutions. However, when using mental ray–specific shaders, you must include all the additional connections, or their functionalities will be missing. For example, if you didn't apply a photon shader when using indirect illumination, that surface would not be active in the simulation.

PHENOMENON SHADERS

It's important to distinguish between monolithic materials and phenomenon shaders, which are shaders that internally comprise a complex shading tree. The complexity derives from the number of options that are provided for controlling illumination characteristics such as ambient, diffuse, reflection, transparency, and other color components, which are all part of the illumination shading model. Thus, when these options are all provided to the user though a single node's interface, the shader is referred to as a phenomenon shader, comprising several component shaders.

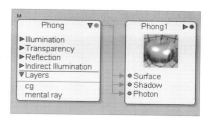

Figure 9.24

XSI demonstrates how a single monolithic shader can drive several different material inputs.

For example, in Figure 9.25 image A you can see a mental ray base Phong shader in XSI, without any additional features. However, in Figure 9.25 image B you can see the XSI host-specific Phong shader, providing several additional "component" options (the upper tabs), all through a single shading node's interface. This process is rather common with host-specific Lambert, Phong, Blinn, Cook-Torrance, and other shaders that are provided as both monolithic and phenomenon material shaders for easy usage. Thus, a monolithic shader may utilize a phenomenon shader for the illumination input.

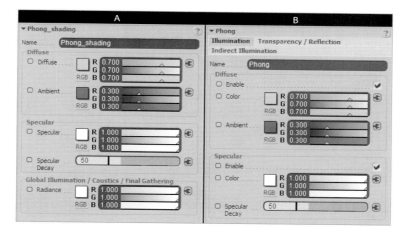

Figure 9.25

Image A shows the simple mental ray Phong shader in XSI. Image B shows the standard XSI Phong shader, which is a "phenomenon" monolithic XSI shader.

All host-centric shaders are basically a mix of both concepts, where the shader is a monolithic shader, and the illumination model is a phenomenon shader that provides robust color control over the surface illumination. Hence, host-specific shaders, such as the Phong shader shown in Figure 9.25 image B, possess phenomenon features, as well as additional (monolithic) functionalities such as a shadow shader with control over color and transparency and a photon shader for indirect illumination control. The photon shader's settings in most cases are derived automatically from the illumination model; thus, you are not required to specify the color values twice, once for direct lighting and once for indirect lighting.

MAYA AND 3DS MAX HOST-CENTRIC SHADERS

Maya-centric and 3ds Max–centric shaders (those not originally intended for mental ray) are a form of phenomenon shaders. All host-centric shaders are exported as mental ray phenomenon shaders during the render.

Maya shaders have additional mental ray tabs that enable further control of mental ray–specific features such as glossy reflections and refractions that are supported only with mental ray rendering. Using the mental ray → Photon Attributes menu, you can also specify different settings for the photon shader with any of the standard (Maya-centric) illumination shaders, as shown in Figure 9.26.

Figure 9.26

Maya shaders have mental ray tabs that enable further control over mental ray–specific raytracing features, subsurface scattering, and the photon shader.

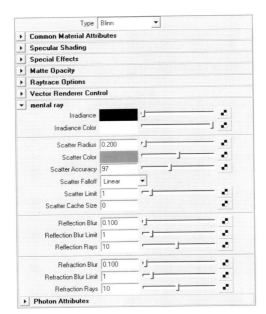

With 3ds Max, once you disable the locked connection for any of the mental ray inputs under the mental ray Connection menu (shown in Figure 9.23), you can then map a new component shader for that function, overwriting the monolithic shaders default output for that feature. Doing so enables you to have separate control over the different shader types that connect to the mental ray material.

Base Shaders and Shader Math

In this section, we examine basic shader settings and shader math using mental ray base shaders. Regardless of whether you use host-specific or mental ray shaders, the shader options (and math) provide similar functionality with the difference in available complexity (robust phenomenon shader vs. base shader). Thus, these calculations are the same for a given shader type in each host application, regardless of the extent of color options it provides (diffuse, reflection, and so on). The primary difference between the shader types (physical, empirical, and so on) is in the level of complexity implemented with their BRDF math—how they calculate illumination and combine the contributions of diffuse, glossy, and specular light scattering.

> With respect to rendering passes and compositing, the internal shader math executed during rendering (described next) acts as a guideline for compositing different color contributions (passes) in 2D compositing applications.

Typically, shaders evaluate color by following the BSDF rules discussed earlier, applying those concepts using shader math internally, as part of the shader's source code. The mental ray base shaders' illumination models all offer ambient and ambience color components (shown in Figure 9.31 later in this section) that together define an ambient light contribution. When ambient color is applied, it acts as an additional light source spreading color uniformly across a surface, regardless of light direction. The ambience color is multiplied by the ambient color so that if you specify a 50 percent gray ambient color, you can then map the ambience color with a texture file that will never exceed 50 percent gray in value (brightness).

To clarify, the ideal is that a texture file applied to one of the two components may include any range of brightness that is then dialed down when multiplied by the other component so that together they balance the total ambient contribution. Essentially, if the ambient and ambience options are both gray values, the lower of the two will prevail as the final ambient light contribution. Host-specific shaders omit the ambience option since you typically map a texture to the ambient color and dial that color down through the texture's color settings. In XSI and 3ds Max there are global (scene) ambience options that correlate to the mental ray ambience color discussed here, and are examined with Final Gather in Chapter 13.

The Diffuse Shading Model

Diffused light reflections (see the section "The Bidirectional Scattering Distribution Function (BSDF)") in shading models obey Lambert's cosine law, as discussed earlier. Hence, a diffuse-only shader (with no specular or glossy reflection) is commonly referred to as a *Lambert shader*. The process for evaluating surface color with a Lambert shader requires two stages, evaluating the ambient contribution and evaluating the diffuse contribution. Once the ambient color (ambient × ambience) is evaluated, the diffuse color is evaluated based on the light's color contribution (color from various light sources) and the light's angle of incidence at a shaded point. Once both contributions (ambient and diffuse) have been evaluated, the results are added together in a nonphysically correct fashion, providing the final surface color. Let's clarify some of these terms and equations.

With respect to mathematically addressing Lambert's cosine law, a dot product is evaluated between the surface normal (vector a) at the sampled point and the directional vector to the light from that sampled point (vector b). See Figure 9.15 earlier in this chapter. The dot product (see Chapter 12 for a dot product example) between the two vectors (a and b) is described with the following equation:

$$\underline{a}.\underline{b} = |a| \times |b| \times \cos\theta$$

The vectors' magnitudes are multiplied by the cosine of the angle between them. This dot product provides a means for evaluating the light influence at a given point based on Lambert's cosine law; however, it neglects the light's spectral energy (all wavelengths reflect at an equal intensity) and light absorption at that point using this simplified (BRDF) function. Thus, the dot product solely provides reflectance information on the relationship between two vectors from the incident sampled point. The dot product result is then multiplied by the light color and then the diffuse color as follows:

(dot product × light color) = light contribution × *diffuse color* = diffuse color contribution

Essentially this means that the diffuse color intensity (reflected radiance) is scaled down along a surface based on the source-light's color (and intensity) and the dot product, providing the final diffuse color contribution. The result is then mathematically added with the ambient contribution to provide the final surface color at a given shading point.

OREN-NAYAR DIFFUSE SHADING

With respect to diffused surface qualities, the typical diffuse component with most shader types (Lambertian diffuse) provides for a very "CG look," rather than a natural look of diffused light that scatters across a surface. One aspect of rough surfaces, such as shown in Figure 9.14 image B, is that the inner reflections that take place on a surface carry more diffused light across the surface as the angle between the surface normal and direction to the light increases. The diffused light doesn't fall off as quickly as with the Lambert cosine law; rather, it maintains its reflected intensity toward more glancing angles (with respect to the light), and then it rapidly diminishes until it reaches a perpendicular angle. For example, consider dirt—it doesn't appear to have a clear falloff as with Lambert's cosine law. Rather, it has a more natural termination of light when it's in shadow, where all other areas (in light) appear relatively uniformly lit.

The Oren-Nayar shader (not part of the mental ray base shaders) is used to accommodate this sort of characteristic. Figure 9.27 compares the typical Lambert diffuse (image A) with an Oren-Nayar diffuse (image B). You can examine the color version of the Oren_Nayar Shading image in the Chapter 9 folder on the companion CD. As you can see, the Oren-Nayar diffuse maintains a relatively uniform intensity leading to the glancing angles. Typically the transition from a standard diffuse (image A) to an Oren-Nayar diffuse is controlled with a roughness parameter, where rougher surfaces lean toward the Oren-Nayar diffuse characteristics. The types of surfaces that are more prone to this sort of diffuse quality are sand, ceramics, paper, powder, dirt, clothes, rough stones, and even skin. Clearly, almost all of these surface types may have a rough or more polished surface, such as glossy paper vs. standard paper.

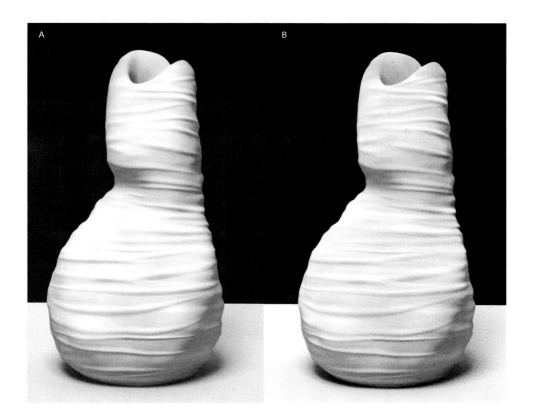

Figure 9.27
A standard Lambert diffuse (A) is compared to an Oren-Nayar diffuse (B), demonstrating the differences in light falloff qualities.

With Maya, XSI, and 3ds Max, the Oren-Nayar diffuse shading is available as part of the mental ray architectural material. In addition, 3ds Max provides a standard Oren-Nayar-Blinn shader.

Specular Shading Models

Specular shading models add a specular color contribution that deals with source light reflections on a surface, providing surface highlights. Essentially, specular light reflections provide mirror reflections across surfaces. With specular shading models the specular reflection is divided into two components, specular color (emulated) and reflection color (and/or reflection intensity), which are typically acquired with raytracing (environment mapping acts as a nonraytraced reflection color). Once the specular contribution (for both components) is evaluated, the results are mathematically added with the diffuse color, typically a Lambert diffuse model, as follows:

[Ambient + Diffuse] + [Specular + Reflection (environment/scene)]

The first pair of brackets represents the diffuse shading models, and the second pair represents the specular shading model.

REFLECTION COLOR

Reflection color provides specular reflections of objects in the environment that are acquired through raytracing secondary rays. With mental ray base shaders, deriving reflection color requires that you add the sample compositing mib_reflect shader. The sample compositing shader can be a reflection, a refraction, an opacity, or any other sample compositing shader, based on the additional functionality you intend on adding, in this case reflections. This sort of network is shown in Figures 9.20 and 9.21 with Maya and XSI and is constructed as follows:

Shading model (Phong, Blinn, and so on) *out color* → sample compositing shader *input* → material *illumination input*

The reflection color provides specular reflections for the environment, whereas the specular component on the base shader deals only with source light reflections. Thus, when using such networks, you can scale the reflection color independently from the specular color. With host-specific shaders, the relationship between specular color and reflection color differs:

XSI With XSI shaders, the specular color contribution is independent of the reflection color contribution. Thus, the properties found for a given shader under its Illumination tab → Specular properties are independent of the properties found under the Transparency/Reflection tab → Reflection properties.

Maya and 3ds Max With Maya (that is, Specular shading → Specular Color) and 3ds Max (that is, Basic Parameters → Specular), the specular color acts as a multiplier for the reflection color (intensity). Thus, if you dial down the specular color to black (zero), then both highlights and scene reflections will be disabled. Essentially, this approach is correct because the total reflection for both components (highlights and scene reflections) represent the specular to glossy reflectivity of a surface, which in real life is not divided into two separate components. However, the additional reflectivity control enables you to control the reflection intensity, which with respect to the specular highlights will either be equal or be lower in intensity.

SPECULAR COLOR

Specular color, as cited earlier, provides only source light reflections (which is not true with the DGS physics shader). To clarify, since 3D light sources are represented as infinitely small light-emission points, they fail to provide information about their physical size, with the exception of area lights. Because of their infinitely small scale, we cannot correctly simulate source light reflections on surfaces merely by evaluating specular reflections, because the light's physical size is misrepresented. Thus, the specular component with base shaders (generally most shaders) addresses source light glossy to specular reflections by providing a means for simulating the size, shape, intensity, color, decay rate, and distance from the light, for a given source light.

> When creating metallic surfaces, the specular color reflects the metal's diffuse color; thus, when creating shaders for metallic objects, you should typically use the diffuse hue (HSV) for the specular color and control the specular intensity using the value.

Figure 9.28 utilizes a rectangular area light to demonstrate how the specular component (raytracing disabled) tries to accurately mimic the source light's shape, distance, and intensity. As you can see, in image A the light is farther away from the surface than in image C (illustrated with the companion screen grabs). As the light gets closer to the surface, the highlight increases in size and better represents the source light's rectangular shape, demonstrating how the shape and size of highlights are defined by the actual source light's size. Thus, when using area lights, the shape of the light is recognizable as part of the specular reflection. With glossier surfaces, the highlight tends to defocus, revealing less of the source light shape and more of a blur. With infinitely small light sources, the specular component options are then used to manually simulate the light's size, shape, and intensity, as well as the surface's glossy nature, as discussed next.

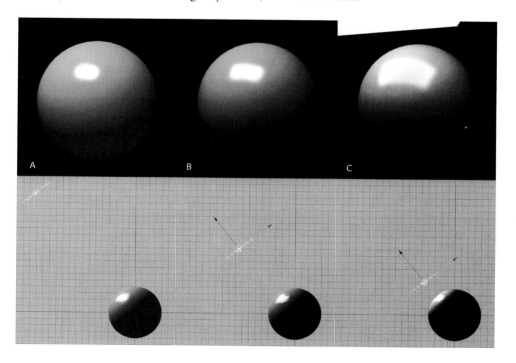

Figure 9.28

The influence a source light shape has on specular reflections

MENTAL RAY SPECULAR SHADING MODELS

The different specular shading models (Phong, Blinn, Cook-Torrance, Ward, and Lafortune) use different mathematical calculations (or scientific data) for defining the shape and glossiness of the specular highlight by using different BRDF approaches. That is, one BRDF model may model light reflectance more accurately than another. It's important to realize that the specular component that is used for simulating highlights typically utilizes a glossy lobe and not a specular lobe (projected light directionality, as shown in Figure 9.11). This characteristic is noticeable as blurred specular rims, rather than sharp mirror highlights. Essentially, the specular color within host application shaders is incorrectly labeled, because it is actually a glossy reflection, not a mirror (specular) reflection. The extent of the glossiness is defined by the specular exponent or other option, depending on the specular shading model. Thus, glossy highlight rims indicate how smooth or rough a surface is. This falls in line with diffuse fundamentals discussed earlier in the chapter, where rougher surfaces are more diffused, as are their (glossy) reflections.

As the approach for generating these highlights differs between shaders, that difference is occasionally misinterpreted as follows: one shader is considered good for sharp highlights (such as plastic) , whereas the other is better for rougher highlights (such as rough, dry wood). Creatively speaking, this approach is correct and allows us to easily construct shaders; thus, we commonly use a Phong shader for sharper highlights and Blinn shader for rougher highlights. However, this approach is a result of convenience and does not consider the physical accuracy of the shader (see the earlier sidebar "Shading Model Types").

When considering physical accuracy, target surfaces are rendered using scientific data and compared with various shading models that attempt to reproduce similar results. To clarify, the target surface, which is based on scientific measurements of light reflectance, compares different shading models that attempt to reproduce the same surface characteristics. Essentially, the shading model that produces the least amount of error (in reflectance) is considered to most faithfully reproduce the physical nature of the target surface. Some of the following websites provide detailed examples and papers on reflectance comparisons between different models, where Cook-Torrance appears to be the most accurate for surface (reflectance) reproduction:

> http://people.csail.mit.edu/wojciech/BRDFValidation/index.html
>
> http://people.csail.mit.edu/addy/research/brdf/index.html
>
> www.graphics.cornell.edu/online/measurements/reflectance/index.html

Phong Specular

The Phong specular shading model is the oldest and least accurate specular model. It calculates the specular intensity based on the dot product between the vector to the viewer (Θ) and the reflection vector (R), raised to the power of the specular exponent (n). The result is multiplied by the specular color (k_s) and the light intensity at that point (f_{att}), as shown in the following equation. Note that f_{att} refers to a fraction of light at a given point assuming that light attenuates over distance.

I (Phong output) = Ambient + Diffuse + $(k_s \times f_{att} \times (R \cdot \Theta)^n)$

The exponent (n) provides the rapid specular light decay (for the highlight), where higher values produce a smaller and sharper highlight. The Phong model neglects some basic BRDF rules, particularly reciprocity, energy conservation, and Fresnel reflections. Thus, the highlight does not appear stronger (or wider) at glancing angles, which is a fundamental specular characteristic. Also, the Phong model does not consider per-wavelength (λ) spectral reflections; thus, all light wavelengths reflect based on an equal IOR. Finally, as the diffuse and ambient contributions are added as separate components using addition, the total color value for a given shading point can easily exceed the total incoming irradiance at that point, and thus the shader will not be physically correct for energy conservation.

The mental ray base Phong shader has an Exponent option for specifying the exponent value. With XSI the Specular Decay property is used, as shown in Figure 9.25 image A. With the Maya-centric Phong, the Specular Shading → Cosine Power is used, and with the mental ray Phong shader, the Exponent attribute is used. With 3ds Max, the Phong shader Specular Highlights → Glossiness is used as the exponent, and the Specular Level attribute defines the highlight intensity, similar to an opacity scale.

BLINN AND COOK-TORRANCE SHADING MODELS

We have already introduced most of the important concepts for specular shading models, including the Phong shader equation, which gets only more complicated with the Blinn and Cook-Torrance models. These models provide more control and sophistication over the specular component by factoring in additional options. With respect to computational efficiency, they improve on the Phong model in that they don't require calculating a reflection vector to define the light intensity seen with the Phong equation cited earlier. Instead, they use a *halfway vector* between the light's position and the viewer, initially introduced with the Blinn-Phong shader. Essentially it provided faster computation times as well as better visual results while comparing reflectance with real surfaces opposed to the Phong model. The modified Blinn model (as with mental ray's shader) later added a roughness parameter that is similar to the Cook-Torrance roughness, providing better control over the highlight appearance based on a microfaceted substructure.

Microfacets

The Cook-Torrance model assumes that a surface's substructure is constructed with an enormous number of Lambertian microfacet reflectors, as shown in Figure 9.29. The microfacets reflect light based on their orientations and densities. They can self-shadow, casting shadows on each other by occluding incoming light, or can mask the reflected light from exiting the substructure, as shown in Figure 9.29. Not all specular shading models actually account for these microfacets, but it is the underlying concept (of their existence) that explains the glossy nature of specular highlights. Specular models that fail to account for these facets will appear to have sharper highlights, such as with the Phong shading model. Shading models that properly account for microfacets better mimic diffuse to glossy surfaces and, generally speaking, most surface types.

Figure 9.29
Microfacets across a surface either mask or shadow each other.

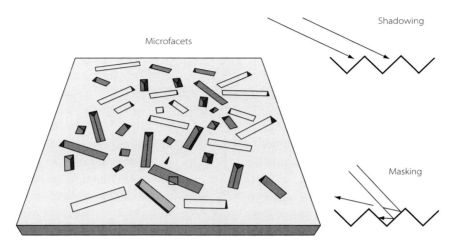

Note that the Cook-Torrance (and Blinn) shader is an isotropic shading model. The orientation of the microfacets is random since if they all flowed in the same direction, the surface would simulate a more anisotropic reflection.

Fresnel Reflections

The Cook-Torrance model considers the reflectivity of a surface, based on the viewing angle and thus factors in Fresnel reflections. As the angle between the viewer and the surface increases, the highlights tend to get larger and more intense, as shown in Figure 9.30 image A (Cook-Torrance). In image A (Cook-Torrance) you can see two renders; the top one is at a glancing angle, where the highlight increases in intensity (and size), and the bottom image shows the highlight at a facing angle. In image B you can see the same renders using the Phong shader, which maintains its relative intensity and size as the angle changes. You can see another comparison between the Phong and Cook-Torrance shading models utilizing an area light in the sidebar "Shading Model Types."

Spectral Reflections

In addition to Fresnel reflections and a microfaceted substructure, the Cook-Torrance model also factors in per-wavelength reflections. Thus, different wavelengths may reflect at different angles based on the surface's index of refraction. Essentially this enables the Cook-Torrance models to render color-fringing effects on the outer rims of the highlight. You can see this effect while trying to simulate the image shown in Figure 9.30 image A on the top, where the outer portions of the highlight will change color based on the shader's settings, as specified by the user.

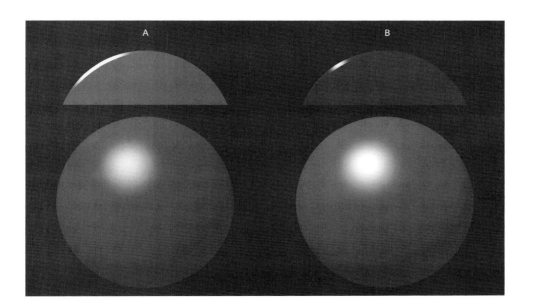

Figure 9.30

Comparing Cook-Torrance reflections with the Phong shading model

Shader Settings

The evaluations of microfacet reflectivity, meaning the intensity, angle, and density, is based on a few different components that are controlled with the Specular Color, Roughness, and IOR options, as shown in Figure 9.31 image A, a Cook-Torrance mental ray base shader. The Roughness option defines the microfacets' slope; larger values provide for more spread-out specular highlights. The IOR option represents the index of refraction for reflected light that is incident on the microfacets; for example, a metal surface's reflection directionality depends on the metal's IOR value, where increasing frequencies of light tend to bend more as they are reflected. Higher IOR values tend to make the highlight appear sharper. As you can see, the IOR parameter for the Cook-Torrance model (Figure 9.31 image A) is provided as an RGB color value, allowing you to specify a different IOR for each wavelength accounting for per-wavelength (λ) spectral reflections.

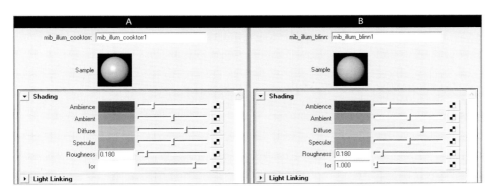

Figure 9.31

Cook-Torrance (A) and Blinn (B) mental ray shading models shown in Maya

The mental ray Blinn shader utilizes a less comprehensive BRDF, removing wavelength dependency. You can see in Figure 9.31 image B (a Blinn shader) that IOR is a scalar value and not an RGB color value. With XSI the IOR is labeled Specular → Refraction, and with 3ds Max the roughness is controlled with the Specular Highlights → specular level and IOR is controlled with Glossiness.

THE WARD SHADER

The mental ray Ward shader is used for simulating anisotropic reflections, as discussed earlier in the section "Anisotropic vs. Isotropic Reflections." Notice that unlike other shaders, the specular color is labeled Glossy, indicating the glossy nature of anisotropic reflections. The shader utilizes two options for controlling the highlights spread:, Shiny U

Figure 9.32

The Anisotropic shader settings in XSI

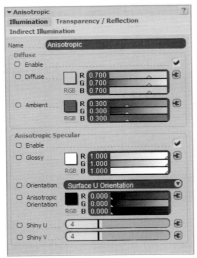

and Shiny V, as shown in Figure 9.32 (the XSI Anisotropic shader). These options apply the ratio, intensity, and length for the highlights, along either the U or V coordinate.

The highlight orientation is based on the U and V surface coordinates, as derived from the surface (first surface derivatives). The surface derivatives are more efficient with NURBS surfaces that use U and V profiles to draw a NURBS patch, and they define the U and V coordinates along those profiles. With polygons, the results can be less predictable, especially with surfaces that have complex forms as there are no predefined U and V profiles that are used by the software to reference U and V coordinates.

Host applications handle defining surface derivates for polygon surfaces automatically. Maya has two versions for the mental ray Ward shader, mib_illum_ward and mib_illum_ward_deriv. You should typically use the mib_illum_ward_deriv shader with NURBS surfaces (further discussed in Chapter 10), which automates deriving the surface coordinates rather than expecting you to provide them. Aside from the mental ray shaders Maya also has its own host specific anisotropic shader. In XSI the Ward shader is Anisotropic, and in 3ds Max you can select anisotropic shading for the Standard material and control the shiny U and V ratio with the Specular Highlights → Anisotropy option.

Anisotropic Orientation and Scale

Highlight orientation (rotating the highlight across the surface) is one of the most significant components of anisotropic shading. First, the Shiny U and V options permit stretching the highlight along only one direction, be it U or V, lacking any control over orientation. Furthermore, the surface U and V coordinates may be unpredictable as cited earlier with polygon objects; hence, you'll require additional control for aligning the highlight. In addition the orientation of the highlight may change based on a brushing direction, as with brushed metals.

To control orientation, mental ray has the mib_texture_rotate component shader that enables rotating the U and V orientation. Similarly, this option is already built into Maya's host-specific shader with the Angle attribute; in XSI, with the Anisotropic Orientation property seen in Figure 9.32 ; and with the similarly labeled Orientation parameter in 3ds Max.

In addition to simulating anisotropic highlights, you can also create effects such as anisotropic dispersion, where the highlight reveals the light wavelengths that manifested the incident light. A simple example such as a CD is achieved by mapping the Glossy color option with a color gradient (spectrum). You then need to apply appropriate U and V settings; typically one coordinate should be set with a value of 1. Thus, if Shiny V is set with a higher value (for example, 6), it will define the thickness of the highlight (making it thinner and sharper as you increase the value), and then Shiny U will define the length along the U coordinate. If U is set to 1, then the highlight will stretch across the entire surface; in contrast, higher values will contract the highlight length. Try applying a value of 1 on a NURBS torus, and notice how the highlight wraps around the entire surface.

Anisotropic Reflections

Since anisotropic shaders (Ward or host-specific) don't provide anisotropic reflections for environments and scene elements, you should consider adding custom anisotropic reflections. To clarify, all the host-specific anisotropic shaders provide anisotropic highlights and isotropic reflections. For anisotropic reflections, you can use the DGS shader or the architectural material, which supports anisotropic highlights and reflections, as shown earlier in Figure 9.16 image C. Alternatively, you can also connect the anisotropic shader with a glossy reflection shader (mib_glossy_reflection) that supports anisotropic reflections. We take a closer look at creating complex shader trees for controlling surface orientation and anisotropic reflections with brushed metal in Chapter 10.

Physical Shading Models

As mentioned earlier, mental ray ships with a collection of physics shaders, as well as the physically correct architectural material (mia). The physics shader library includes DGS, dielectric, parti volume, transmat (a utility more than a shader), physical light, and physical lens shaders. You have already examined the physical lens shader with depth of field (Chapter 4, "Camera Fundamentals") and learned about applying a physical light shader with area lights (Chapter 6). The parti volume shader (participating media) is covered in Chapter 12 with direct and indirect illumination (volume caustics). The architectural material basically renders the DGS and dielectric shaders obsolete, acting as a robust "all-in-one" shader, with superior functionalities for creative, technically complex shading (tweakable BRDF), and optimization options for improved performance.

The physics shaders and the architectural material shading models are intended for use with realistic light simulations, such as with indirect illumination (GI and FG). Regardless of indirect light, these shading models offer a wide range of abilities. Physical shaders accurately model light reflection and transmission while considering energy conservation. Note that different physical shaders possess different levels of physical correctness, as discussed per shader in Chapter 10.

Balancing Light Transport

When using nonphysical shaders, an important consideration deals with energy conservation. Essentially, we already established that light photons are timeless particles of energy that are reflected, transmitted, or absorbed from matter. The total radiant exitance (outgoing energy) at a given point cannot exceed the total incident energy and thus needs to be balanced between the reflected and refracted light, as with Fresnel reflections. Therefore, the different diffuse to specular reflection (and refraction) intensities are all weighed against each other. For example, highly reflective surfaces reflect most of their energy with specular reflections and as a result possess less diffuse reflection.

> Energy-conserving shaders are shaders that limit the total reflected light (radiance exitance) not to exceed the total incident light (irradiance) flux.

For energy conservation, the total combined RGB values for diffuse, glossy, and specular components need to add up to a value of 1 (color normalized to a 0 to 1 range) so that the total radiant flux will not exceed a value of 1. To clarify, regardless of the light's intensity value, the light value is multiplied by the different shader components. Thus, if the total mathematical equation for all the different light-scattering components adds up to 1, that means at the brightest point on the surface the radiant exitance will not exceed 100 percent of the incident light. However, if the total value for all the reflection and transmission components (for RGB channels) adds up to 2, then at the brightest point the light flux would multiply by 2, magnifying the radiant exitance.

When implementing shading models and defining the levels for diffuse, glossy, and specular light reflection, it's up to you to consider how those different light contributions are balanced to better resemble realistic surface characteristics. Typically you shouldn't have a Blinn shader with a bright diffuse and specular, as well as fully reflected (reflection color), because that shader will reach overexposure quickly as well as magnify the light intensity. Note that most BRDF functions evaluate the energy independently for each component. Thus, the overall material output is not energy-conserving once you add ambient light with diffuse light and specular light.

With respect to using standard (base) and physical shaders as well as indirect illumination in the same scene, the likelihood of incoherent results increases for the different shading models. To clarify, the non-energy-conserving shaders typically appear brighter than energy-conserving shaders, because they amplify radiant flux rather than conserve flux based on the irradiance (incoming flux), whereas physical shaders will not allow radiant flux to exceed the irradiance. The topic of energy conservation is further discussed with physical shaders in Chapter 10.

mental ray Shaders and Shader Trees

The main purpose of this chapter is to better acquaint you with shader functionalities and shader trees. Essentially, the in-depth look you've taken at light transport (Chapter 9, "The Fundamentals of Light and Shading Models") and mental ray shaders (throughout the book) should help you recognize and understand similar shader characteristics found in various custom shaders or host-specific shaders, as well as with different rendering software. The aim is to encourage you to design your own shading trees using various component shaders, regardless of the platform (software) and available tools (shaders). After you master this information and understand shaders and shader arithmetic, you will become more productive in your own workflows.

Chapter 9, "The Fundamentals of Light and Shading Models," introduced the common shading models found within the base shader library. In this chapter, I'll further discuss mental ray and host-specific shaders, shader trees, and resources for locating custom mental ray shaders via the Web. All host applications provide most of the base, physics, and architectural shaders that are covered within this book. In this chapter, while examining shader trees, you'll examine other component shaders as required, which deal with particular tasks such as color (or scalar) math, color mixing, and data conversions. Maya provides all the mental ray shader libraries with their "raw" mental ray settings; hence (on occasion), I use Maya UI snapshots for presenting mental ray–specific shader options followed with references to equivalent shaders and options in each host application. This chapter covers the following topics:

- **Installing Custom Shaders**
- **DGS and Dielectric Shading Models**
- **Glossy Reflection and Refraction Shaders**
- **Brushed Metals with the Glossy and Anisotropic Shaders**
- **The Architectural (mia) Material**

Installing Custom Shaders

In addition to mental ray shader libraries and host-specific shaders, there are useful resources on the Web for obtaining custom mental ray shaders. The importance of online resources, particularly for users who aren't coders, is that they greatly extend the mental ray shader collection that ships with these host applications. Table 10.1 lists useful online resources with comments about what each listing offers. These resources provide additional shaders that extend your ability to render complex color effects; you'll find improved procedural shaders (4D fractal, noise, cell, and turbulence shaders) or custom raytracing effects, such as complex lens shaders or shading models that, for example, include within them several specular terms (options for Blinn, Phong, Lafortune, or Ward anisotropic highlights) and empirical data for reflection models, such as the Tek2shoot illumination shader (see Tek2shoot listed in Table 10.1).

	SOURCE	COMMENTS
Table 10.1 **Online Resources for Custom Mental Ray Shaders***	www.binaryalchemy.de and available on the CD**	This is a great collection of custom mental ray shaders for XSI, Maya, and 3ds Max. The shaders are intended for XSI; however, there are additional resources (seen in the following sections) that help implement them in Maya and 3ds Max. Some of this site's best shaders are the ray length (retrieve information on surface edges) texture shader, and oily specular shader. This site offers a great collection of color mixer textures, improved shadow shaders, and more. It also sells some advanced volumetric shaders for special effects.
	www.pixero.com and available on the CD**	Jan Sandström provides a variety of mental ray for Maya and 3ds Max shaders (mostly Maya). Jan provides several include (.mi) and AETemplate files for implementing mental ray shaders (such as the Binary Alchemy or TEK2SHOOT shaders) in Maya and 3ds Max, as shown in the following tutorials. He also has other useful shaders such as a good tone mapping shader (JS_ExposureControl) and output shaders (for glare), amongst several others. If you are a Maya user, this site is for you.
	www.tek2shoot.com and available on the CD**	This site provides a powerful illumination shader that contains several realistic features including an iridescent coating (because of interference) such as with bubbles or oil spills (coating shader on CD). The robust illumination shader also comes with various Fresnel preset files for different types of shaders (on the CD), as well as support for the Lafortune specular shading model. All shaders are available for XSI, and the Illumination (all-in-one) shader is also available for Maya thanks to Jan Sandström (under the TEK2SHOOT folder). This shader is by far one of the most robust illumination shaders available.

continues

SOURCE	COMMENTS
www.Mymentalray.com	This site is a small mental ray community site providing a variety of shaders for download. You can find the P.30 shader collection (from Puppet), which provides robust frame buffer control for pass rendering (see Chapter 3, "mental ray Output"), really fantastic. The same collection includes a Z-depth shader that supports rendering transparency into (RGB) depth pass. You can also find various other shaders for all host applications on this site, such as bump combiner shaders, color mixers, subsurface scattering, and more.
http://www.impresszio.hu/szabolcs/ and available on the CD**	Horvátth Szabolcs offers some great Maya and mental ray shaders (and tutorials), including the lm_2DMV motion vectors shader Maya files covered in Chapter 8, "Motion Blur." He also has shader utilities for custom user frame buffer passes and a ray type shader. The ray type shader very useful for many purposes, a topic discussed in Chapter 13, "Final Gather and Ambient Occlusion." For some of his shaders, such as the reflection utility, 3ds Max users can get an updated .mi file from the www.maxplugins.de site mentioned later in this table.
http://puppet.cgtalk.ru, a switch to English button is on the home page; shaders also available on the CD**	Pavel Ledin (Puppet) provides a collection of shaders for all platforms. His p_MegaTK shader is one of the best alternatives to exporting custom color passes in Maya and 3ds Max (see Chapter 3, "mental ray Output"). He also has various other useful shaders such as custom Z-depth, constant shading, light wrapping, and data conversion shaders to mention a few. Most are available on the CD for all host applications in the CustomShaders/ Puppet folder.
www.alamaison.fr/3d/lm_2DMV/lm_2DMV_ref.htm	La Maison, a studio in France, developed the lm_2DMV shader demonstrated in Chapter 8, "Motion Blur," for motion vectors motion blur. You can get the files for each host application at this site. The files required for each host is discussed in Chapter 8, "Motion Blur."
www.XSIbase.com/	This is a good resource for shaders and links to other useful sites.
http://binaryiris.com/	This is Alan Jones` XSI mental ray shaders.
www.duikerresearch.com/free/index.html	This is a great resource for component shaders for all host applications.
www.maxplugins.de/	This is one of the best resources for 3ds Max mental ray shaders. You can find the include (.mi) files you need for installing several mental ray shaders that come form a variety of other resources, such as those cited above.

* Before using these shaders, you should become familiar with any license agreements that are posted on the sites or included with the downloadable files.

** Find these files on the CD by going to ChapterFiles/CustomShaders and looking for each individual set of files by name.

The TEK2SHOOT, Puppet, Horvátth Szabolcs, Binary Alchemy, and Jan Sandström shaders have been kindly provided by their authors and are available on the companion CD in the ChapterFiles/CustomShaders folder. These shaders can be used in all host applications; see their notes on installation and licensing within their relevant folders and ZIP files.

Besides improving your ability to render visually pleasing results, other resources improve mental ray's functionality, allowing you to export custom user frame buffers from host applications, such as custom passes (that is, the p_MegaTK shaders discussed in Chapter 3, "mental ray Output"; see Puppet shaders in Table 10.1), motion vectors (Chapter 8, "Motion Blur"), and even a transparency supported Z-depth pass (Puppet p_Z shader). Z-depth passes are well known for their inability to represent transparency, and thus installing such a custom shader significantly improves your ability to cope with depth-based effects while compositing.

In the following sections of this chapter, you will primarily look at mental ray physical shaders, as well as using advanced shaders and networks. For the purpose of completing these tutorials, XSI users are required to install the physical shaders from TEK2SHOOT or the XPhysics shader collection (details are provided later in this chapter).

For users who want to install custom shaders from online resources (shown in Table 10.1), the following sections will demonstrate how to install the Binary Alchemy shaders in each host application. The same procedure should be followed while installing most other custom shaders, although some shaders may include specific installation instructions. The Binary Alchemy shaders provide a good example of the involved process with each host application, even though I will not show how to use any of these shaders in the following sections (with one exception).

Installing the Binary Alchemy Shaders

Because these are mental ray shaders, their installation requires merely adding two files into the host root directory, as described next. With XSI on most occasions, shaders are packed in XSI add-on files that are easier to implement. Each host application requires a different set of shaders (provided in CustomShaders/BinaryAlchemy on the CD) to complete the installation, described within the following installation steps:

1. Navigate to the download page (for the most current shaders). Go to www.binaryalchemy.de. Navigate to Development/Software/Shader → Shader Collection – Essential Mental Ray Shaders (under Public Releases) → Download. You should now see the license and download instructions for various collections in the new page that appears.

2. Download the files required for your host application. You can download the current files or use the ones provided on the CD. Each host requires the compiled shaders from this site. XSI users will download an XSI add-on file, Maya users will download all the declaration and DLL files required for Maya, and 3ds Max users will download all the DLL files, as well as download modified declaration files from another source, as described here:

XSI Select "v22.3 XSI 6.01 Addon Linux+Windows, 32+64 bit," which prompts you to download the ZIP file. Once the collection is downloaded, install the XSI add-on file found in the ZIP archive by following the steps in the "Installing XSI Physical Shaders" section. The same file is available on the CD: `ChapterFiles/CustomShaders/Binary Alchemy/XSI`.

Maya and 3ds Max Both Maya and 3ds Max download the v22 Maya Files ZIP file and extract the contents into any folder. The same ZIP file is available on the CD: `ChapterFiles/CustomShaders/BinaryAlchemy/Maya`.

3ds Max 3ds Max users also need to download additional (different) include files. Download the BA_color_mixer shader (or any other BA_ shader will do) from `www.maxplugins.de` → mental ray shaders → Texture shaders; I found it (and other BA shaders) under the third page. To download the include file, click the link in the sentence that says "…the Include file for Max can be downloaded here.…" You will be prompted to save a ZIP file labeled `BA_Shader_Collection_Includes.zip`, which contains all the include files for the BA shader collection, modified for 3ds Max. The DLL files are provided from the Maya collection cited in the previous step.

3. Install the Shaders with Maya and 3ds Max. You now place the correct files in their mental ray directories for each host. Once they are placed correctly, you can launch your host application and find the new BA shaders loaded within the Maya Hypershade window or the 3ds Max Material/Map Browser window.

Here are the steps for Maya and 3ds Max:

1. Open the directory folder where you extracted the ZIP file. You should see three folders labeled Scripts, HTML Files, and mental ray, as well as an HTML page that launches the shader help files.

2. In the mental ray folder, you will find mental ray–specific folders containing all the declaration files and DLL files. The lib folders contain compiled shaders for different computer systems including Windows 32-bit (lib folder), Windows 64-bit (lib_x64 folder), and Linux systems (lib_Linux). Open the appropriate folder for your system, and copy all the DLL (or SO) files.

Here are the steps for Maya only:

1. Open the Maya installation path and navigate to the mental ray directory, as shown for a Windows system with the following path: `C:\Program Files\ Autodesk\Maya8.5\mentalray\`.

2. Open the lib directory, and paste all the copied DLL (or SO) files within that folder.

3. Go back to the extracted ZIP folder directory, and open the `mental ray/include` folder. Copy all the `.mi` declaration files, and return to the Maya installation path and paste all these declaration (`.mi`) files in the `Maya 8.5\mental ray\include` folder.

4. Under the ZIP folder's directory, locate the `scripts/AETemplates` folder. Open the folder and copy all the AEBA MEL files. These files describe the shader interfaces that appear in the Attribute Editor window.

5. Under the Maya installation path, locate the AETemplates directory, and paste there all the MEL files. This directory is typically found under the following path: `C:\Program Files\Autodesk\Maya8.5\scripts\AETemplates`.

6. In some cases, custom shaders will also include XPM files in an icons directory, which you can place in the `Maya8.5\icons` directory.

At this point, if you followed all the steps correctly, you can launch Maya and start using these shaders. You can find the shaders within various rollouts under the Create mental ray Nodes rollout in the Hypershade window.

Here are the steps for 3ds Max only:

1. Open the 3ds Max installation path and navigate to the mental ray directory, as shown for a Windows system with the following path: `C:\Program Files\Autodesk\3ds Max 9\mentalray`.

2. Open the `shaders_autoload/shaders` directory, and paste all the copied DLL (or SO) files within that folder.

3. Open the directory with the include files (BA Shader Collection Includes), downloaded earlier from `www.maxplugins.de`.

4. Copy all the declaration files (`.mi` files), and return to your 3ds Max mental ray directory, as described in step 2.

5. Open the `shaders_autoload/include` directory, and paste within it all the declaration files. These declaration files have been modified to work with 3ds Max.

You can now launch 3ds Max and find the BA shaders in the Material/Map Browser window when mental ray is set as the current (production) renderer.

Installing XSI Physical Shaders

You may have noticed that XSI does not include the physics shader library by default. Before I cover these shaders in the following section, you may want to first install them. There are two options you can choose from:

- Download and install the physics library from Net View. In Net View, select XSI Net → Render, and locate the XPhysics Lib add-on.

- Alternatively (and better), you can use the TEK2SHOOT (`www.tek2shoot.com`) unexposed Mental Ray shaders collection provided on the CD (TEK2SHOOT/XSI_

32_64_bit/T2S_MentalRay1_1.xsiaddon), which provides a wide range of shaders, including the glossy shaders (required for the following sections), physical light, DGS, dielectric, participating media, and others. The add-on file provided on the CD supports both 32- and 64-bit systems and are better implementations than the XPhysics library. You will also find the T2S_Materials_Menu.xsiaddon file, which when installed adds a T2S menu to your Materials menu so you can load them directly.

The TEK2SHOOT shaders are required for various tutorials in this chapter and in Chapter 12; their installation is very easy.

To install the shaders, place the add-on file in your user directory, which on my Windows system is as follows:

```
C:\users\your name\Softimage\XSI_6.0\Addons\
```

In XSI, from the main menu bar, select File → Plug-in Manager. In the Plug-in Manager window, right-click User Root, and select Install .xsiaddon, as shown in Figure 10.1. Navigate to the directory (where you placed the file), and select the add-on file. Once installed, you can then find the shaders in their appropriate directories.

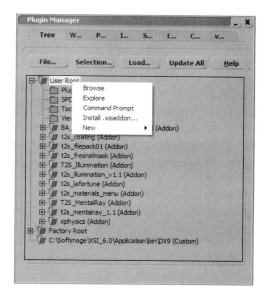

Figure 10.1

Installing add-ons in XSI

From the XSI toolbar, select Get → Material → More, and navigate to the user directory. You can use the Paths shortcut button to quickly navigate to the add-ons path. Note that both libraries provide monolithic shaders that include the illumination and photon shaders, so you don't need to concern yourself with manually connecting a photon shader to the material. See the help files for additional information on installing XSI add-ons.

DGS and Dielectric Shading Models

Chapter 9, "The Fundamentals of Light and Shading Models," discussed diffuse, glossy, and specular (DGS) reflections and mentioned that mental ray provides a DGS shader. In the following sections, I'll first review the DGS and dielectric shaders, and then I'll review mib_glossy_shaders, which greatly improves performance for glossy reflections. Then, in the section "Brushed Metals with the Glossy and Anisotropic Shaders," I'll review a shader tree that implements brushed-metal anisotropic reflections with the mib_glossy_shader and the Ward shading model.

The DGS Shader

The DGS shader acts as a shading model implementation for DGS physical shading functionalities. Its purpose is to present a physically correct shading model that accurately simulates diffuse, glossy, and specular light scattering, accounting for energy conservation. As shown in Figure 10.2, the shader provides three main components: diffuse, specular, and glossy reflections and refractions. The diffuse component supports only diffuse reflectance (diffuse transmission is characterized as subsurface scattering in translucent surfaces). The specular and glossy components support both reflectance and transmission. The incident light energy that is reflected from a DGS shading model is defined by the total color values of all three diffuse, glossy, and specular components. As discussed in Chapter 9, "The

Figure 10.2

The mental ray DGS shader in Maya

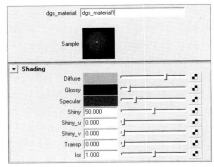

Fundamentals of Light and Shading Models,"— specifically in the "Balancing Light Transport" section—to maintain light reflection up to or less than 100 percent of the incoming light, the color values you specify for the RGB components should not exceed a value of 1. For example, in terms of grayscale (RGB values are equal), the diffuse component is set to a value of 0.4, glossy is set to 0.4, and specular is set to 0.2; hence, the total value when combined equals 1.

The Specular Component

The specular component controls raytrace reflections and refractions only. Thus, with respect to highlights, the specular component does not render highlights; you can see this in Figure 10.3 image A, where only the floor appears reflected on the sphere. In image A the area light visibility option is disabled so that it does not appear reflected, behaving like other source lights. However, when visibility is enabled (image B), the area light geometric shape appears reflected, as shown in Figure 10.3 image B. As you can see (image B), the area light shape renders a raytrace specular (mirror) reflection of the light's geometric shape on the sphere's surface. Thus, unlike other base shaders, the DGS specular component does not control emulated highlights, only raytrace reflections.

Figure 10.3
**Specular vs. glossy
reflections with the
DGS shader**

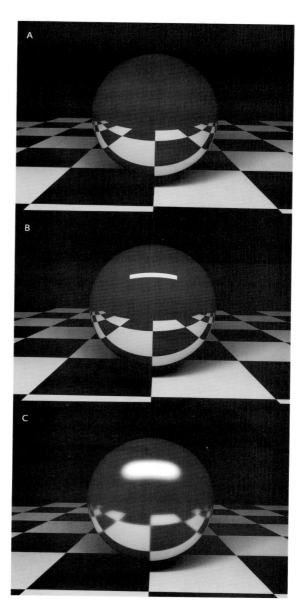

The transparency (Transp) and index of refraction (IOR) attributes shown in the DGS interface enable surface transparency and refraction. When you specify a transparency level and index of refraction, the specular component controls focused refractions, such as with water or glass. When Transp is set to 1, the surface renders full refractions, as shown in Figure 10.4 image A, which uses a 0.8 specular gray. There are a few points to note with respect to specular refractions:

- The specular and glossy components control the surface color and transparency level. Thus, a specular value of 1 (white) will render full transparency, and a 50 percent value with a green tint, will render a semitransparent green surface.

- If the specular color is set to black, even with full transparency, the surface will appear opaque because the transmission is canceled when the specular component is disabled (set to black).

Figure 10.4

Specular vs. glossy refractions using the DGS shader

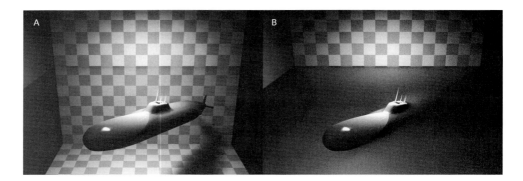

The Glossy Component

The glossy component supports reflections and refractions, just as with the specular component, as well as source light highlights. In Figure 10.3 image C, the specular color is set to black, and the glossy color is set to white. As you can see, the floor is reflected on the sphere, and a highlight that corresponds to the area light's emission area (its rectangular shape) appears reflected. Note that the area light visibility is disabled, and thus the highlights are not rendered as raytrace reflections but as part of a shader emulation of highlights, as discussed in Chapter 9, "The Fundamentals of Light and Shading Models" in the "Specular Shading Models" section. Since we established in Chapter 9 that the term *specular highlights* with base (or other) shaders typically has a glossy nature, in the case of the DGS shader the specular and glossy components are correctly associated (labeled) with that specific function (specular vs. glossy reflections or refractions).

The main benefit of the glossy component is that it provides glossy scattering for both reflections and refractions, distance-based scattering, and anisotropic or isotropic scattering. The following considerations apply:

- The amount of "blurriness" in the reflection or refraction is controlled with the Shiny option, providing isotropic scattering only. Higher values (from 100 to 200) yield sharper (more specular) results, and lower values (below 50) provide glossier scattering. You can see examples for DGS Glossy reflections in Chapter 9, specifically in Figure 9.16 image B (isotropic) and image C (anisotropic).

- As the reflected surfaces get farther away from the reflective surface, the reflection or refraction will appear glossier (also shown in Figure 10.16). Thus, the DGS shader supports distance-based reflections that dictate that as the distance between surfaces increases, their reflections become glossier based on each surface's glossy character, as discussed in the section "Glossy Reflection" in Chapter 9, "The Fundamentals of Light and Shading Models."

- A Shiny value less than 50 provides significant glossiness, as shown in Figure 10.4 image B, where a Shiny value of 5 was used to simulate a deep ocean surface with a highly glossy refraction. Notice how the submarine becomes less recognizable over distance, demonstrating distance-based glossiness. Thus, glossy transparency enables simulating translucent refractions, such as with deep water, wax, or frosted glass, which are typically dense substances that absorb a lot of light while scattering light internally.

- Notice that along the edges of the water surface where the water touches the checkered wall, the checkers in the water appear in focus; they don't appear blurred in close proximity to the water surface. This again demonstrates the distance-based character of glossy refractions (or reflections).

- Note that unlike the dielectric shader and architectural material (discussed later in this chapter), the DGS shader does not support light absorption; however, the glossier and darker the surface, the more it appears to absorb light. Thus, to better simulate glossy absorption, use low Shiny values (such as15 to 25) and darker glossy color values.

The subsurface shaders are better geared toward subsurface scattering effects in highly translucent surfaces, whereas for deep materials (Figure 10.4 image B) or materials that exhibit less translucency, such as with frosted glass and ice (not fully diffused refractions, more of a glossy transparency), shaders such as the DGS, architectural material, and glossy shaders are better suited for rendering the glossy refraction effect.

Glossy Anisotropic Scattering

When the Shiny option is set to a value of 0, it is effectively disabled and the Shiny_u and Shiny_v options are enabled instead. These two options provide the same functionality as with the Ward shader's Shiny U and V options (see "The Ward Shader" in Chapter 9, "The Fundamentals of Light and Shading Models"), accommodating anisotropic scattering by utilizing separate U and V values. Thus, higher values provide sharper reflections (or refractions), and lower values are glossier. As with the Ward shader, the difference between their values defines a ratio for the highlight, as shown in Figure 10.5 image A, where Shiny V is set to 1 and Shiny U is set to 40. Notice that because Shiny V is set to 1, the highlight wraps around the entire surface. If Shiny V is set to a value greater than 1, the highlight will wrap around only a partial area of the surface, as shown in Figure 10.5 image B (Shiny V set to 4). If Shiny V in this case is used to determine the extent of the highlight across the surface, then Shiny U defines its thickness, where higher values will provide for a sharper (thin) effect and lower values will appear glossier (wider-spread highlights). The glossy color has the same purpose as discussed earlier, controlling the highlight brightness and color (the intensity of the glossy effect).

Figure 10.5

Anisotropic shading with the DGS shader

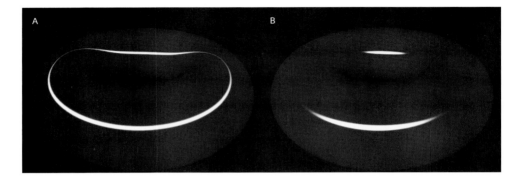

The DGS glossy Shiny U and Shiny V options support rendering both anisotropic highlights and reflections (raytrace), a topic discussed in more detail in the section "Brushed Metals with the Glossy and Anisotropic Shaders," which includes an advanced shader tree example using the Ward shader and the mib_glossy_reflection shader for generating anisotropic highlights and reflections.

The Dielectric Shading Model

The mental ray dielectric shader is a physically correct shader that supports several features discussed in Chapter 9, "The Fundamentals of Light and Shading Models." These include Fresnel equations, which balance the ratio between the reflections and refractions intensity, the Beer-Lambert law for simulating internal absorption within the dielectric, and Snell's law of refraction. The architectural material enhances those abilities with glossy refractions and a customizable BRDF interface providing further control over Fresnel reflections (more on that later in this chapter).

The main purpose of the dielectric shader is to model an interface between two different media, where you indicate the refraction into the first medium and also the refraction when entering the second medium.

This solves one of the conundrums of rendering dielectric surfaces, where the refraction going into the surface is calculated but the refraction upon exiting the surface is not. Typically, an additional surface can be modeled that applies that corrective refraction. For example, a glass of water would require an index of refraction of 1.5 entering the glass and an index of refraction of 0.8 when exiting the glass and entering water based on a water index refraction of 1.3. Recall that Chapter 9, "The Fundamentals of Light and Shading Models," explains how an index of refraction represents the ratio of the speed of light between two mediums; therefore, in this case, the ratio from glass to water is written like this: 1.3 ÷ 1.5. With the dielectric shader you don't need to do the math; just apply the index of refraction value for each medium based on a standard vacuum to medium interface (that is, 1.5 for glass, 1.3 for water, and so on). Using the shader is not clear-cut, and there is room for confusion; the following explanations will help you understand how to resolve such cases.

Dielectric Options and Light Absorption

You can see the dielectric shader's interface in Figure 10.6. Similar settings in each host are reviewed in the following section. The Col attribute defines the color for the glass, and its absorption level based on the Beer-Lambert law. The Col attribute's luminance color value, defined with the V parameter on an HSV color scale, defines an absorption coefficient for the dielectric. The absorption is applied using an exponential rate for light decay through the dielectric. A Black value (a value of 0) corresponds to full absorption, and white (a value of 1) corresponds to a fully transitive dielectric, meaning there is no absorption. Values within that range (from 0 to 1) indicate a percentage of absorption per unit length in world space coordinates, through the dielectric. Thus, at a value of 0.5, there is 50 percent absorption, and at 0.1 there will be 90 percent absorption per unit length through the dielectric.

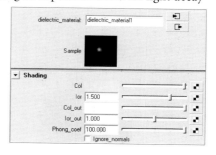

Figure 10.6

The dielectric shader enables you to model an interface between two different dielectrics that have different indices of refraction.

   The Col_out attribute defines the nature of the second dielectric and its absorption level, which will become clearer shortly. The Ior and Ior_out attributes define the indices of refraction for the first and second dielectric interfaces, respectively. Thus, in the case of a simple glass, the Ior attribute is set to 1.5 (glass ior), and the Ior_out attribute is set to 1.0, which is the IOR in vacuum (or air); in such a case it has no effect unless Col_out is set to show the effect of absorption (using a darker color value than white) from the external dielectric. Thus, the second set of options (Col_out and Ior_out attributes) is used to describe an external environment that surrounds the dielectric, whereas the first set of options describes the internal character of the dielectric. The external environment may then be any type of matter, which is a different dielectric substance.

   Phong_coef defines a Phong-based specular highlight using a simple exponent value, as described in Chapter 9, "The Fundamentals of Light and Shading Models." The Ignore_normals attribute ignores the surface normals while defining the front and back-sides of the surface. When enabled, polygons that are facing the camera are considered as the front side of the surface regardless of their normal direction; they are rendered as if their normals were facing the camera. Basically, the direction of the normals is used to define whether a ray is refracting into dielectric, which will use the first set of Col and Ior attributes, or refracting out of the dielectric, which then uses the second set of Col_out and Ior_out attributes.

RENDERING GLASS WITH THE DIELECTRIC SHADER

The dielectric shader is the only shader that provides the ability to model two separate interfaces. Even the architectural material deals with only one interface at a time, so the modeling considerations when using the dielectric are different than in most other cases. Essentially, the approach is a bit easier with the dielectric shader. Figure 10.7 shows a modeling scheme for a dielectric glass with a liquid substance such as water. Slice B shows a split view of the glass and the liquid. Slice A shows the different surface interfaces that are applied with three dielectric shaders. The arrows indicate the surface normals, which are crucial for defining the first and second interfaces.

Figure 10.7

Modeling two different dielectric interfaces for creating a glass with an internal fluid

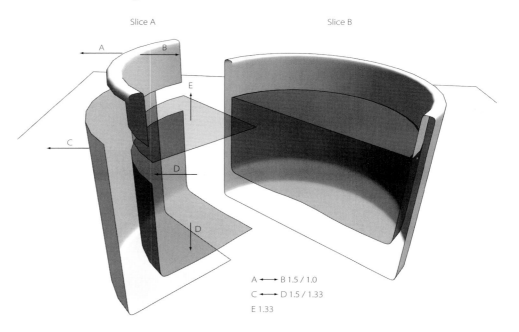

The first surface, shown with the normals A, B, and C, represents the portion of the glass that interacts with air; therefore, the Ior attribute is set to 1.5, and the Ior_out attribute is set to 1.0. Notice how a section of that surface also defines an interface between the glass and the liquid, shown with the normals C and D (D on the liquid surface). With the dielectric shader, you can model only two interfaces. So, the shader for the outer surface (normals A, B, and C) uses an air to glass dielectric shader, because the light travels from air into glass and then back to air as it exits the glass on the other side, aside from were it enters the liquid, which is handled with the next dielectric shader.

The liquid in the glass is divided between two interfaces: the glass-to-liquid interface (normals labeled D) and the air-to-liquid interface (normal labeled E). The surface with the normals labeled D has the Ior attribute set to 1.33 (entering the liquid), and the Ior_out attribute is set to 1.5 (exiting into the glass). The E interface represents the liquid surface that interfaces with air and therefore is an air-to-liquid interface, where the Ior attribute is set to 1.33 and the Ior_out attribute is set to 1.

ABSORPTION IN THE SECOND DIELECTRIC

The second dielectric's Col_out attribute specifies the absorption rate through the external (second) dielectric. The best way for you to visualize its effect is with a glass example. Consider that the base of the glass is a solid (thick) where you can see the absorption through the glass. The glass sides are thin, and between them a volume of air (or other dielectric) exists. The air is represented by the second dielectric using the Col_out absorption and Ior_out attributes. If you set the Col_out attribute to a high absorption rate, you will see its absorption effect (a dark color) between the glass sides (within the empty volume) but not through the base area of the glass, which is never exposed to the second dielectric because it's a contained volume.

FINAL CONSIDERATIONS

When you are not using the dielectric shader, you need to consider the difference in the IOR between different interfaces, something this shader calculates for you. You can refer to the section "Diffuse, Specular, and Glossy Transmittance" in Chapter 9, "The Fundamentals of Light and Shading Models," for a list of common indices of refraction for different dielectric substances. In addition, the dielectric shader does not support transparent shadows, and thus you can use a separate shadow shader (see Chapter 7, "Shadow Algorithms"). Or better yet, you can use caustics, a topic covered in Chapter 12, "Indirect Illumination."

> To help realize the differences of the dielectric shader, consider that in comparison with other refraction shaders, which provide vacuum-to-dielectric interfaces using a single IOR option, the dielectric shader extends that ability by supporting two different dielectric interfaces (such as glass to liquid); the dielectric shader is not limited to a vacuum-to-dielectric interface, which is the common dielectric interface used with most refraction shaders.

You can see comparisons between different types of glass renderings, demonstrating absorption, glossiness (frosted glass), and Fresnel reflections, using the dielectric shader and architectural material in the color inserts under "Glass Shark Comparisons." In the following section, you will see how you need to be resourceful while developing a dielectric shader tree; however, when the dielectric shader is set correctly, it simply provides for nice glass renderings.

Another great shader for rendering glass is the Lume (shader library) glass shader that provides various options for controlling the appearance of glass.

Colored Glass Effects

One of the problems the dielectric shader presents is applying color to glass. Although you can easily specify a color for the glass within the shader, or even map it with a texture that has some color pattern, doing so presents two problems:

- The absorption of the dielectric is defined by the value of the color, as cited earlier. Thus, different colors will have an unwanted effect on absorption.

- You may want to layer a texture on top of the glass, as with a label; however, if white represents full transparency with no absorption, how do you add a white label (or any texture color) that appears opaque or blends with some transparency?

The solution is to use the mental ray mib_color_mix shader (or any color mixers) to mathematically mix color from a texture with the color from the dielectric. This way, the dielectric shader passes its color evaluation to the color mix shader, and then the color mix shader adds (or blends) that result with the texture color, as shown in Figure 10.8. The figure shows a simple shader tree in Maya using the mental ray mib_color_mix shader (labeled C) that adds the color from a texture file (labeled A) with the color from a dielectric shader (labeled D). By doing so, the color values specified with the dielectric shader represent the glass absorption and base color (transparency color), unaffected by the texture color.

Figure 10.8

Creating color glass effects using the dielectric shader and the mib_color_mix shader

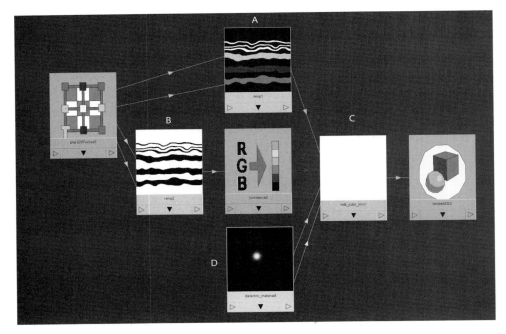

THE MIB_COLOR_MIX SHADER OPTIONS

The mental ray mib_color_mix shader (available in host applications), whose interface is shown in Figure 10.9, can take several color entries and blends them together based on a blending mode. Each color entry has an associated weight option that is used as a masking channel for the color influence. The first attribute, Num, defines how many of the color entries will be used while blending colors. To clarify, when Num is set to 1, only the Color_0 attribute is used, and if Num is set to 2, then both Color_0 and Color_1 will be used, and in both cases they are blended based on their associated mode and weight options with the Color_base attribute. You can use these blending modes like you blend layers in Photoshop.

CREATING THE SHADER TREE

For the color glass effect, I want to apply a simple compositing trick; I want to mask out the color areas of the label, shown as the texture file labeled A in Figure 10.8, from the dielectric shader so that it appears as an opaque labeled on a glass surface and it doesn't show any transparency through the label. To achieve this effect, I use a black-and-white mask (labeled B) derived from the texture file (labeled A) as a hold-out mask for the dielectric shader's color values; the mask is multiplied by the dielectric shader to remove its influence across the surface where the texture has color values (other than black), effectively cutting out a hole for the label. This process is known as an *over* composite in compositing software (discussed further in following chapters). Here are the basic steps:

1. I connect the label texture (labeled A) to the mib_color_mix shader's Color_base attribute and the dielectric shader to the Color_0 attribute.

2. I connect an inverted mask (labeled B) of the texture (A) to the mib_color_mix Weight_0 option using a luminance shader. Since the mib_color_mix weight options use scalar (single channel) values, I use the Maya luminance shader (shown with the large RGB letters) to convert the RGB color values from the mask labeled B to a single scalar value for the Weigt_0 attribute. Similar RGB-to-scalar shaders are available in each host; also, since the mask is already black and white, I could have just used any of the R, G, and B channels instead of a luminance shader. Note that the mask should not have any gray color values; only black and white colors should be used if you want it to complexly mask out an area, as with this example.

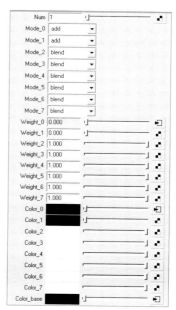

Figure 10.9

The mib_color_mix shader's options

3. With respected to an inverted mask, notice in Figure 10.8 that the mask (labeled B) appears black where the texture (labeled A) has color, and white where it doesn't. The mask is inverted so that areas that appear as white in the mask define the areas where you see color from the dielectric shader, and the black color defines areas where the dielectric shader is masked out. As mentioned earlier, I want to multiply the colors from a mask with the dielectric shader, carving out a hole in the dielectric shader's colors for the texture color. Thus, I use an inverted mask of the texture as a weight value for the dielectric shader; it multiplies the black-and-white scalar values from the mask by the dielectric shader's R,G, and B color values, a typical masking operation.

4. I then set the mib_color_mix shader's Mode_0 attribute to Add. This way colors from the dielectric shader that have not been masked out (the white areas of the mask) are added over the black color values shown in the texture (A).

5. Finally, the mib_color_mix shader is connected to the material shader as an illumination shader, as discussed in Chapter 9, "The Fundamentals of Light and Shading Models" under "mental ray Materials."

MAYA

The mib_color_mix shader is located in the Data Conversion section of the mental ray nodes in the Hypershade window, and the luminance shader is in the Color Utilities section of the Maya nodes. In Figure 10.8, the mib_mix_color shader is connected to the ShadingEngine node's mental ray → Custom Shaders → Material Shader.

XSI

In XSI you can re-create the same network using the dielectric shader from the TEK2SHOOT library (see "Installing XSI Physical Shaders" earlier in this chapter). However, the shader tree presented in this section can be applied in the same way with any other XSI refraction shader. Thus, you don't need the physics dielectric shader to create this type of shader tree; it's a common exercise in masking (combining) different source shaders using a mask.

TAKING IT A STEP FURTHER

The procedure described for colored glass effects can be used with different math operations to add labels or custom effects onto surfaces. For example, you could use grayscale mask values and different blending modes to combine the colors from the texture and shader together. This way you can show some transparency through the label, even a variation in transparency, based on the mask's grayscale values and the blending mode.

Furthermore, the texture map (A) can alternatively be provided as a shader, such as a Lambert shader, instead of a texture file. This way I use one shader to define the material character of the label and another to define the character of the glass. These concepts are at the backbone of complex shader trees, where you apply traditional compositing theories while constructing shader math procedures using various component shaders.

For the mib_color_mix shader, you can use one of the color mixer shaders found in the Render Tree window under Nodes → Mixers → Mix_2colors or Mix_8colors (when mixing more than two colors). The shaders use the same settings as shown in the earlier example; however, in this case the mix_2color will suffice. Just as in the earlier case, the mix shader is connected to the Material → Surface input.

If you look at the Mix_8colors shader, you will see the Base Color property referred to as the Color_base attribute and a list of layers that can be enabled when you click their In Use property; clicking the In Use property is the same as setting the Num attribute discussed earlier with the mental ray shader. Also, you don't need to use a shader to convert RGB values to scalar values since the XSI color mix shaders use RGB values for the Weight properties.

If you do want to apply an RGB to scalar conversion for other purposes, you can use the Color to Scalar shader found under the Render Tree → Nodes → Conversion menu.

3DS MAX

With 3ds Max you can follow a similar process to re-create a similar shader tree; just use the following steps:

1. Open the Material Editor window, and load a mental ray material from the Get Material button into an empty slot.

2. Select the mapping button under the material's Material Shaders rollout → Basic Shaders → Surface parameter to apply a new shader. From the Material/Map Browser window, select the (3ds Max) Mix shader shown mapped in Figure 10.10.

3. Select the Color #1 parameter, and map it with the "Material to Shader" shader from the Material/Map Browser window, as shown in Figure 10.10. Under the Material to Shader Parameters, map the Material parameter with a dielectric shader; you can use the glass (physics_phen) shader. The glass shader should be set with the desired settings for the glass base material characteristics.

4. Under the mix shader's Mix parameters, map the Color #2 input with the color shader. This input may be mapped with a bitmap for a label, a procedural texture, or an illumination shader by using yet another material to Shader shader. Use the Mix Amount mapping parameter to map the cutout mask, as shown in Figure 10.10 and described in the earlier tutorial.

Once you complete all these steps, you have re-created a network similar to that presented in Figure 10.8. The only difference is that you have little influence on how the dielectric and the color texture are mathematically combined, a topic discussed in the earlier sidebar "Taking It a Step Further." To clarify, the mix shader will simply cut out the influence of one shader to benefit the other, based on the masks' values.

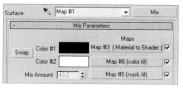

Figure 10.10

The 3ds Max Mix shader is used to combine a dielectric with color based on a cutout mask image.

How can you develop the same type of effect as described previously, where the mask controls the areas with color influence (from the bitmap) and a mode option (as described for the mib_color_mix shader) defines how color is superimposed with the dielectric shader's color? Instead of using the Mix shader as described in step 2, map the mental ray shader's Surface parameter with the Binary Alchemy color mixer shader (the BA Color Mixer is available on the CD in the BinaryAlchemy folder), provided you installed it correctly (described earlier under "Installing Custom Shaders").

You can then apply a dielectric shader (for example, Dielectric Material) to the Layer color parameter without using the "Material to Shader" shader. Apply the color texture (bitmap or texture) to the Base color parameter and the cutout mask to the Weight (color) parameter (for the dielectric shader). The Use scalar weight should be disabled so that the cutout mask image (or texture) RGB values are used; thus, you don't need to apply an RGB-to-scalar conversion as described earlier with the luminance shader. Finally, the BA Color Mixer shader's Mix mode parameter specifies the math function used to combine both layers. However, you can not easily determine the arithmetic for each mode since they appear numbered rather than labeled. Table 10.2 summarizes the mode operations correlating to a mode number.

Table 10.2

The Binary Alchemy Color Mixer Modes

MODE NUMBER	METHOD
01	Screen
02	Multiply
03	Add
04	Subtract (base minus layer)
05	Subtract inverted (layer minus base)
06	Difference [abs (subtract)]
07	Output white
08	Output black
09	Output black (opaque alpha)
10	Use base color (no operation)
11	Use layer color (no operation)

Glossy Sampling and Raytrace Control

The mental ray DGS and depth of field physical shaders base their raytrace sampling qualities on global scene anti-aliasing settings, so to get better quality, you must increase the sampling for the entire scene. To clarify, when rendering depth of field, glossy reflections, or glossy refractions, multiple samples are taken to improve the quality and reduce visible noise. Thus, for good-quality renders, you are required to increase the max sampling level, which significantly increases the render time, rather than just increase sampling for the surfaces in question. For example, Figure 10.4 image B (using the DGS shader) required several hours of rendering for a print resolution image. I discuss a better option for rendering the same image in a matter of minutes later in this chapter.

Another point of consideration involves the length of raytrace rays. As you increase the sample settings for glossy effects (making a surface appear glossier), the number of raytrace rays increases. By limiting the length (reach) of rays, you can significantly reduce the render times while maintaining the quality of the effect. Typically, at the max ray distance, an environment image (or some color value) would be used as a source for distant reflection values so that raytracing is in effect only for a given distance, beyond which the environment image is used.

The greater the distance a ray travels to extract color values for reflections or refractions, the glossier they appear on the surface. The glossier the appearance, the more ray samples are required to produce a better result. By limiting ray distances, you effectively specify a given area in the scene that affects the glossy reflection or refraction colors; anything beyond that distance has no effect. Thus, surfaces that are placed far from the reflective (or refractive) surface that contribute to poor-quality glossy reflections, which visually appear grainy, will not be used (sampled). The result is that your render will use fewer samples (raytrace rays), sample shorter distances, look better in the render (without artifacts), and, most important, render faster.

Fortunately, most host-specific and custom shaders provide shader-dependent sampling (per-shader multisampling), allowing you to increase the render quality at the shader level. Also, some mental ray shaders provide limiting options for defining a max distance for raytrace rays, such as with the glossy shaders, and architectural material, as you will soon see. Per-shader sampling and raytrace distance control are amongst the more sought out features, especially with heavy raytrace shaders. An example would be a depth-of-field lens shader that enables you to increase the sampling only when required (for out-of-focus areas), rather than for the entire scene as with the mental ray physical_lens_dof shader discussed in Chapter 4, "Camera Fundamentals." You can experiment with the Binary Alchemy DOF shader provided in the Binary Alchemy shader collection on the companion CD that has built-in shader sample options (see the earlier Table 10.1).

DGS, Dielectric, and Host-Specific Shaders

Host applications have their own settings that support DGS shading. Both Maya and XSI monolithic shaders have built-in per-shader sampling for glossy reflections and refractions. Also, Maya and 3ds Max ship with the mental ray DGS and dielectric shaders, and with XSI you can easily add the physics library as described earlier in the section "Installing XSI Physical Shaders."

With host-specific shaders, typically Fresnel reflections and light absorption are not supported. However, each host application supports creating custom Fresnel reflections using shaders that control the reflection and refraction intensity along a surface based on a facing ratio between the camera and the surface normal. These shaders enable you to design your own Fresnel shaders for illumination shaders that don't support Fresnel reflections. You can find examples in the Chapter 10 folder for each host on the companion CD. Next I'll cover host-specific shaders and the mental ray dielectric and DGS shaders in host applications.

Maya

The previous sections presented the mental ray DGS and dielectric shaders and their attributes in Maya. In addition to these mental ray–specific shaders, all the Maya-centric shading models have incorporated a mental ray tab that includes blurred reflections and refractions, as shown with a Maya Blinn shader in Figure 10.11. The only advantage of these shaders over the DGS shader is that the samples for the blurred reflection and refractions can be controlled on a per-shader basis, as shown with the Reflection or Refraction Blur, Blur Limit, and Rays attributes. However, the DGS shader is energy conserving and provides for better shading. These attributes also have equivalent global scene limits in the Render Settings window under the mental ray tab → Raytracing rollout, as discussed in Chapter 2, "Rendering Algorithms," in the "Enabling and Controlling Raytracing" section. I'll clarify the shader characteristics with a few points using the scene shown in Figure 10.12.

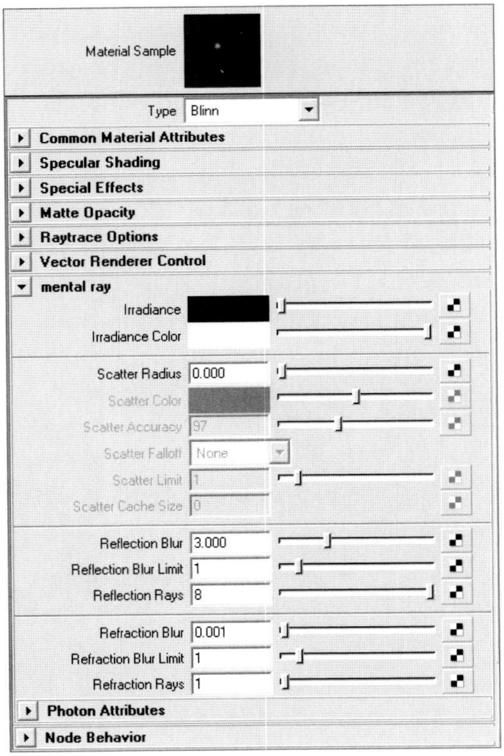

Figure 10.11

Maya host-specific shader settings for glossy reflections and refractions

The scene `reflectionBlurLimits.mb` is available in Chapter 10's Maya folder on the companion CD. You will find Blinn and DGS shaders with appropriate labels that you can experiment with while reading the tutorial.

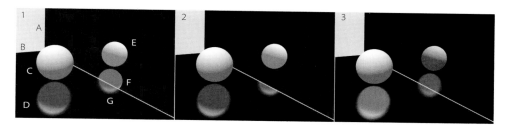

Figure 10.12

Reflection limit attributes for Maya-centric shaders (images 1 and 2) and mental ray DGS shaders (image 3)

Images 1 and 2 use Maya Blinn shaders, and image 3 uses the mental ray DGS shader. The purpose of this example is to demonstrate how surface A reflects the reflection of the sphere (labeled C) on surface B (labeled D); it demonstrates the rendering qualities of the reflection shown on surface A (labeled F) of the reflection on surface B (labeled D). Note that surface A is set with high raytrace limits, and all the changes are applied only to the raytrace attributes of surface B.

In Chapter 2, "Rendering Algorithms," we discussed the raytrace attributes found under a Maya shader's Raytrace Options rollout (shown contracted in Figure 10.11). The Reflection Limit attribute, unfortunately, has a "double" effect that can lead to some confusion:

- It limits the number of raytrace reflections shown on that surface, as discussed in Chapter 2, "Rendering Algorithms."

- It also limits the number of reflections from that surface on other surfaces, as shown in Figure 10.12 image 2. Notice that when the Reflection Limit attribute for surface B (the floor) is set to 2, the sphere's reflection is shown on surface A (the wall), labeled F in image 1. However, after setting the Reflection Limit (for surface B) to 1, the reflection (F) is not shown on the wall in image 2. Thus, the shader limits for surface B have the double effect of limiting reflections on both surfaces, regardless that each has its own shader with its own limits.

The Reflection Blur attribute, under the mental ray rollout of a Maya shader, acts like the mental ray shiny options discussed earlier with the mental ray DGS shader, defining the glossy nature of the surface. Higher values increase the reflection glossiness. When rendering glossy reflections (Reflection Blur greater than 0), the Reflection Rays attribute provides per-shader sampling. Higher Reflection Rays values provide for better-quality glossy reflections (and also increase the render time). The same is true for the Refraction Blur and Refraction Rays attributes, which provide glossy refractions, similar to those shown with the DGS shader earlier in Figure 10.4 image 2.

For the Reflection Blur Limit and Refraction Blur Limit attributes, keep in mind the following points as you examine Figure 10.12:

- The Reflection Blur Limit attribute is supposed to limit the number of times blurred reflections will reflect in the scene, as does the equivalent attribute in the Render Settings window under the Raytracing rollout. The same is true for the Refraction Blur Limit attribute. For this example, the global limit settings are set high (5), and all the following changes are applied to surface B's Blinn shader.

- If surface B has a Reflection Blur Limit attribute set to 0, the reflections (D and G) on surface B will appear sharp, without any reflection blur.

- At a Reflection Blur Limit of 1, the reflections appear glossy, as shown in image 1 with the labels D and G on surface B.

- In image 1, clearly you can see that the reflection labeled F doesn't account for the reflection blur D shown on surface B; it appears sharp rather than glossy.

- Consider that if you increase the Reflection Blur Limit attribute (on surface B) to a higher value (2 or higher), you would expect the reflection blur (D) to appear in the reflection labeled F, on surface A. However, that is not the case as shown in image 1, where all the settings were set high (over 2), yet the reflection on surface A (F) doesn't appear to capture blurred reflections from surface B.

- Currently, the Reflection Blur Limit attribute is not working as expected. I expect Autodesk will correct this "bug." Thus, you should apply similar tests with your version of Maya. Note that you can apply the same blurred reflection settings for the Reflection Blur and Reflection Rays attributes of surface A; however, in such a case, the reflected sphere labeled E would also appear blurred, which is most likely an undesired effect. If you want a mirror reflection of surface B on the wall (A), the reflection should appear blurred only in F, as shown in image 3.

- Image 3 utilized mental ray DGS shaders for both surfaces, and as you can see, the blurred reflection is captured as expected. However, in this case, the scene sampling had to be set high, consequently increasing the render time significantly.

- Note that mental ray shaders are not affected by the Reflection or Refraction Blur Limit global attributes found under the Render Settings window → Raytracing rollout. Thus, even if they are set to 0, glossy reflections or refractions will render correctly.

XSI

The previous sections presented the mental ray DGS and glossy shaders and their attributes in Maya. If you installed the XSI XPhysics or TEK2SHOOT mental ray libraries, you will find those shaders with the similar settings. Note that with the dielectric TEK2SHOOT shader, the Col and Col_out attributes, shown in Figure 10.6, are labeled Inside and Outside Persistence Color, respectively. With the XPhysics library the naming conventions are identical to the previous discussions. Note that both shader libraries provide monolithic shaders that are both illumination and photons shaders, thus with these shaders you don't need to connect a separate photon shader when using indirect illumination, as discussed in Chapter 12, "Indirect Illumination."

For the most part, the DGS reflection and refraction glossiness is already integrated in the options for glossy reflection and refraction in XSI's illumination shading models, as shown with an XSI Phong shader in Figure 10.13 using the Transparency section's Frost and Samples properties and the Reflection section's Gloss and Samples properties. However, these shaders are not energy conserving as with the physics DGS and dielectric shaders; that means they don't limit your reflected light values to 100 percent of incoming light.

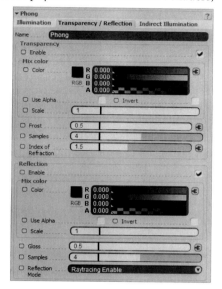

Figure 10.13

XSI Phong illumination shader's glossy reflection and refraction properties

The refraction Frost and the reflection Gloss properties are equivalents to the mental ray shiny options discussed earlier. Thus, these settings apply the extent of the refraction or reflection blur. The advantage of XSI's illumination shaders over the physics DGS shader is with the Samples properties that provide per-shader sampling control for glossy reflections and refractions. Thus, by increasing the Samples property value, the glossy render quality improves, without a need to increase the global sampling level for the scene, as with the DGS shader. Note that blurred reflections are always isotropic, even when using the anisotropic shader.

3ds Max

The 3ds Max mental ray DGS shader is located in the Material/Map Browser window labeled DGS Material (physics_phen). It is a monolithic DGS shader that includes the relevant photon shader for use with indirect illumination simulations, a topic discussed in Chapter 12, "Indirect Illumination." The shader parameters are similar to the ones presented earlier, with the exception that it doesn't support anisotropic shading, omitting the Shiny U and V options. You can use additional complex shaders for DGS reflections or transmissions that support anisotropic shading, which are covered later in this chapter in "Brushed Metals with the Glossy and Anisotropic Shaders" and in "The Architectural (mia) Material."

You can load the dielectric shader from the Material/Map Browser labeled Glass (physics_phen). This too is a monolithic material that includes a photon shader, derived from the Glass (physics_phen) parameters (more on that in Chapter 12, "Indirect Illumination"). The Col and Col_out parameters, shown in Figure 10.6 with the dielectric shader, are labeled Light Persistence and Outside Light Persistence respectively with the

Glass (physics_phen) shader. Basically, all the parameters work as described earlier, with the addition of a Persistence Distance parameter. The Persistence Distance parameter is used with the Light Persistence parameter to define the absorption rate through the dielectric. If a surface is n units thick (world space coordinates), then using that n value for the Persistence Distance parameter defines the correct size of the surface for absorption; it scales the absorption rate to a certain percentage so that after n units the surface will appear to absorb light based on the absorption value defined with the Light Persistence parameter. Trial and error experimentation will help you visualize its effect on absorption.

Fresnel Shader Trees

Most shaders don't account for Fresnel reflections or refractions, and in such cases you want to use simple shader trees to add Fresnel reflections and refractions to a surface. These shader trees can connect to either Maya-, XSI-, or 3ds Max-centric shaders, or mental ray illumination shaders, such as with the mental ray base shaders. Let's examine the steps for creating Fresnel reflections in each host with the purpose of seeing how host-specific shaders can be used to create complex shader effects; it's a thought-provoking exercise based on Fresnel reflections with the purpose of better understanding how shader trees can be connected for various purposes. You can see the shader tree in XSI in Figure 10.14, which is constructed in a similar way in each host application. You can see the rendered result of using this tree in Figure 10.15.

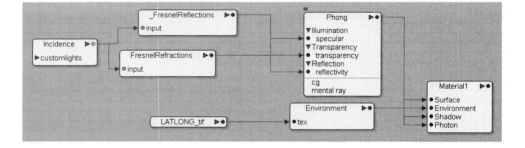

Figure 10.14

The tutorial shader graph for Fresnel reflections and refractions, shown in XSI

You will find a scene file for each host application labeled "FresnelReflections" in the Chapter 10 directory under your host's directory; use the scene to examine the connections discussed in this tutorial. Note that each scene consists of the following:

- A sphere, used for the complex shader tree shown in Figure 10.14.

- A floor surface, used to reflect color on the sphere. It is also intended to show the effect of refractions through the sphere.

- An environment shader is used locally with the sphere's shader tree to provide non-raytrace environmental reflections. The environment shader is also here so that you can see the effect of Fresnel reflections in your host's shader preview: Maya Hypershade, XSI Shaderballs, and 3ds Max Material Editor.

Figure 10.15

An XSI render of three different shapes that are applied with the shader tree seen in Figure 10.14

- The spherical environment image file labeled LATLONG.tif is also provided in each host's tutorial folder in the Chapter 10 folder for the environmental projection.

- A spot light is used with raytrace shadows. Notice how the shadows are affected by the shader in each host.

Once you complete the following steps in your host, look at the section "How It Works (All Users)" for details on this shader as well as additional steps.

MAYA

In the Maya file on the CD I included two sets of shader networks. One shader tree is based on using a Maya Phong shader, and the other network is based on using Maya and mental ray components shaders with the mental ray Phong shader; the mental ray tree includes a shadow shader and sample compositing shaders, which is thus a more comprehensive network. Both shader trees accomplish the same effect.

Here are the steps for the Maya-centric shader tree, equivalent to the shader tree shown in Figure 10.14:

1. In the Hypershade window under the Create Maya Nodes rollout, create the following nodes:

   - An illumination shader such as a Phong shader.

   - A Ramp node from under the 2D Textures rollout without any texture support (disconnect the place2DTexture node or any other projection nodes).

- A Sampler Info shader (found under the General Utilities rollout). It is used in the same way as the XSI Incidence shader shown in Figure 10.14.
- A Env Sphere shader from under the Env Textures rollout.
- Create a Maya File node and load the LATLONG.tif environment image, and assign it to the Env Shader's Image attribute.

2. Connect the Env Sphere shader to the Phong's Reflected Color attribute. Similar to the mental ray environment shader shown in Figure 10.14, it provides local environmental reflection color. The mental ray shader tree provided in the scene file uses an environment shader (mib_lookup_spherical1) to connect to the ShadingEngine node's mental ray → Environment shader input.

3. In the Connection Editor window, connect the Sampler Info's Facing Ratio attribute (output) to the Ramp node's UV Coord → V Coord input.

4. Select the ramp node, and in the Attribute Editor make sure that Type is set to V Ramp. Set the Ramp to a black (top color) to white (bottom color) gradient. The top color correlates to direct angles (facing angles), and the lower color correlates to glancing angles.

5. Connect the Ramp's outColor output to the Phong shader's Specular Color attribute.

If you prefer using a graph (instead of the ramp shader) to define the transition from white to black across the surface, you can use the Remap Value shader found under the Color Utilities rollout. See "How It Works (All Users)." Just make sure you use the Remap Value's outValue to connect to the Specular color attribute and not the outColor output. The Value rollout under the remap value shader's attributes controls the gradation.

XSI
Here are the steps for the XSI shader tree shown in Figure 10.14:

1. In the Render Tree window from the Nodes menu, create the following nodes:
   - An illumination shader (Blinn, Phong, and so on).
   - Illumination → Incidence shader. Mode should be set to Surface/Camera (default).
   - Mixers → Gradient shader.
   - Environment → Environment shader. Set the Environment Mode property to Spherical mapping, and load the LATLONG.tif file.

2. Connect the environment shader to the Material Environment input property as shown in the figure.

3. Connect the Incidence shader to the Gradient shader's Input property (shown labeled "FresnelReflections" in Figure 10.14).

4. Set the gradient to a white to black gradient using the White/Black preset. The gradient shader's leftmost marker (white) correlates to glancing angles, facing away from the camera, and the rightmost marker (black) correlates to facing angles, toward the camera.

5. Connect the gradient output to the illumination shader's Specular and Reflectivity properties as shown in the figure. The gradient shader now controls the intensity of highlights and reflections across the surface based on the viewing angle.

6. You can use a separate gradient shader for each component (specularity and reflectivity) providing you with more control.

7. Use the incidence shader's Bias and Gain properties to further control the gradation extent and its glossiness as follows:

   • Lower values for the Bias property will flatten the effect, whereas higher values push the gradation closer to the surface edge. The Bias defines the location (boundary line) on the surface where the gradation takes place.

   • The Gain acts as a multiplier that further controls the transitions falloff rate along the border line. Higher values provide for a more linear (flat) transition and lower values provide for a faster (exponential) transition, sharpening the effect (explore these properties with the provided scene file).

   • A typical glass Fresnel reflection would have a higher Bias value (such as 0.75) and a lower Gain value (such as 0.25).

In XSI you can also use other shaders such as the Nodes → Raytracing → Dielectric shader instead of the incidence shader to balance the light transport across the surface. The incidence shader provides abilities for controlling color based on the angle between two vectors, such as the camera's perspective and surface normal (used in this example) or the light direction and surface normal.

3DS MAX

Here are the steps for the 3ds Max shader, equivalent to the shader tree shown in Figure 10.14:

1. In the Material Editor window using the standard 3ds Max material, select an illumination shading model (Blinn, Phong, and so on). I used a Blinn in the scene file provided on the CD.

2. Set both Ambient and Diffuse colors to black.

3. Under the mental ray Connections rollout, map the Environment parameter with an Environment (3dsmax) shader. Similar to the mental ray environment shader shown in Figure 10.14, it provides local (for this shader only) environmental reflections.

4. Under the shader's Environment (3dsmax) parameters, map the Map parameter with a bitmap shader and load the LATLONG.tif environmental image. Under the bitmap's Coordinates rollout, enable the Environ radio button, and set Mapping to Spherical Environment.

5. Under the Blinn shader's basic parameters, map the Specular color parameter with a Gradient Ramp from the Material/Map Browser window.

6. From under the Gradient Ramp Parameters, set the ramp as a white (leftmost color, position 0) to black (rightmost color, position 100) ramp.

7. Set the Gradient Type parameter to Normal, which maps the color to the surface based on the angle between the direction to camera and surface normal vector. The ramp now controls the intensity of highlights and reflections across the surface based on the viewing angle.

8. The white color (position 0) defines the color at glancing angles, facing away from the camera. The black color controls the color toward the camera, at facing angles.

HOW IT WORKS (ALL USERS)

In all host applications, gradient shaders are used to map the intensity of the reflection color across the surface based on the viewing angle. To build a dependency on the viewing angle, each host uses an additional shader that provides information on the dot product between the two vectors (see Chapter 11, "mental ray Textures and Projections," for a detailed discussion on dot product math and 3D) that are as follows:

- The surface normal vector
- The direction to the camera vector

The dot product is extracted in each host using the following shaders and parameters:

- In Maya, the sampler info shader's Facing Ratio attribute.
- In XSI, the incidence shader is set to Surface/Camera.
- In 3ds Max, you use the Normal option for the Type parameter, which is built into the gradient shader.

Each of these shader parameters extracts information about the angle between two vectors using values that range from 0 to 1, which is a dot product. A value of 0 refers to glancing angles (perpendicular vectors), and 1 refers to facing angles (parallel vectors).

In 3D, gradient shaders are used to map color onto a surface based on the color's position on the gradient's scale, which is also indicated with 0 to 1 values. In all host applications, the gradient shaders have been set so that the white color is at position 0 and the black color is at position 1. Thus, after the host evaluates the angle between the two vectors (the dot product), it determines which color will be used at that sample location; if the normal is facing away from the camera (glancing angles), the dot product returns a value of 0, and thus the gradient color indicated at position 0 (white) is used for that sample location. In this way, the white to black colors that range from position 0 to 1 are mapped to the surface based on a viewing angle that also ranges from 0 to 1.

For our purpose, we used the gradients to define the intensity of highlights and reflections in each host, where white is fully reflective and black is not. You can now use the color position on the ramp, as well as select different interpolation methods (linear, cubic, and so on), to control the transition rate between both colors, providing controllable Fresnel reflections.

ADDING REFRACTIONS

Ideally with refractive surfaces you want to map the intensity of refractions and reflections based on Fresnel reflections. Thus, as the angle between the camera and normal increases toward glancing angles, the surface becomes more opaque and reflective. To do so, you can use the same connections described earlier to add angle depended refractions. In other words, create another gradient shader with the same connections described earlier, and map it to the shader's transparency color (already applied in the scene files). Figure 10.15 shows the end result of this network rendered in XSI; it shows Fresnel reflections and refractions using three different simple shapes over some text.

You can see the refraction gradient shader (a duplicate of the reflection gradient shader) connection in Figure 10.14, labeled FresnelRefractions. As you can see, it too is connected to the incidence shader that, in this case, drives transparency based on the viewing angle. Also, don't forget to set the index of refraction to a desired value; I used 1.5 for glass with the rendered example and in the scene files.

With Maya and XSI shaders, a black transparency color refers to fully opaque; if you duplicated the reflection gradient shader, you need to invert it for the refraction gradient shader as follows:

- In Maya, under the ramp texture's attributes, labeled FresnelRefractions, I enabled the Invert attribute under the Effects rollout.

- In XSI, under the FresnelRefractions gradient shader properties, I enabled the Invert Direction property.

> Maya users: to see raytrace shadows through the refractions, you need to increase the Shadow Depth Limit attribute (2 or higher) for the source light in the Attribute Editor, in the Shadows → Raytrace Shadow Attributes rollout.

Glossy Reflection and Refraction Shaders

The focus of this section is on the mental ray base library mib_glossy_reflection and refraction shaders. They are among the more important and powerful component shaders that ship with mental ray; they significantly improve render times and enhance glossy abilities, providing higher performance glossy reflection and refraction rendering. In fact, phenomenon shaders such as mi_car_paint_phen build on their abilities (together with other component shaders), offering more robust illumination shading models. Also, the architectural material (reviewed later) has the same abilities and more. Therefore, reviewing these shaders is as an important introductory review for the architectural material. Note the following comments for XSI and 3ds Max:

• 3ds Max does not currently have the mib_glossy shaders, but I expect they will become available in the future. Regardless, the architectural material is present and, as cited earlier, provides even more capabilities. You can also use the Reflection Utility shader provided by Horvátth Szabolcs (available on the CD in ChapterFiles/CustomShaders/Horvátth; get the 3ds Max include files from www.maxplugins.de) that provides several nice features for controlling anisotropic reflections with 3ds Max. See the 3ds Max tutorial in the section "Brushed Metals with the Glossy and Anisotropic Shaders" later in this chapter.

• With XSI, you need to install the TEK2SHOOT XSI add-on (provided on the CD and described earlier). You can then find the mib_glossy shaders in the install path from the T2S_Mentalray path. XSI has two built-in raytracing shaders (Render Tree → Raytracing), Reflection and Refraction Diffuse. These less robust shaders are already implemented with the XSI illumination shaders such as the Phong and Blinn under the Transparency/Reflection properties tab.

We'll begin by reviewing the glossy reflection shader and then make some quick comparisons with the glossy refraction shader.

Maya and XSI users: you can find a file labeled "GlossyReflections" under your host's directory in the Chapter 10 folder. The file has a basic shader tree setup using the glossy reflection shader, assigned to a sphere. XSI users: you need to have the TEK2SHOOT shaders installed, as cited earlier.

The Glossy Connection

The mib_glossy reflection and refraction shaders are basically two illumination shaders that deal solely with specular to glossy reflectance and transmission. Regardless of whether your host categorizes them as illumination shaders or some other component shader type, in my opinion they are not illumination shading models such as the DGS or Blinn. Rather, they're sample-compositing shaders. These shaders are meant to be piped with an illumination shader that provides diffuse color and highlights, just as with any other sample compositing shader, such as an mib_reflection shader. Thus, glossy shaders deal only with raytracing reflections and refractions; they do not provide highlights.

You can see the mib_glossy_reflection shader interface in Figure 10.16, which has a Ward illumination shader connected to the Base_material attribute. The Glossy shader can then be connected to the material's illumination port, as shown in XSI in Figure 10.17 (using a Phong instead of the Ward). You can also see in Figure 10.16 and Figure 10.17 that an environment map has also been connected to the glossy shader, providing glossy environmental reflections.

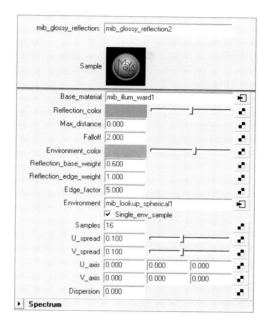

Figure 10.16

The mib_glossy_ reflection mental ray shader Interface

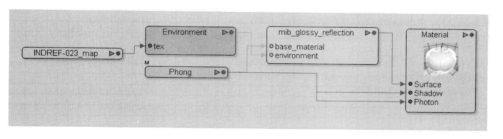

Figure 10.17

A basic glossy shader tree. Phong and environment shaders are connected to the mib_glossy_ reflection shader, which is then connected to the mental ray material.

The environment map should be connected to the shader directly as shown in Figures 10.16 and 10.17, connected to the material's environment input (Maya shading engine and XSI material), or applied as a camera shader as discussed in Chapter 3, "mental ray Output."

In the Maya and XSI scene files, the environment map is connected directly to the mental ray material environment input. The reason for preferring the material connection will become clear after you read the section "Glossiness and Multisampling" later in this chapter.

Reflection Control

The Reflection_color and Environment_color attributes (Figure 10.16) control the reflection intensity (for scene reflections) and environmental reflections (environment maps only), respectively. A white color provides for full reflectivity and black disables the reflections completely. These separate options allow you to balance scene vs. environment reflection intensities, although in theory they should be set to the same value. The biggest difference between the two components is that sampling scene reflections requires raytracing, whereas sampling environment reflections requires only a projection map using an environment shader, as shown mapped in Figures 10.16 and 10.17.

Environment sampling with glossy shaders is not a raytrace process; you can disable raytracing altogether, and you will still see the environment reflect on the surface, but not the scene.

The Max_distance and Falloff attributes increase the render performance by limiting the reach of raytrace rays. When Max_distance is set to a nonzero value, that value represents the maximum distance raytrace rays can query the scene for reflections. Over that distance, as the distance limit is reached, the reflection color transitions from scene reflections to environment reflections, providing a gradual transition of color. This way you don't see a sudden cutoff of scene reflection colors at the max distance, rather a smooth transition from one reflection color to the next. The Falloff attribute defines the rate of change from scene reflections to environment reflections over distance. The value defines a power function so that a value of 2 is equal to a square falloff transition and a value of 1 is equal to linear falloff. Higher falloff values provide more nonlinear (faster) transitions from scene reflections to environment reflections.

Using the Max_distance and Falloff attributes can also help blend scene reflections with environment reflections before a 3D scene suddenly "ends." To clarify, look at Figure 10.18. Image A doesn't use these features, so you see the full scene reflect on the sphere before the environment reflections appear. As you can see, the sphere is placed on a small floor with one spot light so that the floor doesn't provide for nice reflections; along the floor's border there is no light, and you see the dark (black) areas from the floor appear before the environment reflection. However, in image B, by setting the Max_distance attribute to 10 and Falloff to 2, you can see how the environment blends with the scene before reflecting the corners of the floor, providing for a much nicer and more aesthetic reflection effect.

As discussed earlier in the section "Glossy Sampling and Raytrace Control," with distance-based reflections a significant amount of sampling is required to maintain quality. When the sampling is too low, you typically see artifacts such as grainy reflections. Thus, using the attributes discussed earlier to limit the reach of raytrace rays greatly reduces the chance of poor quality glossy reflections and also reduces the overall amount of sampling required for a reasonable result.

Figure 10.18

Limiting the distance of raytrace rays in image B helps blend the environment and scene reflections.

Fresnel Reflections

The mib_glossy shaders enable simulating custom Fresnel reflections, as discussed in Chapter 9, "The Fundamentals of Light and Shading Models" in the section "The Fresnel Equations." The Reflection_base_weight and Reflection_edge_weight attributes (Figure 10.16) are used to balance the reflection intensity at facing angles and glancing angles, respectively. These attributes act as multipliers against the reflectivity across the surface so that a value of 1 provides 100 percent reflectivity and lower values gradually decrease the reflectivity. Edge_factor acts as a bias that controls the transition from the reflection at glancing angles to facing angles. Higher values provide for a narrower (faster) transition from glancing angles to facing angles, meaning the reflection outline is more distinct.

The sphere shown in Figure 10.19 uses a glossy reflection shader with a black Phong shader (no diffuse) that is connected to the glossy shader's Base_material attribute; the Phong's sole purpose is to contribute white specular highlights. Also, a white environment map has been applied to the glossy shader, enabling you to see the reflection area as white gradation along the surface. Notice how in all the images the reflection intensity increases toward glancing angles. All the images use the same base weight of 0 and edge weight of 1 so that ideally there is no reflection at facing angles and full reflections at glancing angles, making it easier to identify the Fresnel characteristics. The Edge_factor in image A has a value of 1 and a value of 4 in image B. Notice how a higher edge factor provides for a tighter reflection along the surface rim. The Falloff attribute discussed earlier affects the transition from reflection to environment colors in the same way, where higher values provide for faster transitions.

Figure 10.19

**Fresnel reflections
using the glossy
shaders and a Phong
specular highlight**

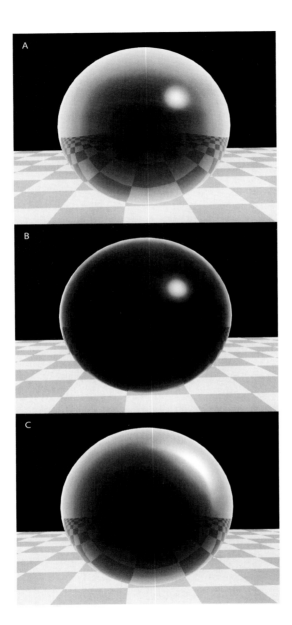

Since the mib_glossy shaders don't provide specular highlights, the highlight shown in
Figure 10.19 is provided by the Phong shader. However, the highlights seen in images A
and B contradict Fresnel characteristics; highlights are also a reflection component, and
thus they too should respect Fresnel characteristics and appear stronger at glancing angles.
To remedy this, a custom shading network was used to add Fresnel characteristics to the
Phong's specular color, as shown in image C, where the highlight intensity is visible along

the rim, toward a glancing angle. I used the same connections described earlier in the "Fresnel Shader Trees" section. The connection is applied to the Phong shader's specular color in the "Glossy Reflections" scene file for Maya and XSI.

Glossiness and Multisampling

The glossy shader supports multiple sampling on a per-shader level, rather than requiring high scene level sampling values, a topic discussed earlier in "Glossy Sampling and Ray-trace Control." The Samples attribute is used to define the per-shader sampling by specifying how many additional raytrace rays (in addition to the initial secondary ray; see Chapter 2, "Rendering Algorithms," for raytracing rays) are used to sample glossy reflection colors. A value of 0 provides a specular reflection, because only one secondary ray (the initial ray) will be cast into the scene, and thus glossy reflections are effectively disabled. A value of 1 or higher will provide glossy reflections. Good values range from 32 to 64.

> The Samples attribute specifies the quality of the glossy reflection only, whereas the U and V spread options (discussed next) define the glossy nature of the reflection.

Anisotropic or Isotropic Glossy Reflections

The glossy shaders U_spread and V_spread attributes (Figure 10.16) act just like the DGS shiny U and V attributes, defining the ratio of anisotropic (or isotropic, a 1 to 1 ratio) reflections, as well as their glossy extent. The difference between these settings and the Ward and DGS is simply the values' usable range. In this case, the usable range is between 0–1 where 0 is specular and 1 is significantly diffused (extremely glossy). Good values typically range from 0.05 to 0.1, so you may want to start low while examining the result. When both U and V are equal, you have isotropic scattering, and again, the larger the value, the glossier the reflection. With glossier reflections, more samples are required to prevent grainy results; thus, with higher U and V spread values, more samples are required to produce a quality effect.

> When the U and V spread values are set with a high ratio (such as 0.01 and 0.1), the reflection appears very anisotropic, and that too requires a lot of samples to produce a quality effect.

Environmental Sampling

An additional optimization option is the Single_env_sample attribute, which allows the environment to be sampled as a specular reflection, meaning with a single environment sample. Remember, as discussed earlier, sampling the environment color from an environment map is not a raytrace process but a shader projection. However, the glossy shader is still required to calculate multiple samples from the environment image to produce a glossy effect, which in many cases can prove to be a waste of time. As an alternative, you can provide an already blurred environment map, which has the effect of improving the quality of glossy reflections from the environment, as well as reducing the render time, as explained next.

Because the environment map is typically farther away from the surface than other objects, it is one of those elements that is more prone to grainy glossy effects, as a result of distant based glossiness (see the section "Glossy Sampling and Raytrace Control" earlier in this chapter). The idea is then to use a blurred environment map that appears glossy and enable the Single_env_sample attribute, which will take only one shader (specular) sample from this preblurred environment map; the reflection will appear glossy because the image is blurred. In such a case you may want to connect a blurred version of the environment image to the shader and use a nonblurred image for other purposes, such as the background image. The environment reflection will be derived from the image mapped to the glossy shader, when one is provided.

USING THE SINGLE_ENV_SAMPLE ATTRIBUTE

As noted earlier, you can connect the environment map directly to the glossy shader or to the mental ray material (Maya shading engine and XSI material), as shown in Figure 10.20 in XSI. As you can see, the Environment shader in the figure connects directly to the Material → Environment property and not to the glossy shader's Environment property, as shown earlier in Figures 10.16 and 10.17. It is also connected in this way in the provided Maya and XSI scene files.

Figure 10.20

Connecting an environment shader directly to the mental ray material, shown in XSI

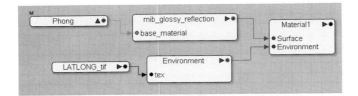

The reason I prefer the material connection is because the Single_env_sample attribute will not function correctly ("broken") when the environment map connects directly to the glossy shader. Thus, when enabled and the environment is mapped to the glossy shader, you won't see environment reflections render at all. When disabled, it will render the environment applying the glossy effect, as dictated by the U and V spread attributes. However, when you map the environment directly to the material and the Single_env_sample attribute is enabled, it will render a specular reflection of the environment as expected, and when disabled, it will apply the glossy effect to the environment, also as expected.

> When using a preblurred environment map, map it directly to the mental ray material, and enable the glossy shader's Single_env_sample attribute, which will then function correctly; it will take only one color sample from the environment projection.

The DGS Shader vs. the Glossy Shader

Unlike the Ward shader discussed in Chapter 9, "The Fundamentals of Light and Shading Models," DGS anisotropic effects apply to highlights, reflections, and refractions. Essentially this solves one of the Ward shader's limitations—that highlights appear anisotropic and reflections isotropic. However, with respect to anisotropic reflections or refractions with the DGS shader, the scattering does not realistically simulate anisotropic reflections. To clarify, DGS anisotropic reflections are a result of extending (stretching) an isotropic reflection across the surface in a specific direction, based on the shiny U and V values and ratio. In contrast, more realistic anisotropic reflections (as shown in Figure 10.16 image C in Chapter 9, "The Fundamentals of Light and Shading Models,") that "stretch" along the surface grooves can be applied with more complex shaders such as the mib_glossy shaders and the architectural material. These shaders recalculate the surface normals to mimic surface grooves along a particular direction, and only then do they calculate the light scattering (glossy) contribution along those grooves. This enhanced ability extends the DGS's anisotropic reflection abilities, providing better anisotropic scattering.

The floor shown in Figure 10.21 image A has a DGS shader applied. The floor under image B has the glossy reflection shader. Notice how the anisotropic reflection under image A appears very blurred and doesn't reach as far as the one seen under image B. To make the anisotropic reflection stretch along the surface (image A), a very low Shiny U value (2) was required, resulting with a very blurred appearance. That means that I had to use a high Max sample level (4) for the scene, which provided a reasonable rendered result but an extremely slow render time. In contrast under image B (the glossy reflection shader), you can see that the object maintains a more focused anisotropic refection; it looks better and more realistic opposed to the one in image A that looks like a large blurred smudge across the surface. In fact, lower U and V spread values for the glossy shader allow you to control the glossiness effect and maintain the anisotropic reflection.

To clarify, with the DGS shader I had to use a very low Shiny U, which significantly blurs the reflection; overblurring the reflection is the only way I could stretch the reflection across the surface so that it looks anisotropic. However, with the glossy shader, the shader determines the microgroove characteristics of the surface by reorienting the normals (perturbing) to simulate rows of surface grooves. By doing so, the reflection can then be calculated based on the perturbed normals applying glossiness to a given extent, as defined by the user. With the glossy shader, the anisotropic reflection will reflect from surface grooves and stretch correctly across the entire surface, as expected (and seen in image B), without requiring you to increase its glossiness to force it to blur (cover) across the surface as with the DGS shader (image A). The only condition is that you specify a ratio for anisotropic reflections, such as 0.05 and 0.1, with the glossy shader's U and V spread attributes.

More important is that at standard sample levels, even at a low max sample level of 1, the glossy shader provides decent results because the sampling is applied on a shader basis; compare that to the DGS shader, which required extreme measures for decent quality.

Glossy Refractions

The glossy refraction shader, shown in Figure 10.22, is similar to the glossy reflection shader, except that it offers IOR (index of refraction) and Refraction Color properties instead of reflection properties. As with the reflection shader, a white Refraction Color provides for full refractions. Also note that the shader provides the same controls for Fresnel refractions that deal with the refraction's intensity based on a viewing angle but does not reflect any color. You can combine both shaders to develop a shader with both reflections and refractions with correlating Fresnel settings; however, for most purposes that may be a bit overkill.

The main differences with the glossy refraction shader are three different color inputs instead of one (Base_material attribute) input with the glossy reflection shader and the Reverse Back Side property. The three color inputs correspond to a top material, deep material, and back material and are not shown in the XSI window in Figure 10.22 (you can see them in Maya's UI implementation for this shader).

Figure 10.23 shows the network where you can see those inputs available in XSI's Render Tree window, where each input is receiving a different illumination shader. These inputs are similar to the base material with the reflection shader. However, in this case, they allow you to specify different colors for controlling the glossy refraction over distance. In XSI, once these properties are mapped with shaders, as shown in the figure, those shaders appear as additional tabs in the shader's interface, as shown with the Phong, Lambert1, and Lambert tabs in Figure 10.22.

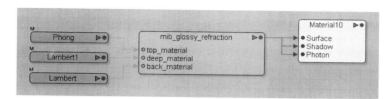

Figure 10.23

The glossy refraction shader network with three illumination shaders connecting to the top, deep, and back material inputs

The scene presented in the following example is available on the companion CD in the Maya and XSI folders under the Chapter 10 directory, labeled "GlossyRefractions." I highly recommend you experiment with the scene while reading through this section. XSI users: you need to have the glossy refraction shader installed using the TEK2SHOOT unexposed mental ray shaders, presented earlier and provided on the CD.

The top material defines the appearance of the surface from the front side, facing the light as shown in Figure 10.24. Note that front and backsides are not dependent on a viewing angle, only relative to the light's position. Label 1 represents the front side of the surface facing the light, and label 2 represents the backside. (The top and sides of the polygon cube are considered as part of the front side.) This scene setup is used in the following examples to demonstrate the glossy shader's characteristics.

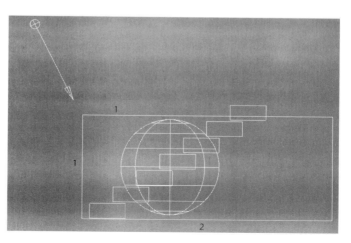

Figure 10.24

The scene used for rendering the glossy example. The placement of the light defines the front surfaces vs. the back surfaces.

In Figure 10.25, the top material has been set to black (diffuse color) using a Phong shader, and the deep material is set to white using a Lambert shader. Essentially, the specular component should be included as part of the top material, and thus a Phong shader was used. (I'll talk about that more later.) Let's clarify the relationship between the top and deep materials with the following points using Figure 10.25 image A:

Figure 10.25

Two examples using the glossy shader where image A demonstrates the effect on the front of the surface and image B demonstrates the effect of translucency seen through the back surface

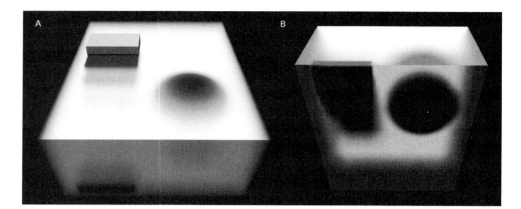

- The top material defines the color on the surface front (described earlier), and the deep material defines the internal color.

- Max Distance defines the distance over which the top material color fades to the deep material color. Lower values will show a brighter deep material color within the surface. The Falloff property defines the falloff rate for that gradation, where higher numbers provide for faster falloff rates. Higher values will transition to the deep material faster, thus also making it appear brighter in the surface. With respect to "brighter," it means that you see more of the deep material's color in the surface. These two options are similar to the glossy reflection shader's Falloff and Max distance options discussed earlier.

- Any surface placed within the glossy volume (a cube in the figure) inherits color from the top and deep materials, based on their distance from the top (front/facing the light) of the surface. In Figure 10.25 image A, notice how the white deep material is more present in the volume as the top (black) material fades to white over the Max Distance value. Consider the following points:

  - The top material shows its dark color along the volume container's edges, where it is close to the container's sides, and on the sphere and stairs as they gradually fade to white.

  - Notice that the topmost outer cube (for the stairs) appears gray (its "natural" color); however, the one placed directly beneath, placed within the volume, inherits the top material color and appears black.

- You can see the stairs reappear as black at the bottom of the cube as they get closer to the front side of the cube, which is also facing the light and thus utilizes the top material.

- If Max Distance is set to zero, the deep material is not used (disabled).

- The Max Distance property is aimed at improving raytracing by limiting the distance raytrace rays can travel in the scene, as discussed with the glossy reflection shader and in the section "Glossy Raytrace Control." However, with the glossy refraction shader, the Max Distance property essentially takes on a new meaning; it enables you to simulate light absorption through matter along the defined distance. Note that light absorption is not physically simulated with this shader (the glossy shaders are not physical shaders) as it is with the dielectric shader, but the effect of light absorption is made possible by means of blending the top and deep materials over a specific distance and with a given falloff rate.

The Back Material

The purpose of the back material is to define the color shown reflected back toward the front from within the surface; it is the color you see internally along the surface walls reflected back towards the camera. To see its effect, I recommend you set the top and deep materials to a black color and then set the back material with a bright diffuse color as well as increase its ambient color. Since the back material refers to polygons that are facing

Figure 10.26

The glossy refraction shader's back material effects

away from the light, by using ambient color you effectively force the shader to show the back material color in the render. Furthermore, if you set the top material to a pure red, disable the deep material by specifying a zero Max Distance value, and set the back material to a pure green, you will clearly see the color separation across the surface, as shown in Figure 10.26 and in the "Back-Mat1," "BackMat2," and "BackMat3" color images provided on the CD in the Chapter 10 folder. Consider the following points based on the color scheme cited earlier, while looking at the color images and Figure 10.26:

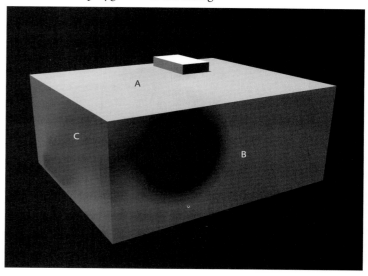

- The volume's sides that are facing the light, labeled A and C in Figure 10.26, will appear red. Basically, the internal objects will inherit the top material color, thus when looking into the cube through the front sides, everything will appear red. You can see this in the color image labeled "Backmat2."

- The volume's sides facing away from the light will appear green (back material), as shown in all the color images and in Figure 10.26 label B. However, in this case, the internal objects will appear black since they inherit color only from the top and deep materials, looking from a frontal side (they don't receive any light).

- Consider the cube has front, left, right, and back sides. The front face, as shown in Figure 10.26 labeled C, is facing the light. If you look through this front face, you can see the left side of the cube. In such a case, the red and green from both front and back materials blend in color, as shown in the color image labeled BackMat2.

- To further clarify the reasons for effect noted in the previous point, consider that every face seen from inside, meaning you are observing it through the volume, will render based on the back material color. You can see this effect in the color image "Back-Mat3." This image looks at the cube from behind so that the front side (labeled C in Figure 10.26) appears through the volume. Notice that it is green and not red, since we are not looking at it from a frontal perspective but seeing it through the volume. Furthermore, the same is true for the top of the surface, which we know is facing the light; however, it too appears green when you see it through the sides, as shown in the color images "BackMat1."

- Finally, if you enable the deep material, it would act in the same way as the top material. The top and deep material will define the appearance of the surface when looking at outer faces that are facing the light. The back material then handles all the faces that are seen internally through other faces.

The Back Material and Through Scattering

Technically, the glossy shader reverses the normals for the faces that are seen through the volume. Those are the faces that render using the back material color. If you look at the surface from the back on the outside, without using any ambient color with the back material, the volume will appear black. The reason is that those faces that reflect light internally, back toward the viewer, are not receiving any light when viewed from the back side (opposite the light's direction); hence, they render black. It is an important point to realize since it tells you that for the back material to contribute color, it needs to receive light from the outside, seen through the volume and reflected back toward the viewer (reflected from the inner faces). Thus, using some ambient color with the back material really helps show a more translucent effect by mimicking light that is reflected internally. It only looks that way; obviously, it doesn't apply any real subsurface scattering.

Keep in mind that while observing the volume from the back, you won't see any of the top or deep material colors appear through the back. However, what if you want to simulate through scattering—the scattering of light seen through the volume, and in the case of the glossy shader, the light scattering from the front (top and deep materials) faces, seen through the volume on the back side, as shown in Figure 10.25 image B. For that effect, the Reverse Back Material property (shown in Figure 10.22) allows you to better simulate translucent effects of through scattering. When enabled, it renders the top material through the backsides, using the back material color. In other words, if the top material is red and the back material is green, the light seen through the bottom of the cube in Figure 10.25 image B labeled 2, will render green. It is the top materials scattering seen through the back, affected by the back material. Technically, when the Reverse Back Material property is enabled, the normals of faces seen through the volume are not reversed; therefore, they allow you to see the effect of light rendered from the front side.

The Glossy Refraction Shader in Action

You can use the glossy shader to create complex effects by using different procedural shaders and shader trees for the top and deep materials. Figure 10.27 shows an example of an ocean render; the color version is in the chapter's folder on the companion CD labeled "OceanShot." The top material has Maya's ocean shader (also used for the displacement mapping), and the deep material has a brighter greenish color. This makes the water appear brighter below the ocean surface. If I decrease the max distance, the top material (the ocean shader) would render a darker top surface. You can use this sort of effect, for example, to create phosphorescent tropical waters or water that is illuminated by bright lights from a nearby hovering helicopter by using local lights (with fast decays) close to the ocean surface that help reveal the deep material. In this case, a low max distance value helped make the ocean appear deep, where the submarine fades out quickly. Also this scene used 32 samples for the glossy refractions, and rendered in only about five minutes on my laptop at a resolution of 2100×1180, which is extremely fast for glossy refractions, compared to hours of waiting for Figure 10.4 image B using the DGS shader.

Figure 10.27

A practical example of using the glossy shader to create a complex ocean effect that is optimized for efficient rendering

Maya users note that the ocean shader tends to cause a crash when connected directly to the glossy shader; therefore, I used an RGB to HSV shader to transfer the color from the ocean shader to the top material. I then used the Connection Editor to connect the ocean shader's displacement output to the shading engine's Displacement Mat. Attribute (the Maya centric displacement input).

As you saw in Figure 10.23, the glossy refraction shader in XSI connects to the material's surface, shadow, and photon inputs. This shader works well with global illumination (using the TEK2SHOOT shader). With respect to shadows, it is not a shadow shader; therefore, shadows cast through the volume appear opaque unless you connect an alternative shadow shader. Furthermore, with Maya you also need to use a different photon shader (try the dielectric or basic photon shaders), as well as leave the shadow shader disconnected or use a transparent shadow shader.

As with the glossy reflection shader, changing the ratio of the U and V spread values renders anisotropic refractions that appear to disperse light internally. Try it with the example scene to observe the effect of anisotropy in refractions.

With both glossy shaders, the max distance is defined in world space units; therefore, surfaces of varying sizes will require different distance values.

Brushed Metals with the Glossy and Anisotropic Shaders

Until now, while discussing anisotropic reflections, we've dealt with simulating highlights perpendicular to grooves that stretch along a direct path, such as along the V coordinate. These reflections assume that the surface grooves travel in straight lines along the selected coordinate. We also mentioned that in XSI and 3ds Max the anisotropic shaders allow for orienting the highlight, so you can think of it as placing a rotational dial in the center of the highlight and turning it until it runs along the path you desire. However, with brushed metals, the highlight orientation changes along the surface, as shown with the rendered example in Figure 10.28 image B. This example is based on the brushed metal shown in the table photo in Figure 10.28 image A. You can see the final color version (Figure 10.28 image B) in the color gallery labeled "Brushed Metal Plate." Note that with metals, the metals diffuse color needs to be present in the specular highlights and reflections, tinting those colors in accordance with the metals diffuse "natural" color.

You can find the scene files and textures for each host application in the relevant host directories in the Chapter 10 folder on the companion CD; the scene file is labeled AnisoTable in each case.

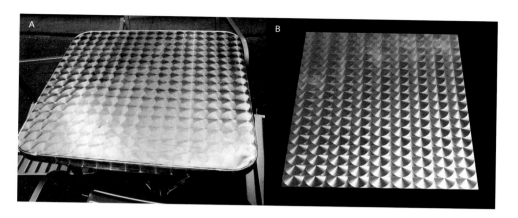

Figure 10.28

An outdoor table (image A) exhibiting anisotropic and Fresnel reflections, and a rendered version of a similar effect (image B)

The purpose of this tutorial is to show you how several component mental ray shaders and host-specific shaders can be used to form a complex shader tree and effect. Thus, through this tutorial you will learn more about mental ray component shaders and how they are used.

Orienting the Highlight

The mib_texture_rotate component mental ray shader, as shown in Figure 10.29 (in Maya), allows you to rotate texture vectors (U and V coordinates) using an Angle option that ranges from 0 to 1. Similarly, in the XSI anisotropic shader, the Anisotropic Orientation property is applied as a color value that ranges from 0 to 1 (black to white). With 3ds Max, the anisotropic shader's Orientation parameter specifies degrees, where basically the usable range spans from 0 to 180. With the component shader (and XSI), to orient a brushed-metal highlight, you then select values from 0 to 1, which are equivalent to 0° to 360° rotations. Basically, any degree greater than 180° repeats the cycle, so that 0°–180° provides the same range as 0°–360°.

Notice that the mib_texture_rotate Angle attribute is mapped with the grayscale scalar value extracted from the texture shown in Figure 10.30 image A, providing white-to-black color information for orienting the UVs, where black is equivalent to 0°, 50 percent gray is equal to 180°, and white is equal to 360°, which is an Angle value of 1. The same image is used to map the orientation in the XSI and 3ds Max's anisotropic shaders. 3ds Max users should note that black to white is equivalent to 0–255 (the RGB color values), so if the image is remapped to a range of 0–180, then it will apply rotations along 180° (more on that later).

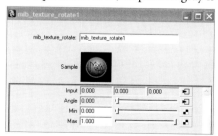

Figure 10.29

The mib_texture_ rotate shader is used to rotate UVs on a surface, enabling you to reorient the anisotropic reflections based on a texture.

Figure 10.30

Black-to-white images used to rotate the anisotropic shader across the surface, providing a brushed-metal appearance

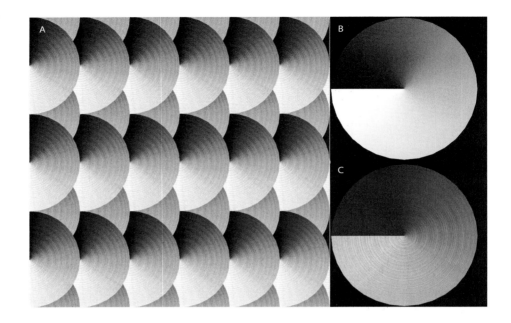

Thus, the use of a black-and-white image provides control over perturbing the UV coordinates along the surface. To clarify, if the anisotropic reflection (highlight) travels along the V coordinate, then by applying this image you rotate the V coordinate several times along the surface. By doing so, the anisotropic shader attempts to follow the new (perturbed) path while "drawing" the highlights. This point is really all you need to understand to come up with several different approaches for creating brushed-metal surfaces. I further discuss the topic of texture coordinates and vectors in the tutorials later in this chapter and in great detail in Chapter 11, "mental ray Textures and Projections."

The Brushed-Metal Texture Map

Figure 10.30 image B and image C show the single plate that was tiled several times for the brushed-metal map. The difference between image B and image C is that image C also uses a stretched fractal shader to form grooves along the rotation, so the reflection breaks up and doesn't appear flat, as shown in the color insert version ("Brushed Metal Plate"). Clearly, you can create different types of maps to define the orientation of highlights on a surface using Photoshop.

> You can use the images "Brushed Intensity1" and "Brushed Mask1" (Figure 10.30 B and C) that are under the chapter folder on the CD to test anisotropic highlights on a surface while viewing the effect on a single cycle (it's not a tiled image). It should help you build a better understanding for the effect values have on the anisotropic appearance.

The Networks

Let's examine brushed-metal networks using anisotropic highlights and reflections in each host. The purpose is to create the effect shown in the "Brushed Metal Plate" image in the color gallery and in Figure 10.28 image B. Since the network is applied using different approaches, you may want to read through the other hosts to get some other ideas or insight. As noted earlier, I'm using these networks to further show other useful component shaders as required by the network in each host application.

Maya

Figure 10.31 shows the graphed network in Maya using the mib_glossy_reflection, Cook-Torrance, and the anisotropic Ward shaders that are all used as illumination shaders, as well as additional component and Maya-specific shaders, such as ramp textures used for remapping color values. I load the image file `brushedMetalPlateTile.tif` (on the CD in `Chapter 10/Maya/sourceimages`) with a Maya file node labeled A (also shown in Figure 10.30 image A). I then convert it to a grayscale scalar value with the Maya luminance shader labeled B and then connect to the Angle attribute of the mib_texture_rotate shader labeled C. To apply this connection, you can either drag and drop the luminance shader over the Angle attribute or use the Connection Editor window. You can see the mib_texture_rotate connections in Figure 10.29 and in the scene file. These connections apply the rotational information based on the texture map's color values, ranging from 0 to 1 (0° to 360° rotation), as cited earlier. To determine the surface's texture coordinates (U and V vectors), a mental ray mib_texture_vector shader labeled D is used.

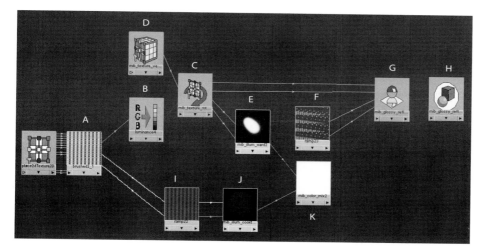

Figure 10.31

The brushed-metal network in Maya

The mib_texture_vector shader's Select attribute is set to 0 (by default), which extracts the UV coordinates from the surface, as they are defined (UV layout) in the UV Texture Editor window (all the attributes should remain at default). The mib_texture_vector → OutValue

value connects to the mib_texture_rotate → Input value (drag and drop), providing the mib_texture_rotate shader with texture coordinates that it can then perturb based on the texture map values. In other words, the texture vector shader is used to extract the UV coordinates from the surface as they appear in the UV Texture Editor. The mib_texture_rotate then deforms those UV coordinates according to the texture map.

> The mib_texture_vector shader provides different methods for deriving or defining (projections) the surface UV coordinates. I discuss texture coordinates using this shader and others in detail in Chapter 11, "mental ray Textures and Projections."

ANISOTROPIC HIGHLIGHTS

mib_texture_rotate (image C) connects to the Ward shader labeled E providing orientation for the anisotropic highlights. Notice that I'm using the Ward shader and not the Ward_deriv shader, which automatically derives UV coordinates from NURBS surfaces (see Chapters 9 and 11 for Ward shading and coordinates). This is a key element for the network. As shown in Figure 10.32 image A, using the Connection Editor I connect the mib_texture_rotate U vector attribute to the Ward shader's U vector attribute (Figure 10.32 image A labeled 1) and similarly connect V to V (Figure 10.32 image A labeled 2). By doing so, mib_texture_rotate provides modified (rotated) UV coordinates to the Ward shader, which will use those coordinates when defining the anisotropic character of highlights across the surface. At this point, the Ward shader will render highlights based on the orientation of the texture map.

Figure 10.32

The Ward shader used for creating the anisotropic highlights (image A) and the Ramp texture (image B)

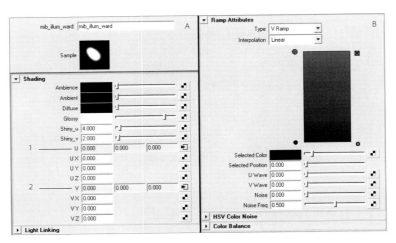

ANISOTROPIC REFLECTIONS

As cited earlier, the new UV coordinates provide information for anisotropic reflections, and until now I've focused on highlights, applying the new coordinates to the Ward shader; the Ward shader only provides anisotropic highlights. We also need to apply the same logic for the glossy reflections. First I connect the mib_glossy_reflection shader (G) to a surface material (Shading Engine) and set its reflection and environment colors to white. Then I also provide an environment map using the Render Settings window, mental ray → Environment → Image Based Lighting node (see Chapter 3, "mental ray Output"), using the LATLONG.tif environment image provided in the Chapter 10/Maya/sourceimages folder. For anisotropy, I set the mib_glossy_reflection U_spread attribute to 0.1 and the V_spread attribute to 0.001. I also set Samples to 32 and render. At this point, I can see default (not perturbed) anisotropic glossy reflections.

Using the Connection Editor window I apply the texture map as an influence for the anisotropic reflections, similar to the process described earlier with the Ward shader. I connect the mib_texture_rotate → U vector to the mib_glossy_reflection → U_axis vector and then repeat the same process for V and V_axis and render. At this point, you should see that the anisotropic reflections try to follow the coordinates provided by the texture map labeled A in Figure 10.31. Now that anisotropy is set for reflections and highlights, you can look at connecting the remainder of the network.

REMAPPING COLOR

Let's look at the connections from image A to image I in Figure 10.31. The same texture map (labeled A) is also connected to the Maya ramp texture labeled I (Figure 10.32 image B), which enables remapping the black-and-white texture colors from the texture map with color for the brushed-metal diffuse component. The diffuse color is applied using the Cook-Torrance shader labeled J, which is further discussed shortly. Using the Connection Editor, I connect the texture map file (a Maya file node labeled brushedMetal in Maya) to the ramp shader using the following connections:

- brushedMetal.OutColorR → ramp.uCoord input
- brushedMetal.OutColorB → ramp.vCoord

The ramp is set as a V ramp, where I apply a darker color at position 0 (Figure 10.32 image B labeled 2), and a brighter color at position 1 (top/labeled 1). The lower position (2) correlates to the black color in the texture file, and the top position (1) correlates to the white color. Thus, the ramp is used to remap the texture's black to white colors with the new (ramp) colors; the remapped colors assure that you will identify some variation in color, based on the texture patterns, in the diffuse shading component. The difference between the darker and brighter colors should not be significant, since they are there only to help establish the brushed metal's pattern, not clearly draw bright and dark circles across the surface. Thus, as you can see in Figure 10.32 image B, the remapped color at position 1 is not that much brighter than the darker color at position 0. Note that these colors should also be tinted to the metals color; they represent the metal's natural (objective) color. The Ramp node (Figure 10.31 labeled I) is then connected to a mental ray Cook-Torrance illumination shader (labeled J) Diffuse color attribute, providing solely diffuse color. In this case, the Cook-Torrance specular component is set to black as the highlights are provided by the Ward shader. However, having an additional specular color can enable you to further customize the shader tree, for example rendering a clear coating highlight across the surface top, such as the one seen in the original photo in Figure 10.28 image A.

FINALIZING THE SHADER TREE

Why use a separate illumination shader for the diffuse color, instead of applying that color with the Ward shader? As you can see in Figure 10.32 image A, the Ward shader's Diffuse is indeed set to black. This enables me to use the anisotropic highlights as an additional intensity mask for the reflection color (environment and scene reflections), as you will soon see. Using the mib_color_mix shader (Figure 10.31) labeled K (located in the Data Conversion rollout in the Hypershade window), I connect the Cook-Torrance (J) shader to the mib_color_mix → Color_base attribute. I then connect the Ward shader (E) to the mib_color_mix → Color_0 attribute using a simple drag and drop. The mib_color_mix shader allows you to mix different colors together using several components, as described earlier in this chapter in the "Colored Glass Effects" section. In this case I am using only one input, so I set Num to a value of 1 and then set Mode_0 to Add, and Weight_0 to 1 (default). Thus, the anisotropic specular highlights from the Ward shader are added with the diffuse color from the Cook-Torrance shader. I then connect the mib_color_mix shader (labeled K) to the mib_glossy_reflection → Base_material attribute (shown mapped with a Ward shader earlier in Figure 10.16).

By separating the highlights from the diffuse color, I can use the Ward shader as a mask. I now connect the Ward shader to the ramp shader (labeled F), enabling me to fine-tune the contrast ratio from the highlights (remapping their color values) for the purpose of a mask, used for the reflection color. I connect the Ward → outValueR and outValueB to the ramp's (labeled F) uCoord and vCoord, respectively, as we did earlier with the texture map and ramp texture. I then connect the ramp (F) → OutColor to the mib_glossy_reflection → Reflection_color and Enviorment_color attributes (connect both attributes independently). As described earlier, these colors control the reflection intensity, where brighter colors are more reflective. Thus, the Ward shader is used with an additional ramp to generate a mask for further control over the reflection intensity, dependent on the directionality of the brushed-metal surface grooves (provided through the Ward shader). Note that these final steps have no influence on anisotropy, which is provided with the mib_texture_rotate shader; they are only an additional tool for controlling reflection intensity.

For the texture map file (A) you can control the initial amount of rotation using the Color Balance → Color Gain attribute; as cited earlier the usable range for rotating highlights ranges from 0° to 360° so that by setting the color gain value to 0.5 you specify a range of 0° to 180° rotations. If you test this effect using the Ward shader while observing highlights you will see that with a range of 0° to 360° (a white to black value) the highlights appear twice on each disk, and when you reduce the range to 180° it appears only once per disk. Experiment with the Color Gain attribute values such as 0.5 and 2 to learn about controlling multiple highlights based on a texture.

XSI

Before you begin, note that you will need to install the TEK2SHOOT T2S_Mental-Ray1_1.xsiaddon, to expose the glossy shader in XSI, as discussed earlier. Figure 10.33 shows the graphed network in XSI using the glossy reflection and anisotropic shaders, as well as gradient shaders for remapping color values. First create an XSI anisotropic shader, and apply it to a surface. Load the shader in the Render Tree window, where we will re-create the network shown in Figure 10.33. For this example, consider that when you map the surface with a projection, you then need to extract that projection (the UV coordinates) to perturb its UV coordinates using the brushed-metal texture, reorienting the highlights across the surface. You can think of it as looking in the XSI Texture Editor window at the surface UVs and then taking those UVs and applying a deformation to them for anisotropic highlights and reflections, based on the brushed-metal texture.

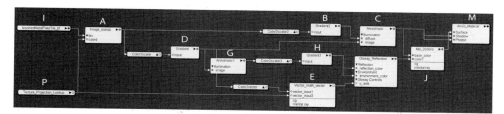

Figure 10.33

The brushed-metal network in XSI

EXTRACTING UVS AND REMAPPING COLOR

Instead of using a standard image loader in XSI that includes the projections within its properties, I use the image lookup shader (labeled A), which can be found in the Render Tree window under Nodes → Map Lookups → Image Lookup. I then create a separate texture projection (labeled P) from Nodes → Texture Space Generators → Texture Projection. I connect the texture projection to the image lookup → coord input. Since the texture projection is an independent shader, I can now extract the projection information (UV coordinates) for further editing, which we will soon use. I load the brushed-metal image (labeled I/brushedMetalPlateTile.tif on the CD) into the image lookup shader from its New → New from File property.

> You can also find Figure 10.33 in the Chapter 10 directory on the companion CD, labeled "XSI Anisotropic Network" so that you can see the inputs more clearly.

At this point, I still can't apply a projection method until the image lookup is connected to the surface. I connect the image lookup labeled A to the input property of the gradient shader labeled D (Nodes → Mixers → Gradient). This gradient provides control over tweaking the amount of orientation for highlights and reflections, as you will soon see. The gradient should be set with a black (leftmost marker) to a 50 percent gray (rightmost marker) corresponding to 180° rotations. As discussed earlier, a black-to-white color range (the texture map) provides 360° of rotation; therefore, this gradient remaps that color range so that the output color now represents 180° of rotation, which is the effective/usable range.

ANISOTROPIC HIGHLIGHTS

I then connect the gradient shader labeled D to the anisotropic shader (labeled C) Orientation property, by connecting to the Illumination → image input as shown in the figure. The image input correlates to the anisotropic shader's Anisotropic Orientation property. Thus, this connection maps the highlight orientation property with the remapped texture colors from the gradient shader. I now return to the texture projection (P) properties, and from under the Texture Projection → New property I specify a UV or Planar XZ projection (texture coordinates are discussed in detail in Chapter 11, "mental ray Textures and Projections"). Consider the following:

- If you are using a simple NURBS plane, you can select the UV projection, as I did in the provided file.
- If your model is a polygonal surface and you defined usable UVs (without overlapping), you should use the Unique UVs (polymesh) option.

> With respect to projecting the brushed-metal image and setting the number of texture repeats (in the projection), you may want to first connect the lookup shader to the anisotropic shader's diffuse color and tweak the projection results visually. You want to see the brushed metal clearly tilling across the surface without distortion.

For the anisotropic shader's Anisotropic Specular → Shiny U and V properties, specify values that provide anisotropic highlights, such as 1 and 8, respectively (equal values would create isotropic highlights). As with the Ward shader, it's important that the lower of the two values is set to 1 so that the highlights extend along each disk's full coordinate range. If you increase the lower value while previewing, you will notice the highlights diminish. Disable the anisotropic shader's reflections (if enabled); the reflections are applied later with the glossy reflection shader.

DIFFUSE AND SPECULAR COLORS

To control the diffuse color, I create another Mixers → Gradient shader (labeled B). The Image_lookup (A) connects to the gradient (B), remapping the brushed metal's grayscale values with color. (The Color2Scalar2 shader shown in the figure is generated automatically; that also applies to other areas of the shader tree where you see these conversion shaders.) Under the gradient properties, the leftmost marker correlates to the brushed-metal texture map's darker colors, and the rightmost marker correlates to brighter colors. The difference between the darker and brighter colors should not be significant, as you can see in the scene file, since they are there only to help establish the brushed metal's pattern, not clearly draw bright and dark circles across the surface. Note that these colors should also be tinted to the metal's color; they represent the metal's natural (objective) color.

After defining the metal's diffuse colors, the gradient (B) connects to the anisotropic shader's Illumination → diffuse color (C). In addition, the anisotropic shader's (C) Glossy color should be tinted to a bright color tinted based on the diffuse color so that the specular highlights reflect the metal's color, an important metal characteristic. At this point, you have successfully created a brushed-metal surface with highlight driven according to the texture, which in most cases will suffice for rendering purposes.

PERTURBING UVS FOR REFLECTIONS

As cited earlier, the anisotropic shader (like other illumination shaders) supports only glossy isotropic reflections without any control over anisotropic reflections. In the following steps, we'll further expand the network for the purpose of adding glossy anisotropic reflections, based on the texture map so that the reflections and highlights follow the same "surface grooves."

First let's prepare the texture vectors for the glossy shader (discussed next). From under Nodes → Math, select the Vector-Vector shader. We will use this shader to perturb the normals across the surface for glossy reflections. Connect the gradient shader (D/the remapped texture values) to the vector math shader's (labeled E) vector input 1 (notice the Color2vector shader is automatically generated). Now connect the texture projection (P) to the vector math shader's (E) second vector input (input 2). Under the vector shader's properties, set the Operation property to Vector input1 – Vector input2 (subtraction). As cited earlier, we needed to extract the texture projection coordinates for perturbing the reflections along the surface. Thus, this process takes the projection UV placement (a range of 0 to 1) and changes its values using the brushed metal's (0–1) range.

This math process is not an accurate means for perturbing the UVs based on the texture, opposed to the anisotropic shader's Orientation property. Since XSI doesn't provide the mib_texture_rotate shader by default, which would provide an accurate effect, this process is a workaround for orienting the reflections based on the texture map. Thus, the effect of using the vector math shader will cause for some distortion in the reflection that is similar to the desired effect. An alternative option is to use the Nodes → Texture Space Controller → Kaleidoscope shader that has an Angle property that can be used to orient the reflection. In such a case, connect the gradient shader (labeled D in Figure 10.33) directly to the kaleidoscope Angle property, leave the Coordinate property disconnected, and set the Number of reflections property to 1. This will generate texture coordinates based on the texture map that are somewhat better than the process described earlier. However, with the vector math shader, the rendered effect is more pronounced.

CONTROLLING THE ANISOTROPIC REFLECTIONS

At this point, you will need the TEK2SHOOT glossy reflection shader from the mental ray library. Once installed, you will find it under the T2S_MentalRay path → Shaders → Texture → mib_glossy_reflection. Take the glossy shader (F), and connect it directly to the material (M) surface input. The glossy shader should not have any inputs at this stage. Set the Reflection and Environment Color properties to white (fully reflective), and disable Single Environment Sampling. Set both U and V Spread to 0.001, and set Samples to 16. Create an environment for the pass (see Chapter 3, "mental ray Output" for camera shaders), and apply a picture that you can recognize clearly in the reflection. You can keep the default image (noIcon) for testing (recommended), or use the LATLONG environment image provided in the Chapter 10 XSI folder. At this point you should see clear reflections of the environment when you draw a render region around the surface.

Set the glossy shader's U Spread to 0.01 and leave V Spread at 0.001. You should see the reflection change to an anisotropic reflection along the U coordinate. The reflected image should still be relatively clear. Let's rotate the direction of the U coordinate several times across the surface, using the brushed metal, as we did with the highlights. Connect the vector math shader (E) to the glossy shader's u_axis input property, as shown in the figure under F. The glossy shader will automatically evaluate the V coordinate based on the U coordinate. At this point, if your image was projected correctly on to the surface, you should see something similar to Figure 10.34, where the reflection is distorted several times across the surface.

You can now swap the vector math shader (E) connection to the glossy shader's u_axis input with the kaleidoscope shader discussed earlier. Notice the different effect each shader has on the anisotropic reflection; both provide good results.

Figure 10.34

The UV coordinates are perturbing along the surface applying the anisotropic directionality to the reflection color, based on the brushed-metal texture.

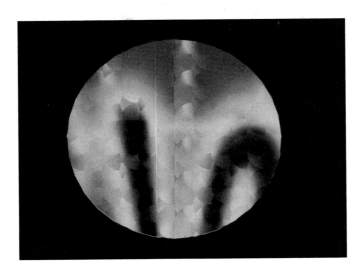

Select the gradient D and change the HSV value for its rightmost marker (the 50 percent gray). If you set it to black, you will see the anisotropic reflection as it appeared before you connected the vector math node (no perturbation). If you set it to white, you should see how the influence increases and forms a "double" effect. Basically at a value of 1 (white), the UVs perform a 360° rotation so that at 50 percent gray in the texture map image (the center of each disk), a new cycle is initiated, shown as "double" directional highlights.

FINAL STAGES

At this point, everything is set up for combining the different color influences and finalizing the shader. However, I want to add a cutout mask to control the reflection intensity based on the highlights. To clarify, the reflection is now oriented correctly; however, it still reflects at 100 percent across the surface (aside from the glossy shader's Fresnel effect). Create a new anisotropic shader (Figure 10.33 image G) and apply the same connections (Orientation property)and values used for the Shiny U and V properties as with the first anisotropic shader. Set its Diffuse and Ambient colors to black, and disable transparency and reflections. This shader acts as a black-to-white mask for the reflection, based on the specular highlight's intensity. Here are some setup tips:

- The specular highlight is the most reflective area on the surface, whereas the reflection color should be set to have a more spread-out effect (glossier) and at a lower intensity. Thus, you reduce the shader's output color contrast using a remapping process.

- Connect the anisotropic shader to a new gradient (Mixers → Gradient) (Figure 10.33 image H), which can be used to remap the color output.

- Set a color range with less contrast, such as from 0.2 to 0.6 (leftmost marker to rightmost marker). A minimum value of 0.2 assures that the surface is always reflective, dependent on the glossy shader's Fresnel effect. In any case, the reflection value won't exceed 0.6 once the connections are finalized; this is your max reflection value control.

- In addition, you can use the (HSV) hue and saturation scales to tint the reflection color according to the metal's diffuse characteristics, which is a required step with metallic reflections.

- You can also decrease the Shiny U option (the higher of the two) slightly so that it appears glossier.

- Connect the new gradient (H) to the glossy shader Reflection and Environment color properties. (In this case, we only have environment reflections so that it is essential to map the Environment color property.)

After the final masks are set, create a Mixers → Mix 2 Colors shader (labeled J). Connect the anisotropic shader labeled C to the mix s colors → base_color input, labeled J. This provides the diffuse color and specular highlights. Then connect the glossy shader to the second input (color 1), and set Mode → Add. Adding the anisotropic shader with the glossy reflection shader in this way superimposes the diffuse and specular highlights with the reflection color. The mix 2 color is then connected to the material (M) Surface input providing the final surface color. At this point, you are all done; you can now use the different gradient shaders for exploring color and value influences on controlling anisotropy.

3ds Max

Until now this chapter reviewed several mental ray base shaders, including the glossy shaders. The base shaders for the most part have equivalents in 3ds Max; however, the glossy shaders are not implemented. Since Autodesk's intention is to increase the compatibility between Maya and 3ds Max, I assume we will see these shaders implemented in future versions. Let's first examine the straightforward approach using the 3ds Max anisotropic shader and then further develop the concept using the architectural material. You can also experiment with the reflection utility shader provided by Horvátth Szabolcs on the companion CD (`ChapterFiles/CustomShaders/Horvátth/for_Max/ReflectionUtil-ity.mi`), which provides similar capabilities to the glossy reflection shaders

ANISOTROPIC SPECULAR HIGHLIGHTS

For creating brushed-metal highlights, in an empty slot in the Material Editor, set a default shader to Anisotropic, as shown in Figure 10.35. Under Anisotropic Basic Parameters, increase the Specular Level parameter to control the intensity of the highlight. Set Glossiness to 0, and set the Anisotropy parameter to 100. You should notice a clear highlight streak in the shader preview. As you can see, the Anisotropic Basic Parameters → Diffuse and Orientation (under Specular Highlight) parameters are mapped with textures.

Figure 10.35
The 3ds Max anisotropic shader enables you to create brushed-metal specular highlights.

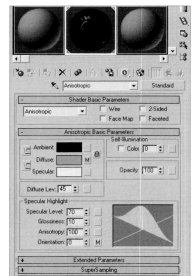

The Anisotropy parameter defines the thickness of the highlight as it stretches along the surface, where lower values produce a more glossy effect. Thus, Anisotropy actually defines the glossiness of anisotropic highlights. The Glossiness parameter defines the anisotropy of the highlight, including the extent to which the highlight wraps around the surface, where higher values produce "shorter" highlights. With this shader, the Glossiness parameter is the equivalent to the mental ray Ward shader's Shiny option, but here you need to specify a value of 0 instead of 1 to render a highlight that wraps around a surface. While tweaking the visual appearance of the highlight, you should reduce the Anisotropy parameters slightly to add glossiness to the highlight.

Create a directional light and simple plane surface in the scene. Aim the light at the surface, and map the surface with the anisotropic shader. Render an image at an angle similar to the one shown in Figure 10.28 image B. See that you can identify the anisotropic highlight on the surface; you may have to change the Orientation parameter to a value of 90, rotating the highlight 90°.

DIFFUSE COLOR

Map the Diffuse parameter with a 3ds Max Gradient Ramp shader from the Material Map Browser. You can use the gradient shader to define diffuse surface characteristics for metal by remapping the brushed metal's black-to-white colors. This allows you to maintain the brushed-metal pattern; however, you need to reduce the contrast so the effect is subtler. Under the Gradient Ramp Parameters rollout, set the Gradient Type parameter to Mapped, which enables the Source Map slot, as shown in Figure 10.36. Next, map the

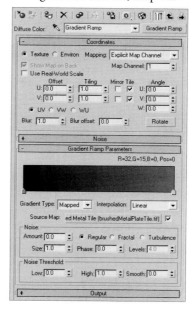

Figure 10.36

The Gradient Ramp used to remap the diffuse color

Source Map parameter with a Bitmap, and load the brushed-metal image (brushedMetalPlateTile.tif from the Chapter 10/3ds Max folder on the CD). Under the Bitmap parameters, set the projection parameters for the surface to Texture → Mapping → Explicit Map Channel (texture projections are discussed in Chapter 11, "mental ray Textures and Projections"), and set the tilling to 2.0 for both U and V (or as required by your geometry). Essentially, you want to test the image on the surface to find the right projection parameters so that the image appears clearly and without distortion. Step back to the gradient ramp shader, and remap the color values by specifying different colors along the gradient ramp, as shown in the figure (notice the reduced contrast). The rightmost flag (Flag#2) corresponds to the brushed-metal image texture map's white value, and the leftmost flag corresponds to its black value (Flag#1).

BRUSHED-METAL HIGHLIGHTS

Back in the anisotropic shaders parameters, map the Orientation parameter. When the Material/Map Browser window pops up, select Browse From → Scene, and find the (Source Map) brushed-metal image you just loaded in the previous steps with the gradient ramp. Select Copy from the pop-up window. If you test render the shader, you should now see the anisotropic highlights orienting accordingly with the texture file, similar to the effect shown in Figure 10.28 image B. The reason you made a copy is so you can control the numerical range that is used to rotate the highlight, independent from the bitmap used for the diffuse color. Navigate to the bitmap image mapped to the Orientation parameter. Under the Output rollout, shown in Figure 10.37, select Enable Color Map. You can use the curve shown under Color Map to control the numerical range of color that is outputted from the image, within (or beyond) the 0 to 1 range. If you decrease the range for the rightmost marker labeled A, it remaps the brightest (white) colors in the image from 1 to the specified value, indicated as 0.7 in the figure (the 1.0 and 0.7 numbers shown below the graph on the left side). If you increase the range beyond 1, you will see additional highlights appear on the surface; this has the effect of repeating the highlight, creating duplicate highlights. You should test higher values such as 2 and 3 to see the effect, but a value of 0.5–1 will provide the best result rendering a wider-spread highlight. Consider that a range of 0–2 will "repeat" a 0 to 1 cycle across the brushed metal's pattern on each disk twice; if the image range is 0 to 1, then at 0 to 2, a 50 percent gray is remapped to 1, and a 51 percent gray initiates a new cycle for orienting the highlights, which is also a 0-to-1 cycle.

> The best way to understand how values beyond the 0–1 range orient highlights, creating additional duplicate highlights, is to test and see the results.

Note that the same curve can be used with the diffuse color map to reduce some of the contrast in the image. You can now add reflections and tweak the color; however, as cited earlier, the reflections will be isotropic rather than anisotropic.

USING THE ARCHITECTURAL MATERIAL

Currently, in the absence of the glossy shaders, the only option to create proper anisotropic reflections with mental ray is either with the architectural material (Figure 10.38) or with external custom shaders such as with Horvátth Szabolc's reflection utility shader mentioned earlier (available on the CD). The workflow is similar to the one described earlier, with the exception that instead of using the gradient ramp shader, you will use the mix shader. Note that the architectural material features are discussed in detail later in the chapter, so I'll focus only on the network connections.

Diffuse Color Mapping

In the Material Editor, load the Arch & Design (mi) material from the Material/Map Browser window. You can select a brushed-metal template and further examine their settings. For now, leave everything at the defaults. Figure 10.38 shows the architectural material parameters used for this example. Follow these steps to prepare the shader:

1. Under the Main material parameters → Diffuse section, map the Color parameter with a Mix shader from the Material/Map Browser, shown in Figure 10.39. This shader will define the diffuse characteristics for brushed metal.

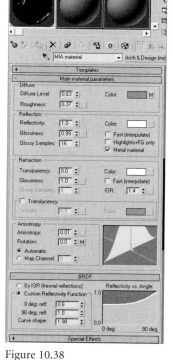

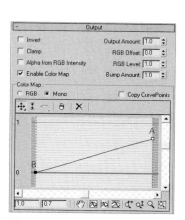

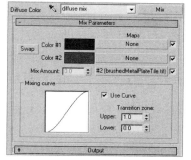

Figure 10.37

Controlling the color output from the brushed-metal texture

Figure 10.38

The architectural material in 3ds Max used for the brushed-metal effect

Figure 10.39

The 3ds Max Mix shader is used with the mia_material to map the diffuse color of the surface.

2. Map the Mix Amount parameter with a Bitmap, and load the brushed-metal image file. Set the bitmap's projection parameters to explicit UVs, and set the U and V Tiling parameter to a value of 2, just as in the first part of this tutorial.

3. Under the mix shader's Mix Parameters, set the color values for metal with small contrast differences, just as in the first case with the gradient ramp shader, as shown in Figure 10.39.

4. Enable Use Curve, which allows you to further specify the transition from one color to the next, based on the brushed-metal image, which in this case defines the transition from Color#1 (black) to Color #2 (white), with the difference of using the new remapped colors.

5. From the main parameters shown in Figure 10.38, decrease the Diffuse Level, and increase the Roughness (Oren-Nayar shading) to further tweak the surface characteristics. Note that this shader will automatically reduce the diffuse in favor of the reflection, because it is an energy-conserving shader (more on that later).

Anisotropic Reflections and Highlights

Follow these steps to set up the anisotropic highlights using the architectural material's parameters:

1. Under the Reflection section, Reflectivity should be set to 1.0 and Glossiness to 1.0 (for now).

2. Under the Anisotropy section, map the Rotation parameter (shown mapped in Figure 10.38) with a bitmap, and repeat the process of loading the brushed-metal file. (The bitmap should have the same projection and tilling settings as with the diffuse bitmap.)

3. Notice that the architectural material's Rotation parameter uses a 0-to-1 range, unlike the Orientation parameter in the previous example with the anisotropic shader. Enable the bitmap's Enable Color Map parameter (shown in Figure 10.37), and set the bitmaps output range (labeled A) to 0.5, corresponding to 180° of rotation.

4. The Anisotropy parameter should be set between 0.01 and 0.2, providing anisotropic highlights across the entire surface. Opposed to the previous section, in this case the Anisotropy parameter affects anisotropy and not glossiness as with the 3ds Max centric anisotropic shader (Anisotropy parameter).

5. Load an environment image for reflections under the architectural material's Special Purpose Maps → Environment parameter. Map it with a bitmap, and load the LAT-LONG image provided on the CD in `Chapter11/3ds Max folder` (or any other environmental image).

6. Under the environment bitmap Coordinates parameters, enable the Environ parameter radio button, and set Mapping to Spherical Environment. This stage generates an environment projection for reflections.

At this point, if you render an image, you should see brushed-metal highlights. To make the reflection appear anisotropic, you need to set the Reflection → Glossiness parameter to a lower value, effectively enabling glossy anisotropic reflections; when the Glossiness parameter is set to 1, the reflections appear isotropic, and once you reduce the value, they appear anisotropic following the brushed-metal pattern. Try values between 0.95 and 0.99, and increase the Glossy Samples to a value greater than 1 (enabling it); you can try values between 16 and 32. With respect to the anisotropic reflections, consider the following points:

- For the architectural material, make sure that under Fast Glossy Interpolation the Single Sample from Environment parameter is disabled, or else environment reflections will be isotropic.

- Metal reflections tint the specular contribution based on the surface's diffuse characteristics. Under the architectural material's Reflection parameters, enable the Metal material check box, as shown in Figure 10.38.

- For the architectural material, under BRDF you can change the Fresnel characteristics of the surface for metal. Try using a value of 0.6 as a starting point for the 0 deg. refl parameter, as shown in Figure 10.39 in the lower portion of the figure.

- It may be hard to see the effect of anisotropic reflections with a normal environment map (the LATLONG image will reflect a blue sky, so you don't really see anything distinguishable). Try mapping a checker texture as a spherical environment, and test the anisotropic characteristics using the Reflection → Glossiness and Anisotropy parameters. It will be easier to experiment with the effect when you can clearly identify the effect on the environment.

> Remove the brushed-metal image, and experiment with the characteristics of anisotropic reflections using the architectural material to learn how they behave.

The Architectural (mia) Material

Maya, XSI, and 3ds Max include the mental ray architectural library, which exposes the mia (mental images architectural) material, as well as the round corners, tone mapping, physical sun, and physical sky shaders. You'll learn about the physical sun, sky, and tone mapping shaders in Chapter 13, "Final Gather and Ambient Occlusion," with Final Gathering as they become more relevant.

The mia material is a monolithic (including shadow and photon shaders), physically accurate shader that emphasizes BRDF functionality with respect to correct light reflection and refraction, as well as energy conservation and light absorption. This shader has two major implementation advantages: physical accuracy and render efficiency. The latter means that several optimization options are built into the mia material. The mia material can be found in each host application, as follows:

- With Maya, in the Hypershade window under Create mental ray Nodes → Materials → mia_material.

- With XSI, in the Render Tree window under Nodes → Illumination → Architectural.

- With 3ds Max, when mental ray is the specified renderer, from the Material Editor window select Get Material, and in the Material/Map Browser window select the Arch & Design (mi) material.

The architectural material offers several options for defining the characteristics of each color component. These range from Oren-Nayar diffuse, glossy isotropic, and anisotropic reflections and refractions, to manually defining BRDF curves and simulating translucency.

> You can learn about the architectural material and round corners shader in the "The Architectural (mia) Material" PDF file on the companion CD.

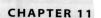

mental ray Textures and Projections

This chapter examines the basics of using image files and procedural textures with mental ray, including image filtering, elliptical filtering, memory-mapped images, and pyramid images. In the same context, it also covers the methods for defining (or deriving) texture coordinates and applying texture placement using mental ray–specific texture shaders. The purpose of this chapter is to show how to use mental ray texture nodes for loading and mapping image files, not to provide an exhaustive review of UV texture mapping techniques with each host application using host-specific nodes. To get the most out of this chapter, you should be familiar with the concepts of applying projections to surfaces and generating UV layouts, as well as the differences between them. In particular, you should understand the concept of "unwrapped" UV layouts, in which each UV has unique placement within the 0 to 1 texture space coordinates, in contrast to overlapping UV layouts, where UVs share texture space coordinates. With mental ray, the process of defining texture mapping coordinates is not as straightforward as within host applications. Fortunately, in most cases, host-centric shaders and mental ray shaders interact correctly, so you do not need to rely on mental ray–specific texture placement nodes. This chapter covers the following topics:

- **Texture Space and Projections**
- **mental ray Bump Mapping**
- **mental ray Projection and Remapping Shaders**
- **Host Application Settings**
- **Memory Mapping, Pyramid Images, and Image Filtering**

Texture Space and Projections

The term *texture space* refers to yet another coordinate system available with 3D applications. In this case, it's a 2D grid with U and V coordinates that range from 0 to 1. Within that grid, UV layouts are constructed to provide a means for mapping a 2D image file or procedural texture onto 3D surface coordinates. The 2D texture space is used to define the relationship between 3D surfaces and 2D images. Mapping is then the process of applying a texture across a surface's U and V (2D) coordinates, where the UV coordinates are encoded with values that correspond to X and Y coordinates within a 2D grid, which is the texture space. Thus, the tasks of rotating, scaling, and translating a texture across the surface are relative to its 2D internal (UV) coordinates and not the 3D scene coordinates.

The UV surface coordinates are defined either through *explicit projections* or *implicit projections*. Explicit projections create (built-in) UV coordinates, such as those you typically lay out within a UV texture editor for polygon surfaces or derive directly from NURBS surfaces. Implicit projections refer to directly projecting images onto the surface during rendering, regardless of the surface's UV coordinates. The mental ray shaders used to apply such projections are one of two primary topics for this chapter, along with image filtering techniques. Even if you are not that well versed with the applications of explicit vs. implicit projections and UV layouts, the chapter covers these topics in enough detail to clarify some of their finer points. Host-specific workflows and tools for assigning and editing UVs are reviewed only in the context of mental ray shaders.

> With respect to explicit coordinates, the UV coordinates of a NURBS surface are derived strictly from the NURBS surface's UV profiles; by contrast, polygonal objects are more flexible in the sense that they allow for customized UV layouts.

Texture Projection Basics

Texture projection tools (and viewport manipulators) are found within all 3D host applications, using 2D planar or 3D (that is, spherical, cubical, cylindrical, and so on) projection shapes, as shown in Figure 11.1. These projections appear within host applications as geometric wireframe objects that have no render properties and thus are merely geometric manipulators that define a projector's shape with UVW coordinates.

The additional W coordinate is always present with UV coordinates. It extends 2D coordinates to 3D coordinates, creating a 3D texture vector. It can be compared to the Z coordinate in 3D space, providing a means to project an image along any of the three UVW coordinates. Thus, UVW coordinates are actually an additional set of vector coordinates, comparable to XYZ coordinates. The difference is that they are used to define texture coordinates along a 2D projection shape or surface. The topic of defining and manipulating texture vectors is discussed in detail in the section "The Texture Vector and Remap Shaders" later in this chapter.

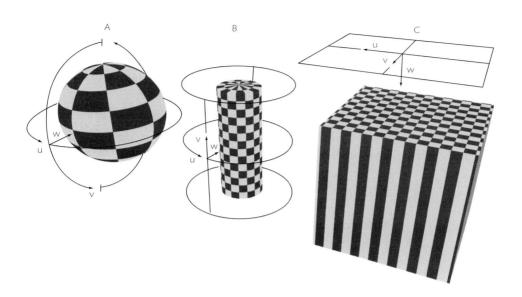

Figure 11.1

Texture projection shapes can be seen as wireframe geometric objects in host applications; they are used to project images on surfaces, acting as 3D projectors.

In most cases, we refer to texture mapping along U and V coordinates, omitting any reference to the additional W coordinate; however, these coordinates are always defined using a 3D vector that has U, V, and W vectors.

The projection shapes shown in Figure 11.1 are then used to set the position, orientation, and size for a given projection, as shown with the spherical (A), cylindrical (B), and planar (C) projections. All these projections are in fact 2D image projections from a 2D or 3D projector shape. They are 2D projections because a 2D image file or procedural texture is mapped across the projector's coordinates and projected toward a given surface point.

Notice how a 2D planar projection stretches the texture across the surface faces that are perpendicular to the projection direction, which is a typical planar projection characteristic. In each case, the projection has its own U and V coordinates (directions) that define how a 2D image or procedural texture will be mapped along those U and V coordinates and then projected onto a surface along the W coordinate. Essentially, these geometric projection shapes are identical to NURBS surfaces in the sense that both define surface coordinates that range from 0 to 1 along U and V profiles, as discussed for NURBS surfaces in the CD excerpt, "Surface Approximation Methods." Also, as cited earlier, polygonal surfaces benefit from an ability to customize UV layouts that are independent of the geometry.

3D Textures

3D texture projections (which are always procedural textures) define color values within a 3D volume area based on XYZ coordinates; they "live" in 3D space (that is, world, camera, or object space) regardless of the surface UV texture coordinates. Therefore, the texture itself is a 3D procedural texture that can uniformly distribute color values along XYZ coordinates. In Figure 11.2, you see one of the benefits of using 3D textures, which is the correct flow of texture from one axis to the next. To clarify, the texture pattern shown on the top of the table flows correctly over the front and side of the table. Thus, 3D textures make it possible to apply projections that are independent of the surface's location and orientation in the scene, acting as a volume effect that applies color at each surface intersection.

Figure 11.2

3D textures project color values along all XYZ axes, effectively maintaining a coherent flow of values across the surface.

To create a 3D texture in this case, I used mental ray's turbulence shader, connected with a texture vector shader. The texture vector shader is set to Select -1 (point in space) and world space. Its output value connects to the turbulence coordinate input. The turbulence output, a scalar (one-dimensional) value, is connected three times—once to each RGB color input of a constant shader. The scene also used an ambient occlusion light to define form. The texture vector shader, its options, and its connections are discussed in detail later in this chapter.

Texture Mapping Basics

Along the projection's UV coordinates, additional texture *remapping* shaders determine how an image or procedural texture is placed within the projector's UV coordinates. The remapping shader utilizes the UVW coordinates to manipulate the texture placement within the projector's surface area, and thus the UVW coordinates are calculated as discussed earlier, in two stages:

1. The first stage defines a projection area, which may take the form of a 2D or 3D projector, as shown in Figure 11.1. This stage also defines or extracts the UVW vectors for texturing.

2. The second stage applies texture remapping within the projection's texture space, based on the UVW coordinates. This stage is used to further transform the vectors, such as scaling or rotating the texture.

In Figure 11.3, a NURBS sphere is contained within a 3D spherical projection labeled A. Within that spherical projection, the remapping process has further optimized the projection region to one quarter of the top hemisphere (the upper-half sphere) of the spherical projector using UV coordinates. Therefore, the projected area, labeled B, projects the image onto the surface only from that region, as shown with the distorted image captured on the NURBS sphere; the same shape as the projection area.

Remapping determines the region, orientation, and scale of the projection itself, within the bounds of the projector object.

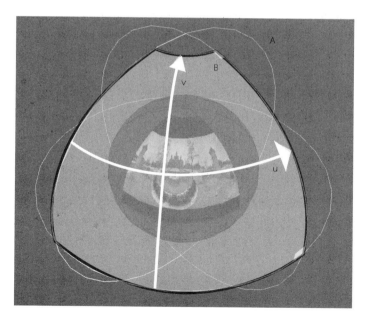

Figure 11.3

Texture remapping controls the 2D texture placement along the U and V coordinates within the projection shape boundaries.

As you will see in the remainder of this chapter, you have a lot of options for projections (projectors) and remapping shaders, such as picking the projector's coordinate space and choosing how to control the *translation matrix* with remapping shaders. The topics of mental ray texture projections and remapping shaders, as well as host-specific options, are discussed next to provide a better understanding of texture coordinates and texture space.

Explicit vs. Implicit Projections

Projections in all host applications are offered as either implicit or explicit. The difference is that explicit projection manipulators act as tools that assist you in laying out a basic UV scheme on a polygonal surface or derive coordinates from a NURBS surface. On the other hand, implicit projections don't require surface UV coordinates and thus can speed up model preparation times, but at the price of render speed and flexibility.

Explicit Projections

With explicit projections, once the projection is applied, you can see the updated UV information in the host application's UV texture editor, where you can then further modify the UV coordinates. Explicit UVs are exported within .mi files as per-vertex UV coordinates. Thus, during rendering, the UV coordinates are derived from the surface and not from a projector as with implicit projection.

One advantage of explicit projections for defining UV layouts is that you can apply these projections on a per-face basis, so you can troubleshoot problematic regions with isolated projections, such as the conversion of faces on the top of a sphere or a character's head. The techniques for using multiple projections to define explicit UV layouts are beyond the capabilities of mental ray's shaders and are instead part of each host application's tool set for creating custom UV layouts. Thus working with explicit projections in mental ray means selecting an existing predefined layout.

> A common technique with all host applications is to use several different projections consecutively to unwrap the texture coordinates while modifying the UV coordinates in a UV texture editor.

Implicit Projections

With implicit projections, as cited earlier, the projection manipulator has the final word on how the image is applied onto the surface, and any manual UV editing in the UV texture editor doesn't affect the rendered result. Implicit projections don't assist you in laying out UVs and then further editing them. Therefore, the scale, placement, and orientation of the projector's shape, along with any additional texture remapping manipulations, provide the only means for manipulating the texture placement during rendering. Thus, with implicit projections, the coordinates are evaluated at render time only, which is a more time-consuming process.

Note the tremendous difference in the amount of flexibility you have as an artist between implicit and explicit projections. With implicit projections, you can place a projector and edit its image placement. In contrast, creating custom-made (explicit) UV layouts that solve complex mapping scenarios, such as with a high-resolution model that has a significant degree of curvature (cars, boats, characters, and so on). In practice, low-resolution polygonal surfaces can benefit from implicit projections when not enough vertices exist to properly define explicit UV coordinates using the texture editor; for example, it may be easier to use a cylindrical or spherical projection to project an image of a character's face onto a low-resolution model opposed to attempting to lay out and map the texture manually in the UV texture editor. As an example, you can look at Figure 11.34 later in this chapter; if both cubes A and B are low-resolution (one face per side), using a spherical implicit projection would result with a good layout as seen under A, and with explicit UV coordinates the texture could not properly wrap around the surface, resulting with the distortion seen under B.

mental ray Bump Mapping

Bump mapping is a well-known technique for simulating geometry that rises or declines from a surface without actually displacing the geometry; it offers a quick and cheap way for simulating geometry using shaders rather than modeling in details. There are two techniques for bump mapping; one is based on using standard textures, and the other uses *normal maps*.

Chapter 9, "The Fundamentals of Light and Shading Models," introduced Lambert's cosine law, and you learned that a dot product determines the intensity of light at a given sampled point, based on the surface normal and direction to the light. Bump mapping is based on changing the direction of the surface normal so that when the dot product evaluates, it returns a result that is based on a modified normal (affected by the bump map) that points in a different direction, not perpendicular to the surface face as with standard shading. Therefore, the normals need to perturb (bend) before the illumination shader evaluates the light influence using these new redirected normals. The topic of dot products and vectors is discussed in detail throughout this chapter.

> Bump mapping is in-fact a method for producing normal maps by converting grayscale images into normal maps for the purpose of shading effects; manipulating the effect of light across a surface.

Standard Bump Mapping

With standard bump-mapping techniques, the grayscale color values of an image influence the surface normal direction; *white* refers to the highest point that is raised from the surface, and *black* refers to the most declined point from the surface. It is common to use resources such as noise textures or manually prepared grayscale images that correlate to a given texture, such as a floor's tiles or wood patterns.

The process to implement standard bump mapping with mental ray is not intuitive and requires using custom shaders that perturb (bend) the surface normals. Thus, the illumination shader needs to use normals after they have been processed using bump map and bump basis shaders.

With XSI and 3ds Max, the bump mapping is straightforward, and you don't need to use any complicated shader trees. XSI and 3ds Max both enable you to easily plug a color texture into the mental ray material bump slot. See Chapter 9 for a review of the mental ray materials in each host.

Bump Mapping in Maya

Maya shaders with Maya-centric bump-mapping shaders work well, so you don't need to use custom trees. With mental ray illumination models, you have little choice and must construct a custom shader tree. The tree needs to utilize both texture projection and remapping shaders, as discussed throughout this chapter, as well as custom bump-mapping shaders.

You will find a scene labeled bump.mb in the Chapter 11 directory on the companion CD. In the file you'll see three examples of bump map networks, one on each display layer:

- Under the Bump1 layer, I provide a simple example that uses a common workflow. The key here is the mib_color_mix shader that takes the bump map as a base color and an illumination model as the color 1 input and passes them to the mental ray material.

- Under the Bump3 layer, using a similar network, I added some mental ray shaders to provide a more elaborate example of mixing several colors and shaders with bump mapping. In this case, I passed the result to an illumination model that is connected to the mental ray material.

- Under the layer Bump2, I used a completely different approach where the illumination shader itself passes through the bump shader and into the Maya shading engine, under the mental ray Custom Shaders (the mental ray material) Material Shader input.

I bookmarked the Hypershade views so you can quickly review these shader trees.

Chapter 10, "mental ray Shaders and Shader Trees," discussed bump mapping using the mia material with the round corners shader, takes another look at bump mapping using the subsurface-scattering shaders.

Normal Map Bump Mapping

Normal maps (and a bump map's output) use a custom color-coded scheme to represent the direction of the normal relative to the surface. In the section "Putting It All Together" later in this chapter, you will see how color can relate to 3D coordinates. In the same way, colors that indicate a given axis are used to redirect the normals on a surface into that direction (of the color-coded axes). Thus, normal maps redistribute the normals across a surface based on RGB color-coded images and not grayscale values as with the texture maps used for standard bump mapping. They are more advanced than standard bump mapping and are used extensively in 3D to define bump mapping, lighting influence, and environment sampling.

Normal maps are typically rendered with one of two color-coded schemes: *tangent space* normals are intended for object deformation, and world space (or object space) normals are encoded based on the scene (or object) coordinate space X, Y, and Z axes. Tangent space normals will stick to an object as it orients and deforms; normals are encoded based on the geometry itself, meaning that a positive Y vector correlates to a normal that is per-pendicular to its face and the X and Y axes correlate to the U and V directions along the surface. In this way, tangent based normals allow modifying the surface shading (bump effect) when deformations or transformations are applied such as with a character's rig (bone-system) or while rotating a surface. Normal maps commonly used with programs such as ZBrush and Mudbox that export maps for representing the fine detail across the surface using tangent space normals without physically displacing the geometry.

World space normal maps are based on the scene XYZ axes and are not bound by any object orientation. This method is better for static objects such as brick walls, fences, or cables that run along a distant wall in a game. All these surfaces need to react to light in a way that provides a visual cue that they have real depth; for example, when the light changes direction, the light across the surface needs to change to reveal the form in the shadow areas, or vice versa. However, the object itself is no more than a simple flat polygon surface that now appears to have more detail.

Several resources on the Web provide tutorials and insight into using normal maps with all host applications, such as in ZBrush forms. Each host application has built-in bump shaders that offer normal bump mapping such as with XSI's Normal Map shader, Maya's 2D Bump Map (tangent space normals option), and 3ds Max's Normal Map bump shader. As cited earlier, with XSI and 3ds Max you simply connect these shaders to the bump map slots.

mental ray Projection and Remapping Shaders

The mental images base shader library, presented in Chapter 9, includes the mib_texture_ vector and mib_texture_remap component shaders, which are used for texture projections and remapping. These are mental ray's primary shaders for applying explicit or implicit projections, as well as remapping the projection. The texture vector shader defines implicit UV coordinates or selects explicit ones. The remapping shader provides a 4 × 4 translation (transformation and translation) matrix, as well as some other common remapping features such as tiling and alternating the texture, all discussed in the following sections.

Also from the base library, the mib_texture_lookup and mib_texture_filter_lookup shaders are used to load images and apply filtering. Both image lookup shaders are discussed throughout this chapter. The following sections focus on the texture mapping shaders and texture coordinates while demonstrating basic shader trees that use the image lookup shaders to load images and connect to a base illumination model.

mental ray Network Connections

Figure 11.4 demonstrates two simple mental ray shader graphs in Maya. Both graphs use a base illumination shader (C), with texture and image lookup shaders to apply an image (D) onto a surface. Note that only one network is connected to the material, and the other network is present only for illustrative purposes. Each network uses a different image lookup shader: the standard lookup shader (B) and the elliptical filtering lookup shader (A). You can also see that the texture vector shader (E) and the texture remap shader (F) are used with both lookup shaders, and therefore they can be shared with various shader trees. This process is commonly found in complex shader trees where a given portion of the network defines texture coordinates and placement, which are then shared by several other shaders throughout the network or even across networks, as shown in Figure 11.4.

Figure 11.4

A standard mental ray network for texture projection and placement shown in Maya using mental ray–specific shaders

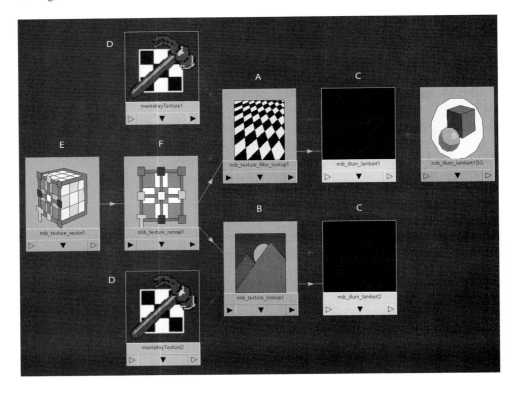

You can see a similar network with XSI in Figure 11.5, which shows an image lookup shader connected to the Lambert shader's diffuse color property. The image lookup shader receives two inputs: a texture file and a texture projection. The texture projection shader incorporates the mental ray texture vector and texture remap shaders discussed in the following sections, and the image file is a simple mental ray image loader shader with standard filtering options.

> In XSI, the commonly used image shader found in the Render Tree window under Nodes →
> Texture → Image (c) is a more user-friendly shader that has built-in options for specifying ellip-
> tical filtering, selecting a texture projection, and getting texture support; these correspond to
> equivalent options in the mental ray component shaders examined throughout this chapter.

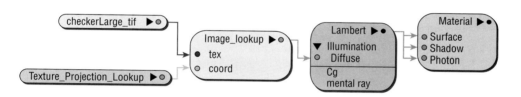

Figure 11.5

A basic mental ray network in XSI. Ordinarily you would use the Image shader, which has more features built into its options.

Let's focus on the networks shown in Figure 11.4 using mental ray base shaders. As cited earlier, both networks share the same texture coordinate shaders, labeled E and F. Note that if remapping is not required, it would suffice to connect only the vector shader (E) directly to the image lookup shaders (A and B), omitting the remap shader (F). The following section describes the shader connections shown in Figure 11.4. Our purpose is to further understand the relationship between these shaders and to demonstrate how you can connect such shaders in any host while relying solely on mental ray–specific shaders.

Basic Texture File and Coordinate Connections

The texture vector shader (E) outputs texture coordinates to the texture remapping shader (F) with the following connections:

```
texture_vector.outValue→ texture_remap.input
```

The remapping shader (F) transfers the texture coordinates to the lookup shaders (A and B) coordinate input with the following connection:

```
texture_remap.outValue→ texture_lookup.coord
```

Doing so provides the lookup shaders (A and B) with modified texture coordinates based on any additional remapping settings such as translation or tiling. We will discuss the differences between the two lookup shaders momentarily. The mental ray texture (D) connects to the texture lookup shaders using the following connection:

```
mentalrayTexture.message→ texture_lookup.tex
```

The mental ray texture shader is merely an image loader shader providing the path to the image file, as well as enabling standard (simple) filtering. If you look at the declaration of such a shader in an .mi file (exporting the same shader graph), you'll see the following:

```
filter 20 color texture "mentalrayTexture" "C:/path/checker.tif"
```

Therefore, the shader provides a filter option and a file path. When the elliptical filtering lookup shader (A) is used, it overrides the standard filtering option shown as `filter 20` in the excerpt.

The lookup shaders (A and B) connect to the illumination shader's (C) diffuse input, as shown with the following connection:

```
texture_lookup.outValue→ mib_illum_lambert.diffuse
```

Filter Lookup vs. Standard Lookup Shader Connections

Notice that although the same remapping shader connects to both image lookup shaders, both receiving the same texture coordinates, the elliptical filtering lookup shader (A) requires an additional connection:

```
texture_remap.message→ texture_lookup.remap
```

This connection provides insight into the remapping features so that the elliptical filtering process can recognize any transformations that have been applied to the texture, such as resizing or rotating the texture. It is important for elliptical filtering to determine the relationship between the camera's perspective and the current texture point orientation (at the sample location) for properly projecting (defining) the elliptical filter shape. The topic of elliptical filtering is discussed in more detail in the section "Memory Mapping, Pyramid Images, and Image Filtering" later in this chapter; however, these required shader connections are covered only in this section.

To recognize the differences between both lookup shaders, let's look inside an .mi file at the different code entries for both shaders. The following block is used with the standard lookup shader (B):

```
shader "mib_texture_lookup"
    "mib_texture_lookup" (
    "tex" "mentalrayTexture",
    "coord" = "texture_remap"
    )
```

Notice how both connections described earlier are present. The `"tex"` option receives the mental ray texture (D) input, using the same name shown in the previous excerpt. The `"coord"` option receives the texture remap input, providing the texture coordinates. With elliptical filtering, notice in the following excerpt the additional options in the filter lookup declaration:

```
shader "elliptical_filter_tex"
        "mib_texture_filter_lookup" (
        "tex" "mentalrayTexture",
        "coord" = "texture_remap",
        "eccmax" 30.,                    // A: elliptical filter options
        "maxminor" 12.,
        "disc_r" 0.1,
        "bilinear" on,
        "space" 0,
        "remap" "texture_remap"
        )
```

You can see the `"coord"` and `"tex"` options with both lookup shaders, providing the texture file and texture coordinates. In addition, you can see all the elliptical filtering options from the point labeled A and below. All these options are discussed in the section "Elliptical Filtering Options" later in this chapter. Notice that the additional `"remap"` option (the last entry) is also connected with the texture remap shader. This additional connection refers to the elliptical filtering requirements cited earlier on texture remapping options.

The Texture Vector and Remap Shaders

Now let's examine the texture vector shader, labeled E, and the texture remap shader, labeled F in Figure 11.4. This section focuses on the differences between explicit and implicit coordinates, projection methods, and coordinate spaces (that is, world, object, camera, and so on), which all affect texture mapping and are all controlled with the texture vector shader. A texture vector shader is always required for texture mapping; however, the optional remapping shader enables further mapping options, including transformation, repetition and alternation options for procedural textures, or texture files. Some custom shaders may have built-in texture vector options, such as the Binary Alchemy shaders (see Table 10.1 in Chapter 10), as part of their shader interface. In all cases, texture vectors are required for texture mapping. The following sections introduce the relevant mathematical concepts and terminology before reviewing the mental ray shaders. The purpose is to help visualize why things are the way they are in 3D. This introduction plays two roles:

- It presents mathematical terms and equations on a "need-to-know" basis; I'll leave a full, in-depth coverage to the math books.

- It helps you understand how mental ray texture mapping shaders deal with texture coordinates, as well as how you can use them to your advantage.

Introduction to Matrices, Vectors, and Coordinate Systems

With 3D applications, arrays and vector variables are used to express multidimensional data. A typical 3D vector variable stores three scalar values, and each may be a fractional or whole number (a float or integer variable). Note that vectors can also store characters (strings), which are non-numeric values. A vector is then a collection of data contained within a single row or column and with a dimension, such as 2D, 3D, and 4D vectors. For example, a 2D vector stores X and Y scalars, and a 3D vector stores X, Y, and Z scalars. In 3D we constantly (but not exclusively) utilize two primary types of 3D data sets: coordinate vectors and color values. As a result, a vector variable can store data such as the following:

- XYZ coordinates, where each scalar is a *position vector*

- RGB colors, where three scalar values define some color combination

Vector notation uses lowercase bold letters, and components (values) are encompassed within square brackets using row vectors that look like $\mathbf{n} = [x\ y\ z]$ and column vectors that look like this:

$$\mathbf{n} = \begin{bmatrix} i \\ j \end{bmatrix}$$

You can also think of a column vector as an array with one column and n rows. A matrix is a form of array that has a given number of columns and rows and is used extensively to solve problems such as the transformation of objects and textures within a given coordinate system. Matrix notation is written using uppercase letters, and their components are provided in square brackets, as shown here.

$$M = \begin{bmatrix} r_{11} & r_{12} & r_{13} \\ r_{21} & r_{22} & r_{23} \\ r_{31} & r_{32} & r_{33} \end{bmatrix}$$

The letter r and its subscript number refer to the row number and column number so that r_{22} means "row 2, column 2." The topic of matrices is discussed in more detail in the section "The Texture Remap Shader." For now, consider that each row of a matrix can represent a vector of any dimension, such as a position vector with three scalar values, that is, a 3D vector.

VECTOR DIRECTION AND MAGNITUDE

Vectors have two primary attributes: *magnitude* and *direction*, as shown in Figure 11.6. The direction of a vector is defined by the location of the vector's head (the arrow) relative to its tail. The direction tells us whether a vector is pointing, for example, southeast (along the X and negative Y axes) as with vector **j**, or is pointing northeast (between the positive X and Y axes) as with vector **k**.

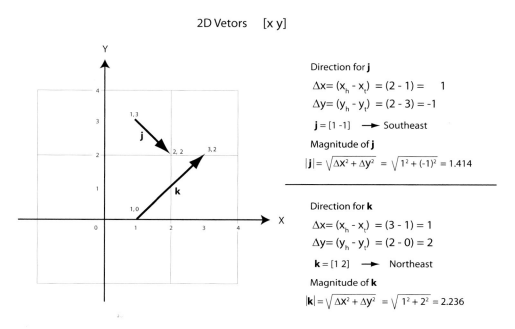

2D Vetors   [x y]

Direction for **j**

$\Delta x = (x_h - x_t) = (2 - 1) = 1$
$\Delta y = (y_h - y_t) = (2 - 3) = -1$

j = [1 -1] ➜ Southeast

Magnitude of **j**

$|\mathbf{j}| = \sqrt{\Delta x^2 + \Delta y^2} = \sqrt{1^2 + (-1)^2} = 1.414$

Direction for **k**

$\Delta x = (x_h - x_t) = (3 - 1) = 1$
$\Delta y = (y_h - y_t) = (2 - 0) = 2$

k = [1 2] ➜ Northeast

Magnitude of **k**

$|\mathbf{k}| = \sqrt{\Delta x^2 + \Delta y^2} = \sqrt{1^2 + 2^2} = 2.236$

Figure 11.6

The mathematical equations for deriving vector direction and magnitude of the two vectors graphed in a 2D Cartesian coordinate system

Both vectors are shown graphed on a 2D Cartesian coordinate system; however, their locations on the graph are irrelevant as long as you can determine their direction (arrow) and magnitude (length). As you can see, the delta (Δx and Δy) for the direction on each axis is adjusted to represent the per-axis length of the vector along the X and Y axes, regardless of the origin. It is achieved by subtracting the vector's head coordinate from its tail coordinate along both axes, as shown in the figure under "Direction for." The result represents the vector's aim direction. If you redraw the vector from the origin of coordinate system, where the tail is at the origin [0, 0], then you can say that the head is X and Y units away from the origin.

This form of representation, as you will see, is used to express position vectors relative to a coordinate system's origin.

Magnitude describes the distance of a vector from head to tail. The vector notation for magnitude is typically written like this: |**a**|. It can represent several characteristics such as physical forces, distances, amplitudes, and so forth. For example, the distance to the camera is 20 units. Magnitude is calculated with the theorem of Pythagoras as shown in Figure 11.6 under "Magnitude for." To apply this theorem, you must first extract the vector's directions as unit vectors for each axis, which is the delta distance. Magnitude is essential for solving texture transformations with matrix multiplication.

BASIS VECTORS AND IDENTITY MATRICES

Coordinate spaces define Cartesian XYZ coordinates, where each axis is perpendicular to the next, a 90° difference. The alignment of the coordinate system may differ based on the selected space, as you will see. To use coordinate systems effectively with vector (and matrix) math, such as for deriving texture coordinates, surface normals, and the direction to the camera, we must first define the term *basis vector*. In mathematics, the basis vector is used to solve equations by representing the coordinate system using three *unit vectors*. Each unit vector is linearly aligned with a different axis (that is, the vectors are axially aligned) on the coordinate system and has a magnitude of 1. Basis vectors are then the basis for mathematically representing a coordinate system with three unit vectors that align with the different axes of a given coordinate system. You can write **p**, **q**, and **r** basis unit vectors using row (or column) vectors this way.

$$\mathbf{p} = [1\ 0\ 0]$$
$$\mathbf{q} = [0\ 1\ 0]$$
$$\mathbf{r} = [0\ 0\ 1]$$

The term *unit vector* means that the vector's magnitude is normalized to 1. In the context of texturing, basis vectors are then a form of normalized vectors where each component has a magnitude of 1 on its X, Y, or Z axis. Basis vectors allow you to easily relate a vector to a coordinate system. For example, if you take the vector **k** [1 2] (Figure 11.6) and relate it to the basis vectors **p** and **q**, you can express this relationship as follows:

$$\mathbf{k} = [1\mathbf{p}\ \ 2\mathbf{q}]$$

This form of vector representation helps us visualize a unit-based relationship between vectors and coordinate systems using basis unit vectors such as **p** and **q**. They allow us to identify the per-axis displacement (distance) of a vector's head relative to the coordinate system's origin (its tail). You will see the importance of unit vectors while rotating textures with the texture remap shader.

Position Vectors

A 3D *position vector* (mentioned earlier) is then a vector that has X, Y, and Z components that displace a vector a given distance from the coordinate space origin. Thus, unlike the examples shown in Figure 11.6, position vector components already identify the delta distance (per axis). The fact that each component can be viewed as an independent displacement along an axis from the origin and relative to the coordinate space enables easy transformations such as rotating or scaling textures. These transformations are demonstrated in the following sections with the texture vector and remap shaders.

Transform Matrices and Identity Matrices

A 3×3 transform matrix that looks like this represents a coordinate system using three basis vectors, one in each row:

$$M = \begin{bmatrix} 1 & 0 & 0 \\ 0 & 1 & 0 \\ 0 & 0 & 1 \end{bmatrix}$$

Transform matrices are used to transform a texture's UVW coordinates. A matrix like the one shown here, with a diagonal line of ones and zeros everywhere else, is referred to as an *identity matrix*—a matrix that when multiplied by a vector will result in an unchanged vector, similar to multiplying a number by 1. Thus, multiplying a vector with an identity matrix means that all the vector components are linearly aligned with the basis vectors; the coordinate system and (UVW) position vectors are aligned.

Let's examine Figure 11.7 to better understand identity and transform matrices. Under label A, you can see the procedure for multiplying a vector **r** by the matrix M. The vector **r** can represent a texture vector shader's output vector. The matrix M can represent the texture remap shader's transform matrix. When multiplied, the result is a new texture vector output **s**, which is a transformed vector. So, $\mathbf{r} \times M = \mathbf{s}$ is the process of transforming vector **r** to vector **s**.

A

Transform Matrix (M)

Texture vector output (r) $\begin{bmatrix} x & y & z \end{bmatrix}$ × $\begin{bmatrix} r_{11} & r_{12} & r_{13} \\ r_{21} & r_{22} & r_{23} \\ r_{31} & r_{32} & r_{33} \end{bmatrix}$ = $\begin{bmatrix} xr_{11} + yr_{21} + zr_{31} & xr_{12} + yr_{22} + zr_{32} & xr_{13} + yr_{23} + zr_{33} \end{bmatrix}$

Transformed vector / output (s)

dot product

B

Identity Matrix

$\begin{bmatrix} 2 & -2 & 3 \end{bmatrix}$ × $\begin{bmatrix} 1 & 0 & 0 \\ 0 & 1 & 0 \\ 0 & 0 & 1 \end{bmatrix}$ = $\begin{bmatrix} xr_{11} + yr_{22} + zr_{33} \end{bmatrix}$ = $\begin{bmatrix} 2 & -2 & 3 \end{bmatrix}$

output vector = input vector

Figure 11.7

Under A, an example for matrix multiplication of a vector by a matrix. Under B, the equation demonstrates with an identity matrix.

An important characteristic of matrix multiplication is that the transformed components of **s** are each a dot product of the vector **r** components with the matrix M column components. Therefore, you can consider vector **s** a result of three separate dot product equations of vector **r** with each column of matrix M.

Under label B, you can see this process applied using scalar values for all the components, where the matrix in this case is an identity matrix. If you multiply the texture vector **r** by the transform matrix M, the output vector **s** remains unchanged, as in **s** = **r**. You will see later that the texture remap shader's default transform matrix is an identity matrix. Thus, when connected to a texture vector shader, it merely passes the texture coordinates unchanged, unless of course you specifically define a texture transformation by changing the transform matrix components.

In this section, you have been exposed to a lot of the inner workings of coordinate systems with vectors and matrices. One of the more important realizations should be that without defining basis vectors we could not operate simple transformations between vectors and a transform matrix. Earlier, in Chapter 9, we used a dot product between two 3D vectors to determine light intensity. A basis vector is used to interpret the magnitude and direction of each vector (light direction and surface normal) before determining the light intensity based on Lambert's cosine law. You can see a complete dot product example in the section "Fresnel Reflections and Dot Products" later in this chapter.

The Texture Vector Shader

The texture vector shader is responsible for defining whether UV coordinates are explicit or implicit, as well as what type of projection is applied to those coordinates. After evaluating the implicit or explicit coordinates and projections for a surface, the shader outputs texture vectors for each sample point during rendering. Those vectors' coordinates are then used with the remap shader to further adjust the placement of the texture across the surface.

THE SELECT OPTION

Figure 11.8 shows the mental ray mib_texture_vector shader options. You can find similar options in XSI and 3ds Max, which are discussed in the section "Host Application Settings" later in this chapter.

The Select attribute (shown in Figure 11.8) defines whether the coordinates are derived from the surface, as with explicit coordinates, or whether they are applied implicitly. If implicit, it also determines a projection method within a given coordinate system (that is, world, camera, object, and screen space). In this way, the Select attribute defines how an intersection point (point being sampled) locates its respective UV coordinate within the 2D texture space for deriving a color value.

Figure 11.8

The mental ray texture vector shader options in Maya

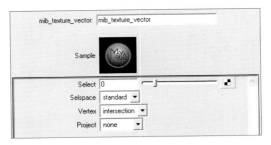

Explicit Coordinates

When the Select attribute value is set to 0 or higher (positive numbers), the UV coordinates are referred to as *explicit* and derived from the surface's predefined UV layout and from a given *UV set*, as shown in Figure 11.9. In this figure, the same shader has been applied to both surfaces. You can see that both surfaces utilize their own predefined UV coordinates.

Figure 11.9

Explicit UV mapping using the predefined UV layout

Commonly, with polygonal surfaces, you might specify more than one UV set of texture coordinates. For example, one set is used for the surface color (a texture map), and the other UV set is used with a baked indirect illumination map. When the two textures are layered together with a shader tree, each texture requires its own UV layout to define texture placement. In such cases, the Select attribute determines which UV layout will be selected (used) with each texture. Hence, positive numbers correlate to UV sets, where a value of 0 refers to the default (first) UV set, and a value of 1 selects the next UV set. If you specify a value for a UV set that doesn't exist, the render will provide garbage values. We look at using separate UV layouts in the following per-host sections. The article "HDRI_3D_Issue7_Mental Ray" on the companion CD (HDRI 3D magazine) examines using UV sets in detail with Maya. The concepts presented in the article are true to all host applications.

Implicit Coordinates

Negative values implement implicit projections that are not dependent on any predefined layout. In this case, the Select attribute determines the relationship between a surface intersection point and the texture space, without any assistance from predefined UV coordinates. The more commonly used functions of negative values are listed in Table 11.1 and further demonstrated with their relationships to coordinate spaces and projection methods in the following sections. For a complete list, refer to the mental ray documentation.

	VALUE	PURPOSE
Table 11.1 **The Select Option Values and Purposes**	0 and higher	This selects a predefined UV layout (UV set).
	-1	This selects an intersection point directly in the 3D scene (at the sample point). This method is commonly used with (implicit) projections such as spherical or planar projections and in object, camera, or world space.
	-2	The texture vector coordinates are aligned with the surface normals and are based on world space coordinates by default (see the section "The Selspace Option" next). In other words, for a given implicit projection, the surface normal orientation defines how the shader locates its texture space coordinates. You can use this method to extract normal maps.
	-3	The intersection point is derived from motion vectors; thus, motion blur needs to be enabled and set to motion vectors so that they are generated during the render. The vectors are based on the Selspace option.
	-4	The intersection point is derived based on the direction to the camera and thus depends on the camera's orientation in the scene. This is similar to Select -2, but it's dependent only on the camera's orientation. The vectors are based on the Selspace option.
	-10	This specifies a screen projection such as with a background image. The image is locked down to the corners of the render screen regardless of any other options.

THE SELSPACE OPTION

The Selspace attribute shown in Figure 11.8 defines the coordinate space used for the projection, offering World, Camera, Object, Screen, and Unchanged (standard) options. This attribute applies a coordinate space transformation; it takes the extracted coordinates (a texture vector) and multiplies them by some basis vector that represents the selected coordinate space. Doing so transforms the initial texture coordinates from one space to the next. When set to Unchanged, these vector coordinates are typically extracted in world space.

Once transformed, the texture vector's magnitude and direction are relative to the coordinate system. In world space, the vectors are aligned in the same way as they appear in your viewport for XYZ directions. In object space, the vectors are aligned relative to the object's pivot point. In camera space, the basis vectors are aligned with the camera. With mental ray, the negative Z axis aims forward (outward) from the camera. Later in the section "Putting It All Together," you will see a shader technique to visualize transformations in color.

THE PROJECTION OPTIONS

The Project attribute offers a variety of projections that include Unchanged (none), UV (based on the UV layout), Spherical, Cylindrical, Planar (XY, XZ, YZ), and Lollipop.

Let's examine the relationship between the Select, Selspace, and Project attributes with a few figures. A Select value of -1 is common with most implicit projections, using a given projection method and with a given coordinate space. Both images in Figure 11.10 use a Select value of -1, and the Project attribute is set to spherical projections. In image A, the Selspace attribute is set to world space coordinates; notice how the spherical projection appears to initiate from the center of the screen, which is in fact the 3D scene origin. With world space coordinates, the texture is centered at the scene origin and projected from there, using the given projection method. Thus, if the object moves, it will appear to swim underneath the texture.

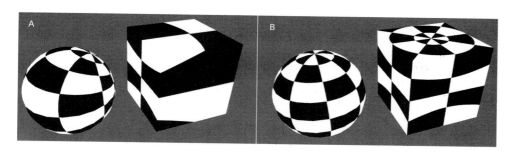

Figure 11.10

World space vs. object space spherical implicit projections

In image B, Selspace is set to object space (also known as *internal space*), and as expected, the spherical projection initiates from the center of each object—their object space origin. Therefore, with object space, textures are mapped from the center of the object and attached to the object regardless of its rotation, scale, and location within the scene. As the object animates, the texture follows along with it. As a result, image B would be more appropriate for animation purposes using implicit projections, whereas image A is more appropriate for environmental projections such as with the mental ray environment shaders.

In Figure 11.11, you can see four images that have similar appearances. Images A and B are both rendered with Select set to -4 (direction to camera), Selspace set to camera space, and Project set to XY planar projection. The result is a camera-based XY projection into the scene along the Z coordinate. When the camera changes, so does the projection. In this case, the camera's focal length changed between images A and B, and the texture scaled down proportionally with the surfaces (actually with the camera). Therefore, with camera projections, as the projection is subject to change based on camera transformations, any additional transformations applied with the remap shader will also have an influence on the texture appearance.

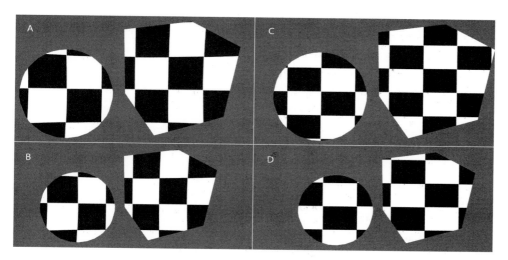

Figure 11.11

Camera space vs. screen space implicit projections

In images C and D, the Selspace attribute is set to screen space. In this case, the remaining settings (Select, Project) have no effect. The image will stretch to fit the screen regardless of the changes applied to the camera. You can see that in this case as the focal depth changed between images C and D, the texture maintained its size and placement, so the surfaces appear to swim under the texture. This method is ideal for projecting a background plate in the scene. Note that in images A and B, the texture will also appear to swim if the camera changes orientation or the surfaces move.

PUTTING IT ALL TOGETHER

You know that the Select attribute defines how coordinates are extracted and that Selspace defines how those coordinates are transformed to align with a given coordinate system, which is a coordinate space transformation. To see the coordinates relative to the coordinate systems as color, you can connect the texture vector output to the color input of a constant shader. Doing so forces XYZ texture vector coordinates to interpret as colors.

Basic Connections

In Maya I connected the outValue of the texture vector to the Out Color attribute of a Maya surface shader. With XSI I used the texture space generator shader (a texture vector shader) and connected its output to a constant shader's Color property, as shown in Figure 11.12. Note that the texture generator shader must have a texture projection internally that is set to implicit projections. Also, the texture generator's Space Transformation property should be set to world or object space, depending on the desired result. The topic of adding and controlling these shaders is further discussed in the XSI sections later in the chapter. The section "Normalizing the Color Output" discusses adjusting the color value to output a coherent range of color.

For both Maya and XSI, you can find the scene files in the in the Chapter 11 host directories on the companion CD with the scene file labeled "Normal Projection".

Figure 11.12

Connecting a 3D coordinate vector as a color output to a constant shader, enabling you to see a normal map render

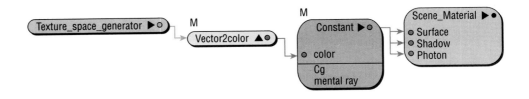

Color-Coded Normals

If you set the Select attribute to -2 (surface normals) and you set Selspace to object space, you output color-coded coordinates based on object space. To clarify, consider the coordinate output is [0 1 0] for a sampled point, which means that when converted to RGB values, that surface point renders as green. Regardless of the settings you use, the following relationship exists between XYZ coordinates and RGB colors:

X=R, Y=G, Z=B

So, when the Select attribute is set to -2, the outputted coordinates will render normal maps color-coded based on the current Selspace selection. With all spaces, the Y axis renders as green, the X axis renders as red, and the Z axis renders as blue. If you select camera space, then normals are color-coded based on the camera's coordinates, and if you select world space, the result is a world space normal render.

> Conduct several test renders while changing the coordinate space and the cameras angle; notice how the color scheme across the surface changes with different coordinate spaces.

Normalizing the Color Output

The first stage of directly connecting the texture vector to color will not suffice for a coherent (readable) result. When you connect UVW texture coordinates to RGB colors, you need to remap the vector values to positive numbers that range from 0 to 1. Essentially, texture vector output coordinates can range from -1 to 1 correlating to positive and negative XYZ axes. Furthermore, the texture vector may actually output values that exceed that range or, alternatively, are much smaller than that range.

If you consider that the primary RGB colors correlate to positive values with each color component, as cited earlier, what happens to CMY (cyan, magenta, and yellow) subtractive colors? You can assume that the subtractive colors correlate to the negative output values, such as the negative Z axis.

Therefore, negative XYZ coordinates need to paint subtractive CMY colors, and if you don't remap the range correctly, those subtractive colors will appear as black instead of color; negative values are clamped at 0. The solution is to remap the coordinate output range to a 0 to 1 normalized range before connecting it to the shader's color. This allows vector coordinates to output a correct combination of color values that can redraw any color from the color wheel, relative to their axes, which is a key element for generating useful normal maps when baking textures.

> You can visually assess that you've done a good job when you don't see any black and white colors appear across the surface.

Consider the following per-host points for normalizing values and remapping the range, because the process differs between hosts:

Maya I connect the texture vector output to the set range shader. Doing so allows remapping the input range, for example from -1 to 1, to an output range of 0 to 1. I found these values work well with world space. However, with object space the vector output range is much smaller, so I remapped the range from the -0.1 to 0.1 range to the 0 to 1 range. You can examine the Maya scene cited earlier.

XSI With XSI I used a chain of three vector-vector (vector math vector) shaders. I connected the texture generator to the first vector (input 1) and set the Operation property to Normalize (Vector Input). This assures that the range remains between -1 and 1. To remap the negative range to a positive range, I connect the vector output to another vector shader input and set the Operation property to Vector Input 1 + Vector Input 2. For the Vector Input 2 property, I manually specified a value of 1 to each of its numerical values. Doing so adds a value of 1 to the range, pushing the range from -1 to 1 to the new range of 0 to 2. I then use the last vector shader with a multiply operation. I set the Operation to Vector Input 1 × Scalar Input 1, and I set Scalar Input 1 to 0.5, assuring that the values are all multiplied by this scalar. This remaps the 0 to 2 range to a 0 to 1 range. I then connected the output of this vector to the color property of the constant shader via a vector2color shader. You can examine the XSI scene cited earlier.

FRESNEL REFLECTIONS AND DOT PRODUCTS

As an example of using texture vector implicit coordinates, you can look at one of the most common practices in 3D: defining color based on the angle between the sample point's surface normal and its direction to the camera (a Fresnel reflection). This sort of effect is already integrated in shaders within each host application using host-specific shaders (see Chapter 10) and mental ray shaders such as the glossy shaders and the architectural material.

The Dot Product

The dot product equation, shown in Figure 11.13, is a form of vector multiplication that results with the relationship of an angle between two vectors. The equations in Figures 11.13, 11.14, and 11.15 examine the dot product between two vectors; **a** is the direction to the camera, and **b** is the surface normal. To solve for the angle between both vectors using the equation in Figure 11.13, we use the following four steps, as shown in Figure 11.14:

1. The dot product of vectors **a** and **b** is calculated and results with the scalar value of 3.

2.–3. The Pythagorean theorem calculates the magnitude of each vector.

4. The angle is calculated with the following steps:

   a. The $\cos(\theta)$ is equal to the dot product result, which is divided by the (multiplied) magnitude of both vectors, resulting with the value 0.387.

   b. The inverse of the cosine is then calculated and equal to an angle of 67.23° between both vectors.

In 3D you can benefit from using vectors that are unit vectors (normalized). In such cases, the magnitude is always known (equal to 1). It allows for easier interpretation of the angle between the vectors, as shown next.

Vector Dot Product ($\mathbf{a} \cdot \mathbf{b}$)

Direction to camera $\quad \mathbf{a} = \begin{bmatrix} x\ y\ z \end{bmatrix}$

Surface normal $\qquad \mathbf{b} = \begin{bmatrix} i\ j\ k \end{bmatrix}$

$|\mathbf{a} \cdot \mathbf{b}| \cos(\theta) = ix + jy + kz = $ Angle between two vectors

Figure 11.13

The dot product equation

$\mathbf{a} = \begin{bmatrix} 1\ \text{-}2\ 5 \end{bmatrix}$

$\mathbf{b} = \begin{bmatrix} 0\ 1\ 1 \end{bmatrix}$

Figure 11.14

The steps for solving the angle between two vectors

Step 1 $\quad \begin{bmatrix} 1 \\ \text{-}2 \\ 5 \end{bmatrix} \times \begin{bmatrix} 0 \\ 1 \\ 1 \end{bmatrix} = (\mathbf{a}_x \times \mathbf{b}_i) + (\mathbf{a}_y \times \mathbf{b}_j) + (\mathbf{a}_z \times \mathbf{b}_k) \longrightarrow 0 + (\text{-}2) + 5 = 3$

Step 2 $\quad \mathbf{a} = \sqrt{\mathbf{a}_x^2 + \mathbf{a}_y^2 + \mathbf{a}_z^2} = \sqrt{1 + 4 + 25} = 5.477$

Step 3 $\quad \mathbf{b} = \sqrt{\mathbf{b}_x^2 + \mathbf{b}_y^2 + \mathbf{b}_z^2} = \sqrt{0 + 1 + 1} = 1.414$

Step 4 $\quad \cos(\theta) = \dfrac{3}{5.477 \times 1.414} = 0.387 \quad \theta = \cos^{-1}(0.387) = 67.23^\circ \longleftarrow$

Normalized Vectors

Figure 11.15 shows two examples, one using parallel (labeled A) and one using perpendicular (labeled B) unit vectors.

Figure 11.15

Two examples of dot products between parallel and perpendicular normalized vectors

A

$\mathbf{a} = \begin{bmatrix} 0\ 0\ 1 \end{bmatrix}$

$\mathbf{b} = \begin{bmatrix} 0\ 0\ 1 \end{bmatrix}$

$\mathbf{a} \cdot \mathbf{b} = 0 + 0 + 1 = 1$

$\mathbf{a} = \sqrt{0 + 0 + 1} = 1 \quad \mathbf{b} = \sqrt{0 + 0 + 1} = 1$

$\cos(\theta) = \dfrac{1}{1} = 1 \quad \theta = \cos^{-1}(1) = 0^\circ \longleftarrow$

B

$\mathbf{a} = \begin{bmatrix} 0\ 0\ 1 \end{bmatrix}$

$\mathbf{b} = \begin{bmatrix} 0\ 1\ 0 \end{bmatrix}$

$\mathbf{a} \cdot \mathbf{b} = 0 + 0 + 0 = 0$

$\mathbf{a} = \sqrt{0 + 0 + 1} = 1 \quad \mathbf{b} = \sqrt{0 + 1 + 0} = 1$

$\cos(\theta) = \dfrac{0}{1} = 0 \quad \theta = \cos^{-1}(0) = 90^\circ \longleftarrow$

Notice that with normalized vectors, the dot product result gives a quick indication of the angle between two vectors. Under image A, using the same steps cited earlier, a dot product between the two unit vectors $\mathbf{a}$ and $\mathbf{b}$ is calculated resulting with a value of 1. That indicates that the angle between both vectors is equal to 0°. You can see that after calculating the inverse cosine, this results in a 0° angle between both vectors and thus parallel vectors (with the same direction and magnitude).

In image B, the dot product of two vectors results in a value of 0, which is a 90° difference between the vectors. You can see that with greater dot product values (the result) vectors are more parallel (similar) and smaller values indicate more perpendicular vectors. Consequently, the dot product returns the cosine for the angle between two vectors and is very useful in solving several lighting and texturing problems, such as those presented in Chapter 9.

The Shading Networks

To re-create this equation using the shading networks shown in Figure 11.16 (Maya) and Figure 11.17 (XSI), I use two texture vector shaders. One shader has the Select attribute set to -4, which is the vector to the camera. The other shader has the Select attribute set to -2, which is the normal vector. With both shaders, the Selspace attribute is set to camera space. Thus, these networks are used to define color based on the dot product between two vectors in camera space.

Two examples are presented; one re-creates the dot product using math shaders, and the other utilizes a dot product shader option. You can find both examples in the Chapter 11 directory for each host on the companion CD. Each network is attached to a different sphere in the scene files (labeled "Dot Product").

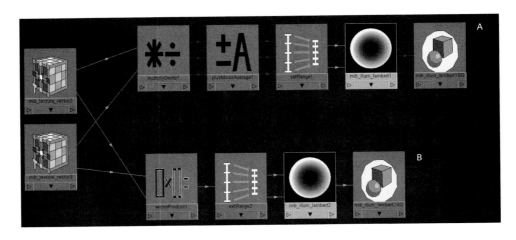

Figure 11.16

Two texture vector shaders are used to create a custom Fresnel reflection shader using a dot product in Maya.

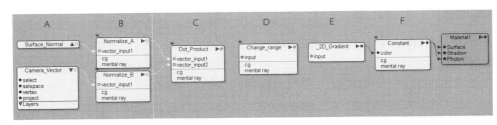

Figure 11.17

Two texture vector shaders are used to create a custom Fresnel reflection shader using a dot product in XSI.

In both cases, using a more mathematical approach, I connect the output from each vector shader to a math shader that multiplies two vectors together. So, I first multiply the vector components as follows:

$$a_x \times b_p, a_y \times b_q, a_z \times b_r$$

I then add together the resulting vector components using another math shader with an addition operation. Note that in both hosts I individually connect each X, Y, and Z output from a multiply shader to three scalar inputs in an addition shader, adding the three together. By adding them in this way, I finalize a dot product equation between two vectors, as shown in step 1 in Figure 11.14. You can see this process in the shader tree labeled A in Figure 11.16. With XSI, you can examine this approach in the scene file since the shader tree is too large to display as a figure in this book.

After applying the dot product, I remap the range, similar to the process shown in the section "Normalizing the Color Output" earlier in this chapter. In Maya I use the setRange shader and in XSI I use the Change Range shader to specify a range of 0 to 1 instead of -1 to 0 (their output is typically negative), assuring that only positive values convert to color.

I use the scalar output from the range changing shaders to define color along the V coordinate of a gradient shader. By doing so, I remap the color output for a sampled point based on a scalar value that represents the angle between both vectors. Thus, one color appears at facing angles (the ramp's position 1) and gradually transitions to the other color (the ramp's 0 position) at glancing angles. The gradient shader then connects to the color of a constant shader, which is the resulting Fresnel shader.

For the second approach, shown in Figure 11.16 image B and in Figure 11.17, I use a similar process, but this time I use a math shader that calculates the dot product between two inputs, rather than using math shaders to compute it manually. If you compare the shader previews or renders in both hosts for both methods, you will see that the results are the same. With respect to the stages presented here, note the following comments for Maya and XSI:

Maya For the first example, I connected the mental ray texture vector shaders to the MultiplyDivide shader. I then connected each of its outputs to a separate 1D input of a Maya PlusMinusAverage shader. Using the Connection Editor window, I connect the output of the PlusMinusAverage shader to the V coord input of a Maya ramp shader. The ramp needs to be set as a V ramp.

For the second example, I used a Vector Product shader and enabled its Normalized Output attribute that assures the values are within the 0 to 1 range, which are easier values to work with, as discussed in the section "Normalized Vectors" earlier in this chapter.

XSI In both cases I connected the XSI Generator shader, labeled A in Figure 11.17, to a vector-vector shader (labeled B) and normalized the output before proceeding to the multiplication and addition shaders, providing easier values to work with, as discussed in the section "Normalized Vectors" earlier in this chapter.

The two texture generator shaders labeled A have the Space Transformations property set to Camera. Each shader has an implicit projection applied to its Texture Space property using the following settings:

- The UV Generation property is set to implicit.
- The Coordinate property is set to surface orientation with one shader and is set to direction to camera on the other shader.
- The Space Transformations property is set to None.

For the second example shown in Figure 11.17, I connected the two vector-vector shaders' normalized output to the inputs of a vector-scalar math shader labeled C. The Operation property is set to Dot product. For D, I use the change range shader to remap the range as cited earlier.

Using a 2D gradient shader, found under Nodes → Texture Generators → Gradient, I connect the change range shader (D) output to the gradient shader (E) input. Under the gradient shader's Input tab, I set the Input Type property to Scalar input.

The Texture Remap Shader

The texture remap shader is used for applying texture *transformations* and *translations* across a surface, as well as defining common tiling features. Figure 11.18 shows the mental ray texture remap shader options in Maya. You can see the Input attribute is mapped with a connection from a texture vector shader, and thus the coordinates (a 3D vector) from the texture vector shader are passed to the remap shader for further processing. You can see the same input within the following excerpt from an .mi file marked as A:

```
shader "mib_texture_remap3"
    "mib_texture_remap" (
        "input" = "mib_texture_vector",   // A: texture vector input
        "transform" 1. 0. 0. 0. 0. 1. 0. 0. 0. 0. 1. 0. 0. 0. 0. 1.,
        "repeat" 50. 50. 1.,
        "alt_x" off,
        "alt_y" off,
        "alt_z" off,
        "torus_x" on,
        "torus_y" on,
        "torus_z" on,
        "min" 0. 0. 0.,
        "max" 1. 1. 1.,
        "offset" 0. 0. 0.
        )
```

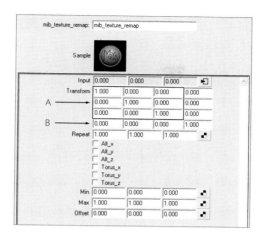

Figure 11.18

The texture remapping shader options in Maya

Let's begin reviewing the easier options shown in the excerpt and in Figure 11.18. The Repeat attribute defines the number of times a texture is tiled along the different XYZ coordinates. The Alt_x, Alt_y, and Alt_z attributes define whether the surface alternates every time it repeats, meaning that each repeated tile is flipped vertically or horizontally based on 3D coordinates.

The Torus_x, Torus_y, and Torus_z attributes define texture wrapping so that the texture will continue to repeat outside the projection boundaries. To clarify, every projection (projector shape) can be specified to a given size, location, and orientation. In addition, the remap shader can further orient, scale, and translate the texture within the projection's area, as shown earlier in Figure 11.3. The Torus attributes further enable it to tile (repeat) outside the projection borders and across the entire surface (to infinity). Note that spherical projections that project 360° around a surface are not affected by the Torus attributes.

The Min and Max attributes are used for cropping the texture based on its 0 to 1 texture space, and the Offset attribute defines a placement offset for the texture in X, Y, and Z directions. All of these attributes are common to all host applications and with some hands-on experimentation can be fully understood.

> Consider texture remapping as additional texture support that defines the projection region within the projector's UV boundaries. Each host application has options for manipulating texture support within the boundaries of the projector.

Rotating or scaling textures is relatively simple with all host-centric 2D placement shaders. However, with mental ray, no magic sliders enable you to easily rotate a projection, as you will see with the following practical examples. Maya users in particular are required to manually specify values that define the rotation, scale, and translation for a texture using a translation matrix. In Figure 11.18, as well as in the earlier excerpt, the translation matrix is referred to with a Transform attribute. This matrix is traditionally referred to as a *translation matrix*, the term I will use here. The following sections provide an easy approach to manually configuring this 4 × 4 matrix without using complex math equations, as well as understanding its mathematical foundation with respect to our previous discussions on vectors and matrices.

THE TRANSLATION MATRIX

The Translation matrix provides for three important functions, which are rotations, scaling, and translations. The values encompassed within the box labeled A (Figure 11.18) control a transform matrix (rotation and scaling), and the values within the box labeled B control the translation vectors. Both transformations and translations are applied along X, Y, and Z coordinates relative to a coordinate system. Each row of the matrix corresponds to a specific axis on the coordinate system. The first three rows of the matrix are X, Y, and Z transformation vectors, and the last row is an XYZ translation vector. Technically (in linear algebra terms), factoring in the translation vector with the transform matrix is described as appending a notation to a 3 × 3 matrix, resulting in a 4 × 4 matrix, or a *4D vector*.

If you consider that the transform matrix and translation vector (four vectors) both utilize three components, why do we have a fourth column? The fourth column is the result of combining four vectors together that mathematically enable expressing rotations, scaling, and translations using one matrix. There are two primary reasons for this 4 × 4 matrix representation. When conducting matrix multiplication by vectors or matrices, linear algebra rules require that when multiplying a vector **v** by the matrix M (**v** × M), the number of columns for **v** must align with the number of rows in M. Therefore, a 1 × 4 vector can be multiplied only with a 4 × *n* matrix when written as **v** × M. Note that if you switch the order, the same rule applies so that an *n* × 4 matrix can be multiplied only with a 4 × 1 vector and, thus in this case, a column vector (4 rows). In both cases, you can see that as a condition of matrix math, a 4 × 4 matrix is required.

The fourth component also has a more technical implication, besides enabling matrix multiplication. This additional fourth component in the vector and matrix (r_{44}) is referred to as a *homogeneous coordinate* that is typically set to a value of 1 (but not always). So, typically a 4D vector is expressed as **v** = [x y z 1]. The fourth homogeneous coordinate enables texture translations and transformations without distorting the image; this topic is further discussed soon.

HOMOGENEOUS COORDINATES AND TRANSLATIONS

Transformations are always applied relative to the coordinate system's origin point with position vectors, so if we factor in translations, theoretically it requires moving an entire coordinate system along with the origin point. So, you can think of it as repositioning the basis vectors themselves relative to the coordinate system and then executing the transformation there, relative to the new origin point. Consequently, mathematically translating a 3D vector as a whole (with its unit vectors) presents an additional variable into the equation. To remedy this, we extend the 3D vector with the additional homogeneous coordinate notation using the 4D vector [x, y, z, 1].

In a nutshell, the homogeneous coordinate is typically set to 1. It defines a virtual plane on which each XYZ component of a 4D vector has a coordinate relative to the plane. The idea is that for every XYZ coordinate in Cartesian space, there is a new X ÷ W, Y ÷ W, and Z ÷ W on that plane. This enables transforming XYZ coordinates along the coordinate system while uniformly scaling the projection using the homogeneous coordinate, as you will soon see.

If you divide the vector components by W, you will see that the result maintains their physical integrity (relationship to each other) but projects them at a new scale (coordinate) relative to the homogeneous coordinates size. You now have a way of preserving proportions relative to this virtual plane that enables transformations at a different coordinate from the coordinate system's origin.

> The topic of 4 × 4 matrices and 4D vectors is mostly a matter of linear algebra alongside 3D practices for manipulating surfaces and textures coordinates within a given space. To learn more about the topic of 3D math, you can look at books that teach math fundamentals such as *3D Math Primer for Graphics and Game Development* by Fletcher Dunn and Ian Parberry (Wordware Publishing, 2002) or *Essential Mathematics for Computer Graphics* by John Vince (Springer, 2001).

In the following sections, we examine the translation matrix with the remap shader, as well as see how matrix math characteristics control texture placement.

CONTROLLING THE TRANSLATION MATRIX

Let's look at controlling texture placement with the transform matrix using a simple polygon plane and gray background. A black-and-white checker texture file is being used.

The texture is applied based on explicit surface UVs, which is why the Select attribute is set to 0. Selspace is set to standard and Project to none. Therefore, this example is aimed at showing you how to rotate, scale, and translate a texture for a given explicit UV layout. Repeats are set at 2, and the Torus and Alt attributes are disabled so that the texture does not repeat outside the projection borders. Areas that appear black (outside of the texture border) are surface areas that don't receive any color.

Translation and Scaling

Figure 11.19 shows four examples using different values for the Transform attribute. Image A is set with the default matrix options. For image B, the translation values of the matrix (row B in Figure 11.18) have changed to 0.1, 0.2, and 0. Notice that the texture shifted 10 percent along the X axis and 20 percent along the Y axis. Also notice that translations are applied as a relative percentage of the current texture size. A full translation (one full cycle) is equal to a transform value of 1.

Notice that in this case (and most cases), we require only U and V coordinates since we are dealing with a 2D coordinate system, which is the surface texture space. The W axis is pointing upward from the surface, similar to the normal direction illustrated in Figure 11.1. These coordinates are prone to change based on the coordinate space and texture vectors, so in some cases, such as with environment projections, you may need to experiment with the values to determine which coordinates you want to adjust.

Image C demonstrates a scale transformation. The upper rotation matrix labeled A received the following values (note that the translation values have been reset to 0):

$$\begin{bmatrix} 2 & 0 & 0 & 0 \\ 0 & 2 & 0 & 0 \\ 0 & 0 & 1 & 0 \\ 0 & 0 & 0 & 1 \end{bmatrix}$$

As you can see, only the two relevant axes are changed from a value of 1 to 2. Notice that we don't use (change) the Z coordinate (r_{33}) because it is irrelevant to UV (2D) coordinates unless it is part of the projection plane (projections may utilize XY, XZ, or YZ axes). The texture appears to scale down 50 percent, aligned along the bottom-left corner of the plane (the coordinate system's origin point). In image D, the translation values changed to negative 0.5 for X and Y like this:

$$\begin{bmatrix} 2 & 0 & 0 & 0 \\ 0 & 2 & 0 & 0 \\ 0 & 0 & 1 & 0 \\ -0.5 & -0.5 & 0 & 1 \end{bmatrix}$$

As you can see, the texture shifted 50 percent along both coordinates, aligned in the center of the plane. Remember that the translation value ranges from 0 to 1, representing a percentage of the actual size of the texture. Thus, a value of 0.5 shifted the texture to the center, which is a 50 percent translation along each axis based on the new scaled-down texture size, however, that's only 25 percent of the overall surface area (on the polygon plane).

Homogeneous Scaling

I've mentioned that the homogeneous coordinate can be used for uniformly scaling the matrix. Set the translation matrix back to its default settings (diagonal line of 1s), and change the homogeneous coordinate (r_{44}) to 0.5 and 2, each time testing the result. You will see that a value of 0.5 scales the texture down by 50 percent, and a value of 2 doubles its size. This character is exactly the opposite of what we saw with the previous examples where we changed the transform coordinates to 2 and the texture scaled down. When the homogeneous coordinate is set to 2, the texture scales up. Furthermore, if you set the transforms (X and Y) to 0.5, you will restore the texture size relative to the surface plane. Here are the settings I used for the matrix to demonstrate the homogeneous coordinate scaling the texture down and the transform coordinates scaling it back up:

$$\begin{bmatrix} 0.5 & 0 & 0 & 0 \\ 0 & 0.5 & 0 & 0 \\ 0 & 0 & 1 & 0 \\ 0 & 0 & 0 & 0.5 \end{bmatrix}$$

Nonuniform Scaling

Figure 11.20 shows a nonuniform scale where the following values were used:

$$\begin{bmatrix} 1 & 0 & 0 & 0 \\ 0 & 3 & 0 & 0 \\ 0 & 0 & 1 & 0 \\ 0 & -1 & 0 & 1 \end{bmatrix}$$

As you can see, the X axis (U coordinate) is set at its normal scale of 1 (first row), and the Y axis (V coordinate) is set to 3, scaling it to one-third its size (second row). So, the transform value along the Y axis is set to -1, translating the texture to the center of the surface based on the texture's current size; a 100 percent translation along the V coordinate using the scaled down texture.

Figure 11.20

Nonuniform scaling with the rotation matrix

Understanding Scale Transformations

The mental ray texture 4D vector X, Y, Z, and 1 (the W homogeneous coordinate) output components are multiplied with the 4D transformation matrix labeled A in Figure 11.18, using matrix multiplication (shown earlier in Figure 11.7 A).

> When the transform matrix is set at the default, which is a square matrix with a diagonal line of 1s and 0s everywhere else, the matrix acts as an identity matrix that does not transform the incoming texture vector, as discussed earlier in this chapter.

The transform matrix can be considered a basis for vector transformations (rotation and scale) using the three unit vectors X, Y, and Z that are relative to a coordinate system. In Figure 11.21 a 2D coordinate system is drawn with a texture placed one unit away from the origin on the X and Y axes. The position vector is $\mathbf{v} = [1\ 1]$. It defines the distance from the origin to the texture boundaries on both X and Y axes using unit vectors.

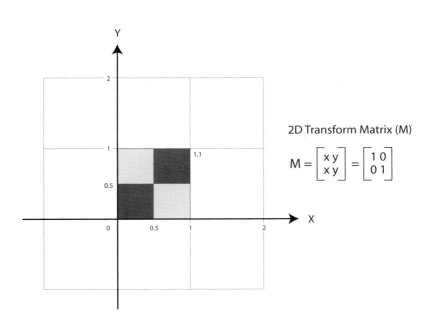

2D Transform Matrix (M)

$$M = \begin{bmatrix} x\ y \\ x\ y \end{bmatrix} = \begin{bmatrix} 1\ 0 \\ 0\ 1 \end{bmatrix}$$

Figure 11.21

The position vector [1, 1] relative to the 2D coordinate system defines the distance from the coordinate system's origin to the texture boundaries using two unit vectors.

If the matrix is set as an identity matrix (as shown in Figure 11.21), each component of the matrix represents a unit vector that is linearly aligned with an axis on the coordinate system. When the vector $\mathbf{v} = [x\ y]$ (equal to [1 1]) is multiplied by the matrix M ($\mathbf{v} \times M$), like this:

$$\mathbf{v}' = \begin{bmatrix} 1\ 1 \end{bmatrix} \times \begin{bmatrix} 1\ 0 \\ 0\ 1 \end{bmatrix} = \begin{bmatrix} (x \times 1) + (y \times 0) & (x \times 0) + (y \times 1) \end{bmatrix} = [1\ 1]$$

the result is a one-to-one mapping between the vector's X and Y components and the coordinate system unit vectors. In this case, when $\mathbf{v}$ transforms to $\mathbf{v}'$, it maintains its size. In all cases, a position vector ($\mathbf{v}$) defines a relative displacement from the origin using component vectors for each axis. These components are transformed using a matrix, or they remain unchanged. If we transform the vector $\mathbf{v}$ with a value of 2, we scale the texture relative to the coordinate system so that the vector $\mathbf{v} = [1\ 1]$ is multiplied by the transform matrix M like this:

$$\mathbf{v}' = \begin{bmatrix} 1\ 1 \end{bmatrix} \times \begin{bmatrix} 2\ 0 \\ 0\ 2 \end{bmatrix}$$

$$\mathbf{v}' = \begin{bmatrix} (1 \times 2) + (1 \times 0) & (1 \times 0) + (1 \times 2) \end{bmatrix} = [2\ 2]$$

This results in the transformed vector **v**′ that has doubled its magnitude while uniformly scaling the texture, as shown in Figure 11.22. Thus, if the magnitude of $|\mathbf{v}| = 1.414$ (based on the Pythagorean theorem), after matrix multiplication it proportionally increased to $|\mathbf{v}|' = 2.828$.

Figure 11.22

Transforming a position vector scales the vector components relative to the coordinate system's origin while proportionally increasing their magnitudes.

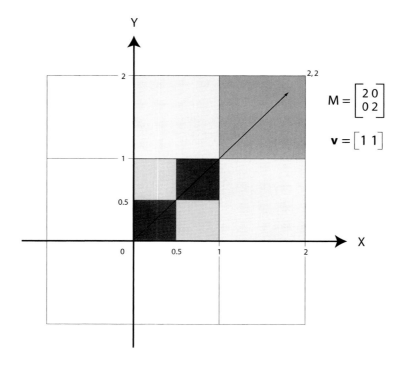

$$M = \begin{bmatrix} 2 & 0 \\ 0 & 2 \end{bmatrix}$$

$$\mathbf{v} = \begin{bmatrix} 1 & 1 \end{bmatrix}$$

Note that the examples presented here doubled the texture size. With mental ray, a value of 2 scaled the texture by half. This is a matter of implementation that should not concern you; as long as you understand that the relationship is reversed, you can control texture placement.

Rotating the Texture

To rotate the texture, you need to apply certain mathematical equations (discussed next) to derive the correct values for the transformation matrix. We will examine the rotation along the Z axis (pointing up from the plane) so that the texture rotates 45°. Remember that the axis you may require for rotating might differ with surfaces.

For rotations, you need to apply cosine and sine values for the desired angle of rotation as part of the translation matrix (Figure 11.18 image A). To rotate along the X, Y, and Z axes, use the following equations, where θ is the angle you require:

X rotation:

$$\begin{bmatrix} 1 & 0 & 0 & 0 \\ 0 & \cos(\theta) & \sin(\theta) & 0 \\ 0 & -\sin(\theta) & \cos(\theta) & 0 \\ 0 & 0 & 0 & 1 \end{bmatrix}$$

Y rotation:

$$\begin{bmatrix} \cos(\theta) & 0 & -\sin(\theta) & 0 \\ 0 & 1 & 0 & 0 \\ \sin(\theta) & 0 & \cos(\theta) & 0 \\ 0 & 0 & 0 & 1 \end{bmatrix}$$

Z rotation:

$$\begin{bmatrix} \cos(\theta) & \sin(\theta) & 0 & 0 \\ -\sin(\theta) & \cos(\theta) & 0 & 0 \\ 0 & 0 & 1 & 0 \\ 0 & 0 & 0 & 1 \end{bmatrix}$$

Figure 11.23 uses the following settings for a 45° Z rotation. As a result, the values used are the cosine and sine of 45°, which is 0.707 in both cases. Based on the equation shown above for Z rotations, I placed the values in the translation matrix as follows:

$$\begin{bmatrix} 0.707 & 0.707 & 0 & 0 \\ -0.707 & 0.707 & 0 & 0 \\ 0 & 0 & 1 & 0 \\ 0 & 0 & 0 & 1 \end{bmatrix}$$

As you can see, the texture has rotated 45°; however, we still need to fix the size and placement since the rotation pivoted around the bottom-left corner (the 0, 0 UV coordinate).

Figure 11.23

Rotating a texture using purely numerical input values

The transform matrix can rotate and scale a texture only relative to the coordinate origin and not from the center of the texture.

Understanding Matrix Rotations

If you consider magnitude as a shape of a curve on a coordinate system, then in the previous examples the curve increased its size proportionally relative to the origin while maintaining its form. The proportion of a vector's magnitude is the key element of rotations. Let's examine basic vector rotations in Figure 11.24.

Figure 11.24

2D rotational transformations of unit position vectors on both X and Y coordinates while maintaining their magnitudes

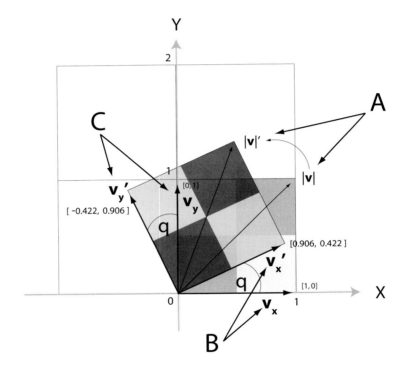

Consider the vectors **v** and **v**′ (labeled A), where the components of **v** are linearly aligned with the coordinate system. If we transform **v** to **v**′ with a 25° rotation, the component vectors ($\mathbf{v_x}$ and $\mathbf{v_y}$) labeled B and C change position, each graphed with new X and Y coordinates shown in Figure 11.24 (labeled B and C) with the transformed vectors $\mathbf{v_x}′$ and $\mathbf{v_y}′$. For **v** to maintain its form after the transformation, its magnitude should remain the same while transforming from **v** to **v**′; thus, the magnitude of **v** and **v**′ needs to stay the same so that you have this:

$$|\mathbf{v}| = |\mathbf{v}′|$$

To clarify, consider that the component vectors of **v** are in-fact unit vectors on the coordinate system, as shown in Figure 11.24, where each component vector has a magnitude of 1 on its relative axis; $|\mathbf{v}_x|$ = 1 on the X axis, and $|\mathbf{v}_y|$ =1 on the Y axis. After the transformation you see that the new component vectors of v´ ($\mathbf{v}_x$´ and $\mathbf{v}_y$´) have varying units on both X and Y coordinates (not linearly aligned with the coordinate system). In order for the newly transformed vector **v´** to maintain its shape after the transformation (rotation), the magnitudes of both component vectors also need to maintain the same value, in this case equal to 1; the transformed component vectors $\mathbf{v}_x$´ and $\mathbf{v}_y$´ magnitudes should also equal 1. As you can see in Figure 11.24, the new X and Y coordinates for **v´** component vectors are not equal to 1 on either axes, however, these values are not just erroneous values. In fact, by using basic trigonometry rules, the relationship between the rotation angle (25°) and the two component unit vectors magnitudes $|\mathbf{v}_x´|$ and $|\mathbf{v}_y´|$ are provided with the *cosine rule* that dictates the following:

$$\sin(\theta)^2 + \cos(\theta)^2 = 1$$

Based on the cosine rule you can see that the component vectors $\mathbf{v}_x$´ and $\mathbf{v}_y$´ are both equal to 1; the magnitude of 1 is preserved after the transformation and thus the texture will maintain its form, without distortion. Breaking these rules—when values (component vectors) don't maintain the same magnitude—will lead to distortion in the newly transformed shape. Thus selecting the correct values for component vector rotations becomes a matter of using cosine and sine values that when examined with the cosine rule add up to a value of 1. If we apply this rule to each unit vector's components ($\mathbf{v}_x$´ and $\mathbf{v}_y$´), we can preserve the magnitude of the unit vector **v´** while rotating the vector using correct XY coordinates for its components. So, the following equation is used to rotate (transform) **v** to **v´**:

$$\mathbf{v} \times M = \mathbf{v'}$$

$$\begin{bmatrix} x\ y \end{bmatrix} \times \begin{bmatrix} \cos(\theta) & \sin(\theta) \\ -\sin(\theta) & \cos(\theta) \end{bmatrix} = \mathbf{v'}$$

$$\mathbf{v'}_{x1,\,x2} \qquad \mathbf{v'}_{y1,\,y2}$$

$$\mathbf{v'} = [\, x \times \cos(\theta) + y \times (-\sin(\theta)) \quad x \times \sin(\theta) + y \times \cos(\theta) \,]$$

You can see that after transforming a vector with the matrix of **v´** are actually dot product equations (see Figure 11.7). Thus, each component vector ($\mathbf{v}_x$' and $\mathbf{v}_y$') has its own X and Y coordinates as subcomponents of the vector **v´**. You can see these in the dot product of each component, and for clarity they are referred to in the equations using two lines from $\mathbf{v}'_{x1, x2}$ and $\mathbf{v}'_{y1, y2}$. While examining them as separate components, their numerical values, based on the cosine and sine of 25°, result in the following:

$$\sin(25) = 0.422$$
$$\cos(25) = 0.906$$

$$\mathbf{v_x}' = [\, x \quad y \,] = [\, \cos(\theta) \quad \sin(\theta) \,] = [\, 0.906 \quad 0.422 \,]$$
$$\mathbf{v_y}' = [\, x \quad y \,] = [\, -\sin(\theta) \quad \cos(\theta) \,] = [\, -0.422 \quad 0.906 \,]$$

If you refer to Figure 11.24, you can see that these coordinates are used for both the unit vectors $\mathbf{v_x}'$ and $\mathbf{v_x}'$, placing them correctly while maintaining a magnitude of 1 for the vector $\mathbf{v}'$ and thus maintaining the texture size. We can see that the magnitude is preserved when we solve the magnitude of each component vector and then the magnitude of $\mathbf{v}'$ like this:

$$|\mathbf{v}'_x| = \sqrt{0.906^2 + 0.422^2} = 1 \qquad |\mathbf{v}'_y| = \sqrt{0.422^2 + 0.906^2} = 1$$

$$|\mathbf{v}'| = \sqrt{|\mathbf{v}'_x|^2 + |\mathbf{v}'_x|^2} = \sqrt{1^2 + 1^2} = 1.414$$

Notice that each component vector is a unit vector based on the cosine rule. If we perform the dot product equation for the two unit vectors of $\mathbf{v}'$, the result reflects on the angle between them, and based on the Pythagorean theorem, it should prove to be 90° since they should be perpendicular axes that define the bounding box of a square texture, as shown here:

$$\mathbf{v}'_x \bullet \mathbf{v}'_y = (0.906 \times (-0.422)) + (0.422 \times 0.906) = (-0.382) + 0.382 = 0$$

$$\cos(\theta) = \frac{\mathbf{v}'_x \cdot \mathbf{v}'_y}{|\mathbf{v}'_x| \times |\mathbf{v}'_y|} = \frac{0}{1 \times 1} = 0$$

$$\theta = \cos^{-1}(0) = 90° \quad \longleftarrow$$

A key character of matrix math based on the cosine rule is as follows: if you square all the values along any of the rows or columns of a matrix, you always end up with a value equal to 1. Therefore, you have $r_{11}^2 \times r_{12}^2 \times r_{13}^2 = 1$ and $r_{12}^2 \times r_{22}^2 \times r_{32}^2 = 1$. If we check it with our example, we can see that it is true:

$$\begin{bmatrix} 0.906^2 + 0.422^2 & = 1 \\ + \qquad + & \\ -0.422^2 + 0.906^2 & = 1 \\ \| \qquad \| & \\ 1 \qquad 1 & \end{bmatrix}$$

This matrix characteristic is important in selecting correct values for the transform matrix rotations. If your values don't add up correctly, they are inaccurate, and you will get the wrong results. These values may exceed 1 when we factor in scaling and translations, as discussed soon. In the earlier examples, the cosine and sine values are not displayed at full numerical precision so that the equation adds up to less than 1; however, at full precision (for cosine and sine values), they do add up to 1.

Rotation and Scaling

To change the size of the texture (after rotations) shown in the previous examples (Figure 11.23), you need to apply matrix multiplication. I will show you two approaches, one based on evaluating the numbers yourself and the other based on piping additional texture remap shaders consecutively for a more simplistic approach. Let's make the texture 50 percent smaller, as when specifying a value of 2 for the X and Y axes, as in the previous examples, using the following equation. Note that s is the new scale multiplied by the cosine or sine of a given angle (a uniform scale and rotation), and the example shown here skips many stages to present a simplistic approach that works:

$$
\begin{bmatrix}
s \times \cos(\theta) & s \times \sin(\theta) & 0 & 0 \\
s \times (-\sin(\theta)) & s \times \cos(\theta) & 0 & 0 \\
0 & 0 & 1 & 0 \\
0 & 0 & 0 & 1
\end{bmatrix}
$$

Since the cosine and sine for 45 is 0.707, the same number has been used in all cases, based on the Z rotation equation presented earlier. When multiplied by 2, the result is 1.414, as used in the following matrix:

$$
\begin{bmatrix}
1.414 & 1.414 & 0 & 0 \\
-1.414 & 1.414 & 0 & 0 \\
0 & 0 & 1 & 0 \\
0.45 & -0.85 & 0 & 1
\end{bmatrix}
$$

Notice that the third row's scale value can remain at one, because it doesn't affect orientation and scaling in this case (the Z axis). Figure 11.25 shows a 45° rotation and a 50 percent scale after applying the new matrix. Also, notice the transform values added in the bottom row are used to push the texture to the center of the surface. Because combining different matrices (translation and rotation) with matrix multiplication is not commutative ($a \times b \neq b \times a$), you will always need to find the correct translation values after applying the rotation and scaling, as discussed next.

Figure 11.25

Rotating, scaling, and translating a texture using the translation matrix

Figure 11.25

Rotating, scaling, and translating a texture using the translation matrix

Translation After Rotation and Scaling

Consider that the translation evaluates after the matrix rotates and scales the texture. As a result, if the X, Y component vectors for the texture transform with the texture, just as with local space axes of an object in 3D, then the textures translation axes actually change direction after rotations. So, the component X and Y vectors that push the texture along U and V coordinates, as shown in the previous examples, will now (after a 45° rotation) translate the texture in diagonal lines across the surface.

> Look at Figure 11.30 (an XSI screenshot) in the section "The Translation Matrix in XSI" later in this chapter to see a 3D visual representation of the texture projection and remap shaders. Notice that the translation arrows labeled C and D have rotated with the texture placement labeled B.

Combining Rotations and Scaling with Individual Shaders

As cited earlier, you don't have to apply matrix multiplication manually to rotate, scale, and translate the texture; instead, you can connect individual texture remap shaders, as shown in the shader graph in Figure 11.26. Each shader provides some form of transformation or translation. The outValue from one texture remap shader connects to the coordinate input of the following one. In this way, they form a chain of matrix operations that initiate with a texture vector shader (labeled A), extracting the initial coordinates, and then gradually transform the coordinates as they are passed through four texture remap shaders consecutively, labeled B, C, D, and E. To make the example a bit more advanced, we also consider that we want to rotate the texture from the center of the image, offsetting the origin point for the transforms. This enables us to rotate the image as if it is locked in place (from its center), rather than estimating a translation value (or doing the math) as we did in the previous example.

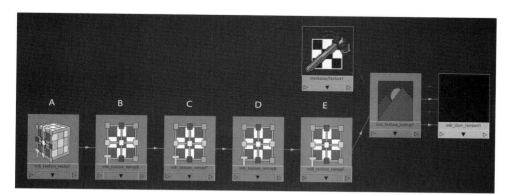

Figure 11.26

Applying consecutive texture remap shaders in a shader network, letting mental ray handle the matrix multiplication for you

If you look at Figure 11.27, you can see the result of each step using labels that correspond to the same labels (steps) in Figure 11.26. The values used for the translation matrix are shown in Figure 11.27 for each step. The first texture vector shader, labeled A, derives the explicit UVW texture vectors, providing a one-to-one mapping between the texture and the polygon surface. The following remap shader, labeled B, applies a translation moving the texture 50 percent on both the X and Y coordinates so that the origin is centered in the plane. Areas that appear black on the polygon surface are outside the projection region. The remap shader labeled C applies a 50 percent scale using a value of 2 for the X and Y coordinates. Currently, you can see the texture in the upper-right corner and its origin point located at the center of the polygon plane. The step labeled D applies a Z rotation of 45°. The cosine and sine are equally set to 0.707. We can see that the texture rotated from the center of the polygon 45° to the left. The final texture remap shader, labeled E, applies the inverse translation of the first translation (B), which pushes the texture back so that it is centered.

You can see that if you want to rotate a texture with the translation matrix around a given point, you first need to place the origin (for the transformations) at that point, the new center of rotation. You then apply the transformations, and when you are done, you backtrack and push the texture to its place using the inverse of the first translation. If you test this with different rotational values, saving an image each time, you will see the texture rotate around the center point.

As you can see, you may apply several shaders consecutively so that they apply the matrix math internally. In such cases, you need to make sure that only the last shader (that connects to the image lookup shader) applies repeats, alternating, and torus wrapping. Therefore, the remap shaders B, C, and D all have their repeats set to 1, and the Alt and Torus attributes are disabled.

Figure 11.27

Viewing the rendered result of each texture remap shader's transform with the values used for the translation matrix

Host Application Settings

The following sections cover each host's relevant texture vector and remapping options, as well as their methods for defining UV sets. The goal is to outline the relationship between mental ray texturing and host applications. Note that the sections devoted to UV sets are a critical prerequisite for texture / light baking, a topic discussed in the "HDRI_3D_Issue7_ Mental Ray" article on the CD.

Maya

With Maya, a problem arises when you want to use mental ray–specific textures. For example, there are image loaders, procedural textures, or custom shaders that all require texture coordinates and remapping (2D placement). These textures don't always cooperate with Maya-specific shaders (the Maya 2D and 3D placement nodes and projections), so you are forced to use the mental ray texture vector and remap shaders, such as with the brushed metal tutorial in Chapter 10.

The earlier examples demonstrated the process of using mental ray textures.

Note that you can use Maya textures (and an image loader) to connect to any mental ray shader, such as mib_illum_lambert, Phong, and so forth, using Maya-specific 2D and 3D texture placement shaders. The differences discussed here refer to using mental ray textures as opposed to Maya textures. For example, a mental ray mib_texture_polkadot shader requires you to connect the mib_texture_vector to a mib_texture_remap and then the remap to the Coord input of the mib_texture_polkadot, as demonstrated earlier in this chapter in the section "mental ray Network Connections."

In most cases, you can avoid using the mental ray image loader with mental texture coordinates by using Maya's File shader. However, if you want to use elliptical filtering, which is discussed in the following section, you would have to create the same network shown earlier in Figure 11.4.

Maya UV Sets

When you create UV coordinates in Maya in the Polygons menu set under the Create UVs menu, you can select various types of explicit projection methods (that is, planar, spherical, automatic, and other projections). If you open the options window for any projection method, you will see the Create New UV Set checkbox and text input, as shown in Figure 11.28.

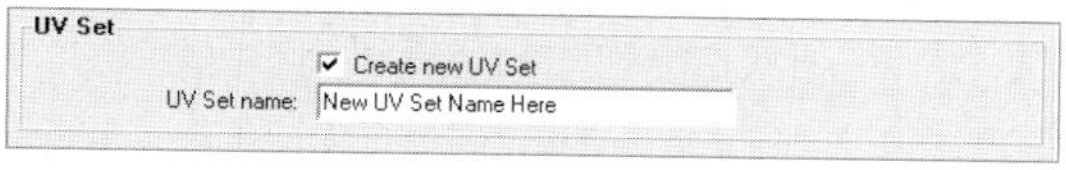

Figure 11.28

Creating new UV sets in Maya with projections

When this option is disabled, the projections always override the default layout; however, if you specify a unique name, then an additional projection is created. You can see the projections by selecting Window → Relationship Editors → UV Linking → UV-Centric or Texture-Centric for a selected polygon surface. You can also see them, and their layouts, in the UV Texture Editor window when selecting a specific set from the UV Sets menu. Their order of appearance under the UV Sets menu is based on the order of creation and directly corresponds to the mib_texture_vector Select attribute number. Therefore, the first default set is specified with the default value of 0 (first explicit UV set), the next set uses a Select value of 1, and so forth.

XSI

As you can see, the mental ray shaders are not very intuitive, so XSI has wrapped around them more user-friendly options that make them more readable. In the following sections, XSI shaders are covered with references to their properties, and the equivalent mental ray options are discussed throughout the chapter.

XSI integrates the texture vector and remapping shaders by means of projection shaders into most texture shaders and the image shader (image loader). The Texture_space_generator shader found in the Render Tree window under Nodes → Texture Space Generators → Generator (v) offers the same properties as the texture vector shader but is not commonly used. You already saw an example for using this shader in the section "The Texture Vector and Remap Shaders" earlier in this chapter. Under the same menu you can find the Projection (v) shader, shown in Figure 11.29, which is a far better implementation for applying texture vectors and remapping in XSI.

Figure 11.29

The XSI texture projection shader is equivalent to the mental ray texture remap shader.

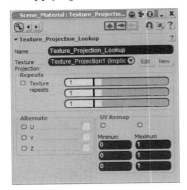

As a matter of convenience, the projection shader is already implemented into most XSI texture shaders. However, if you want to access texture coordinates for other purposes, such as those shown in the brushed metal tutorial in Chapter 11, you can use this projection shader to define texture coordinates and then manually connect it to other shaders, as shown in the shader graph in Figure 11.5. In Figure 11.12 and Figure 11.17 (labeled A), the generator shader is used in a similar fashion to extract implicit coordinates.

Texture Coordinates

A surface material may have several textures that require independent texture coordinates, as cited earlier. The projection properties enable you to specify, on a per-texture basis, independent texture coordinates.

In Figure 11.29 you can see that the projection shader offers most of the properties found with the mental ray texture remap shader, including texture repeats, alternating, and cropping. The torus (wrapping), offset, and rotation matrix that are missing can be accessed after you define texture coordinates using the Texture Projection property (labeled Texture Space with other shaders).

The mental ray Select option is controlled with the Texture Projection drop-down list. When you click the New button, a texture projection (with texture support) is created and added to the list. This list represents the different UV layouts (UV sets) that are available for a given shader. By default, projections are explicit UV coordinates that can be further edited in the projection's properties window after clicking the Edit button (see Figure 11.31 in the next section). With explicit projections, the UV placement can also be manually edited in the Texture Editor window.

Essentially, every new texture projection acts as a separate UV set that can either be explicit or implicit. The Texture Projection property allows you to select which UV set should be used for a given texture, as does the mental ray Select option. The only difference is that you then further control the explicit or implicit properties (equivalent to the Select option's negative values) internally, within the projection's properties, as you will soon see.

The Translation Matrix in XSI

When you create a new projection (by clicking the New button), a geometric projection is created within the 3D viewport, as shown in Figure 11.30 label A. The projection also includes a texture support, labeled B. To see the texture support, select the projection, and press the J shortcut key. The texture support controls the translation matrix, enabling you to adjust the texture placement within the projection boundaries. While you're manipulating the texture support (B), the texture coordinates (shown in the Texture Editor) maintain their same UV layout. Thus, the image itself scales, rotates, and translates. However, when you move the texture projection (A), the UVs update in the Texture Editor window, redefining their explicit layout.

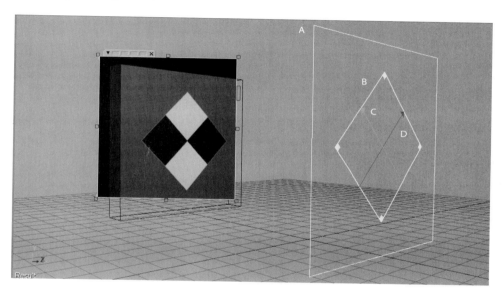

Figure 11.30

A planar projection with its projection support displayed in the XSI viewport

Notice how a checkered image file is scaled down, oriented, and centered (as with the examples in the section "The Texture Remap Shader" earlier in this chapter) using the XSI texture support, which is the translation matrix.

As a follow-up to the discussion of translation after orientation in the section "The Texture Remap Shader" earlier in the chapter, notice how the texture support translation arrows labeled C and D indicate diagonal translation directions for the X and Y axes, which is a result of rotating the texture support 45°. So, the texture support now translates diagonally. The gray color shown outside the texture support borders in the render region is derived from a mix shader that is masked to affect areas outside the texture region.

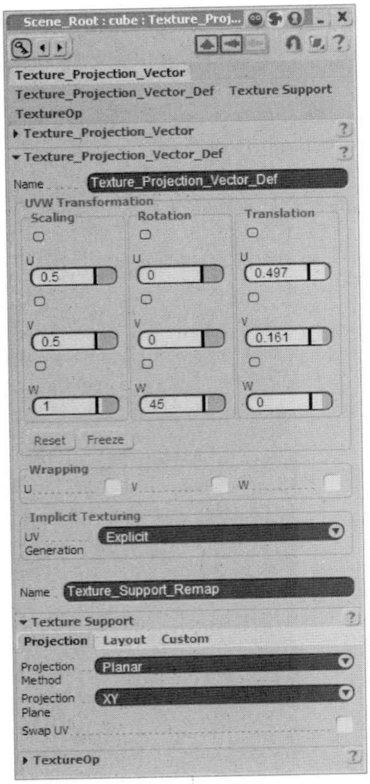

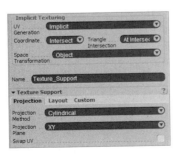

Figure 11.31

The XSI projection properties used to define explicit vs. implicit properties and the translation matrix

In Figure 11.31 you can see the texture projection options used in this case. One method for viewing these settings is to click the Edit button under the projection shader's Texture Projection property. Notice the UVW Transformation properties section. This section is equivalent to the translation matrix discussed earlier. The values you see for the Scaling, Rotation, and Translation properties are derived based on the manipulations you apply visually in the viewport, and they update automatically. Thus, you can adjust the translation matrix either using these properties or manually in the viewport (only with explicit projections). The values you enter here for rotation are easier to interpret then those discussed in previous sections with matrix math. For example, you can see that the Rotation → W property is set with a value of 45 providing a 45° rotation—which is much easier than using sine or cosine values with the mental ray remap shader. Notice that you can also see the Wrapping property in this window (torus XYZ).

Explicit vs. Implicit Properties

You can find most of the mental ray texture vector shader's options for explicit and implicit projections in the Implicit Texturing section and in the Texture Support rollout shown in Figure 11.31.

The Implicit Texturing → UV Generation property defines whether the projection is implicit or explicit. By default, all projections are set to Explicit. If you create a new projection from the projection shader's Texture Projection → New property, you can then set the UV Generation property to Implicit. You are not required to create a new projection in order to select Implicit; however, if you manually edit a texture support in the viewport or Texture Editor window, those coordinates must remain explicit, and hence a new projection is required.

IMPLICIT PROPERTIES

Implicit projections don't have the texture support that explicit projections have. You can change the projector's shape by transforming it in the viewport (Figure 11.30 image A) and manually entering values for the UVW Transformation properties; however, you will not have a texture support manipulator in the viewport as you do with explicit projections.

When the UV Generation property is set to Implicit, you can see that additional properties appear, as shown in Figure 11.32, that correlate to our previous discussions of the mental ray texture vector shader. These properties include the Coordinate property equivalent to the Select option's negative values. If you look in the drop-down list, you can see the same options as listed in Table 11.1 earlier in this chapter. The Space Transformation property corresponds to the Selspace option discussed earlier, offering the same options for defining the coordinate space (world, object, and so on) for a projection.

Figure 11.32

Implicit texture projections properties for a given projection shown in XSI

The mental ray Project option is implemented as the Texture Support → Projection tab → Projection Method property that defines the type of projection. The Projection Plane property is used to define the projection plane (axis). This option is mostly used for defining XY, XZ, and YZ planar projections.

XSI Textures

XSI textures, such as the Checkerboard and Image textures, allow you to define explicit or implicit texture projections from their Texture tabs using the Texture Space → New button (the Texture Projection property discussed earlier). When you create a projection, you can see the same properties shown in Figure 11.31 that encompass the options for both mental ray texture vector and remap shaders. Essentially, this enables creating projections internally within a texture rather than with an external projection shader; delete, they are the same.

3ds Max

In 3ds Max you apply and use textures solely via native 3ds Max shaders. In fact, 3ds Max texture coordinates are built into the image loader (bitmap shader) and texture shaders, including most of the options found with both mental ray texture vector and remap shaders. Thus, you are not required to use mental ray–specific shaders while defining texture coordinates and placement. When you export a 3ds Max scene for rendering, or as a .mi file, the 3ds Max UV generator shader provides all the same functionalities as those discussed throughout the chapter, supporting all the mental ray textures that ship with 3ds Max, as well as custom shaders for 3ds Max (from online resources).

Essentially you are not required to specifically use the UV generator (3ds Max) shader, which can be found in the Material/Map Browser window. This shader, however, is always exported as a custom shader that provides mental ray texture coordinates and remapping options.

Built-in Explicit and Implicit Coordinates

Let's first examine the straightforward approach, using the parameters found in the Material Editor window for a given texture (bitmap or procedural texture) under the Coordinates rollout parameters, as shown in Figure 11.33.

With 3ds Max, the choice of explicit or implicit projections respectively correlates to using a texture map or environment map. The Texture radio button shown selected in Figure 11.33 defines explicit coordinates, such as with the mental ray texture vector Select option. If you select the Environ radio button instead, then the projections are implicit. Once you select a projection method, the Mapping drop-down list offers additional parameters for selecting the

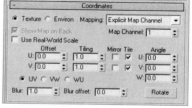

Figure 11.33

3ds Max projection options for a given texture in the Material Editor. These parameters are similar to the texture vector and remap shaders; they provide a straightforward approach for selecting UV coordinates and mapping textures.

projection type. When Environ is selected, the Mapping list includes some common implicit projection methods such as spherical or cylindrical.

With respect to the texture remap shader, notice how all its options are found under the Coordinate rollout. These include the Offset, Tiling (repeats), Mirror (alternating), and Tile (torus) parameters. You can also easily rotate the texture using the Angle UVW parameters, which correlates to the translation matrix discussed earlier.

Explicit UVW Mapping and UV Sets

When you select a polygon object (Editable Mesh), you can add explicit UV coordinates using a variety of modifiers from the modifier stack. The same modifiers are also available from the menu by choosing Modifier → UV Coordinates. All these modifiers use the same parameter to select a UV set, labeled Map Channel or just Channel. This parameter defines the UV sets in numbered sequences, corresponding to the texture vector Select option. Conveniently, the sequence is numbered from 1 and up, similar to the Select option that uses values from 0 and up.

Under the Coordinates rollout, when the Texture parameter is selected, you can specify the Explicit Map Channel option from the Mapping drop-down list, as shown in Figure 11.33. This allows you to select a UV set number with the Map Channel parameter. Therefore, every UV modifier that is added to the modifier's stack can be set with a unique UV channel that provides a given UV layout (texture coordinates), for a texture map or image file. These options become more relevant when you want to combine textures using separate UV layouts.

The two modifiers I want to discuss are UVW Map and Unwrap UVW. Both modifiers allow you to select a map channel, so you may create several modifiers and assign each with a different map channel. Also, both modifiers create explicit UV coordinates; however, one has a more implicit approach, and the other has a more explicit approach.

THE UVW MAP MODIFIER

With the UVW Map modifier, under the Parameters rollout, you can select a type of implicit projection (planar, spherical, box, and so on). A projection gizmo that identifies the selected projection shape appears in the viewport, similar to the shapes shown in Figure 11.1 earlier in this chapter.

These projections, their scale, their orientation, and their placement define the UV coordinates that will be exported as explicit UV coordinates. To clarify, where a solely implicit projection can project an image without distortion across a surface with few polygon triangles, as shown in Figure 11.34 image A, an explicit projection will try fitting the projection onto the available polygon faces. And, when not enough are available, the image is distorted as shown in image B. Thus, both images A and B used the same UVW Map modifier, with the difference that the cube labeled A has a high-resolution mesh, and the cube labeled B has a single face for each side. You can see that the UVW Map modifier exports explicit coordinates. If it were solely implicit, the result for a low vs. high resolution model would appear the same; as with label A.

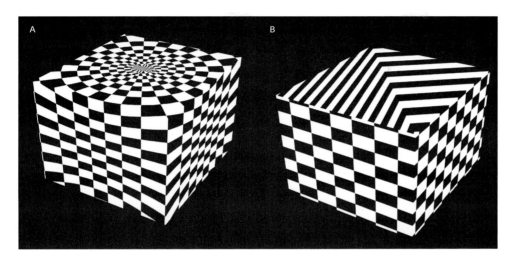

Figure 11.34

Projecting with the UVW Map modifier on a high-resolution cube (A) and low-resolution cube (B)

THE UNWRAP UVW MODIFIER

The Unwrap UVW modifier provides a more common approach to specifying UV coordinates, where you can select a base projection technique and then further modify its UVW coordinates in the Edit UVWs window. To open this window, click the Edit button in the Parameters rollout. You can use the Map Channel parameter to define the UV set number, as discussed earlier. When the Face mode is enabled, under the Unwrap UVW modifier in the modifier list, you can then specify a base projection method for the selected face (you must select the faces in the viewport) under the Map Parameters rollout. The result is automatically updated in the Edit UVWs window, where you can see the selected faces, and their respective UVW coordinates unwrap.

So, the Unwrap UVW modifier provides a means for creating and editing UVW layouts within a UV texture editor, opposed to the UVW Map modifier that is aimed at using a more implicit approach to define explicit UVW coordinates.

The UV Generator

When you export an .mi file from 3ds Max, you can then examine the different custom shaders that export for a given surface. In this case, I will compare the two explicit modifiers discussed earlier (UVW Map and Unwrap UVW) and an implicit environment projection, selected under the Coordinates rollout shown in Figure 11.33. As cited earlier, every time a file is exported (or rendered), the 3ds Max UV generator shader is used to define the texture coordinates. As you can see in the following excerpt, the `"max_base_UVGenerator"` shader is created and labeled `"UVGen_Shader"`. I have included only a few lines that demonstrate explicit or implicit options.

```
shader "UVGen_Shader" "max_base_UVGenerator" (
            "MapSlotType" 0,
            "EnvType" 1,
            "MapChannel" 1,
            "UVWSource" 0,
            "UOffset" 0,
            "UScale" 10,
            "UWrap" on,
            "UMirror" off,
            "UAngle" 0,
```

The `MapSlotType` parameter defines whether the coordinates are explicit or implicit. A value of 0 refers to the Texture parameter (explicit), and a value of 1 selects the Environ parameter (implicit), both shown in Figure 11.33. The `EnvType` parameter simply selects the type of projection when using implicit projections, as with the Mapping parameter, so in this case (explicit), it has no effect. `MapChannel` selects the explicit UV set, with the Map Channel parameter. If you look at some of the following parameters in the excerpt, you can see how they relate to remapping options, such as tiling, alternating, rotating, and so forth. Thus, this shader encompasses texture vector and remap options, geared for 3ds Max shaders.

In the following excerpt, you can see how the UV generator shader connects to the coordinate input (`"Coords"`) of a texture file, just as with the shader trees demonstrated earlier in the chapter. The following excerpt excludes the other options for simplicity. Of course, you can export .mi files and see the full range of options and how they export.

```
shader "Map #3|Texmap" "max_Bitmap" (
            "Parameters" {
            "Coords" "|UVGen|Shader",
```

Let's take a brief look at the following excerpt, another UV generator used for implicit projections:

```
shader "|UVGen|Shader" "max_base_UVGenerator" (
            "MapSlotType" 1,
            "EnvType" 1,
            "MapChannel" 1,
```

Notice that in this case the `MapSlotType` parameter is set to 1 and selects the Environ parameter, and the `EnvType` selects a spherical projection using a value of 1. In this case, it has an effect because the projection is implicit.

Examining these shaders should give you a clearer picture of how 3ds Max and mental ray interact with respect to texturing; fortunately, their compatibility allows you to easily define coordinates within the host.

Memory Mapping, Pyramid Images, and Image Filtering

The following sections look at image filtering techniques, pyramid images, and memory-mapped images. The mental ray image loader and lookup shaders allow you to load and filter images. Pyramid images are precalculated multiresolution images that are used for improving image filtering processing. Memory-mapped images simply improve memory handling during rendering, particularly when loading pyramid image data into memory. In some cases, these techniques are intended to improve on the default *point sampling* approach for acquiring surface shading values; in others, the purpose is to improve the general workflow with respect to image processing and memory optimization. Typically you would use a memory-mapped pyramid image with standard or elliptical filtering for the purpose of texture mapping.

Point Sampling

During rendering, when textures or image files are used to provide color values for a surface, those value are evaluated using *point sampling*. This term refers to how each sample block (discussed in Chapter 5, "Quality Control") looks up color values for a given shaded point within a texture file and at specific texture space coordinates. Each sample point interpolates color values using four nearby pixels at the sample location in texture space, determining a color value.

Figure 11.35 illustrates the process of point sampling values from texture files and passing them to the frame buffer pixels. Under the "Camera view" label, you can see the resolution for this shot (exaggerated for the purpose of discussion). Each illustrated square is equal to one pixel in size, and each square in the checkered texture on the floor represents a pixel in the texture file, so theoretically you are looking at this scene at a microscopic level. The point samples (white circles) illustrated in the four rows (numbered 1 through 4) can be seen under the scene layout, in the camera view, and at their 2D (UV) texture space coordinates in the texture file, under the "Texture space/sample spread" label.

Render and Texture Pixel (Texel) Ratios

Point sampling provides an efficient approach to interpreting color values from a texture file, but only if the texture pixels, known as *texels*, occupy roughly the same amount of pixels in the rendered image. When there is roughly a one-to-one mapping between texture pixels and render pixels, then point sampling, combined with a render filtering technique (reviewed in Chapter 5), can provide fairly decent consistent color results. The relationship between render pixels and texture pixels directly influences the sample accuracy and color consistency in animations. When a single render pixel corresponds to several pixels within an image file, as illustrated in Figure 11.35 along the third and fourth rows, certain problems arise.

Figure 11.35

Point samples are
taken at increasingly
farther distances on
a texture.

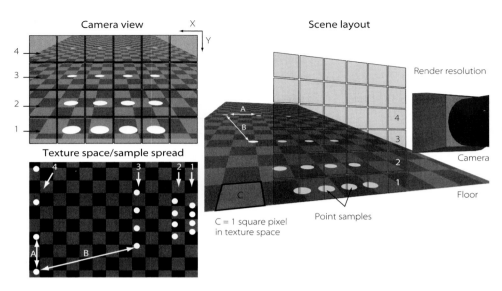

Notice how the texels (checker squares) shown in the camera view for the first and second rows have a relatively close mapping. To clarify, there are roughly four pixels for each render pixel, and because point samples interpolate values using four adjacent pixels, the results are fairly accurate, meaning they are derived using all the texels found within that pixel's line of sight. However, in the third and fourth rows, the point samples don't account for several other texels that are seen within a given render pixel's perspective. Poor mapping between texels and render pixels has two primary results:

- The sample point locations cover a limited amount of texels per render pixel, as cited earlier.

- The sample locations are spaced too far apart to provide accurate results on the values between them, as indicated with the distance labeled A. The distance labeled B demonstrates an even larger gap between the samples along the third and fourth rows. Since point sampling samples the color only directly at sample coordinates, when the next closest (neighboring) sample location is several pixels away, accuracy is significantly compromised, not accounting for entire regions (between samples) of the texture. Essentially, important color information will not be interpolated, and the image is prone to all sorts of motion and visual artifacts (moiré patterns).

When surfaces appear at glancing angles, as shown in the figure, transitioning in depth away from the camera increases the ratio between texels and render pixels. As a result, at a given distance, a render pixel may encompass more than 100 texels but contributes only four texels for the sample's color interpolation. The result of poor sample coverage leads to inconsistent color artifacts, such as sampling a checker texture's white checkers along a given row and constantly missing the black checkers. Clearly, the result is not an accurate representation for the appearance of a checker texture converging in depth.

Motion Artifacts

When we factor in motion, we consider that during the next animation frame, a new set of samples may look up different texture coordinates, because something is in motion (surfaces or the camera) and the sample location aligns with new UV texture coordinates, such as along the distances labeled A and B in Figure 11.35. Therefore, the next set of samples will most likely interpolate completely different texture values, providing a color that does not follow up on the previous sample values (from the previous frame). The result of poor sample consistency between frames is typically shown as texture shimmering during the animation. Thus, because point sampling looks up only a very small pixel region in the texture file, the point sampling process becomes "unstable" for animation, returning erroneous inconstant values for each frame.

Because resolving image artifacts with motion or still images is not entirely dependent on antialiasing and filtering techniques (discussed in Chapter 5), increasing the sampling quality may provide for better results, but it typically will not suffice for eliminating artifacts such as moiré patterns or motion artifacts (flickering and jittering of the texture pixels). By now you should have a clearer picture of antialiasing sampling and its relationship to point sampling.

> When you increase the antialiasing sampling (oversampling), you improve render quality, but that still leaves room for several missed texture pixels. The answer is a combination of good sampling settings, as well as using image filtering to interpolate larger texture pixel regions on a per-sample basis.

Image Filtering

Filtering is a means for averaging (interpolating) color value within the texture file across several pixels. Note the difference between image filtering (discussed here) and the render filtering process discussed in Chapter 5. With image filtering, point samples are given a radius (filters are round) that interpolates color across several texels. Because more texels are used, the result is a more accurate color value that decreases the chances of shimmering in animation.

As surfaces in the scene get farther away from the camera, they require larger filter sizes to interpolate the result. Fortunately, filter sizes tend to scale up with distance, as shown in Figure 11.36. By doing so, the filtering process ideally tries to maintain the relationship between texels and render pixel sizes by filtering a number of texels that correlate to a given render pixel size.

Figure 11.36

Image filtering offers an alternative to point sampling, utilizing round filters of varying scales and interpolating color from several texture pixels

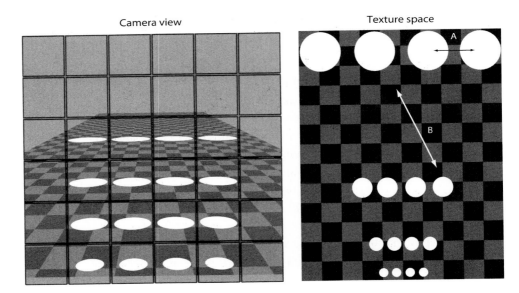

Camera view   Texture space

In the camera view, you can see that for each row, the filter size increases to try to encompass all the texels within that row (along the U coordinate). Therefore, if you look at the same samples in the texture space image, you see that the round filters are significantly larger with distance, containing more texels. If you look at both images, you can tell that the filter radius scale better represents the increased ratio between texels and render pixels, leaving fewer gaps between samples in a given row (U coordinate), as shown with the label A. However, these round filters still have significant gaps between the rows along the V coordinate, as illustrated with the distance labeled B.

Since the floor in the image is at a steep glancing angle, these larger filters cope effectively with pixels only along the U coordinate. However, they can't effectively deal with the gaps along the V coordinate, because the distances are nonuniform. Round filters can cope effectively only with uniform distances. Thus, filtering, as with point sampling, copes well with images that have some proportional uniform relationship between texels and render pixels. At glancing angles, with nonuniform relationships between texels and render pixels, round filtering fails. For coping with nonuniform ratios along U and V coordinates, mental ray provides an alternative filtering technique known as *elliptical filtering*.

mental ray Filter Options

With mental ray, standard filtering is applied through the mental ray texture shader, which simply loads images from files. A filter option determines the size of the filter, where a value of 1 determines a best-guess size automatically. If the filter option is disabled, then only point sampling is used. The filter size value is meant to provide mental ray with additional insight into the relationship between texels and render pixels, where the filter size ideally represents the relationship between one render pixel and the number of texels contained within it (in the render pixel).

Essentially, you may use a texture image that has been tiled several times using the remapping shader. So, as the ratio between the texture and render pixels increases, so should the filter size. In such cases you would want to specify a filter size that represents the new resized texture. For example, if the checker texture has a one-to-one mapping with render pixels (not tiled), then after tiling it 50 times, effectively scaling it down by 1 ÷ 50 of its size, you should specify a filter radius of 50 correlating to the new proportions. By default mental ray assumes that one texel corresponds to one render pixel; it has no knowledge of tilling. As a surface gets farther away, a larger filter size is used. By manually specifying larger filter sizes, you provide information about the relationship between texels and render pixels, such as after tilling an image several times.

> Although 3ds Max provides an option to enable or disable filtering (via a bitmap shader's Bitmap Parameters → Filtering), it does not offer mental ray's elliptical filtering with the options discussed in the following sections.

You can find the filter attribute for each host as follows:

Maya With Maya, in the Hypershade window, select the mental ray texture shader (shown in Figure 11.4 labeled D) from under the Textures rollout. The Filter checkbox attribute enables filtering, and the Filter Size attribute specifies the filter radius as discussed earlier.

XSI With XSI, when you load a new image, under the Image Clip → Texturing tab → Mental Ray Multi-Resolution Texture section, you can use the Blurring property to define the filter size. The Enable Multi-Resolution Texture checkbox property also needs to be enabled, turning on pyramid filtering.

> When filtering is enabled, mental ray automatically generates pyramid (multiresolution) images.

Elliptical Filtering

Elliptical filtering is an alternative to standard filtering that is more effective at reducing texture shimmering and moiré pattern artifacts in highly detailed (or tilable) textures, particularly with surfaces seen at glancing angles. In Figure 11.37, notice how the filter shapes seen in the scene layout appear as ellipses at increasing scales. Also, notice that the filter shape shown in the camera view appears relatively round, opposed to the shapes shown in Figure 11.36 where the filter shape looks like an ellipse. Essentially, round filters projected on surfaces that are at glancing angles, appear as horizontal ellipses in the camera view; they are aligned with the surface orientation. If we force round filters to encompass a render pixel, while projecting on a surface that is at a glancing angle, the round filter projects an elliptical shape as shown in Figure 11.37, maximizing its coverage in the render pixel; the filter maintains a round shape in the camera views and projects as an ellipse on the surface, as shown in Figure 11.37.

Figure 11.37

Elliptical filtering is used to cope with a nonuniform relationship between texels and render pixels.

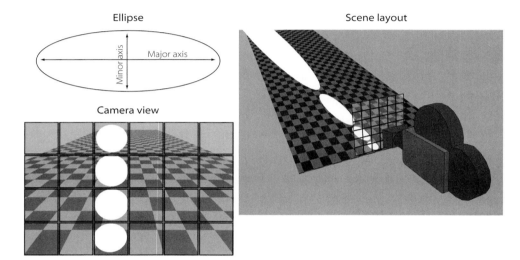

Elliptical filtering extends your abilities to control filtering by using additional options that cope with nonuniform relationships between texels and render pixels. These options provide you with a means to define the size of the minor axis (see "Ellipse" in Figure 11.37), as well as the maximum ratio between the minor and major axes, defining the elliptical shape extent. The latter limits the shape from forming too narrow and long ellipses. Note that the ellipse shapes are camera-projected ellipses; thus, the directionality of the ellipse may change from horizontal to vertical ellipses, based on the circumstances.

Elliptical Filtering Options

You can find the options that control elliptical filtering in the mental ray mib_texture_ filter_lookup shader. You can see the filter lookup shader (Figure 11.4 labeled A) and its shader tree connections using mental ray–specific shaders in the section "mental ray Network Connections" earlier in this chapter.

Figure 11.38 shows the filter lookup shader options in Maya. You can find the equivalent XSI options after loading a new image (using the Texture → Image shader) under the Image → Image Filtering tab. We'll review the mental ray options here, as well as refer to their host-specific settings:

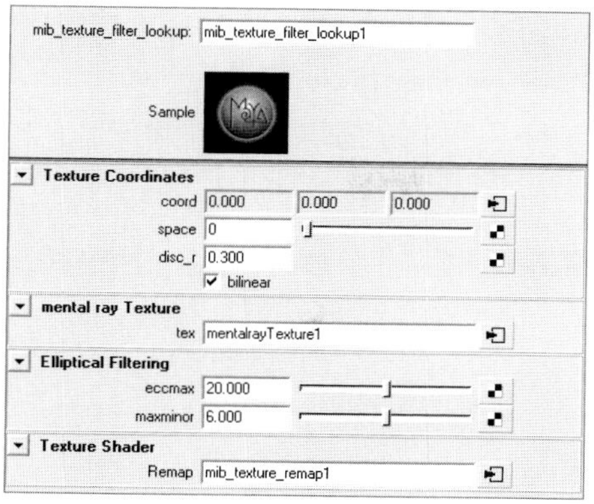

Figure 11.38

The mib_texture_ filter_lookup shader options for elliptical filtering shown in Maya

- The Space option (Maya only) needs to be set using a positive value (selecting explicit UVs) and should be set equally with the mib_texture_vector shader → Select option (discussed earlier).

- The Disc_r attribute is used to resolve aliasing artifacts that are caused during the conversion from screen space to texture space with surfaces that exhibit a lot of curvature. The valid range is from 0 to 0.3. A value of 0 uses the default 0.3 value. Higher values (within that range) are better for highly curved surfaces, whereas lower values are intended for flat surfaces. If you see aliasing artifacts, use a trial-and-error process to identify the right values.

- The Eccmax attribute defines the maximum ratio between the minor and major axes. Setting a limit can prevent extremely long ellipses, referred to as *runaway projections* that are less efficient, and may even slow down the render progress. In XSI, this option is the Maximum Eccentricity property.

- The Maxminor attribute defines the maximum length for the minor axes. This option is similar to the filter size option with standard filtering, defining a relationship between texels and render pixels. In XSI, use the Maximum pixels for Min Radius property.

- The bilinear interpolation option, found in both applications, defines how values in texture space are interpolated. Basically, bilinear interpolation means that two values interpolate in both directions. Each direction is a linear interpolation, and the final result, a product of both linear interpolations, is a nonlinear result. Bilinear interpolation then refers to X and Y coordinates in texture space that are interpolated in both directions.

When enabling elliptical filtering with XSI, you can select whether the filtering is applied to RGBA color channels, bump mapping, or both, using the RGBA and Bump Mapping property checkboxes.

Memory Mapping and Pyramid Images

Whenever filtering is enabled, mental ray automatically creates a prefiltered multiresolution image, known as a *pyramid image*, also known as *mip-map* textures in various host applications. Pyramid image files store a single image at multiple levels of resolution as a means for accelerating filtering and rendering. The benefit is that the renderer can use lower-resolution images to acquire color values for a sample block that correlates to several texels.

Essentially, a pyramid image makes it easier for the renderer to acquire the correct interpolated (filtered) color value, because it's provided with a "road map" for color values from several different resolution steps. Consider that for a given sample point, with filtering enabled, mental ray interpolates values that occupy a 512×512 texture pixel region. In such a case, a pyramid image that has already prefiltered those pixels into lower resolution images can provide the renderer with fewer pixels for the filtering process, such as a 2×2 pixel region. Therefore, lower-resolution levels (images) represent already interpolated values for the same higher-resolution images. Doing so allows mental ray to interpolate four color values rather than 512—a much larger region and clearly more render expensive as well as more prone to artifacts.

Let's look at Figure 11.39 to learn more about pyramid images. Here I use a collection of checker images to create a multiresolution pyramid image starting at 1024×1024 pixels and decreasing to 1×1 (32×32 in the figure) pixels. Each image (resolution) is color-coded and cropped rather than scaled down. By cropping, I assure that in the following Figure 11.40 you can easily identify the different resolutions. In Figure 11.39, I placed each resolution with a small offset so you can easily distinguish between the different levels. Pyramid images scale the larger resolution image into smaller resolutions, creating a collection of "prefiltered" images using fewer texture pixels (lower resolution), which can be thought of as the higher-resolution filtered pixels.

Figure 11.39

A pyramid image's layout, where each half resolution is stored in an empty quadrant

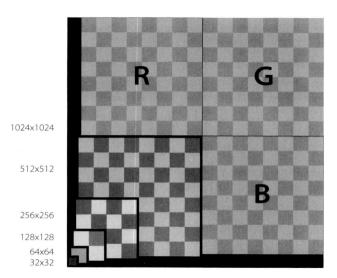

As you can see in Figure 11.39, the pyramid image stores the RGB color channels in separate quadrants of the image, leaving one quadrant empty. Each quadrant is effectively half the resolution of the previous (higher-resolution) quadrant. Thus, the pyramid image stores successive half-resolution images starting at the highest resolution, and down to 1-square pixel, as shown in Figure 11.39, from 1024-to-32-square pixels.

If you look at Figure 11.40, you can see this pyramid image being used with elliptical filtering. Because the images are cropped, you can clearly see when lower resolutions are used. Remember, the concept of pyramid images is to use fewer pixels (lower resolutions) for filtering areas that occupy more pixels (larger resolutions). The section labeled A is closest to the camera, where the smallest relationship between texels and render pixels exists. In this case, the highest resolution (1024) is being used. As the plane recedes away from the camera, the filter occupies larger texel regions; thus, B utilizes the next level, a 512×512 resolution. From C to E the following resolutions are used in this order: 256, 128, and 64. As you can see, as the surface recedes in depth, lower resolutions are used to provide prefiltered interpolated colors. You can see the pyramid.map image used with this example and the color version of Figure 11.40 labeled "ellipse_pyramid" in the the Chapter 11 folder on the companion CD.

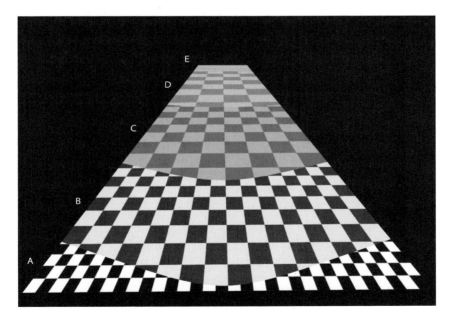

Figure 11.40

Elliptical filtering using a pyramid image, where you can identify when the different resolutions are used

Memory-Mapped Pyramid Images

Memory-mapped images improve memory handling with texture files. What they do is enable mental ray to read the texture data, as required, from the file directly, without loading the entire image into memory. If you render scenes with large texture files, you will see how the memory usage significantly increases every time an image is loaded, shown in the verbosity output and the RAM reader, as discussed in Chapter 1, "Introduction to mental ray." Therefore, using memory-mapped images can significantly reduce memory usage, as well as improve render times.

One of the more advantageous aspects of memory-mapped images relates to filtered images. When rendering with filtering (elliptical or standard), mental ray automatically generates a pyramid image. Effectively, the pyramid image is a larger image file with several resolutions, as discussed earlier. By using memory-mapped pyramid images, mental ray can simply access the relevant resolution, rather than precomputing the pyramid image and storing it in the immediate memory. Some applications allow you to define whether memory-mapped images are generated for textures and how they are stored. However, some preparation is always desirable when you attempt to render highly detailed high-resolution images, particularly in texture-intensive scenes.

> Memory-mapped images are byte order dependent, based on the system on which they are created. They cannot utilize their memory-mapping abilities on systems that don't have the same byte order (little or big endian); thus, memory mapping is disregarded. Most Windows machines use the same byte order, so you can move a file freely from one system to the next. However, you can't transfer it to a Mac OS X system.

We can conclude that memory-mapped pyramid images have three main benefits: they allow a faster render as a result of using fewer pixels for interpolation, they improve memory handling, and they ensure that there is less chance for flickering or shimmering over animation. Regardless of memory mapping, pyramid images still improve render performance; however, when memory mapped, it's a more significant improvement.

Creating Memory-Mapped Pyramid Images

To create memory-mapped images and pyramid images, you can use the mental ray imf_copy utility. Let's create the memory-mapped pyramid image used in the previous examples. In all cases, you should run the terminal, shell, or command prompt on Windows (select the Start menu → Run, type **cmd**, and press Enter), and then run **imf_copy -h**. If you see the help flags, then the system knows where to find the utility. If you don't see the help flags, you need to locate the utility in your host application's directories (see Chapter 1) and then enter the full path before specifying the command.

CREATING MEMORY-MAPPED IMAGES

To convert a texture to a memory-mapped image, simply enter the following:

```
imf_copy path\textureName.tif path\newName.map
```

You can force the new image to maintain the same format and extension. Doing so allows your host to recognize the texture file without requiring you to reload it under the texture shader (within the host). This makes it easier to replace all the textures in a given directory with memory-mapped images, without relinking (renaming) all the textures within the host. Thus, mental ray will identify the image as memory mapped regardless of the extension. So, you can specify a new path for the resulting images so that they are stored under another directory using the original texture name and extension. Make a backup copy of your original images before overwriting them with the new memory-mapped images. Type the following to maintain the format extension and apply memory mapping:

```
imf_copy "path\texName.tif" "newpath\ texName.tif" map
```

Note that the quotes are optional; however, they are required when paths contain spaces. If you open the resulting image using the imf_display utility (run **imf_disp** in the prompt), select the Image → Info option. In the Image Info window, you will see that the Image Format reads *map*, confirming the image as a memory-mapped format.

> You can simply drag a texture file into the command prompt that then applies its path and name within quotes, which is a nice alternative to typing a full path.

CREATING MEMORY-MAPPED PYRAMID IMAGES

To create pyramid images, you simply add the pyramid flag, as shown next:

```
imf_copy -p path\textureName.tif path\newName.tif
```

If you want the result to be a memory-mapped image, simply follow the previous examples, adding the map flag as shown next:

```
imf_copy -p path\textureName.tif path\newName.map
```

You can extract any given resolution for viewing the result in an image viewer, as follows:

```
imf_copy -x resolution path\textureName.map path\extracted.tif
```

The -x flag defines the resolution level you want to extract. If you specify 0, the highest resolution is extracted, and as you specify higher values, you extract lower (filtered) resolutions.

You can manually load individual images at the different resolution levels using the collate flag (-c) like this (several stages are skipped between 256 and 1):

```
imf_copy -c 1024.tif 512.tif 256.tif 1.tif output.map
```

Start at the highest resolution, and then add decreasing half-resolution images until you eventually reach a 1×1-pixel resolution. You can use the images provided in the Chapter 11 directory "pyramid resolutions" folder on the companion CD.

> I've omitted some of the lower resolutions, which means that running the example will return an error; however, you can ignore this message, and the example will still work.

## CHAPTER 12

Indirect Illumination

Indirect illumination significantly impacts our ability to draw more realistic images using 3D software. Essentially, it adds the ability to calculate *light paths* that occur after the direct light scatters in the scene. By doing so, indirect illumination focuses on reflected radiation between different surfaces in the scene. In addition, there are also volumetric indirect illumination effects, which tackle illumination of particles suspended in air; these particles absorb, transmit, and reflect light.

This chapter builds on the previous discussions of light characteristics in Chapter 9, "The Fundamentals of Light and Shading Models." Be sure to complete that chapter prior to reading this chapter, which demonstrates how indirect illumination handles the simulation of indirect diffuse, specular, and glossy (DGS) light paths while considering energy conservation, using simulated photon energy packets.

All host applications offer identical options for controlling indirect illumination. This chapter first covers mental ray's indirect illumination options and the host application settings and then examines their effect on controlling indirect light paths. This chapter covers the following topics:

- **mental ray Indirect Illumination**
- **Photon Shaders and Photon-Casting Lights**
- **Indirect Illumination Options and Fine-Tuning**
- **Participating Media (PM) Effects**

mental ray Indirect Illumination

mental ray indirect illumination simulates the distribution of light in a scene using theoretical photons as a means for measuring and scattering light. Light energy is then quantified using photons—small energy packets that are emitted from light sources and absorbed, transmitted, or reflected from surfaces in the scene. At each instance they transfer properties like real light, as discussed in Chapter 9, "The Fundamentals of Light and Shading Models." The transferable properties of light between surfaces are stored in a data tree known as a *photon map*. To understand what a photon map is and how it is used by mental ray for global illumination, see the sidebar "3D Photon Maps and Kd-Trees."

3D PHOTON MAPS AND KD-TREES

This sidebar presents an overview of photon mapping. The topics introduced here are discussed in detail and demonstrated using mental ray throughout this chapter and Chapter 13, "Final Gather and Ambient Occlusion."

A photon map stores photons in a three-dimensional data structure known as a *Kd-tree*, which is a space-partitioning storage technique that, in this case, records the distribution of photons in a three-dimensional space. Once these trees have been generated, you can search inside them for values of nearby points at a given location.

Global illumination is a two-step process. The first stage handles the distribution of photons in the scene, recording RGB (per wavelength) energy values for a given photon in a photon map Kd-tree. It records energy only when a surface that interacts with a photon (a photon hits it) has some diffuse light reflection applied through a photon shading model. (Photon shaders were introduced in Chapter 9, "The Fundamentals of Light and Shading Models," and are further discussed in this chapter.) Global illumination simulates diffuse light reflection, so to be recorded in a photon map, a surface must have some diffuse character; it must reflect diffuse light. If it is either purely specular or black (absorbing all the light), the location doesn't contribute any data to the Kd-tree since there is no diffuse light reflection. The photon is then reflected, refracted, or absorbed.

The advantage of a Kd-tree photon map is its ability to search over a certain radius at a given location in the tree, which is essential to the second stage of global illumination—rendering. That is, the first stage of global illumination handles the distribution and storage of photons in a Kd-tree data structure, and the second stage deals with averaging the energy values over a given radius in the Kd-tree, interpolating the color (energy) effect in the scene using whatever photons fall within a given radius. The photons' energy values are extracted from stored data at each point within the photon map Kd data tree.

When you reuse a photon map, essentially you choose to skip the first stage of generating photons, saving time by avoiding the precomputation and storage stage of points within the photon map. During rendering (the second stage), you can still change how photons, from within the photon map, are interpolated for color. Specifically, you can control how many photons are to be considered for each interpolation and in what *n* radius nearby photons can be "seen" for interpolation. To further clarify, interpolation is initiated during rendering with each render sample that is taken in the scene (sampling is discussed in Chapter 5, "Quality Control"); each render sample requires an interpolated color value derived from the RGB energy values stored within the photon map, and by doing so (interpolating color from several photons), it defines the indirect illumination effect in the scene. The interpolation process is handled by global illumination, and that data is then passed to mental ray for use with the render equation to add direct illumination with indirect illumination.

When Final Gather (FG) is also enabled and specifically set to precomputed irradiance during the photon map generation, the Kd-tree also stores irradiance values (from photons) across surfaces in addition to global illumination photon energy values. The irradiance data used for FG reflects the total irradiance from various photons at a given point (see Chapter 13, "Final Gather and Ambient Occlusion,"). Essentially it enables FG to extract irradiance at a given point with a single sample (lookup for an RGB irradiance value at a given point in the Kd-tree) without requiring it to sample several photons to determine their contribution to irradiance (using several samples/lookups in the tree).

mental ray carries color as RGB energy values from one surface to another. At each point of incidence (irradiance), the energy carried by a photon to the surface partially affects that surface color, based on the surface's photon shader settings (that is, whether it's a specular or diffuse surface). At the same time, photons may acquire color information from that surface's photon shader, representing its reflected color, carrying that reflected light color to the next point of incidence. The process of transferring reflected color properties (light) from one surface to the next is referred to as *color bleeding* in mental ray and other global illumination simulations. Color bleeding resolves the transferable color properties between surfaces in the scene using photon shaders. For example, a green sphere on a white floor will bleed some of its green color onto the floor. You can see samples of color bleeding in the color gallery images labeled "Photon Shaders and Color Bleeding," as well as in several other images in the gallery.

In addition, the loss of energy over distance (the inverse square law) is accounted for at each point of incidence. Therefore, indirect illumination simulates the transfer of color and energy, until either all the energy has been absorbed (stored in a surface) or a photon is cast into "empty space," theoretically traveling infinitely. Recall that light spreads over distance based on the inverse square law, in which relative light intensity is a factor of the light spread over a given distance. Photons in mental ray also simulate energy decay characteristics, as you will see throughout this chapter. Essentially photons are conveniently used with indirect illumination simulations to transfer intensity (radiance flux/energy) as RGB per-wavelength color properties in small photon packets, mimicking the light's real-world behavior.

Each photon acts as a temporary data container that carries RGB energy values corresponding to long, medium, and short wavelengths of light that are stored within the photon map file. Obviously, some physical light characteristics, such as an actual pair of oscillating waves, are not really simulated in 3D; however, the geometric optics mathematical equations that are based on the particle accretion of light are used to calculate the emission, absorption, transmission, and reflection of indirect light contribution in a scene. Ultimately, by considering direct and indirect light, as well as surface shading characteristics, mental ray can determine the equilibrium of light in the scene using a rendering equation. Rendering is then the process of using a wide range of geometric optics equations that describe light within a synthetic environment. Each component (direct vs. indirect and diffuse vs. specular) is evaluated independently of the other, and at the end they are all balanced together using the rendering equation.

The only real caveat with respect to photons is that in real life an infinite number of photons exist, whereas in 3D, the number of photons represents a very small percentage of real-world conditions. So, photons in mental ray are used to average the result over a given area, as discussed in the earlier sidebar "3D Photon Maps and Kd-Trees."

Indirect Illumination Features

mental ray *photon mapping* differs from radiosity (discussed briefly in Chapter 13, "Final Gather and Ambient Occlusion") in that it is independent of the scene geometry. It does, however, deal with the same topic of resolving diffuse indirect light paths in the scene. The photon mapping technique used with mental ray also adds the ability to calculate the contribution of specular and volume indirect light reflection. Thus, there are two types of indirect illumination techniques used to resolve indirect light: global illumination and caustics. Both can be used to illuminate geometry or participating media (particles) in the scene.

Global illumination deals with the diffuse properties of indirect light, as they reflect, absorb, and transmit photons from surfaces. *Caustic* light deals with the additional interaction of specular reflection and transmission, which have an ability to amplify the light intensity and thus possess very different visual characteristics. *Participating media* volume effects are a subset of global illumination that is used to illuminate diffuse substances that are not considered solid surfaces. The term typically refers to smoke, dust, mist, and light rays that enter a room; see "Participating Media (PM) Effects" later in this chapter. Note that participating media can be applied as direct or indirect light.

Photon Mapping and Light Paths

Photon mapping is a two-step process, introduced in the sidebar "3D Photons Maps and Kd-Trees," that first involves emitting photons from a source light and then rendering the scene while weighing in both direct and indirect light. Global illumination (GI) and caustics are raytrace features that are somewhat different from the raytrace algorithms discussed in Chapter 2, "Rendering Algorithms." Typically, primary rays (direct lighting) initiate at the camera, traveling to a surface and then to the light source. With indirect lighting, the first stage of emitting photons is reversed, a process known as *forward raytracing*. Therefore, rays carry photons from the source light into the scene and then from one point of incidence to the next, where photons are used to transfer energy and rays are used to reflect or refract the photon's path.

Figure 12.1 illustrates some of the different paths light may take as it travels in the scene. As a user you can define the number of times each ray type (photon) may bounce or transmit in the scene, as discussed in this chapter. The arrow labeled A shows the process of global illumination where diffuse light reflects from the floor to the wall and then back to the ceiling, adding light in areas where the direct light has no effect. At each point of contact it stores radiance (energy) using photons, as described in the sidebar earlier.

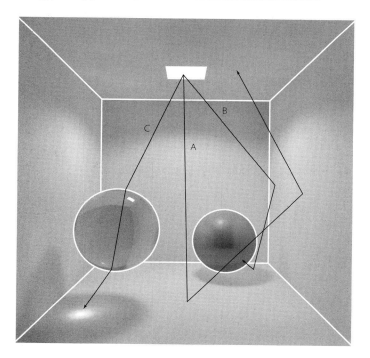

Figure 12.1

Some photon light paths for global illumination and caustics

The arrow labeled B carries diffuse light from the wall to the floor and then to a sphere illuminating the sphere using the floor's diffuse reflected light. The sphere has a mix of diffuse and glossy surface properties, so it is affected by indirect light because it has diffuse values. The arrow labeled C is shown refracting through a dielectric sphere that does not possess any diffuse characteristics. Thus, in this case, the photons will not store any information as they transmit through the sphere; they are merely redirected by rays that carry them through the sphere. When caustics are used, the arrow labeled C will magnify the intensity of light after refracting through the sphere and form the caustic region shown at the tip of the arrow labeled C.

You'll learn more about all of these characteristics throughout this chapter.

Balancing Light

If direct illumination is independent of indirect illumination, how do they interact during rendering? Here are a few points to consider:

- If both photons and direct light influence the same surface points within a direct line of sight (from the light), then the light influence at those points would be mathematically added (combined). To remedy this, photons for a given light source are not stored within its direct line of sight, where the direct light illuminates the surface. However, when using multiple lights, areas within a direct line of sight for one light may be in an indirect line of sight for another.

- Indirect light is intended to omit the process of creating fill or back lights in the scene. Its main purpose is to provide the same effect as those solutions (fill light from reflected radiation), simulating realism.

- Since both direct and indirect light are evaluated independently, the direct light characteristics should be set to match the indirect light characteristics, with respect to energy and falloff (light decay). Failing to do so can produce incoherent results in the final rendered image. This assumption is primarily based on your approach to indirect lighting. You may decide to use physical shaders that simulate light transport realistically according to the laws of energy conservation, such as for architectural rendering. Or, for a more creative approach, you may use nonphysical shaders and lights that provide a visually pleasing end result with indirect illumination.

We also need to consider that photons that are cast from a source light may end up reflecting back to the direct light's area of influence, as shown in Figure 12.2 image A. The result is overexposure, because the direct lighting is not balanced with the indirect lighting and the two together create very bright regions of light around the source light. The reason for the overexposure is a result of using energy values that are too high. If you use correct values, then this sort of artifact should not appear; however, creatively speaking, the room may appear too dark for your purposes. So, you increase the energy and get more light but also overexposure. To remedy this, I use a second spot light that is placed farther away from the source light and doesn't affect direct lighting but does emit photons. Figure 12.2 image B shows the result.

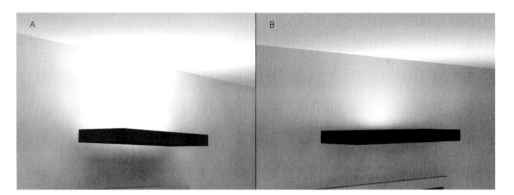

Figure 12.2

Photons can reflect back on the light emission area (direct light) leading to overexposure in the direct light area.

Rendering Indirect Illumination

Once the photon map is evaluated, the scene is then rendered using the standard backward raytracing approach for primary eye rays. So, the photon map provides additional color that is weighed in during rendering and additively combined with direct lighting.

Photons can store color values only on diffuse surfaces; they may leave some energy or be fully absorbed only on surfaces that possess some diffuse color (regardless of global illumination or caustics). Thus, with specular surfaces, photons are reflected or refracted but not stored; they are stored only when they eventually hit a surface that has some diffuse characteristics.

Figure 12.3 demonstrates a global illumination solution where the direct light is negligible so that you can clearly see the photons in the scene. Each photon that appears on a surface (the walls) is there because the surface stored some of the energy from a photon, and thus the color you see represents the reflected energy cast onto that surface from the surroundings, using photons. If the surface completely absorbs the photon, there is no color, so you do not see a photon. A plane is placed through the center of the room and is fully specular, meaning it has no diffuse characteristics. In this case, I used DGS illumination and photon shaders (see "Photon Shaders and Photon-Casting Lights" later in this chapter) where the diffuse color is set to black and the specular color is set to white. The result is that the photons are reflected from the surface and never penetrate the plane, and they don't deposit any energy on the plane surface. On the right, you can see the photon map illustrated in a host application. The dots represent the stored photons (from the photon map Kd-tree) shown in the rendering, and as you can see, there are no photons placed on the center plane.

Figure 12.3

Photon paths are reflected from pure specular surfaces that have no diffuse color and are stored on diffused surfaces only.

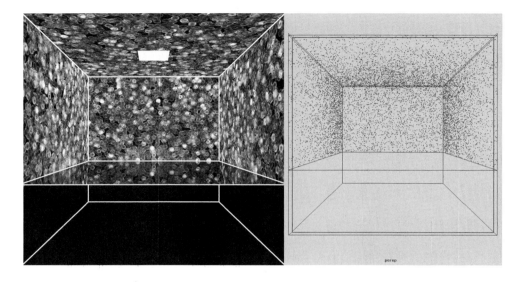

Figure 12.4 demonstrates the same room with a surface that is purely refractive (100 percent transparent). In this case, you can see in both the rendered version and the screen grab that photons transmit through the surface without depositing any energy on that refractive surface.

Figure 12.4

Photon paths are reflective from a purely specular surface that has no diffuse characteristics and are then stored on a diffused surface only.

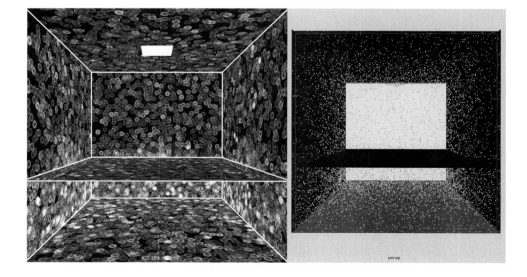

In both cases, it's important to note that in the rendered image all the photons that are stored on the walls are seen on the reflective surface (Figure 12.3) or through the refractive surface (Figure 12.4). This emphasizes the point that once the indirect contribution is distributed in the scene, it is rendered as visible light on surfaces that may appear in reflective surfaces or through refractions. However, there are no stored photons on the mirror or glass surface, because it reflected or refracted all the photons that interacted with it.

As mentioned earlier, caustics handle the specular nature of light, whether it is reflection or refraction. However, the global illumination solution shown in these two figures reflects and transmits from the center plane. Thus, the difference between global illumination and caustics is that caustics actually account for the effect specular surfaces have on light, magnifying their intensity, as I will discuss in the "Caustics" section later in this chapter. And with global illumination, the light paths interact correctly in the scene, reflecting and refracting through surfaces, but the energy they transfer is not influenced by the specular surface, only their color. In a similar way, direct lighting also inherits color from specular surfaces; however, neither direct light nor global illumination simulate the effect these surfaces have on the photon's energy (intensity).

Photon Shaders and Photon-Casting Lights

The following sections cover lights and photon shaders that are used for indirect illumination and their host-specific settings. They are for the most part named and distributed in the same way with each host application.

Photon Shaders and Settings

As noted previously, direct light and indirect light are calculated separately during the render, and their combined contributions are added up mathematically using a render equation. The photon map is evaluated based on a separate set of shaders so that direct light uses the illumination shaders to evaluate light, and photon maps use the photon shaders. Effectively, each surface has two types of illumination shaders that are used independently of each other to calculate direct and indirect light. Thus, a blue illumination shader will reflect blue light (direct lighting), and a red photon shader will reflect red indirect light, as shown in the color gallery labeled "Photon Shaders and Color Bleeding."

> You can see the effect of *bleeding* in some amateur green-screen visual effects. If the object is too close to the green screen, a green glow appears on it.

To fully understand how everything (direct light, indirect lighting, and photon shaders) comes together, let's examine the "Photon Shaders and Color Bleeding" image in the color gallery. It shows a red sphere and red wall that share the same green photon shader as the green sphere. This green photon shader is responsible for reflecting green indirect light in the scene, shown with the green color bleeding from the green and red surfaces in the image. The blue wall and sphere have a blue photon shader that reflects blue light. The reason for this strange setup is to demonstrate that illumination shaders are completely detached from photon shaders and global illumination. The only interaction between illumination shaders and global illumination is when the global illumination light contribution is added with the direct light illumination while solving the rendering equation. From this you can draw two important conclusions:

- Global illumination extracts the light energy values (color) from photon shaders.

- It then uses those values to illuminate a surface's illumination shader.

Thus, values from global illumination represent the indirect light contribution applied to illumination shaders, acquired by the process of reflecting and transmitting indirect light using global illumination with photon shaders. This means that for proper results you will need to match the two shaders so the overall lighting makes sense, avoiding errors such as the one demonstrated in the color gallery where the red sphere and wall reflect green light.

If a surface does not have a photon shader, it will not participate in the photon emission stage and thus will not affect indirect illumination.

mental ray Photon Shaders

A photon shader's diffuse color is used with global illumination, and the glossy and specular colors are used with caustics. From the physics shader library the DGS and dielectric illumination shaders have corresponding photon shaders that have identical color options so that it is easy to match their settings. The base shader library has one

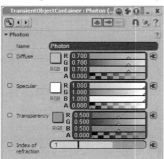

Figure 12.5

The mental images base (mib) shader library photon basic shader options seen in XSI

default photon shader (mib_photon_basic) that is used with the different illumination models (Phong, Blinn, Cook-Torrance, and so on). The basic shader offers the important components used with indirect illumination, including Diffuse, Specular, Transparency, and Index of Refraction options, as shown in Figure 12.5, which shows a base photon shader in XSI. Effectively, in this way it covers the different types of light paths that may be used to absorb, transmit, or reflect photons.

I discussed the topic of applying mental ray shaders to surface materials in Chapter 9, "The Fundamentals of Light and Shading Models." In that chapter, you saw that each host has a material connection for a photon shader in addition to all the other connections (illumination, volume, displacement, and so on). There is really nothing more to say about photon shaders (as a shader type) beyond that they are identical to standard shaders and are used during indirect illumination only, which is why they don't need to be as complex as standard shading models. The photon shader dictates only the appearance of reflected indirect light from a surface and does not handle rendering the highlights or reflection colors, so all the information it really needs about a surface is whether it is diffuse or specular and its color.

Selecting Diffuse Colors

In real life a surface's color is based on two main components: the incident light's spectrum of color and the wavelengths that the surface predominately reflects, filtering light between absorption and reflection or transmittance. Typically, red surfaces reflect a "redder" spectrum of light while absorbing other wavelengths so that the red portion of the visible spectrum is more predominant to the observer. With CG you can use pure colors such as red, green, and blue. In such cases a surface will reflect only the pure color it is assigned. Thus, if it's red, it will absorb the green and blue colors completely, since those color components are set to zero and reflect only red color. In real life the red would still be partially affected by the other wavelengths in a number of ways (different wavelength combinations can form similar red tints) and not a pure color; however, in CG you can break the rules and use pure colors, but that is not recommended.

The use of pure colors has influence on the appearance of overexposure and color bleeding:

Overexposure   When a surface has a color defined using one predominant color, such as red, and some blue and green, then as you increase the intensity of light, the reflected light increases for each wavelength. Eventually all three components will reach a value greater than one, and you will see white, which is overexposure. However, with pure colors, two components are set to black (zero), so as they multiply by an increasing light, they always cancel it out and never increase in their intensity. This characteristic actually simulates full absorption for a given color channel that is set to zero. Thus, with pure colors, overexposure will always appear as a strong pure color and never transition to white.

Color bleeding   A pure color surface that absorbs the two other color components makes it impossible to affect that surface with color bleeding, which typically is undesirable; you do want to see the effect of color bleeding on surfaces. Thus, with pure colors, you will not see color bleeding because they always render only the pure color.

Color and Absorption

Color defines how much absorption occurs on a surface. Thus, a white color will reflect all the incoming indirect light, and black will absorb all the indirect light. The result is that photons will not store (deposit energy) where a shader has black diffuse color. Essentially, the diffuse RGB color channels act as multipliers against the incident photon RGB energy values so that a black color cancels out any indirect illumination, as shown in Figure 12.6. Here the rendered image A utilizes a checker pattern on the back wall, and the screen-grab image B shows the photon distribution in the scene (in Maya you can load the photon map into the scene for viewing) where you clearly see that the black checkers don't have any photons stored at their locations. Thus, if you want to avoid this sort of effect, you may want to leave some value so that it is dark but not completely black. In that way, you guarantee that the photons will not disappear as they transition to black colors. In real-world conditions even very "black" objects have some diffuse light effect. A theoretical purely black surface was already discussed in Chapter 9, "The Fundamentals of Light and Shading Models," with respect to black body radiation experiments used to derive color temperatures.

Figure 12.6

Black diffuse color will completely absorb photons as shown in the rendered image (A) and in the screen grab (B), thus there is no indirect light influence on the black checkers shown in the figure.

When you choose colors for a surface, you need to keep in mind that different combinations of wavelength frequencies, at different amplitudes (brightness), depict color. The objective is to use some variation with RGB colors and value so that you can better simulate light transport without completely omitting a light wavelength such as red, green, or blue, if one of them is set to zero.

Host Application and mental ray Photon Shaders

In Figure 12.7 you can see two shader trees in XSI. In image A you can see that I connected the mib photon base shader to a material's photon input directly. In image B you can see that the Cook-Torrance shader connects to the photon input. Chapter 9, "The Fundamentals of Light and Shading Models," discussed the difference between host-specific monolithic shaders and mental ray base shaders. All host-specific shaders have been compiled in a way that they have a built in photon shader. Thus, all the color information is directly taken from the surface's illumination shader and used with the photon shader, referring to the diffuse, specular, transparency, and index of refraction options.

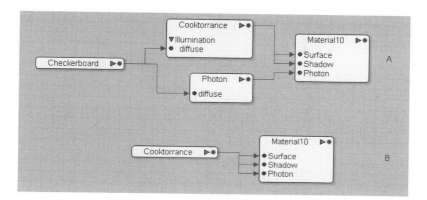

Figure 12.7

A photon shader tree in XSI in A and a monolithic shader shown in B

An important consideration is that you can map the diffuse or specular components of a photon shader with the same texture you use for the illumination shader. Essentially they both share the same color information as shown in A, where a checker texture is attached to the diffuse component of both the Cook-Torrance and photon shaders. However, some complex textures may cause artifacts in the render with indirect illumination if they are too detailed, so you may want to just map it with a simplified version of the surface texture that has approximately the same colors. In this way you guarantee that the indirect illumination colors will appear to inherit the correct color from the surface.

CONTROLLING SURFACE IRRADIANCE

Maya and XSI monolithic shaders also have an irradiance option that acts as a multiplier against the irradiance on the surface, as shown for Maya in Figure 12.8 image A and XSI in image B. These options enable you to fine-tune the amount of irradiance cast on a surface point. In Maya you can find it in a Maya-centric shader under the mental ray rollout. In XSI-centric shaders, it appears on the Indirect Illumination tab, as shown in the figure.

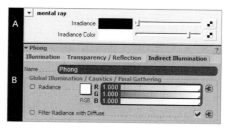

The following considerations apply:

Figure 12.8

Irradiance options on host-specific monolithic shaders

- If the surface receives too much color bleeding or energy (if it appears too bright), you can reduce the Irradiance Color attribute in Maya or the Radiance property in XSI to decrease the indirect illumination effect.

- Reducing the irradiance can solve problems such as the blown-out regions shown in Figure 12.2 earlier. Doing so may also cause an imbalance between surfaces. For example, if you try to reduce the irradiance on the wall to resolve the blown-out regions shown in Figure 12.2, the entire wall would appear darker than the remaining walls, so it is not always an ideal solution.

- When changing the irradiance for a surface, you typically need to change the irradiance across that entire object, regardless of how many independent surfaces the object comprises. For example, reduce the irradiance for an entire room (all the walls if they have the same color), all the surfaces that build a cabinet, or the entire car. In this way you are more likely to have coherent results.

Let's briefly look at host-specific shaders and the process of assigning photon shaders in host applications.

MAYA

In Maya, when using Maya-centric shaders, you don't need to apply a photon shader as cited previously. You can break the connection between the illumination shader and photon shader with the attributes found under a Maya-centric shader's mental ray → Photon Attributes rollout. The Derive from Maya Attribute check box breaks the dependency; when it's disabled, you control the photon shader using the settings in the Photon Attributes rollout.

When using mental ray shaders, you can find the photon shaders in the Hypershade window under the Create mental ray Nodes → Photonic Materials rollout, as shown in Figure 12.9. Notice that you have DGS, dielectric, mib_photon_basic, and transmat (discussed in the "Participating Media (PM) Effects" section later in this chapter) shaders. When using shaders other than the DGS or dielectric shaders, which have their own photon shader, you should use the mib_photon_basic shader. To apply these connections, follow these steps:

Figure 12.9

mental ray photon shaders in Maya

1. Apply a mental ray illumination shader to a surface from the Create mental ray Nodes → Materials rollout.

2. Graph the network in the Hypershade window so you can see the shading engine node, for example, mib_illum_blinn1SG.

3. Select a photon shader from the Photonic Materials rollout.

4. Under the shading engine, expand the mental ray rollout (the mental ray material discussed in Chapter 9, "The Fundamentals of Light and Shading Models").

5. Drag and drop the photon shader over the mental ray material's Photon Shader input.

6. Set the diffuse and specular colors for the illumination and photon shaders to the same values.

Your material is now ready to participate in indirect illumination. Note that as cited previously and illustrated in Figure 12.7 image A, you can apply the same texture map to both the illumination shader and the photon shader.

> When using the architectural library (labeled as *mia material* under the mental ray illumination shaders) material, you should drag and drop the mia material onto three inputs: Material Shader, Shadow Shader, and Photon Shader. Sometimes these connections may already be present.

You can also see the participating media photon shader (parti_volume_photon) in the Photon Volumetric Materials rollout, as shown in Figure 12.9. You'll use it later in the "Participating Media (PM) Effects" section for volumetric effects. In that section you will also use the transmat_photon shader shown in Figure 12.9.

XSI

I've already reviewed the differences between XSI-centric shaders and mental ray shaders with the shader tree graphs shown earlier in Figure 12.7. You can also see the photon shader properties for an XSI monolithic shader in Figure 12.8 image B. You can find the mental ray base photon shader in the Render Tree window under Nodes → Raytracing → Photon. Once a connection is created, applying it is as simple as dragging the shader to the material's Photon input, as shown in Figure 12.7 image A.

I discussed adding custom shaders to XSI in Chapter 10, "mental ray Shaders and Shader Trees," where you saw the Tek2Shoot and XPhysics shader library add-ons. You'll need to have one of these libraries installed for the "Participating Media (PM) Effects" section later in this chapter, where you'll use the transmat and parti_media photon shaders for volumetric effects; both shaders and their photon equivalents are included with both libraries.

If you added the Tek2Shoot Unexposed mental ray shaders (from their home page) library, you will find a Photon directory with DGS, dielectric, and transmat photon shaders. You will also find a volume directory with the parti_volume participating media shader and photon shader. With the Xphysics library all thee shaders are constructed as monolithic shaders that can be attached to the material's Surface and Photon inputs. The Xphysics_volume (participating media) shader is also a monolithic shader that is attached to the Volume and Photon Volume inputs.

Note that XSI already incorporates the participating media shader using the volume effects shader found in the Render Tree window under Nodes → Volume → Volume Effects.

3DS MAX

In 3ds Max when using 3ds Max–centric shaders, you don't need to apply a photon shader, as cited earlier. You can break the connection between the illumination shader and photon shader with the parameters found in the Material Editor under the shader's mental ray

Figure 12.10

3ds Max–centric shaders can have independent photon shaders applied.

Connection rollout in the Caustic and GI section, as shown in Figure 12.10. When you disable the lock for the Photon connection, you can then map it with a photon basic

(base) shader from the Material/Map Browser window. You will find a collection of photon shaders that include the DGS, dielectric, photon basic (base), and transmat photon (physics), as well as some photon shaders for the lume shader library.

Once the Photon parameter is mapped, as shown in Figure 12.10, you then control the photon shader using the settings found under the photon shader's parameters rather than having them automatically update from the 3ds Max shader. The color or texture used for the 3ds Max shader's diffuse parameters should also be mapped to the photon shader's diffuse parameter unless, as discussed earlier, you specifically want to use a simplified version of the settings such as a simple color for the photon shader diffuse color, opposed to a texture map.

When you select to use mental ray material (see Chapter 10, "mental ray Shaders and Shader Trees") instead of 3ds Max's standard material, then under the Material Shader rollout there is no automation that drives the Photon shader. Instead, in such cases you must connect the Photon parameter with a photon shader in addition to the surface shader input if you want that surface to participate in both direct and indirect lighting simulations, as cited earlier.

You can also see in Figure 12.10 and under the mental ray material's Material Shader rollout the photon Volume and Volume parameters. You'll use these connections later, in the "Participating Media (PM) Effects" section, for volumetric effects. In that section, you will use the parti volume (physics) and transmat (physics) shaders and their correlating photon shaders; you can find all of these in the Material/Map Browser window when you select to map any of these inputs.

Photon-Emitting Lights

Just as with surfaces that have an independent photon shader for indirect illumination, light sources also have a separate statement block that deals with emitting photons, as shown in the following excerpt from a photon-emitting light shader:

```
light "pointLightShape"
    = "physical_light"
    origin 0. 0. 0.
    rectangle 0. 2. 0. 2. 0. 0.
    3 3 0
    visible
    energy 5000. 5000. 5000. # photon energy
    exponent 2.              # photon decay
    caustic photons 10000    # caustic photons (stored)
    globillum photons 10000  # GI photons (stored)
end light
```

This light declaration statement has four parts, three of which were discussed in detail in Chapter 6, "Lights and Soft Shadows":

- The light shader, in this case a physical light that is used to define direct light characteristics.

- The light type; in this case the `origin` option defines the light as a point light.

- The area light options; in this case creating a rectangular emitting area light.

- The remaining options (labeled with respect to their purpose) are all photon-related options that add a photon-casting ability to the light.

The *energy* and *exponent* Options

One of the most important options with indirect illumination is the `energy` option. It defines the light's energy using three RGB values. These are the RGB values (wavelengths) that are stored within a photon as it travels in the scene, as discussed at the beginning of this chapter. Here lies the difference between standard direct lighting and physically correct simulations of light. Direct lighting doesn't deal with real energy values; you simply use a 0 to 1 range to define the light's brightness for visually pleasing results. Here the energy corresponds to physically correct energy values for the purpose of simulating real light characteristics. Topics such as gamma correction and overexposure, as discussed in Chapter 9, "The Fundamentals of Light and Shading Models ," become more important with physical simulations of light; see the "Indirect Illumination and Gamma Correction" sidebar later in this chapter.

In addition to the energy values, light falloff should also mimic realism, following the inverse square rule of light decay. The `exponent` option defines the falloff rate, and when set at the default (a value of 2), the falloff is physically correct; an inverse square falloff ($1 \div radius^2$). If you change the value to 1, the falloff is linear ($1 \div radius$). In 3D, an inverse square falloff may appear too rapid because it does not deal with real-life scales. Thus, for visually pleasing results, without overthinking correct energy values and distances, you can occasionally use linear falloff rates and still render compelling images that appear to have realistic lighting. For example, if you are simulating sunlight entering a room, it is clear that you will not see a rapid falloff of light energy. In such cases you may prefer using a linear falloff rate for a source light that simulates the sun.

DIRECT AND INDIRECT LIGHT ENERGY AND FALLOFF

When preparing indirect illumination scenes, photon-casting lights should have the same energy for direct light as with the photon's energy. Thus, with light simulations, it is better to use the mental ray physical light shader, which accepts energy values as light color and enforces an inverse square falloff rate. In this way, you assure that the photon's energy and the light energy are coherent. For example, you would set both RGB color values and the photon energy RGB values to 1000.

In some cases you will want to set the photon energy to a higher value than the light shader's energy, such as when a room appears too dark and you want to try increasing the indirect lighting. Another approach is to use Final Gather to add irradiance, as discussed in Chapter 13, "Final Gather and Ambient Occlusion."

Besides using mental ray's physical light shader for specifying real energy values and inverse square falloff, you can use host-specific lights. Host application lights have a color option as well as an intensity multiplier to specify direct light intensity and color. You should set either the multiplier or the color to the same energy value used with the photons. If you set energy using the light's color, the intensity multiplier should be set to 1 so it doesn't reduce or amplify that energy.

The falloff rate of both direct light and photons should also match, as cited earlier. Thus, you also need to set their falloff to quadratic (or inverse square) if the exponent option is set to 2. See the following sections for host-specific settings.

The *globillum* and *caustic* Options

The globillum and caustic options define how many photons are cast for global illumination and caustics, respectively. Each simulation is independent of the other, as cited earlier, and thus so are their photons. That is, photons used for global illumination are not shared or used with caustics, and vice versa. So, if you intend to use both simulations, you need to set both options with values that are efficient for each purpose. The following section discusses the differences and decision-making process of how many photons you should use.

Regardless of their purpose, these two options behave in the same way, dictating the number of photons that are stored for each solution (global illumination and caustics) in the photon map. Essentially they control how many photons are stored rather than how many photons are emitted in the scene.

The globillum and caustic options accept two values:

```
globillum  [store n] [emit n]
caustic   [store n] [emit n]
```

The first number (store n) defines the number of photons that are eventually stored in the photon map. The following number (emit n) is optional and specifies the maximum number of photons that can be emitted. If the store option is set to zero, then the photon map will store as many photons as possible until the emit limit is reached and the photon emission terminates.

It is the store option that you commonly specify in host applications, which is commonly misinterpreted as the number of emitted photons in the scene rather than the number of stored photons in the photon map.

Not all emitted photons are stored. Some photons may be absorbed, and others may escape the scene (travel to infinity), never reaching a target surface. Thus, the store value indicates that at minimum a given number of photons will be stored and used for indirect illumination regardless of how many are emitted. Doing so guarantees that the energy specified with the energy option is properly distributed within the scene, and none is lost in empty space. Thus, the purpose of the photon emission is to distribute a given amount of light in the scene, utilizing all its energy. By specifying the number of photons to store, mental ray can determine the correct energy value for each photon that it emits. To clarify, the energy is divided by the number of stored photons (flux ÷ stored photons) so that when all the photons are stored, they equally distribute the total energy in the scene. Any lost photons are then irrelevant because they didn't reduce the energy.

Although you typically want to match the light shader's energy with the photon energy, you can also use higher photon energy values to add more light. Keep in mind that the number of photons stored reflects the total energy value, possibly including photons in distant areas of the scene or runaway photons that store externally outside the scene. For example, suppose you are using a source light to emit photons into a room, such as with the sun, where a given percentage of the photons will store outside the room, externally on the room's walls. In this case, a lower amount of energy is distributed in the scene, and you would need to increase the photons' energy to add more light internally.

Host applications only provide an option to define the stored amount of photons and don't provide the additional (optional) emit number.

TROUBLESHOOTING PHOTON EMISSIONS

Since photons are initially cast into the scene, you can follow the photon emission stage within each host application. If this stage takes excessive time, or even aborts, it is likely that photons are being cast but few are actually interacting with surfaces that store photons. Thus, the photon map has a hard time reaching its target number of stored photons efficiently, and the next stage cannot commence. Two primary reasons can lead to an unnecessarily long photon emission stage: light framing and photon shaders.

For light framing, examine the scene from the light's perspective. Make sure the light doesn't emit photons into large empty areas, where the scene represents a small percentage of the light's perspective.

With photon shaders, if you cast photons and don't see any indirect light influence on some or any of the surfaces, it is likely they are not assigned with photon shaders. Remember, surfaces that don't have a photon shader are invisible to photons and will not store photons at their locations.

Relatively speaking, photon casting should not take too long. Even with 1 to 2 million (several photon-emitting lights) photons, the process should take a few minutes at most, not hours.

Host Application Photon-Emitting Lights

Host application source lights have the same settings discussed earlier in this section. Here I briefly point them out with some additional relevant comments. There are two common-alties to all hosts worth mentioning before I cover each host independently.

With respect to the energy option discussed previously, all hosts offer an RGB color option that defines the initial color for photons and uses an additional multiplier to define the photon's intensity for higher values (realistically simulating light energy).

Hosts do not offer one energy option with three values, rather a multiplier and color option that together define the photon's initial color and intensity as with chromaticity and brightness. In the same way, direct light settings in host applications specify the light's color with a color option and the light's intensity with a scalar (single float value) multiplier. When setting these values, the photon color option should be set to the same color used for the direct light so the light emits direct and indirect light using the same tint. Effectively it means all the photons that are cast into the scene will apply that tint to surfaces they interact with, because they transfer color properties. That initial color is subject to change, because photons also inherit color from surfaces, as discussed previously with respect to color bleeding.

In addition, with Maya and XSI note that specifying the number of stored photons (the globillum and caustic options) requires you to first enable that particular feature under the render settings, as discussed next with the options block options. Thus, you first enable global illumination or caustics under the render settings, and only then you can specify a photon count under the light's options.

> You should typically use area lights when possible with indirect lighting, which is always better because photons are emitted over a given area (radiant exitance) rather than from an infinitely small point. The result will provide for better illumination.

MAYA

For a selected light (point, spot, or directional), you can find the photon emission attributes under the mental ray rollout → Caustics and Global Illumination rollout shown in Figure 12.11. To enable photon emission, simply check the Emit Photon attribute box. You then use the remaining settings to control the light's contribution to indirect illumination.

As cited earlier, use the Photon Color attribute to define an initial color for photons and the Photon Intensity attribute to define the energy intensity. Both these attributes correlate to the energy option discussed earlier. The Exponent attribute is the same as the exponent option; it is set to 2 by default, providing an inverse square falloff. Both Caustic Photons and Global Illum Photons clearly define the number of photons that are stored with each simulation, and they are editable only after the corresponding attributes have been enabled in the Render Settings window, as cited earlier.

Notice that a physical light shader is also attached to the same source light. The physical light Color attribute should have RGB values that correspond to the Photon Intensity attribute so that as a starting point they emit the same light intensity into the scene. You then can increase or decrease either one, as discussed earlier for improving photon illumination. The light is also set as an area light, so overall this is the sort of light you typically set up for indirect illumination.

XSI

Under the light properties you can find the photon emission properties on the Photon tab shown in Figure 12.12. To enable photon emission, check the Caustics or Global Illumination property boxes. When both are enabled, you will emit both global illumination and caustic photons into the scene if those features are also enabled globally in the Render Options property window. You then use the remaining settings to control the light's contribution to indirect illumination.

The Energy color property defines an initial color for photons, and the Intensity property defines the energy intensity. Both properties correspond to the energy option discussed earlier. The Exponent property is actually located on the General tab so that it is shared with direct lighting; essentially both will have the same falloff rate. Just note that with direct lighting you need to check the Light Falloff property box and set Mode to Use Light Exponent in order to enable direct light decay. A value of 2 provides inverse square falloff, as cited earlier.

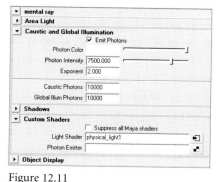

Figure 12.11

Maya light options for indirect illumination

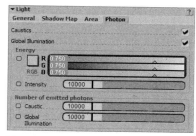

Figure 12.12

XSI light options for indirect illumination

Both Caustic and Global Illumination properties under Number of Emitted Photons control photon emission. In spite of their names, they actually control the number of *stored* photons, as discussed earlier. Both properties become editable only after the equivalent properties have been enabled in the mental ray Render Options property window, as cited earlier. The light can (recommended) also be set as an area light on the Area tab, so overall this is the sort of light you typically set up for indirect illumination.

Figure 12.13

3ds Max light options for indirect illumination

3DS MAX

For a given light in the Modify panel, you can find the photon emission parameters under the mental ray Indirect Illumination rollout, as shown in Figure 12.13. To enable photon emission, simply check the Automatically Calculate Energy and Photons parameter box, or alternatively, you can check the On parameter box under Manual Settings. Both enable indirect illumination, but the parameters under Manual Settings include all the options discussed earlier, and the former provides fewer settings by automating some of the process.

The automation technique is based on parameters that are defined globally in the mental ray Renderer parameters window. I'll cover them later in this chapter with indirect illumination. The Energy, Caustic, and GI Photons parameters act as multipliers for the global parameters. Ideally it is aimed at setting all the lights with the same parameters for indirect light, and then you can fine-tune these settings on a per-light basis using these multipliers.

Under the Manual Settings parameters, the Color parameter defines an initial color for photons, and the Energy parameter defines the energy intensity. Both parameters correlate to the energy option discussed earlier. The Decay parameter is the same as the exponent option cited earlier; it is set to 2 by default, providing an inverse square falloff. Both Caustic Photons and GI Photons define the number of photons that are stored with each simulation. Typically it is better to use area lights unless you are using photometric lights, as discussed in Chapter 6, "Lights and Soft Shadows," so overall this is the sort of light you set up for indirect illumination.

Indirect Illumination Options and Fine-Tuning

To use indirect illumination, you need to define two sets of options, as cited earlier. The light options define the photon-scattering characteristics on a per-light basis, and the option block options are used to enable and tweak global illumination, caustics, and participating media effects on a global level. The option block options for global illumination and caustics are shown here:

```
## Global illumination options
globillum [on | off]
globillum accuracy [photons] [radius]
globillum scale [RGBA color]
```

```
        "globillum merge" [distance]

        ## Caustic options
        caustic [on | off]
        caustic filter [type] [size]
        caustic accuracy [photons] [radius]
        caustic scale [RGBA color]
        "caustic merge" [distance]

        ## General options
        photon trace depth [reflections][refractions] [max trace]
        photonmap rebuild [on | off]
        photonmap file "filename"
```

All these options are global to the scene and are used to enable and fine-tune global illumination (GI) and caustics, based on which set of options are included in the options block. These options define how mental ray will use GI and caustic photons during the second phase of indirect illumination, which is rendering. They define how photons are averaged and scaled when added with direct illumination. By looking at the previous excerpt, you can tell that the options divide into three categories: GI, caustics, and general settings. Some of these features are quality control features, and others are optimization features that improve render times.

Note that some of these options can also be specified on a per-object level, overriding global settings; but they are functional only when GI or caustics are enabled. You'll learn about per-object options in the host sections later in this chapter.

General Options

The general options shown in the previous excerpt are used to define how photons are traced in the scene and whether mental ray should generate a photon map or reuse an existing map. In addition to these options, mental ray also has two photon diagnostic techniques that help troubleshoot photonic emission counts and energy levels. Let's review the general options and then examine the diagnostic modes.

Controlling Photon Reflections and Refractions

The `photon trace depth` option limits the number of times photons can bounce in the scene, similar to the raytrace limits discussed in Chapter 2. Since real-world photons are not limited to a given number reflections or refractions, when you increase the photon trace depth values, you enable mental ray to conduct a more realistic simulation of light. Earlier in this chapter I mentioned that photons bounce in the scene until they are fully absorbed or cast into empty space. That statement is only partially true, because they are also limited by the number of bounces permitted with this option.

As you see in the excerpt, you can specify reflections, refractions, and a max trace depth, just as with raytrace limits. The max trace depth defines the total reflections and refractions combined that a given photon can occur. If you consider reflections, which is the primary type of trace a photon undergoes as it bounces in the scene, too low a value can significantly reduce the amount of light and color bleeding in the scene. Thus, increasing the reflection trace value helps better illuminate the scene by allowing more photons to interact with surfaces. An increase in value also provides for more color bleeding between surfaces. In the color gallery, "Photon Trace Limits" shows two images side by side. Image A has a reflection limit of 3, and image B has a reflection limit of 6. As you can see, image B appears brighter and also demonstrates more color bleeding across the surfaces.

Photon Maps

The `photonmap file "filename"` option defines a file name on disk that is used to store a photon map. Typically each host defaults to a mental ray photon maps directory (see the "host application" section later in the chapter). Once the file is stored you don't need to generate photons again, unless of course objects in the scene are in motion, or you change (or animate) the settings of the photon light options or photon shader options. Specifically, if you change the light photon energy or photon count, you need to generate a new photon map.

The `photonmap rebuild [on | off]` option defines whether a new photon map is generated (when set to on) or a preexisting one is used (when set to off). Thus, when you render a scene for the first time, photons are generated. For subsequent renders, you can choose to set this option to off and continue tweaking the camera, direct lighting intensity and color, and some of the indirect illumination global options without regenerating a new photon map every time you render, reducing the render time particularly with large photon counts. Photon maps are based on the light's location in the scene; because they are not dependent on the camera, you can generate a light solution (photon map) and render it from any angle or even with an animated camera while reusing the same photon map without taking the time to generate a new one unless you move the photon source light itself.

> If for some reason the photon map is set to off and you render, either you will see the result from an old photon map or you won't see anything at all. Make sure to keep track of this option while using GI or caustics, as discussed in detail throughout the remainder of the chapter.

Also, the indirect illumination options shown in the previous excerpt for caustics and global illumination define how photons are rendered; thus they too can change without requiring you to rebuild a photon map. It is a common practice to generate a photon map and then set `photonmap rebuild` to `off` while adjusting the GI or caustic accuracy, radius, and scale. However, if you change the trace depth, you need to rebuild a new photon map, because the trace option influences the spread of photons in the scene, not just how they appear when rendered. At some point you may decide to change the photon count, exponent, photon color, or energy (under the source light's options), which also requires generating a new photon map as their first phase (emission) properties have changed.

In other words, every time you change options that influence the first phase of indirect lighting, you need to regenerate a new photon map file. Obviously, if you change direct light settings or illumination shader settings, you don't need to create a new photon map because those settings are not used with indirect illumination photons.

Photon maps are especially beneficial for animated scenes that have static objects where only the camera changes, as with fly-through animations. If you have a large scene that is static but a character interacts within it, consider rendering first the background and then the character as separate passes to avoid rebuilding photon maps. You could also just reuse the same photon map while the character interacts in the scene; the character will not influence the indirect light in any way, similar to using passes. Remember that direct and indirect lighting are rendered as separate components and then added with a render equation so you can achieve the same results when adding the two lighting solutions together in compositing, See the sidebar "Compositing Light Passes." An advantage with photon maps is that you can create a few different solutions and then just enter the name for your favorite one as well as disable the rebuilding option.

Photon Diagnostics

There are two modes for diagnosing the distribution of photons in the scene. One is based on density, and the other is irradiance intensity. Both options enable you to see a color transition from blue (minimum), cyan, green, and yellow to red (maximum). The command-line option used to enable photon diagnostics is as follows:

```
-diagnostic photon [off|density|irradiance] [max]
```

The image "Photon Density" in the color gallery shows the photon density diagnostic mode and then the result after applying photon merging (discussed next). As you can see, the location of the light is between the upper column and the ceiling, projecting light upward. The result is a higher photon density, shown in red in that area of the ceiling, while other areas of the scene appear blue. In the same way you can visualize the irradiance across surfaces.

COMPOSITING LIGHT PASSES

With compositing passes, you need to add the direct light and indirect light passes together and then multiply them against a color pass. Alternatively, you can multiply each one by the color pass and then add them together, since light is multiplied by color, as discussed in Chapter 9, "The Fundamentals of Light and Shading Models." Thus, areas that do not receive light will appear black and areas with a light value of 1, for example, will show the surface's full color.

A color pass needs to be a full ambient pass without any shading, only texture color, since the light passes add the diffuse character of light. You can set the ambient color on shaders to white or alternatively use an ambient light (if your host provides one) without any shading to generate a color pass. In all cases, you should delete or disable any light sources, including the default light from the scene. Here are some host-application specifics:

- In Maya the simplest approach is to create an ambient light and set the Ambient Shade attribute to 0 so that it's pure ambient light. In this way you don't need to set ambient color on a per-shader level. Disable the default light in the Render Settings window on the Common tab.

- In XSI and 3ds Max you need to replace the shades with a constant shaders (no shading; simple color output) or use custom passes.

These are basic guidelines, and as discussed in Chapter 3, "mental ray Output," each host has various options for outputting custom passes more effectively. Consider that such a color pass doesn't include diffuse characteristics, such as bump mapping (and the Diffuse attribute in Maya). The diffuse effect of bump mapping needs to be present in the light passes that define the intensity of light based on the surface normal, which may be perturbed by a bump map. Thus, light passes also include per-surface diffuse characteristics.

Furthermore, you then need to add additional passes such as specular, reflection, and shadow color passes, to mention a few. In a nutshell, the math behind the composite tree, at the most basic level, is as follows:

Indirect light pass × color pass = indirect color and light (A)

Direct light pass × color pass = direct color and light (B)

((A + B) × shadow pass) + Specular highlights pass + Reflection color pass

This topic warrants a book on its own; the information presented here is only enough to get you started and to help you understand the internal workings of adding light passes. Chapter 13, "Final Gather and Ambient Occlusion," covers some additional passes with ambient occlusion.

The max value used with both options defines how the maximum limit is set, defining what density level or irradiance intensity appears as red. With density it defines a number of photons per-surface area, and with irradiance it defines the irradiance intensity. Higher values tend to reduce the visible transition from red to blue, as you permit more photons (density) per-surface area or accept higher irradiance values. The following section shows one example of using diagnostics to fine-tune photon merging. You should experiment with these modes to learn more about them.

Global Illumination (GI)

This section examines the global illumination options and defines each option's purpose so you can better understand how they relate to the light options discussed earlier, particularly photon counts. After reviewing these options, you will look at fine-tuning them with a few simple examples that are easy to visually interpret.

Global Illumination Options

The globillum [on | off] option enables or disables GI. When the option is disabled, a source light will not emit photons, even if it is set to do so. Thus, you don't need to concern yourself with disabling photon emission on a per-light basis when GI is disabled at the global scene level.

The globillum scale [RGBA color] option acts as a global color multiplier for global illumination. Decreasing the value reduces the total irradiance across surfaces in the scene. Note that you can also render a 32-bit global illumination light pass and then have more control over the irradiance (overexposure) in compositing without the overhead of rendering times; however, that affects the entire image, whereas this option influences only GI.

The "globillum merge" [distance] option merges photons in near proximity, within the given distance in scene units. As discussed in the sidebar "3D Photon Maps and Kd-Trees," one of the advantages of a Kd-tree, such as a photon map, is that you can conduct searches within a given area or radius. In this case, that radius is used to define a distance where points in the tree will be combined into an individual point, reducing the density of points in the Kd-Tree. Thus, it reduces the number of photons stored in the photon map, decreasing its file size. It also has an effect on the rendered appearance of photons; as you increase the merge distance, you can eliminate artifacts that occur when too many photons with different colors are interpolated over a small distance. The image "Photon Density" in the color gallery shows photon density in a diagnostic mode and the result after applying a small distance value for photon merging.

Consider the case that you have a very dense distribution of photons in a small portion of the scene, whereas the remainder of the scene doesn't receive enough photons. Naturally you increase the light's photon count to force more photons into sparse areas of the scene; however, at the same time you also increase the density of the photons in the denser areas. In such extreme cases you may want to use the merge option to reduce the density of photons in a given area, improving render performance. In the "General Options" section earlier in the chapter, you looked at the options for diagnosing photon distributions.

The `globillum accuracy [photons] [radius]` option is the most significant option for quality control. This option determines how photons are interpolated to produce a final color and look for the image. Most of the work with GI is based on balancing this option along with the light's photon count and energy. With all host applications, the `globillum accuracy` option is divided into two separate options: `accuracy` and `radius` (labeled similarly in each host). The `radius` option does not have to be specified; if it's not, mental ray will derive a best guess value based on 0.01 percent of the scene size. With hosts, specifying a radius of 0 has the effect of forcing the default settings.

The `accuracy (photons)` setting defines how many photons are used to extract color within a given radius from the sample point. With higher accuracy values, more photons are considered during sampling and the render time increases. Larger radius values enable more photons to overlap based on their distribution in the scene. You can see how these options fall in line with Kd-trees and conducting searches in a given area.

Note that here is one of the major differences between real-life photons and simulation of indirect light in CG. In real-world conditions, photons exist in infinite numbers, not limited to 100,000 or a million. Thus, the accuracy and radius options allow for simulating photons within a region, where each mental ray photon is equivalent to an area of photon spread. The more photons you use, the finer the color and light detail distributed in the scene. Let's discuss balancing photon counts with the accuracy and radius options.

Fine-Tuning Accuracy, Radius, and Photon Counts

The first step is recognizing the effects of the `radius` and `accuracy` options. You can then examine how to balance them effectively. In the following examples, GI is enabled in the host's global render settings, and a top-down area light emits photons into the scene.

The workflow for fine-tuning indirect illumination is to create an initial photon map and then disable the Rebuild Photon Map option (set it to `off`). You then reuse that map while tweaking the `accuracy` and `radius` values. At some point you may decide to cast more photons into the scene, so you need to change the light's photon count and rebuild a new photon map and then again test different `accuracy` and `radius` values until you are satisfied with the result.

The scene in this example, shown in Figure 12.14, is based on a *Cornell box* scheme. A Cornell box is typically a square room with one red wall and one blue wall, and the center wall, floor, and ceiling are white. A Cornell box room can be used to examine how indirect illumination color bleeding affects objects in the room and examine light distribution using different accuracy, radius, and photon counts. In this case, the scene is populated with a kitchen and a wooden floor. Some of the objects in the scene have color textures, and the right wall is red and the left wall is blue, as with a Cornell box. Let's look at some different settings and their effect on the rendered image and then derive some conclusions on how to fine-tune global illumination.

Figure 12.14
Casting 5,000 photons into the scene with a small radius value of 2 and accuracy set to 10

In Figure 12.14 you can see the spread of 5,000 photons in the scene. Direct lighting is set to a negligible value so that it does not affect the scene and you see only the effects of indirect light and photon shaders. Note that you can see specular reflections of photons, as demonstrated earlier with Figures 12.3 and 12.4; for example, the reflection of the door appears on the floor. You can see the color version for this image on the companion CD in the Chapter 12 folder. In color you will notice the effect on the white ceiling, which acquires a multitude of color photons from various objects in the scene.

In this case, the photon accuracy is set to 10, and radius is set to 2. The radius defines the search area for photons when sampling a point in the scene. Any photons found in that area are averaged based on the accuracy value. In other words, the accuracy determines how many photons will be used to define the color within that radius. The result is a circle of colors that blend to provide the final color seen within that radius. In this case, you can see that there are too few photons in the scene, and several areas in the scene are not covered with photons. Thus, a radius of 2 with 5,000 photons leaves several areas unaffected by indirect light. If you increase the radius, you can then blend more photons over a larger region, affecting more areas in the scene such as in the corners of the room.

In Figure 12.15 (also available on the CD), the radius has been increased to 4, and you see more indirect light coverage in the scene. Note that there are still areas in the scene that don't receive any contribution from indirect lighting and are marked with the arrows shown in the figure. One of your goals with indirect light is to balance the photon distribution in a way that affects the entire scene.

Figure 12.15

Increasing the radius to 4 blends more photons over a larger region

I also increased the accuracy to 200 in Figure 12.15. However, you can clearly see splotches of color (in grayscale), so clearly the photons are not blending in a way that provides aesthetic results. Thus, even though I increased the radius, there are still far too few photons in the scene to blend properly, and therefore increasing the accuracy has no effect. I could increase the accuracy to 1,000 and still the render will appear the same; it is already using all the photons found within the provided radius. That point is one of the most important indications for determining when you need to increase the photon count or increase the radius. If you increase the photon count, you will provide more photons in the scene, and thus a higher accuracy setting will have more of an effect in smoothing out the result. If you increase the radius, you force mental ray to use larger regions in the scene while smoothing the effect. So, what's the difference?

INCREASING RADIUS

Suppose you have a fine detailed scene, where using a larger radius forces photons from distant locations to be considered over a larger area. The result is a more uniform distribution of color rather than a localized one, appearing less realistic with little detail and contrast around scene elements (flat lighting). In other words, it's like blurring color across the entire scene uniformly, as shown in Figure 12.16 (available on the CD, labeled "Photon Spread low"). In color you can see a red tint across the entire scene, because red tints from the wall, wood floor, door, and kitchen provide for a predominant red color, where the blue wall's effect becomes negligible, even within close proximity to it.

Figure 12.16

Direct and indirect lighting using an area light with soft shadows and a low photon count

In Figure 12.16, I increased the radius to 40 and set accuracy at 300, the point where higher values had no effect. You can see that even with a small photon count I was able to optimize the scene so that all the photons are interpolated to provide a smooth result. However, it's not a very satisfactory indirect illumination solution, because it lacks any detail such as fine light qualities and color bleeding in close proximity to the objects; it is thus a "flat" solution. Note that in this case I added the direct lighting so the only nice effect is from the area light that creates the transition on the wall and provides for soft shadows. This example demonstrates the combination of a low photon count GI solution combined with direct lighting.

The "Photon Counts" images in the color gallery provide a more detailed scene using higher photon counts to demonstrate the differences of low vs. high photon counts. Image A corresponds to this example, providing flatter lighting with less detail. The radius was set to 15, and the accuracy was set to 300. The photon count was set to 100,000 photons specified for each of the two source lights in the living room area.

INCREASING PHOTON COUNTS

If you increase the photon count significantly, you can get away with using much smaller radius values, which will ensure that you will see more local color bleeding effects and thus more detail. Look at the color gallery "Photon Counts" image B. Image B compares with image A only using a photon count of 2 million cast from the two living room lights and the two lights above the stove (combined 2 million). The radius was decreased to 4. There is a nicer feel to the lighting around objects displaying a more natural feel opposed to the synthetic feel shown in image A.

With this example (large photon count), I was able to use accuracy settings of up to 2400 and still see a change in the lighting; therefore, the renderer has a significant amount of photons to blend within a smaller radius value (value of 4). The higher accuracy values essentially leveraged several color samples (photons) from the scene to interpolate color, providing better detail, particularly around corners such as on the walls in the kitchen area.

On the companion CD in the Chapter 12 folder you will find the image shown in Figure 12.16 labeled "Photon Spread Low" and the same image using a higher photon count and lower radius labeled "Photon Spread High." In that image, you can see some of the splotchy artifacts on the ceiling as well as more local color bleeding; the red tints from the red wall don't stretch as far as with the low photon count image.

There are a few more points of consideration with respect to fine-tuning GI. With lower radius values, even with higher photon counts and accuracy settings, you will see splotchy artifacts as seen on the CD with the image "Photon Spread High". To remedy such artifacts, I can increase the radius using a lower photon count, as I did for the example in Figure 12.16; however, I start to lose the detail around the smaller objects. You should consider that a large object, such as the wall, may require a different radius than the furniture in the kitchen. To avoid ruining the effect of GI on the smaller objects, I can use per-object radius and accuracy options, increasing the radius only on the ceiling. You'll look at these options later in this chapter. At this point, a better solution would be to use Final Gather to remove splotchy artifacts from GI, as discussed next.

FINAL CONSIDERATIONS

The ideal with indirect illumination is to blend enough photons within a given radius so that they appear to form a visually pleasing light simulation. You may take the approach of few photons using a larger radius setting to blend photons. One problem with this approach is that areas in the scene will not receive any light, so when you increase the photon radius, they receive the same amount of light as other areas of the scene, which are more exposed to light. This approach flattens out the lighting across the wall into the corners of the scene, so you don't see any natural transition in light intensity.

On the other hand, you can use a large number of photons, where a million or more photons are reasonable with highly detailed scenes. In such cases you will see more detail because photons are likely to spread everywhere in the scene so that you are not required to increase the radius to force color into the corners, such as around the furniture or between walls. As a result, you use smaller radius settings and have more color bleeding and variation in the irradiance across surfaces.

High photon counts really only take time during the first render when you generate a photon map. You then reuse that map while rendering an animated sequence. Essentially, you should not regenerate photon maps with animation, because the true benefit of photon mapping is reusability. Having said that, a larger photon count usually will use higher accuracy values and provide for slower render times, aside from generating photons during the first phase, which is photon emission.

GI, Final Gather, and Ambient Occlusion

Using Final Gather (discussed in Chapter 13, "Final Gather and Ambient Occlusion") provides a means for removing splotchy artifacts in the scene. On that topic, both Final Gather (an indirect lighting technique) and ambient occlusion (a shader) provide a means to add detail in nooks and crannies so that ideally GI can be used with smaller photon counts to provide the overall indirect lighting. This approach means that GI tackles multiple diffuse bounces in the scene, handling most of the color bleeding, and then Final Gather adds diffuse lighting and color bleeding to improve the GI result, as well as improve some of the detail near surfaces in close proximity. Furthermore, if Final Gather is used with low settings so that it doesn't expose all the fine detail (occlusion near objects), ambient occlusion or an ambient occlusion pass (preferable) can be used to add a lot of occlusion detail such as self-shadowing and light occlusion from nearby surfaces. Combining these techniques and more information about Final Gather and ambient occlusion can be found in Chapter 13, "Final Gather and Ambient Occlusion." See the image "Physical Lighting" in the color gallery, which combines all these techniques (GI, Final Gather, and an ambient occlusion pass).

Physical Shaders

Also note that the "Physical Lighting" image in the color gallery was rendered solely with physical shaders. If you choose to use physical shaders, you should use them for all the surfaces in the scene. This is because they deal with energy conservation, as discussed in Chapter 10, "mental ray Shaders and Shader Trees," and thus will appear darker than nonphysical shaders such as Phong or Blinn shaders. Using both types will produce inconsistent shading on surfaces so that one surface may appear overexposed, while neighboring surfaces under the same light will appear underexposed. Mostly, it is easier to follow this approach from the beginning rather than realizing at the final stages of rendering that several shaders are inconsistent and that you need to start converting them to physical shaders, or vice versa.

TONE MAPPING AND GAMMA WORKFLOWS

Indirect illumination deals with linear light (radiance) values that are meant to represent real-world energy values. They can easily exceed the 0 to 1 range of color and overexpose. Using 32-bit images allows you to adjust the exposure in compositing software, without losing detail in overexposed areas, as discussed in Chapter 3, "mental ray Output." You may apply a tone-mapping operation to remap the values from the brightest and darkest areas in the scene so that the final result better simulates human perception under those conditions. Chapter 9, "The Fundamentals of Light and Shading Models," discussed tone mapping, and Chapter 13, "Final Gather and Ambient Occlusion," presented a tone-mapping shader.

With respect to workflow, I typically test render the scene using an 8-bit image with a gamma correction of 1.8 to 2.2. I use a gamma of 1.8 since it better resembles the gamma for film, giving a more cinematic appearance. When I am satisfied with the GI solution, I render the final image as a 32-bit image using a gamma of 1 (linear, unchanged), so I can apply the gamma correction in compositing or Adobe Photoshop. Note that with 32-bit images, gamma correction is disabled with mental ray, so it always renders a linear gamma. This approach provides more control over color correction, exposure, and gamma using a high bit depth so that color artifacts caused by image processing don't appear in the image.

When you open an OpenEXR or HDR 32-bit image (or 8-bit RGBE; see the discussion on data types in Chapter 3) in Photoshop, it automatically applies a gamma correction of 2.2 so that even though you rendered a linear image, it appears gamma corrected. To see what the image looks like without gamma correction, you can select View → 32-bit Preview Options. In the window that opens, set Gamma to 2.2, removing the gamma correction and displaying the image with a linear transition from black to white. The same window appears when you convert a 32-bit image to an 8-bit (or 16-bit) image using Image → Mode → 8 Bits/Channel. You will clearly see that some level of gamma correction is required to finalize the rendered appearance, as discussed in the sidebar "Indirect Illumination and Gamma Correction."

INDIRECT ILLUMINATION AND GAMMA CORRECTION

One of the most important considerations with respect to indirect illumination rendering is gamma correction, as discussed in Chapter 3, "mental ray Output," and Chapter 9, "The Fundamentals of Light and Shading Models." If you don't apply gamma correction, then the light will get too dark too fast, so you'll end up increasing the energy and getting blown out areas around the source light similar to those shown earlier in Figure 12.2 image A. In the image shown here you can see a very large area light at an entrance to a room, casting direct and indirect light. The direct light and indirect light are both set with the same energy values and falloff rate. Gamma is set to linear (unchanged). You can see the light falloff is rapid and unnaturally fast for a source light of that scale.

To fill the room with more light, you may attempt to increase the light's energy, as I have done for both direct and indirect light in the next image. Notice how the entrance to the room reaches overexposure, yet the far side of the room still receives very little light. Thus, increasing the energy was not an adequate solution to render a more realistic appearance to light scattering.

continued

continues

Instead of increasing the energy as with the previous example, in the next image I applied a gamma correction of 2.2. With mental ray I used a gamma value of 0.454 for the render settings (see Chapter 3, "mental ray Output," for details on gamma correction). As you can see, in this image the light scatters more realistically in the room, filling it with light. It reaches the far side of the room without creating overexposure near the entrance, closer to the source light. However, creatively speaking, it may appear too flat for your purposes, which in such cases you can use a lower gamma correction.

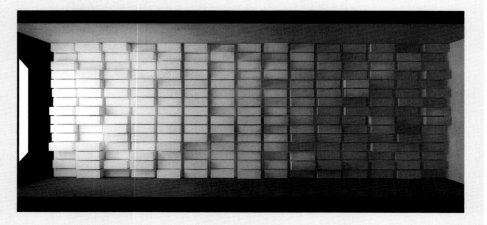

Gamma correction is required when using indirect light, just as much as when you bring images from a digital camera into the computer. With digital photographs it's done for you automatically; most digital cameras use the sRGB color space (discussed in Chapter 9, "The Fundamentals of Light and Shading Models"), which resembles a gamma correction of 2.2. Although the image after gamma correction may appear flatter, meaning there is less contrast, the distribution of light is correct. To remedy the loss of contrast, some artists prefer using a gamma correction of 1.8 (a gamma setting of 0.555) instead of 2.2, which provides a more cinematic look with more contrast. In all cases some gamma correction is desirable, or you end up rendering images with blown-out regions that rapidly and unnaturally transition to black.

The workflow of testing with gamma correction before rendering a high-bit-depth image enables you to see what the lighting should look like while adjusting direct and indirect light settings.

Caustics

Caustics deal with focusing light through refractive and from reflective surfaces. One of the primary differences you'll see when using caustics is in how they manage light energy and shadows. As light transmits or reflects from surfaces, it tends to create more focused patterns of light on the surroundings that magnify in intensity or simply reflect very intense light with minimal absorption, as with a magnifying glass or a mirror. The process of combining caustics with direct lighting using the rendering equation is not the same as when combining GI with direct lighting. GI is influenced by shadows, whereas caustics are used to add light in opaque shadows (for refractive surfaces). Let's look at some of the examples of caustic rendering in the color gallery. The image labeled "Glass Shark Comparisons" shows two glass sharks, one with the dielectric shader (top) and the other using the mia material (bottom). In both cases you can see the caustic patterns on the floor. Notice that the intensity of the caustics is influenced by the thickness (absorption) of the refractive shark, and thus you see more light passing through the fins than through the thicker body regions, particularly with the mia material image on the bottom. You can also see the image labeled "The Water Bottle." Notice the interesting patterns that are formed by the bottle on the wall. One of the nicest effects you gain with caustics is patterns that are formed by caustic light as it passes through shapes that have a more complex form when compared to simple shapes such as spheres or windows.

GI and caustic options are similar; you can see that by comparing the caustics options shown here to the GI options:

```
caustic [on | off]
caustic filter [box|cone|gauss] [size]
caustic accuracy [photons] [radius]
caustic scale [RGBA color]
"caustic merge" [distance]
```

Aside from the `caustic filter` option, the remaining options are the same as with GI. They all have the same functionality as with the equivalent GI options discussed earlier with the difference of controlling caustic photons; see that section (GI) for the option details. With respect to using these options, the main difference is in the approach to selecting values while fine-tuning caustic effects.

The `caustic filter` option defines how the intensity from the center of the sample point transitions outward within the radius. With caustics, the filter option provides additional control in smoothing or sharpening the caustic effect. Typically it should be set to `cone` or `gauss`, where cone will appear sharper. The filter size has the effect of increasing the blurriness with larger values, where the minimum is 1. Typically you would not change it from its default value of 1.1.

The following sections discuss the characteristics of caustics and examine some of the considerations while choosing accuracy and radius values, similar to the earlier discussion with GI.

Shadows and Stained Glass

With respect to transparent (refractive) surfaces, shadows appear brighter based on how much light transmits through the surface. In that respect, caustics are used to add visible light in shadow. With physical shaders, when using the mental ray dielectric shader or the mia material, the shadow renders opaque, as shown in Figure 12.17 image A using the dielectric shader. Caustics are then used to add the "brightness," as shown in the shadow in image B. It also inherits color from the surface color defined with the surface's photon shader. You can also see scattered caustics on the ceiling from reflections as the dielectric surface maintains Fresnel reflections and thus possesses both reflective and refractive characteristics.

Figure 12.17

Caustics add light to opaque shadows while transmitting through refractive surfaces.

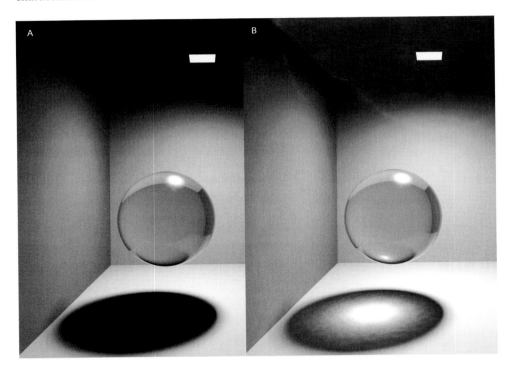

Note that the mia material provides an option for choosing whether you want to define the shadow transparency using caustics or a shadow shader, as discussed in Chapter 10, "mental ray Shaders and Shader Trees." Thus, if you select the shadow shader, the shadow will appear transparent, but the light will not amplify. If you select caustics, the shadow renders opaque, and then caustics define the light intensity in the shadow.

Surfaces that have a transparent shadow from a shadow shader (discussed in Chapter 7, "Shadow Algorithms") and are also affected by caustics doubling up the effect of shadow transparency. To clarify, the shadow is already transparent, and caustics then add even more light on top of that. Creatively speaking (not physically accurate), caustics don't always provide the detail you want to see in transparent shadows since they're harder to fine-tune than a shadow shader. You can use both, but you then need to reduce the intensity of the caustics so they don't create large blown-out areas in the shadow. One problem users typically need to address is stained glass transmission, where you want to see the color of the glass appear in the shadow regions, as shown in the color gallery image "Stained Glass."

In that image you can see patterns of color transmit through the surface. The glass is applied with a dielectric shader. To create the effect of color patterns, I connected the stained glass (checker) texture to the dielectric shader's color input (see Chapter 10, "mental ray Shaders and Shader Trees") and then connected it to the photon shader's color out input. In this way, the color of the glass appears in the direct lighting render (the illumination shader) and also in caustics using the photon shader. You can find the Maya scene file in the Chapter 12 folder on the companion CD. This image is a great example for making the point that caustics are meant to simulate the appearance of light as it transmits or reflects from surfaces, not just a tool to create cool looking patterns.

Note that when using host-specific shaders that already provide shadow color, as discussed in Chapter 7, "Shadow Algorithms," you can override their shadow shader by attaching a separate shadow shader to the material, generating an opaque shadow rather than a transparent one. Consider that if the surface doesn't have the same texture applied to its photon shader's transparency, the caustics will generate a uniformly colored caustic effect that is superimposed over the direct lighting shadow shader effect. Ideally you should use one method for generating shadow color, which also makes it easier to tweak because you don't have to manage two completely different and separate components (caustics and shadow shaders).

Caustic Accuracy and Radius

When you tweak the accuracy and radius values with caustics, you typically try to generate a sharp effect, not a smooth transition of color as with GI. You can see that in the color gallery with the image "The Water Bottle" where the caustic patterns have some rough edges. Therefore, with caustics you will use smaller accuracy or radius values generating sharper patterns. Let's look at an example to see the influence values have on caustics. As with GI, I first generate a photon map and then disable the Rebuild option so I can examine accuracy, radius, and caustic scale (intensity) without rebuilding a photon map each time I render.

The scene shown in Figure 12.18, a Cornell box, has four refractive spheres that are contained within a reflective ring. The spheres demonstrate refractive and reflective caustics using a dielectric shader, and the ring demonstrates reflective caustics using a DGS shader (fully specular). Caustics are enabled on the global level and a photon-casting light is present at the top of the scene, casting 100,000 photons. Gamma correction is set to 0.454 (a standard 2.2 gamma correction for PC monitors) so that the caustics don't fade to black rapidly, as discussed in the sidebar "Indirect Illumination and Gamma."

Tweaking GI and caustics requires a trial-and-error approach to resolve the right look. Also, energy values may differ based on the scene scale as energy is simulated with an inverse square falloff.

Figure 12.18

Examining the effects of caustics using dielectric and DGS shaders

In Figure 12.18 the accuracy was set to 32, and the radius was set to 1. As you can see, there are some nice patterns in the figure, but there is a lot of grain and artifacts everywhere in the image. With caustics, light doesn't spread everywhere; it's based on the surfaces and their reflective or refractive character. The result is that some areas of the scene will receive few photons that are sparsely spread. You can remove or improve their effects in sparsely spread areas in a few ways:

- Increasing significantly the accuracy and radius values until they blend in with the other photons. This has an effect of blurring the patterns, which defeats the purpose.

- Increasing significantly the photon count, which is not always efficient because they still form patterns; however, it provides for better blending when you increase the accuracy.

- Decrease the per-surface irradiance using the surface's shader (discussed on a per-host basis next).

- Decreasing the `caustic scale` option so that there is less visible irradiance in areas with low irradiance value is probably the best approach (discussed shortly).

In Figure 12.19 image A you can see the result of reducing the caustic scale, which has the effect of removing some artifacts—those that were not very bright. By reducing the scale, I keep the detail, reveal more detail that was overexposed, and remove artifacts in the low-intensity areas. In addition, the radius was increased to 2, and the accuracy was increased to 100. As you can see, there is still some grain, but the image has some nicer caustic qualities to it.

Figure 12.19

Increasing the accuracy with caustics has an effect of removing the fine detail seen in the patterns.

The roughness or graininess of caustic can have a visually pleasing appearance, but if you want to remove them completely, you need to continue adjusting values such as increasing the photon count and then changing the accuracy and radius. In image B, the accuracy was increased to 500. As you can see, the result was to blur the caustic effect as well as remove more artifacts. The process of tweaking caustics is usually based on using as low an accuracy as possible to maintain the sharpness of the effect.

Consider rendering a 32-bit caustic pass and then fixing its exposure and sharpening its appearance in compositing, which is an easier and more intuitive approach.

Caustic Irradiance and Merging Photons

The caustic scale option acts like a threshold that can remove irradiance below a certain intensity. In actuality, it is a multiplier that darkens the overall effect. As mentioned earlier with GI, you are not dealing with values between 0 and 1 so that the brightest areas typically possess higher values and will not lose their intensity as you decrease the caustic scale, while artifacts such as those shown in Figure 12.19 are removed.

The photon scale option for GI or caustics, a color option, not only can reduce irradiance, but it can also force a given tint so it can be used to further tweak photon color influence after a photon map is generated.

In Figure 12.20 you can see a glass that has been rendered with caustics enabled, and the caustic scale is set to white (RGB values of 1). The result is a blown-out caustic effect that possesses very little detail. By reducing the scale, you reveal the fine detail that was overexposed. In image B the scale has been reduced to 0.14 for the RGB values, a very significant reduction; however, all the detail stands out. In the same way, you can reduce the light's photon energy; however, that requires you to generate a photon map every time you change that value.

You should always test lower scale values to see if you're losing details in overexposed areas.

Figure 12.20

Revealing caustic patterns by decreasing irradiance.

Note that in the case of Figure 12.20 I used 300,000 photons to bring out the detail; however, the result appeared very grainy, as shown in Figure 12.21. Figure 12.20 (image B) and Figure 12.21 have the same settings. The only difference is that in Figure 12.20 (image B) I also used the `caustic merge` option with a value of 0.5 to merge photons in the denser areas. The result is a significant reduction of the noise shown in Figure 12.21; it also reduces some of the sharpness of the effect.

Figure 12.21

The caustic effect used for Figure 12.20 before photons are merged

All these methods can be used together to find the best solution for each case. Typically you want to compromise with some grain while maintaining the sharpness of the effect shown in the color gallery images "The Water Bottle" and "Glass Shark Comparisons."

GI and Caustics Workflow Considerations

When you want to use GI and caustics in the same scene for diffuse and specular indirect light, there are a few points to note. Most important is that each is an independent solution that stores photons in the photon map. Thus, GI photons are used only for GI, and caustic photons are used only for caustics. Here are a few considerations (in no particular order) for you to contemplate while using indirect illumination:

- Use separate photon-emitting lights for GI and caustic photons. This approach allows you to change the energy level for each solution independent of the other, as well as use better scene framing for the caustic light (further explained in a moment). The following considerations and consequences should be noted.

- When both GI and caustics are enabled on the global level, GI and caustic photon emission is automatically enabled with each photon-emitting light, using default photon emission values (typically 10,000). Thus each light will cast both GI and caustic photons, so you must remember to set the caustic photons to 0 for the GI light, and vice versa, for the caustic-emitting light. See the section "Photon-Emitting Lights" earlier in this chapter.

The GI direct lighting should apply diffuse and specular light since it is cast on all the surfaces in the scene. However, the caustic photon-emitting light should be set to cast specular light only. Better yet, reduce its light intensity to zero so that it casts only photons and doesn't participate in direct lighting. With caustic emitting lights, it is particularly important to remove any direct diffuse light influence. As cited earlier, this approach allows you to focus the caustic emission light only on specular reflective or refractive surfaces that participate in generating caustics. In Figures 12.20 and 12.21 an area light provides the direct lighting, and a spot light, placed at the same location as the area light, casts caustic photons onto the glass. The spot light's perspective (cone) is set to encompass only the glass so that all the photons are being used efficiently. In this way, none is being wasted in the remainder of the room. This approach is particularly important with caustics because they don't need to fill the room with photons before they interact with a specular surface. However, after they reflect or refract on a surface, their influence is applied everywhere in the scene.

Don't forget to rebuild a photon map every time you do the following:

- Change the source light's GI or caustics settings
- Change photon shader settings
- Change the trace depth settings on the global level
- Change the merge photons value

Host Application Settings

The following sections identify the global illumination and caustics options discussed in the previous sections in host applications. The mental ray options are almost identical to those found in each host.

In addition to controlling the radius and accuracy on a per-surface level, as cited earlier, surfaces can also be set as GI or caustic receiving only, casting only, or casting and receiving surfaces. This option allows you to tweak which objects participate in the photon-generating phase and to what extent.

Maya

Except for photon merging, you can find all the global options cited previously in the Render Settings window → mental ray → Caustics and Global Illumination rollouts, as shown in Figure 12.22. The Caustics and Global Illumination attribute checkboxes enable that feature. Once enabled, you can then specify a photon count for a photon-emitting light, as

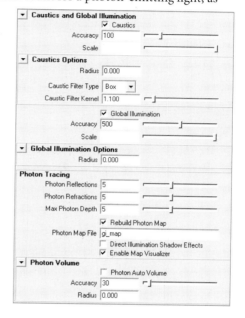

Figure 12.22

Maya indirect illumination attributes in the Render Settings window

cited earlier. Each of these features has default settings that can be changed when you expand the Caustics Options or Global Illumination Options rollout. In the Photon Volume rollout at the bottom of the figure, you can change how participating media effects render in a similar way to GI and caustics, a topic further discussed in the "Participating Media (PM) Effects" section.

You can see the Accuracy, Radius, and Scale attributes for both features that correlate to the `globillum accuracy [photons] [radius]` and `globillum scale [RGBA color]` (or caustic) mental ray options. Under the Caustics Options rollout, you also find the Caustic Filter Type and Caustic Filter Kernel attributes that select the `caustic filter` type and size, respectively.

Under the Photon Tracing rollout, you can find the Photon Reflection, Refraction, and Max Photon Depth attributes, which control the number of photonic reflections and refractions, as discussed earlier.

When the Rebuild Photon Map attribute box is checked, a new photon map is generated with every render. When it's not checked, the photon map is reused. The Photon Map File attribute specifies the name for the photon map. You should omit any extension when entering a name. Typically for a given project the photon files are stored in `\projects\project_name\renderData\mentalRay\photonMap`.

THE MENTAL RAY MAP VISUALIZER WINDOW

The Enable Map Visualizer attribute checkbox creates a Maya MapViz node (listed in the Outliner window) in the scene. As shown in Figures 12.3 and 12.4 earlier in this chapter, it provides an easy way to diagnose the photon distribution in 3D. You can easily see how photons interact in the scene, as well as the photon color when the view is in shaded mode. To control the appearance of these photons in 3D, you can use the mental ray Map Visualizer window shown in Figure 12.23. You can open this window from under the main menu by selecting Window → Rendering Editors → mental ray → Map Visualizer.

> If you want to remove the map from your viewport, you can delete the MapViz node in the Outliner window or press Delete in the mental ray Map Visualizer window.

When you enable the Enable Map Visualizer attribute in the Render Settings window, the photon map is automatically specified under the Map file name attribute shown in Figure 12.23. You can load a different preexisting map and click the Refresh attribute button to see it update in the scene. One of the best features of this window is the attributes

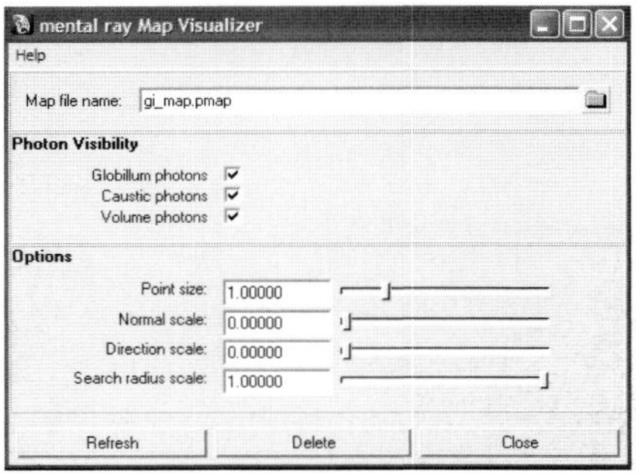

Figure 12.23

Maya's mental ray Map Visualizer window enables you to see photons in the 3D viewport.

under the Photon Visibility heading. Disabling or enabling any of these attributes allows you to see the effect of only GI or caustics in the scene, making it easy to troubleshoot the photon distribution for each component (GI, caustics, and participating media). It is especially helpful when you want to see participating media distributions in the scene; in such a case, you can clear the Globillum Photons and Caustic Photons attribute checkboxes.

MERGING PHOTONS

You have already been introduced to the miDefaultOptions node, which can be found in the Outliner window after you disable Display → DAG Objects Only. Once you select the miDefaultOptions node, you can examine its rollouts and attributes in the Attribute Editor window. Note that mental ray needs to be set as the current renderer for the node to exist in the scene.

> You can also access the miDefaultOptions from the Render Settings window mental ray tab → Framebuffer rollout → User Framebuffer → Open Editor attribute button.

The miDefaultOptions node has all the mental ray options that are included in the Render Settings window and then some. You already used this window in Chapter 8, "Motion Blur," with motion blur. Under the Extra Attributes rollout you will find the Caustic, Photon Volume, and Global Illum Merge attributes (in that order), which were discussed in previous sections.

DIAGNOSING PHOTONS

In the Render Settings window under the mental ray tab → Diagnostics rollout, you can find the Diagnose Photon and Photon Density attributes. Diagnose Photon selects whether you want to render density or irradiance (applied after the image renders), and Photon Density specifies the max value for each option, as discussed earlier in the "Photon Diagnostics" section and shown in the image "Photon Density" in the color gallery.

PER-SURFACE ATTRIBUTES

You can find per-surface attributes within two different nodes for a given surface. Under the transform node → mental ray rollout → Flags, you find the Caustic and Globillum attribute overrides. To use them, you need to first clear the Derive from Maya attribute checkbox, as shown in Figure 12.24. As you can see in the figure, I changed the Caustic attribute to Cast+Receive and set Globillum to Cast Only. These options define how surfaces participate in indirect illumination. In this case, the surface would both receive and cast caustic photons and cast (reflect) only GI photons. Thus, the surface would not receive any indirect diffuse (GI) light, but it would affect other surfaces with indirect diffuse light, because it is set to cast.

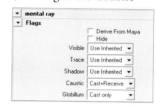

Figure 12.24

Overriding per-surface attribute under a surface's transform node

Under the shape node of a given surface, you find another mental ray rollout, as shown in Figure 12.25. In that rollout you can define per-surface accuracy and radius options overriding the global option values. Both Global Illumination Override and Caustic Override attribute checkboxes are checked in the figure. Thus, when rendering, the surface will use these values to define the radius and accuracy. It can be used to fine-tune areas with a lot of artifacts so that you increase the radius and accuracy only for a particular object, such as the ceiling in a room. This ensures the remaining areas of the scene maintain their detail, but the ceiling will look smoother, as discussed earlier in this chapter.

Figure 12.25

Overriding accuracy and radius per-surface attributes under a surface's shape node

SHADER IRRADIANCE

You can fine-tune the irradiance across a surface when using Maya-centric shaders. Each of the Maya shaders (Blinn, Phong, and so on) has a mental ray rollout, as shown in Figure 12.26, which contains the Irradiance Color attribute. Reducing the color from white to black has the effect of decreasing the irradiance effect on the object, as cited earlier.

Figure 12.26

Shader irradiance controls the light intensity on a per-shader basis.

XSI

You can find the global mental ray options in the mental ray Render Options property window (or in the Render Manager) → mental ray → GI and Caustics tab. The Global Illumination and Caustics Enable property checkboxes enable those features. You will then see all the options for each feature appear in the window, as well as the general options used with both of them, such as photon map name and trace properties, as shown in Figure 12.27. Also, when either option is enabled, you can then specify a photon count for a photon-emitting light, as mentioned earlier. Notice the Photon Volume Accuracy section near the bottom of the window, where you change how participating media effects render in a similar way to GI and caustics, a topic further discussed in the "Participating Media (PM) Effects" section.

You can see under the Global Illumination and Caustics properties the Accuracy, Search Radius, Merge Factor, and Photon Color properties for both features; these correspond to the `globillum accuracy [photons] [radius]`, `globillum merge`, and `globillum scale [RGBA color]` (or caustics) mental ray options, respectively. Under the Caustics properties you can see the Sharpness Filter Type and Size properties; these select the `caustic filter` type and size.

> You can easily fine-tune accuracy and search radius properties while viewing a constant update within a render region.

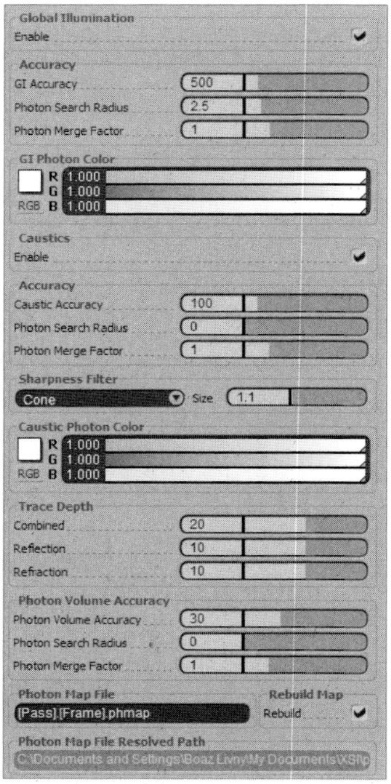

Figure 12.27

XSI indirect illumination properties shown in the Render Manager window

Under the Trace Depth section you can find the Combined, Reflection, and Refraction properties that control the number of photonic reflections and refractions and the total for both, as discussed earlier.

When the Rebuild Map → Rebuild property box is checked, a new photon map is generated with every render. When it's disabled, the photon map is reused. Use the Photon Map File property to specify the name for the photon map. You should omit any extension when entering a name. You can see the path where the photon map is stored in Photon Map File Resolved Path; typically it uses the active project's Render_Pictures directory.

DIAGNOSING PHOTONS

On the Render Options window → Diagnostics tab, you can find the View Photons and Maximum properties, shown in Figure 12.28. The View Photons drop-down list specifies whether you want to render density or irradiance (applied after the image renders), and the Maximum property specifies the max value for density, as discussed earlier in the "Photon Diagnostics" section and shown in the image "Photon Density" in the color gallery. You can easily view these diagnostic modes in a render region while troubleshooting indirect lighting.

Figure 12.28

XSI diagnostic properties for photon density and irradiance

PER-SURFACE PROPERTIES

You can find per-surface properties in a surface's Visibility property window, as shown in Figure 12.29. You can access this window from the Explorer window under the surface's stack or from the Main Command Panel (on the right) Selection → visibility.

As you can see in the figure, under Caustic I disabled the Caster property, and under Global Illumination I left all three properties enabled. These properties define how surfaces participate in indirect illumination. In this case, the surface is visible to GI photons

Figure 12.29

Overriding per-surface attributes in the Visibility window

and will receive and cast GI photons. The Visible property defines whether the GI or caustic photons interact (reflect or refract) with a surface. When it's disabled, the photons pass through the surface, ignoring its existence. It differs from the Caster property in that casting means the surface actually reflects or refracts (redirects) photons and Visible means they merely pass through it.

With respect to caustic photons in the scene, in this case the object will only receive caustic photons. Thus, the surface would not cast any caustic photons into the scene, even if it has specularity defined in its photon shader. However, it would be affected by caustics from other surfaces in the scene.

SHADER IRRADIANCE

You can fine-tune the irradiance across a surface when using XSI shaders. Each of the XSI shaders (Blinn, Phong, and so on) has an Indirect Illumination tab, as shown in Figure 12.30. On this tab you can find the Radiance color property shown in the figure. Reducing the color from white to black has an effect of decreasing the irradiance on the surface, as cited earlier.

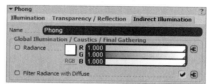

Figure 12.30

Shader Radiance controls the surface irradiance on a per-shader basis.

3ds Max

You can find the global mental ray options cited earlier in the mental ray Renderer window → Indirect Illumination tab. The Global Illumination (GI) and Caustics Enable parameter checkboxes enable those features, as shown in Figure 12.31. Notice the Volumes section, where you change how participating media effects render in a similar way to GI and caustics, a topic further discussed in the "Participating Media (PM) Effects" section.

Figure 12.31
XSI indirect illumination parameters in the Render Manager window

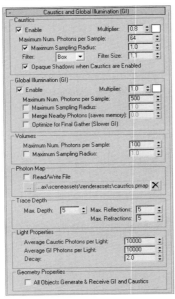

Under the Global Illumination (GI) and Caustics parameters, the Maximum Num. Photons per Sample parameter refers to the mental ray accuracy option, and the Maximum Sampling Radius parameter refers to the radius option. When the Maximum Sampling Radius parameter is disabled, the radius is derived automatically from the scene size. The Multiplier parameter and color swatch refer to the globillum scale[RGBA color] (or caustics) mental ray options. Both the multiplier and color swatch are used together to define the GI and caustics irradiant influence in the scene, as discussed earlier.

Under the Global Illumination (GI) parameters, the Merge Nearby Photons parameter corresponds to the globillum merge mental ray option. Under the Caustics parameters, you can see the Filter and Filter Size parameters, which select the caustic filter type and size, respectively.

Under the Photon Map parameters, when the Read/Write File parameter checkbox is enabled, a new photon map is generated with every render. When it's disabled, the photon map is reused. Select the browsing button below this parameter to specify a photon map file and directory, as shown in the figure. You should omit any extension when entering a name.

Under the Trace Depth parameters, you find the Max. Depth, Max. Reflection, and Max. Refraction parameters, which control the number of photonic reflections and refractions and the total for both, as discussed earlier.

The Light Properties parameters are used to set scene global values for photon count and decay. As discussed in the 3ds Max instructions in the "Photon-Emitting Lights" section, each light has two sets of options for defining the photon emission. The automatic technique described in that section uses these values as base settings. You can then use the multipliers under the light's parameters to amplify or decrease each component. Thus, all the lights will have the same starting point for photon emission and decay when set to automatic. When you set a light to Manual Settings, these settings are not used with that light. Ideally, with a large number of photon casting lights, it becomes easier to find a good balance of light by using a global starting point and then increasing or decreasing photon emission counts locally.

DIAGNOSING PHOTONS

In the mental ray Renderer window → Processing → Diagnostics rollout, you can find the photon diagnostics parameters, as shown in Figure 12.32. The Enable parameter enables diagnostics. When it's enabled, you can then select the Photon parameter radio button and select Density or Irradiance from the drop-down list, as discussed earlier in the "Photon Diagnostics" section and shown in the image "Photon Density" in the color gallery.

Figure 12.32

3ds Max diagnostic parameters for photon density and irradiance

PER-SURFACE ATTRIBUTES

You can find per-surface properties in a surface's Object Properties window → mental ray tab, as shown in Figure 12.33. You can access this window by right-clicking over an object and selecting Object properties.

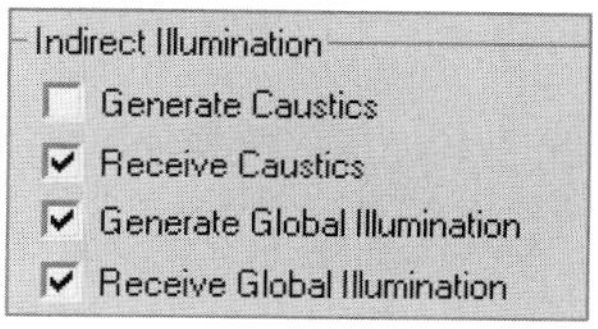

As you can see in the figure, Generate Caustic is by default disabled. These parameters define how surfaces participate in indirect illumination. In this case, the surface will receive and cast GI photons, and with respect to caustic photons, in this case the surface will only receive photons. Thus, the surface would not cast any caustic photons into the scene, even if it has specularity defined in its photon shader. However, it would be affected by caustics from other surfaces in the scene. Also, under the mental ray Renderer window → Indirect Illumination tab → Geometry Properties parameters, shown in Figure 12.31, the All Objects Generate & Receive GI and Caustics forces all the objects to participate in indirect lighting regardless of their per-surface parameters, as shown in Figure 12.32.

Figure 12.33

Setting per-surface parameters in the Object Properties window

> To use a surface as a caustic-generating surface, you need to first enable the Generate Caustics parameter in the Object Properties window or enable the global All Objects Generate & Receive GI and Caustics parameter.

Participating Media (PM) Effects

Participating media effects are used to simulate any type of atmospheric effect that absorbs and scatters light, as well as the effect on shadowing (with segmented raytrace shadows only; see Chapter 7, "Shadow Algorithms"). The environment we usually deal with in CG can be thought of as a vacuum; atmospheric particles are nonexistent. When such effects are needed such as haze, mist, and so on, mental ray uses a PM shader with certain variables (provided by the user) to determine how to simulate the existence of an atmosphere. Calculating the influence of suspended particles in air requires a technique known as *ray marching*.

> The term *particles* as used in this discussion does not refer to CG particles but to molecules or water droplets that are present in the atmosphere.

PM effects are applied using the parti_volume and parti_volume_photon shaders (see the host application sections in the "Photon Shaders and Settings" section), which illuminate nongeometric particles that are suspended within a volume; these shaders support both direct and indirect illumination simulations.

In contrast to other volumetric lighting techniques, PM is independent of source lights. It is not a volume effect that is added to a light. Rather, it is an effect applied within a given region (volume). Therefore, participating media utilize all the illumination sources that have influence within that volume. (You can define which lights will be associated with the shader, but by default all lights that have influence in the volume will be used.) Varying sources of illumination will affect participating media at varying colors and intensities, where the strongest effect appears in close proximity to the source lights, where you see a lot of light absorption and scattering that decays over distance, as shown in the color gallery images "Participating Media Effects" and "Photon Counts." Obviously, for PM effects, you must have at least one source light that has influence in the volume.

> I recommend using physically correct lights, such as the mental ray physical light, which provides more realistic participating media simulations by accounting for realistic light decay and energy.

In the color gallery image "Participating Media Effects," you can see the two large spot lights on the ship provide a strong source of light that is responsible for illumination most of the scene. Aside from that, you can see rays of light casting out from the windows. Since light absorbs fast, I also used an area light above the front of the ship to light up the canon. As you can see, various light sources at various intensities provide for variation in the PM effect's color and intensity.

I then set all the surfaces in the scene with a constant black shader and removed the windows (hidden layer) for the purpose of rendering participating media as an independent pass. The PM pass was then multiplied by the color pass so that I could tweak the intensity of PM effects in compositing. I'll briefly return to the topic of PM passes later in this chapter.

PM effects are expensive to render (slow); therefore, when you're making subtle changes in intensity, you should apply them in compositing with more control and while viewing immediate feedback (the result).

There are three categories of PM effects:

- Direct light PM handles the effects seen in a direct line of sight from source lights; for this the PM volume shader (direct lighting) is always required regardless of whether you use GI and caustics.

- When a PM photon shader is added and GI is enabled, the PM effect handles multiple photon scattering in indirect lines of sight.

- When a PM photon shader is added and caustics are enabled, the PM effect handles illumination of particles that transmit through or reflect from caustic surfaces.

The following section examines all these categories.

Ray Marching and Light Scattering

Light spills into a room in a particular direction, illuminating visible dust particles in its path. The observer can look at that light and recognize the interaction between suspended particles and light. Ray marching calculates the path light takes between these visible particles from the camera's point of view, and the PM shader settings determine the frequency (interval for ray marching rays), illumination, and absorption at those points of contact. Essentially, ray marching casts rays between suspended particles in a given path, evaluating the light's influence at those locations, as shown in images A, B, and C in Figure 12.34 A. Thus participating media simulates eye-rays that are cast into the scene (from the camera's point of view), and collide with illuminated particles within their paths as seen under labels A and B in the figure. At each point of collision (with a theoretical particle) the illumination is calculated with the PM shader, providing perceivable particles that reflect and absorb light in the scene.

Anisotropic and Isotropic Scattering

With respect to the scattering characteristics of PM, there are four fundamental aspects of light that are considered: emission, abosorption, out-scattering, and in-scattering.

Emission The emission of light (photons) from suspended particles that are not dependent on incoming light; self-illumination properties. It has the effect of increasing radiance scattered from particles. For example, fire is a self-illuminating type of participating media.

Figure 12.34

Ray marching in participating media evaluates the light path between particles that are seen from the observer's point of view and reflect light from a given source light.

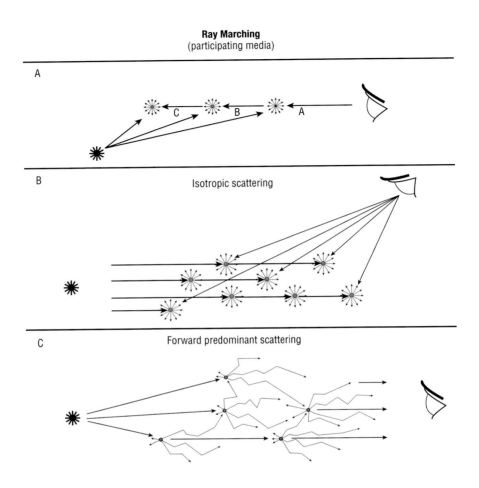

Absorption This deals with decreasing radiance by absorbing light. For example, the sky molecules or clouds absorb light on its way to Earth; this is further discussed shortly.

Out-scattering This deals with light that is reflected outward from the particles (perturbed from the light path), as with the example of the sky cited earlier. It has the effect of decreasing radiance while absorbing and reflecting light. For example, as discussed in Chapter 9, "The Fundamentals of Light and Shading Models ," the Beer-Lambert law of absorption is used to determine how much light is absorbed and scattered through a dense medium such as fluids, clouds, or the sky.

In-scattering This determines how much light (how many photons) enter and scatter internally in a medium. It has the effect of increasing radiance while scattering light within the medium, such as with subsurface scattering.

Typically you can pair out-scattering and absorption, which both define how a medium decreases radiance, and you can pair in-scattering with emission because they both define the increase of radiance due to internal scattering and emission.

With respect to the scatter intensity and directionality, participating media can scatter light in a particular direction, referred to as *anisotropic scattering*. Chapter 9, "The Fundamentals of Light and Shading Models," discussed anisotropic scattering in the context of surface grooves flowing in a particular direction, as with brushed metals. But in this case there is no surface, and the scattering characteristics are based on a *phase function* that models the probability of light scattering (its intensity in a given direction) in a hemisphere around the incident light point of contact on the particle and based on some predefined parameters. It is, as with BSDF functions, based on the particle's characteristics, primarily the particle size that dictates the absorption and scattering characteristics and the angle of incidence (incoming radiance). The particle size provides different scattering characteristics that are defined by two well-known functions, known as *Rayleigh* and *Mie* scattering. These phase functions describe the anisotropic vs. isotropic character of the scattered light based on the medium's character.

RAYLEIGH SCATTERING

The effect of light scattering through molecules in the atmosphere or gases is described as Rayleigh scattering. The Rayleigh function describes a more uniform (diffused) light scatter from each particle in 360°, as illustrated in Figure 12.35 image A, where each light particle emits an equal amount of light in all directions over the hemisphere around the incident light. The Rayleigh phase (p) scattering intensity, in a given scatter angle (θ), is described by the following equation:

$$p(\theta) = 3 \div 16\pi \times (1 + \cos^2\theta)$$

Essentially Rayleigh scattering is a result of particles that are smaller than wavelengths of light and mostly scatter higher frequency wavelengths. To clarify, the violet-blue (higher frequencies, see Chapter 9, "The Fundamentals of Light and Shading Models") wavelengths of light that interact with molecules in air are scattered more than larger frequencies such as green and red. In a nutshell, it explains why the sky is blue, because direct light from the sun travels through the atmosphere predominantly scattering higher frequencies of light on its path to Earth. Furthermore, during sunsets and sunrises, the distance light travels to the viewer is significantly larger (the sun is not directly above, rather farther away), so that more light gets scattered in the atmosphere before we see it. Eventually only the lower frequencies remain visible, because the higher ones have already been absorbed and scattered, and thus we see a warmer color in the sky. Rayleigh scattering is then characterized as selective scattering that predominantly scatters higher frequencies of light. Another example is gases that scatter mostly blue or green frequencies of light.

Figure 12.35

Rayleigh vs. Mie scattering

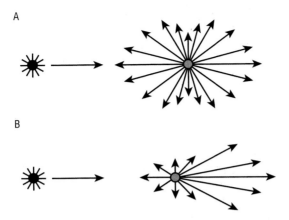

MIE SCATTERING

The Mie scattering function deals with light scattering through particles or droplets of water that are equal or a bit larger then the size of visible wavelengths of light, typically providing more forward scattering as shown in Figure 12.34 image C and 35 image B. If the particles are much larger, then we start to deal with geometric optics, which is the scattering of light on solid surfaces. Mie scattering is not selective (wave dependent) as with Rayleigh scattering, and it scatters all wavelengths of light so that it is not seen as blue or red. For example, clouds that appear gray absorb some of the light internally and scatter the rest outward (scattering all wavelengths equally). It's the type of scattering you see in mist, fog, liquids, clouds, smoke and so forth. Larger particles typically produce more forward scattering. You can see an example for complex environmental conditions that encompass different scattering characteristics in Figure 12.36. The sky is scattered based on Rayleigh scattering, and the clouds and rays of light possess more Mie scattering characteristics.

The Henyey-Greenstein Phase Function

Participating media can favor forward or backward scattering, as with Mie scattering, or Rayleigh scattering referring to anisotropic vs. isotropic scattering. The *Henyey-Greenstein* (HG) and Schlick (HG mathematically simplified) phase functions are typically used in CG to model anisotropic or isotropic light scattering. You will learn about phase functions while referencing only the HG phase function.

The HG works well with empirical data collected thorough experimentation, and thus it can be fit with data that is representative of the scattering characteristics for a given medium. The HG phase function (p) scattering intensity in a given angle (θ) is given with the following equation:

$$p(\theta) = 1 - g^2 \div (4\pi \times (1 + g^2 - 2g \times \cos\theta)^{1.5})$$

Figure 12.36

You can see both Rayleigh and Mie scattering in this photograph.

Without getting into the math, the *g* parameter is used in the function to define the relative intensity of light in a given direction (θ), relative to the light's angle of incidence (the center of the hemisphere for the phase function) and dependent on the cosine of the scattering angle. In Figure 12.37 you can better understand the basics of a phase function. As you can see, a ray forms a hemisphere around a center point, and then the phase function dictates the scatter intensity in each angle (θ) from that center point. In this case, it shows isotropic scattering.

It is similar to how a dot product is used in shading models to define the light intensity relative to the surface normal and direction to the source light. In this case, the phase function $p(\theta)$ is used to describe the scatter intensity in all possible directions within the hemisphere around the center point, as shown in Figure 12.37. Since the HG phase function provides only for a single hemisphere, it can represent scattering in only 180° in the hemisphere, thus either forward or backward scattering. To remedy this, a two-term HG phase function is used, one for forward scattering using a g_1 term and the other for backward scattering using a g_2 term. Essentially the HG function is then used twice to combine two separate lobes (see Chapter 9, "The Fundamentals of Light and Shading Models," for lobes) of light scattering together. An additional *r* term is then used to balance the two together, blending them together. Thus, the two-term HG phase function for a given scatter angle (θ) considers two *g* terms and an *r* term like this ("HG" refers to the HG equation shown earlier):

$$HG(g_1) + (1 - r) \times HG(g_2)$$

Figure 12.37
A ray of light defines
a center point
for a hemisphere
that defines the
scattered light
intensity in each
angle over the hemi-
sphere center.

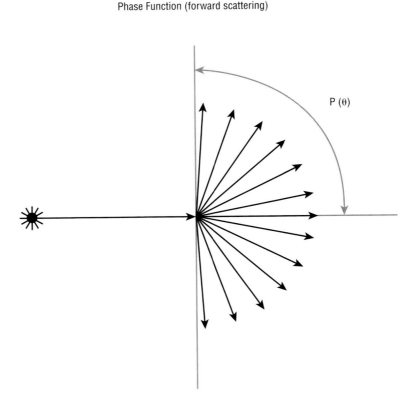

Phase Function (forward scattering)

$P(\theta)$

In this way it considers the probability of light scattering at a given intensity in all directions (360°) around a particle, relative to the light's center point (the two hemispherical origins). If the r term is set to 1, you can see that the intermediate equation of $1 - r$ will result with zero, which is then multiplied by the second term, resulting with zero. Thus, if r is set to 1, only the g1 term is used.

In a following section, you will look at how the mental ray PM shader uses this two-term approach with two g parameters and an r parameter to model isotropic or anisotropic PM light scattering.

PM and the concepts discussed here for forward and backward scattering deal with the same concepts of subsurface scattering. In fact, participating media effects can be used to simulate volume scattering such as with subsurface scattering in skin, volume effects such as fire, and rendering deep scattering mediums such as liquids. Thus, the PM volume shader, although typically used in hosts for lighting particles of light, is not limited only to that purpose.

I continue to discuss the HG phase function, and empirical data for light scatter characteristics in Chapter 14 with the mental ray physical subsurface shader.

Direct Light Participating Media

The mental ray participating media shaders are part of the physics library. The options found on the parti_volume and parti_volume photon shaders for the most part are identical, just as with illumination and photon shaders (DGS, dielectric, and so on). The shaders can be found in each host under the locations specified earlier in the "Photon Shaders and Settings" section. XSI users should also see the section "PM Shaders and XSI" later in this chapter. In this section, you'll examine the parti_volume shader options shown in Figure 12.38 with direct lighting; then, in following sections I'll review the differences when using GI and caustics with the parti_volume_photon shader. Note that when using these shaders, you need to set up the scene in a particular way as discussed in the "Scene Setup" section later in this chapter.

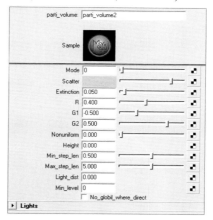

Figure 12.38

The parti_volume shader in Maya. The same shader options are seen with this shader and the photon shader in each host.

The Scatter and Extinction Options

Standard volume light effects in 3D applications allow you to attach a volume effect to a light source. The volume light is relatively detached from the direct light in the sense that volume light appears to acquire the light's intensity but does not absorb direct light and reduces radiance from the scene. Thus, you typically use additional settings to better match the intensity and decay of direct light and volume light. They are merely two different and detached components of rendering. PM effects, by contrast, deal with a realistic simulation of light within a volume that handles direct and volume light absorption and scattering. That means the direct light and volume light are influenced by the PM shader; they are not two separate components.

The Scatter color attribute shown in Figure 12.38 defines the color and intensity of the scattered light. With higher scatter values (closer to white), the light reflection intensity increases, and you see more volume light scatter in the environment. The Extinction attribute defines the level of absorption. Higher Extinction values produce more light absorption, and lower values will allow more light to travel through the scene. At a value of zero the scene is in vacuum, and there are no participating media particles to render. At high Extinction values the light absorbs rapidly in near proximity to the light source, and the remainder of the room will receive very little or no light; the radiance in the volume decreases. Because the Scatter and Extinction attributes are closely tied together, while adjusting them you need to consider how you balance these two attributes in a way that does not remove all the direct light from the scene.

Let's look at an example that examines different values and their effect on the lighting in a Cornell box. In Figure 12.39 you can see a Cornell box with an area light as the light source and a sphere in the center that is used to occlude some of the light from reaching the floor. The sphere has a dielectric shader, and so you need to use caustics to reveal transparency in the opaque shadow area. The scene is contained within a volume that has the transmat and parti_volume shaders attached, as discussed in the "Scene Setup" section later in the chapter.

Figure 12.39

Examining the effect on PM while changing the Scatter attribute's color value

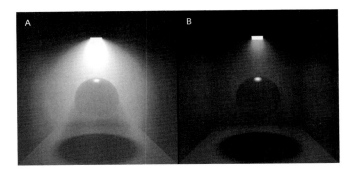

In Figure 12.39 image A, the Scatter attribute's RGB values are set to 0.8, and the Extinction attribute is set to 0.05. This is a relatively high Extinction value, and the room becomes significantly darker. You can also see that there is a high level of light scattering near the source light, because this Extinction value rapidly absorbs light. Since the scatter value is relatively high, you can see a lot of particles reflect light in the scene; in some cases, they may reflect too much light. Thus, the Extinction attribute absorbs light rapidly, making the room very dark, but the Scatter attribute reflects a lot of light from each particle in the environment within the direct light's perspective, including through the dielectric sphere.

In Figure 12.39 image B, the Scatter attribute has been decreased to a value of 0.05 for the RGB colors. You can see that less light is being scattered by the participating media. Thus, it decreases the radiance of the particles. However, as the extinction remains the same (0.05), the direct light is still absorbed at the same rate and the room remains dark. To show more light in the room, you could either increase the area light's intensity or reduce the decay rate (extinction value).

The Scatter attribute defines the radiant intensity of light scattering from a given particle, and the Extinction value defines the rate of absorption in the atmosphere.

In Figure 12.40 image A, the Extinction attribute has been set to 0.001 and the Scatter attribute's RGB values are set at 0.45. As you can see, there is more visible light in the room. Thus, by reducing the Extinction value from 0.05 in Figure 12.39 to 0.001 in Figure 12.40, you allow more direct light to travel in the scene. The room is brighter because less light is absorbed per unit distance. However, as a result, the Scatter attribute's influence increases, as the PM doesn't absorb as much of the direct light radiance. Notice that in Figure 12.39 image A the Scatter attribute is set to 0.8, and in Figure 12.40 it is set at 0.45, almost half of the former value, and yet you see much brighter light scattering from PM in the room. After I reduced the Scatter value to 0.02 (Figure 12.40 image B), you can see the room clearly because the light isn't fully absorbed, and there is a decent amount of PM scattering for a visually pleasing result.

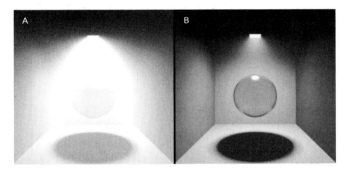

Figure 12.40

Examining the effect on PM while changing the Extinction and Scatter attribute values

You can see a similar balance in the color gallery with the image labeled "Photon Counts" where some PM effects are seen for the light that enters the room from outside, as well as the two lights above the stove. The purpose was to add a subtle effect without reducing the overall intensity of light in the scene, at least not significantly.

You should always examine very low Extinction values that range from 0.001 to 0.1; higher values tend to absorb too much light and create very dark scenes.

PHYSICAL LIGHTS AND PM DENSITY

In the case of Figure 12.39 and Figure 12.40, the physical light's intensity (Color attribute) is set to 1000 for the RGB color channels. Participating media functions better when the source light's range is not set to a 0 to 1 range, as with physical lights. You can use the Extinction and Scatter attributes along with the physical light's energy (Color attribute) to balance the density and intensity of PM effects in a volume. If you set low energy values for the light, then you need low extinction rates to maintain lighting in the room. You then adjust the scatter value so that PM effects appear in the room as with Figure 12.40; however, it will typically appear bright so you use lower values and show less PM scattering (not very dense). If you significantly increase the light energy, you can then use much higher extinction rates that absorb a lot of light and form a denser effect. In such cases, the scatter value will need to be set higher to reveal the dense volume light. Thus, higher physical light energy values provide more light that may be absorbed by the PM shader in a way that will still introduce enough radiance in the scene and a dense volume light effect.

As mentioned, in the color gallery image labeled "Participating Media Effects," you can see various physical lights used with different intensities and colors. The PM effect accounts for each light in the volume area and shows its effect relative to the other lights, based on the light's energy settings and the light's decay rate (inverse square falloff).

Figure 12.41

Mapping the Scatter attribute with a 4D texture to render nonuniform volume light

ANIMATING LIGHT SCATTER AND NONUNIFORMITY

You can use a 3D texture such as turbulence to create patterns in volume light. In this way you can animate the effect by using 4D shaders (the fourth dimension is time) or by using host-specific 3D projections that are translated in the scene, moving from one point to the next.

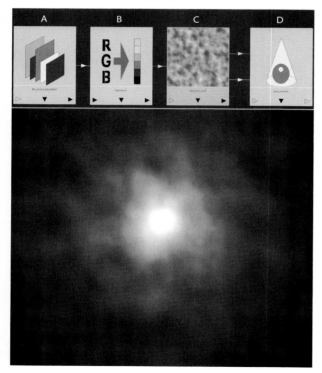

In Figure 12.41 you can see a small shader network in Maya. I used the Binary Alchemy (BA) 4D fractal texture (see Chapter 10, "mental ray Shaders and Shader Trees") labeled A to generate 3D turbulence. Since PM effects produce very different results with small changes in value, you should use an additional texture that can limit the output range of the 3D texture to a given range such as 0.2 and 0.6. In this case, the BA texture is connected to a Maya luminance shader (B) that converts the RGB values to a scalar grayscale value so you can use it as a mask. Note that you could use the alpha output from the BA shader, but in Maya it caused the render to abort, so I used the luminance as a conversion shader. I connected the luminance shader to a mental ray mib_color_mix (C) shader's Weight_0 attribute input and set Mode_0 to mix. This way it acts as a mask that mixes the Color_base and Color_0 color attributes. I set the darkest value using the Color_base attribute and the brightest value using the Color_0 attribute. If you map the texture to the Scatter attribute, then brighter values scatter more light and darker values scatter less light, as discussed earlier, only based on the mib_color_mix texture output values. I connected the mix shader to the parti_volume (D) Scatter attribute. I then rendered a point light within a boxed volume, and you can see the result in the figure. You looked at using the mix shader and limiting ranges in the tutorials in Chapter 10, "mental ray Shaders and Shader Trees," with brushed metal.

PM Isotropic or Anisotropic Scattering

The intensity of light scattering based on a direction relative to the source light's incident ray, discussed in the section "Anisotropic and Isotropic Scattering," can be modeled using lobes. Lobes are used to outline on polar coordinates the relative intensity of scattered light in a given direction, as shown in Figure 12.42, also shown with arrows that depict intensity in Figure 12.35 and Figure 12.37.

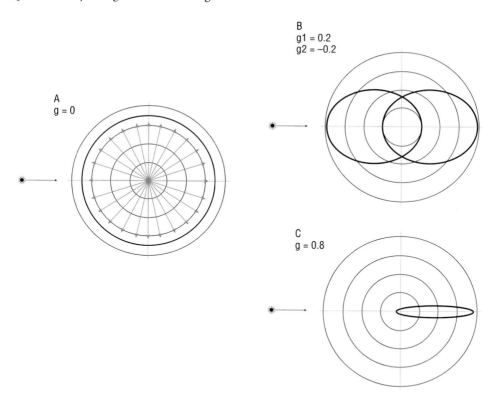

Figure 12.42
Lobes depict the intensity of light based on the scatter direction relative to the source light.

The mental ray PM shader has three attributes that handle the intensity of scattered light based on the scatter direction; they are shown in Figure 12.38 earlier and are the R, G1, and G2 attributes that directly correspond to the r, g_1, and g_2 terms discussed earlier in "The Henyey-Greenstein Phase Function."

As discussed earlier, the Henyey-Greenstein (HG) and Schlick phase functions define the probability of scattering in a hemisphere around the incident light origin (see Figure 12.37) using the g term. Furthermore, the two-term phase function uses two g terms and one r term that correlate to the PM shader attributes cited earlier. Thus, these attributes enable you to utilize a two-term phase function to model forward and backward scattering (each in a separate hemisphere) using two lobes, one for forward scattering and the other for backward scattering. The r attribute is used to blend the two together (selecting a predominant lobe).

The lobe shown in Figure 12.42 labeled A demonstrates isotropic scattering, where there is an equal amount of scattering in each direction. In this case, the r, g1, and g2 attributes are set to 0. Under label B you can see two overlapping lobes for forward scattering (g1) and backward scattering (g2) using a value of 0.2 for g1 and negative 0.2 for g2. Both create the same lobe, just in opposite directions. Note that forward scattering is applied in the same direction as the light, as noted in the figure. Thus, when the mental ray g1 or g2 parameters are set with negative values between 0 and -1, the lobe represents backward scattering, and when using positive values from 0 to 1, it represents forward scattering. Thus, either lobe can be set to handle forward or backward scattering. Essentially you specify one that defines backward scattering and the other forward scattering, and then use the r parameter to balance the two together. When r = 1, the g1 lobe is used, and when r = 0, the g2 lobe is used. Any value between 0 and 1 defines a blending factor between both lobes.

Note that the r parameter defaults to 0, which means that only the g2 parameter is used unless you increase the r value. And, use g values less than 1 or negative 1 (that is, 0.99); a value of 1 will "break" the effect, and it will appear black.

To understand how g values influence the intensity of the scattered light based on direction, under label B you can see a g1 value of 0.2 and under label C you can see the g value of 0.8. As the value increases, the scattering intensity increases significantly for forward or backward scattering, as shown with the more elliptical shape under label C; it demonstrates predominant forward scattering. By contrast, when g1 and g2 are set with values closer to 0, the function provides more isotropic scattering, as shown under label B and with full isotropic scattering under label A.

The illustration shown in Figure 12.42 is drawn to visually "ballpark" the phase function with those values; it was not generated by a scientific application.

REFLECTANCE DATA AND RESOURCES

Andrew Glassner has written several books on computer graphics. His *Principles of Digital Image Synthesis* (Morgan Kauffman, 1995) is a thorough two-volume set on all matters concerning programmers, shader writers, and software developers who work with CG. In his documentation, he recommends values that represent the reflectance character of Rayleigh scattering and Mie scattering using the Schlick phase function based on empirical data acquired by experimentation. They are as follows:

FUNCTION	R	G1	G2
Rayleigh	0.5	-0.46	0.46
Hazy Mie	0.12	-0.50	0.70
Murky Mie	0.19	-0.65	0.91

The same values are also presented to you in the same context in the mental ray help documents. You can see the different results of these settings in the images shown here. Each one renders a point light within a boxed volume with the parti_volume shader assigned. The Rayleigh scattering (A) produces a relatively linear decay of light from the center in all directions. Both the hazy (B) and murky (C) Mie have a stronger forward scattering intensity and thus appear to have a brighter region close to the light, where the camera is looking directly at the light source (which is why the "white circle" is larger). However, their transitions away from the light, meaning the transition from forward to backward scattering, decay faster. The murky Mie (C) demonstrates the fastest decay because the light is predominately forward scattering, exhibiting the strongest intensity in a direct line of sight from the light.

XSI users will find the values shown in the previous table as presets in the Tek2Shoot parti_volume shader implementation. Note that there is an enormous amount of information on the Web that details the scattering properties of dielectric media, but not so much on atmospherics that can easily be implemented using the parameters shown in the table and discussed in this section. As cited earlier, the process of light scattering, its directionality, and its intensity represent the subsurface character of light that interacts with molecules and water droplets that are relatively smaller or a bit bigger than the wavelength of perceivable light. Thus PM concepts apply to all sorts of liquids and atmospheric effects, as cited earlier, that exhibit subsurface scattering. On that topic you can find a lot of research online about the reflectance properties of materials.

One very useful paper is "Acquiring Scattering Properties of Participating Media by Dilution" compiled by various researchers and universities. You can find the PDF downloadable file at the following address:

    http://graphics.ucsd.edu/~henrik/papers/acquiring_scattering_properties/

Note the paper is advanced and will only bring your attention to how PM effects can be used for subsurface scattering effects. The values you will find in such papers are not easily implemented with the PM shader.

Uniform vs. Nonuniform Scattering

In addition to the scatter directionality, different environments may provide for more uniform or nonuniform scatter characteristics; for example, a smoky shaft of light will appear to scatter light rather nonuniformly, compared to a source light in a uniformly dense fog or underwater. Clearly, it all depends on the environment and how the particles interact with light, because their general distribution will define how uniform they appear. You can see some examples of different participating media nonuniform atmospheres in the color gallery.

You saw a method to create nonuniform volume light in "Animating Light Scatter and Nonuniformity" earlier, using 3D textures. However, the PM shader offers a more visually pleasing (but more render-expensive) technique for nonuniform PM effects using the Nonuniform attribute shown in Figure 12.38. This attribute utilizes values from 0 to 1 for controlling uniformity. At a value of 0, the PM appears uniform, as shown in Figure 12.43 image A, a deep-sea example using murky Mie scattering. As you increase the Nonuniform value toward 1, the PM takes a more nonuniform appearance as shown using a value of 1 in image B. In both cases, only one point light is present in the scene.

Figure 12.43

Uniform (A) vs. nonuniform PM effects (B)

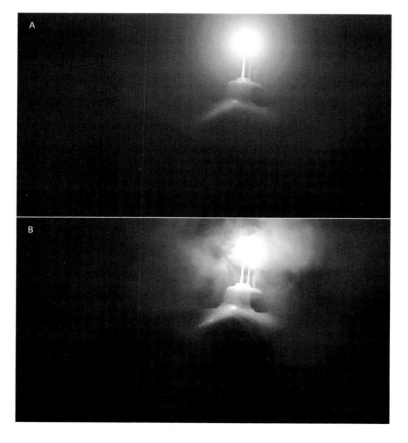

Note that increasing the value can take a significant toll on render times, so the more nonunifrom the PM, the longer the render time. Also, with uniform PM, the ray marching sample settings (discussed next) can be lower (higher values) than with nonuniform effects. Also note that it is much slower to render than when using a 3D texture and that with a 3D texture you can easily animate the volume light.

Ray Marching Sample Level

The Min and Max_step_len attributes shown in Figure 12.38 control the sample interval for ray marching (discussed earlier). These values define a minimum and maximum length for ray marching rays. Essentially by doing so, they are the primary attributes that define the appearance and quality of PM effects; they control how often rays simulate nonexistent participating media in the volume. Higher values will lead to grainy results, and lower values produce fine detailed effects by visualizing participating media in close proximity, again resulting in more detail and slower render times.

Values such as 1 (min) and 5 (max) can be used for quick testing Although the appearance is very low quality; with PM effects the low values are enough to allow you to identify the pattern and intensities of light in PM effects, which makes this an effective means for working fast without waiting for slow renders. Values between 0.1 and 1 usually suffice to produce high-quality PM effects, but you can use even higher-quality settings such as 0.01 and 0.1 (not recommended). Typically the Min_step_len value should be set to 10 percent of the Max_step_len value.

Also note that you should use lower quality sampling values, such as -2 and 0 for min and max sample levels (see Chapter 5, "Quality Control"), for anti-aliasing while testing ray marching values. Then when you see that the quality is relatively sufficient, increasing the sampling will produce a final high-quality image. With some hands-on experimentation you will learn to recognize when PM length settings will appear smooth once the anti-aliasing for the scene is also increased, allowing you to work with lower anti-aliasing during the testing phase without specifying too high-quality ray marching length settings.

Additional Options

The Height attribute controls the height from the scene floor (the Y axis floor) at which PM effects appear. This attribute merely enables you to select the highest point in the scene where PM effects appear. In this way you can force the PM effects to apply their influence closer to the floor, removing absorption near the source light. For example, you can use it to create a low-level fog. For the Height attribute to function, the Mode attribute needs to be set to 1, which is the only reason for you to change the Mode value from 0 to 1.

The Light_distance attribute is used to optimize the sampling quality from area lights. When the area light has a low sampling level defined (see Chapter 6, "Lights and Soft

Shadows"), those lower sampling values will be used at a given distance from the light. Thus, the Light_distance attribute specifies a distance at which lower sampling values are used for calculating an area light's influence on PM effects.

Under the Lights rollout (shown contracted in Figure 12.38), you can drag and drop particular lights that will interact with PM effects. If you don't manually connect any lights to the light list, the PM shader will use all the lights in the volume. However, once you connect lights to the light list, only those lights will be used. After you connect the first light, an additional option will appear, enabling you to connect an additional light. You can accomplish these connections in each host application.

Scene and Shader Setup

The only conditions for rendering participating media effects are that a light source exists in the scene and a given volume is defined with a geometric object such as a sphere or box. The volume may be visible geometry such as a room or an invisible (fully transparent) container applied with a transmat shader (as an illumination shader), as shown in Figure 12.44.

> With PM effects for both direct and indirect lighting, the global shadow option should be set to segmented shadows (see Chapter 7, "Shadow Algorithms").

Figure 12.44

Scene setup using two transmat planes

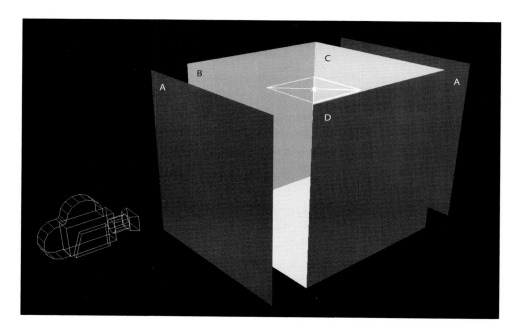

You can see the two planes marked A that are used for specifying the volume area. Notice that they don't have to encompass the entire scene; they just set a near and far region relative to the camera. Any lights within that region will be affected by the PM shader. You don't have to use these containers; they are merely a means of defining a particular area for volume light that may not correspond to existing scene geometry. If you omit them, you can apply the PM shader directly to the walls labeled B, C, and D that define the room. However, it is easier to use transmat surfaces, because you don't have to apply the PM shader to various shaders (for each surface); you have to apply it to only one shader that is assigned with the transmat shader and the parti_volume shader.

One important consideration is that the containers need to cover the entire render region seen from the camera's perspective. To clarify, the far container needs to be scaled up so it covers the entire view from the camera's perspective. If it doesn't, the PM effects will cut off at the container's borders and not fill the entire room. An alternative to scaling the containers so that they cover the render region is to use floor and ceiling containers to ensure that the defined volume area, applied with the parti_volume shader, bounds the entire scene. I usually prefer to use two near and far planes and just scale them up.

Surfaces used to set volume regions should have their surface normals pointing inward, facing into the container.

THE TRANSMAT SHADER

The transmat shader is a transparent shader that doesn't affect the direct lighting; it does not have any options and is intended purely for assisting in rendering PM effects. Note that you should disable the transmat surface's shadow-casting abilities, or it will cast opaque shadows. Disabling shadow casting is only significant if the transmat surfaces are occluding light based on their placement in the scene, which is the case with setup discussed next for indirect PM effects.

SETUP FOR GI OR CAUSTIC PM RENDERING

With caustics and GI PM effects, a *photon collector* surface (Figure 12.45 labeled B) needs to be placed below the photon-casting light and assigned the transmat, transmat photon, and PM volume and volume photon shaders, as shown in Figure 12.46. Note that the photon collector surface has shadow casting disabled and it's facing the light; that is, its normals are pointed upward. Thus, to generate GI and caustic PM effects, you need to have at least one surface assigned with the transmat and PM shaders, which I will refer to as the *PM material*. The other surfaces that define the container, labeled A in the figure, should also be assigned with the same PM material, or alternatively you can omit the containers and use the walls (shown in wireframe labeled C). In such a case you need to apply the PM shader to those surface materials' volume and photon volume inputs.

Figure 12.45

**Scene setup using
two transmat planes**

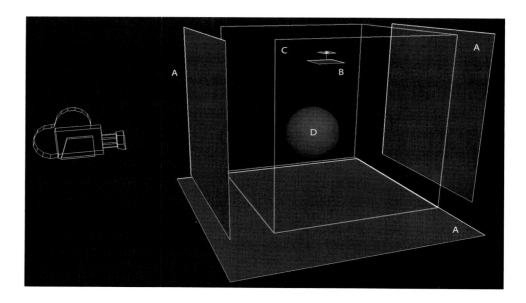

Notice that in this case an additional transmat surface is placed below the room along the floor. You will need this surface to define the near and far boundaries of the container seen from the light's perspective. Thus, the photon collector and floor surfaces are added for indirect illumination PM effects and assigned with the PM material. With GI or caustic PM effects, the photon collector object must be set to cast GI or caustic photons into the scene, based on your intentions. Note that in XSI and 3ds Max for PM caustic effects you need to enable caustic photon casting (disabled by default). I discussed per-object settings earlier in this chapter in "Host Application Settings."

There are a few additional considerations for setting the scale of the photon collector surface and the light type when creating PM caustic effects. I discuss the topic in more detail in the "GI Participating Media Effects" section later in this chapter.

THE SHADER NETWORK

In Figure 12.46 you can see a typical setup for PM effects using the parti_volume shader and transmat shader, which is the PM material. You also see the transmat photon and parti_volume_photon shaders that are required when rendering indirect PM effects. As cited earlier, the transmat and transmat photon shader are optional (with the exception of

Figure 12.46

**Shading network
shown in XSI using
the transmat and PM
illumination and
photon shaders**

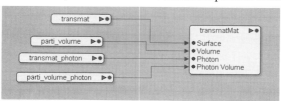

a photon collector surface for GI and caustics) as long as bounding surfaces exist that define the volume area and are assigned with the PM shader.

PM SHADERS AND XSI

In XSI you can use the PM shaders described here after installing the Tek2Shoot mental ray shader library or the Xphysics shader library, as cited in the "Photon Shaders and Settings" section earlier in this chapter. However, the PM shader is already built into XSI using similar settings and can be found in the Render Tree window → Nodes → Volume → Volume Effects shader. When you create this shader, you simply attach it to the volume input on a material as you would with the PM shaders.

The volume effects shader has all the options discussed in this section as well as several additional options, such as defining nonuniform texture-based PM effects, as discussed earlier in "Animating Light Scatter and Nonuniformity." You can find this on the Fractal tab. If you review the help files for the properties, you can easily identify the corresponding options discussed here. Furthermore, most of them are labeled in the same way, so they clearly stand out. Note that you must attach scatter and shadow-casting lights to the shader on the Lights tab.

> The volume effects shader does not include a photon shader; it is meant to be used only with direct light PM effects.

Indirect PM Effects

When participating media effects are combined with indirect illumination techniques, the parti_volume_photon shader is used to define the illumination of suspended photons within the environment that are part of the indirect illumination simulation. The indirect illumination of PM is divided into GI and caustic effects, just as with indirect light simulations. Thus, for PM indirect effects, at least one of the two indirect (GI and caustics) techniques needs to be enabled. To clarify, unlike GI and caustics you do not specifically cast PM photons into the scene. PM photons are separate from GI and caustic photons; however, they are generated only when one of the two techniques is enabled.

PM Options and the PM Photon Shader

Controlling the rendered appearance of indirect PM effects is similar to using GI and caustics (but more like caustics). The global options for PM effects are added in the options block, as with GI and caustics, and are as follows:

```
photonvol accuracy [photon] [radius]
photonvol scale [RGBA]
photon autovolume [on | off]
```

As you can see, the accuracy, radius, and scale options are present and function exactly as they do with GI and caustics. You can find these options in host applications under their render settings, and I discussed them in the chapter's earlier coverage of GI. As with caustics, you are interested in revealing the detail between the different PM particles. Thus, you'll tend to use lower accuracy and radius values, as when fine-tuning caustics. The autovolume option enables mental ray to keep track of multiple volumes. It should be enabled if the camera is going to transition through different volumes during an animation. Typically you should leave it enabled, the default in host applications.

With respect to the photon shader, it has the same attributers as with the parti_volume shader shown in Figure 12.38, with a few minor exceptions that should be considered:

- The Min_level attribute is used only with the photon shader and defines when PM caustic photons are stored (don't confuse this option with the Min_step_len attribute). Caustic PM photons are stored only after refracting or reflecting as many times as specified with this attribute. Note that with GI and caustics, the number of times a photon can refract or reflect in the scene is based on the general options that define the max reflection, refraction, and max trace of both combined, as discussed earlier in "Controlling Photon Reflections and Refractions."

- The Min and Max_step_len attributes for ray marching are the same as with the parti_volume shader. When using GI or caustics, they can be set to high quality (low values) while generating a photon map. After that you can reuse the photon map (disable rebuilding) without the overhead of recalculating the PM photons.

- The Extinction attribute contributes to the density of PM photons in the scene. When the extinction is set to a high value, a larger number of PM photons will be stored on "particles" in the scene (volume). As noted, the photon shader primarily influences the distribution of photons, and thus you can use higher extinction rates to generate more photons that provide for better photon blending in indirect areas of the scene. It is particularly useful with caustics where you may want to generate a sharper dense beam of light as shown in Figure 12.49.

- The parti_volume shader has to be present. If you attach only a PM photon shader, PM photons will be generated, but they will not be visible in the render. Essentially you can think of the PM photon shader as a tool that spreads more participating media particles in the scene that are then rendered with the PM shader.

- Thus, for fine-tuning PM effects, the photon shader is really used only for distribution and absorption; the appearance of PM effects, such as their scatter color and extinction, is primarily a result of fine-tuning the parti_volume shader settings more than the photon shader settings. Decreasing the scatter value decreases the photon radiance in the scene, so you may use it to lower the radiance of PM photons if they appear too bright. Also, PM photons may absorb too much light, making the indirect lighting look dark. To fix this you may need to reduce the extinction, a topic further discussed shortly. If the scene is set up for physical correctness, where the physical light's energy and the photon casting light's energy are set at the same value, you have a better chance of getting away with a white scatter value for the photon shader, adjusting only the scatter value on the direct light's parti_volume shader.

- The Light_distance and light list are not functional with the photon shader. The photon shader doesn't use direct lighting, only indirect lighting photons generated during GI or caustic simulations.

GI Participating Media Effects

The GI effect deals with enhancing the indirect effect of PM around the source light, referred to as *multiple scattering* effects. Multiple scattering reflects light from particles that are outside the light source's direct line of sight and provides a more realistic effect, as well as a brighter region around the source light. It helps explain why the approach of assigning PM shaders to a volume makes more sense if you consider that volume light should scatter within both direct and indirect lines of sight in a given volume and not from a particular light source. If an environment is dense and reflects a lot of light, it will do so everywhere light can be seen.

In Figure 12.47 image A you can see a spot light casting direct light into the scene as well as PM effects using the parti_volume shader. In image B, GI was enabled, and a PM photon shader was added. Note the difference in the distribution of the volume light in image B in indirect areas of the scene and around the source light, compared to image A.

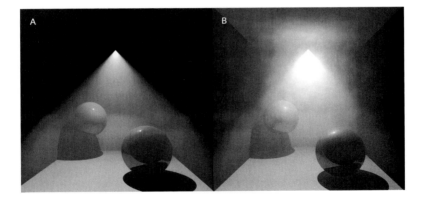

Figure 12.47

GI participating media effects for direct and indirect light

To generate GI PM effects, all you need to do is follow the scene setup instructions discussed earlier and have at least one photon casting light with GI enabled. Note that because GI photons are stored in air on theoretical particles, you may need to increase the photon count to account for a high-quality distribution for both PM and GI photons in the scene. With respect to the photon shader, a lower extinction value and brighter scatter value will reveal more indirect light in the scene. To clarify, if the extinction is set high, then the scene will not reflect a lot of light from surfaces that are influenced by indirect light, because the light is absorbed before it reaches them. This has the effect of creating denser PM effects near the source light. Balancing these values is based on the scene scale, so they differ in each case; for example, you may need to use very low values such as an extinction of 0.002 and a scatter of 0.5 to see indirect light in the scene. In this way you allow GI photons to interact with the scene rather than absorb within a short distance from the source light.

Caustic Participating Media Effects

The caustic component deals with scattering focused light through surfaces that amplifies in intensity, just as with caustics only for suspended particles. You can see in Figure 12.48 the same scene used previously with caustics with the addition of PM effects and PM caustic effects. As you can see, the parti_volume shader (direct light) handles the PM effects down from the source light, within its line of sight. The PM caustics effects contribute the light beams seen through the refractive spheres, as well as the light beams projected back toward the light by the specular ring and the spheres.

Figure 12.48

PM effects with the addition of caustic PM effects using the parti_volume_photon shader

If you use an area light to illuminate the scene and use a spot light to cast caustic photons, as in Figure 12.49, then the photon collector surface will cast caustic photons based on the spot light's perspective and form a ring of bright light in the scene, as shown in image A. To remedy this effect, you should cast caustic photons from the point or point area light in the scene so that these caustic photons are cast everywhere and don't form a clear ring around the spotlight's terminator line (along the transition to shadow). Alternatively, you can try scaling down the size of the photon collector surface, as I did in this instance in image B, so the influence remains within a specific region without affecting areas outside the sphere yet still maintains the caustic beam effect.

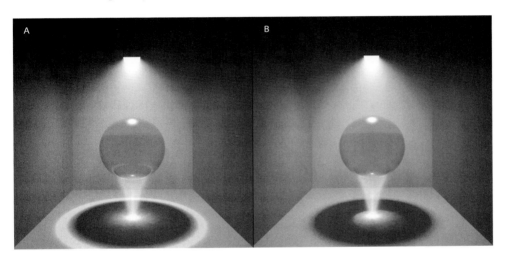

Figure 12.49

The photon collector object adds caustic photons to image A, and in image B its influence has been removed.

FINE-TUNING CAUSTICS

Let's look at Figure 12.50 to examine some of the parti_volume_photon characteristics and how they can be fine-tuned with the parti_volume shader. In image A you can see the caustic beam exiting the sphere. The parti_volume shader is set with an extinction value of 0.05 and a scatter (RGB) value of 0.05. The parti_volume_photon shader has an extinction of 0.02 and a scatter value of 1 (white).

For image B I increased the parti_volume_photon extinction to 0.12, which yields a stronger caustic beam, because more PM photons absorb light near the sphere and enhance the effect. For both images C and D I left the extinction at the same value of 0.12, reusing the same photon map.

In image C I changed the extinction for the parti_volume shader to 0.1 from 0.05. As you can see, there is less light in the room, and the caustic beam has decreased in intensity. The only difference with respect to the beam between A and C is that there is more detail inside the beam, shown as a more intense line that runs through the center of the beam. Thus, by increasing the photon count and reducing the overall radiance, I increased detail.

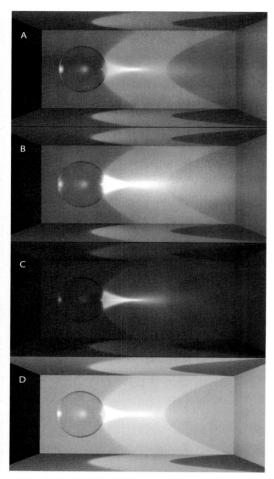

Figure 12.50

Comparing different settings using the PM and PM photon volume shaders

To introduce more light into the room and maintain a strong beam in image D, I reduced the parti_volume extinction to 0.02 and set the scatter value to 0.005 instead of 0.5 as with the previous images. The result is that there is more light and a strong beam; however, some of the detail appears overexposed. At this point, I would continue to reduce the parti_volume scatter to try to reveal the detail that is already there. Or better yet, I would render a 32-bit image and manage the exposure in compositing.

Rendering Efficiently

PM effects are extremely processor intensive, leading to very long render times. It is better to render PM effects as a separate pass and then superimpose it over the image, allowing you to tweak the two passes independently of each other in the host application. You can accomplish a PM pass by applying a constant black shader to all the surfaces in the scene so that they mask out the effect of PM in the scene and can superimpose over the image in compositing, as I mentioned earlier with respect to rendering the color gallery "Participating Media Effects" image. Note that you may need to use semitransparent shaders for objects that display transparency in the scene.

With indirect light passes you need to consider generating the photon map while the shaders are intact, and then you need to change all the shaders to the constant shader and render using the prebuilt photon map. In this way, the photons acquire the correct color values before you render a PM pass for compositing.

## CHAPTER 13

Final Gather and Ambient Occlusion

The Final Gather (FG) and ambient occlusion techniques discussed in this chapter overcome some limitations of using GI indirect illumination to account for diffuse-reflected radiation in the scene. These techniques add more detail, improve the spread of light, and account for environmental sampling. In fact, FG is a hybrid of indirect lighting techniques, and the ambient shader is a subset of FG. FG deals with color-bleeding effects across surfaces from directional irradiance, whereas ambient occlusion mostly deals with the effects of occlusion in nooks and crannies in the scene.

In this chapter, we examine both of these techniques and look at using Final Gather alongside indirect illumination photon casting. We also look at using the architectural library's physical sun, sky, and tone mapping shaders, as well as using HDR images. This chapter covers the following topics:

- **Final Gather Fundamentals**
- **Final Gather Options and Techniques**
- **Advanced Final Gather Techniques**
- **Ambient Occlusion**

Final Gather Fundamentals

Final Gather, also referred to as Final Gathering, is an additional tool for indirect illumination. As with global illumination (GI), FG calculates diffuse irradiance from indirect light in the scene without considering caustic effects on glossy to specular surfaces. Unlike global illumination, FG does not rely on photons to calculate indirect illumination; it uses raytracing to trace rays from a surface outward into the scene, a topic explored throughout this section.

The most significant difference between FG and GI is that FG does not solely depend on light sources for illumination; it reflects light from various sources that either are affected by a light source or that generate their own radiance by means of a shader. To clarify, in 3D the diffuse and specular color components of a shader require a light source in order to appear visible when rendered. Aside from that, you can use background images or constant shaders that are not affected by lighting, and render as is, displaying a texture or constant color. These colors appear as indirect reflected light when used with FG. Any of the following elements are used by FG to generate indirect diffuse lighting:

- Surfaces that are lit by light sources
- Surfaces that reflect ambient light (a shader's ambient color)
- Surfaces that have constant shading such as bounce cards (light reflectors) and light-emitting surfaces (surfaces acting as light sources); texture color is rendered as is, without utilizing a light source that affects its shading (more on that later)
- Environment images or constant background shading

You will see examples of each of these elements in the following sections. Let's start by examining FG rendering to demonstrate a few common FG techniques. You'll then learn in depth about FG basics, about the differences between FG and global illumination (GI), and finally about FG mental ray options and advanced techniques with HDR images.

The FG algorithm and its mental ray options have significantly changed in mental ray 3.4 and 3.5 from previous versions; this is further explained throughout the chapter.

Final Gather Rendering

FG provides two main components, which are ambient occlusion and irradiance sampling (scene and environmental), both demonstrated in Figure 13.1. Irradiance sampling, a topic discussed in detail throughout the following sections, refers to the process of sampling irradiance (diffuse reflection) across a surface, as affected by other scene elements (listed earlier). As a result of irradiance sampling, FG renders color-bleeding effects from nearby surfaces, similar to GI.

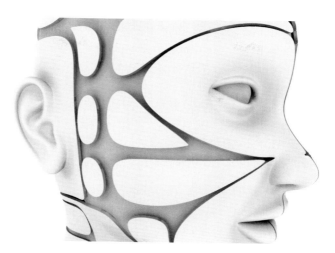

Figure 13.1

FG applied with a constant background shader

As cited in the earlier list, FG can use several resources for extracting and interpolating diffuse indirect illumination. In Figure 13.1, you can see the simplest form of FG. The background color is set to a constant color (white), providing FG with a source of illumination (360° around the model) that affects the model. Thus, there are no light sources in the scene so that when FG is disabled, the scene renders as black. However, with FG, the entire model appears lit by a constant light because FG extracts the same irradiance values (constant intensity) that are reflected from everywhere in the scene. Constant background shading can be applied either with an environment shader (see Chapter 3) or by means of a bounding surface such as a sphere with a constant shader.

Throughout the chapter, the term *background* refers to a spherical environment that projects color into the scene from 360°, regardless of how it's applied on a per-host basis.

Since certain areas of the model occlude light from penetrating between the various surfaces (cracks, folds, and so on), some areas appear darker than others; light is occluded from reaching deep into those areas. Thus, the irradiance across the surfaces varies based on occlusion and the irradiance source, in this case a constant background color. If you change that color to blue or red, for example, the irradiance across the surface would naturally inherit that color. Furthermore, if you apply a texture or image file as a background, you will see a variation in the irradiance across the surface from various color intensities displayed in that background.

Light-Emitting Surfaces

As noted, FG is sensitive to any color value that appears in the scene, whether lit by a source light or reflecting its own ambient light. Thus, you can use various surfaces as light emitters (one of the key advantages of FG) by applying a constant shader to them with a color, texture map, or image file. The same is true with illumination models, that if you increase their ambient (and ambience when applicable) color or map it with a texture, they too act as light sources (with XSI you also need to use the scene ambience, discussed later).

> Color values with FG don't need to remain within the 0 to 1 range. As discussed in Chapter 9, "The Fundamentals of Light and Shading Models," HDR images and lighting in general are not bound by a specific range. Thus, in the following sections, I occasionally refer to values that exceed the 0 to 1 range by specifying color using an HSV color picker. The V (value) parameter controls the intensity (luminance) of the light, and the H (hue) and S (saturation) parameters control chromaticity, which is the color of light. It is easier to specify value in this way than independently for each RGB channel.

In Figure 13.2, you can see a simple scene with various surfaces acting as light emitters. The label A points at a plane that has a constant shader with a texture applied. The texture has two white stripes that run across the surfaces, and all the remaining areas are set to a very dark gray. As you can see, these stripes reflect diffuse light into the scene in areas that are closest to them, within a given spread beneath them. The stripe numbered 2 is narrower than 1 and is also set with a brighter value. The value for that stripe is set to 12 (HSV, V parameter), and the stripe numbered 1 is set to 1. As you can see, the intensity of the light reflecting downward from the stripe numbered 2 appears to cast brighter irradiance across the cubes and floor, whereas the stripe numbered 1 appears to cast a softer, more natural light that spreads out more, because it's a broader stripe with a lower intensity value.

Figure 13.2

Using surfaces as light sources with FG

Label B points to various surfaces that are also used in a similar way, only without a texture; they all have a constant shader applied. As you can see, there are three spheres, where one appears bigger, and all cast light into the scene. The largest sphere is set with a value of 2, and the two smaller ones are set with a value of 5. You can see that even though the largest sphere has a lower value, it produces more light because it's larger and closer to the surrounding surfaces. These sorts of spheres can be used as lightbulbs to cast radiance into the scene. You can also see that the label B points to a thin, curvy surface that reflects its shape on the floor. This demonstrates how you can use custom shapes for effects such as neon lights using constant shaders and FG.

Under label C, you can see one of the more common practices of using flat planes to reflect light as bounce cards. Some are placed between the cubes indicated with the arrows. As you can see, they reflect light upward from their location. These sorts of surfaces can be used as bounce cards or as light fixtures. For example, they can mimic light fixtures that emit light upward onto a ceiling and then reflect (bounce) back into the room, providing softer indirect lighting.

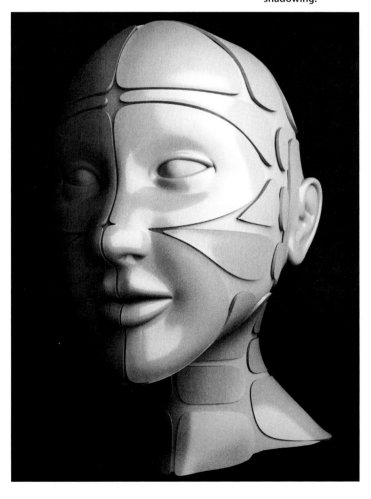

Figure 13.3

Soft light with large bounce cards provides a lot of light wrapping and soft shadowing.

STUDIO LIGHTING

In studio conditions or on film sets, it is common to use large diffuse light reflectors that reflect soft light onto actors or subjects. The source lights are pointed toward the light reflector and then bounce back at the subject. FG is particularly good at simulating these sorts of lighting conditions, reflecting light from simple flat surfaces that have a constant shader. This effect results in soft shadows and a lot of light wrapping in the scene. Both topics were discussed in Chapter 6, "Lights and Soft Shadows," using area lights.

In Figure 13.3, you can see a model that receives light from a single bounce card that's placed in close proximity. There are no additional light sources in the scene. The bounce card is fairly large, providing a lot of light wrapping and soft shadowing on the character's face. You can see how light wraps around the face across the nose, providing a very soft and diffused effect.

All the surfaces are set with a white diffuse color so that you can see the influence of the lighting without any texturing. In addition, the panels on the face have been set with a low glossy reflection value using the architectural material. The purpose of the reflections is to add specular highlights, in this case the reflections of the bounce card across the surface. Without the raytrace reflections, FG would not produce any specularity; it solely deals with diffuse reflections, as discussed next.

Specular Highlights

FG lighting doesn't produce specular highlights; therefore, for specular highlights, you must have light sources that cast specular light. However, if the light source is visible, such as with a visible area light or a bounce card (Figure 13.3), raytrace reflections will provide for specular highlights. As discussed in Chapter 9, "The Fundamentals of Light and Shading Models," the specular component on base shaders emulates the effect of specular highlights, because 3D light sources are infinitely small.

In Figure 13.4, you can see a standard setup for FG; again, simple shading models are used so you can focus on the effects of FG. Image A shows the scene with direct lighting using a physical light. As you can see, the scene is very dark and primarily reflects specular highlight with a Cook-Torrance shader. Image B shows the FG effect without any lighting; the physical light has been removed, and you don't see any specular highlights. You do see some soft shadows under the model, as well as the effect of occlusion in various areas of the model, such as inside the engines, intakes, and panels. There is one exception that is inside the tail where you see specular reflections from a chrome shader (a purely reflective DGS shader). As you can see, it reflects the environment, showing how raytracing is the only means for specular highlights in absence of light sources in the scene. Image C shows the combination of FG with the physical light (images A and B), providing both specular highlights and indirect diffuse reflections with FG.

Figure 13.4

Combining specular highlights (image A) with FG (image B) in image C

It's a common practice to use source lights to produce highlights with FG.

In the following sections, you'll learn about the technical aspects of FG, as well as FG mental ray options. While examining the options, you'll learn more about the techniques you can use to control FG and the effect it has on lighting.

Final Gather Basics

The purpose of FG is to provide a final pass that gathers irradiance values in the scene before rendering commences, which is why it's called Final Gathering. Similar to GI, it too is implemented as a two-stage process:

1. Preprocessing *FG points* in the scene (distributing FG points and gathering irradiance).

2. Interpolating the irradiance (color and brightness) values from various FG points during the rendering phase. Furthermore, during the rendering phase, FG has the ability (optional) to add additional FG points as required.

FG uses raytracing rather than photons, meaning it's a *backward raytracing* technique, not *forward raytracing* as with GI (see Chapters 2 and 12). In Figure 13.5 (the color version is on the CD in the Chapter 13 folder as "FG primary rays"), you see an illustration of the FG process where you can see two eye rays (see Chapter 2) cast into the scene from the camera's perspective. Once they hit a surface in the scene, an *FG point* is generated, and *FG primary rays* are cast into the scene to look for the incident illumination cast on that FG point, as shown for both FG points labeled A.

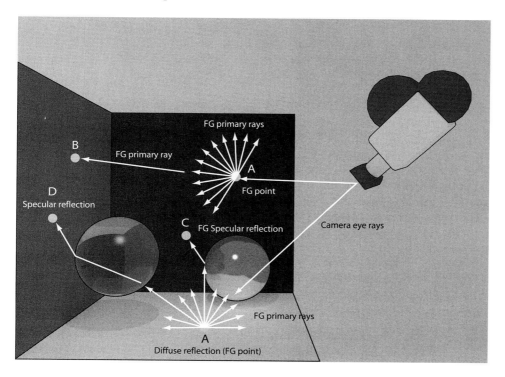

Figure 13.5

The FG process casting FG rays from FG points in the scene

FG initiates as a result of an eye ray that interacts with something in the scene; it could be either hair geometry, surfaces of all types, and software-rendered particles such as fluid effects.

Unlike GI, which deals with one photon at a time, FG deals with several rays cast from each FG point, one point at a time. In other words, GI traces the path each photon takes throughout the scene from the source light, whereas FG looks at the entire scene from a given FG point. At each FG point the diffuse irradiance is then calculated by casting several *FG primary rays* in the hemisphere around that shading point's surface normal, as illustrated in Figure 13.5 with the FG points labeled A. These rays are used to gather irradiance values from various entities in the scene by extracting their radiant exitance (see Chapter 9, "The Fundamentals of Light and Shading Models" for radiometry) values as follows:

1. With geometric surfaces, their material illumination shader is used to provide radiant exitance from the surface based on its interaction with direct lighting in the scene. Thus, FG utilizes the surface's illumination shader and does not require a photon shader as with GI effects.

2. If GI is enabled, additional illumination influences from GI photons are sampled from the photon map. When GI is enabled, FG has an ability to leverage photons to accelerate the process of sampling radiance from photons by storing FG irradiance values with photons, a topic further discussed with mental ray options later in this chapter.

3. Environment maps such as HDR images are commonly used to extract luminance values from a nongeometric environment. This practice uses images as diffuse illumination sources in the scene. In a similar way, *image-based lighting* techniques use an array of source lights to cast light into the scene based on the luminance values from an image file.

Another image based lighting technique can be applied using the architectural library's portal light shader (mia_portal_light). This shader (with Maya 2008) is also used to further optimize GI and Final Gather rendering; after completing the chapter you should refer to the architectural library's help files for more details on using the portal light shader with HDR environments and indirect lighting techniques.

FG Points and Paths

The first set of rays cast from an FG point are FG primary rays. When a ray hits a diffuse surface, it extracts the diffuse-reflected illumination from that surface and terminates. You can see that with the FG primary ray on the wall that travels from A to B. Because both walls have Lambert shaders (purely diffused surfaces), the primary ray that reaches the point labeled B initiates a material shader call at that point to evaluate its (point B) illumination. The values derived from the material shader are then cached with the FG point as explained in the section "FG Maps."

If a surface exhibits specular to glossy reflection or transmission, a secondary ray is cast, as with standard raytracing, reflecting and refracting through the scene. In Figure 13.5, you can see that the ray at the point labeled C reflected from a glossy sphere in its path. In a similar way, the ray that hits the point D first refracted through a refractive sphere. In each case the FG primary rays eventually hit a diffuse surface (the walls) where irradiance values are extracted from the illumination shader, as cited earlier.

The number of times a ray can bounce (reflect and refract) in the scene is based on a user-defined maximum trace depth as with all raytrace techniques. With FG, primary rays are cast from FG points in the scene with the purpose of evaluating indirect diffuse light paths, and secondary rays perturb (reflect or refract) the FG primary ray's direction, carrying it through the scene to a final destination.

It's important to note that influence from reflections or refractions is irrelevant; FG deals only with diffuse indirect light. Thus, those reflective and refractive secondary rays are only a means for redirecting the FG primary ray to a diffuse surface (final destination), if any exists.

> Each FG point emits a set of first-generation FG primary rays, which is a single indirect diffuse reflection that can be reflected or refracted in the scene.

GENERATING FG POINTS

The FG points that are created in the scene are dependent on the surface's material. FG will not generate an FG point on a surface that has purely reflective qualities, as shown in Figure 13.6, which is an FG diagnostics render (we discuss FG diagnostics later in the chapter). In the figure, FG points are shown as small dots across the surfaces (green).

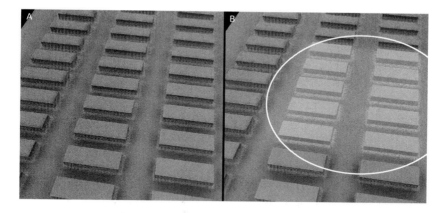

Figure 13.6

FG points are created only on surfaces that possess diffuse qualities (A), omitting surfaces with purely reflective (glossy to specular) qualities (B).

For now, notice that under label A, FG points are generated everywhere across the surfaces, which all share the same Lambert diffuse shader. Under label B some of the cubes (circled in the figure) are applied with a purely reflective DGS shader. As you can see, the FG points omit those surfaces, generating FG points around them where they intersect with the floor; the FG points are generated on the floor, not on the cubes. Thus, you can see how a surface's material shader has influence on the generation of FG points in the scene.

> With partially diffused surfaces, FG points are generated.

SINGLE AND MULTIPLE DIFFUSE BOUNCES

FG is primarily intended for extracting a single indirect diffuse bounce, even though you can specify multiple diffuse bounces. Unlike GI, which deals with casting and bouncing a photon several times within the scene, FG is mostly used with one or two diffuse bounces as a means of improving the indirect illumination solution. For this reason FG is known for acquiring a final pass of irradiance influence in the scene that provides first-generation diffuse indirect lighting effects.

If you specify more than one diffuse bounce, a secondary FG ray is cast after the primary FG ray hits a diffuse surface, as shown in Figure 13.7. In the figure you can see an eye ray cast from the camera to point A. At that point, an FG point is generated, and primary FG rays are cast into the scene. If you track one of these rays, you can see that it hits point B. If you increase the diffuse bounces to 2 (trace depth for FG rays), a secondary FG ray is cast from point B to C. And if you allowed for three or more diffuse bounces, an additional secondary FG ray will cast from point C to D, and so forth. Note that if a reflective or refractive surface existed along any of these secondary FG ray paths, as shown in Figure 13.5, the FG secondary ray would reflect or refract from it as described earlier with primary FG rays.

> You need to distinguish between FG primary and secondary rays that are used for diffuse bounces and raytrace secondary rays that are used to redirect FG rays from reflective and refractive surfaces.

Figure 13.7
Secondary diffuse bounces with Final Gather

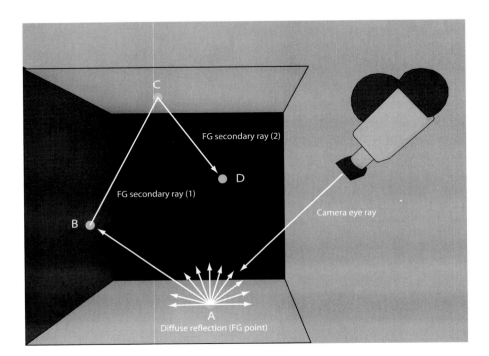

Typically you should not use more than two diffuse bounces with FG, because that would be inefficient. If you need several diffuse bounces in the scene, you should prefer GI. That's because FG casts an enormous number of raytrace rays from each FG point, and if each of those rays bounces multiple times in the scene, it increases the rendering time and reduces efficiency. Furthermore, the influence of FG illumination in the scene decreases as you increase the diffuse bounces. Two bounces will show more color bleeding between surfaces in the scene than a single bounce. If you increase the diffuse bounces to 3, you will not see a significant change in the illumination on the floor; however, you will reduce the rendering efficiency. You can see the color version of Figure 13.7 (rendered with two diffuse bounces) in the Chapter 13 folder on the CD, named "FG secondary rays," where you see red and blue color bleeding from the walls on the floor and ceiling.

> Consider that GI photons are cast from light sources and behave differently than FG. Their sole purpose is to simulate multiple bounces and thus produce better (more realistic) results, whereas FG has the sole purpose of improving GI renders with an additional set of first-generation (single) diffuse bounces.

FG Maps

The FG point stores irradiance information within a special KD data tree (see the "3D Photon Maps and Kd-Trees" sidebar in Chapter 12, "Indirect Illumination"), known as an FG *map*, and uses it for color interpolation during the rendering phase. That information includes directional dependent color and luminance values from the surroundings that are stored with each FG point. The cached FG map file can then be reused to reduce the overhead of recalculating FG points for each frame. However, the way FG maps are used and implemented are very different from GI, as you will see throughout this chapter.

FG Sampling

To extend our discussion of FG efficiency (see the earlier "Single and Multiple Diffuse Bounces" section), we need to discuss FG sampling, which is the distribution of precomputed FG points during the first stage of FG. You already know how adaptive sampling works with mental ray (see Chapter 5, "Quality Control"), and how the sample density exponentially increases with high maximum sample values (that is, 64 samples per pixel with super-sampling). With FG it would be very expensive to calculate hundreds of FG rays per shading point (if each shading point is also an FG point) for each sample in the scene.

To avoid excessive calculations, FG utilizes its own sample pattern (and user-defined density) to evaluate incident illumination, shown in Figure 13.8. The distribution of FG points during the precomputation stage within the 3D scene is based on a raster space distribution (2D pixel space). To clarify, it distributes points by projecting eye rays through a hexagonal 2D grid of potential FG points from the camera's perspective. When these eye rays intersect with geometry in the scene, actual FG points are generated in 3D space at those 3D world space coordinates.

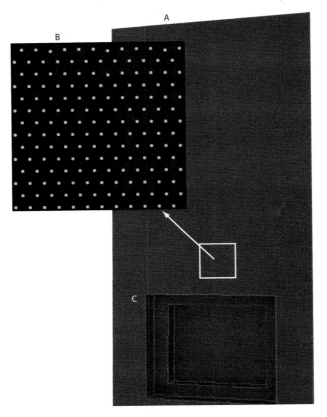

In Figure 13.8 label A, you see a rendered surface where FG points appear distributed across the entire surface. In label B, you can see a zoom on a small portion of the surface. Since the surface is simple (mostly planer), you can easily identify the hexagonal sample pattern. When the surface curvature shifts, particularly at the corners, the FG sample density appears to increase, as shown under label C. Typically, round corners and sharp edges produce more FG points for interpolation, depending on the FG mode used and other FG options. We will discuss the FG modes and controlling the density of FG points in more detail in the "Final Gathering Options and Techniques" section.

> Since FG points are generated in raster space, their distribution is dependent on the camera's perspective and thus subject to change when a camera animates; by contrast, GI photons depend on the location of source lights in the scene and do not change because of a camera animation.

The fact that FG is a camera-dependent solution, not a scene-based solution like GI, has two important implications:

- The solution is optimized for rendering performance by avoiding the generation of FG points everywhere in the scene; FG points are created only on surfaces that are in a direct line of sight from the camera's perspective (see Figure 13.9).

- When rendering animations, the fact that each frame has its independent FG solution results with FG flickering. Consider that raster-based FG sample patterns may distribute differently (and at different densities) on objects as the camera pans and dollies around them. These different FG distributions produce flickering artifacts, a well-known issue with FG. To resolve flickering in animations, there are a few well-developed options based on the usage of FG maps, which are discussed in detail in the section "Final Gathering Options and Techniques."

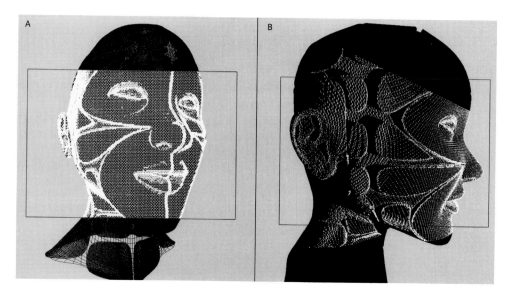

Figure 13.9

Viewport snapshots of the FG distribution in 3D based on the camera's perspective (A) and after rotating the camera (B)

In Figure 13.9, you can see the distribution of precomputation FG points within a 3D scene. (In Maya, after executing a render, it is possible to view and analyze the distribution of precomputation FG points within the viewport). In image A you can see how the FG points are distributed within the boundaries of the resolution gate, which is the rendered perspective. As you can see, geometry outside the resolution gate does not receive any FG points. In image B I rotated the camera's perspective to better illustrate how FG points are glued to the surface in 3D, illustrating that the 2D raster space sample pattern projects FG points within the 3D space.

Render-Time Interpolation of FG Points

As cited earlier, the FG point distribution is independent of shading samples in order to avoid generating too many FG points in the scene as a matter of render efficiency. Similar to GI photons, FG can leverage existing FG points within a given area to interpolate color across the surface, applying FG influence to areas that didn't receive FG points during the precomputation stage (sample locations between FG points).

Thus, FG interpolates irradiance values by using existing FG points within a given radius in world space units or raster (pixel) space, a concept illustrated in Figure 13.10. As you will see in the "Final Gathering Options and Techniques" section, two radius values are used to depict the area of influence for neighboring FG points at render time. A min radius value defines a region; all FG points within that radius must be used for interpolation or extrapolation. The max radius extends that region where a given number of FG points may be used. To clarify, the radius is "activated" with each sample taken in the scene (shading point), where irradiance values from nearby FG points (within the radius regions) are then used to apply FG shading. As with the GI photon search radius, smaller radius values produce finer details and increase the render time.

> The methods for specifying and controlling min and max radius values, as well as those values' relevance to FG, differ between the different FG modes, as discussed in the "Final Gathering Options and Techniques" section.

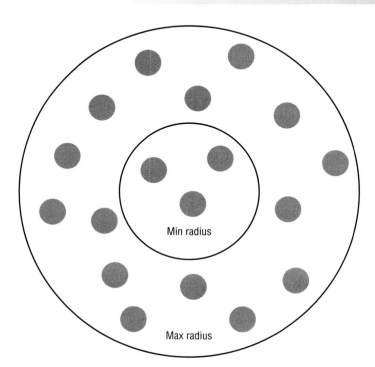

Figure 13.10

The min and max radius for interpolating FG points

Precomputed and Render-Time FG Points

As discussed earlier, FG is a two-stage process that includes precomputing FG points and render-time FG interpolation with additional FG point distribution (on demand). The precomputation stage handles the generation of FG points through the hexagonal sample pattern cited earlier.

During the interpolation stage, FG may decide to add other points when necessary. Basically, if there are too few FG points for interpolating color within the influence area (the min or max radius), FG is required to cast additional render-time FG points. Thus, render-time FG points are added where they are needed, on demand. Typically, you see them around sharp corners where nearby FG points are lacking. For example, if you place an imaginary circular plane (the radius) at an object's corner, because of the curvature, very few FG points will exist within that circle; hence, additional FG points are generated at corners, increasing the FG point density locally.

> With mental ray 3.5, the FG algorithm differs between the different modes. The automatic and multiframe modes do not produce additional render-time points.

FG Point Diagnostics

When FG diagnostics is enabled, the precomputed FG points appear as green dots, and additional render-time FG points appear as red dots. In Figure 13.11 under label A, you can see only precomputation points (correlating to green dots). Under label B, you can see precomputation FG points and render-time FG points (red dots). The green dots appear as brighter and larger circles opposed to the red ones in the black-and-white image. For generating the additional render-time FG points, I decreased the radius discussed earlier, forcing additional render-time FG points. One thing to notice in this figure is that the precomputed sample pattern has not changed; it remains the same under both images. Thus, the only difference is that additional render-time FG points have been added locally around the precomputed sample pattern.

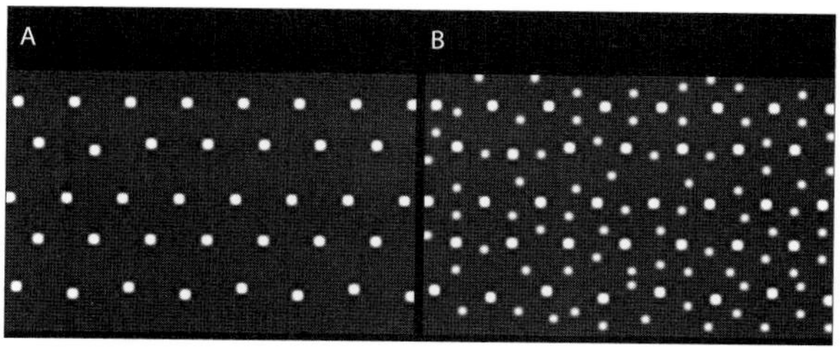

Figure 13.11

The distribution of precomputed FG points (A) and precomputed with render-time FG points (B)

If you look at the color image "Final Gather Diagnostics" on the CD in the Chapter 13 folder, you can see a color version that illustrates the two types of FG points. In that image under label A, you see the full diagnostic of the head model. Under label B, you can see a zoom of the nose area where you can identify a mix of green and red dots. Label C is an additional zoom that clearly displays their distribution. As cited earlier, the green dots are distributed based on the projection of eye rays through the hexagonal grid. Render-time FG points are added at random locations around those points based on demand.

In the color insert under label D, you can see that the distribution of FG points along some of the panels appears denser than the rest of the model. This demonstrates per-object FG settings. In this case, I used different setting for the panels, producing more pre-computed FG points along their surface. In previous versions of mental ray, per-object FG points rendered as blue dots.

So the distribution of FG points is based on the initial hexagonal grid, where render-time FG points may be added (based on the FG mode) around those initial points. Furthermore, per-object FG settings can be specified in each host.

FG STATISTICS (VERBOSE OUTPUT)

In addition to visualizing the diagnostics, mental ray outputs straightforward FG statistics from the RCFG module as verbosity info messages, as follows:

```
RC 0.4  info : rendering statistics
RC 0.4  info : type                    number    per eye ray
RC 0.4  info : eye rays                442904    1.00
RC 0.4  info : fg points interpolated  441491    1.00
RC 0.4  info : on average 86.44 finalgather points used per interpolation
```

You can learn from these output statistics more about the FG process. If you use different modes, such as the 3.4 modes (discussed in a moment), you will see two additional lines (in addition to interpolated):

```
RC 0.4  info : finalgather rays        2219500   4.87
RC 0.4  info : fg points computed      22195     0.05
```

These provide information on the total computed FG points (`fg points computed`) and the total number of FG rays cast in the scene.

ENABLING DIAGNOSTICS IN HOST APPLICATIONS

When FG diagnostics is enabled, the color dots appear after the render has completed, superimposed on the image as shown in the earlier examples. You can enable FG diagnostics in each host under the following paths:

Maya In the Render Settings window under the mental ray tab → Diagnostics → Diagnose Final Gather attribute check box.

XSI In the Render Manager window mental ray tab under the mental ray Render Options rollout → Diagnostics tab → View Final Gather Points property check box.

3ds Max In the Render Scene: mental ray Renderer window under the Processing tab → Diagnostics rollout, enable the Enable parameter check box, and then select the Final Gather parameter radio button.

PER-OBJECT FG SETTINGS IN HOST APPLICATIONS

This section covers the FG per-object options in host applications. You can find per-object FG options in each host for a selected surface under the following paths:

Maya In the Attribute Editor window under a shape node's mental ray rollout, the Final Gather Cast attribute check box enables a surface to cast influence (FG) on other surfaces. The Final Gather Receive attribute check box enables a surface to generate FG points and thus receive influence from FG. When either attribute is disabled, the surface will not cast or receive FG influence.

The Final Gather Override attribute check box, when enabled, enables additional attributes that appear directly below it. These per-object options have equivalent global options and are discussed later in the "Final Gathering Options and Techniques" section.

XSI In the Explorer window, select the Visibility node to open the Visibility property editor. In the Rendering tab → Final Gathering section, you can specify how an object participates in FG with the following properties:

- The Caster property enables generating FG points on that surface.
- The Visible in Sampling and Sampled properties both make the object visible to FG rays cast from other surfaces. When disabled, the Visible in Sampling property makes the surface invisible to FG rays (does not influence FG) so that they pass through the surface and can hit surfaces that are farther back. The Sampled property also makes it invisible; however, it stops the rays at the surface.
- Local FG Map allows you to specify a per-object FG map.

3ds Max Currently 3ds Max does not have per-object FG parameters.

GI and FG

Since both GI and FG evaluate diffuse indirect illumination, why use both? To answer that question, you need to consider the following points:

- High-quality GI renders typically require an enormous number of photons (millions), resulting in slow render times.
- Even with high-quality GI, artifacts may appear such as splotchy color smudges (noise) in the render, as shown with the kitchen sample on the CD in the Chapter 13 folder labeled photonSpread_high; look at the ceiling.
- To resolve artifacts in GI renders, you typically increase the search radius for photons; this has the effect of reducing the detail in the scene, such as in tight corners, by smoothing out the GI effect, as with the image on the CD in the Chapter 13 folder labeled photonSpread_low.

The purpose of FG is twofold: it improves the GI quality and improves rendering times by significantly reducing the number of photons required for GI as well as requiring fewer FG rays from each FG point. Thus, the reason you use both solutions is to remove GI splotchy artifacts, enhancing the quality of the image as well as improving the rendering time. Having said that, FG is extensively used as a single diffuse pass without GI, in which case it requires more rays to produce good results resulting with slow render times.

The effect FG has on the rendered image is more than just a means to remove GI artifacts; it's also a means for generating finer detail around and between surfaces (occlusion). Occlusion greatly improves realism by adding finer detail such as darkening in nooks and crannies, unlike GI, which is smoothed out over a search radius. In the same context, it also adds irradiance in nooks and crannies that may have been missed with GI photons. To clarify, in Chapter 12 you saw how the distribution of photons, its coverage in the scene, may miss certain target areas in the scene that are hard to access, such as along a corner or inside a recessed crack on a surface. FG compensates for the lack of photons in those areas by sampling irradiance from the FG points themselves (from the surfaces) rather than based on the distribution of photons from a source light.

In Figure 13.12, you can see a GI render under image A and the combination of both GI and FG under image B. Notice the increased irradiance, particularly around corners between image A (only GI) and image B (GI with FG), demonstrating how FG improves the render quality of GI. You can see a color version of this image in the Chapter 13 folder on the CD, labeled "GI and FG," where the influences on color are more apparent. Particularly note the increase in color bleeding on the cubes from the walls. The cubes are set as white diffuse surfaces so that they clearly show the color bleeding effect from the surroundings.

All in all, FG adds some nice qualities to GI rendering but reduces realism. For pure realism such as CAD rendering, you should use GI and caustics only with very high photon counts. For most creative purposes, a combination of GI with FG provides aesthetic results.

Figure 13.12

Comparing GI (A) and the effect of GI and FG combined (B)

Final Gather Options and Techniques

In this section, we review the mental ray FG options and discuss their effect on rendering. By doing so you will learn more about the techniques for using FG; however, in this case the techniques are more geared toward optimizing the render for efficiency. In the following section, we will further discuss more creative usages of FG. After reviewing the options, I'll identify them in each host application, as well as note some per-host specifics for environment mapping and constant shading.

The mental ray options for FG are applied in the options block of a .mi file. The options are mostly dependent on the selected FG mode; some are required, and others are optional (some options are only for version 3.5). The FG options are as follows:

```
finalgather [on | off | only | fastlookup]
"finalgather mode" "[automatic | multiframe | 3.4 | strict 3.4]"
"finalgather points" n (number of interpolation points)
finalgather presample density n (sample density)
finalgather accuracy [view] [n rays] [max radius] [min radius]
finalgather rebuild [on | off | freeze]
finalgather file "file name"
finalgather filter n (filter size)
finalgather falloff [start] [stop]
finalgather trace depth [reflection] [refraction] [diffuse] [total
combined]
finalgather scale [RGBA (color values)]
finalgather secondary scale [RGBA (color values)]
```

In mental ray 3.5 the automatic and multiframe modes have been added and utilize a different approach to FG rendering. Mostly they don't generate render-time FG points (the red dots discussed earlier) and use an option for point interpolation rather than a radius value. All these differences will be thoroughly clarified throughout this section. Let's start by examining some of the more straightforward options, and then look at the more complex and influential options in more depth.

The `finalgather [on | off | only | fastlookup]` option is used to enable or disable FG. It also provides two alternative "on" options: `fast lookup` and `only`. The `fast lookup` option leverages photons when GI is also enabled by storing irradiance values with photons during the photon distribution stage. As a result, when mental ray examines photons to determine their contribution to FG, it can extract the irradiance from one photon lookup rather than sample several photons to determine irradiance from GI. Using this option slows down the GI photon distribution process but accelerates FG. Overall, it provides for a faster render.

The `only` option is used to render solely FG without rendering the scene (a color image is not rendered). Its purpose is to generate FG maps that store information for several frames (with camera animations). We'll return to the topic of generating multiframe FG maps later in this section.

The `finalgather presample density` option is used to control the density of the pre-computed FG points. As discussed earlier, the hexagonal sample pattern (precomputed FG points) is a fixed grid in raster space. This option acts as a multiplier for the grid density, where values less than 1 decrease the density and greater than 1 increase the density. Typically, a density of 1 to 2 will suffice for most purposes. The density has the effect of improving detail in nooks and crannies, similar to the examples presented in Figure 13.14 while changing the radius sizes.

> Since the distribution of FG points is based on projected eye rays through the grid, from the camera's perspective, higher render resolutions will provide for better quality because more FG points will distribute in the scene.

The `"finalgather points"` option specifies how many FG points should be used for interpolating color when the automatic or multiframe modes (discussed shortly) are used. It's similar to the accuracy option with GI that defines how many photons will be used within a search radius for interpolating color.

The `finalgather trace depth` option is rather redundant; we have discussed similar trace options with raytracing, GI, and caustics in previous chapters, as well as earlier in the "FG Points and Paths" section. It simply limits the times an FG ray may reflect, refract, and a total for both combined. The only difference here is that an additional diffuse option exists that is unique to FG. This option refers to how many times an FG ray can reflect from diffuse surfaces to acquire color samples for irradiance, as discussed earlier with secondary bounces; the diffuse reflection is the sole purpose of FG that collects indirect irradiance from the scene. A value of 0 means there will be only one diffuse FG bounce (primary FG rays), and a value of 1 enables secondary FG rays, which is a secondary diffuse bounce. Thus, the reflect and refract options merely redirect rays, whereas the diffuse actually acquires color values from shading points. The total combined is the total of all three reflection types. As cited earlier, you should not use more than two diffuse bounces, even though you can. For more bounces, GI is a better solution.

The `finalgather scale` option is simply an RGBA color multiplier for FG primary rays. It reduces the intensity of FG primary rays based on the value you specify. When the color value is set to 1 for all four channels (white), the irradiance is multiplied by a value of one and thus maintains its original intensity. The `finalgather secondary scale` option is the same only for all secondary rays, for all diffuse bounces greater than 0. Thus, you have a color control for the primary rays and another for all secondary rays. Typically when a scene appears too bright, such as when using an HDR image, you can either scale down these color values or scale down the environment image's intensity (luminance) using a color multiplier, for example, with a color gain option, more on that later.

The `finalgather filter` option is used to reduce artifacts when rendering with HDR images, referred to as *speckle elimination*. A filter size of 0 means that no filtering is applied, and values of 1 and 2 are typically sufficient (you can use higher values). The purpose and benefits of filtering HDR images are discussed in detail in the "Final Gather Options and Techniques" section.

FG Falloff Distances

The `finalgather falloff` option defines the start and stop falloff ranges for FG rays. It's an important option that you should use to decrease render times by limiting the distance FG rays may travel in the scene. When an FG ray reaches the stop distance, it looks for an environment image (camera environment shader; see Chapter 3) to extract a final color value. The start value defines a starting point for a linear transition to the environment color, and the stop value defines the end point of that transition. From a creative perspective, it can be used to prevent FG from extracting irradiance influences from objects that are too far away in the scene so that they don't get darker or brighter (based on the target objects), as shown in Figure 13.13. Thus, it adds "creative" control over which objects influence FG.

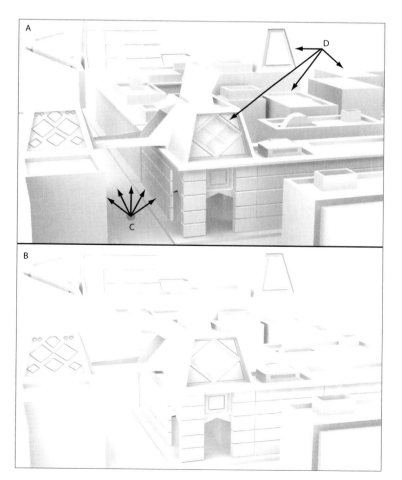

Figure 13.13

Influences of limiting the distance FG rays can travel in the scene

In Figure 13.13, the entire scene has the same Lambert shader applied using a white diffuse color, and the environment is set as a constant white color. For all purposes, this setup is an ambient occlusion pass using FG, a topic discussed in detail in "Ambient Occlusion" later in this chapter. In both images A and B, the influence of nearby occluding objects causes certain areas to appear darker, such as those labeled C and D in image A.

For image A, the falloff start and stop options are set to 0 (limitless), and for image B the falloff stop has been changed to 15, which is the maximum distance FG rays can travel to look for irradiance influence. Any value past that distance returns the environment color, which is white.

As you can see, under image A the point labeled C shows how the walls on both sides of the street and the overpass influence each other, as well as the floor, occluding some of the constant light from passing underneath the overpass. The same areas appear almost completely white in image B. They are completely white because the FG rays from the walls and overpass are not long enough to have influence on each other. For example, the floor emits rays that never reach the overpass; therefore, the overpass is more than 15 units away from the point labeled C. After the ray travels the distance of 15 units, it looks at the environment and extracts a white color for the floor's irradiance (for that ray only). In other words, in image B the rays "see" through surfaces in the scene, such as the overpass, and extract the background color.

To provide an extremely ridiculous analogy, light that hits the Empire State Building in New York will not influence the Eiffel Tower in Paris, and because mental ray has no idea as to the real scale of the scene, by using these falloff distances you can prevent objects that should not affect each other from doing so. But, there is a catch; if the environment is set to white, or any other color other than black, that color will be extracted by FG and add illumination. Consider these two scenarios when using an environmental image of a sky and FG:

- In the case of the Empire State Building and Eiffel Tower example noted earlier (an outdoor scene), limiting the distance is fine since FG will extract color from the sky after a given distance.

- Inside a closed room with an open window, the window is open so FG can sample the environment and "cast light" into the room. If you limit the distance in this scenario, the objects in the room might see through the walls and sample the environment if the distance is too short, which would be an undesired effect.

In Figure 13.13, the label D points to some more areas of interest in both images that show significant differences between the images. Note the farthest arrow from D points at four diamond-shaped windows at the top of the building. In that area, the detail is lost in image B because the rays within that encompassed area (on the diamond-shaped windows) don't extract influence from the surrounding four walls. In this case, clearly the falloff is set too low.

FG Accuracy

The `finalgather accuracy` option specifies the number of FG rays cast from each FG point (the n rays parameter in the previous excerpt). Values such as 100 are good for testing your scene and keep the render times relatively fast, whereas values from 500 to 800 provide for high-quality FG rendering.

> Note that higher ray values will also produce more FG precomputed points that may show more irradiance.

THE MIN AND MAX OPTIONS

The min and max radius parameters (found only with the "3.4" and "strict 3.4" modes) were discussed earlier in the section "Render-Time Interpolation of FG Points." If left unspecified, the max radius is automatically calculated based on the scene size and the min radius is set to 10 percent of the max radius. When manually specifying these values, for the max radius, typically 10 percent of the scene size is a good starting point, and then use 10 percent of that size for the min radius. The influence of min and max radius on rendering is significant. When set to low values, such as 0.1 and 1 for min and max radius, respectively, it has the following influences:

- It increases the render time.
- It adds more precomputed FG point sites.
- It enhances the level of detail around corners.
- It typically forces render-time FG points to generate.
- It can produce splotchy artifacts because of the shift in irradiance at close proximity, as with GI artifacts, requiring higher-accuracy settings (more FG rays per point) to improve the quality.

As discussed earlier, the hexagonal sample pattern for precomputed FG points is a fixed grid based on a given density. If the max radius is too small to encompass enough points for FG interpolation, then additional points are generated. Thus, small radius values act as an additional method for increasing the FG density, in this case using render-time FG points rather than precomputed FG points. Precomputed FG point density can be increased with the FG density option discussed earlier.

You saw in Figure 13.11 image A an example of precomputed FG points, and you saw in image B precomputed and render-time points. I forced the render to include the render-time FG points by decreasing the max radius (and min, respectively) value from 10 to 1.

You should use a simple scene to test these characteristics with FG diagnostics while using the 3.4 mode (discussed next).

Render-time FG points should be kept to a minimum because they can cause flickering. As you will see, an FG map can store precomputed FG points so that the objective is to get as many of those precomputed points into the map so that they remain static over a given number of frames. As cited earlier, when using the "automatic" and "multiframe" modes, render-time FG points are irrelevant.

In Figure 13.14 image A, the min and max radius are set to 1 and 10, respectively. In B they were set at 0.1 and 1. As you can see, there is more detail in the areas indicated with the arrows in image B. Thus, when the radius is set smaller, you can see better occlusion effects within cracks and neighboring surfaces. With lower values the occlusion effects are more pronounced and the render times increase.

Again, lower radius values also means that you see faster shifts in irradiance across the surface. By increasing the number of rays cast from each FG point, you also increase the likelihood that FG points in near proximity (which don't affect each other during the interpolation) will receive relatively similar irradiance values by taking an enormous amount of FG ray samples (about 400 to 800) in the scene and reducing artifacts.

With mental ray 3.4 and newer, 1,000 rays is considered excessive because it can now use approximately half as many rays to produce similar results as with the preceding mental ray versions (that is, typically users used approximately 1,000 rays so they can now use only 500 rays). Some users consider values of more than 1,000 rays, which in my opinion (in most cases) will prove inefficient (unnecessary). If you use FG in that way for high production quality, it should be used only when you have the support of very powerful machines.

Figure 13.14

Decreasing the min and max radius from image A to B provides the enhanced detail shown.

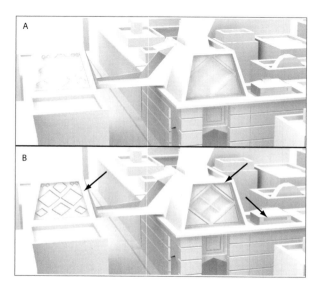

THE VIEW PARAMETER (ALL FG MODES)

The view parameter of the finalgather accuracy option defines whether the radius sizes are measured in 3D world space or in 2D raster space. When view is enabled, these distances basically become view dependent, regardless of the mode, so that objects that are close to the camera have more detail than those placed farther back. Consider that an object can encompass a pixel space of 64×64 pixels, so that when you specify a max radius of 10 pixels, several FG points need to be spread across the surface for interpolation. However, if you translate the object farther back in the scene so that it encompasses an area of 10×10 pixels, that object will receive fewer FG points.

When you enable view, the min and max radius values used for pixel space may differ drastically than those used for world space, so you should not assume that the current values (world space values when view is disabled) are correct; you should specify appropriate values based on the level of detail in the scene and the render resolution size.

Consider that higher resolutions can use higher radius sizes, and vice versa.

FG Modes

The FG algorithm has improved its handling of modes in mental ray 3.5. Aside from the difference in how many FG rays are required for producing good results, as noted earlier with mental ray 3.4, in version 3.5, the quality of the data (irradiance values) stored with FG points has been improved. Each FG point now stores colors with directional information, which improves FG in general and particularly with normal or bump mapping. In previous versions, for bump mapping, FG had to generate new FG points based on the bump map, similar to the increased density around sharp corners discussed earlier. Now FG stores directional color (irradiance) information so that it can simulate bump mapping without increasing the FG density. Thus, mental ray can interpret the influence bump mapping has on irradiance at a given FG point without adding additional FG points, because each FG point possesses within it directional information on the sources of irradiance.

There are four optional modes for controlling FG. They are specified with the following option:

```
"finalgather mode" "[automatic | multiframe | 3.4 | strict 3.4]"
```

The automatic, multiframe, and 3.4 modes are new to mental ray, whereas the strict 3.4 forces mental ray to function exactly as it used to in previous versions, without leveraging any of the enhanced features of mental ray 3.5; it's intended for backward compatibility so that existing scene files will render the same as with earlier versions of mental ray. One difference between modes is that the automatic and multiframe modes do not generate render-time FG points, thus they use only precomputed points. The 3.4 mode does allow render-time points to generate; it also leverages the enhancements to the FG algorithm. Let's look at each mode in more detail.

The Automatic Mode

With the automatic mode, you specify a number of points that should be used for interpolating color, rather than use the min and max radius parameters with the `finalgather` accuracy option; mental ray extracts FG points automatically from the scene determining on its own the adequate distance for interpolation (the influence area), regardless of a specified radius. Note that the accuracy statement is still used to specify the number of FG rays (the `ray` parameter) and enable the view dependent mode (the `view` parameter); however, the radius parameters have no effect. Thus, our discussions on min and max radius values and interpolation are based on mental ray 3.4. Those concepts still apply, but they are handled internally without user control, aside from specifying view dependency. The following points sum up the most relevant options to control quality when using the automatic mode:

- The `finalgather presample density` option defines the initial distribution of FG points. Values from 1 to 2 provide adequate quality.
- The `finalgather accuracy [view] [n rays]` option is used to specify view dependency and the number of rays.
- The `finalgather points` option is used to define the number of FG points for interpolation.
- The `finalgather scale` and `secondary scale` options are used to control the intensity of the FG irradiance contribution, as discussed earlier.

The Multiframe Mode

Multiframe is aimed at improving FG solutions with motion cameras. It's an extension of the automatic mode, functioning in a similar way. The difference is in how you approach rendering and how points are computed. The render should be divided into the two stages of FG map generation and rendering. The FG map is generated to cover the entire sequence and then used by mental ray during rendering. Also, during the first stage (point generation), the multiframe mode ensures that the same number of FG points will be used for each frame. With this approach, the multiframe mode reduces the likelihood of flickering in animation. This technique is further demonstrated in the "FG Maps and the fg_copy Utility" section.

In addition, this mode utilizes the max radius parameter from the `finalgather accuracy` option. It uses the max radius to define a maximum distance at which FG points can influence each other during interpolation. This is because with the automatic and multiframe modes, FG points can be extracted from anywhere in the scene, based on how mental ray decides to handle the interpolation internally. With multiframe, mental ray knows that FG points are spread out to cover a larger area of the scene, based on the camera's animation.

Thus, by allowing you to define a max distance for interpolation, it prevents mental ray from pulling influence from points that are placed in remote areas of the scene from the point in question. If FG cannot find enough FG points within that max radius for interpolation, it fades whatever irradiance results it has to black.

Thus, the multiframe mode utilizes the same options as the automatic mode, with the difference of also accepting a max radius value with the `finalgather accuracy` option.

> The multiframe mode is geared toward camera animation only. If objects are animated in the scene, you should not use this mode.

The 3.4 Mode

The 3.4 mode is similar to the previous implementation of FG in that it utilizes the `finalgather accuracy` option radius parameters and not the `finalgather points` interpolation option, while it also leverages the enhancements to the FG algorithm. In other words, you can specify values using the min and max radius parameters as with previous versions of mental ray but benefit from the advances in the technology.

The 3.4 mode does generate precomputed and render-time FG points. The reason render-time FG points are so significant is that they are not stored in FG maps and are less predictable, which is cause for flickering. On the other hand, they allow finer detail when needed based on demand. Fine-tuning FG with the 3.4 mode is then divided between the following options:

- All the parameters of the `finalgather accuracy` option
- The `finalgather presample density` option
- The `finalgather scale` and `secondary scale` options

> One benefit of using the 3.4 mode is that seasoned users may prefer to fine-tune the scene manually, using radius values, rather than rely on the automatic mode.

Choosing a Mode

With the automatic and multiframe mode, the only option you have to increase the detail in the render is the precomputation FG point density, opposed to defining min and max radius values to specify the influence area. The ideal is that these modes simplify the usage of FG while providing adequate results. Furthermore, in XSI the 3.4 mode is labeled "Expert" in the XSI options, showing that it is regarded as a more manual approach. Finally, as a personal preference, I prefer using the radius option and thus the 3.4 mode; however, that may be because I'm used to it.

You should typically use the 3.4 or automatic modes for still images and use multiframe or 3.4 for animation (discussed next).

FG Maps and the fg_copy Utility

As cited earlier, FG caches irradiance values in a KD data tree that can be saved to disk in an FG map for reusability. As long as the FG rays remain the same (as specified by the finalgather accuracy option), you can reuse the FG map without recalculating the precomputed FG points. Also, only precomputed FG points can store in FG maps. FG maps become useful with animation sequences as a means to reduce flickering, especially when using the multiframe or 3.4 modes, and to decrease render times. The mental ray options used for controlling the FG map are as follows:

```
finalgather rebuild [on | off | freeze]
finalgather file "file name"
```

As you can see, the finalgather rebuild option provides three optional modes for controlling FG. You will see in Figures 13.15 to 13.17 the different characteristics of each mode. Note that the scene consists of a camera attached to a motion path (the curve shown in each figure) that travels over time between the spheres.

Rebuild Option Set to On

When set to On, the FG map is regenerated with each rendered frame, storing precomputed FG points. Thus, if an FG map exists, it's overwritten. Typically you will use this option while experimenting with different FG settings to tweak the rendered appearance. In Figure 13.15 rebuild is set to on, and you can see that two separate frames have been rendered with the same FG map. The FG points can be seen projected from the camera in the scene (in Maya you can see FG points in the viewport) as white dots, and as you can see, each frame has a completely different scatter pattern for FG points and hence a different FG map. Thus, the first frame was rendered in image A, and then when the next frame was rendered in image B, the previous FG points were deleted and new ones created.

Consider that with a slow-moving animation, each frame will have a new FG map (its FG points recalculated) that differs slightly from the previous frame. The result is flickering in the FG during animation.

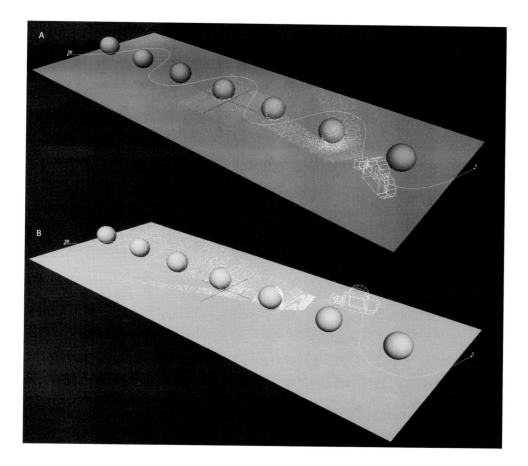

Figure 13.15

FG points projected at different camera angles when rebuild **is set to** on, **overwriting any pre-existing FG points**

Rebuild Option Set to Off

When the rebuild option is set to off, FG points in the map are reused instead of being regenerated. However, if FG requires additional precomputed points for interpolation, for example because the camera has moved, then additional precomputed points will be calculated and appended to the FG map, as shown in Figure 13.16. In image A you can see frame number 13 rendered as a single frame; the FG points appear in the scene. I then changed to frame 20 and rendered another frame, so as you can see, there are two scatter patterns that appear in image A. I then switched to frame 3 and rendered another frame, and a third projection of FG points is added to the scene, shown under B. Thus, appending FG points is independent of a frame sequence; you can append points manually by moving the camera and rendering a frame, each time other FG points are added to the FG map, and if sufficient FG points exist, such as rerendering the same camera angle, the precomputation stage will be skipped.

Figure 13.16

FG points are appended to the FG map each time a render is executed when the rebuild option is set to off.

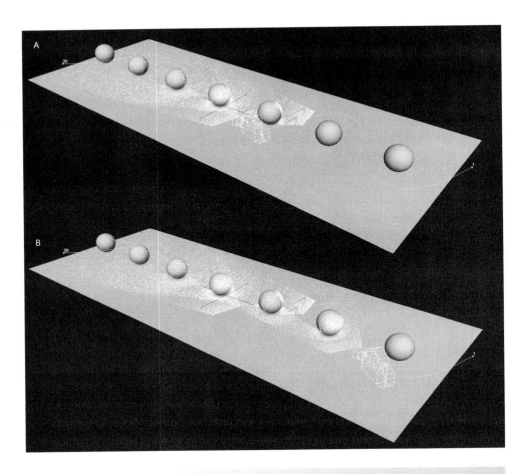

Figure 13.16

FG points are appended to the FG map each time a render is executed when the `rebuild` option is set to `off`.

One important point is that when objects animate in the scene (aside from the camera), the FG points will remain static so that irradiance will appear where it shouldn't; you will see FG effects for an object that is no longer there, similar to reusing shadow maps with moving objects. You can't reuse an FG map with animated surfaces such as characters.

FG maps work well over networks (render farms), even when several machines need to access the same file, reading and writing information into the file.

Rebuild Option Set to Freeze

When the `rebuild` option is set to `freeze`, precomputation is skipped, and the current FG map is reused regardless of whether there are sufficient FG points for interpolation. This mode is aimed at reducing flickering during animation by freezing the FG map to a given distribution. Note that with the automatic and multiframe modes, the map is completely frozen; however, in the 3.4 and strict 3.4 modes, render-time FG points may still be calculated. When render-time points are generated, they are not added to the FG map so that they are essentially temporary points that assist FG with a given frame. Of course, having fewer render-time points reduces the likelihood of flickering.

There is an additional mental ray stand-alone option, `rebuild deep freeze`. It prevents render-time FG points from generating in 3.4-compatible modes.

Flicker Control

As you can see, when `rebuild` is set to `off`, you can reduce the chances of flickering by reusing FG points over a sequence of frames. Nonetheless, regardless of the mode (automatic, multiframe, and so on), flickering can still occur during interpolation. The FG map guarantees only that the distribution of FG points does not change; however, it does not control how FG interpolates those points during rendering, that is, which points FG decides to use with each frame. Thus, with the 3.4 and strict 3.4 modes, if you interpolate over a larger radius, you can reduce some of the chances of flickering. With the automatic mode, you can specify how many points are used for interpolation, but you can't control where those points are extracted from; the maximum radius for the influence area is determined by mental ray.

As a solution to this limitation with the automatic mode, the multiframe mode (as cited earlier) uses the `finalgather accuracy` option max radius parameter to add more control over the influence area with animation. Thus, multiframe is an extension to the automatic mode that uses the new approach to FG (no longer dependent on radius values) with mental ray 3.5 and higher with some added functionalities for animation, such as the max radius parameter.

Generating FG Maps

Regardless of whether you want to render with the 3.4 or multiframe modes, the approach to generating and using FG maps is identical. Personally, I get better results with the 3.4 mode than with the multiframe mode. The process has two stages: generating the FG map and then rendering the sequence.

In the first stage, you use the `finalgather only` option and set `rebuild` to `off` so that you generate an FG map for the entire animation sequence without rendering the color frames. You don't need to render every frame; you can set it to render every other frame instead, depending on the distance the camera travels between frames, as shown in Figure 13.17. If the difference between one frame and the next is significant, you need to render frames at higher intervals. This stage produces an FG map using the `finalgather rebuild off` option that covers the camera's motion using a constant number of FG points. Thus, when FG renders, it will have the same FG point distribution across the entire camera animation as shown in the figure, where you see FG points everywhere in the scene.

Figure 13.17

Rendering a sequence of frames with the rebuild **option set to** off **produces an FG map for the entire animation.**

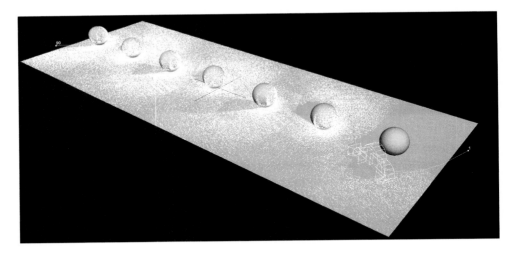

At the second stage, render time, you render the animation sequence using the final-gather rebuild freeze option, which is a frozen FG map. In this way, you avoid adding new precomputed FG points to the scene. Again, this only reduces the likelihood of flickering as the interpolation stage (render time) may still provide for some flickering. However, with a good distribution of FG points and the correct max radius values, you can get good results.

> When the rays parameter of the finalgather accuracy option changes, the FG is rebuilt and not reused.

As noted earlier, if you look at Figure 13.17, you can see the importance of max radius whether with the 3.4 modes or the multiframe mode. It prevents FG from extracting values from distant areas in the scene during rendering.

As an example for this method, I've included under the Chapter 13 directory in the companion CD a movie clip of a camera animation for the scene shown in Figure 13.17, with additional walls and windows, solely lit with FG and an external environment image (casting light into the room). It was rendered using the 3.4 mode. There is no FG flickering in the animation; however, you may see some compression artifacts because I had to compact 1GB of images into 4MB. The scene was rendered with rather low accuracy settings and large radius settings (1 and 10), and yet the FG doesn't flicker.

The fg_copy Utility

In addition to these techniques, an FG utility exists that allows you to combine individual FG maps. You run the `fg_copy` utility in a command prompt; for example, on Windows, open the Start menu, choose Run, and then type **cmd** to open a command prompt. At the command prompt, type **fg_copy**, and click Enter; a list of options appears. The idea is to list all the maps you want to combine and, as a last entry, provide a path and name for the output file. Remember that you need to specify paths that have spaces, such as "My Documents" in quotes (the entire path with the filename in quotes). It should look like this (you don't need to specify an extension):

```
fg_copy "path\fgmap1" "path\fgmap2" "path\outfile.fgmap"
```

To make life easier, you can simply type **fg_map** and a space and then drag and drop all the FG maps you want to combine one after the other, applying a space between each of them. Eventually you enter the output path with the filename and click Enter. You will have a new FG map with all the data appended.

For 3ds Max users, it's especially important to get the utility since the `finalgather rebuild off` and `finalgather only` options are not available. Thus, you want to render separate FG maps (change the FG map name for each rendered frame) for certain frames and then combine them with this utility. In XSI and 3ds Max 9, I noticed that the utility doesn't ship with the software; maybe their Support department can help you get a copy. For Maya users, the utility is located in the `Maya/bin` folder.

FG in Host Applications

As discussed in Chapter 3, "mental ray Output" (see the "mental ray Cameras" section for host application specifics), mental ray cameras accept environment shaders. These shaders enable mapping the environment with an exterior environmental image that encompasses the scene, be it a standard image (low dynamic range) or HDR image, and using a spherical, angular, cubical or other projection method. The following sections briefly recap some of these options for FG; however, applying connections, applying projections, and finding the shaders were covered in Chapter 3.

Let's look at the host application options for FG and then applying environment images for FG. In all cases, the FG options have similar names as those presented throughout the chapter. In addition, all hosts allow you to preview Final Gather tiles while they are being generated, which are the irradiance values from precomputed FG points. These tiles enable you to quickly estimate the influence of irradiance from FG and appear darker than the final rendered image since it displays only the FG irradiance that is then added with the illumination in the scene.

Maya

You can find the FG attributes in the Render Settings window under the mental ray tab →
Final Gathering rollout, shown in Figure 13.18. You can find additional options under the
miDefaultOptions and mentalrayGlobals nodes in the Attribute Editor.

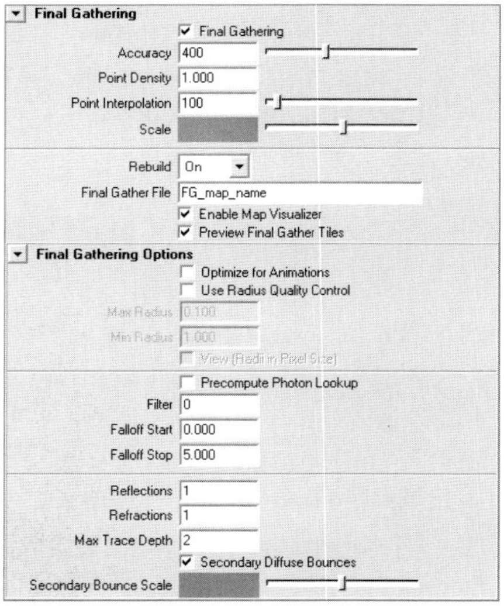

Figure 13.18

**The mental ray Final
Gather attributes in
the Render Settings
window**

When mental ray is enabled, you can select these nodes in the Outliner (disable the
Display → DAG Objects Only option) window or by executing the following commands in
the Script Editor window:

```
select -r miDefaultOptions
select -r mentalrayGlobals
```

These commands will reveal the .mi default options and render globals nodes in the
Attribute Editor. I refer to some attributes that are not found in the Render Settings window but only in both of these nodes in the following sections.

Under the Render Settings window's Final Gathering rollout, shown in Figure 13.18,
you can find most of the FG settings discussed in the earlier sections. Let's quickly review
each attribute referring to its corresponding mental ray option or its functionality:

The Final Gathering attribute check box is used to enable FG.

The Accuracy attribute is used to define the number of FG rays cast from an FG point
as with the finalgather accuracy option *n* rays parameter.

The Point Density attribute refers to the precomputed FG density as with the mental
ray finalgather presample density option.

The Point Interpolation attribute is used to specify the number of FG points used for interpolation, as with the mental ray `finalgather points` option.

The Scale color attribute controls the irradiance intensity as with the `finalgather scale` option for FG primary rays. The Secondary Bounce Scale color attribute is used for all secondary FG rays as with the `finalgather secondary scale` option.

The Rebuild attribute drop-down menu is used to select the different FG map rebuild options, including On, Off, and Freeze as with the `finagather rebuild` option. You can specify the FG map filename below in the Final Gather File attribute text box. Do not specify an extension for the file; just type the name. By default, the file is stored in the current project directory in *project name*\renderData\mentalray\finalgMap\FG file.fgmap.

The Enable Map Visualizer attribute, as with GI, enables you to see only precomputation FG points in the viewport after you render an image in the Render View window. You can control the size of the FG points using the Point size attribute in the mental ray Map Visualizer window, found under Window → Rendering Editors → mental ray → Map Visualizer.

You can load other FG maps to display using the browsing option in the Map Visualizer window.

The Preview Final Gather Tiles attribute displays the precomputation FG tiles as they are calculated before the render commences, as noted earlier.

The Max and Min Radius attributes correspond to the `finalgather accuracy` option min and max parameters. And, the View (Radii in Pixel Size) attribute check box corresponds to the view parameter where radius values are specified in pixel sizes when enabled.

The Precompute Photon Lookup attribute check box corresponds to the `finalgather` option using the `fastlookup` parameter. When enabled, GI photons also store irradiance to assist FG in sampling the influence from photons, as discussed earlier.

The Filter attributes correspond to the `finalgather filter` option for speckle elimination typically when using HDR images. By default, it's set to 0, which has no influence on rendering. We further discuss filtering with FG and HDR images later in this chapter.

The Falloff Start and Stop attributes limit the distance FG rays can travel in the scene in world space units, as discussed with the mental ray `finalgather falloff` option's `start` and `stop` parameters.

The Reflection, Refraction, Max Trace Depth attributes are straightforward and correspond to the `finalgather trace depth` option reflection, refraction, and total combined parameters. The Secondary Diffuse Bounces attribute check box corresponds to the `diffuse` parameter of the `finalgather trace depth` option. When enabled, the `diffuse` parameter is set to 1, allowing one additional bounce of secondary FG rays, as discussed earlier. If you want to specify additional secondary bounces such as 2, you need to open the Attribute Editor window and reveal the miDefaultOptions cited earlier. In the Final Gather rollout, you will find all the trace depth attributes shown

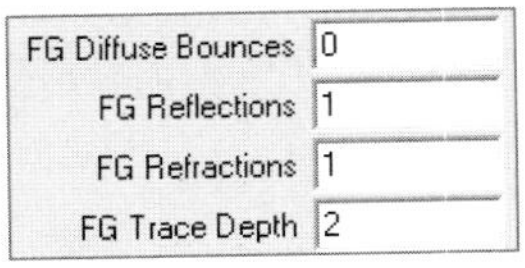

Figure 13.19

Although it's not usually recommended, you can increase the number of secondary diffuse bounces to greater than 1 by using the FG Diffuse Bounces attribute, found under the miDefaultOptions node attributes.

FG Diffuse Bounces	0
FG Reflections	1
FG Refractions	1
FG Trace Depth	2

in Figure 13.19. As you can see, an FG Diffuse Bounces attribute exists (only in this window), allowing you to increase the number of secondary diffuse bounces. As discussed earlier, typically you should not use more than two diffuse bounces (primary FG rays and one pass of secondary FG rays). Therefore, you should not increase it to a value greater than 1 (two diffuse bounces), which is the same as enabling the Secondary Diffuse Bounces attribute in the Render Settings window.

Under the mentalrayGlobals node in the Attribute Editor you can enable the mental ray `finalgather only` option using the Render Mode attribute drop-down list → Render Final Gather Maps option. When it's enabled, mental ray will render only an FG map, avoiding any actual rendering as discussed earlier.

SELECTING FG MODES

The FG modes are set in the Render Settings window (Figure 13.18) as follows:

- By default the automatic mode is enabled.

- The Optimize for Animations attribute check box enables multiframe mode. When it's enabled, you can use the Max Radius attribute to specify the max radius for multiframe FG points as discussed earlier.

- The Use Radius Quality Control attribute check box enables the 3.4 mode (not strict 3.4). When it's enabled, use the Min and Max Radius attributes below to control the `finalgather accuracy` option min and max radius values.

- To select the strict 3.4 mode, you need to open the Attribute Editor window and display the miDefaultOptions node attributes cited earlier. Under the Extra Attributes rollout you will find the Final Gather Mode attribute drop-down menu shown in Figure 13.20. The Original option corresponds to the strict 3.4 mode. Notice that the

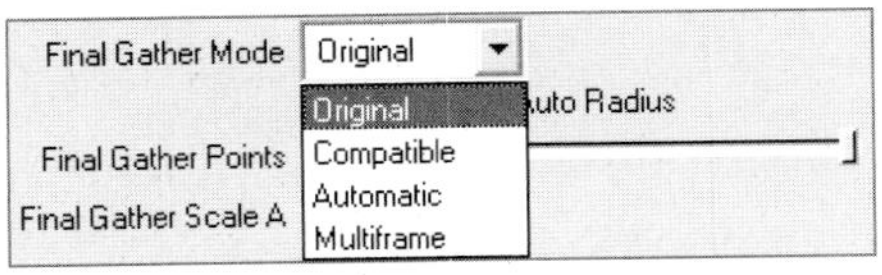

Figure 13.20

To select the strict 3.4 mode, use the Final Gather Mode attribute under the miDefaultOptions node attributes.

Final Gather Mode	Original ▼
	Original uto Radius
Final Gather Points	Compatible
Final Gather Scale A	Automatic
	Multiframe

three additional modes are also present: Compatible (3.4), Multiframe, and Automatic. Thus, you can select any mode using this attribute instead of through the Render Settings window. If, for example, you select the multiframe option (Optimize for Animations attribute) from the Render Settings window, you will see this attribute update to read multiframe.

APPLYING ENVIRONMENTS FOR FG

With Maya there are four common approaches for specifying backgrounds for FG, whether using a constant color, procedural texture, or image file. You can apply them by using one of the following methods:

- Applying a mental ray environment shader to a camera's shape node in the Attribute Editor window under the mental ray rollout → Environment Shader attribute (see Chapter 3, "mental ray Output").

- In the same window, you could alternatively use the Background Color attribute under the Environment rollout, applying a constant color or texture for FG. For example, if you specify a white color, FG will sample white irradiance in 360 around an FG point. I always use this technique for specifying a constant color.

- The mental ray *image-based lighting* (IBL) node, discussed in Chapter 3, "mental ray Output," is the preferred method for applying an environment image with Maya and mental ray. It's found in the Render Settings window, under Environment rollout → Image Based Lighting. Once you click the Create Attribute button, an IBL node is added to the scene.

- You can also use a geometric sphere, such as a NURBS sphere, with a constant color or spherical projection applied to a constant shader, such as the Maya surface shader. Because it's a surface shader, it renders as is without any influence from lighting. However, it is not the most practical technique, because you force mental ray to deal with additional geometry in the scene, which is not the case with all the other techniques cited above.

The techniques for applying environment shaders for reflections were discussed in Chapter 3, "mental ray Output," in the "mental ray Cameras" section, particularly some important IBL node attributes. In addition to the points cited in that chapter, you need to consider the following points for using the IBL node with FG.

The IBL node should always be used to load background images. It's basically a nongeometric environment shader with additional advanced options for light and photon emission for image-based lighting (not for FG). Because it can be used to specify light and photon emission, it's categorized as a Maya light shader that can be found on the Lights tab in the Hypershade window. Regardless of those advanced abilities, it's a great environment shader for loading images or HDR images for FG rendering.

In the Attribute Editor window, under the IBL nodes Image Based Lighting Attributes rollout, the following attributes are important for FG:

- The Mapping attribute is used to select a specific type of panoramic environment image. You will most commonly use spherical images. The types of images are further discussed in the section "Advanced Final Gather Techniques" later in this chapter.

- The Type attribute selects whether you want to use an image file for an environment or a texture, specified with the Texture attribute. If you set it to the Texture option, the Texture attribute's color acts as a constant color for the background, unless mapped with a procedural texture. For images, use the Image Name textbox attribute to load an environmental image. HDR images are supported, and you should always prefer using HDR images for FG environments, as discussed in the section "Advanced Final Gather Techniques."

- The Infinite attribute defines whether the environment image (the IBL node itself) is always placed outside the scene, encompassing the entire scene. When enabled, it has infinite scale, always casting light from outside the scene inward. You can rotate it so that it aligns with the scene in a particular way, for example, the sun placed facing west. When disabled, you can also translate and scale the node so that the placement of the node in the viewport defines its rotation, scale, and position. For example, you can wrap the node around a crystal ball in a room and cast light from there into the ball when Infinite is disabled. This option is mostly for light or photon casting. With FG, in most cases, you want to leave it enabled.

- When an image is loaded, the Hardware Exposure and Alpha attributes define the visibility of the image in the viewport, mapped on the IBL node. You will need to see the image clearly when you position a light source that aligns with the light source in the image, as further discussed in the section "Advanced Final Gather Techniques."

- The Color Gain attribute is multiplied against the environment image or texture. Use this attribute to increase or decrease the intensity of an HDR image. You can use values that exceed the 0 to 1 range so that FG samples a brighter light for the FG effect. For example, you can specify using HSV color a V value of 2.

Under the Render Stats Rollout you have a Visible in Final Gather attribute that defines whether the IBL node affects FG in the scene. You always want to leave it enabled when rendering with FG; however, you may want to disable Primary Visibility so that it doesn't appear rendered in the background, as a background image. You may also want to disable Visible in Secondary Reflections so that it affects only FG lighting and does not appear to reflect from surfaces in the scene. Typically, if it affects the lighting, you would expect to see the environment reflecting on glossy to specular surfaces.

HDR IMAGE EXPOSURE

The Color Gain attribute cited earlier is currently the only method for setting the exposure of an HDR image with Maya; however, it doesn't really set exposure values. Rather, it multiplies the entire dynamic range by the specified value. To set exposure, you should use an external tool such as HDR Shop to specify the default exposure, a topic discussed in more detail in the section "Advanced Final Gather Techniques."

The techniques discussed in the section "Advanced Final Gather Techniques" are based on using the IBL node with HDR images.

XSI

When using FG in XSI, you must have at least one light source in the scene, whether it's the default light generated with each new scene or a light source you've created. In addition, XSI has a default ambient light that controls the overall (max) intensity of the Ambient color property for all the shaders in the scene. Thus, a shader's Ambient color property is multiplied against the global Ambience property similar to mental ray base shader's ambient and ambience options. With FG, you may want to remove any influence from shader ambient lighting. You can do so by opening the Ambient Lighting property editor from the main menu bar by choosing Render → Modify → Ambience, and then dialing down the Ambience property RGB colors to 0. Figure 13.21 shows the Ambient Lighting property editor.

Figure 13.21

XSI has a global Ambience property that is used to control the overall influence of the Ambient color property in XSI shaders.

As discussed in the "Final Gather Options and Techniques" section, you may want to render without any light influence; however, you must maintain at least one light source. Thus, instead of deleting the light source, simply reduce its intensity value to 0 so that it has no influence on the scene.

If you want to use ambient light with a shader for FG, forcing brighter values for FG lighting, you can further specify per-object ambience values. In this way, the ambience color doesn't affect all the shaders in the scene. You can do so by selecting the Ambient Lighting node for a given surface in the Explorer window. When the Confirm Make Local window pops up, select the Yes option to make the Ambience property local for that surface. By doing so, you can, for example, specify a white Ambience color that will affect only that surface shader's Ambient color property.

Based on the points cited earlier, a good starting point setup for using FG with an environment image is as follows:

1. Select the default light (labeled "light" and hidden) from the Explorer window, and reduce its Intensity property to 0.

2. Open the Ambient Lighting property editor, and reduce the Ambience property to black.

If you render a scene it should appear black, and ready for FG testing.

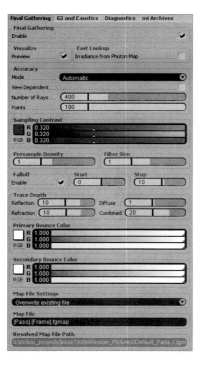

You can find the FG properties in the Render Options window under the mental ray Render Options rollout → Final Gathering tab, shown in Figure 13.22. Once you enable the Enable property, FG is enabled, and all the FG properties appear below the property, as shown in the figure.

Let's quickly review each property referring to its corresponding mental ray option or its functionality:

The Visualize → Preview property check box displays the precomputation FG tiles in the render view as they are being calculated, before the actual render commences, as noted earlier.

The Fast Lookup → Irradiance from the Photon Map property check box corresponds to the finalgather option using the fastlookup parameter. When it's enabled, GI photons also store irradiance to assist FG in sampling the influence from photons as discussed earlier.

The Accuracy properties section provides all the properties that control the mental ray finalgather accuracy and finalgather points options. Here are a few points for this section:

- From the Mode property you can specify which of the four modes you want to use: Automatic, Multiframe, Expert (3.4), and Legacy (strict 3.4).

- Based on the selected mode, the relevant properties for that mode appear below the mode.

- In all cases (modes) the View Dependent property check box is available, corresponding to the mental ray finalgather accuracy option view parameter where FG interpolates FG points based on pixel sizes rather than scene distances (when enabled).

- Also, all modes use the Number of Rays property corresponding to the mental ray finalgather accuracy option *n* rays parameter (number of rays per FG point).

- When the Automatic or Multiframe mode is selected, the Points property corresponds to the number of FG points used for interpolation, as with the mental ray finalgather points option.

- If you selected Multiframe, you will also see the Max Radius appear, corresponding to the mental ray finalgather accuracy option max radius parameter.

- If you select Expert or Legacy (both based on radius values for interpolation), the Points property disappears (as it's irrelevant), and the Min and Max Radius properties appear, corresponding to the `finalgather` accuracy option min and max radius parameters.

The Sampling Contrast property controls the amount of color bleeding between objects, increasing or decreasing the FG effect. Higher values produce more color bleeding. The effect of this property is very subtle; for example, when set to 0, it does not remove color bleeding; it just reduces the effect slightly.

The Presample Density property corresponds to the precomputed FG density as with the mental ray `finalgather presample density` option.

The Filter Size property corresponds to the `finalgather filter` option for speckle elimination typically when using HDR images. By default it is set to 1. I further discuss filtering with FG and HDR images later in this chapter.

The Falloff → Enable property enables the Start and Stop properties, which limit the distance FG rays can travel in the scene in world space units, as discussed with the mental ray `finalgather falloff` option start and stop parameters.

The Trace Depth → Reflection, Refraction, Diffuse, and Combined properties are straightforward and correspond to the `finalgather trace depth` option reflection, refraction, diffuse, and total combined parameters. To enable secondary diffuse bounces, the Diffuse property should be set to a value of 1, allowing one additional bounce of secondary FG rays, as discussed earlier. At the default value of 0, only primary FG rays are cast in the scene, which is one pass of FG indirect illumination. You can increase the Diffuse bounces to more than 1. But as noted earlier, it is not recommended; you should use GI for multiple bounces.

The Primary Bounce Color property controls the irradiance intensity, as with the `finalgather scale` option for FG primary rays. The Secondary Bounce Color property is used for all secondary FG rays as with the `finalgather secondary scale` option. Note that their influence on rendering does not take effect while rendering tests in a viewport render region, only when you render an actual frame (output a file).

The Map File Settings drop-down menu is used to select the different FG map rebuild options, including Overwrite existing file (on), Append new FG points to file (off), and Only use FG points from file (freeze) as with the `finagather rebuild` option. You can specify the FG map filename under the Map File property text box or use the default path.

In the mental ray Render Options → Optimization tab → Render Type section, you can enable the mental ray `finalgather only` option using the Render Type property drop-down list → Finalgathering Only option. When it's enabled, mental ray will render only an FG map, avoiding any actual rendering as discussed earlier and demonstrated in the "FG Maps and the fg_copy Utility" section.

APPLYING ENVIRONMENTS FOR FG

With XSI there are two common approaches for specifying backgrounds for FG, whether using a constant color, procedural texture, or image file. You can apply them by using one of the following methods:

- Applying a mental ray environment shader to a camera from under Render → Render → Pass Options property. You can also access the pass options in the Render Manager window → Current Pass tab → Pass Output tab → Pass Shaders tab. From the Environment shader list, select Add to add an environment shader to the list, typically selecting the Environment shader shown in Figure 13.23 and discussed in Chapter 3. You can specify an image file or texture as an environment. If you use a texture, you could use a texture that has one color value to provide constant shading, such as white.

- You can also use a geometric sphere, such as a NURBS sphere, with a constant color or spherical projection applied to a constant material shader. Because it's a constant shader, it renders without any influence from lighting. However, it is not the most practical technique as you force mental ray to deal with additional geometry in the scene, which is not the case with the other techniques cited earlier.

The techniques for applying environment shaders for reflections were discussed in Chapter 3, "mental ray Output," in the "mental ray Cameras" section. Consider the following points when using environment images and FG with respect to the environment shader's properties shown in Figure 13.23 (supports HDR images).

- The Environment Mode property is used to select a specific type of panoramic environment image. You will most commonly use spherical images. The types of images are further discussed in the section "Advanced Final Gather Techniques" later in this chapter.

- Consider that the environment image is always placed outside the scene, encompassing the entire scene. You can rotate it so that it aligns with the scene in a particular way; for example, the sun shown in the image needs to be placed facing west. Using the Transformation properties → R (rotations) property X, Y and Z (axes) inputs, you can specify the degree of rotation on each axis. It's straightforward; a value of 180 for the R property Y axis will turn the image 180°. The S and T (scale and translate) properties also work, but they are mostly irrelevant because the image always encompasses the scene.

- When an image is loaded, you will need to see the image when you position a light source that aligns with the light source in the image, further discussed in the section "Advanced Final Gather Techniques." Use a Render Region view to control the position of the light source while you rotate the environment image without FG enabled (just as a background image).

- The Image property defines whether the environment affects FG in the scene. The specified value is multiplied against the environment image or texture so that if set to 0, the environment does not affect FG. Use this property to increase or decrease the intensity of an image. Note that you can use values that exceed the 0 to 1 range so that FG samples brighter color values for the FG effect. For example, you may specify a value of 2. See the next section, "HDR Image Exposure."

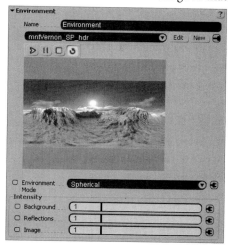

Figure 13.23

The Environment shader in XSI allows you to load any type of image or texture for background color and FG lighting.

- The Background property, if left at a value of 1, renders the background visible in the image. Thus, with FG, you may want to set it to 0 so that you don't see the environment image render as a background. You may prefer to use compositing to add the environment with more control over the foreground (the rendered image) and background images.

- You may also want to disable the Reflections property by setting it to 0 so that the environment affects only FG lighting and does not appear to reflect from surfaces in the scene. Typically, if it affects the lighting, you would expect to see the environment reflecting on glossy to specular surfaces.

HDR IMAGE EXPOSURE

When you use an HDR image as an environment image, you need to set the current exposure for rendering. The exposure defines the effect the HDR image has on the scene irradiance. In the Environment shader properties shown in Figure 13.23, first click the Inspect property and load an HDR image using the New property. Then click the Edit property button. Navigate to the Adjust tab in the Clip property window that opens, shown in Figure 13.24. In the HDR and OpenEXR section, the Exposure property allows you to set the current f-stop value used for FG rendering. Higher values provide brighter irradiance across surfaces in the scene, and lower values decrease the irradiance. You can use negative values, since a value of 0 refers to the default exposure of the HDR

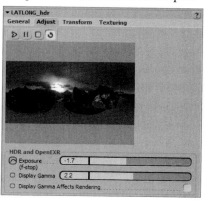

Figure 13.24

Editing the exposure of an HDR image in XSI

image. You should prefer using this Exposure property to control an HDR image's exposure over the Image property discussed
earlier and shown in Figure 13.23.

> The techniques discussed in "Advanced Final Gather Techniques" are based on using the Environment shader with HDR images.

3ds Max

With 3ds Max there are a few limitations to FG that I hope will be resolved in future releases. By default FG is set to the automatic mode, and in addition you can specify the 3.4 mode.

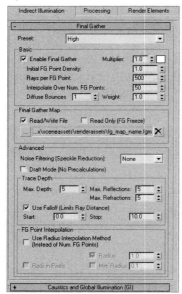

Figure 13.25

The mental ray Final Gather parameters in the Render Scene: mental ray Renderer window

You don't have any parameters for enabling the multiframe or strict 3.4 modes. If you use the stand-alone mental ray renderer, you can edit the "finagather mode" option in the .mi file, enabling any mode. Also, with FG maps, 3ds Max doesn't provide the finalgather rebuild off option. As a workaround for that limitation, use the workflow for generating custom FG maps with the fg_copy utility as discussed in the "FG Maps and the fg_copy Utility" section. Also, the finalgather only option for rendering solely FG maps is not available. (It would be pointless without the finalgather rebuild off option.)

You can find the FG parameters in the Render Scene: mental ray Renderer window under the Indirect Illumination tab → Final Gather rollout, shown in Figure 13.25. This is also where you find most of the FG settings discussed in the previous sections.

Let's quickly review each attribute, referring to its corresponding mental ray option or its functionality:

The Enable Final Gather parameter check box enables FG.

The Initial FG Point Density parameter refers to the precomputed FG density as with the mental ray finalgather presample density option.

The Rays per FG Point parameter defines the number of FG rays cast from an FG point as with the finalgather accuracy option *n* rays parameter.

The Interpolate Over Num. FG Points parameter specifies the number of FG points for interpolation, as with the mental ray "finalgather point" option.

The Multiplier and Color chooser parameters (at the top) control the irradiance intensity as with the `finalgather scale` option for FG primary rays. The Weight parameter (across from the Diffuse Bounces parameter) is used for all secondary FG rays as with the `finalgather secondary scale` option.

The Diffuse Bounces parameter controls the maximum number of secondary rays, where a value of 0 provides for one level of FG diffuse bounces (casting primary FG rays) and a value of 1 or higher provides for secondary FG rays, as with the `finalgather trace depth` option diffuse parameter.

The Read/Write File parameter check box enables the `finalgather rebuild` option for generating FG maps. When enabled, it is set to On, and when Read Only (FG Freeze) is enabled, it sets it to the FG freeze mode. Unfortunately, you don't have an Off option as cited earlier. You can specify the FG map filename below in the text box field. Do not specify an extension for the file; just type the name in the browser window that opens.

The Noise Filtering parameter drop-down list corresponds to the `finalgather filter` option for speckle elimination, typically when using HDR images. By default it's set to Standard, which is a filter value of 1. None is equal to 0, which has no influence on rendering. High equals 2, Very High equals 3, and Extremely High equals 4. We further discuss filtering with FG and HDR images later in this chapter.

When the Draft Mode (No Precomputation) parameter check box is enabled, FG skips precomputation and renders only with render-time FG points. By doing so it allows you to see a fast draft for the FG result without talking the time to precompute the FG points. Since the automatic and multiframe modes don't support render-time FG points, this parameter is applicable only when the 3.4 mode is enabled.

If you leave the Draft Mode (No Precomputation) parameter enabled with automatic mode, you won't see any FG render since it skips precomputation.

Under the Trace Depth section, the Max. Reflection, Refraction, and Depth parameters are straightforward and correspond to the `finalgather trace depth` option reflection, refraction, and total combined parameters. The Diffuse Bounces parameter corresponds to the diffuse parameter of the `finalgather trace depth` option, as cited earlier. Typically you should not increase it to a value greater than 1, which provides one level of secondary FG ray diffuse bounces.

The Use Falloff (Limit Ray Distance) parameter enables the Start and Stop parameters that limit the distance FG rays can travel in the scene in world space units, as discussed with the mental ray `finalgather falloff` option start and stop parameters.

The Use Radius Interpolation Method parameter check box enables the 3.4 mode (not strict 3.4) instead of the automatic mode. When enabled, use the following parameters to control the `finalgather` accuracy parameters:

- The Radius parameter corresponds to the max radius parameter.
- The Min Radius parameter corresponds to the min radius parameter.
- The Radii in Pixels parameter check box corresponds to the view parameter where radius values are specified in pixel sizes when enabled. Note that in 3ds Max you can use it only with the 3.4 mode.

Under the Caustics and Global Illumination (GI) rollout, the Optimize for Final Gather (Slower GI) parameter check box corresponds to the `finalgather` option using the fastlookup parameter. When enabled, GI photons also store irradiance to assist FG in sampling the influence from photons as discussed earlier.

APPLYING ENVIRONMENTS FOR FG

With 3ds Max there is only one method for applying backgrounds for FG, whether using a constant color, procedural texture, or image file. Unfortunately, the Environment Map and Color parameters found in the Environment and Effects window do not affect FG, even though they should. In future versions of 3ds Max this problem may be corrected, so you should test it with the current 3ds Max version you use.

You can apply an environment for FG by creating a geometric sphere, such as a NURBS sphere, that encompasses the scene. You then need to apply a constant color or texture using a spherical projection. A constant shader renders as is, without any influence from lighting. Since you don't have a constant shader in the shader library, there are two easy workarounds for applying a color or image to the surface as a constant color, as follows:

Option 1 In the Material Editor using a 3ds Max standard material, set the Ambient and Diffuse color parameters to white (or the color you prefer for the background), and set the Self-Illumination parameter to 100. If the Ambient and Diffuse parameters are locked together, that's fine; they both need to have the same value.

As an alternative to using a color value with the Ambient and Diffuse parameters, you can map the Diffuse parameter with a bitmap shader. It should be locked with the Ambient parameter so that the image is applied to both parameters.

In the bitmap's Coordinates rollout, the Environ radio button parameter should be enabled, and the Mapping parameter should be set to Spherical Environment. Texture projections with 3ds Max are discussed in Chapter 3, "mental ray Output," and Chapter 11, "mental ray Textures and Projections."

In this way you force the object to self-illuminate using a constant color, texture map, or image file; however, it will also be affected by source lights in the scene. Option 2 solves for that discrepancy.

> The background color can be set to any intensity from 0 to 100 using the Self-Illumination parameter.

Option 2 In the Material Editor window, create a mental ray material by selecting a mental ray material shader from the Material/Map Browser window.

Figure 13.26

Direct mapping of the Surface parameter (the illumination shader input) with a bitmap, providing constant shading for the background color

Under the Basic Shaders parameters, map the Surface parameter with a bitmap shader from the Material/Map Browser, as shown mapped in Figure 13.26, mapped with an HDR image file. Apply the same projection coordinates as cited for option 1.

In this way the mental ray material acts as a constant shader, outputting the mapped texture or bitmap file color as is, unaffected by scene lights. Thus, it provides a constant color for the background that is used for illumination with FG.

With both options, you don't have to use a bitmap shader; alternatively, you can use any procedural texture, but it is more common to use images with FG rendering. In addition, the bitmap shader supports HDR images, shown mapped in Figure 13.26. Therefore, you can use this approach for loading HDR images or standard images.

HDR IMAGE EXPOSURE

When you select to load an HDR image to a bitmap shader in the Select Bitmap Image File window's browser, an HDRI Load Settings window appears, shown in Figure 13.27. Under the Internal Storage section when using HDR images, the Real Pixels (32bpp) parameter radio button should be enabled. If the Def. Exposure is enabled, then the exposure will be set automatically; otherwise (when it's disabled), under the Exposure section, the Log and Linear parameters allow you to set the black and white point for the image using either one. Notice that if you change the linear

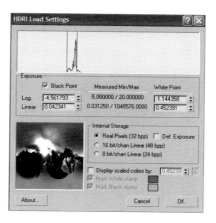

Figure 13.27

When loading HDR images, the HDRI Load Settings window allows you to specify the exposure.

values, the log values update simultaneously. Doing so sets the exposure of the HDR image used with FG. For example, the White Point value shown in Figure 13.27 (the right vertical line in the graph) is set below the maximum white point value charted for the image in this Exposure histogram, which increases the exposure value used for FG.

> You can set the Log or Linear parameters to encompass both ends of the histogram and then increase the exposure using the RGB Level parameter under the bitmap's Output rollout. Higher values (greater than 1) increase the exposure used for the FG rendering.

Advanced Final Gather Techniques

In this section, I'll extend the discussion of using environment image files, particularly HDR images, and of generating 3D-based HDR environments using the architectural library's sun and sky shaders.

The topic of HDR imaging was covered in detail in Chapter 9, "The Fundamentals of Light and Shading Models"; see the "High Dynamic Range (HDR) Concepts" section there. In fact, Chapter 9 covered all the light concepts you need for understanding HDR lighting with FG, particularly HDR images and photometric light measurements (luminance/lux); that discussion is an essential preparation for using FG with HDR lighting and images.

HDR environments with FG serve the purpose of rendering using realistic photometric light measurements. Of course, if you render with realistic light measurements, you will be using light and reflection values that exceed the 0 to 1 range, and therefore, the output image, a low dynamic range (LDR) image file, is prone to overexposure. As a means of dealing with overexposure, you need to use tone mapping techniques to calibrate the image so it provides a lot of detail within a low dynamic range. The approach for dealing with high dynamic range differs between the sun and sky shades and when using an HDR image. Mostly, the HDR image exposure is set while rendering, as discussed per host earlier, and if it appears too bright, additional measurements are taken to reduce the dynamic range exposure. However, with the sun and sky shaders, you generate a high dynamic range environment in 3D and then tone map the rendered image; your output image acts as an HDR image that need to be remapped to a low dynamic range. These different approaches are presented in detail in the following sections with respect to using HDR images for environments and when using the physical sun and sky shaders.

Physical Sun and Sky Lighting

This section covers most of the physical sun and sky shader options in detail with an overview of using them in each host application. In the mental ray help files you can find additional explanations and rendered examples.

The purpose of three shaders is to provide a realistic environment for HDR lighting in 3D using an environment shader (the mia physical sky shader) and a light shader (the mia physical sun shader). As with real cameras, you can capture only a given exposure at a time, so you need to calibrate the exposure of the camera for maximizing the detail in the image. Since 3D cameras don't have a real camera exposure setting for light, you can use some of the shader options to calibrate the exposure. Also, as discussed in Chapter 9, "The Fundamentals of Light and Shading Models," tone mapping techniques allow you to maximize detail without overexposure. For that purpose, a camera tone mapping lens shader is provided; it is the mia exposure simple shader, giving you additional control over the exposure using tone mapping.

The upgraded architectural library available in Maya 2008 (also expected to appear in XSI and 3ds Max) includes an improved exposure lens shader called mia exposure photographic shader as well as an improved depth of field lens shader called the mia lens bokeh shader. The exposure shader is an alternative to the mia exposure simple shader and provides additional control over camera f-stop exposure as well as better tools for simulating real camera characteristics. When coupled with the mia lens bokeh lens shader for depth of field effects you can produce more realistic camera effects with mental ray.

> The physical sun shader provides real-world conditions that should be used with physical shaders, such as the architectural material that ships with the same shader library.

In Figure 13.28 you can see a shader graph that illustrates the connections between these shaders in Maya, which is applied in a similar fashion in each host application. I'll review each of these connections in the following sections, as well as on a per-host basis.

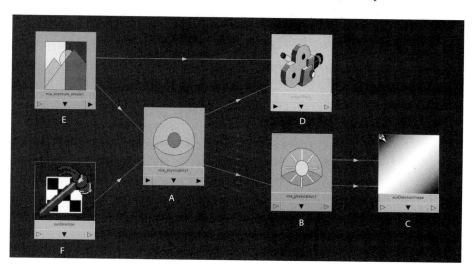

Figure 13.28

Physical sun, sky, and simple exposure shader connections

The Physical Sun Shader

The physical sun shader (B) connects as a light shader to an infinite (directional) light source (C) in the scene (see Chapter 6, "Lights and Soft Shadows," for light shaders). It generates a source light that defines the characteristics of sun lighting based on the sun's directionality, which is the angle of the sun relative to the horizon, as shown in Figure 13.29, where the infinite light source is rotated to a different angle for each image. You can tell by the directionality of the shadows from one image to the next as I increase the angle between the horizon and the light source (the sun). You can see the influence of these shaders on light intensity and colors in the Chapter 13 folder on the CD with the image "Sun and Sky Lighting."

As you can see, in the color image, the purpose of the physical sun and sky shaders is to provide realistic light simulations based on the sun's angle relative to the horizon, simulating the time of day automatically based on the sun's direction.

Figure 13.29

The angle of the sun relative to the horizon affects the intensity of light.

If you look at the physical sun declaration in a .mi file, you will see all of the physical sun's options and connections, as shown in the following excerpt:

```
## Light Shader Decleration
shader "mia_physicalsun1"
        "mia_physicalsun" (
                "on" on,
                "multiplier" 0.5,
                "rgb_unit_conversion" 0.0001 0.0001 0.0001 1.,
                "haze" 0.,
                "redblueshift" 0.,
                "saturation" 1.,
                "horizon_height" 0.,
                "shadow_softness" 1.,
                "samples" 8,
                "photon_bbox_min" 0. 0. 0.,
                "photon_bbox_max" 0. 0. 0.,
                "automatic_photon_energy" off,
                "y_is_up" on
                        )

## Light Decleration
light "sunDirectionShape"
        = "mia_physicalsun1"
        emitter = "mia_physicalsun1"
        direction 0. 0. -1.
        end light
```

The physical sun shader is declared under the "Light Shader Declaration" label, with all the options for controlling the light's influence in the scene. Notice that a mental ray directional light is then declared under the label "Light Declaration" using the physical sun shader as a light shader, shown in this statement:

```
light "sunDirectionShape"
        = "mia_physicalsun1"
```

Also, the light shader has a photon declaration so that it can be used for GI, shown in the following declaration:

```
emitter = "mia_physicalsun1"
```

All these connections are handled automatically for you in host applications.

The sun shader, a mental ray light shader, is in fact calibrated to the sun's intensity, providing realistic photometric measurements based on lux (more on that shortly). The problem with that is distance and absorption; real-world sunlight decays before it reaches the earth. That is, a lot of the sun's energy is absorbed with atmospheric effects such as Rayleigh and Mie scattering, which are both topics discussed in Chapter 12, "Indirect Illumination," with the participating media shader.

Clearly, using the sun's real photometric intensity (illuminance) is too bright for the purpose of rendering. To deal with that, you have certain options that allow you to calibrate the illuminance units so that you can use the shader more efficiently. The most significant option is `rgb_unit_conversion`, which is a multiplier against the sun's illuminance intensity. In a way, this option is your exposure control. When set to 1, it's calibrated to real-world sun light intensities outside the earth's atmosphere, a value that produces too much light in the 3D scene, causing significant overexposure. Typical values are in the range of 0.001 and 0.0001, as shown in the earlier excerpt. By using these values, you have more control with the tone mapping (mia_exposure_simple) shader over the final result (see the "The MIA Exposure Simple Shader" section). In other words, the unit conversion option scales the scene down with respect to light intensities while providing a high dynamic range environment using suitable values.

A value of 0 acts as a preset that sets the sun light intensity value (applied automatically) to represent a bright sunny day using 8000 lux (a measure of illuminance in photometry, see Chapter 9, "The Fundamentals of Light and Shading Models" for photometry). Table 13.1 shows common measurements of lux.

I use the terms *illuminance* and *luminance* often with respect to FG and HDR lighting. Illuminance is the photometric term that refers to the intensity of light over a given area on the surface, as with the radiometric term, irradiance. Luminance is the photometric term that refers to the intensity of light projected from, or passing through, a given area and in a specific angle. See Chapter 9, "The Fundamentals of Light and Shading Models," for more on photometry and radiometry.

	LIGHT SOURCE	PHOTOMETRIC ILLUMINANCE VALUE
Table 13.1		
Common Illuminance Measurements	Average sunlight	32,000-10,000 lux
	Candle light	10 lux
	Interior lighting	50 to 400 lux
	Sunrise or sunset	400 lux
	Full moon	0.25 lux
	Starlight	0.0005 lux

The `shadow_softness` and `samples` options simulate soft shadows, such as with area lights. These options allow you to simulate softer shadows during sunrises and sunsets and sharper shadows during daytime. The `samples` option defines the quality of the shadow, similar to area light shadow samples, as discussed in Chapter 6, "Lights and Soft Shadows."

Aside from the shadow and photon options seen in the excerpt above, all the other sun options are automatically driven by the same options found under the sky shader, as discussed next.

The Physical Sky Shader

In Figure 13.28 you saw how the physical sky shader (A) connects to the camera (D) as a camera environment shader, providing the following three components:

- A background image of the sky and horizon.
- The background is used for raytracing reflections.
- The background is used for FG to provide indirect HDR lighting from the sky, 360° around the scene.

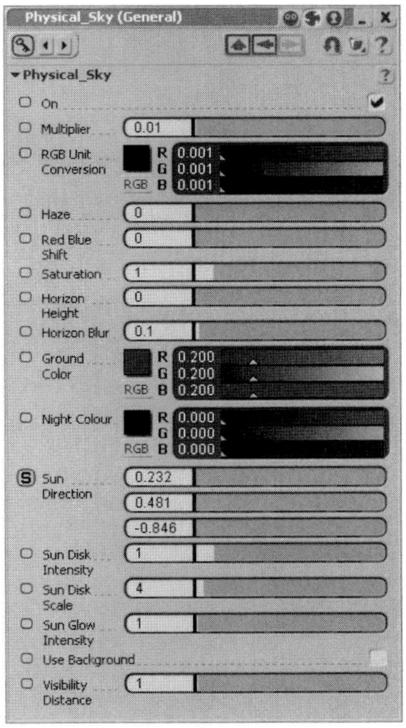

In addition, it can also connect to the camera as a volume or lens shader, a topic further discussed shortly. As cited earlier, the physical sky and sun shaders share several options such as the unit conversion option cited previously. You can see the XSI physical sky options in Figure 13.30.

The options found on both shaders have the same effect, only one applies it to the light source (the sun), and the other applies it to the environment (the sky). In host applications, the two shaders are incorporated in a way that the sky's options automatically drive the sun's options as shown in Figure 13.28 with the connections from A (sky shader) to B (sun shader); doing so assures that the sun and sky illuminance values are consistent.

For example, when you set unit conversion values, it assures that both the sun and sky shaders are calibrated to the same atmospheric conditions (intensity).

As you can see in Figure 13.30, the Sun Direction option in XSI is automatically driven by the infinite light's position in the scene. You can also see the sunDirection node (F) connects to the mia_physicalsky node (A) in the shader graph shown in Figure 13.28 in Maya. In this way, the environment shader knows where the sun is so that it can simulate the environment correctly. For non-Maya users, note that the node labeled F is a transform node that positions the light labeled C in the 3D scene; the two together define a Maya infinite light source and its location in the scene.

Figure 13.30

The physical sky shader properties shown in XSI

The purpose of the sun is to cast HDR direct lighting, and the purpose of the sky is to reflect HDR indirect light with FG. Thus, these shaders are intended for use with FG. The fact that they operate in a high dynamic range environment provides for richer lighting in 3D.

The sky shader has a few additional options shown in Figure 13.30 that deal solely with the environment and how it affects FG:

The Sun Disk Intensity option defines the intensity of the sun in the environment image. It doesn't affect FG, but it does affect the visual appearance of the sun in the rendered image. For example, if you use a lot of haze and you can't see the sun but want to, you can increase this value to try to restore some of the sun's appearance.

The Sun Disk Scale and Sun Glow Intensity options define the visual appearance of the sun, as well as its size. For example, the sun will become smaller at lower altitudes, so if you want a large sun in a sunset environment, you will need to increase the scale.

The Use Background option applies a background image for the environment, such as an HDR image, instead of the physical sky environment.

Suppose you want to export a panoramic HDR image of an environment using the physical sun and sky shaders. For that purpose, the Sun Disk Intensity option has influence on the sun's intensity in the exported HDR environment image. You can see an example of a spherical HDR image in the Color Gallery image labeled "Sun and Sky Lighting."

THE PHYSICAL SKY SHADER AS A VOLUME OR LENS SHADER

The physical sky shader can also be used as a volume or lens shader that provides more realistic *aerial perspective*. Thus, you can connect it to the camera's volume or lens shader inputs, as discussed with other shaders in Chapter 3, "mental ray Output." Note that the Sun Disk Intensity, Scale, and Glow options mentioned earlier solely deal with the appearance of the sun in the environment and have no influence when used as a volume/lens shader.

If you use the physical sky shader as a volume or lens shader, you should also apply it as an environment shader, as discussed earlier. That way, the sky will appear in the background, and the volume or lens shader will deal with aerial perspective in the scene.

AERIAL PERSPECTIVE AND HAZE

The most significant purpose for using this shader as a volume or lens shader is to better simulate haze over distance and by doing so better simulate aerial perspective. The term *aerial perspective* refers to the effect the atmosphere has on the scene. It is dependent on the distances between the camera and the surfaces in the scene. When surfaces in the scene appear farther away from the camera, they are more influenced by the atmosphere, blending with the atmosphere's color. In other words, the contrast between surfaces and the background decreases as a surface gets farther away from the camera.

The sky shader's Visibility Distance option shown in Figure 13.30 defines the decay of haze over distance in the scene, defining the aerial perspective. In Figure 13.31 image A was rendered using the physical sky shader solely as an environment shader without any haze; the Haze option shown in Figure 13.30 is set to 0. The only difference with image B is that the Haze option is set to 15. You can see how the visibility of the sun decreases in the background, and in black-and-white print you can also tell that there is some change in the tonality of the image; the background and physical sun colors adjust to better mimic haze. However, there is still a lot of contrast between the colors of the spheres in the scene and the background. For image C, the physical shader was also applied as a volume shader to the camera's volume shader input. As you can see, aerial perspective is now properly simulated; the contrast between the background and the spheres decreases over distance, fading out because of the high haze value. In image C, the haze affects the 3D scene as with volume effects.

Figure 13.31

Simulating aerial perspective using the physical sky shader as a volume shader

With haze, higher Haze values provide the visual effect of reducing the sun's intensity and provide appropriate coloration to the scene, based on the time of day.

When the sky is used as a lens shader, it provides better lighting and shadows than when used as a volume shader; try using it as both shaders to see these effects. Also note that when it's used as either type of shader, with the Haze option set to 0, it will still render aerial perspective effects based on the Visibility Distance value.

The MIA Exposure Simple Shader

The mia_exposure_simple lens shader (labeled Simple_Tone_Mapping in XSI) is used to apply tone mapping to the rendered image (tone mapping is discussed in Chapter 9, "The Fundamentals of Light and Shading Models"). Unlike tone-mapping techniques that are applied on a per-pixel basis, this shader is a lens shader and thus applied during sampling on a per-sample basis (see Chapter 3, "mental ray Output," for more information on per-pixel operations). In this way, the quality of the tone mapping process is better than postprocess tone mapping. Having said that, there are some good tone mapping tools in 2D applications, so you need to decide when you want to tone map an image based on production considerations. For example, if you want to process the image as HDR or 32-bit images in compositing, you may prefer to apply the tone mapping there, at the end of the composite tree.

The mia_exposure_simple shader connects to the camera's lens shader input as shown earlier in Figure 13.28 with the connection from E to D. It is also shown connected to the physical sky shader (A) exposure input; however, that's a "Maya" thing. The shader is designated as a lens shader, and that's how you should use it for any rendering purposes, regardless of the physical sky and sun. For example, you can use it with any GI simulation.

SHADER OPTIONS

Let's review the mia_simple_exposure shader options with some figures and the following points. You can see the shader options in Figure 13.32 in 3ds Max. These options are

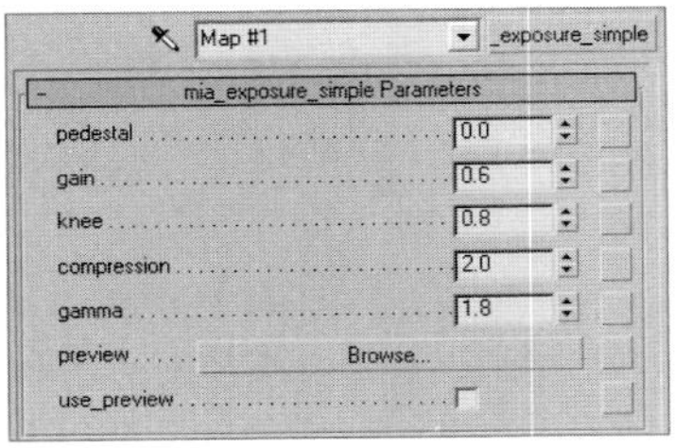

Figure 13.32

The mia_simple_ exposure lens shader options in 3ds Max

labeled in the same way in all host applications.

As discussed in Chapter 9, "The Fundamentals of Light and Shading Models," HDR images have a virtually unlimited range of color, exceeding the 0 to 1 range. To demonstrate the influence of this shader on tone mapping values, I'll show the range a waveform displays of rendered images in Fusion, which is a compositing package from Eyeon software. In Figure 13.33 image A, you can see an HDR render of an image using the sun and sky shaders, without any tone mapping. The values from the HDR render by far exceed the 0 to 1 range. For convenience, in image A the 0 to 1 range is marked with an arrow from 0 to 1, which is black to white. Those bounds are the same in all the following waveform figures.

We want to tone map this HDR image using the exposure simple shader in the host application so that the output values better fit into the 0 to 1 range indicated in the figure. That way, the images will show more detail from overexposed values.

Figure 13.33

A waveform displaying values of an HDR rendered image (A) and values after applying gamma correction with the mia exposure simple shader (B)

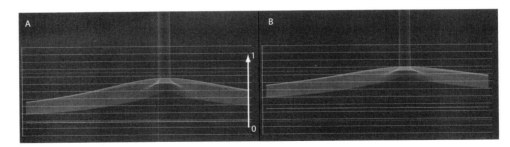

In Image B, you can see a gamma correction applied to the image by changing the Gamma option shown in Figure 13.32 to 1.8. As you can see, the gamma correction increases the brightness of the image by shifting values between the 0 to 1 range higher up (see Chapter 3, "mental ray Output," for more about gamma correction). However, gamma is intended for dealing solely with correcting values that are already between the 0 to 1 range, and thus it's the last operation applied by the tone mapping shader. In other words, after the image is tone mapped using the other options, gamma correction is then applied; the assumption is that the tone mapping operation distributes (compresses) values between the 0 to 1 range, and then gamma correction adjusts their appearance for monitor display.

> For illustrative purposes, all these images are rendered as HDR images and not LDR images so that you can see values that exceed the 0 to 1 range. Typically tone mapping is applied when the output format (rendered image) will be an LDR image.

The Pedestal option is used to offset the color of the sample. Positive values are added and negative values are subtracted. Thus, it's a simple add/subtract operation on color before all the other options take effect.

Let's discuss the effects of the Gain, Knee, and Compression options (shown in Figure 13.32) with Figure 13.34. In image A, the Gain value has been decreased to 0.5 from the value of 1 (no effect) used in the previous step (Figure 13.33 image B; gamma correction is already taking effect). As you can see by comparing Figure 13.34 image A to Figure 13.33 image B, the values have been pushed down because each sample is multiplied by a value of 0.5. Thus, the Gain option is used as a multiplier and can significantly decrease the range of values. However, it also has the effect of flatting the low color values as you decrease the value so that there is less contrast visible in the image (in dark areas). If an image appears too bright, you should start by testing gain values such as 0.5 to 0.2.

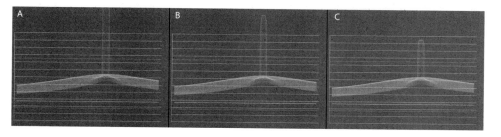

Figure 13.34

Effects of the Gain option (A) and the Knee and Compression options (B and C)

After the Gain option takes effect, the Knee and Compression options further compress values greater than a certain range. The Knee option defines that range; it defines a starting value where any value greater than that is compressed based on the Compression option. In Figure 13.34 image B, the Knee option is set to 0.7 and Compression is set to 10. As you can see, the illuminance values are significantly reduced, and you can finally see the peak of the highest values. However, it is still greater than a value of 1; all the values greater than 1 appear overexposed. To force it into the 0 to 1 range, the Compression value is increased to a value of 30 in image C. As you can see, the peak is now just over the line that indicates a value of 1. Thus, the image has been tone mapped so that all its values are within the 0 to 1 range and gamma correction has been applied.

You don't necessarily want to force all the values into the 0 to 1 range; doing so will flatten the image, losing significant contrast. For example, the sun in this case was set very high so that it may be better to have left this image as shown in image B, without any additional compression; values that are within the sun's area can be overexposed.

> This example is not a common practice in that you don't see a waveform while tweaking these values. It is intended only to visually illustrate the effects of the shader options. Your decisions with respect to choosing values should be determined visually, based on the output.

The additional Preview option allows you to use a rendered HDR image of the scene, mapped to the Preview option so that you can see the effects of tone mapping immediately. In such a case the shader is used to test values without rendering the scene. Every time you render, the preview image will be used until you disable the preview option and render your final pass. It helps speed up the decision-making process when dealing with render-intensive scenes.

Host Applications

This section covers creating the physical sun, sky, and exposure shaders in host applications. For more information on shader options, refer to the help files.

MAYA

In the Render Settings window under the mental ray tab → Environment rollout, click the Physical Sun and Sky Create button. All the required shaders are automatically generated and connected as shown earlier in Figure 13.28. The mia_exposure_simple is automatically connected as a lens shader, and FG is automatically enabled. You may prefer to disable FG while placing the sun and defining the direct light intensity. You can also find all these shaders in the Hypershade window under the Create mental ray Nodes rollouts.

You can graph the camera in the Hypershade window and then connect the physical sky shader as a volume or lens shader by dragging the physical shader over the camera and applying the connections with the Connection Editor window. Alternatively, you can drag and drop the physical sky shader directly onto the Camera shape's Lens or Volume Shader attributes under the mental ray rollout in the Attribute Editor window. If you want to attach the physical sky as a lens shader, assuming the mia_exposure_simple lens shader already occupies the Lens Shader attribute in the Attribute Editor, you can use the Connection Editor as follows to append another lens shader:

1. Load the physical sky shader under Outputs and the camera shape node under Inputs. Note that it must be the camera shape, not the transform node (for example, perspShape).

2. From the Output list select the physical sky's Message attribute (the first one listed).

3. Under Inputs, scroll to the last input, and expand the Mental Ray Connections rollout. Select the MI Lens Shader List.

In this way, you add a lens shader. You can see the result in the Attribute Editor window under the camera shape attributes → mental ray rollout → Lens Shaders, as shown in Figure 13.35. In the figure you can also see that the physical sky shader is connected as an environment shader.

Figure 13.35

Appending lens shaders to a camera with Maya

XSI

In XSI you can manually create the physical sun and sky shaders in the Render Tree window under Nodes → Environment and Light menus. Alternately, an easier method is by selecting the Initialize Sky Shader option under the Render menu → Edit menu. The window shown in Figure 13.36 opens, allowing you to automate the process of creating all the shader connections. After you click the Apply button, an infinite light is created in the scene applied with the physical sun shader.

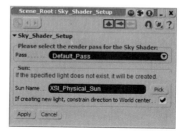

Figure 13.36

The Sky_Shader_ Setup window allows you to automatically generate the physical sky and sun shaders with all the connections in XSI.

You can find all the shared options discussed earlier in the physical sky shader, which has automatically been added to the current pass Environment shader list. You can find the list in the Render menu; choose Edit → Edit Current Pass. Look on the Pass Shaders tab in the Passes property window. You can select the Physical_Sky shader in the list, and click the Inspect property button to modify the physical sky properties shown earlier in Figure 13.30.

To add the Simple_Tone_Mapping shader (mia_exposure_simple) to a camera, select the camera, and under its properties navigate to the camera's Lens Shaders tab. Click the Add button, and locate the Simple_Tone_Mapping shader in the browser window under Lens Shaders. It's typically located in the installation path, for example, in `C:\Softimage\ XSI_6.0\Data\DSPresets\Shaders\Lens`. You can also apply the same connection after loading the camera into a Render Tree window and importing the tone mapping shader.

Figure 13.37

The mental ray sun and sky parameters in 3ds Max

You can set the sun's location using the infinite light, tweaking the direct lighting properties. Once you are satisfied with the direct lighting, enable FG for rendering indirect lighting cast from the physical sky shader. The section "FG in Host Applications" that focused on ambient light is also relevant in this case; you don't want any additional ambience influence in the scene. Furthermore, in this case, the default light can be deleted, because the physical sun generated its own infinite light source.

3DS MAX

In 3ds Max you can create the physical sun and sky shaders manually by selecting them from the Create panel → Lights → Photometric Lights → mr Sky and mr Sun. When you do that, you need to draw both in the scene with the same placement, because they are not tied together. Alternatively, a better and more convenient approach is to create a daylight system using the mental ray physical sun and sky. I cover only the latter in this section. The following steps present the workflow and considerations for using these shaders in 3ds Max:

1. From the Create → Systems → submenu, select the Daylight System.

2. A Daylight Object Creation window asks whether you want to use Logarithmic Exposure control. Select No so that you can first see the default results of rendering, and then manually enable Logarithmic Exposure control in the Environment and Effects window under the Exposure Control rollout.

3. Click in the top view to draw the compass rose in the scene that defines the global coordinates (north, east, and so on). The first click creates the compass, and the second click (holding down the left mouse button) allows you to place the physical sun and sky lights in the scene defining their distance from the scene objects only. Their direction is defined based on the specified time of day.

4. After the first click, a mental ray Sky window opens, asking whether you want to add a mental ray Physical Sky environment map; select Yes.

5. On the right under the Create panel → Systems tab (opens automatically), you have a few options under the Control Parameters rollout for setting the time of day. You can always set that later.

6. After creating the daylight system, you can now modify the parameters shown in Figure 13.37 in the Modify panel.

With respect to these parameters, note the following:

- Under the Daylight Parameters rollout shown in the figure, the Sunlight and Skylight parameters should be set to mr Sun and Sky, respectively.

- In the same rollout under Position, you can choose the Manual parameter to manually place the sun in the scene. If the Date, Time, and Location parameter is enabled, you can click the Setup parameter to change the location and time. It switches from the Modify panel to Motion panel → Parameters.

- In the Modify panel under the mr Sun Basic Parameters, you have the parameters discussed earlier for specifying soft shadows.

- Notice that under mr Sun Parameters, the Inherit from mr Sky parameter is enabled so that shared options are controlled only by the mr Sky Parameters roll-out, also shown in the figure.

- You can also find all the parameters for indirect illumination. The only new parameter is under the mr Sun Photons rollout. When the Use Photon Target parameter is enabled, you can set the radius for casting photons into the scene by increasing the Radius parameter. Notice how it gives you a visual representation in the scene as you increase the value. It is used to optimize the distribution of photons so that they are not wasted in empty space.

Now that everything is set you can enable FG in the Render Scene: mental ray Renderer window on the Indirect Illumination tab to see the effect of indirect light from the atmosphere in the scene. There are a few additional points to consider with respect to FG and the daylight system setup in general. 3ds Max divides the physical sky shader into two components: the mr sky light (created with the daylight system or manually, as cited earlier) and the mr physical sky environment shader. From the previous discussion of FG in 3ds Max, you already know that the environment maps don't affect FG. Therefore, for the purpose of FG, the mr sky (created with the daylight system) is used for FG indirect atmospheric lighting, and the mr physical sky shader appended as an environment map is used only for background color. If you selected to create the mr physical sky in the mental ray Sky window, you can see that the shader has been added in the Environment and Effects window. If you open the Material Editor window and drag and drop the mr Physical Sky shader Environment Map onto an empty slot in the Material Editor, you can edit its parameters (select to Instance the map from the prompt). You will notice that in the mr Physical Sky Parameters rollout, the Inherit from Sky option is enabled so that it derives those values from the daylight system's mr sky that you created in the scene (shown in Figure 13.37). The additional parameters that are used solely for defining the sun's appearance in the background are also present. The Distance parameter for aerial perspective, found at the bottom of the map parameters, is applied only when the shader is also a volume or lens shader.

If you want to use the mr Physical Sky map as a volume shader, open the Render Scene: mental ray Renderer window, and drag and drop (select instance) the map from the Material Editor slot to the Renderer tab → Camera Effects → Volume parameter, as shown in Figure 13.38.

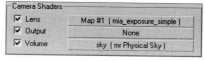

Figure 13.38

Mapping the camera with the physical sky as a volume shader and the exposure simple as a lens shader

With respect to the mia_exposure_simple lens shader (tone mapping), if you enabled the Logarithmic Exposure control in the Environment and Effects window → Exposure Control rollout, you may not need to add tone mapping to the render. If you want to use the tone mapping shader, particularly when the exposure control is disabled, under the Render Scene: mental ray Renderer window Renderer tab → Camera Effects, select the mapping option for the Lens parameter to add the exposure shader, as shown mapped in Figure 13.38. From the Material/map Browser window, select the mia_exposure_simple shader. You can then drag and drop the shader from the Lens parameter to an empty slot in the Material Editor (select Instance when prompted) to edit its parameters.

If you want to use the mr Physical Sky map as a lens shader in addition to the mia_exposure_ simple shader, use the Shader List (Lens) shader discussed in Chapter 3, "mental ray Output," to stack both shaders.

Environmental Images and HDR

You already know how to use FG and apply environment images with your host application. In the following sections, I'll cover the differences between using LDR (low dynamic range images, which are standard image files) and using HDR images. Applying them as a projection is the same in each case; both are image formats. I'll also cover the different types of panoramic environmental images, which may be LDR or HDR images. You will also learn about tools for creating and editing panoramic HDR images.

LDR vs. HDR Lighting

The purpose of FG is to sample the luminance values from the environment and apply them to surfaces in the scene. As discussed in Chapter 9, "The Fundamentals of Light and Shading Models," HDR images contain within them realistic photometric measurements of light. These light values provide FG with a realistic source for illumination in the scene. Most important, it provides FG with a lot of contrast between the brightest and darkest sampled colors in the environment, which is a topic discussed in detail in Chapter 9. Since LDR images contain only a range of luminance from 0 to 1, they don't provide a high dynamic range for FG, as well as don't provide for a lot of contrast. As the purpose of indirect light simulations is to mimic realism, when using LDR images you don't use realistic light measurements and thus don't mimic realism. With HDR images, the luminance values stored in the image enable FG to work outside a 0 to 1 range, providing for much richer shading, more contrast, and more realistic lighting, as you will see in this section.

In the color gallery, the image labeled "LDR versus HDR" shows two images that have been rendered with the same environmental image using solely FG (no source lights are used). In image A an LDR (TIF) image is used, and in image B the HDR version of the same image is used. The surfaces in the scene are shaded as follows:

- The leftmost apple is a fully specular surface that is not affected by FG. As discussed earlier in the chapter, FG doesn't affect fully specular surfaces.

- The apple in the middle is set with the architectural material as a glossy surface with FG emulated reflections.

- The rightmost apple is a purely diffuse surface.

- The floor is a semiglossy surface.

You can clearly see the differences in contrast between image A and B. In image B, notice how the diffuse apple on the right appears somewhat overexposed from the bright intensity in the image, projected from one of the windows from within the HDR image. Also notice how rich the reflections are on both the specular apple and the floor. Finally, you can see some gradation in the emulated reflection on the middle apple. In contrast, in image A the lighting and reflections appear flat and without detail. For example, by looking at the image, you can't tell that the light from the right side (hitting the diffused apple) has a higher intensity than that found in other areas of the scene. Thus, using an LDR environment image to render image A provided for poor reflections and reduced contrast.

HDR lighting with FG provides for brighter light, as shown in image B, because the sources of illumination have a high dynamic range providing for a lot of variation in luminance value, outside the typical LDR range of 0 to 1. The variation in luminance means that FG can accurately simulate the intensities of different light sources in the scene based on the HDR values stored in the image. Unlike GI, which only deals with indirect lighting, FG has the effect of also simulating direct light influence sampled from actual light sources (sun, light fixtures, and so on) in the HDR image. However, as discussed earlier with FG and specular reflections, there are a few reasons for using FG as well as a light source in the scene:

- To generate specular highlights.

- To cast clear shadows; FG usually only "hints" at the shadows by occluding light from reaching the umbra region, which in most cases is not enough shadow.

- To cast volume light (participating media) projected through an HDR image. This technique has the effect of creating high-quality volume light effects.

With respect to source lights and HDR environment maps, you will need to position the light source so that it aligns with the brightest light source in the image for consistency. For example, try placing a directional light where the sun appears in an HDR image so that you cast shadows and have specular highlights from the right angle in the scene.

HDR SPECKLE ELIMINATION

There are a few points to consider with FG and HDR images that deal with the current exposure of an HDR image and the contrast between the brightest and darkest areas. In Figure 13.39, you can see three images rendered with the same HDR environment image. Image A used an accuracy setting of one ray per FG point, and the point interpolation was set to 1. Thus, you see the scatter of individual irradiance values in the scene with the dots. You can use these techniques to get an idea for the spread of the irradiance across surfaces in the scene. Some areas stand out in particular where the white dots appear particularly bright, especially the square "dots" that appear below the diffused sphere. You can also see that the chrome sphere is not affected by FG and reflects only the scene. For image B, the accuracy rays were increased to 200, and the point interpolation was set at 50. As you can see, the dots blend together to form widespread overexposed artifacts in the image. Simply put, there are several white circles that have extremely high luminance values and provide overexposure.

Figure 13.39

Examining speckle artifacts with HDR images that are caused by extremely bright luminance sources

When FG was designed, its purpose was to improve GI rendering as an additional tool for acquiring indirect light influence. As cited earlier, with HDR images and FG, source lights in an HDR image, such as the sun, actually make FG provide both direct and indirect light influence, because it samples the source light's projected radiance. When the sun in particular appears in an HDR image, the luminance value at the sun's location is significantly higher than in the rest of the image. The result is that only a given number of FG rays actually hit that target, which may be only a few pixels wide. Those values are then interpolated with neighboring sampled FG points, whereas other points never "see" the sun and are interpolated based on the atmosphere only, which is the indirect light reflected from the atmosphere. The result is what you see in all three images in Figure 13.39, where a sudden change in illuminance across the surface provides for extreme variation in intensity.

To resolve these artifacts, you might try decreasing the intensity of the HDR image using a color multiplier, as discussed earlier per host in the section "FG in Host Applications." Doing so multiplies all the values of the HDR image by a given value, such as 0.5, a technique that is occasionally used to "change/reduce the exposure." However, typically it will not suffice for removing speckle artifacts, as shown in image C. For image C, the HDR image is multiplied by a value of 0.1, and as you can see, the entire image appears darker, but the speckle artifacts (bright dots) still appear. Thus, even the value of 0.1 was not enough to reduce their luminance enough to provide a good result. Furthermore, by using this method, you lose a lot of detail in the HDR image, because all the areas considered as indirect light (from the atmosphere) now possess significantly lower values, probably within a low dynamic range. Clearly, by doing so, you flatten the image and lose the primary advantage of using an HDR image, which is contrast and detail.

THE SOLUTIONS

There are three practical solutions for dealing with speckle artifacts:

- Using the `finalgather filter` option discussed earlier.
- Creating a convolved HDR image in HDR Shop or another tool. This method blurs the image and interpolates the sun's values over a larger area, as well as decreases its overall intensity.
- Cutting a hole in the image by drawing a black spot over the brightest spot in the HDR image. You can do so with HDR Shop. See the HDR Shop tutorials online at HDRShop.com.

The first option is the most practical option and is similar to the second one listed. Filtering reduces the luminance values in the HDR image and assists in removing speckles. Typical values range from 1 to 4. Remember, it also makes the scene look darker because it reduces luminance, so you want to use the lowest value possible. In Figure 13.40 you see the same image used in Figure 13.39 after applying a filter value of 1. As you can see, all the speckle artifacts have disappeared—simple and fast.

Figure 13.40

Using the FG filter option allows you to remove speckle artifacts from the rendered image.

GLOSSY REFLECTIONS, FG, AND HDR IMAGES (RAY TYPES)

An additional consideration refers to glossy reflections regardless of FG. HDR images also affect the reflection providing for richer reflections, as discussed earlier. However, luminance values that create speckle artifacts with FG will typically also cause glossy reflection speckle artifacts, as shown in Figure 13.41. (This does not happen with pure specular reflections.) The problem is that the FG filtering option applies its influence only with respect to FG and does not reduce glossy reflection speckles. To remove the speckles, you can decrease the amount of glossy reflection until they disappeared—not the most desirable solution if you want a specific glossy characteristic. The alternatives are to apply a correction to the HDR image as mentioned earlier with blurred (convolved) HDR images or by cutting a hole in the image. In addition, you can render the reflections as a separate reflection pass using an LDR image, or vice versa, you can render the FG as a separate lighting pass.

Figure 13.41

Glossy reflection speckle artifacts caused by high luminance values in an HDR image

A more advanced approach is to designate specific environment images for specific ray types. This means you define one environment image that is used for FG and another for glossy reflections (or refractions). In this way, when glossy artifacts appear, you can use a lower dynamic range image for the reflections but still use an HDR image for FG. In Figure 13.42, you can see such a shader tree in XSI's Render Tree window. The Ray Type shader labeled C (available in the Nodes → Switch menu) is used to break up the environment shaders used for a given XSI pass. (XSI users can graph the pass network after selecting it in the Explorer window.) In other words, it utilizes two different environment images, labeled A and E, that are used with the environment shaders labeled B and F. These shaders represent mental ray camera environment shaders, as discussed in Chapter 3, "mental ray Output." However, in XSI they are applied per pass.

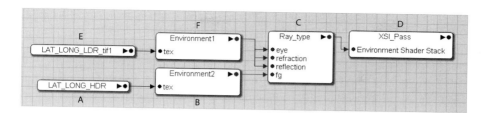

Figure 13.42

An XSI shader tree that shows how different environment images can be used for different purposes (FG, reflection, eye rays, and so on)

The HDR image (A) connects to an environment shader (B), which is then connected to the ray type shader's (C) fg input. This network designates that environment shader (B) as a source for FG for the entire scene. The LDR environment image (E) connects to another environment shader (F), which is then connected to the ray type shader's eye, refraction, and reflection inputs. Thus, the LDR image will be used as a source for all ray-trace reflections and refractions and as a background image, whereas the HDR image is used as a source for FG sampling only. In this way, you can customize a scene on a ray-type basis.

With Maya and 3ds Max you can find various shaders that deal with separating rays in this way (commonly referred to as *control shaders*). The Ray Type shader is provided by Horvatth Szabolcs on the CD: ChapterFiles/CustomShaders/Horvath/RayType1.1.zip. 3ds Max users will need to download a 3ds Max specific include file from www.maxplugins.de.

FG SHIMMERING

One thing to note about these types of shaders is that they are more commonly connected to the mental ray materials illumination shader slot. Then different illumination shaders connect to each of the inputs. Using it on a per-shader basis allows you to remove FG shimmering artifacts that appear in animation because of highly detailed textures. In other words, background images or textures from other surfaces can be a source for animated noise (shimmering) especially when FG samples high frequency fractal shaders. Using this technique allows you to detach a noisy shader from FG and use just a flat color instead, reducing the shimmering effect. The only other alternative for solving shimmering artifacts is to increase the FG accuracy rays number, sampling the scene with more accuracy and, of course, significantly increasing the render times, which is not the most desirable approach.

For our purpose, when using FG, you would not want to manually remap each shader network in this way. That's why I demonstrated how it can be used globally as a means to define separate environment shaders (applied as camera environment shaders) applied to an XSI pass. A similar network can be created for Maya or 3ds Max shaders using the Horvátth Szabolcs shader or other shaders from online resources such as www.mymentalray.com.

Common Practices

A common production practice is to generate an HDR image of a lighting set, whether inside a studio or an outdoor environment. Then, that HDR image is used as a source of luminance to light a subject in 3D so it appears realistically placed within an environment when composited over that background. The same is true for reflections regardless of FG, where you want a glossy-to-specular subject to accurately reflect the environment using realistic light measurements, which are available only with HDR images. In the color gallery you can see the "3D HDR Color" and the "2D HDR Color" images; both are generated using HDR images. The only difference is that for the 3D color plate I used 3D software to generate the HDR environment images, and for the 2D color plate I used photographed HDR images. You can see that all of them provide variation in illuminance and color values based on their environment HDR image.

Whether you generate HDR images by means of photography or using software, in both cases you are required to take several photographs at different exposures and then combine them into a single HDR image. To generate a panoramic image, you would need to take each "slice" of the panorama at several exposures so that they can be converted into an HDR panoramic image.

PHOTOGRAPHY AND HDR

With photography you can use Photoshop or HDR Shop (www.HDRShop.com) to combine multiple exposures into a single HDR image. It is best to use a digital camera with a high pixel resolution so that you have a lot of detail in the HDR image. The HDR Shop site has several useful links to resources where you can learn more about HDR imaging, HDR and 3D, and HDR Shop.

> HDR Shop provides a noncommercial free version that you can use to experiment with HDR images; see the site for details. You will see some examples shortly.

2D AND HDR PANORAMAS

An HDR photography technique I'm not a big fan of is known as the *mirrored ball*, where you photograph a chrome sphere (mirrored ball) to obtain almost 180° of the scene in a single photograph. You can see an example of a mirror ball HDR image in the section "Environment Image Types and Construction Techniques." The problem is that you need to stay far away from the sphere so that you don't reflect in a large portion of the image, and you also need the entire sphere to appear in focus so that it doesn't cover a large portion of the frame. Thus, you lose a lot of detail and resolution, wasting valuable pixel real estate.

A much better technique is to use a fish-eye lens to obtain three to four images of the environment. Better yet, use a normal to wide-angle lens and take several photographs using a custom pan head and tripod, such as the Manfrotto panoramic QTVR head (not the cheapest solution). The Gnomon Workshop (`www.thegnomonworkshop.com`) has a series of DVDs on spherical panoramic photography that covers the topic of generating panoramic images with different techniques.

3D AND HDR PANORAMAS

An additional option is to use software to generate 3D HDR environment images; you can use either your host application or a terrain-specific 3D application.

If you use your host application, you can, for example, create an HDR image using the physical sun and sky shaders discussed earlier. In such a case you need to render an HDR image using the RGBE framebuffer data type (see Chapter 3, "mental ray Output"). You also need to decide how you want to create the panoramic image; for example, 3ds Max has a panoramic exporter that ships with the software. In other hosts, you may need to render six images for each direction (cubic), as you'll see in the examples in the "Environment Image Types and Construction Techniques" section. (You can also use a panoramic lens shader.)

An alternative for generating complex terrain HDR images is by using terrain-generating software, such as Terragen from Planetside software. It allows you to create complex terrains, cloud coverage, and realistic sun and atmospheric conditions that can be rendered out to an HDR format and as six cubic images that are then combined into a panoramic image. For the "3D HDR Color" color insert I used different HDR environment images that I generated with Terragen.

Planetside Software (`www.planetside.co.uk`) provides a noncommercial free version of Terragen with some minor limitations.

Environment Image Types and Construction Techniques

Let's look at the different formats used for environment panoramic images. Here are the common types used with each host:

- Maya supports using spherical and angular maps with the IBL node.
- XSI supports spherical and cubical (six images) mapping with pass environment shaders.
- 3ds Max supports mostly spherical mapping with the bitmaps environment projection.

All host applications can also use mental ray environment shaders, which ship with the mental ray base shader library. You can manually connect them as environment shaders to a camera (see Chapter 3, "mental ray Output").

When you render an HDR environment image, as discussed in the earlier "3D and HDR Panoramas" section, you need to obtain six HDR rendered images for each camera projection: front, right, back, left, top, and bottom. You need to set the camera to a field of view of 90° as well as set the render resolution to a square resolution such as 800×800 pixels. You can see an example for six HDR images I rendered using Terragen in Figure 13.43. If they were combined in this layout into a single image, it would be considered a horizontal cross environment image.

Figure 13.43

Six camera projections rendered with Terragen and used to create a panoramic HDR environment image

To compile a single panoramic HDR image, I used a very useful and free tool (Windows OS) called Cube2Cross that you can find on the Terragen page:

`http://www2.cs.uh.edu/~somalley/hdri.html`

The tool takes six images (depending on the format) regardless of Terragen and outputs one vertical cross HDR image; you can see the HDR version in the HDR Images folder on the CD labeled "Vertical Cross Panorama" and an LDR (for preview) version in the LDR folder (all the image types presented here are available in those directories). Once you have a vertical cross image, you can then convert the image into the more common spherical HDR image format (on the CD) using a program such as HDR Shop, which is a necessary tool for working with HDR images. Alternately, you can use the six image projections using the mental ray cubic 6 environment shader that takes six separate images.

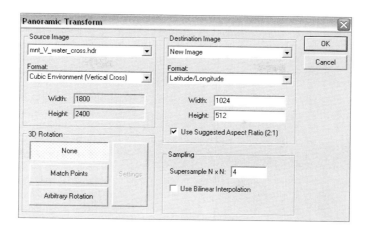

Figure 13.44
The HDR Shop Panoramic Transform window

In HDR Shop, after loading a vertical cross HDR image, select from the main menu Image → Panorama → Panoramic Transform, which opens the window shown in Figure 13.44. As you can see, this window allows you to take a source format, in this case the vertical cross generated with Cube2Cross, and output a new image with a different panoramic format, in this case set to Latitude/Longitude, which is the spherical format supported by all host applications.

Figure 13.45 shows the spherical panoramic image; the output image generated from the vertical cross. This type of HDR panoramic image format is the most common format for environmental images in 3D.

Figure 13.45
The spherical panoramic format is the most common format for HDR environments.

The last two formats shown in Figure 13.46 are mirrored ball (image A) and angular map (image B, also known as a *light probe*). A mirrored ball image typically provides almost 360° of the environment. Typically by using two fish-eye photographs or two photographs of a chrome sphere (at 90° angles), a 360° mirrored ball image can be generated. A mirrored ball image or fish-eye photographs can be converted to the angular map, which is better suited for our purposes, and overall is a better format. The angular map, as shown in the figure, starts to "bend" the environment farther away from the sphere's edge. In this way it does a better job at distributing the image data, using more pixels for representing the environment along the sides of the sphere. Many of the HDR images you download from the Web come as either angular or spherical images. If you want, you can always use HDR Shop to convert an angular image to a spherical one for your host application.

Figure 13.46

Mirrored ball (A) and angular (B) panoramic images providing 360° of coverage

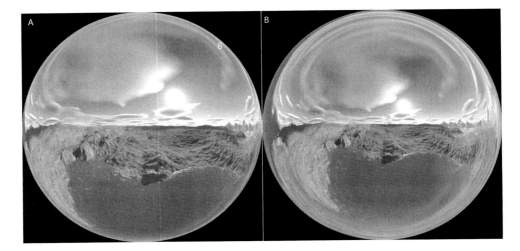

It's not necessary to have perfect environment images for FG lighting.

In the context of FG, the purpose is to sample the light intensities from the image and apply their influence on the scene as indirect lighting. Thus, the purpose is not for image display such as when creating panoramic images for compositing backgrounds or for photographic display. For that reason, you can use partial environment images. The only concern is that they include the information you want within them, which is a high dynamic range.

In most cases you want to render the environment so its primary visibility is disabled so that it will affect only the FG lighting without appearing in the frame. Then composite the rendered frame over a well-prepared background image using a compositing application. That way you also have more control over fine-tuning the foreground or background images.

Controlling HDR Exposure Values

This section will help you understand how to use HDR images in HDR Shop and how to prepare them for FG rendering.

HDR images are stored at a default exposure that is used when the image is viewed as well as with FG lighting. You can manually increase or decrease that exposure value, as specified per host in the "FG in Host Applications" section. You may prefer to leave the image intact and just change the default exposure.

In HDR Shop, the plus and minus keys on the numeric pad allow you to view the different exposures. Select the preferred exposure, and from the main menu under Image → Pixels select Scale to Current Exposure. Then save the image. This will set the current exposure as the new default exposure, which will also affect how the image is used with FG.

In addition, HDR Shop shows you the RGB intensity values stored at each pixel as you drag the mouse over the image. Leaving the mouse at a given pixel, look at the lower bar of the HDR Shop interface. You can easily identify areas with problematic exposures, like the speckling you saw how to eliminate earlier. Also note that the current f-stop value is displayed on that lower bar.

REMOVING HOTSPOTS

As a follow-up to the speckle elimination discussion, you can use HDR Shop to remove a problematic area by painting over it in an external program. You can do so by selecting Edit in Image Editor from under the File menu. It will automatically launch an external image-editing program, such as Photoshop, and it opens a temporary image so that you can paint over that area. When you're done, select Save (not Save As), and return to HDR Shop. The updates will take effect automatically, removing that area from all the exposures.

The external editing program is selected based on the file association for bitmap images on your Windows system. You can set it if you examine the file properties for a bitmap image in a Windows browser.

To easily identify a problematic area, use the minus key to reduce the exposures until only that area remains visible, and then edit it in an external program.

You will find the image Spherical_speckle in the HDR Images folder on the CD. In it you can see a hole (black spot) that was used to remove the hot spot in the "Spherical" HDR image in the same folder.

Ambient Occlusion

Ambient occlusion provides a way of adding realism to images by taking into account the influence of occluding objects while determining the color at every given point on a surface. Occlusion is the process of blocking or the blocking of a passageway, for example, blocking a flow of air. In our context, it is the process of objects blocking the flow of light from each other, which has an effect of darkening the surface area on an object as it gets closer to another surface. This also affects how a surface reacts to its own geometry such as around folds or creases (self-shadowing).

This section examines how you can easily improve the detail in images using the mental ray ambient occlusion texture. The great benefit of rendering with occlusion is the ability to achieve aesthetically pleasing renders to show off a model using a simple shader, which is the ambient occlusion texture.

With respect to indirect lighting techniques, consider that GI provides multiple bounces distributing photons indirectly in the scene, and FG adds the ability to improve those results using primary and secondary FG (diffuse) rays. When both are used together, you can use fewer GI photons and FG rays, improving the render time as discussed earlier. However, some of the fine occlusion details you saw earlier with FG in Figure 13.13 and Figure 13.14 may be lost when you use low FG settings such as a large radius. For that purpose, using the ambient occlusion texture provides a means of maintaining detail around corners, and by doing so, it allows you to use even lower FG quality values so that FG mostly contributes color bleeding and irradiance to surfaces in the scene, whereas the occlusion texture adds all the occluding detail where needed.

The ambient occlusion shader can also be used with the mental ray mib_fg_occlusion shader. This shader has only one option: result_when_fg_is_off. If you connect the ambient occlusion shader to this option, mental ray will render using the ambient occlusion shader when FG is off. When FG is on, mental ray will extract occlusion values from FG and use them instead, reducing the overhead of calculating both FG and ambient occlusion.

The Ambient Occlusion Texture

An occlusion texture examines the distance between different occluding surfaces and uses those distance values to determine the influence they should have on the resulting occlusion (darkening) effect at each point on the surface. The occlusion texture determines how much light is blocked from the surface based on the distances between surfaces—in other words, how much light is occluded by other objects. As surfaces get closer to each other, the occlusion influence rises, and the surfaces become darker in the neighboring regions; light is occluded from penetrating between them.

The most apparent use for the occlusion texture is to retrieve self-shadowing values, as well as influence from surfaces within close proximity, as a simple grayscale image that describes the diffusive occlusion color values across the surface, as shown later in Figure 13.51. You can choose to bake the diffusive ambient occlusion calculation into an image file, use it within a shader, or use it as a separate render pass for compositing (most common).

The ambient occlusion texture can be used to retrieve diffusive and reflective occlusion, normal maps, and environmental sampling. We will examine all of these within this chapter. In each host application you can find the Occlusion shader in the following paths:

Maya You can find the ambient occlusion shader, shown in Figure 13.47, in the Hypershade window under Create mental ray Nodes → Textures rollout → mib_amb_occlusion.

XSI You can find the ambient occlusion shader, shown in Figure 13.48, in the Render Tree window under Nodes → Illumination → Ambient Occlusion.

3ds Max You can find the ambient occlusion shader, shown in Figure 13.49, when mapping an illumination shader's color parameter, such as diffuse color, in the Material/Map Browser window → Ambient/Reflective Occlusion (base).

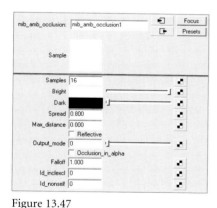

Figure 13.47

The Ambient occlusion shader in Maya

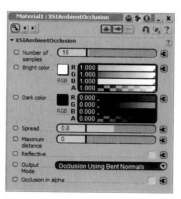

Figure 13.48

The Ambient occlusion shader in XSI

Figure 13.49

The Ambient occlusion shader in 3ds Max

The Ambient Occlusion Options

Let's start by examining the purpose of the options found in the occlusion textures. The option labels are almost identical in each host, so I don't refer to them on a per-host basis.

You can set the quality of the occlusion by increasing the Samples option. A higher value will improve the quality of the render but also increase the render time. Typical values range from 32 to 64. The Samples option defines how many rays are cast into the scene to sample for occluding surfaces over a shading point.

Figure 13.50

Examining a sample point on a surface with ambient occlusion

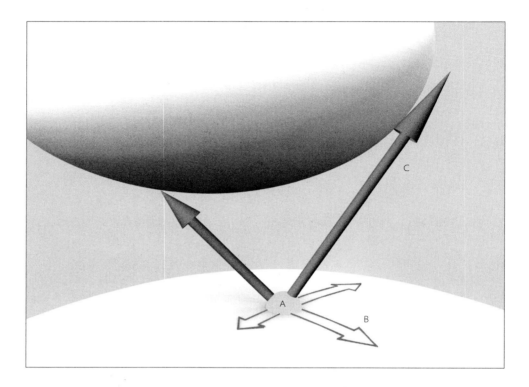

Spread defines the falloff distance of the effect from the sampled point as shown in the figure with the arrows labeled B. Note that the Spread option acts in a similar way to the glossy options in the architectural material or DGS shader; however, in this case higher values produce a glossier effect, and lower values produce a more specular (focused) effect. This effect is mostly seen with environment sampling, discussed later in this section. Thus, higher Spread values will darken and blur a larger region across the surface from a given sample point. In Figure 13.51 you can see two identical images rendered with different spread values. Image A has a spread of 0.5 and image B has a spread of 1.5. As you can see, the areas, particularly along the back wall and ceiling, appear to spread the occlusion effect farther away from the corners in image B.

The Mode option determines what type of effect the occlusion texture will calculate; at 0 it is used for diffusive or reflective occlusion, at a value of 1 it renders environment sampling (see "Environment Sampling" later in this chapter), and at values 2 and 3 it renders bent-normal images in world and object space, in that order (see the "Bent Normals" section). In XSI the Output Mode property labels these options with names rather than numbers, and in 3ds Max you can see the corresponding numbers with the Type parameter.

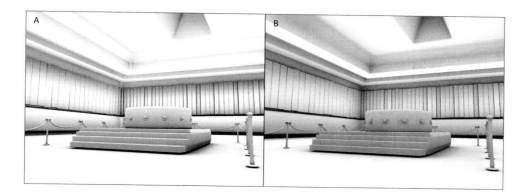

Figure 13.51

Comparing a low spread value (A) with a higher spread value (B)

Reflective Occlusion

The ambient occlusion texture lets you do much more than calculate *diffusive* ambient occlusion; it also allows you to calculate *reflective* ambient occlusion. To mimic realism, we would simulate the properties of natural light being scattered off an object, and this would include diffuse reflected light as well as specular reflected light. Both are influenced by occluding objects so that when we render without occlusion we always get unnatural results; the surface appears evenly diffused or reflective across the board, for example 100 percent reflective, without considering the effects of occlusion on the diffuse or reflection intensities. Having said that, we can control Fresnel reflections, as well as map color options with textures, but that still doesn't account for the influence of occluding surfaces.

Reflective occlusion provides a way to control the amount of reflection color along a surface based on the reflection rays so that it reduces the reflection intensity where surfaces are in close proximity, based on occlusion effects. The technical difference between rendering a diffusive occlusion versus a reflection occlusion pass is in how the occlusion is calculated. With the diffusive occlusion the influence is calculated based on the surface normals, whereas with reflected occlusion it's calculated based on the reflection rays. To clarify, with ambient occlusion the effect is calculated based on shooting rays evenly from a hemisphere above the shaded point, as with diffuse light reflection. With reflective occlusion, a glossy lobe (see Chapter 9, "The Fundamentals of Light and Shading Models") is used to cast rays based on the reflection directionality, not uniformly in all directions above the shaded point. In doing so, it builds a dependency with the viewing angle (using reflection rays). So if the camera changes its viewing angle, the effect of the reflective occlusion will adjust accordingly.

In Figure 13.52 you can see in image A an ambient occlusion render and in image B a reflective occlusion render. Image B looks glossy; it has a reflective feel because the reflective occlusion is applied based on glossy rays that hit polygons in near proximity to each other adjusting the reflection intensity accordingly. Areas that appear darker would reflect less light.

Figure 13.52

Comparing ambient occlusion (A) with reflective occlusion (B)

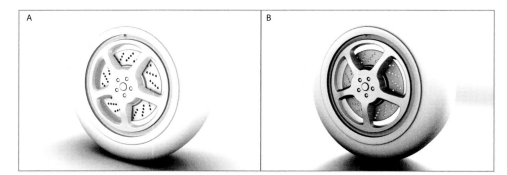

The occlusion texture provides a grayscale output that can be used to vary the reflection values along the surface. To leverage the occlusion shader's output, you need to multiply it with the reflectivity value of a given shader so that it affects the overall reflection intensity across the surface. The result would be a reflection shader that scales the amount of reflection across the surface based on reflective occlusion, rather than an overall linear value. If the reflectivity is already mapped with a texture, you can always multiply the occlusion shader with that texture and then map the result to a shader's reflection color or intensity options.

Ambient Occlusion Shading Networks

Ambient occlusion is usually used as a compositing pass. Thus, you want to render the scene with only ambient occlusion influence, without taking any source lights or shading effects into account, and then use that pass in compositing to control the intensity of the effect (more on that soon). To use the ambient occlusion texture for generating an occlusion pass, you connect the out value from the occlusion node to the ambient color of any shader, typically a Lambert shader as shown for Maya in Figure 13.53 image A. Another and better approach to rendering occlusion passes is to connect the value directly to a constant shader that outputs the texture color as is, without any influence from scene lighting, as shown in image B.

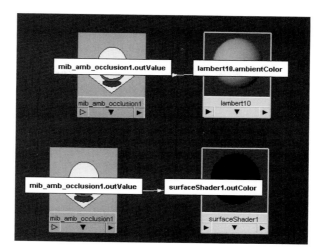

Figure 13.53

Connecting the ambient occlusion texture to a shading network for rendering diffuse occlusion effects

The surface shader in Maya and Constant shader in XSI provide you with a way of viewing the exact color on an object without any shading influence such as light.

3ds Max users, you can connect it to the mental ray material Surface parameter as shown earlier in the chapter with background environment images for FG.

With respect to using a Lambert shader or any other shading model (Blinn, Phong) and connecting an occlusion texture to the ambient color on the shader, consider the following points:

- An ambient color value acts as a multiplier for the diffuse color value.

- The occlusion texture that is connected to the ambient color value will render out details of darker/brighter based on occluding objects and then multiply it with the diffuse color values to determine color for each shaded point in the rendered image.

- The rendered image will have also been influenced by the shading model characteristics, such as the diffuse and specular color values that are influenced from lights in the scene, as shown in Figure 13.54 image A.

- In the case of a mental ray Lambert shader, if you set the diffuse value to zero, map the ambient color with the ambient occlusion texture, and set the ambience color to white, then the result will be the same as using a constant shader. Image A used this technique with a Lambert shader, and image C used this technique with a constant

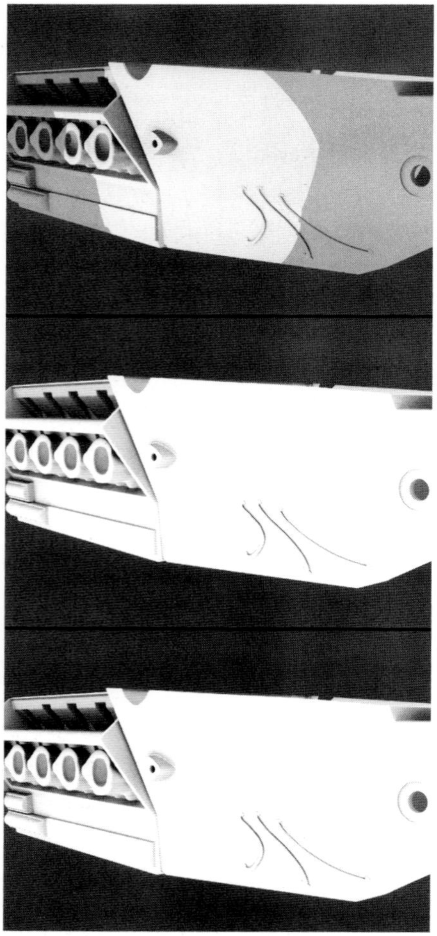

Figure 13.54

Comparing the effects of using different shader setups with the ambient occlusion texture

shader; they both look the same because a shader with a zero diffuse value will not be influenced by any lights in the scene. Note the following host-specific considerations:

- For Maya users, it works this way only with the mental ray Lambert shader. With the Maya Lambert shader, set the Diffuse attribute to 0 and the Color attributes to white. The Ambient Color and Color attributes are multiplied together.

- XSI users should map the Ambient property of a Lambert shader and set the global scene Ambience property to white, as discussed earlier in "FG in Host Applications."

- 3ds Max users should map the Ambient parameter of a standard shader with the occlusion texture and set the Specular and Diffuse color parameters to black. Then, in Environment and Effects → Global Lighting, set the Ambient color parameter to white.

As you can see, the constant shader occlusion pass (image C) looks much more like the kind of pass you could use in a compositing tree opposed to a Lambert shader that is influenced by lights (image A). Note that you might want to adjust the occlusion texture's dark value so that when multiplied by the color value in a composite, the result won't completely darken the colors at the fully occluded areas. However, if you are using it as a pass, you can always correct the color values in compositing. For example, you can decrease the spread by contracting the values or sharpen the falloff effect. The bright value should always remain white so there won't be any influence at unoccluded areas.

Compositing Occlusion

This demonstration of compositing is brief, for the purpose of understanding the theory behind compositing grayscale occlusion passes over color passes. While compositing a standard color pass with a reflection pass, the reflection pass is a combination of both a fully reflected pass (shown in Figure 13.55 image A) multiplied by the reflected occlusion pass (B) to give the reflection more variation on the surface. Then the resulting reflection pass, shown in Figure 13.55 image C, is added to the color pass, which is also multiplied by a diffusive occlusion pass as follows:

$$((color \times diffusive\ occlusion) + (reflection \times reflected\ occlusion))$$

To clarify, a fully occluded point from the reflected occlusion pass that is multiplied by the same fully reflective point in the reflection pass would yield a reflection value of zero for that point; no reflection will render for that point in compositing. The same is true for the diffuse color and ambient occlusion (diffusive occlusion) passes.

Methods for Rendering Ambient Reflective Occlusion

Rendering reflective occlusion is as simple as enabling the Reflective check box in the occlusion texture node; you can then render reflective occlusion in a number of ways.

You can render a reflective occlusion pass with the same network shown earlier using a constant shader just with the ambient occlusion texture's reflective option enabled. The resulting render is a reflective occlusion pass that can be multiplied with a reflection pass in compositing, as noted earlier.

You can multiply the reflection color with reflective occlusion in a shader tree, driving the reflection intensity across the surface in some of the following ways:

- In Maya and XSI, connect the output from the occlusion texture to the shader's reflectivity scalar value as follows:

  - In Maya, connect the occlusion shader to a Maya Luminance shader, and use that output for the shader's Reflectivity attribute.

  - In XSI, connect the occlusion shader to a Color2Scalar shader, and then connect that to the shader's Reflection → Scale property (scalerefl input in the Render Tree window for a given shading model).

- In Maya and 3ds Max, you can connect the occlusion texture output to a shader's specular color, which also affects the reflection intensity.

- In all hosts, you can create a specular shading model that is multiplied with an occlusion texture and then connected to the color input of a constant shader or directly to the material as follows:

  - In Maya, use the Multiply/Divide utility to multiply the shading model with the occlusion texture. Then connect the multiply divide node to a surface shader Out Color attribute.

  - In XSI, connect the occlusion shader and the specular shader (such as a Phong) to the inputs on a Color_Math_Basic shader and set it to multiply. Then connect

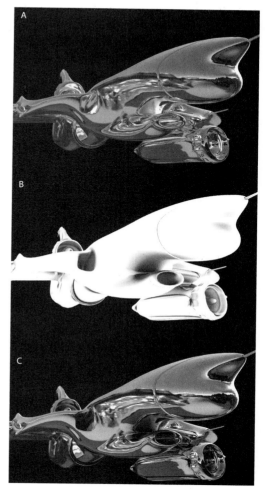

Figure 13.55

A reflection pass (A), reflective occlusion pass (B), and the result of compositing the two together (C)

the color math shader directly to the material's Surface input. Note the Phong shader reflection Color property should be set to white.

- In 3ds Max, for any of the standard shaders under the Maps rollout, map the Reflection parameter with the RGB Multiply shader. Then map the occlusion shader to one color parameter and the Reflect/Refract shader to the other color parameter. Alternatively, you can apply the same steps to a mental ray material Surface parameter, mapping it with the RGB Multiply shader.

All of these methods provide a way for controlling the reflection value across the surface, and their purpose is the same: the scaling of the reflection value at each point across the surface based on the occlusion texture output. The main difference is whether you plan to composite the reflection and reflective occlusion pass within a compositing package or would rather create a single shader tree that has the occlusion texture multiplied with the reflection values at render time as described earlier. With the later the difference is in how the shading network connections are applied rather than the end result.

Environment Sampling and Bent Normals

The ambient occlusion texture also provides a way to render bent normals and environment sampling. You enable these by choosing different rendering modes from the ambient occlusion texture mode option discussed earlier.

Environment Sampling (Mode 1)

Environmental sampling is extremely useful for retrieving the environment's light influence on an object, similar to a single diffuse bounce with FG. This is useful for controlling the appearance of a model or digital set that is superimposed on a live action plate, and you have the appropriate HDR environment image for the background.

With the occlusion shader, the process of retrieving the influence from the environment is based on the diffuse or reflective occlusion sampling. This means you can choose whether to examine the environment influence for a diffused surface based on the surface normals (diffusive occlusion) or for a reflective surface based on the reflection rays (reflective occlusion).

In practice, using the ambient occlusion texture for extracting environmental sampling, rather than taking the time to calculate FG, simply speeds up the render process; it gets the environment's influence on shaded point without any FG precomputation or FG maps. Furthermore, you can use an advanced mental ray shader that utilizes baked (light maps) occlusion and bent-normal image files to render environment sampling without any raytracing, which is significantly faster than raytracing every frame. (You can read about that in an article I wrote for the HDRI 3D magazine about texture baking in Maya, included on the companion CD.)

It's important to note that environment sampling will pick up color influence only from the environment map, not from nearby surfaces; nearby surfaces will affect only the occlusion, meaning they will make certain areas darker or brighter. Thus, this differs from FG in that it doesn't look for color influence from surfaces in the scene, as does FG.

In the case of environment sampling, you retrieve color values from the environment and multiply them by your surface color; this in return can be used as a render pass or part of a procedural shading network used in the same way as described earlier with the different shader trees. The only difference is that you want to multiply the environment sampling output with the diffuse color (it acts as fill/ambient lighting). Figure 13.56 shows two examples of environment sampling using different HDR images on a model with the occlusion texture and a constant shader. It's essential to see this effect in color; see the color version in the Chapter 13 folder on the CD labeled "Environmental Sampling."

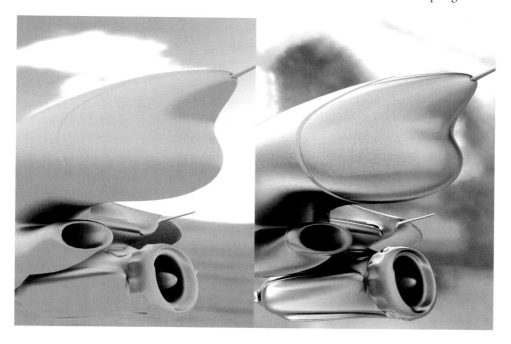

Figure 13.56

The effect of using environment sampling with the occlusion texture and two different HDR environment images

The most important fact to know about environment sampling is that the Spread option controls how glossy the environment sampling appears, and lower values provide more specular (mirror) reflections. Thus, the glossier the sampling (higher spread values), the more rays (the Samples option) are needed to produce a quality effect, increasing the render time.

Bent Normals (Modes 2, 3, and 4)

The mode option when set to 2, 3, or 4 enables rendering bent normal-maps as follows:

- *Mode 2*: It's based on the world space coordinates.
- *Mode 3*: It's based on the camera space coordinates.
- *Mode 4*: It's based on object space coordinates.

You already know that normal maps can represent a given coordinate space in color, color coding the coordinates where the Y axis is green, the Z axis is blue, and the X axis is red, as discussed in Chapter 11, "mental ray Textures and Projections."

What *bent normals* means is that the direction of the average unoccluded vector is used rather than the shaded point's standard normal direction (which is perpendicular to the surface face). Thus, bent normals differ from standard normal maps in that they color code the imaged based on the average area that represent the least occlusion, in other words, pointing away from nearby surfaces—which is why they're considered "bent." They too use the same color-coding scheme for the three axes but derive the normals based on the average result from sampling rays over a shading point's hemisphere.

They are mostly used for internal shader purposes and don't really assist you in other purposes. The best option is to bake them into a texture map, as cited earlier, and use them with the mental ray mib_ bent_normals shader that provides for nonraytrace environment sampling using a baked occlusion texture and baked bent normal map texture as cited earlier and demonstrated in the HDRI 3D mental ray texture baking article found on the CD.

## CHAPTER 14

Subsurface Scattering

Subsurface scattering refers to characteristics of light as it penetrates and scatters within surfaces. Once light penetrates a surface it can refract and exit, as with glass; or it may hit several "layers" within that surface, essentially bouncing until it either exits the surface or is fully absorbed, as with jade, milk, emeralds, wax, opals, and many other such materials.

To simulate subsurface scattering, mental ray offers shaders it describes as both physical and nonphysical. The second group is more extensive; these shaders don't attempt to calculate the physics of deep scattering. There is also one physical shader, which does calculate deep scattering. This chapter examines both mental ray techniques. The chapter includes the following topics:

- **Advanced Shading Models**
- **Nonphysical Subsurface Scattering**
- **An Advanced Shader Tree**
- **Physical Subsurface Scattering**

Advanced Shading Models

The BSDF light transport models discussed in Chapter 9, "The Fundamentals of Light and Shading Models," are a simplification of a more advanced approach to modeling light transport known known as the *Bidirectional Surface Scattering Distribution Function* (BSSRDF). The BSSRDF model primarily describes subsurface scattering and has been developed for use in computer graphics by Henrik Wann Jensen (`http://graphics.ucsd.edu/~henrik`). Jensen introduced it in 2001 at Siggraph.

You saw that in BSDF shading models a mathematical function accounts for various characteristics of light scattering without using volumetric simulations (which are used with participating media photon casting). BSSRDF shading models are similar to BSDF models but more complex.

BSSRDF is a model for light transport that has few CG shading model implementations. They are only beginning to emerge in the field, mostly thanks to custom in-house development for feature films (for example, see Gollum's skin in *Lord of the Rings 2* and *3*). BSSRDF shading models support rendering internal light diffusion such as in jade, marble, milk, juice, or any other form of matter that exhibits a lot of translucency, including realistic skin shading.

mental ray shaders apply subsurface scattering using two different methods: nonphysical shaders use light maps based on a standard BSDF model, and the physical shader models physically accurate light transport by casting photons for the purpose of addressing the principles of BSSRDF light transport.

The physical shader is in fact Jensen's motivation for developing BSSRDF shading models. His efforts are aimed at removing the dependency on photon casting while providing a good solution for rendering surfaces that display some level of internal scattering (almost every material other than metal). Thus, the advantage of BSSRDF shading models over the mental ray shaders is that they render faster without a need to cast photons (as the mental ray physical shader does) and are more accurate shading models and easier to use than the nonphysical shader.

After a brief conceptual discussion of the BSSRDF model for subsurface scattering, this chapter then looks at how mental ray implements these concepts using the two techniques cited earlier.

The BSSRDF Light Transport Model

Jensen's BSSRDF scattering model is a complex light model that describes subsurface absorption and light scattering (diffusion) using two terms: *single scattering* and *multiple scattering*. These concepts are mathematically implemented in the form of a shading model that resolves light transport inside translucent materials where subsurface scattering is key to their natural (soft/diffused) appearance, as with skin.

The concepts discussed in this chapter are an extension to the discussion in Chapter 12's "Participating Media (PM) Effects" section. They deal with rendering light that interacts within matter (volume rendering), following the same principles presented with the Henyey-Greenstein phase function for anisotropic and isotropic scattering as well as the concepts of emission, absorption, in-scattering, and out-scattering.

As shown in Figure 14.1, BSSRDF light transport accounts for the fact that incident light does not reflect directly from the point of contact on a surface (externally), but actually transmits through the surface, where it may bounce around internally (in-scattering) before it is either absorbed or exits the surface (out-scattering).

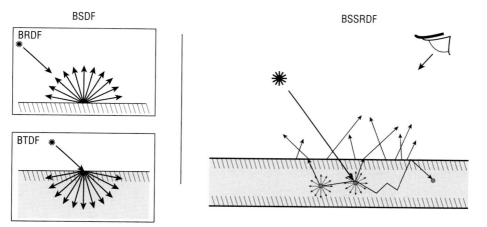

Figure 14.1

The BSSRDF light transport function

The figure also shows the difference between BSDF light transport models and the BSSRDF model. You can see that with the BSSRDF model, incident light may exit the surface at an offset location after carrying out several internal reflections; this is the *multiple scattering* term cited earlier. It can also refract through the material and exit on the opposite side without bouncing around internally (low scatter conditions); this is *single scattering*.

The primary effect BSSRDF has on shading is that surfaces appear more natural, conveying a realistic (diffused) feel across the surface. The ability to account for internal single and multiple scattering is a significant advantage for rendering natural-looking surfaces, compared to the harsh, "computer-generated" appearance most standard shading models provide.

BSSRDF shading models and the mental ray physical shader provide an accurate simulation of light. But to simulate subsurface characteristics properly, you also need to know about the diffusive qualities of the surface, precisely how it scatters light internally. For that purpose, empirical data from experiments can be applied to these models for greater realism. At the following links, you can learn more about BSSRDF light transport by reading papers that describe subsurface scattering and list empirical data for absorption and scattering coefficients. You can implement these values with the physical shader discussed later in this chapter:

```
http://graphics.ucsd.edu/~henrik/images/subsurf.html

http://graphics.stanford.edu/papers/bssrdf/

http://graphics.ucsd.edu/~henrik/papers/skin_bssrdf/

http://graphics.stanford.edu/papers/bssrdf/bssrdf.pdf

http://www.tml.tkk.fi/Opinnot/Tik-111.500/2002/paperit/kalle_koutajoki.pdf
```

(The first and last links may be the best places to start.)

Rendering Subsurface Scattering Effects

mental ray provides two solutions for simulating subsurface scattering; choosing one of them will primarily depend on whether deep scattering is required. Other considerations include ease of use and memory usage. The first method is nonphysical; that is, it does not attempt any realistic calculation for determining light scattering. This method provides faster results and fewer artifacts and is not as processor intensive. It is used to simulate shallow scattering in surfaces that possess some level of internal scattering. Thus, the nonphysical approach is a more creative and time-efficient approach. The other, physically correct method uses photons to simulate how light scatters within a deep surface, making it obviously more expensive to render and harder to control.

As with all surfaces, subsurface-scattering effects are based on certain factors that define the scattering characteristics of the surface. Figure 14.2 (also found on the companion CD in the Chapter 14 folder as "Subsurface Scattering in Real Surfaces") demonstrates some of the properties of different materials and how their interaction with light differentiates them from a common CG look. The surface properties that define their appearance relate to how light scatters through the surface; such considerations are as follows:

- How much light penetrates through a thin surface? The surfaces shown in images B (balloon), D (plate), and F (cloth, a seat cover) can be rendered using the nonphysical shader.

- What about deep scattering? Does light penetrate a thick surface such as A (marble), C, and E? Both C and E show candle wax, which can be simulated only with the physical shader. With marble (A), the surface is thick; however, does light travel into its depth as with the wax? With marble you can use both nonphysical and physical shaders depending on the type of surface you are rendering; for example, the tile shown in the figure could be rendered with either method, but a statue that displays more internal scattering would require the physical shader.

- How much light is absorbed within the surfaces? This property applies to all the surfaces in the figure.

- Does the back side appear to transmit light through the surface (through scattering) as shown in B, D, E, F, and the first thin layer (liquid state) of the candle wax under image C?

These are all essential questions you should consider before determining an approach to simulating subsurface-scattering effects.

Figure 14.2

Common surfaces that exhibit subsurface scattering

The most significant use of subsurface scattering in 3D has been to simulate skin characteristics. This feature has ignited a whole new era, in which the CG artist's ability to simulate realistic skin shading has greatly improved. Another ability (somewhat undervalued) is that even a small amount of scattering at shallow layers provides for softer diffused light, making surfaces appear much more natural, as illustrated in Figure 14.3 as well as various images in the color gallery and in the Chapter 14 folder on the CD with the image "Cardboard Subsurface Scattering." In Figure 14.3 you see an "out-of-the-box" render, using only the nonphysical subsurface shader without any additional surface mapping. Thus, subsurface scattering is a valuable effect for simulating all types of natural surfaces that may span from translucent materials to skin shading, from wax to stone, and so forth. Note that for some purposes you can use the architectural material discussed in Chapter 10, "mental ray Shaders and Shader Trees," for translucency without taking the time to set up the nonphysical shader; however, the nonphysical shader will produce better results.

Figure 14.3

The nonphysical shader used with "out-of-the-box" settings assigned to simple geometry

Nonphysical Subsurface Scattering

mental ray ships with the subsurface shader library, which includes several component and phenomenon shaders specifically designed for nonphysical subsurface-scattering (SSS) effects. In addition, the SSS library ships with one photon-based shader for physically correct subsurface scattering; this shader is discussed later in the chapter.

Using component shaders requires a process of developing a shader tree that defines the subsurface-scattering effect. Chapters 9 through 11 included discussions of mental ray component shaders; based on those discussions and examples, this process sounds just right. Each component shader is aimed at solving a particular task. There are shaders for calculating the scattered light, color, region, and effect, as well as shaders providing control over external light contributions such as diffuse, specular, and bump shading. When these subsurface component shaders, along with other shaders (Lambert, DGS, and so on), are combined, they form a subsurface shader tree that controls both the external and internal shading contributions. With nonphysical subsurface scattering, these shader trees greatly rely on mental ray light maps and depth maps, which provide essential information for determining the light's influence across the surface, front and back, based on the cameras position in the scene.

Most significant is that you are not required to know how to combine all these different shaders. As a matter of convenience, certain preset shaders have already been combined as phenomenon shaders, essentially forming four easy-to-use subsurface-scattering shaders. These phenomenon shaders are as follows:

- misss_fast_simple
- misss_fast_skin
- misss_fast_skin_d (misss_fast_skin with displacement)
- misss_fast_lmap

Not all hosts offer all four shaders; it depends on how the SSS shader library is implemented in host applications, as described per host next. The *miss* portion of each name stands for "mental images subsurface scattering" library. As discussed in Chapters 1 and 9, the phenomenon node is a complex shading network compiled into a single shader node and interface with access to options within that hidden network. These four shaders are compilations of the different component shaders found in the SSS library. In the following sections, I'll cover all the component shaders and their options, as well as the phenomenon shaders, to show how to construct custom shaders or use these preset shaders. You can find these shaders in host applications as follows:

Maya In the Hypershade window under the Create mental ray Nodes → Materials rollout, you will find the first two shaders listed earlier. In addition, you will see the component shaders (all the SSS shaders begin with the *miss* prefix), as shown in Figure 14.4. You will find the fourth phenomenon shader listed earlier (a light map shader) under the Light Maps rollout and the misss_lambert_gamma shader (another component shader) under the Textures rollout, as shown in the figure. The disadvantage with Maya 8.5 and lower is that you need to configure the light map shader manually, which at times requires some troubleshooting. In Maya 2008 the process of creating the shader tree is automated using the shaders described throughout this chapter.

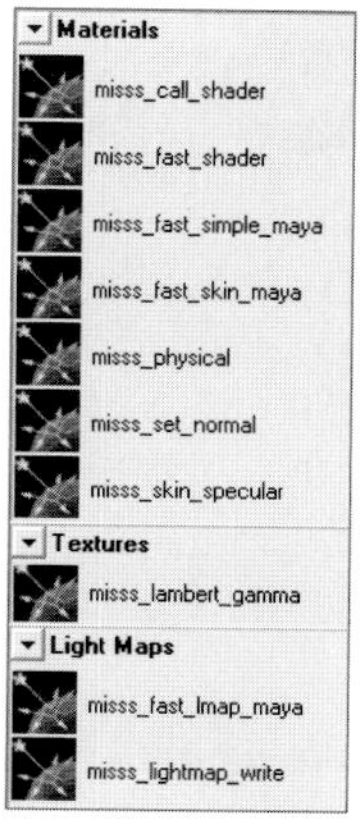

Figure 14.4

All the SSS shaders in Maya have the *miss* prefix, as shown in the Hypershade's Create mental ray Node panel.

XSI In XSI you have the two phenomenon shaders listed earlier (1 and 2), and the light map shader (4) is already built into the first two phenomenon shaders. Thus, in XSI the SSS shaders are provided as monolithic materials that are the subsurface phenomenon shaders (1 or 2) as well as the light map shader required by each of the phenomenon shaders.

As we review the SSS shader purposes, it will make more sense. You can find both materials in the Render Tree window → Nodes→ Illumination menu, where Fast Sub-surface Scattering Shader corresponds to misss_fast_simple and Fast Skin Shader corresponds to misss_fast_skin. Note that because these are monolithic materials, both shaders connect to the material input of an XSI material, as shown in Figure 14.5.

Figure 14.5

The misss_fast_ simple shader connected to the material input of an XSI material

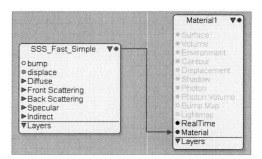

3ds Max In 3ds Max you will find three nonphysical shaders that correspond to the first three shaders in the earlier list. You can locate them by selecting a new material in the Material Editor window, and then under the Material/Map Browser window you will find SSS Fast Material (mi), Fast Skin Material (mi), Fast Skin Material + Displace (mi), and the SSS Physical Material (mi), which is discussed later in this chapter. The Fast Skin Material and Fast Skin Material + Displace shaders both correspond to the misss_fast_skin shader with and without support for displacement mapping. The light map shader is already implemented in all three monolithic materials, and therefore you do not have to deal with manually configuring them. These phenomenon shaders are provided as monolithic shaders that encompass the SSS shader as well as the required light map shader. The component shaders used to create these shaders are not provided; however, as you learn about SSS in the following sections, you will learn how these shaders work in detail through their component shaders.

> In all hosts, if you enable info verbosity (see Chapter 1), you will see mental ray output information on the light map generation process so that you can see that it didn't fail.

In Maya and XSI the misss_fast_skin_d phenomenon shader is not required to extend support for displacement mapping. In each host you can attach a displacement map directly to the material shader's displacement input and the SSS phenomenon shader to the material input, which is the Material Shader attribute in Maya and the Material property in XSI. Essentially, when exported to mental ray, the material is translated as one material that will have the SSS shaders as well as the displacement map, as with a misss_fast_skin_d phenomenon shader.

The Component Shaders

As mentioned earlier, mental ray includes a set of component shaders that when used together form a subsurface-scattering effect. The following are detailed descriptions of the component and phenomenon shaders, some of which are presented in more detail in the instructions for host applications.

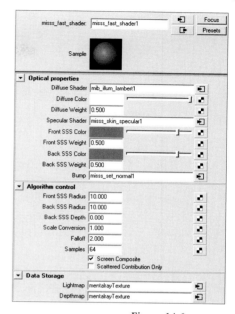

misss_fast_shader

This component shader, whose Maya interface is shown in Figure 14.6, is the "brain" behind subsurface scattering. It is used to calculate the scattered light effect for the internal subsurface layers. Because it's implemented internally as part of the phenomenon shader's (listed earlier) shader trees, its options can be found in each of their shader interfaces. This shader controls two internal layers of subsurface scattering, *front* and *back*, and provides inputs that accept an additional illumination shader that provides the external BRDF light contribution. Figure 14.6 shows these shading inputs mapped with mental ray shaders that provide additional components for rendering external diffuse, specular, and bump contributions.

Figure 14.6

The misss_fast_ shader UI seen in Maya

THE DIFFUSE AND SPECULAR COMPONENTS

The misss_fast_shader Diffuse Color and Diffuse Weight attributes provide for a Lambertian shading model, so this shader does not require other shaders for rendering external diffuse light reflection. You can map the Diffuse Shader input with a different shading model, such as an Oren-Nayar model (recommended for skin shading); however, that shader will be subjected to a diffuse multiplier that will reduce some of the Oren-Nayar effect; the Diffuse Color and Weight attributes are multiplied by the diffuse input shader. To clarify, the misss_fast_shader provides a Lambert shading model that is multiplied by whatever else is mapped to the Diffuse Input attribute. If set as color, it also influences the color of the mapped shader.

In this case, you can see a mental ray base Lambert shader attached to the Diffuse Shader input in Figure 14.6 for the purpose of adding a complex shader tree, such as diffuse shader with various texture maps that enhance the diffuse reflection appearance, which is more than possible using the weight and color options. Thus, the Lambert shader acts as a pipeline shader that bridges between a complex diffuse shader tree and the misss_fast_shader. Furthermore, consider that the purpose of the Diffuse Color and Weight attributes is to balance the diffuse shading contribution (the mapped diffuse shader) with the subsurface effect. Thus, they act as an additional tool for balancing how much of the diffuse shader is combined (influences) with the subsurface effect during rendering.

If the Diffuse Color and Weight attribute is set to zero, the mapped shader is also affected and will not contribute any color. In such a case, you could use this shader solely for the purpose of internal scattering (without a mapped shader); the diffuse component has no effect. You could then layer the misss_fast_shader with other shaders in a shader tree (using add or screen math composite operations) that provide the diffuse contribution, such as an Oren-Nayar shader, without the limitation of having it multiplied with the Diffuse Color and Weight attribute. This approach can also be implemented with the more complex phenomenon shaders when setting their diffuse contribution to zero.

For specular reflection, the misss_skin_specular shader is attached to the Specular Shader input, as shown in Figure 14.6. You are not required to use the misss_skin_specular shader; however, it is a robust shader that provides multiple layers of specularity, as discussed later in this chapter. As an alternative, you can use (for example) a Blinn shader that has the ambient and diffuse colors set to black so it contributes only specular reflections.

ALGORITHM CONTROL

When rendered, the misss_fast_shader is responsible for combining the different external and internal light contributions into a final result. Another factor in this calculation is the Algorithm Control attributes shown in Figure 14.6. These attributes provide control over fine-tuning the scattered light measurement units and the shader compositing method (internal shader math), all discussed in more detail throughout this chapter.

LAYERING SHADERS

One powerful approach to subsurface shader tree construction is that you can connect an additional misss_fast_shader to the Diffuse Color attribute of a "base" misss_fast_shader, providing more layers that simulate internal light scattering, essentially stacking one shader on top of another. This type of shader stacking is applied internally in the misss_fast_skin phenomenon shader, which offers three layers of internal scattering.

misss_lightmap_write

The light map shader is responsible for collecting depth and irradiance values from the camera's perspective. These values are stored in one or two (depending on how it is set up) 32-bit floating point light map files. You can see in Figure 14.6 how two mental ray texture shaders, the results from the light map shader, are mapped to the misss_fast_shader under Data Storage. When only one map is used, the RGB channels store RGB light intensities, and the alpha channel is used to store depth values.

Light map shaders look at each surface's front and back from the camera perspective and store the overall diffuse light contribution across a surface as well as the distance from the camera so that the shader can determine the thickness of the surface. The light map is then used by misss_fast_shader to determine subsurface scattering through a surface. This means that light maps are essential for any subsurface-scattering effect; without them, it won't work because they provide critical information on the front and back surfaces' external illumination and the depth. As cited earlier, light maps are integrated in the XSI and 3ds Max monolithic SSS shaders and generated automatically in Maya 2008.

misss_skin_specular

The misss_skin_specular shader, whose interface in Maya is shown in Figure 14.7, provides two separate layers of specularity, shown as First Layer of Specularity and Second Layer of Specularity. If you look at the misss_fast_skin phenomenon shader later in the chapter, you will see that misss_skin_specular is implemented within the phenomenon shader using the same options as shown here; the options in each host are presented in the same order and have similar labels. Thus, by reviewing the misss_skin_specular shader in this section, you are in fact reviewing the specular options of the misss_fast_skin phenomenon shader, which can be seen under the following rollouts / tabs in each host:

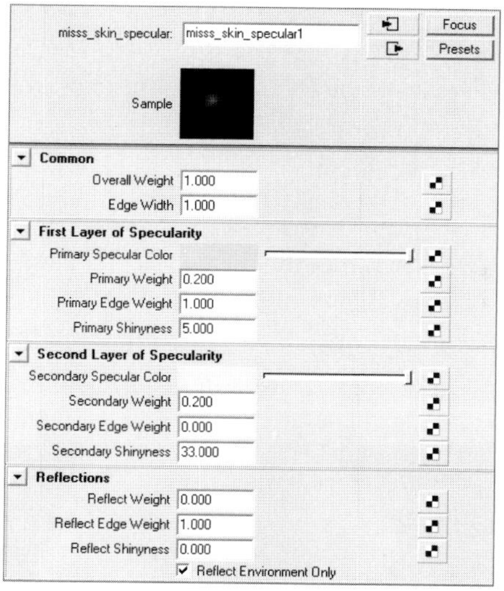

Figure 14.7

The misss_skin_specular shader UI

- In Maya look at the misss_fast_skin_maya shader in the Specularity rollout.

- In XSI look at the SSS_Fast_Skin material shader on the Specular tab.

- In 3ds Max look at the SSS Fast Skin Material (mi) material shader under 2-Layer Specularity and Reflections.

Each layer has options that specify the glossy nature of the highlight using a Shinyness attribute and a means to define Fresnel reflections using the Primary or Secondary Weight and Edge Weight attributes. The shader is also used as a reflection shader, providing the same set of attributes for reflections as with the highlights shown in the Reflections rollout. In Figure 14.8 you can see a render using only this shader (attached to a constant shader) demonstrating glossy reflections and highlights, two layers of highlights, and Fresnel characteristics. Notice how a glossier highlight appears below a more specular highlight, corresponding to the first and second layers of specularity. Also note that each layer can have a different highlight color.

The Reflect Shinyness, Reflect Weight, and Reflect Edge Weight attributes function exactly as with their correlating attributes found under each specular layer, so we can briefly examine their effect on reflections and highlights. In Figure 14.9 image A the Reflect Shinyness attribute is set to 0 providing a fully specular reflection. In image B the Reflect

Shinyness attribute is increased to 15 and provides a glossy reflection. The Reflect Shiny-ness attribute functions exactly like the DGS Shiny attribute discussed in Chapter 10. Thus, as with the DGS shader, improving the quality of glossy reflections requires increasing the scene sample settings.

Figure 14.8

The misss_skin_specular shader provides multiple glossy highlights, glossy reflections, and Fresnel reflections.

Figure 14.9

Specular and glossy reflections using the misss_skin_specular shader

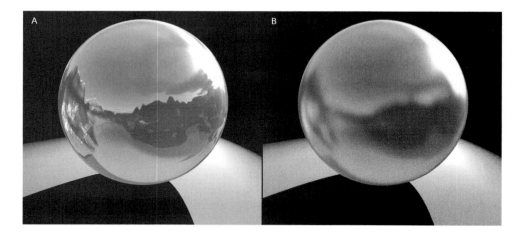

In Figure 14.10 image A and image B the Reflect Weight property (facing angles) is set to 0 and the Reflect Edge Weight property (glancing angles) is set to 1, providing Fresnel reflections. The difference between the two images is in the transition from facing to glancing angles, as discussed for various shaders in Chapter 10, "mental ray Shaders and Shader Trees." In this case, the Edge Width attribute (shown in the Common rollout in Figure 14.7) defines the transition rate. In image A, the Edge Width attribute is set to 1, and in image B it is set to 5. As you can see, the increase in value provides for a narrower edge and faster transition, compared to the linear transition produced by a value of 1. These attributes function exactly as with the architectural material, discussed in Chapter 10, where you define the reflectivity at both angles and specify a curve value to define the transition. In addition, the Overall Weight and Edge Width attributes are used as a multiplier that can decrease or increase the overall reflection and highlight effect as well as the transition (Edge Width attribute).

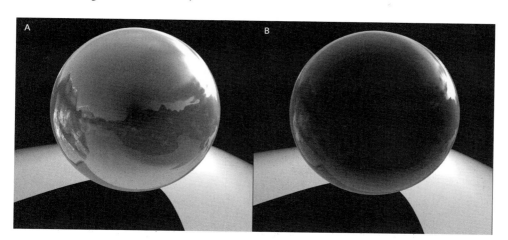

Figure 14.10

Controlling Fresnel reflections and falloff rate

You can use this powerful specular shading model in any network regardless of subsurface scattering, providing enhanced control over layering glossy to specular reflections and highlights.

Because this is only a specular shader, it carries no diffuse qualities and must be mathematically added to a diffuse shader. An easy way to add this shader to a network is simply to use an Add operator to superimpose this shader on top of a diffuse shader. For example, you can use the mental ray color mix base shader, where the diffuse shader connects to the base color, the specular shader connects to the first color input (color 0), and the mode is set to add.

SKIN SPECULARITY

All these specular shader options are useful for skin shading, because they allow you to separate skin specularity into two components. One component deals with the specularity of skin at facing-to-glancing angles, which is typically very glossy and full of noise, because the specular highlights break up within the skin's microstructure, especially around wrinkles. The second component deals with the Fresnel reflection of increasing highlight intensity at glancing angles. Here the highlight also increases in noise, distinguishing the "broken" structure of skin. Furthermore, at glancing angles specularity typically also shifts from the warmer specular color it has at facing angles to a cooler color (unless a warm source light, such as a fire, is in close proximity). One of the reasons for this color shift is that the glossy specular highlight across the skin (at facing to glancing angles) reflects primarily the skin's microstructure surface, which has a warmer tint. By contrast, at glancing angles the Fresnel effect increases in intensity, and the reflections from hair (fuzz) produce cooler highlights whose color is not as affected by internal scattering from within the skin's microstructure.

For skin shading you should use specular texture maps that break the reflections and highlights according to skin characteristics, as discussed earlier, mapping both the Primary and Secondary Specular Color attributes and the correlating reflection attributes with high frequency noise texture maps. Skin reflections should be very glossy so that the shader primarily deals with environmental sampling—sampling the color influence of an environment without drawing a distinguishable reflection across the character. Also, the global scene anti-aliasing sampling doesn't need to be increased significantly because you are not trying to create a smooth glossy reflection like metal. Skin is a very rough surface with a lot of bumpiness so that you are more likely to want a lot of "noise" in the skin (broken highlights), and thus you can get away with using lower sampling values while rendering very glossy reflections.

misss_lambert_gamma

The misss_lambert_gamma shader is a light-sampling utility used to define the gamma level and light linking of light maps. It provides control over the gamma as well as additional color multipliers such as ambient color, enabling you to add light to the light map. Hence, this shader is a tweaking device for controlling the light map's colors and intensity values. All its attributes are built into the misss_fast_lmap phenomenon light map shader and the XSI and 3ds Max monolithic SSS shaders, as discussed in detail later in this chapter.

misss_call_shader

The misss_call_shader is a pass-through shader used when creating phenomenon shaders. In a nutshell it allows you to specify inputs in a phenomenon shader that would receive external shaders. Hence, this shader is used to link external shaders into a phenomenon network. It can be used to construct SSS phenomenon shaders.

misss_set_normal and Bump Mapping

The misss_set_normal shader is used to perturb the surface normals as with a bump map using normal maps. (See Chapter 11, "mental ray Textures and Projections," for a discussion of normal maps and bump maps.) You can use this shader to drive a texture into the

Bump attribute of the misss_fast_shader, but it will not actually simulate a bumped surface unless you use a normal bump map; instead, it applies its effect visually as a color change, which is not the desired result with a bumped surface. Also note that even if you use a normal map, you still need to use an intermediate bump shader to define the intensity of the bump, referred to as *bump factor* with mental ray bump shaders. In the absence of an intermediate bump shader, the bump value (how bumped it appears) is defined solely from the normal map, which may suffice.

There are two world-space normal map example images, "normals_1" and "normals_2" in the Chapter 14 folder on the companion CD, that you can test on a NURBS sphere. Both maps were baked from the same fractal texture but just at different bump intensities; therefore, each map will produce a different amount of bump. You'll also find an example, Zaxis_wall, of a normal map that was generated from a procedural shader tree; it shows a tiled bump map with different bump intensities. This example can be tested on a plane facing the Z axis only. Note that all these examples are world-space normal maps, which require you to view them under the same conditions as those used to generate them.

> With the nonphysical shaders, the bump effect does not affect the subsurface layers; it affects only the external diffuse layer.

It's important to note that you can use this shader for the purpose of assigning normal maps to any shader, regardless of subsurface scattering. In Figure 14.11 you can see a normal map, labeled A, attached to the Normal attribute of the misss_set_normal shader, labeled B. The shader is then connected to the bump input of architectural material and assigned to a flat surface. You can see the rendered result in Figure 14.12, where I also added a sphere in the center for comparison; it has the same mia material without a normal map. The amount of the bump in this case is solely defined by the normal map, because the normal map connects directly to the misss_set_normal _shader.

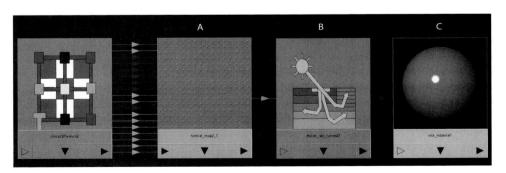

Figure 14.11

Using the misss_set_normal shader to connect normal maps to a mia material

As you can see, some of these shaders have additional purposes that can be handy. Note that if you install the Binary Alchemy shader library, some of its shaders, such as the fractal shader, provide a bump map output-only option. When enabled (also bump mapping needs to be enabled), the output is in the form of a normal map, so you can connect the BA shaders through a misss_set_normal shader to apply it as a bump normal map to any shader. The normal maps on the CD were created with the BA fractal 4D shader.

Since the misss_set_normal shader is currently made available only in Maya, the following section demonstrates how it can help create bump map effects in Maya, using mental ray shaders and Maya textures.

MISSS_SET_NORMAL BUMP MAPPING IN MAYA

A practical approach for bump mapping in Maya is to use the misss_set_normal shader in conjunction with Maya shaders or other custom mental ray shaders. In Figure 14.13 you can see two shader trees, labeled A and B. The scene file labeled "normal bump mapping" is available in the chapter directory on the companion CD. Both shader trees show a Maya solid fractal (3D texture) connected to a bump 3D node. The bump3d node connects to the misss_set_normal shader as follows:

bump3d.outNormal → misss_set_normal.normal input

Under the shader tree labeled A in Figure 14.13, the misss_set_normal connects to the misss_fast_shader as follows:

misss_set_normal.message → misss_fast_shader.bump input

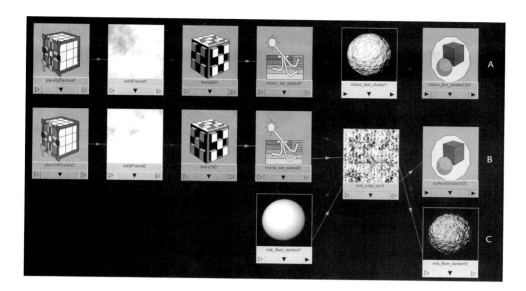

Figure 14.13

Using Maya bump nodes to pass normal data to through the misss_set_normal shader into two different shader trees

You can apply the connection by dragging and dropping the misss_set_normal onto the Bump attribute shown in Figure 14.6 earlier. As you can see, the shader appears bumped by the Maya 3D texture. If you want to use this shader with other shader trees and not the misss_fast_shader, you can use the mental ray mib_color_mix shader to apply a similar connection (discussed in a similar context in Chapter 11, "mental ray Textures and Projections"), as shown with the shader tree labeled B.

In the shader tree B, the misss_set_normal is applied to the Color_base attribute of the color mix shader, and mib_illum_lambert shader is applied to the Color_0 attribute, and Mode_0 is set to blend (both connections applied with drag and drop). The color mix shader can connect directly to the Material input of a shading group node, as shown in the figure. I also connected the color mix shader to an additional Lambert shader labeled C for illustrative purposes (you can't see the bump effect in the color mix shader preview) so that you can see how the bump effect is influencing shading.

The Maya bump 2D and 3D nodes deal with perturbing normals, which is the objective of bump mapping. Thus, the output from bump nodes is in the form of world-space normals. The misss_set_normal can leverage that type of data correctly for bump mapping. As an exercise, I recommend you connect the outNormal output from the bump3d or bump2D nodes to a surface shader's color input and render. You will see the world-space normals color scheme render (see Chapter 11, "mental ray Textures and Projections"), as affected by the bump texture. (You did a similar exercise in Chapter 11 with the mental ray vector shader to visualize surface normals.) It's an effective way for you to test the output; for example, try it with bulge, checker, and fractal shaders that connect to the bump

2D node and then to the surface shader. You can find good examples for all these shader trees in the scene file.

> Remember, if you have normal maps, you can apply them directly using the misss_set_normal shader without using Maya bump nodes, but using the bump nodes (as a normal map bump) enables you to control the bump factor.

The SSS Phenomenon Shaders

As mentioned earlier, the phenomenon shaders pack the component shaders into three easy-to-use subsurface-scattering shaders. There are two subsurface phenomenon shaders (with an additional displacement version) and one light map phenomenon shader.

The misss_fast_simple phenomenon shader is primarily used for most subsurface-scattering effects other than skin. The misss_fast_skin shader provides special features that better resemble skin characteristics, such as skin-like specularity (using the misss_skin_specular shader) and three layers of light scattering. The shaders are otherwise identical, internally relying on the misss_fast_shader component shader to define the effect of SSS; hence, once you have mastered one shader, you've mastered them all.

In all cases, the misss_fast_simple and misss_fast_skin shaders are used either with the component light map and gamma shaders discussed earlier or with the misss_fast_lmap phenomenon shader, which includes the light map and gamma shader options internally. With Maya you actually use both shaders (an SSS shader and light map shader) in the shader tree, as discussed later in this chapter. With XSI and 3ds Max, the options for SSS shaders and the light map and gamma shaders can be found in the misss_fast_simple and misss_fast_skin SSS monolithic shaders. Essentially, the subsurface phenomenon shaders are prepared for you as monolithic shaders, so all you need to do is assign them to a surface and they will work. With Maya, if you don't correctly connect the phenomenon light map shader (or equivalent component shaders), the subsurface shaders will not work.

The misss_fast_simple Phenomenon Shader

Figures 14.14 to 14.16 show the misss_fast_simple shader in Maya, XSI, and 3ds Max. If you look at options under the misss_fast_simple shader in each host, you will recognize the misss_fast_shader options shown earlier in Figure 14.6, with slight differences in how they are organized. For subsurface-scattering effects, the misss_fast_simple shader (in each host) has front and back radius, weight, and color options, as well as a back depth option. These scattering options are all derived from the misss_fast_shader internally, within the phenomenon shader, and thus function in the same way. All these options are discussed further in the section "How Does It All Work?" For now, just note where they are located in your host:

- In Maya you can find these options in the Subsurface Scattering Layer rollout shown in Figure 14.14.

- In XSI you find them on the Scattering tab shown in Figure 14.15.
- In 3ds Max you can find them in the Diffuse Sub Surface Scattering rollout shown in Figure 14.16.

External Shading

As discussed earlier, a Lambertian shading model is used for the diffuse color contribution, implemented with diffuse color and weight options in each host. A Phong shading model is used for specularity, and that is controlled with the specular color and shinyness options. The misss_set_normal shader is applied internally within the phenomenon shader tree and provides a connection for normal map bump mapping using a bump option without a need to pipe the normal map or bump shader through a misss_set_normal shader, as discussed earlier. These attributes are located in each host as follows:

Maya In Maya you can find the diffuse attributes under Unscattered Diffuse Layer. The specular attributes are in the Specular Layer rollout, and a Bump attribute is in the Bump Shader rollout. Figure 14.14 shows all of these. Note that to use the Bump attribute you simply attach a Maya 2D bump node to the Bump attribute as discussed earlier.

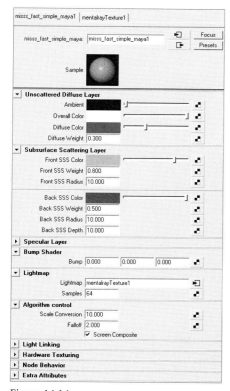

Figure 14.14

The Maya misss_fast_simple_maya shader UI

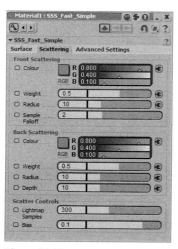

Figure 14.15

The XSI misss_fast_simple shader UI showing the Scatter tab

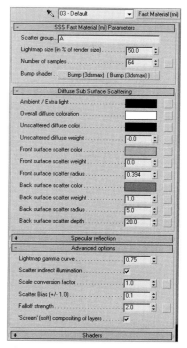

Figure 14.16

The 3ds Max SSS Fast Material (mi) shader UI

XSI In XSI you can find the diffuse properties under the Surface tab → Diffuse section and the specular properties under the Specular section, both shown in Figure 14.17. Because this is a a phenomenon material, it has a bump input, shown in Figure 14.5, where you can simply attach an XSI bump shader.

3ds Max In 3ds Max you can find the Diffuse parameters in the Diffuse Sub Surface Scattering rollout and the specular parameters in the Specular Reflection rollout. In the first SSS Fast Material (mi) Parameters rollout, you can find a Bump shader parameter where you simply map a bump map as with all 3ds Max shaders. Figure 14.16 shows all of these parameters.

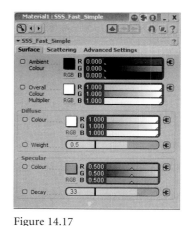

Figure 14.17

The XSI misss_fast_simple shader UI showing the Surface tab

Additional Options

The additional options reviewed here are key to generating good results with subsurface scattering. After you finish reading the chapter, you may want to quickly review these options and experiment with them in your host application.

LIGHT CONTRIBUTION

The ambient color option is used to add light to the overall external light influence, so it is added with the diffuse component just as with other shading models.

An overall color option acts as a color multiplier for all three color layers (diffuse, front, and back). Thus, the overall color affects the scattered and unscattered layers equally and can be used as an overall scaling factor for the color values across the surface. The image "Cardboard Subsurface Scattering" in the Chapter 14 folder on the CD utilizes texture and bump maps for several of the misss_fast_simple shader options. It shows the effect of a worn-out cardboard box that is placed on a source light, showing localized light transmission through the surface. In the case of the overall color, the texture map is used to scale the shader's influence across the surface, similar to a diffuse map in other shading networks. You might consider mapping it with an occlusion shader or grayscale shader to reduce the subsurface scattering in dense areas across the model and particularly in areas that exhibit indentations.

> The effect of light is not as pronounced in areas of indentation, and thus using a texture map to reduce the lighting effect within the indentations is warranted. You should use one global texture with the overall color and then use separate per-layer textures for each layer that also has variation in color.

CONTROLLING SCALE AND FALLOFF

A Scale conversion option is used to convert units of measurement to adjust for scale (volume). It is used to convert from scene units to a target unit. For example, to convert from inches to feet (12 inches = 1 foot) specify a value of 0.083, which is the conversion factor from inches to feet. You can find several conversion calculators online; you can find one of them here:

www.onlineconversion.com/length_common.htm

You can use the Scale conversion option "creatively" to control the distance-based options scale using a single option rather than adjusting each independently. It divides all the distance-based option values by the specified factor, which includes the front and back radius and the back depth options. In Figure 14.18, also placed in the color gallery and on the CD labeled "Subsurface Scale and Falloff", you can see the effects of changing the Scale conversion from a value of 1 in image A to a value of 10 in image B. As you can see, image B is brighter and shows more through scattering where you see more translucency. Figure 14.18 has a green color for front scattering and a red color for back scattering. In the color version you will notice that image B also appears predominantly red because the change in scale permitted more back scattering to penetrate. Since I increased the scale conversion to 10, I effectively changed the measurement for distance to one tenth of that shown in A, making the volume (distance through the surface) smaller.

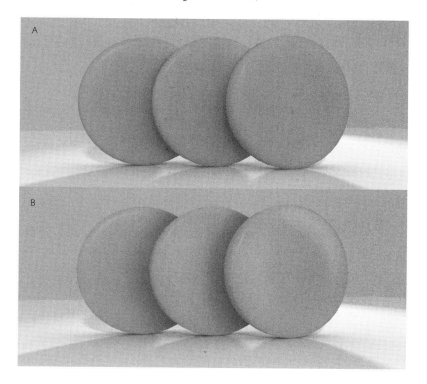

Figure 14.18

The effect of scale conversion on subsurface-scattering depth

An additional Falloff option is used to further define how light transitions from the sample point to the extent of a given radius distance, a topic discussed in more detail in the following section.

> When you are satisfied with all the settings and think the object should appear a bit smaller to show more scattering, or vice versa, rather than change each option's value, just scale the surface up or down using the scale conversion option, which is more manageable.

SSS SAMPLING

A Samples option is used to improve the quality of the SSS effect during rendering. It defines how many samples will be taken from the light map during rendering; higher values are used to eliminate artifacts caused by the subsurface layers. Specify values in powers of 2 that should range from 16 to 128. Typically a value of 32 is sufficient for most purposes. In Figure 14.19 you can see the same surface using 16 samples (image A) and 64 (image B). Even in grayscale, you can see that along the side of the surface in B the values appear brighter than in A, demonstrating more subsurface scattering. Thus, an increase in samples not only removes artifacts such as grain, but it also enhances subsurface scattering.

Figure 14.19

Increasing the samples from 16 (image A) to 64 (image B) improves the qualities of subsurface scattering.

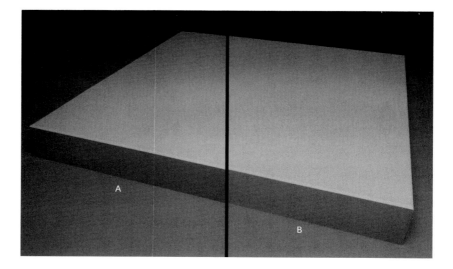

COMPOSITING THE LAYERS

Once the external and internal light scattering influences have all been calculated, they are combined using either a regular add operation (a+b) or a screen compositing operation (a+b − (a×b)). On the CD you can find the "Nuke Compositing" article from the *HDRI 3D* magazine that discusses the topic of math compositing in detail. When screen compositing is enabled, it essentially prevents overexposure by assuring values don't easily exceed a value of 1, if initially each individual component is not greater than 1, including the light source. Note that different light intensities in the scene and external shading influences also weigh in on the final result.

HOST APPLICATION OPTIONS

The options discussed earlier are located in each host application as follows:

Maya In Maya you find the Ambient and Overall Color attributes in the Unscattered Diffuse Layer rollout and the Scale Conversion, Falloff, and Screen Composite attributes are in the Algorithm Control rollout, as shown in Figure 14.14. The Sample attribute is in the Lightmap rollout, where you also see a light map texture file connected to the Lightmap attribute, supplied by the misss_fast_lmap shader as discussed earlier and in more detail later in this chapter.

XSI In XSI you find the Ambient Colour and Overall Colour Multiplier properties on the Surface tab, shown in Figure 14.17. The Scale (scale conversion) property is located on the Advanced Settings tab → Miscellaneous → Scale property. On the same tab when using the SSS_Fast_Skin material (it's not available with the SSS_Fast_Simple material), you will find the Use Screen Compositing for Colors property. On the Scattering tab, the Sample Falloff (falloff) property is on the Front Scattering section, and the Lightmap Samples property is in the Scatter Controls section, both shown in Figure 14.15.

3ds Max In 3ds Max you find the Ambient/Extra Light and Overall Diffuse Coloration parameters in the Diffuse Sub Surface Scattering rollout. The Number of Samples parameter (set to 64) is in the first rollout, and the Scale Conversion Factor, Falloff Strength, and Screen (soft) Compositing of Layers parameters are in the Advanced options rollout, as shown in Figure 14.16.

The Shader Math

When rendering, this shader composites the final result based on either screen compositing or an add function, as discussed earlier, depending on whether the screen composite option is enabled. I recommend using screen compositing for better results. The way this shader mathematically adds all the components is as follows:

1. The front and back layers are multiplied against the light map values to determine their influence on subsurface scattering.

2. The results from calculating the color values for the diffuse (ambient + diffuse), back, and front scattering components are added together based on the screen compositing option. If bump mapping has been applied, it will affect only the diffuse and specular color components.

3. The overall color is multiplied against the result of combining the three color components. When set to white, it has no effect because all the RGB colors (per layer) are multiplied by a value of 1.

4. Specular color is then added into the final result, providing the specular highlights. Again, it is affected by the bump map if present.

As cited earlier, both misss_fast_simple and misss_fast_skin are used with light maps. The light map provides even more options for adjusting how the light maps are rendered and thus also influence the final result. All in all, there are several ways to tweak the final result. Light maps are discussed in more detail shortly.

How Does It All Work?

When preparing your scene for subsurface scattering, you must consider how mental ray will calculate the results. Different lighting scenarios, scene scales, light intensities, and indirect illumination all influence the final result. All the light contributions are balanced against the shader settings for internal and external shading.

External Scattering

Figure 14.20 examines how nonphysical subsurface scattering works. The diffuse and specular shading components occur at the top level of the surface, externally as shown in the figure under "Diffuse to specular light reflection." Another component is bump mapping, which also occurs only at the top level of the surface, and hence has no influence on internal layers. You may also use displacement mapping with these shaders, which influences the different subsurface layers, external and internal, as it generates additional geometry during rendering (see the CD excerpt, "Surface Approximation Methods"). See the color gallery image labeled "SSS Displacement Mapping." It shows simple primitive cylinders that are displaced with a procedural texture, demonstrating how the SSS effect influences the displaced geometry.

Figure 14.20

The mental ray sub-surface layers

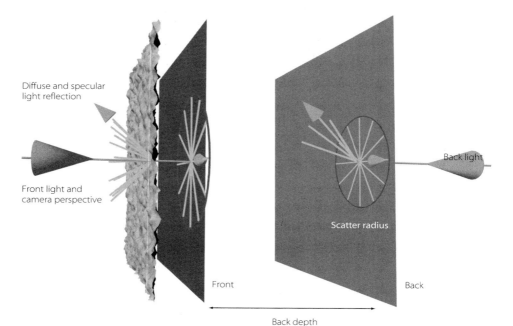

In Maya and XSI, you simply connect the displacement to the displacement input of SSS material (Maya shading engine using the Displacement Mat. attribute and in XSI using the SSS_Fast_Simple displace input shown in Figure 14.5). In 3ds Max you use the SSS Fast Skin Material + Displace (miss_fast_skin_d) shader to apply displacement mapping under the shader's parameters.

Internal Scattering

SSS shaders simulate light transmission that penetrates a surface, front and back, reflecting light internally and thus providing additional diffused light reflection beneath the surface's top level. The options in the SSS shaders labeled with the terms *front* and *back* always relate to the internal layers of the surface. The front layer is used for diffuse light transmission penetrating the front of the surface from the camera's point of view, as shown in Figure 14.20. The back layer refers to diffuse transmission that occurs from light penetrating the back of the surface toward the camera, hence illuminated by backlighting. Backlighting is then seen through the surface front. Thus front and back layers are relative to the camera's perspective.

It is important to note the back layer does not reflect light that transmits through the front layer and reflects from the back layer (toward the front) but instead reflects only light that transmits through the back side of the surface, as shown in Figure 14.20. An example would be a strong backlight illuminating a character causing its ears to appear reddish when viewed from the front. Thus, both front and back layers are based on the influence of source lights on their side of the surface. In this way, the nonphysical shader simulates subsurface scattering without actually calculating any internal reflection of bounced light. For this reason, light maps are used to provide information on the irradiance across the surface.

Next you'll look at the front and back Color, Radius, and Weight options, as well as the additional Back Depth option, to see how they operate while referencing the illustration shown in Figure 14.20 and some sample renders.

The front and back options in each host application are presented under the "misss_fast_simple" section earlier, illustrated in Figures 14.14 to 14.16.

FRONT AND BACK COLOR AND WEIGHT

The Weight option acts as a multiplier applied to the Color option's RGB value of each layer (front and back), providing control over color and intensity just as with diffuse color and weight. If the weight for either scattering layer is set to zero, that layer will not affect the render. The weight is used to balance how much each layer is affected by source lights that are aimed in its direction (front or back). If you have only backlighting in the scene, the front layer will not contribute any reflected light, because it does not receive any light. Thus, each of the layers, as well as the diffuse layer, can be perceived as shading models where the color and weight define their diffuse color and reflection intensity.

Once these layers have been calculated, they are added to the color from the diffuse layer based on each layer's weight and whether screen compositing is enabled. A layer with higher weight values will show more of its color. Thus, by balancing their weights, you also balance how much of the layer's color appears in the render. This should not be confused with balancing how much light can transmit through the surface, a topic discussed shortly in the "Back SSS Depth" section.

> For front and back layers you can use weight values that exceed 1, providing more intense subsurface scattering.

Aesthetics

The front layer acts as a shallow scattering layer that enhances standard shading models by providing you with a means to render much more natural-looking surfaces. The back layer adds to that effect by allowing you to simulate translucency. That is, the back layer allows you to reveal light and surfaces that are placed behind the SSS surface, showing through scattering. With surfaces that need to exhibit deep scattering with multiple reflections in a dense medium, the only solution is the physical shader.

The color section includes various examples of subsurface scattering. In "SSS Displacement Mapping," the displaced surfaces show a nice level of shallow scattering in a matte surface. This sort of render is impossible if you don't use SSS effects or have a BSSRDF shader as discussed at the beginning of the chapter. Another practical example is with marble tiles, discussed later ("The Marble Shader Tree").

> Even the simplest surfaces gain a great deal of realism when using SSS effects.

Using Lights to Control Transmission

Lights in the scene can be used as multipliers of the shader values for both internal layers; hence, a stronger light will greatly increase the scattering influence for the side to which it's applied. This means you can achieve a more "through" scattering either by adjusting the shader values, such as increasing the back layer's weight value, or by increasing the backlight intensity.

As discussed later in this chapter, you can select which lights affect the shader. In that context, aside from the mental ray shader option (Mode) that is used to specify which lights influence a shader, in each host there are host-specific tools that can be used to select which lights affect a surface. By doing so, you can manually adjust the effect of subsurface scattering using a light that affects only the SSS surface. In this way, you can increase its intensity significantly to show more through scattering without influencing other surfaces in the scene, such as the floor.

FRONT AND BACK RADIUS

The Radius option for both front and back layers defines the distance light will scatter from each point of contact, as illustrated in Figure 14.20. For each sample point, light values from the light map are sampled within that given radius. Higher sample values will acquire more color values and provide better sample results, as illustrated with the sampling example in Figure 14.19. With surfaces that exhibit a lot of curvature and back scattering, such as a sphere, increasing the radius will push the back layer's scattering color forward, literally wrapping around the sphere. Thus, lower radius values can provide for a finer effect, and higher values can be used to exaggerate the effect.

In Figure 14.21 you can see the same sphere rendered three times. The diffuse and front layer color and weights are set to zero, so they have no effect. The back layer color is set to white, and the weight is set to 1. In this way, you can examine the effect of radius with back scattering only.

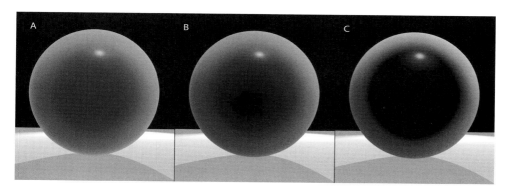

Figure 14.21

Controlling the spread and sharpness of the scatter effect using the Radius options

In image A the radius value is set to 50. As you can see, the white color from the back covers most of the front side of the sphere. In image B the radius value is 25, and you can see that the center of the sphere is darker, because the back scattering doesn't spread as far. In C the radius is set to 10, in this case demonstrating the other characteristic of radius, which is the "sharpness" of the effect. You can see that from images A to C the effect not only spreads less but also increase its sharpness along the sphere (the radius outline), and thus, with a smaller radius you will see more detail when using highly detailed models.

Why didn't the white color recede farther back toward the top of the sphere? That's because of the back depth value. Basically in label C you can see how far light penetrates through the sphere based on the depth, as discussed next. Thus, at the max transmission depth, lower radius values will not pull the color back; it will just further sharpen the effect.

With large radius values, you will need to increase the samples to remove grain. For example, in Figure 14.21 image A, I used 256 samples for rendering; in images B and C, which have smaller radii, I set Samples to 64.

The Falloff Option

The Falloff option, presented earlier for the host applications, defines how light transitions from the sample point outward within the radius region of effect. Thus, it is a radius sub-component that affects only the front layer. The higher the value, the sharper the falloff will appear along the outer edge of the radius. Lower falloff values, such as 1, provide a more linear gradation from the center of the radius to its outer edge. In Figure 14.22 you can see a sphere that is set up to show only front scattering. In this case it's a top-down view that examines the transition from the front to the back (bottom to top of the figure) using a large radius. In image A you can see that the transition is linear, because I set the falloff option to 1, and in image B the falloff is set to 15, where you see more light fill the radius region before it begins to transition toward the edge of the radius. Thus, this value sets a rate of falloff for the front layer's scattering along the radius distance.

Figure 14.22

Examining the effect falloff has on the front radius color transition from the center toward the outer edge. In image A the value is set to 1, and in image B the value is set to 15.

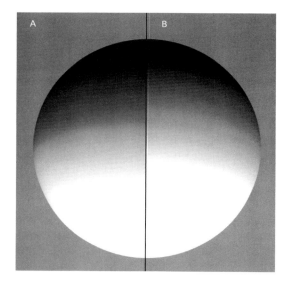

The falloff option affects only the front layer's radius falloff.

BACK SSS DEPTH

The Depth option (back depth) refers to a distance in scene units to which "through" scattering will be visible, as illustrated earlier in Figure 14.20. This means it defines the maximum distance scattered light from the back layer will appear through the front layer (facing the camera). Any distance beyond the depth value will not show "through" scattering. In Figure 14.23 you can see two renders of spheres, where the depth in image A is 10 and the depth in image B is 150. As you can see, in image B the spheres in the back penetrate through the frontmost sphere. However, in A they are not seen, because the depth distance is too low for them to transmit through the back. All we see is the front scattering influence, which appears as a darker color in the grayscale image.

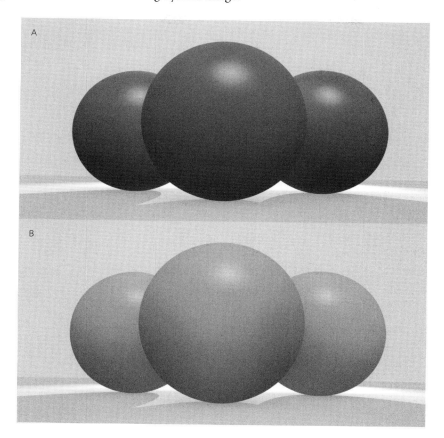

Figure 14.23

The effects on "through" scattering when changing the back SSS depth option

As these effects are more pronounced in color, if you look in the color gallery at the image "Back Scatter Transmission," you will see the same figure with an additional in-between step. In the color version, image A has a depth of 10, image B has a depth of 50 (the additional step), and image C has a depth of 150. The spheres share the same SSS shader, in which the front layer's color is set to green with a weight of 0.8, and the back layer's color is set to red with a weight of 1.

As you can see in image A, all the spheres appear green, showing only front-layer scattering. In image B you can see how the green and red colors begin to blend based on the front and back layer colors. In C you will notice that the spheres predominantly exhibit back scattering, showing much more orange. The higher the depth, the more pronounced the back scattering effect; however, it also depends on the weights set for each color.

Notice that the two back spheres occlude some of the backlight from reaching the front sphere. You can tell by looking at the areas along the front sphere, where you see the back spheres' shapes transmit through the front sphere. Those areas appear green because those back spheres are blocking the backlighting from passing through them and reaching the front sphere, essentially outlining their shapes through the front sphere. Thus, you can see how the front layer color is more predominant in those areas where backlighting is occluded.

BALANCING THE OPTIONS

Tweaking these values is a balancing act. Consider first that a weight of zero will force a color to be negligible. For example, a Diffuse weight of zero and Overall weight of 1 will show only the scattered light effect, assuming ambient and specularity are set to black. Also consider the following points when fine-tuning SSS effects:

- Fine-tuning SSS is a trial-and-error process with each surface. There is no "magic" value that always works; you need to experiment by first finding the right values and then enhancing the shader. You should start by setting the diffuse and front layer weights to zero and then work solely on the back layer. This process has the following advantages:

  - It provides a means to verify that the back light and back layer are providing "through" scattering. In the same context, Maya light maps may fail based on a poor setup; working in this way enables you to verify that the shader is operational.

  - By first working on the back layer, you can find the right settings for depth and radius, which become harder to fine-tune after you've texture-mapped the different components. Thus, first find the right values and then continue to enhance the shader.

- Follow the same process described earlier with the front layer after reducing the back layer weight to 0.

- More weight on the back layer instead of the front will make the back layer more pronounced (depending on the back light's intensity); as you increase the light's intensity, you will see more transmission through the surface.

- Increasing the sampling values will remove grain and enhance the subsurface effect by using more data from the light map.

- Final Gather (Chapter 13) works well with SSS effects; remember to enable the option in the SSS shader, as discussed in the following section.

- As discussed earlier, the scale conversion changes the way measurements are handled for SSS effects. Clearly it has a significant effect on the front and back radius and back depth options. If the values are not sensitive enough, you can increase the scale conversion to mimic a smaller volume that will show more "through" scattering.

In host applications, particularly 3ds Max, the default settings may not suffice to show any subsurface scattering at all. You should significantly increase the radius and depth values until you see the SSS effect; then work your way down. In 3ds Max I had to increase the default radius and depth values significantly to around a value of 50 before I saw the effect appear while testing a scene.

The Misss_Fast_Skin Phenomenon Shader

The misss_fast_skin phenomenon shader is an extension of the misss_fast_simple shader. It provides an additional layer of front scattering to simulate light that scatters within deeper layers of flesh, as illustrated in Figure 14.24. This shader handles three front-based layers:

- The skin's external diffuse and specular character, such as oily in nature.
- A shallow layer of scattering within the skin (*epidermis*).
- A deeper scattering within the flesh (*dermis*).

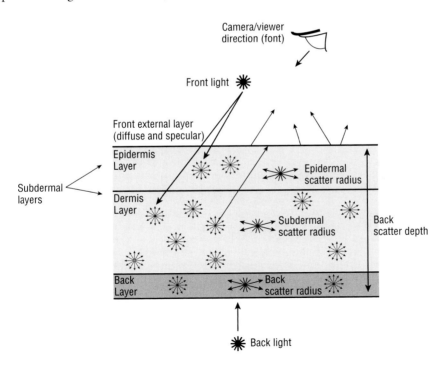

Figure 14.24

The misss_fast_skin shading components for skin shading

These layers account for front lighting only and are not affected by backlighting. In addition, as with the misss_fast_simple shader, you have the same back layer that provides through scattering. As you can see in the figure, the front external layer (diffuse and specular) handles external shading characteristics using diffuse color and weight, as well as the misss_skin_specular component shader options discussed earlier in this chapter.

The Epidermis and Dermis layers, which are subdermal layers, provide the appearance of internal scattering based on the front light's color and intensity, as discussed with the

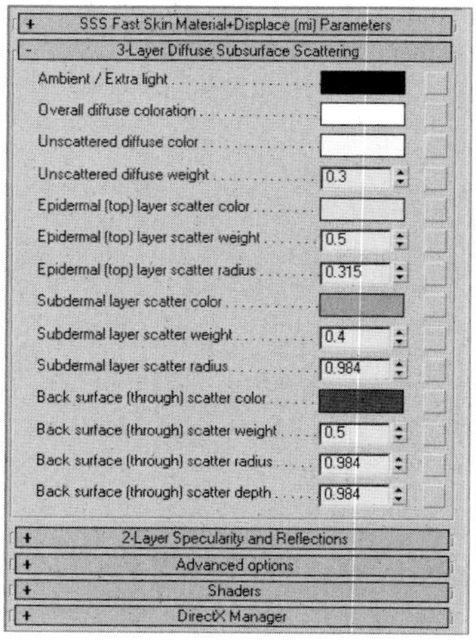

Figure 14.25

The misss_fast_skin shader options seen in 3ds Max

front layer in the previous section. Both have a radius option that depicts a 2D radius along the surface front. Thus, the radius does not expand vertically; it expands only horizontally along the surface. Remember, these shaders don't physically simulate internal scattering; instead, they use light map values to blend color values across a surface using, in this case, the epidermis, dermis, and back layer scatter color, radius, and weight options.

As you can see, the back scatter depth defines the distance required to transmit backlighting through the surface. Note that backlighting does not affect the epidermis and dermis (deep flesh) layers as with the simple shader.

Figure 14.25 shows the misss_fast_skin shader options in 3ds Max; they are the same in each host. As you can see, they look similar to the simple shader's options with the difference that you don't see any reference to a "front." The equivalent in this case consists of two layers (epidermis and dermis) that are labeled Epidermal (Top) Layer and Subdermal Layer Color, Weight, and Radius options. You also see the Back Surface (Through) Scatter layer options, which provide the "through" scattering. As noted earlier, all these options function exactly as with the front and back layers with the simple shader.

You can also see in the figure a rollout labeled 2-Layer Specularity and Reflections. It provides all the settings you need to control two layers of specular highlights and environmental/scene reflections, as discussed earlier in this chapter with the misss_skin_specular component shader, where you looked in detail at the characteristics of skin specularity.

The topic of preparing textures for skin is beyond the scope of this book and is covered in several online resources. Note that the Ballistic Publishing *Character Modeling* book has some great examples for different types of skin textures, how to prepare them, and for what purpose they are used. Such textures should be incorporated with all the color and weight options in the misss_fast_skin shader.

The next section shows how to control all the options associated with light map and gamma shaders.

Light Maps and the Light Map Phenomenon Shader

The misss_fast_lmap shader, shown in Figure 14.26, is used for light baking light maps using a mental ray texture node. The misss_fast_lmap shader is a combination of the misss_lightmap_write and misss_lambert_gamma component shaders discussed earlier. With the misss_fast_lmap shader, both depth and irradiance values are rendered into a single light map file, labeled mentalrayTexture1 in Figure 14.26 (connected to the Lightmap attribute), utilizing the RGB channels for irradiance and the alpha channel for depth. The light map stored with the mental ray texture shader (an image file) is connected to the SSS shaders for rendering SSS effects as shown in Figure 14.27, which is a subsurface shader tree in Maya.

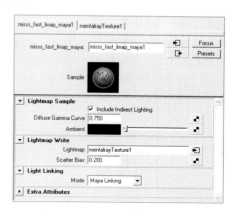

Figure 14.26

The misss_fast_lmap phenomenon light map shader

In Figure 14.27 you can see that the mental ray texture labeled B connects to the misss_fast_lmap shader's Lightmap input labeled A. You also see that the same mental ray texture connects to the misss_fast_simple shader (C) Lightmap attribute (shown connected in Figure 14.14). The misss_fast_simple shader is connected to a mental ray material as an illumination shader, as shown in Figure 14.27 and Figure 14.28, which is a mental ray material. You also see the misss_fast_lmap shader connected to the Light Map Shader input of the material. Thus, both shaders are connected as independent components of a mental ray material, just as with volume shaders, environment maps, and photon shaders.

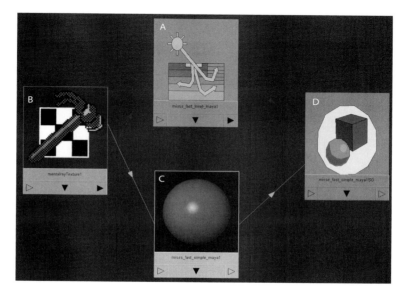

Figure 14.27

A SSS shader tree shown in Maya

Therefore, when rendering SSS effects, you are actually baking light maps before the rendering process can commence. Notice that the light map shader does not connect directly to the SSS shader; instead, the result of baking a light map (the mental ray texture) is connected to the SSS shader. Hence, both SSS and light map shaders are independent of each other. Essentially, you can divide the process of using light maps with SSS shaders into two stages:

1. The first stage is accomplished with a light map phenomenon shader or by using a combination of the light map write and gamma shaders that sample the light contribution across the surfaces, front and back.

2. The second stage uses the image generated (Figure 14.27 image B) with the light map shader as a texture file assigned to the SSS shader.

> SSS light maps do not require a surface to have unwrapped UVs, and thus light mapping (in this case) does not depend on surface UVs. By contrast, baking light maps such as those for indirect illumination require unwrapped UVs so that you can use them as textures. See the mental ray with Maya texture baking article on the CD. It covers techniques and concepts true to any host application.

With XSI and 3ds Max you don't need to concern yourself with this setup because the component light map and gamma shaders are applied internally within the SSS monolithic shaders, as discussed earlier. With Maya, you must apply these connections as illustrated in Figures 14.27 and 14.28 and further discussed in the sidebar "Creating SSS Shaders in Maya." Let's review the misss_fast_lmap shader options shown in Maya and then identify those options (from the component shaders) in XSI and 3ds Max SSS shaders.

THE MISSS_FAST_LMAP SHADER OPTIONS

The misss_lambert_gamma contribution to the misss_fast_lmap shader is shown in the Lightmap Sample rollout in Figure 14.26. It provides control over additional light contribution, light map gamma, and light linking (shown in the Light Linking rollout).

The Ambient color attribute adds ambient light to the light map itself (when generating light maps); note that this is different from the ambient color option discussed earlier with the misss_fast_simple shader, which is added with the diffuse color, determining the external light influence across the surface. In the same context, the Include Indirect Lighting attribute will account for the effect of Final Gather (if enabled) in light maps.

> You should choose to apply Final Gathering influence when enabled; it improves the quality of SSS effects.

Gamma Correction

The Diffuse Gamma Curve attribute will apply a gamma correction to the light map. See the section "Gamma Correction" in Chapter 3 for an explanation on gamma. Creatively speaking, it has the effect of flattening the light when using values less than 1, and values greater than 1 will increase contrast, as with gamma correction, which is applied globally to a render. Hence, gamma correction with light maps is used in the same way as with rendering to help tweak the gamma curve used while storing light values in a light map file. Note that these values typically should not exceed a range between 0.4 and 1.6.

Light Modes

mental ray light linking is applied with a Mode option. You typically find the "raw" mode option with custom mental ray shaders, mostly from online resources. Shaders implemented in host applications either offer more user-friendly options to link or detach lights from a surface or omit the option altogether.

With mental ray shaders, when you do see the Mode (or similar) option, a value of 0 uses all the lights in the scene, a value of 1 will use only the lights in the light list, and a value of 2 will use only lights that are not in the light list. Thus, if you select 1 or 2, you need to connect lights to the shader light list. With SSS shaders, XSI and 3ds Max handle it internally, linking all the lights that are assigned to affect the SSS surface based on the lights you added to the light list.

> In some previous versions of Maya, you can simply drag and drop the lights onto the Lights rollout → lights[0] attribute, which is a light list array.

The misss_lightmap_write Options

The misss_lightmap_write attributes are implemented on the Lightmap Write tab shown earlier in Figure 14.26. They provide an input for the light map file as well as control over a Scatter Bias attribute. The shader also handles another option derived from misss_lightmap_write, namely, the scatter group, which is not shown in Figure 14.26 because it is generated automatically with this light map phenomenon shader. The scatter group is particularly important and discussed in more detail for each host; it is available in the XSI and 3ds Max SSS monolithic shaders.

Scatter Bias is used to depict whether the light map will favor front or back scattering. Values less than zero favor back scattering ("through" scattering), and values greater than zero favor front scattering. Thus, the Scatter Bias attribute will affect how the misss_fast_simple front and back layers are balanced based on values that range from −1 to 1, where values closer to zero are recommended. It applies its effect while generating the light map file, not during the render stage, and hence is a light map-related feature.

In Figure 14.29 (available on the CD as "Subsurface Bias"), you can see the difference of using a negative bias value of -0.5 (B) and a positive value of 0.5 (A), where a stronger light is present behind the cylinders, displaying more through scattering. As you can see in image A, they appear darker and not as translucent as with B.

Figure 14.29

The effect bias has on subsurface scattering

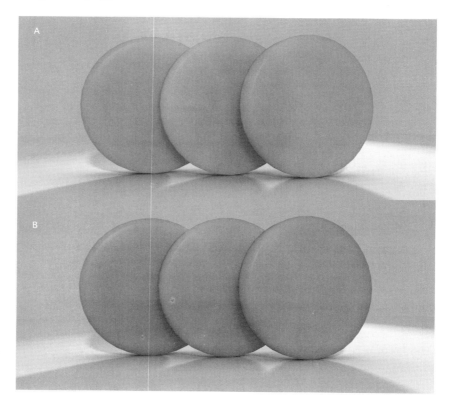

XSI and 3ds Max Light Map Options

In the next sections, I'll briefly point out the light map options in XSI and 3ds Max and then cover how you use them in the following section. In Maya you have already seen these attributes in the figures presented earlier.

XSI

In XSI under the SSS_Fast_Simple material or the skin material you can find the light map and gamma shader properties on the Advanced Settings tab, as shown in Figure 14.30.

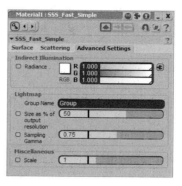

Figure 14.30

The light map and gamma properties for the SSS_Fast_Simple material in XSI

The Indirect Illumination → Radiance property defines the effect Final Gather (FG) will have on the surface when FG is enabled. It's a simple color multiplier so that as you decrease the color value from white, the Final Gather effect will decrease across the SSS surface. In the Lightmap section you can see the Group Name property text box, which is used to specify a scatter group name, as discussed further in the following section. The Size as % of Output property defines the ratio between the render resolution and the light map file; you should use values that range from 50 percent to 80 percent. The Sampling Gamma property refers to the gamma correction discussed earlier. Note that the Scale property refers to scale conversion as discussed earlier; it is part of the misss_fast_simple shader properties, not the light map properties.

On the Scattering tab you will find the Bias property, which implements the light map's scatter bias, as discussed earlier.

3DS MAX

In 3ds Max under the SSS Fast Material shader or the skin materials you can find the light map and gamma shader parameters in the SSS Fast Material (mi) Parameters and Advanced options rollouts, as shown in Figure 14.31.

Under SSS Fast Material (mi) Parameters, the Lightmap Size [in % of Render Size] parameter defines the ratio between the render resolution and the light map file; use values that range from 50 percent to 80 percent. The Scatter group parameter text box is used to specify a scatter group name, as further discussed in the following section.

In the Advanced Options rollout, the Lightmap Gamma Curve parameter implements gamma correction as discussed earlier. The Scatter Indirect Illumination parameter checkbox is used to enable Final Gather effects with the SSS shader as discussed earlier. The Scatter Bias [+/- 1.0] parameter refers to the light map's scatter bias, also discussed earlier.

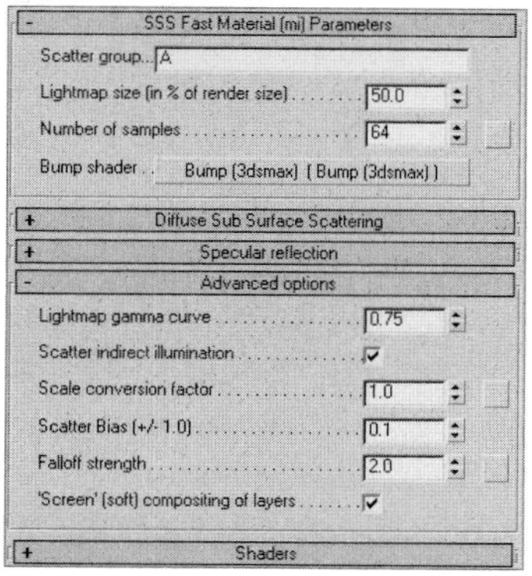

Figure 14.31

The light map and gamma parameters in the SSS Fast Material shader in 3ds max

Light Occluding Surfaces

Figure 14.32 shows an example of a sphere that contains additional primitive shapes that occlude light passing through the sphere. In such cases you may not want to use the SSS shader for internal surfaces, only the external SSS surface. For example, in this case I don't want to calculate SSS effects for the primitive shapes inside the sphere; I instead apply a Lambert shading model to them. To guarantee that internal surfaces influence the SSS effect, regardless of their shader, those surfaces must affect the light map. To clarify, the light map must consider all the surfaces that influence light scattering, and thus the internal surfaces must be connected to the light map shader so they are "seen" during the light map generation phase. Again, the illumination shaders for these additional surfaces are irrelevant. We are not interested in showing their SSS character; they are used only to block light from passing through the surface.

You can use this technique, for example, to render an X-ray image using internal surfaces that represent bones.

Figure 14.32

Using internal surfaces to occlude light from transmitting through the SSS surface

Internal surfaces need to conform to one of the following conditions, depending on the host application, so that the light map considers them during the generation phase:

- They are assigned with the same SSS (and light map shader in Maya) used for the external surface (less desirable).

- They are connected with the same misss_fast_lmap shader while using different illumination shaders (available only in Maya, as shown in Figure 14.33).

- They are assigned to the same scatter group in XSI and 3ds Max but are assigned with different SSS shaders. The same is true when using the light map and gamma component shaders in Maya, which have the scatter group attribute.

Specifying scatter groups enables mental ray to use several light map shaders (light map texture files) to provide adequate resolution and coverage for complex surfaces. Thus, the scatter group links the surfaces that influence each other together so that the surfaces influence light map files assigned to different surfaces.

Consider the steps in the following sections with each host application when you want to create internal occluding surfaces.

MAYA

With Maya you need to connect the same misss_fast_lmap light map shader (used with the subsurface shader) to the occluding surface's shading group's Light Map input. Follow the same workflow for creating and assigning light map shaders presented earlier (and further discussed in the "Creating SSS Shaders in Maya" sidebar). Thus, the only relevant factor is that the phenomenon light map shader is connected to their individual or shared shading group nodes as well as to the SSS shading group node, as shown in Figure 14.33.

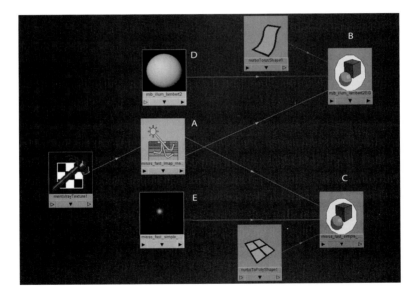

Figure 14.33

Connecting the misss_fast_lmap light map shader to different shading groups

As you can see in the figure, the misss_fast_lmap light map shader (A) connects to both shading groups B and C. The shading group B is connected with a Lambert shader (D) and thus used for the occluding surfaces. The shading group C is connected with the misss_fast_simple SSS shader (E), which is used for the external SSS surface and thus also assigned with the mental ray texture shown connected to both the miss_fast_lmap and misss_fast_simple shaders (A and E).

XSI AND 3DS MAX

Both XSI and 3ds Max have the same scatter group name option presented earlier and shown in Figures 14.30 and 14.31. You may assign an SSS shader (the misss_fast_simple or skin phenomenon shaders) to the external surface and a different SSS shader to the internal surfaces. For the internal surfaces, you can set the front layer and back layer weights to zero so they don't receive any internal shading. However, for them to influence the light map, you need to set both SSS shaders' scatter group names with the same name. Thus, the scatter group defines which group of surfaces influences the light map or several light map files as noted earlier. If you set both scatter groups with the name A, then the internal surfaces will affect the SSS effect. However, if you assign the external surface the name A and the internal surfaces the name B, those internal surfaces will not occlude any light from passing through the external SSS surface.

Note that you must use the SSS shader for the internal surfaces since you don't have access to the light map shader. Therefore, you can't choose to connect it to a material along with a simple shading model as with the Maya example earlier. You can apply the light map connection manually if you import the "raw" SSS shaders into your host application; however, the approach presented here accomplishes the same purpose. The only time it may not be adequate is if internal surfaces themselves have a custom shader that is aimed at showing specific external shading characteristics through the SSS surfaces, which becomes harder to accomplish when using the SSS shaders for internal surfaces.

CREATING SSS SHADERS IN MAYA

Maya connections for SSS are more complex than with XSI and 3ds Max. Basically you need to generate a simple shader tree that includes a SSS shader and a light map shader. You have already seen the shader tree and its connections in Maya in Figures 14.27 and 14.28. In Maya 2008, when you assign a surface with one of the SSS shaders, it automatically generates a shader tree with the SSS lightmap shader and lightmap texture for you. It also will ask you which lightmap shader you want to use when more than one exist in the scene. This process only simplifies the creation process as well as removes some of the problems of using mental ray textures in previous versions of Maya as discussed below. However, you should still know how to manually create and manage these shader trees for more control over your scene. Let's briefly go over a few steps that are required for building the shader, referring to those figures:

1. Create a simple scene that consists of a front light and a back light, a plane, and a simple primitive such as a sphere for SSS.

2. In the Hypershade window, create a misss_fast_simple_maya shader, and assign it to the SSS surface. Then select the SSS surface, and graph its network in the Hypershade window by choosing Graph → Graph Materials on Selected Objects. If you are using Maya 2008, delete the additional nodes (lightmap and texture) aside from the SSS shader.

3. In the Hypershade's Light Maps rollout, create a misss_fast_lmap_maya shader.

4. Connect the light map shader to the misss_fast_simple_maya shading engine (SG) in the mental ray rollout → Light Map Shader input, as shown in Figure 14.28.

5. Under the misss_fast_lmap_maya shader, click the Lightmap attribute's checkered box to automatically map it with a mental ray texture shader, as shown mapped in Figure 14.26 and Figure 14.27.

6. Next drag the mental ray texture node into the misss_fast_simple_maya → Lightmap Write rollout → Lightmap attribute, as shown connected in Figure 14.27. Note that you are not connecting the light map shader, just the mental ray texture node. The light map shader connects only into the shading group node, as discussed earlier.

You have now finalized all the crucial connections for the SSS shader tree. The following sidebar section deals with setting the mental ray texture shader attributes.

The mental ray Texture Shader Attributes

The mental ray texture shader needs to be set so that it can write a light map file to disk when you render. It is important you select a directory that has file write permissions. Usually in Windows it's not a problem, but with Mac OS X or Linux it is more likely you may select a directory that does not have write permissions.

You must apply the settings shown in this sidebar for subsurface scattering to work. If these attributes are not set appropriately, the shader will not render back layer scattering. Note that you will see front layer scattering render without a light map; however, it is not as effective as when you have a light map. Thus, the only guarantee the shader is functional is when you see the back layer's color appear.

In the mental ray texture shader attributes shown here, you must set the Texture Type attribute to Color, enable the Writable attribute, and under the File Size Depth attribute select 32 bits. The File Size Width and Height attributes are based on your render settings. Light maps are generated to account for both front and back sides of the surface. The light map wraps around the scene horizontally; hence, the width should be set to the size of the rendered width, and the height should be set to about half of the rendered height. These are not values that are set in stone; using larger light maps may improve quality, and lower values will improve render times.

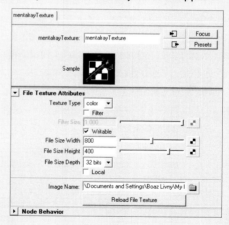

Finally, let's talk about the bug that gets us all, the light map filename. The best workflow is to leave the Local attribute disabled. Local will look for the file in the local project directory. In my experience, it is better to enter the root directory for the light map file without specifying a file extension; just specify the filename. You can copy and paste the path from a file browser for accuracy. Note that once you paste the path in the Image Name text box, continue to type a light map filename before you press Enter.

continued

Here is an example for a path on Linux or Mac OS X:

//users/yourUser/documents/maya/projects/myProject/mentalRay/lightMap/LightmapName

Here is an example for a path on Windows:

```
\Documents and Settings\user name\My Documents\maya\projects\project name\
renderData\mentalRay\lightMap\lightmapName
```

If you are using the default drive, for example the C drive on a PC, the best workflow is to leave the Local attribute disabled. If you use another drive such as D, however, you should copy and paste the path as shown earlier; after you enter the path, enable the Local attribute. You should see that the local path only remains in the text box with the filename you specified. I store Maya projects on an S drive and not in the standard C project directory, which has always worked for me.

Test-render your scene. You should see subsurface scattering. If you don't see the SSS effect, review the notes in "Balancing the Options." If you still see no effect, delete the texture file node and create another. Sometimes if this node fails, it is best to create a new one (it's just one of those troubleshooting things). Most likely there is a problem with the path and mental ray can't access or navigate that path.

Reusing Light Map Files

Once a light map is calculated, you don't need to reevaluate it with each render. Thus, if the light intensity and camera angles don't change, you can disconnect the light map from the shading group and disable the Writable attribute under the mental ray texture (the texture is still assigned to the SSS shader). By doing so, you will use the existing light map with each render and save time by not recalculating light maps every time you render. You can do that while tweaking the SSS weight, radius and depth values; however, if you are going to render an animation, you should reconnect the light map and enable the Writable attribute, because the relationship between the camera, lights, and surface will change with each frame.

When Using the Component Shader

If you use the misss_fast_shader component shader for designing your own subsurface shader, you should still use the misss_fast_lmap light map shader instead of the misss_lightmap_write and gamma component shaders. In this case, follow the steps shown in this sidebar for creating the misss_fast_lmap light map shader and mental ray texture shader, and then connect the mental ray texture to the misss_fast_shader→ Data Storage rollout → Lightmap and Depthmap attributes shown here, applying the same mental ray texture to both inputs.

An Advanced Shader Tree

This example should give you some insight into the importance of color mapping as well as value mapping (weight option) for controlling the appearance of SSS shaders. It also demonstrates how you can expand on SSS shaders with other shaders, and thus you'll see that you are not limited to simple SSS networks. The example is a shader tree for marble, such as for tiled floors.

In most cases, marble is better simulated with the physical shader since it's a thick and dense surface. However, with surface tiles (such as floors, bathrooms, and so on) most of the scattering can be simulated using a shallow layer and not a deep level of internal scattering. You definitely don't see "through" scattering from the back to the front.

In the color gallery, look at "Marble SSS Plate," where the same misss_fast_simple shader was used for both images. In image A, the front and back layers are set so they have no influence (weight of zero), which is the same as using a standard shader, such as the architectural material. In image B, the front layer is set to have influence. The back layer is irrelevant because the surface is a floor and doesn't receive any backlighting. (Also, light cast through the back layer would give the appearance of a translucent surface and lose the feel of a thick heavy tile.) For deep scattering, I could use only the physical shader, as cited earlier. Notice that the bump is softer and you see more light from a warmer texture reflecting through the external layer, particularly along the side of the tile.

To generate the feel of a surface that shows more scattering in certain areas as well as bump and the very glossy reflections, I use several shaders in a shader tree.

The Marble Shader Tree

The shader tree shown in Figure 14.34 is an example of the approach you can take when designing SSS shaders. It is based on mental ray and host-specific shaders that are discussed in Chapters 9 through 12 in detail. Instead of using letters to label the nodes, I used shorthand names so it will be easier for you to examine the tree. Each label indicates the purpose of the shader.

The SSS Connections

The *misss* label refers to the misss_fast_simple phenomenon shader, which is at the heart of this shader tree. You can see that the misss_fast_lmap phenomenon light map shader (labeled Lmap) connects to the material's light map input (not required in XSI and 3ds Max). The lmap shader is responsible for producing the light map file, labeled Lmap file. The lamp file is then connected to the SSS (misss) shader light map input. I discussed all of these connections earlier in the chapter with light maps and SSS shaders on a host basis.

Figure 14.34

The shader tree used
to generate the
marble illustrated
in the color gallery
as "Marble SSS"
image B

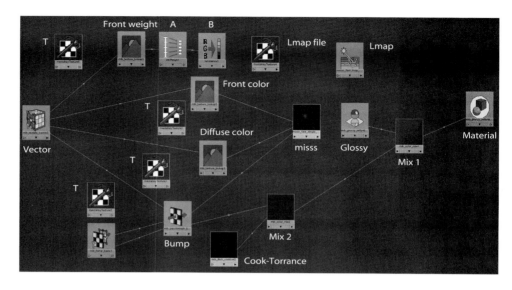

The diffuse color, front layer color, and front layer weight on the SSS shader are
mapped with color textures of marble using mental ray lookup shaders (image loaders),
each connected with a mental ray texture file that loads the relevant texture file (mental
ray texture files are labeled *T*). You can also see that all the lookup shaders and bump
pass-through shader share the same texture vector node, labeled Vector. Thus, they all
share the same UV mapping properties.

The front color is mapped with a darker version of the diffuse color image, and its color
is somewhat warmer for the purpose of internal scattering. You can see cutout sections of
the textures in Figure 14.35. Note that because you can't see color, only the diffuse texture
(labeled A) is displayed without including the front color texture.

Figure 14.35

A portion of the tex-
ture maps used for
the shader tree

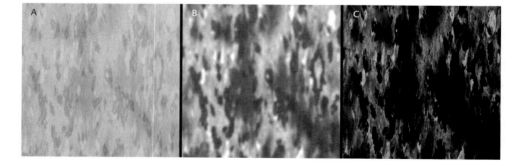

At the top of Figure 14.34 you can see the lookup shader labeled Front Weight, which is
a grayscale version of the diffuse color texture that has been adjusted in Adobe Photoshop,
shown in Figure 14.35 image B. This texture is passed through a set range shader (labeled
A) to adjust the maximum and minimum value for the front layer weight so that the

weight is not entirely dependent on the texture's color values. I set the low and high ranges to 0.1 and 0.45. Thus, the front layer weight will not exceed those values. Also, because the weight is a scalar value, the set range is passed through a luminance shader (labeled B in Figure 14.34) that outputs a single value, much like an alpha channel. That value is then mapped to the SSS shader's front weight value. In Chapter 10, "mental ray Shaders and Shader Trees," the brushed metal example demonstrated using these types of host-specific support shaders with XSI and 3ds Max; you should be familiar with the equivalent shaders in XSI and 3ds Max.

> The front weight is one of the most important shaders in the tree. It maps various intensities that are used to define how much SSS we see through the marble. Areas on the marble that are brighter will show more scattering than areas that are darker. Thus, grayscale values passed with the weight texture map will control the internal scatter intensity (weight) based on the marble's brightness. It provides a richer mix between the external and internal scattering values. This type of mapping benefits from using 3D textures, such as the mental ray turbulence shader, that apply random texture values across the surface using a 3D projection.

Specular Highlights and Bump Mapping Connections

The last texture, shown in Figure 14.35 image C, is used for the external bump mapping shown in the lower portion of the figure. In the shader tree, you can see that the bump texture (lowest T) connects to the mib_passthrough_bump shader labeled Bump, which is also connected with the mib_bump_basis (below the bump texture T) shader and the texture vector shader, which is a typical bump map tree with mental ray shaders.

I connected the bump shader to the SSS shader's bump option, providing external bump mapping. Since it's a mental ray bump shader that produces perturbed normal outputs (see the "misss_set_normal and Bump Mapping" section) and the misss_set_normal is integrated within the SSS phenomenon shader, as discussed earlier, the bump shader can connect directly to the SSS phenomenon shader. I also use the bump map with a Cook-Torrance shader to provide better specular highlights for the surface, rather than relying on the SSS shader specular option, which is a Phong model. To apply it, I connected the Cook-Torrance shader to the Color_0 input of a mib_color_mix shader (labeled Mix 2) and connected the pass-through bump shader to the Color_base input of the color mixer with the mode set to blend. In this way, the Cook-Torrance highlights will also be affected by bump mapping.

Only Maya requires these complex mental ray shader trees for bump mapping; other hosts offer alternative means that are easier to use for bump mapping. In XSI you simply connect to the SSS shader's bump input shown earlier in Figure 14.5, and in 3ds Max you apply the bump mapping internally using the Bump shader parameter shown in Figure 14.31. The example is aimed at helping you design your own shader.

With Maya the mib_bump_basis U and V attribute outputs connect to the mib_passthrough_bump_map shader's U and V attribute inputs; use the Connection Editor window to apply these connections. The mib_texture_vector output connects to the mib_passthrough_bump_map shader's coord input. The mental ray texture is then mapped to the mib_passthrough_bump_map tex attribute. See Chapter 11, "mental ray Textures and Projections," for more details and example files.

Glossy Reflections and the Material Connection

I connected the misss shader to the mib_glossy_reflection shader labeled "Glossy" to obtain glossy environmental reflections. Thus, the SSS (misss) shader connects to the Base_material input of the glossy shader (see Chapter 10, "mental ray Shaders and Shader Trees," for glossy shaders). I then connected the glossy shader to Color_base input of another mib_color_mix shader, labeled Mix 1. The other color mix shader (Mix 2) is then connected to the Color_0 input (in the Mix 1 shader), and the mode is set to add the two colors together. Finally, the color mix shader (Mix 1) connects to the material as an illumination shader.

In this way, I layered the Cook-Torrance highlights with glossy reflections and subsurface scattering, where all the significant color components have been mapped with appropriate shaders. You can see the result in the color gallery as "Marble SSS" image B.

Physical Subsurface Scattering

In Chapter 12's "Participating Media (PM) Effects" section, I discussed how light that passes through a turbid medium exhibits different levels of absorption and scattering as well as anisotropic or isotropic transmission. Realistic characteristics of light transmission through turbid media such as in liquids or through highly translucent surfaces (such as marble or jade) are simulated using the physical shader. The difference between participating media (PM) effects and the physical shader is that the physical shader is better geared (optimized) toward addressing internal scattering within a medium such as a drink (milk, beer, grape juice, and so on) or through a more solid surface (such as jade, opals, wax, and so on). Both shaders deal with simulating realistic light transmission through a given medium, accounting for internal isotropic or anisotropic scattering, in or out scattering, and absorption levels.

See "The Water Bottle," "Candle Physical SSS," and "Jade Physical SSS" in the color gallery for example renders using the physical shader and caustics.

Essentially, all the previous discussions about light characteristics (reflection and transmission), shading models (BSSRDF vs. BSDF), ray marching, and rendering volume effects using PM effects can be thought of as an ongoing introduction to the physical SSS shader. The physical SSS shader, which is a wavelength-dependent shader (see Chapter 9, "The Fundamentals of Light and Shading Models"), is the most accurate shader available within host applications for simulating realistic subsurface scattering with mental ray, but it should be used only when you require rendering highly realistic (accurate) translucent surfaces that exhibit deep scattering such as with liquids.

> The physical SSS shader is not an easy to use shader; you will need to base values on empirical data more so than "guesstimating" ad hoc values.

Overview of the mental ray Physical Shader

This section presents a general overview of using the physical shader, along with scene setup considerations. The following sections will then present a detailed review of the physical shader's options and approximation algorithms.

The mental ray physical shader uses photons to record the transmission of light through a surface, and thus it requires enabling one of the indirect illumination techniques (GI or caustics) that generate photons in the scene. As with indirect illumination PM effects, a ray marching technique is used to determine the influence of light at each photon intersection. To clarify, photons are scattered within the surface volume relying on certain user defined parameters, and ray marching is used to evaluate the photon's contribution to light along the path it takes from the point of entering the surface.

The physical shader also casts GI and caustic photons back into the scene just as with other surfaces that participate in indirect light simulations, with the difference that several photons are also stored internally within the surface. Thus, the purpose of photons is divided between two tasks:

- Photons are stored within the volume and are not affected by GI or caustics global scene options, only by the options set with the physical shader.

- Photons that are reflected from or refracted through the surface into the scene are handled with their corresponding indirect illumination method (GI or caustics). These photons carry energy that has been influenced by the volume back into the scene.

Typically you should use caustics if you want to render an image that displays the effect of light transmitting through a liquid in addition to the caustic effect generated through the liquid's container (the glass itself). Otherwise, it does not really matter which method you select (GI or caustics) for the physical shader, just that it receives a decent amount of photons from a photon emitting source light.

In the color image "Candle Physical SSS," you can see the increase in irradiance along the walls in areas that are in shadow (from the candle top and down). The warm light patterns are a direct result of caustic photons that are emitted from the candle after transmitting through the candle's volume. As you can see, caustic photons have acquired color properties (photon energy) from the candle, realistically mimicking the visual effect of a candle as a source for illumination after light transmits through it. In addition, global illumination was used, which provides the diffused indirect lighting in those areas that are then enhanced with the caustic photons.

> You should first gain some experience with managing indirect illumination scenes before attempting to use them with this shader; see Chapter 12, "Indirect Illumination."

Scene Setup

Because the physical shader is based on casting photons into a volume that represents the turbid medium, the volume should be a closed surface with normals aimed outward, as with a default cube or cylinder in each host. As cited earlier, you should enable either global illumination or caustics. You may decide to enable both features, using GI to apply indirect lighting globally in the scene and caustics for controlling the photon distribution within the physical shader's individual surface. In this way you can provide a general distribution of photons in the scene with GI in addition to a more focused distribution of photons in the turbid medium with caustics. Ideally you will cast caustic photons through a spot light that encompasses within its perspective the SSS surface, similar to the approach with caustic scene setups discussed in Chapter 12, "Indirect Illumination." You will guarantee a high distribution of photons within the SSS surface.

If you look at Figure 14.36, also available in color on the CD as "Milk and Ketchup," many photons are required to simulate light within a liquid (milk) that possesses a lot of deep scattering. The ketchup, however, absorbs more light and shows less internal scattering so that fewer photons are required.

In the figure, a dielectric shader is used for the outer glass surfaces, and the physical SSS shader is used for the milk and ketchup surfaces. In Figure 14.37 you can see the outlines used for the glass and milk surfaces. Notice how the milk surface is placed near the glass outline, but it does not overlap with the glass surface (inner) outline. It's important that the physical shader's surface does not overlap with other surfaces, such as the glass surface in this case, or you will see artifacts appear in the rendered image. The same is true when using transmat shaders with PM effects. For the color render, the liquid's outline was much closer to the glass than illustrated in Figure 14.37, maintaining a minimal gap between both surfaces. You can also see the normal direction marked with the letter N for both surfaces.

Figure 14.36

Physical shader renderings of milk and ketchup using empirical data

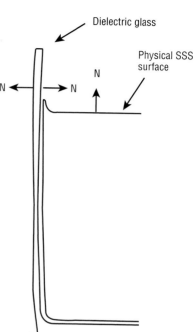

Figure 14.37

Surface outlines for a glass surface and its liquid content (physical SSS surface)

Host Application SSS Physical Shaders

Before we examine all the physical shader options, let's first locate the shader in each host application. As with other examples, these options are labeled in a similar way in each host. Maya and 3ds Max use the mental ray naming conventions, and XSI has renamed some of the options. I'll review the physical shader using the mental ray shader options in Maya and refer to other host specific comments (naming conventions) when necessary. You can find the shaders in each host application as follows:

Maya In Maya, in the Hypershade window, you can find the physical shader in the Create mental ray Nodes rollout → Materials → misss_physical shader. Figure 14.38 shows the shader attributes.

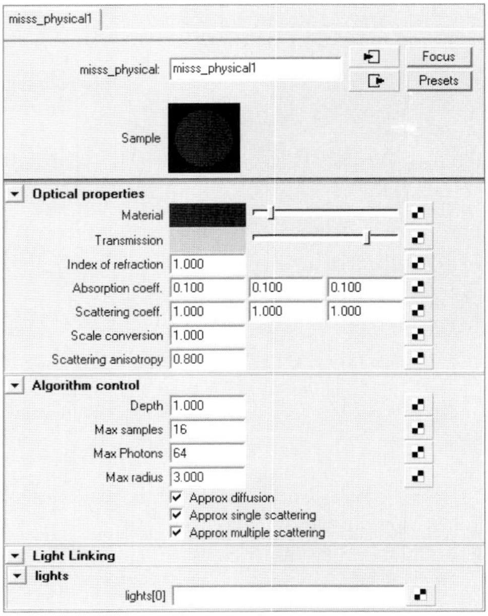

Figure 14.38

The mental ray physical SSS shader options in Maya

XSI XSI provides two preset physical shaders (the same shader in both cases) where one is preset for rendering a liquid (milk) and the other set for rendering jade. You can find both preset shaders by navigating from the Render Tree window and choosing Nodes → Illumination → More, which opens the file browser. In the Subsurface directory you will find both shaders (Jade and Skim_Milk). Basically, both shaders provide a good starting point for rendering but are not constrained in any way to a particular material type. Thus, you can change the values to represent any material type. Figure 14.39 shows the physical shader properties (Skim_Milk shader).

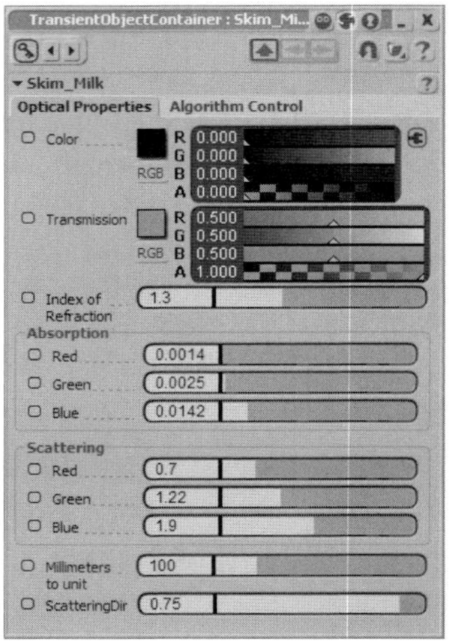

Figure 14.39

The mental ray physical SSS shader properties in XSI with the Skim_Milk preset shader

One difference between the skim milk and jade shaders, apart from their shader values, is that the jade also is created with an additional Phong specular shading model that is connected to the material input, as discussed in the following sections.

3ds Max In 3ds Max you can find the physical (monolithic) shader in the Material Editor → Get Material → SSS Physical Material (mi). You can see the mental ray physical shader parameters in Figure 14.40.

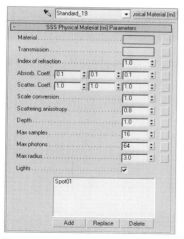

Figure 14.40

The mental ray physical SSS shader parameters in 3ds Max

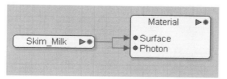

Figure 14.41

The physical shader needs to be connected to both illumination (material) and photon shader inputs in host applications.

In all host applications the mental ray physical shader needs to be connected to the illumination and photon shader inputs of a mental ray material, as illustrated in XSI in Figure 14.41. In XSI and 3ds Max this connection is applied automatically (by default), and in Maya you need to drag and drop the misss_phyiscal shader onto the Shading Engine's Photon shader attribute, as with other GI shader setups.

Scattering Approximations and Photons

In the section "The BSSRDF Light Transport model" earlier in this chapter, I introduced some of the concepts for simulating physically correct subsurface-scattering effects, such as single and multiple scattering. The physical shader uses these concepts internally for simulating subsurface scattering and also divides multiple scattering into two separate components—multiple scattering and diffusion approximation. Thus, the physical shader uses three separate approximations to calculate the internal transmission of light—single scattering, multiple scattering, and a diffusion approximation, as illustrated in Figure 14.42. Each focuses on a different aspect of light transmission, and collectively they provide for robust subsurface-scattering effects.

As you can see in the figure, single scattering deals with direct refractions through the material, and multiple scattering deals with simulating internal scattering within the turbid medium using photons (bouncing light around) until the photons are either fully absorbed, exit the surface, or penetrate the deep layer. If a photon penetrates the deep layer, the diffusion approximation is used to calculate isotropic scattering without simulating any additional light scattering (no additional bounces). I'll discuss each approximation in detail in the following sections.

Figure 14.42

The three different approximation algorithms used to render subsurface effects with the physical shader

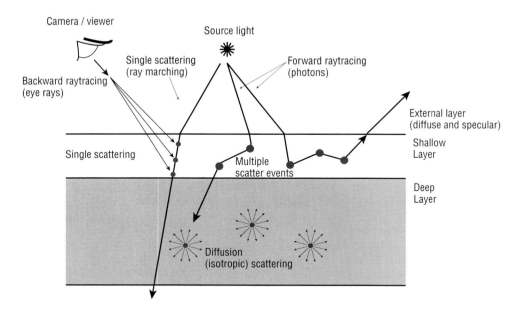

Figure 14.42

The three different approximation algorithms used to render subsurface effects with the physical shader

It's important to note that different materials display different levels of multiple or single scattering. For example, a surface that exhibits a lot of internal scattering, such as skin, pasta, or ketchup, will make more use of the multiple and diffusion scattering approximations than the single-scattering approximation. The *single scattering* term is for more translucent materials that refract a lot of light through the surface while maintaining a more glossy to specular appearance than a fully glossy appearance, such as with plants (leaves), dirty water, oil, or paper. I'll first show how these approximations are enabled or disabled in host applications and then review each approximation as well as other related options.

Figure 14.43

XSI physics shader Algorithm Control tab where you can enable the different internal scattering algorithms

I recommend you read the entire section on physical SSS while identifying the shader options in your host, before using it for rendering.

Enabling Scatter Algorithms

You can enable any of the three algorithms in Maya and XSI using the checkbox options labeled Approx Diffusion, Approx Single Scattering, and Approx Multiple Scattering, which refer to diffusion, single, and multiple scattering algorithms, respectively. Figure 14.37 showed these attributes for Maya, and Figure 14.43 shows them enabled in XSI (on the physical shader's Algorithm Control tab). 3ds Max uses a phenomenon shader that omits these options; all three are always enabled.

By enabling or disabling either algorithm, you can isolate the effect in a way that allows you to better fine-tune each component without being distracted by the overall effect of using all three approximations at once.

There are some slight differences when you enable or disable the diffusion or multiple scattering approximations. For example, when multiple scattering is enabled, if you disable just the diffusion approximation and render again, the result will appear slightly different.

Single-Scattering Approximation

Single-scattering approximation deals with the refraction of light through a turbid medium, where the path of light remains constant, as illustrated in Figure 14.42. In other words, light doesn't bounce around; it only transmits through the surface. Thus, with single scattering, light perturbs (changes direction) only once as it refracts into the surface. Consider that when single scattering is predominant, multiple scattering and diffusion are naturally less predominant, allowing a more focused beam of light to transmit through the surface.

Figure 14.44 shows a rendered example of the single approximation algorithm. As you can see, a spot light with a small cone angle is focusing light through the candle from the top (image A; the arrow represents the spot light direction). You can then see the light reappear on the opposite side of the surface (B) as it exits the surface. (Note that an additional light source with some ambient light from the shader is used so that you can see the entire surface.) Since the single-scattering approximation does use photons, it can't simulate a "beam" of light transmitting through the surface (illuminating particles suspended within a volume); it can only draw the light intensity along the surfaces' (inner or outer) geometry, as shown in Figure 14.44. In other words, single scattering applies its effect across the geometry, whereas the multiple and diffusion approximations apply their effects using photons anywhere internally within a volume area (the geometry), illuminating suspended particles within matter. Since Figure 14.44 is used for demonstrating only single scattering, the other two approximations and photon casting (caustics or GI) are disabled.

Photon casting is irrelevant with single scattering just as direct lighting is irrelevant with the multiple and diffusion approximations.

SINGLE-SCATTERING SAMPLING

As noted earlier, the single-scattering approximation is a raytracing technique that does not utilize photons. It acts like standard refractions with an additional ability to draw the attenuation of light through the surface using ray marching to determine irradiance over a given distance. In this way, it can calculate the intensity of light on the other side of the surface, based on the distance it passes through the surface. Segmented shadows use a similar approach to evaluate the effect of shadows through volumes, as discussed in Chapter 7, "Shadow Algorithms." In Figure 14.44 you don't really see a decay of light through the surface because I used a strong source light to exaggerate the effect for illustrative purposes; otherwise, the light intensity would appear much lower on the opposite side.

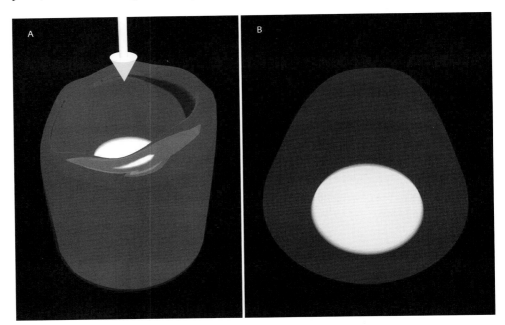

Figure 14.44

The single-scattering approximation focuses light on a candle (A) and transmitting through the candle (B).

The Max samples option, shown in each host (Figures 14.38, 14.39, and 14.43), affects both single scattering and multiple scattering. With single scattering, it defines the number of samples taken (ray marching) per eye ray. It improves the quality (appearance) of light attenuation on the surface. The higher the value, the more samples are taken; typical values range from 5 to 30. You'll look at this option in more detail with multiple scattering.

> Since Max samples is used with both single and multiple scattering, you should prioritize the value for multiple scattering because its effect on single scattering is rather subtle.

Multiple Scattering and the Diffusion Approximation

The multiple and diffusion approximations are tied closely together both in the physical shader's options and in how they share (pass) photons. The following section examines multiple scattering and the diffusion approximation characteristics with the physical shader options that define the surface's optical properties and control photonic distributions.

The multiple-scattering approximation deals with bouncing photons internally within a given depth, referred to as the *shallow layer* in Figure 14.42. Eventually, the photon will be completely absorbed internally, penetrate the deep layer, or exit the surface where the photon may continue to affect the scene. Again, the color image "Candle Physical SSS" demonstrates how caustic photons emit into the scene from the candle (photons that exit the volume area) and affect the walls.

The significant technical difference between single scattering, multiple scattering, and the diffusion approximation is that the multiple-scattering and diffusion approximations rely solely on photons to determine irradiance within the volume. Thus, you tweak photons as with global illumination and caustics using the following physical shader options, shown in Figures 14.38, 14.39, and 14.43 (as well as the photon-emitting light's photon energy and count):

- Max samples (in this context it defines the amount of bounces in the surface)
- Max Photons
- Max Radius (Maximum Photon Search Radius in XSI)

Once photons enter the surface's volume, they reflect internally (bounce around) based on the following physical shader options (labeled the same in Maya and 3ds Max), shown in Figures 14.38, 14.39, 14.40, and 14.43.

- Scattering coeff. (Scattering → Red, Green, and Blue in XSI)
- Absorption coeff. (Absorption → Red, Green, and Blue in XSI)
- Scatter anisotropy (ScatteringDir in XSI)
- Depth (Deep Layer Depth in XSI)
- Scale conversion (Millimeters to unit in XSI)
- Max samples (in this context it defines the appearance of internal scattering)

All these options contribute to internal scattering, defining the material's substance. However, the most significant options that define the probability of a photon being absorbed or scattered within the material are wavelength dependent (RGB) absorption and scattering coefficients (discussed shortly); they define the material's optical properties, particularly its translucency level (amount). Controlling optical properties is covered in the "Optical Properties" section later in this chapter.

In Figure 14.45 you can see a box placed on a floor; this scene is used with the physical shader in several of the following examples. A spot light is placed on top of the box

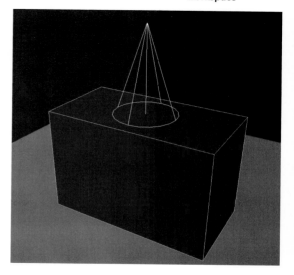

Figure 14.45

The scene used for several of the following examples, as it appears in the workspace

and focuses light onto a small portion of the box. Note that although the floor appears bright, it's affected by a separate point light that doesn't influence the box (and is not used with the physical shader).

Figure 14.46 displays three renders of the scene (color version available on the CD). In image A you see solely the diffusion approximation, and in image B you see solely the multiple-scattering approximation. In image C you see the combination of both approximations. Notice that the diffusion approximation's irradiance appears darker than the multiple-scattering irradiance, because it deals with photons that have already lost energy and are located deep within the material. In many cases, the diffusion contribution to the overall effect appears as small subtleties that extend the irradiance internally, providing more coverage within the surface. These differences between multiple scattering and the diffusion approximation will become clearer after you've reviewed the following examples.

Figure 14.46

The multiple scattering (A), diffusion (B) approximation, and the total of both approximations (C)

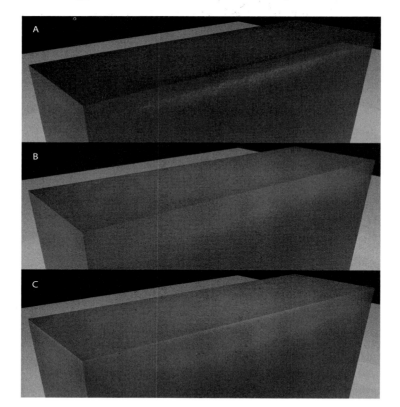

SCATTER DEPTH

First I need to define exactly how depth influences the transition from multiple scattering to the diffusion approximation. In other words, how exactly does it work, and why even bother using a diffusion approximation?

If you're using a diffusion approximation, the assumption is that after a given number of internal reflections and past a given transmission depth, you can calculate more efficiently (in render time and thus processor efficiency) the subsurface effect using a diffusion approximation. This approximation provides solely isotropic light scattering, enhancing the feel of irradiance deep within the material while benefiting from the fact that the diffusion approximation is a faster more efficient rendering approximation than multiple scattering. With respect to isotropic scattering, I'll further discuss isotropic and anisotropic scattering with single and multiple scattering in the "Optical Properties" section later in this chapter.

The Depth option, shown within each host in Figures 14.38, 14.39, and 14.43, defines a critical depth; past that depth, photons are handled solely with the diffusion approximation. This distance reflects the total depth a photon may travel into the surface before the diffusion approximation is used. In Figure 14.47, you can see the same scene used for the earlier example, this time displaying solely the diffusion approximation. The figure is rendered so you are looking at the box from a frontal view, and thus it appears flat; the purpose is for you to see how photons scatter from a frontal perspective. In image A depth is set to 2, and in image B depth is set to 5. As you can see, there is a clear line along the top that defines where the diffusion approximation initiates, controlling photons from that point and downward to the bottom of the box.

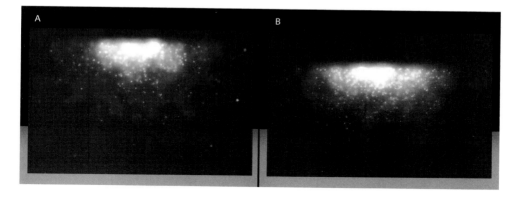

Figure 14.47

Changing depth from a value of 2 (A) to 5 (B) pushes the diffusion approximation deeper into the surface.

Depth is a scale-dependent option; see the discussion on scale conversion in the "Optical Properties" section later in this chapter.

MULTIPLE-SCATTERING DEPTH VS. DIFFUSION DEPTH

If you render the same image used in the previous example solely with multiple scattering (diffusion approximation disabled), you may see an image like Figure 14.48 (the color version is available on the CD). Notice that in image A, multiple-scattering photons reach the lower portion of the box. In image B you see a higher-quality version, where the multiple-scattering photons have been smoothed out (interpolated) making the light appear to wrap around the box like a table cloth. When you render solely multiple-scattering effects and see this sort of result, you may ask yourself two similar questions:

- Why do multiple-scattering photons reach the bottom of the box past the depth level?
- Isn't the diffusion approximation supposed to handle photons only from a depth of 5 (in this case) and lower (as shown in Figure 14.47 image B)?

Figure 14.48

Multiple-scattering photons with a low photon radius (A) and a high photon radius (B) that reach the bottom of the box, past the depth level

When you first use the physical shader, this sort of result may leave room for confusion. For example, when trying to push multiple-scattering photons deeper into the surface (a greater depth distance), you may notice that increasing the depth doesn't really appear to make the photons go any deeper into the volume; it merely increases their spread.

In the photon path shown in Figure 14.49 (A), you can see why multiple-scattering photons reach the bottom of the box in Figure 14.48. As you can see in the illustration, for multiple scattering the scatter depth defines a distance from the surface's exterior (into the surface) regardless of the location of the source light. Thus, depth is not the depth into the surface based solely on the light's physical placement but rather a volume container at a given depth within the surface, which is itself a volume container (the surface). Essentially, a photon that enters the surface from the light's direction may bounce around internally and "fall down" toward the bottom of the box along the surface's sides (shown with a few photons at the bottom of the box in Figure 14.48 image A), as long as it doesn't enter the deep layer.

> Although I have no technical verification for this explanation, from trial-and-error experimentation it appears to be a rational explanation for why multiple-scattering photons travel everywhere within a given envelope from the surface's exterior.

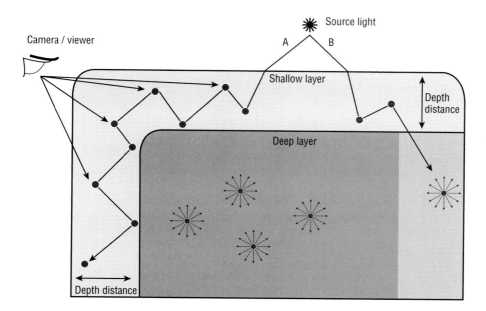

Figure 14.49

The depth defines a given distance from the surface's exterior regardless of the light's location.

> The only way to see a clear-cut indication of where depth initiates is by using only the diffusion approximation, as in Figure 14.47, because with multiple scattering, photons may appear at all depths. As discussed shortly, you can also refer to the SSS diagnostics output to see the actual depth values used.

You may conclude that with thicker surfaces that exhibit a lot of absorption (discussed later in the "Optical Properties" section), photons are less likely to reach the corners and travel around the surface. (In the case of Figure 14.48, the absorption was set to a negligible amount.) If you want to prevent multiple-scattering photons from traveling deep into the surface, as with the example in Figure 14.48, you can set a higher absorption rate with the

Absorption Coeff. option, or you can decrease the depth value so photons are more likely to transition to the diffusion approximation after penetrating the surface. On the other hand, by increasing depth, you increase the likelihood of multiple-scattering photons traveling around the surface within a given distance. Also note that the higher the depth value, the farther away diffusion photons (diffusion approximation) appear from the surface's exterior on the side that they enter (closest to the light), which has the effect of reducing the likelihood of seeing diffusion photons through the surface, a topic I'll further discuss next.

With respect to the diffusion approximation, consider that photons that enter from the top of the surface must travel to a minimum n depth before entering the deep layer. However, once they enter the deep layer, they are "in the hands" of the diffusion approximation regardless of their final destination. Thus, the path photons take may transmit them through that depth (from the top of the surface in these examples) to a location that appears closer to the surface exterior on a different side. In other words, the photon labeled B in Figure 14.49 takes a path that transmits it through the material into the deep layer, for example a depth of 5, landing near the outer border of the container along its side, which is theoretically at a depth of 1 from that side. In this case, that photon will be clearly seen on the outer side of the container, but not necessarily from the top of the container, because it is located deep within the material from that (top) side. This characteristic becomes important later in this chapter when you examine the Max Radius effects in Figure 14.54.

While experimenting with the physical shader, use focused lights on thin and thick objects to see how the physical shader values and the surface's thickness affect the SSS effect independently with each approximation.

Controlling Photons

Tweaking the physical shader's SSS effect by smoothing out the result (blending photons) is similar to working with any of the indirect illumination techniques discussed in Chapter 12, "Indirect Illumination." Let's look at photon control with both approximations and various shader options.

MULTIPLE-SCATTERING PHOTON CONTROL

This section uses Figure 14.50 to examine various shader options and values with the physical shader using multiple scattering. You can see the color version on the CD labeled "Multiple Scattering." The physical shader options examined in Figure 14.50 are initially set to the following values (depth is set to 4, and only multiple scattering is enabled):

OPTION	VALUE
Max Samples	1
Max Photons	1
Max Radius	2

In the scene a spot light is casting 4,500 caustic photons onto the shark's surface top. You can see some of the caustic photons penetrate through the shark and exit on the other side, influencing the shadow area on the floor and transferring the shark's internal color properties into the scene (outside the volume).

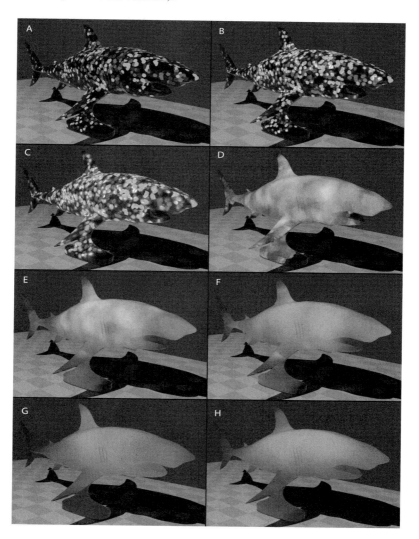

Figure 14.50

Comparing photon-related options to multiple scattering

Max Samples

The Max Samples option affects both the optical properties of the material and the distribution of photons, as discussed earlier. With multiple scattering, it defines how many times a photon can change direction (reflect) internally before being fully absorbed, entering the deep layer, or exiting the surface. Increasing the Max Samples value provides for more stored photon locations in the photon map, similar to the photon trace options used with indirect illumination simulations, only in this case it is more common to use high sample values so that the photons scatter multiple times.

In image A, you can see the basic distribution of photons without any photon blending. Since the Max Samples option is set to 1, the photons don't bounce around; they only store at their initial location as they hit the surface. Notice how the photons are stored externally only on the surface, not exhibiting any internal reflections.

In image B the Max Samples value is increased to 30, and you see several additional photons appear in the image, representing additional sites within the geometry where photons are stored. A visual cue that photons are storing internally is the blurred photons. The deeper the photons are stored, the more blurred (faded) they appear. Comparing images A, B, and C, you can clearly see that in image A all the photons are stored solely on the surface exterior. This is unlike B and C, which both have a Max Samples value of 30, which adds several internally stored photons. If you look at the color version on the CD, you can see the increased variation in color within the surface.

The higher the Max Samples value, the more irradiance you will see from within the surface, as well as increased influence from the material's substance. In other words, the more photons interact within the material, the more they are influenced by the wavelength-dependent (RGB) transmission color, absorption, and scattering coefficients, producing variation in color (all discussed shortly).

The Max Samples option works hand in hand with the Depth option, because the depth defines the total distance a photon may travel within the surface before entering the deep layer, and the Max Samples option defines how many times along that distance mental ray can sample its location (perturbing the photon's path) defining more locations for storing photons before they enter the deep layer.

A Max Samples range of 15 to 30 samples is typically sufficient.

Max Photons and Max Radius

Similar to the GI (and caustics) Accuracy and Radius options, the physical shader's Max Photons and Max Radius options define the number of photons sampled for color within a given radius (search area) to interpolate color. Thus, in Figure 14.50 images A and B, one photon is sampled within a search radius of 2 units with each eye ray cast into the scene. In image C, the Max Radius was increased to 10, and everything else remains as with image B (Max Samples at 30, Max Photons at 1). You can see that the increased search area provides more irradiance coverage across the surface; there is more color across the surface, yet the photons don't appear to blend well.

The Max Photons option increases the number of photons used within a given search radius to blend photons together. It has the effect of increasing the light intensity and quality while using more photons with both approximations (multiple and diffusion). In image D, the Max Photons value is increased from 1 to 100, and you can see how photons within the 10-unit search radius blend together, covering most of the surface.

As with indirect illumination, when blending photons together, if the results appear splotchy, you can always increase the radius, forcing a larger interpolation region, or you can increase the number of photons used with that radius using the Max Photons option. In image E, the Max Radius is increased to 20, doubling the search radius area. As you can see, the result appears somewhat smoother, particularly on the shark's fins and stand. However, it's not enough to provide a visually pleasing SSS effect. In image F, the Max Photons value is increased from 100 to 1,000. As you can see, the result is smoother, providing a smoother gradation in color and intensity based on the shark's surface thickness across most of the surface.

Fine-tuning the result is thus a balance between using the right radius with a sufficient number of photons. In image G, the radius was increased to 50 and the result appears much better, without any significant spottiness. The image now demonstrates a lot of variation in color and intensity based on the shark's surface thickness. It appears better because there are enough photons for interpolation within a relatively large area (radius) across the surface.

Photon Count

Finally, as with indirect illumination, there comes a point where it is not enough to fine-tune the Max Radius and Photon values, and you need to increase the overall photon count on the photon-emitting light. In image H, the light's caustic photon count was increased from 4,500 to 100,000, and the Max Radius was decreased from 50 to 30. As you can see, the result improves on image G, where using a smaller radius with more photons provides better detail—notice the variation in intensity shown in the mouth and on the fins, as well as the smooth gradation along the body. You may have to look at the color image cited earlier (on the CD) to see these subtleties.

Balancing the Option Values

As rules of thumb, consider the following:

- When increasing the Max Photons option (how many photons are used), there will come a point where an increase in value does not provide any change in the rendered result. At that point, you can increase either the radius or the overall photon count emitted into the surface.

- While increasing the radius, if you find you need to use very high values that cover the entire surface, then clearly you lose detail and variation. You should first increase the Max Photons, and if that doesn't suffice, you can increase the photon count emitted into the scene.

- When Max Photons is set to 1, each radius will use only one photon for color. You can use this approach to measure the radius size visually while testing the result. For example, a radius of 100 appears to blend all the photons together, but if you reduce the Max Photons to 1, you will clearly see the radius outlined, visually determining the scale of the search radius in comparison to the surface's size.

DIFFUSION APPROXIMATION PHOTON CONTROL

Controlling the diffusion approximation is not the same as with the multiple-scattering approximations, even though they share the same options. Furthermore, the mental ray support (help) files indicate that the Max Radius option doesn't influence the diffusion approximation; however, it does influence the rendered result. Let's first look at how the Max Radius option influences SSS effects with the diffusion approximation; you'll also learn more about the diffusion approximation characteristics.

Diffusion Radius of Influence

You can think of the deep layer (the diffusion approximation) as a point volume light that emits diffused (isotropic) light within a given area (radius), attenuating with distance. This theoretical point light is located internally within the surface in an opposite location (direct line of sight) from the actual source light and within a given depth distance, as illustrated in Figure 14.51. In the illustration you can see two source lights, each creating a radius of influence within the surface at the depth level defined with the Depth option; this is the depth distance from the surface top to the deep layer. Each light's influence is based on the surface material properties (its optical properties) balanced against the light's photon energy.

The approach for using a theoretical source light internally as a diffusion light source is applied within the BSSRDF multiple-scattering term, introduced with Jensen's shading model (discussed earlier in the chapter). I base the following discussions on that approach to the physical shader's diffusion approximation, which functions in the same way (aside from the ability to use photons as a source for energy).

In Figure 14.52 image A you can see a screen grab with the same scene used to illustrate multiple scattering earlier in the chapter, only in this case two spot lights are located directly above the box with small influence areas (cones). In image B you can see the rendered result using only the diffusion approximation. You can see that each light has a corresponding (opposite) area of influence within the volume (box) that displays bright light within a given radius. This area of influence (the radius) is defined by the Max Radius option and has the effect of decreasing the light intensity from the center (directly opposite the source light's location) and outward along a given radius, as in Figure 14.51.

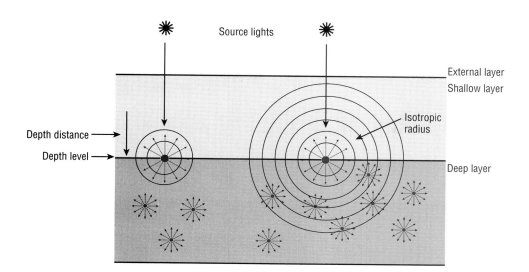

Figure 14.51

The diffusion approximation's radius of influence

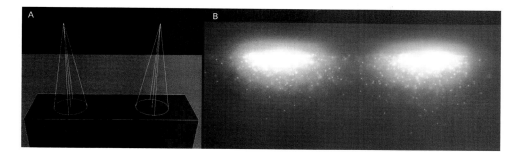

Figure 14.52

Source lights create local regions of influence directly opposite their location within the surface and at the specified depth distance.

Thus, with respect to diffusion approximation, the Max Radius defines the light intensity from the diffusion center (where more photons are located) outward so that as you increase the radius it blends over and utilizes more photons, which are located within the deep layer, creating a larger diffused area. The diffusion center is located exactly at the specified depth opposite the light's location; however, diffusion approximation photons are located anywhere within the deep layer.

> Unlike other global illumination techniques, as well as the multiple-scattering approximation, the Max Radius in this case is not a per-sample search radius that looks up photons; instead, it is a search area based on the source light's location and its corresponding location within a volume at the specified depth.

As an additional example of the Max Radius influence on the diffusion approximation, you can also look at Figure 14.53, where you can see the effect of the Max Radius using one spot light. The Max Radius value is set to 2, 10, and 50 in images A, B and C, respectively. As you can see, it increases the search radius for photons, only in this case forming an increased radius light region from the center of the isotropic source outward (not around each sample point, as with multiple scattering). It is located directly beneath the spot light location (which is not seen in the figure) and at a Depth value of 5 (as with Figure 14.47 image B).

Figure 14.53

Increasing the radius creates a bright isotropic region from the center of influence.

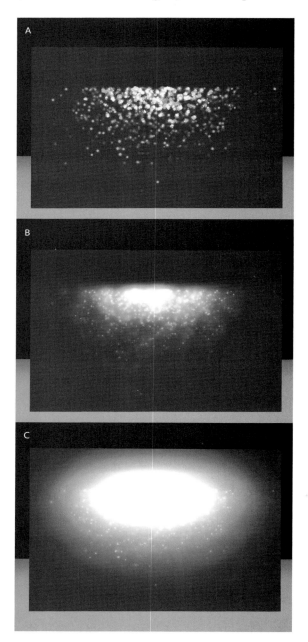

Diffusion Photons Artifacts

Notice the colorful dots (diffusion approximation photons) that appear within the radius closer to its outer rim and even beyond that distance. The Max Radius doesn't influence photons themselves; it just defines an area of increased influence from the isotropic source. This point has two significant implications for fine-tuning the render. One deals with removing these dots, since you don't want spotty renders. The other deals with where you can see the diffusion approximation (deep scattering).

To remove these dots (diffusion photons) that appear in the render, you should reduce the overall radiance or just the amount of internal scattering within the material. You can do so in a number of ways:

- Decreasing the light's photon energy value
- Reducing the Max Photons count (as discussed with multiple scattering)
- Increasing the Depth value
- Decreasing the Transmission color value (discussed shortly)
- Increasing the Absorption coefficient (discussed shortly)
- Decreasing the Scattering coefficient (discussed shortly)

> In most cases, with all the different influences that come to play, the "dots" blend in well with the multiple scattering and the material's color.

Deep Scattering Distance

The visual appearance of diffusion photons through the surface (deep scattering) is significantly affected by the depth level and the surface thickness. The Max Radius defines to what extent diffusion photons can influence the visual perception of the surface. That is, it defines how far diffusion photons' color influence will reach from within the deep layer.

In Figure 14.54 you see the same scene as in the previous example, where in image A the Max Radius is set to 2 and in image B it's set to 50. As you can see in image A, diffusion photons are not seen through the top of the surface, but in image B you can clearly see their influence also from the top of the surface. Thus, the Max Radius option has the effect of defining the distance that diffusion photons can be seen from within the deep layer on the surface exterior.

From the discussion of the Depth setting and Figure 14.49 earlier in this chapter, recall that the diffusion approximation handles any photons that pass a given depth. However, once the photon passes that depth, it may land close to the surface exterior on another side (other than the side from which it entered). If you compare images A and B in Figure 14.54, you can see that the diffusion photons are seen in image A along the side of the surface because they landed close to that side of the surface after entering from the top. However, the same photons are not seen through the top side until you increase the radius enough so that they can be seen through the surface top in the deep layer.

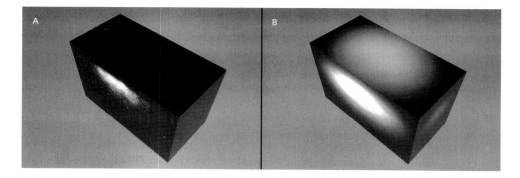

Essentially, you don't fine-tune the Max Radius based on the diffusion approximation but on the multiple-scattering approximation. Because the two are tied together, a larger radius for multiple-scattering will also increase the size of the isotropic source within the surface. Also, consider that when multiple scattering is enabled, photons in the deep layer blend with multiple-scattering photons when those areas are searched for irradiance. For that reason, the diffusion approximation is mostly used to enhance (help) multiple scattering by blending deep scattering with multiple scattering and providing additional subtle irradiance from deep within a surface.

Basic Material Properties

Aside from internal scattering, the physical shader also accounts for external color and Fresnel (raytrace) reflections, as shown in the color gallery candle and shark images (cited earlier) that demonstrate Fresnel reflections. It also provides bump mapped diffuse and specular highlights, as shown on the ketchup's surface in Figure 14.36 (and on the companion CD). In Figures 14.38, 14.39, and 14.40 you saw that the first two physical shader options are the Material (Color property in XSI) and Transmission RGB color options. The Material option defines the material's external properties, and the Transmission option defines the transmission color and intensity through the surface.

> Note that the single, multiple, and diffusion approximations are not affected by the Material color; their colors are defined by the Transmission, Absorption, and Scattering coefficient options. Thus, the Material option solely affects the external color properties of the surface. It does, however, blend with the subsurface colors when all the different components are combined, but not as part of their color-sampling phase.

The Material Option and Reflections

The Material option is used as an overall ambient color when left unmapped (at default). It is not affected by lighting in any way, enabling you to specify an overall ambient color as with the milk and candle examples cited earlier. In each case I specified a base color that represents the material's natural color, as shown in Figure 14.55. Images A, C, and D demonstrate solely the effect of the Material option and Fresnel reflections, and thus all three approximations (single, multiple, and diffusion) are disabled. Image B has all three approximations enabled and is the same as Figure 14.36 presented earlier.

Figure 14.55
The material color defines an ambient color that can also be mapped with a shading model.

In these examples, the material colors for the candle and shark are set with dark values (Figure 14.55 images C and D), and then the subsurface-scattering effect added color and brightness to the surface, making it appear brighter (see the color versions). The milk surface had an overall brighter material color, as shown in image A; then the subsurface-scattering effect added the translucency color and additional brightness to the surface, as shown in image B (using all three approximations). In color the SSS effect also adds a color shift through the material based on the material's scattering properties (its absorption and scattering coefficients).

> When you use the material color in this way (as an ambient color), typically the initial material color should be set to a low value, or else it will overpower the scattering color and reflections using a bright ambient color.

With respect to Fresnel reflections, notice the reflections in Figure 14.55 images C and D, particularly with the shark in image D. The darker the material color and SSS scattering effect appear, the stronger the reflection color (think energy conservation). You can see with both color images (shark and candle) how the reflections blend in well with the SSS effect. With images A and B, the material is initially very bright, providing more diffusion and less Fresnel reflection.

MAPPING THE MATERIAL OPTION

The Material color option can be mapped with a shading model (or custom shader tree) that adds the external diffuse and specular reflections (highlights), as shown in Figure 14.56. In this way, you effectively layer a standard shading model (diffuse color and specular highlights) along with the subsurface-scattering effect.

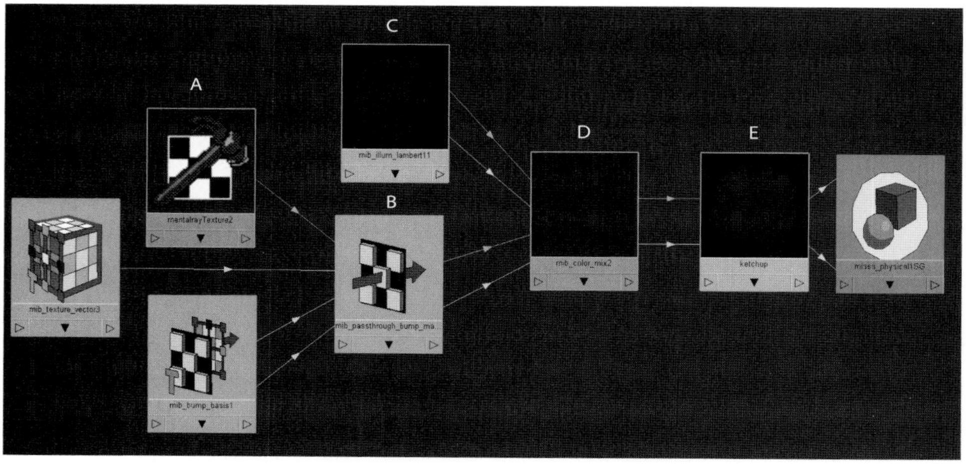

Figure 14.56

The shader tree for the ketchup example using the physical shader with additional bump mapped Lambert shader

For the ketchup's material, a slightly reddish color would suffice as an ambient base color (Material option); however, the surface would appear smooth without any diffuse and specular bumpiness, unlike the subtle roughness shown in Figure 14.55 images A and B.

To generate a diffused bump mapped surface with the ketchup material, I used a custom tree that blends bump mapping (using the texture file labeled A and the mib_passthrough_ bump shader labeled B) with a reddish Lambert shader labeled C using the mib_color_mix shader labeled D. The color mix shader connects to the physical shader's (labeled E) Material color option.

You should use specular shading model instead of the Lambert shader so that specular highlights would also be considered with bump mapping. However, in this case the physical shader's reflection color (Fresnel reflections) is affected by the material's bump mapping, and thus the appearance of broken reflections is present. To clarify, I used a visible area light; thus, the physical shader renders highlights as raytrace reflections of the source area light shape (see Chapter 6, "Lights and Soft Shadows").

> In XSI and 3ds Max you can use a shading model with bump mapping without a need to construct this sort of mental ray–specific custom tree for bump mapping, which is a topic discussed in Chapter 11, "mental ray Textures and Projections."

MATERIAL CONSIDERATIONS

Based on the earlier discussions, you need to keep a few points in mind with respect using the Material color option as well as mapping it with a shading model:

- The purpose of the physical shader is to provide the internal subsurface effect. Providing the Material option as ambient color is an advantage, allowing you to use any custom shader to define the external properties of the surface. In other words, it's good that it does not include all sorts of color options that would constrain you to a specific BRDF shading model.

- Remember, all ambient color options (the Material color) are not affected by lights, so once they are mapped with a standard shading model, the diffuse and specular components from that shading model add in the external influence from the light.

- Not all surfaces require a diffuse component; thus, with some surfaces the color is mostly handled with the subsurface-scattering effect and Material color option, as with the milk and candle examples that have some ambient (Material option) color as a base color for the surface, as shown in Figure 14.55 images A and C.

- The physical shader already provides Fresnel reflections as shown in Figure 14.55 so that when you map a shading model that adds its own reflections, they double up with the physical shader reflections. You should consider using a shading model that adds only specular reflections (highlights), which are not included with the physical shader.

- The only additional consideration with respect to reflections is with visible area lights that appear in both specular raytrace reflections (the physical shader) and in specular highlights (the specular shading model; that is Phong, Blinn, and so on). You may want to use nonvisible area lights, which are not raytraced in reflections, or a Lambert shading model, as noted earlier in Figure 14.56.

The Transmission Option

The Transmission option affects all three scatter approximations, enabling you to tweak their intensity (brightness). It should not be confused with absorption, a topic discussed next with the Absorption coefficient. The sole purpose of the Transmission option is to decrease or increase the overall brightness of the SSS effect, which is a typical color multiplier. It can be used creatively with a texture map or 3D procedural texture to tweak the intensity across the surface.

For the shark color image I utilized the mi architectural material as a shading model (Figure 14.57 label B). The diffuse color has been mapped with a painted texture (label A) that defines the base material color. As you can see, the texture file passes through a multiply/divide shader before connecting to the architectural material, enabling me to tone down the texture color using multiplication; it was multiplied by a value of 0.2 so that the material's brightest color effect does not exceed a value of 0.2.

Figure 14.57

Mapping the Material and Transmission options on the Shark's physical shader

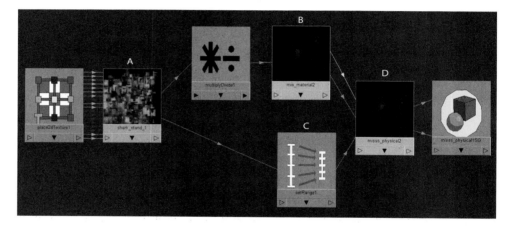

The architectural material connects to the Material option of the physical shader (D). The texture file is also used for the physical shader's Transmission option, passing through a range setting shader (C) and then connecting to the physical shader. The range setting shader allows me to compress the texture values, which range from 0 to 1, to a new min/max range of values.

I use it to decrease the overall brightness of the SSS effect, remapping the output values to a specified range of 0.1 to 0.6. To clarify, the texture is used for varying the intensity of transmission through the surface using a black-to-white color range, and thus I need to remap the initial values to a smaller range so that the transmission is not completely dark or bright at any point across the surface.

Whenever the SSS effect appears too bright, you can reduce the transmission color, for which in some cases very low values (0.1 to 0.01) can help produce compelling results. As with correcting overexposure, reducing the transmission color can have the effect of rein-troducing color variation and detail into the effect.

Index of Refraction

As with all refractive surfaces, the direction of light as it transmits through the surface is based on the material's index of refraction (IOR). As you can see, the physical shader has an IOR option that defines how light refracts through the surface with the SSS approxima-tions. You can see examples of refraction through a shark's fin in Figures 14.58, 14.59, and 14.60 in the following sections.

Optical Properties

The internal scattering options define a surface's optical properties, preferably using real-istic values that have been acquired by experimentation. These options define the proba-bility for absorption and scattering of a given photon that transmits internally within the surface and are controlled with the following four options: Absorption and Scattering coefficients, Scattering anisotropy, and Scale conversion. The host application options for these were shown in Figures 14.38, 14.39, and 14.40. Additional options discussed earlier also have an effect on the rendered appearance of the surface; however, these four options are the keys to defining the material's optical character, its absorption, and scattering characteristics.

Absorption and Scattering Coefficients

The Absorption and Scattering coefficient options define wavelength-dependent (RGB) characteristics for a given photon through a surface. With respect to the distance a photon transmits through a surface and its rendered appearance, consider that a *mean free path* length represents an average distance a photon will travel within a surface without exhibit-ing any absorption or scattering. The greater the distance, the more translucent the surface appears, whereas shorter distances exhibit more absorption and scattering, depending on the values used for each coefficient.

The mean free path length for absorption (a) and scattering (s) is dependent on their combined coefficient values for each RGB color (R_a+R_s, $G_a + G_s$, $B_a + B_s$ = mean free path length for R, G, and B). It is equal to the reciprocal of their combined coefficient values ($1 \div coeff.$)

The distance measurement (units through the medium) and the actual size of the object become very significant when specifying values for these coefficients. In other words, real-world values will represent a real-world mean free length, and thus the CG scene should be based on the same real-world units. Setting the units (discussed further shortly) is accomplished with the Scale Conversion option.

THE ABSORPTION COEFFICIENT

The Absorption coefficient defines the attenuation rate of light through the turbid medium, where higher values provide for more absorption. With high absorption rates, photons are affected at shorter distances, meaning they lose energy more frequently where the mean free path length is shorter. In Figure 14.58, you can see two images that are set as follows: for both images the Scattering coeff. Option is set to 0.01 so that its effect is fairly negligible, and the Absorption coeff. is set to 0.1 in image A and 0.5 in image B. As you can see, image B appears much darker as more light is absorbed through the medium. Also note that decreasing the absorption to a lower value (from B to A) will show more transparency through the surface.

> You can examine the absorption coefficient without casting photons in the scene, similar to examining the absorption with the dielectric shader.

Figure 14.58

Comparing an Absorption coefficient value of 0.1 in image A with a value of 0.5 in image B

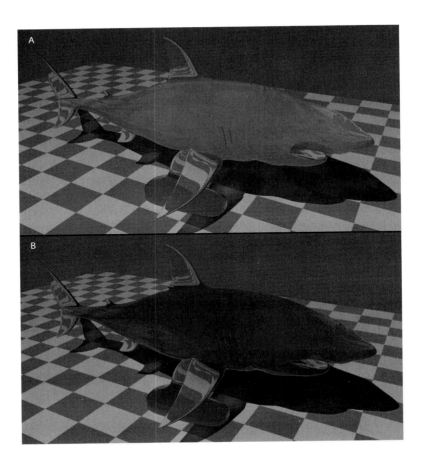

To examine the effect of absorption without using photons as well as learn more about the role the Material option plays, use the following steps:

1. Create a sphere and stretch it a bit so that it's oval with some variation in volume. Place it over a floor surface that has a texture, such as a checker. Place a source light above the sphere.

2. You can disable all three approximations, although that's irrelevant; as long as photon casting is disabled, you will see quick rendered results.

3. Apply the physical shader to the sphere, and set the material color to black. The Transmission color is irrelevant in this case; you are examining absorption of the material without using the approximations that are affected by the Transmission color.

4. Set the R, G, and B Scatter coefficient values to 0.001.

5. Set the Absorption coefficient to 0.01 and render. Then change the value to 0.1 and render and then to 0.5 and render. Make note of the transparency you see with each image.

After executing these renders, you will see how the surface mimics absorption, based on the Beer-Lambert law discussed in Chapter 10, "mental ray Shaders and Shader Trees," with the dielectric shader. Higher absorption values will show more of the material color in the surface, at a more frequent rate. Note that if the material color is initially set to white, then the surface reflects all the light and doesn't show any transparency. That happens because it acts as an overall ambient light. Therefore, the brighter the material color, the less transparent the surface. If you set the material to a dark green, you will see a greenish tint appear as you increase the absorption rate, as with step 5 cited earlier.

THE SCATTER COEFFICIENT

The Scattering coefficient defines the frequency for scattered light in a turbid medium; higher values provide for more frequent scattering. More frequent scattering produces shorter mean free path lengths (as with absorption) and increased intensity (brightness). In Figure 14.59 the Absorption coefficient is set to 0.01 in all cases so that its effect is fairly negligible. In image A the Scattering coefficient is set to 0.001, in image B the Scattering coefficient is set to 0.1, and in image C the Scattering coefficient is set to 0.8. As you see, the increased value has two noticeable effects: less transparency and more out-scattering (increased radiance).

Use the earlier tutorial for examining absorption to examine scattering. Set the Absorption coefficient to 0.01 and then change the Scatter coefficient in the same way as with the Absorption coefficient noted in step 5.

Figure 14.59

**Comparing Scatter-
ing coefficient val-
ues where image A
is set with a value of
0.001, image B 0.1,
and image C 0.8**

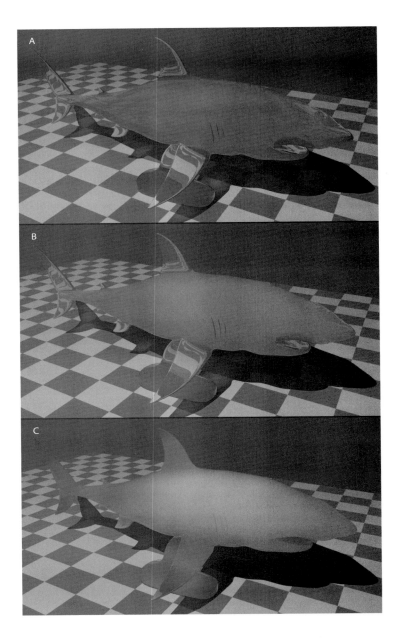

As the scatter coefficient value increases, you can see less transparency through the surface as more light is scattered internally. Notice how in images A and B the fins are fairly
transparent; however, in image C they too exhibit subsurface scattering. Thus, the higher
the value, the more frequent light scatters, and in other words, the probability of a photon
scattering within a given distance increases. With surfaces that exhibit a lot of internal

scattering such as marble, the scattering coefficient is typically set high (I further discuss values shortly). Also, since the scattering is more frequent, more light is reflected internally resulting in increased radiance in thicker areas of the surface. As you can see, the body of the shark, which is the thickest area in the surface, shows the brightest radiance through that region because there are several more instances of light-scattering events.

> Notice that without using the shader to its full abilities (photonic scattering), you can still hack into subsurface scattering by simulating scattering and absorption within the surface; however, it will not handle realistic transport of light and glossy refractions through the surface. It's more like the dielectric shader's ability to mimic absorption through the surface, without the added ability to increase irradiance using the Scatter coefficient.

SCATTERING AND ABSORPTION COEFFICIENTS IN PRACTICE

When setting RGB values for each coefficient, you can use empirical data or try to "guesstimate" ad hoc values. If you look at the values for empirical data provided in the mental ray help files (on the misss_Phyiscal shader Optical properties page), such as for skim milk, marble, and ketchup while comparing their numerical values, you will notice that values are significantly different and some are significantly low values (several values past the decimal point). For example, Marble is set with these coefficients: 0.0021, 0.0041, and 0.0071 for R, G, and B, respectively.

Clearly, it's not practical to guess these sorts of values. You can, however, get more acquainted through trial-and-error experimentation with the effect that higher vs. lower values have on the visual appearance, as shown in Figures 14.58 and 14.59. While doing so, you should consider the effect of absorption and scattering on each wavelength of light. For example, ketchup has a distinct red color that scatters and absorbs a lot of light. Thus, the red component has a very low absorption coefficient in comparison to the green and blue coefficients. Also, the red scatter coefficient is significantly higher than the green and blue scatter coefficients. Thus, most of the red wavelengths of light scatter with little absorption compared to the blue and green wavelengths of light that possess the opposite character.

When guessing values, your approach to controlling the appearance is based on visually attempting to match the optical properties (visual appearance) of the surface with the visual cues of real-world surfaces. It is recommended that you have the actual surface and can examine it under different light conditions such as under a strong light, near a window, in more ambient light conditions, and so forth.

You can find empirical values derived by experimentation (using the same unit measurements) in the mental ray help files for milk, jade, ketchup, and other materials, as well as rather extensive lists of material optical properties in the online PDF documentation cited earlier in this chapter. See the BSSRDF PDF file titled "A Practical Model for Subsurface

Light Transport" (http://graphics.stanford.edu/papers/bssrdf/). These online data lists typically provide RGB (wavelength dependent) scattering coefficients (σ_s) and RGB absorption coefficients (σ_a). They also may include indices of refraction and anisotropic scattering values such as with the Henyey-Greenstein *g* parameter discussed in Chapter 12, "Indirect illumination," for anisotropic scattering.

> Both coefficient options together define the optical properties (appearance) of the surface, based on the distance a photon travels through the medium and the effect each coefficient has on that photon's appearance.

Units and Scale Conversion

The units for absorption and scattering coefficients with the physical shader, as well as those provided in various online resources such as those cited earlier, are set using inverse measurements of millimeter units (mm^{-1}). When specifying values for coefficients, you need to convert the current units you use in the scene to millimeters. Thus, if you model in inches or centimeters, you then need to convert those units to millimeters by specifying a conversion factor with the physical shader's Scale Conversion option. Consider that the model should be modeled to real scale so that when you convert, you get the real transport properties of light in inverse millimeters. In a way, it's similar to the Scale Conversion option discussed earlier in this chapter with the nonphysical shaders, where in that case you want to convert from scene units to the object's real size, for example from inches to feet or any other unit of measurement. In this case, you always want to convert from the scene units (assuming it's modeled to scale in those units) to millimeter units, as described earlier. Table 14.1 shows some common values that may help you.

Table 14.1	SCALE CONVERSION VALUE	SCENE UNIT TYPE (1 UNIT)
Unit Conversions for the Physical Shader	10	Centimeter
	304.8	Feet
	25.4	Inch
	1000	Meter

All the physical shader options discussed throughout these sections are affected by scale conversion, such as the search area radius size and the depth a photon passes before entering the deep layer (diffusion approximation). If you look at Figure 14.60, you can see the effect that Scale conversion has on the Absorption and Scattering coefficient options. In the examples shown earlier, as well as in Figure 14.60 image B, the scale conversion is set to 10. Thus, the shark was modeled in centimeters and converted to millimeters with a value of 10. In image A the Scale conversion value is set to a lower value of 5, which means the shark's body is smaller. As a result, you can see there is less absorption and scattering because a smaller surface provides less volume for scattering and absorption events.

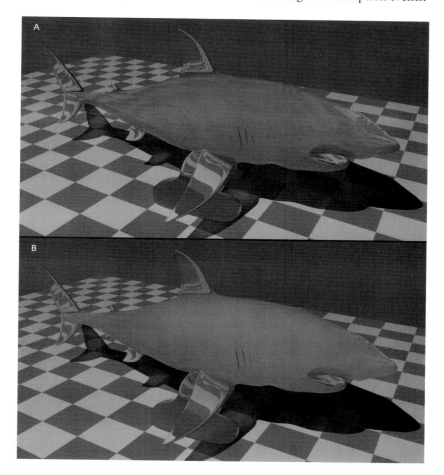

Figure 14.60

Comparing a Scale conversion value of 10 (A) with a value of 5 (B)

Isotropic and Anisotropic Scattering

For anisotropic vs. isotropic scattering, the same g parameter (the Henyey-Greenstein phase function discussed in Chapter 12, "Indirect Illumination," in the "Participating Media (PM) Effects" section) is used. In both cases (PM shader and the physical shader), I'm simulating the transmission of light as it interacts with particles within a turbid medium. As discussed in Chapter 12, "Indirect Illumination," back scattering means that more light reflects backward toward the source light, forward scattering transmits more light through the particle, and isotropic scattering refers to a relatively equal (diffused) amount of light scattering in 360° around a particle.

With the physical shader, isotropic or anisotropic (forward or backward) scatter settings are defined with the Scattering anisotropy option shown in Figures 14.38 to 14.40 (called the ScatteringDir property in XSI) using values from -1 to 1. Values from 0 to 1 are used for forward scattering, and negative values between 0 and -1 are used for backward scattering, just as with the PM shader's g1 and g2 options. A value of 0 provides isotropic scattering.

In Figure 14.61 you can see an example of single scattering (only the single-scattering approximation is enabled). A point area light is located in the center of the candle where the flame should appear. As you can see, light transmits through the surface where it is most pronounced at the top of the candle. In image A the Scattering anisotropy is set to 0.65 (forward scattering), and in B it is set to a negative value of -0.65 (backward scattering). In this case I wanted the candle to appear brighter internally where the light source appears so that more light reflects back toward the source light than through the candle as with forward scattering. You can see a more polished example with the candle in the color gallery that used the same backward scattering value of -0.65.

Figure 14.61

Single scattering with an area light acting as the candle's flame (illumination source) showing forward scattering under image A and backward scattering under image B

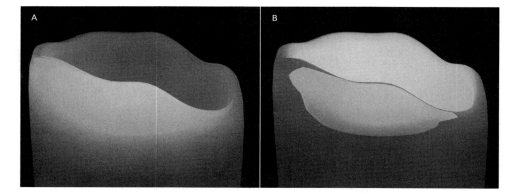

As a general rule of thumb, most turbid materials possess more forward scattering than isotropic or back scatter characteristics, such as with values that range from 0.6 to 0.95.

Scattering Diagnostics

For multiple and diffusion SSS approximation, the mental ray verbosity info messages provide a lot of insight for diagnosing and troubleshooting the SSS effect. These messages are divided into the different scatter algorithms covering the shader optical properties, the raytrace properties from ray marching, photon statistics, and more. They are also presented on a wavelength basis (RGB) telling you more about the mean free path length for each component as well as the number of photons used in each instance for each RGB channel. Here is an example of photon diagnostic output (numbers cropped to fit):

```
PHEN 0.4  info : "misss_physical1" photon statistics:
PHEN 0.4  info : received:      44499
PHEN 0.4  info : channels:       0      1       2
PHEN 0.4  info : stored:       16874  15382  14511
PHEN 0.4  info : stored:         0     56     211 isotropic
PHEN 0.4  info : propagated:    5127   3117   684
PHEN 0.4  info : scatter depth:
PHEN 0.4  info : minimum:       0.0    0.0     0.0
PHEN 0.4  info : maximum:       7.0    7.0     4.0
PHEN 0.4  info : mean:          0.16   0.060   0.011
PHEN 0.4  info : variance:      0.28   0.096   0.019
```

If you look at this output, you can learn the following (in the same order as presented earlier):

- The title tells you that these are photon statistics, informing you on how they interacted with the surface.

- received is the total number of photons that hit the surface.

- channels tabulates the data to RGB channels as 0, 1, and 2 so that anything listed—for example, under 1—refers to the green channel.

- stored lists the per-channel number of photons stored within the volume and used with the multiscatter approximation.

- scatter is the same for the diffusion approximation. You can tell because it's postfixed with the word *isotropic* (after 211 earlier), which indicates it's the diffusion approximation.

- propagated is the number of photons that exit the volume back into the scene. As with the candle example presented earlier, it indicates how many caustic photons illuminated the walls below the source light after passing through the candle.

- The scatter depth title indicates that the following information relates to how photons behave within the volume. That information includes the following:

  - minimum and maximum depth photons penetrate for the RGB channels.

  - The average mean free path length (mean) of each photon before absorbing or scattering.

  - variance indicates the difference for the mean free path length showing the maximum mean free path length for each channel.

Once you are comfortable with the physical shader options, I recommend you experiment with the shader while looking at different diagnostic messages output in the log. If you use the tutorial noted earlier for testing absorption and scatter coefficients (when the approximations and photon casting are off), you will see only the optical properties' output data update as you test different values, showing the RGB values for the mean free path length and the extinction coefficients through the material. It's an easy and fast approach for experimenting with this shader and its output. With the photon output shown earlier, it can help identify problems such as too few photons being absorbed or scattered, as well as the distances they pass before a scatter or absorption event takes place.

About the Companion CD

In this appendix:

- ■ **What you'll find on the CD**

- ■ **Customer care**

What You'll Find on the CD

The following sections are arranged by category and provide a summary of the software and other goodies you'll find on the CD. If you need help with installing the items provided on the CD, refer to the installation instructions in the "Using the CD" section of this appendix.

Some programs on the CD might fall into one of these categories:

Chapter Files

All the files provided in this book for completing the tutorials and understanding concepts are located in the ChapterFiles directory and work with Maya 8.5, XSI 6, and 3ds Max 9 and later (some files will also work with other versions, depending on the program's own forward- and backward-compatibility).

Because this book is focused on using mental ray and the mental ray options, most of the chapters don't require tutorial files. In the case that a complex shader network is presented, appropriate scene files and textures are provided for each host applications in the relevant chapter folder. Note that some of these files are only provided for the host applications that support that type of shader tree. In addition, some figures that require viewing in color are made available in their relevant chapter folder. The additional content on the CD includes custom shaders, HDR images, and articles that are aimed at assisting you to explore mental ray and learn more about rendering and compositing 3D images.

Remember you need to load scene and texture files from the CD into the project folder of the software application you are using.

Custom Shaders

In the Custom Shaders directory you will find a collection of custom shaders as ZIP files that are kindly provided by their creators. These shaders are also distributed freely over the internet from their web pages. The usage of these shaders is unrestricted; in the ZIP files you will find additional licensing information from the authors of these shaders, particularly when the source code is included. These authors do not provide technical support nor any guarantee that the shader will function correctly on your system; it is up to you to properly install and use these shaders. In these files you will also find help files, where provided. Some of these shaders, including installing shaders, are covered in the book, particularly in Chapters 1 and 10. Note that most of these shaders are provided solely for Windows 32-bit systems. Some are also provided for 64-bit systems, as noted below and in the relevant folders on the CD.

The Custom Shaders folder includes the following folders:

Binary Alchemy

The Binary Alchemy shaders (www.binaryalchemy.de) are provided by Holger Schönberger. The folder includes Maya and XSI folders that include shaders for each application.

3ds Max users, see Chapter 10 for installing these shaders in 3ds Max. The help files for these shaders are also included; open the help_BA_Shader_Collection_essential.html file found in this folder. These shaders support both 32-bit and 64-bit Windows systems.

Puppet Shaders

The Puppet shaders (`http://puppet.cgtalk.ru/index_e.shtml`) are provided by Pavel Ledin. The folder includes Maya, 3ds Max, and XSI ZIP files with shaders and source code. The help files are in the docs folder, open the index.html file. These shaders support both 32-bit and 64-bit Windows systems as indicated with the ZIP file titles.

Pixero

The Pixero shaders (`www.pixero.com`) are provided by Jan Sandström. The folder includes Maya and 3ds Max, and Maya (only) folders that include shaders for both applications. The Maya and 3ds Max folder includes shaders authored by Jan Sandström with appropriate install files for each host. The Maya folder includes shaders from Jan Sandström and AETemplate files for Maya. They do not include the complied shader (DLL). You will need to get the DLL file from the shader authors and then use these additional files to install the shaders. For a complete listing of web pages see Chapter 10 Table 10.1. Note that for the T2S_Illumination_1.1.ZIP file, the DLL can be found in the TEK2SHOOT folder. Some of these shaders support both 32-bit and 64-bit Windows systems as indicated with the info text files included within the ZIP files.

LMV

This folder has the Maya and AETemplate files provided by Horvátth Szabolcs (`www.impresszio.hu/szabolcs`) that are required for installing the lm2DMV shader discussed in Chapter 8. The DLL file for Maya and XSI can be downloaded from La Maison at `www.alamaison.fr/3d/lm_2DMV/lm_2DMV_ref.htm`.

Horvátth

These shaders are provided by Horvátth Szabolcs (`www.impresszio.hu/szabolcs`). The folder includes Maya shaders for all platforms that can also be installed in XSI and 3ds Max. 3ds Max users can find appropriate include files at `www.maxplugins.de` or `www.mymentalray.com`. The ForMax folder includes the file required for installing the reflection utility shader in 3ds Max.

TEK2SHOOT

The shaders provided by TEK2SHOOT (`www.tek2shoot.com`) include Maya and XSI folders with shaders for each application. They support 32-bit and 64-bit systems, as indicated with the ZIP file titles. XSI users will find the unexposed mental ray shaders required for the tutorials in Chapter 10 in this folder. The T2S illumination shader (32-bit systems only) is also included; Maya users can get the DLL here and the include files are in the Pixero folder. The T2s_illum_files&presets folder includes Fresnel files and presets for the T2S illumination shader.

HDR Images

In this folder you will find HDR images that are discussed in Chapter 13. There is also an LDR (low dynamic range) folder that contains standard image files that you can view while reading Chapter 13. It's there so you won't have to open \ HDR images in Photoshop or HDRSHOP to view them. These images have been created by the author and you may use them for any purpose. If you distribute them please credit the author, Boaz Livny.

HDRI Articles

This folder includes articles written by Boaz Livny for the *HDRI 3D* magazine, kindly provided with permission by DMG publishing. You will find two PDF files that include an article on compositing OpenEXR images with Nuke, and mental ray texture baking with Maya. Even though the article is specific to Maya, XSI and 3ds Max users can gain a lot of insight on special-purpose mental ray shaders and texture baking.

Surface Approximation Methods

A bonus chapter, SurfaceApproxMethods.pdf introduces you to the tessellation process that converts 3D surfaces into polygons during rendering.

Customer Care

If you have trouble with the book's companion CD-ROM, please call the Wiley Product Technical Support phone number at (800) 762-2974. Outside the United States, call +1(317) 572-3994. You can also contact Wiley Product Technical Support at http://sybex .custhelp.com. John Wiley & Sons will provide technical support only for installation and other general quality control items. For technical support on the applications themselves, consult the program's vendor or author.

To place additional orders or to request information about other Wiley products, please call (877) 762-2974.

Index

Note to the Reader: Throughout this index **boldfaced** page numbers indicate primary discussions of a topic. *Italicized* page numbers indicate illustrations.